Women, Resistance and Revolution

Woman's Consciousness, Man's World

Hidden from History

Dutiful Daughters: Women Talk about Their Lives
(with Jean McCrindle)

Socialism and the New Life: Essay on Edward Carpenter
(with Jeff Weeks)

A New World for Women: Stella Browne, Socialist Feminist

Beyond the Fragments: Feminism and the Making of Socialism
(with L. Segal and H. Wainwright)

Dreams and Dilemmas: Collected Writings

Friends of Alice Wheeldon

The Past is Before Us: Feminism in Action since the 1960s

Women in Movement: Feminism and Social Action

Homeworkers Worldwide

Dignity and Daily Bread: New Forms
of Economic Organization Among Poor Women
(edited with Swasti Mitter)

Women Encounter Technology:
Changing Patterns of Employment in the Third World
(edited with Swasti Mitter)

A Century of Women

THE HISTORY OF WOMEN IN BRITAIN AND THE UNITED STATES

Sheila Rowbotham

VIKING

VIKING
Published by the Penguin Group
Penguin Putnam Inc., 375 Hudson Street,
New York, New York 10014, U.S.A.
Penguin Books Ltd, 27 Wrights Lane,
London W8 5TZ, England
Penguin Books Australia Ltd, Ringwood,
Victoria, Australia
Penguin Books Canada Ltd, 10 Alcorn Avenue,
Toronto, Ontario, Canada M4V 3B2
Penguin Books (N.Z.) Ltd, 182–190 Wairau Road,
Auckland 10, New Zealand

Penguin Books Ltd, Registered Offices:
Harmondsworth, Middlesex, England

First American edition
Published in 1997 by Viking Penguin,
a member of Penguin Putnam Inc.

3 5 7 9 10 8 6 4 2

Page 714 constitutes an extension of this copyright page.

ISBN 0-670-87420-5

This book is printed on acid-free paper.

(∞)

Printed in the United States of America
Set in Monotype Bembo

Contents

List of Illustrations

PICTURE ACKNOWLEDGEMENTS (numbers refer to pages): Abraham Lincoln Brigade Archives: 202; The Advertising Archive, London: 250; Archive Photos, London: 206, 450, 461, 534, 562; British Film Institute, London: 142; Brown Brothers, Sterling, PA: 46, 163 bottom; Communist Party Picture Library, London: 12, 124, 180; Corbis UK, London: 38, 40, 48, 56, 57, 94, 99, 105, 110, 112, 148, 152, 163 top, 167, 199, 210, 215, 252, 255, 265, 269, 315, 316, 319, 326, 373, 379, 442, 456, 516, 519, 521, 531; Format Photographers, London: 402, 476, 482, 483, 490, 502, 545, 549, 552, 554, 558, 559; Glasgow Museums & Art Galleries, Glasgow: 21; Harry Goodwin, Manchester: 383; The Hulton Getty Picture Collection, London: endpapers, 24, 34, 65, 122, 138, 144, 178, 185, 188, 195, 223, 226, 231, 233, 239, 285, 289, 340, 344, 347, 351, 355, 362, 369, 400, 411, 418, 438; *Illustrated London News*, London: 308; Lee Miller Archives, East Sussex: 232; Mary Evans Picture Library, London: 13, 27, 70, 75; Paul Mattsson, London: 573; Mirror Syndication International, London: 221; Robert Miller Gallery, New York: 322; Rox-a-tronic Publishing, San Francisco: 567; Mark Rusher, London: 409; Solo Syndication, London: 143; The Vintage Magazine Co., London: 72, 283, 295, 299, 423; Justin Williams, London: 570; Yaffa Licensing, London: 214

Acknowledgements

I am extremely grateful to Rosalyn Baxandall, who acted as my American consultant on *A Century of Women*, sending me books, copies of articles and references, as well as commenting on the text and contributing valuable suggestions from her great store of knowledge. When I felt overwhelmed and my morale sagged, she restored my faith and spirits with her passionate interest in women's history. My agent, Faith Evans, and my editors, Margaret Bluman and Caroline White, have sustained me with their enthusiasm and encouragement over the years of research and writing. They also made useful criticisms of the various drafts. Thanks are due to John Stokes, who drew the lack of a general history of twentieth-century women in Britain to my attention, to Lily Richards for her picture research, to Lesley Levene for her copy-editing and to the workers at Penguin who contributed to the design and production of the book.

I was helped by a Simon Research Fellowship, 1993–4, and a University Research Fellowship from 1995 in the Sociology Department at Manchester University and by assistance from the Royal Literary Fund during 1995. I was a visiting professor at Carleton University, Ottawa, in the Political Economy Department in the summer of 1993 and was able to use the library for my research. I would like to thank the staff there, as well as those at the British Library, Duke University, North Carolina, the Fawcett Library, Manchester University Library, the Museum of Labour History, the Marx Memorial Library, and Hackney and Wellfleet public libraries.

Thank you to Juliet Ash, Barbara Bair, Lucy Bland, Eileen Boris, Elizabeth Ewen, Dana Frank, Hermione Harris, Delia Jarrett-Macauley, Sheila Jones, Fuyuki Karasawa, Cecilia Mackay, Jean McCrindle, Jacquetta May, Polly Pattullo, Lynne Segal, Ken Weller, Barbara Winslow and Rochelle Wortis for sending me material. For help in my search for data for the biographical section, thanks to Sally Alexander, Jill Craigie, Linda Gordon, Aileen Hernandez, Ann Firor Scott, Gertie Roche, Citizens' Clearinghouse for Hazardous Waste, *News and Letters*, Lucy Fielden of the Conservative Party Central Office, Nigel Fountain and Seumus Milne of the *Guardian*. For reading and commenting on parts of the manuscript, thanks to Alix Anderson, Anne Cottringer, Alana Dave, Monica Henriquez, Marc Karlin, Jean McCrindle and Sylvia Stevens.

Repetitive Strain Injury (upper limb disorder) made the early stages of *A Century of Women* particularly difficult. I owe a profound debt to the kindness of all those who enabled me to keep working. Lisa Vine typed the original proposal for the book, and Faith Evans and Rosie Mortimer helped with its presentation. Sonia Lane helped me with the typing of sections of the manuscript. Not simply adept at deciphering my handwriting, endlessly resourceful and reliable, she has expressed interest in the subject matter which has made it all seem worthwhile. Thanks also to the North East London PACT team of the Employment Service, Les Kingham of Dragon Dictate, Rob Stuthridge, ergonomic adviser, Toni Russell, Alastair Greetham and Elizabeth Maskell, physiotherapists, Bunny Martin, work-related injuries therapist of Back to Back, Dr Richard Pearson, Janet Forsyth, who lifted things for a crucial ten days, and Lynne Segal, Liz Heron, Cynthia Cockburn and Celia Weston for advice and support. I came belatedly to a computer and in my various panics have been rescued by Dragon Dictate, Trevor Griffiths, David Ruccio, John Peepul, Paul Atkinson, Radha Kumar, Manchester University Information Centre, Paul Fallows of Copley High School and the Employment Service.

Last but not least, thanks to Sian Clarke and Tom Blishen, for instruction on magazines for the eleven–thirteen age group. Large stretches of the manuscript were written to a background of jungle music provided by Will Atkinson and Owen Benn Williams Clarke – but I'm not sure if that really gets them into the thanks!

Introduction

The span of a century is vast. How can the multitude of events which become daily news, decade after decade, along with all those submerged personal experiences which women's history has sought out – births, betrayals, ecstasy or even the washing day – be encompassed between two covers? The answer is, of course, that all history is a compromise – a grappling between evidence and consciousness. The writer selects, condenses and moves through the past from a particular vantage point. This is as true for history which starts from women's lives and actions as for any other.

Another way of conceiving this stretch of time is to realize that a century is approximately two lifespans. As one generation overlaps with the other, individuals actually carry the memories of others along with their own. Personal memory thus lifts the decades along and several pasts can coexist in the present. For instance, as I was growing up in Leeds during the 1950s, I listened to my mother's repeated stories of her life. She told me of her girlhood in Sheffield early this century, of the Conservative Primrose League and of her sexually and intellectually adventurous friend Connie Copley, who went off to teacher training college during the First World War. In the early 1920s my mother accompanied my father to India when he got a job as a mining engineer in Bihar. Her accounts of her life there during the 1920s and early 1930s conveyed the claustrophobic isolation of the bungalow, her sexual restlessness, the romance of dances at the club and an implicit questioning of the racist assumptions of the Raj. The Depression, back in Leeds in the 1930s, in contrast, was a grim, tight time, when a packet of Wood-bine cigarettes spelt delight. Her descriptions of wartime Leeds merge with my own earliest hazy memories of Union Jacks and Home Guard helmets.

Did I ever really hear the sirens or just remember that I liked wearing my 'siren suit' with its leggings and zip? Through all my mother's stories weave lines from the songs she sang: 'If you were the only girl in the world', 'When the red red robin comes bob bob bobbing along', 'The sun has got his hat on, hip hip hip hooray'. They were to be drowned out by Tommy Steele and Elvis; rock 'n' roll and adolescence broke the pattern of the past. The colours all changed in the 1950s too. My early recollections of green and dark brown turn into pastel pink, blue and yellow. All that complacent, comfy modernity in its turn came to seem intolerable when I reached my late teens and donned beatnik black. Nonetheless, I had a toehold in the first half of the century, and, through my mother's recollections, traces of perception which stretch further back, a kind of borrowed sensibility. My own memories from the 1950s in their turn have folded into history. I am conscious of them as part of 'the past', while retaining a persistent and perplexing sense that they are contemporary.

Occasionally and incredibly a whole century can be a lifetime. In 1993 Bessie Delany was 104 and her sister Sadie was 106. Their story in *Having Our Say: The Delany Sisters' First 100 Years* describes 'Jim Crow' segregation in North Carolina, studying at Columbia in New York and life in Harlem as professional women in the 1920s. They survived the Depression and the war to support (in old age) the Civil Rights movement. They reflect on American society in the 1980s and 1990s from the vantage point of 100 years and, through their inherited memories, their grasp of historical change reaches back to the mid-nineteenth century; their father, born into slavery, became the first black Episcopalian bishop. Only at birthdays did this heavy load of history really hit them. As Bessie says, 'Turning 100 was the worst birthday of my life. I wouldn't wish it on my worst enemy. Turning 101 was not so bad. Once you're past that century mark, it's just not so shocking.'[1] But even past that century mark life brings surprises: Bessie observes wryly, 'Truth is, I never thought I'd see the day when people would be interested in hearing what two old Negro women have to say.'[2]

Few of us are likely to be having our say 100 years hence. Women's history serves instead: we inherit other lives and memories and hopefully hand them on. The growth of women's history in the last twenty-five years has fused personal memories and oral testimony, shifting the focus of interest and highlighting women's experience. This has been part of an ongoing recasting of historical 'knowledge'; who and what gets into the record of the past are contentious political matters and women's history, like labour history or black history, has contributed to the argument.

Women's history has been part of a pervasive impulse which has characterized the twentieth century to document everyday life and culture. The result has left much less to be taken for granted. As the images of femininity came to be seen as socially created, so did those of masculinity – from Valentino to John Wayne. Not simply gendered identity but the interaction of gender relationships in society have raised new questions about the organization of work, the structure of the family and attitudes towards sexuality. And by applying a gender lens to a whole range of issues, from social policy to industrial relations, from religion to the forms of protest in social movements, new historical perspectives have emerged. A mounting pile of historical studies of women's activism on the left – and on the right – continues to question the myth of passivity. These are currently raising a new set of issues about the contradictory views and responses of the category lumped together as 'women'. 'Women's history' is thus in the process of transcending its own boundaries by reaching outwards to contest how the existing topics of 'history' are interpreted. This is as it should be, for if history is a compromise with time, the demarcations we impose are equally artificial. 'Women' are no more apart than 'labour', for example, from life, from society and thus from history.

Such a realization becomes evident, however precisely, because women's history has been shifting the contours of inquiry over the last three decades. An assumption that women's lives mattered, or that what women have done has shaped this century, was not self-evident in the autumn of 1969, when I sat in a student bedroom at the trade union college, Ruskin, in Oxford with a small group of young women planning the first Women's Liberation conference. Around the same time, women in many countries were inspired by the beginnings of Women's

Liberation to ask questions of the past that we could not find answered in books. It is often the case that a reorientation in scholarship is stimulated by a perception of a crisis in contemporary society, and the initial writing was affected by the turmoil of the 1960s. However, research takes time. If it is to be sustained and flourish it needs a material and institutional context, and it has been in the United States, where women's studies have had an extensive impact, that the books have really burgeoned. One compelling reason for looking at America as well as Britain is the depth and extent of this work.

Another, however, is more personal: my own complex affair with the US. As for most of my generation, American popular culture was part of my teens. Over the course of the 1950s I abandoned *Carousel* for Johnny Ray, for rock 'n' roll, for blues and then for jazz. 'America' was both mythic and a muddle – a land of cowboys and bobby-soxers. After Betty Macdonald's *The Egg and I*, I read John Steinbeck's *The Grapes of Wrath* and was to discover 'the other America' through TV footage of civil rights protests. I was introduced to American history through this 'other America' of Pete Seeger's records and the blues, and my interest in American women's history was awakened, before the term existed, by Richard Drinnon's biography of Emma Goldman, *Rebel in Paradise*, in the early 1960s. So when the Women's Liberation groups first appeared and the impulsive internationalism of late 1960s radicalism brought ideas, journals and books across the Atlantic, the connection of 'women's history' did not seem so strange. Barbara Winslow was among a group of American feminists who played an influential role in the start of the British women's movement, and when I set about writing *Women, Resistance and Revolution* in 1969, she told me about the radical organizer Elizabeth Gurley Flynn and the miners' leader 'Mother' Jones. Along with Emma Goldman, I took to these unladylike characters as women after my own heart.

In 1974 I went on a speaking tour to America and met Rosalyn Baxandall, who was a member of one of the first radical feminist groups in New York. From then on she sent me books, copied articles and wrote innumerable letters and cards in which her own life and politics were interwoven by her fascination with women's history, as well as black history and labour history. Through her, and through other friends in the US who are feminist historians, I became more and more involved in trying to understand women's past in North America, as well as in Britain. Without really realizing it, I was assimilating the culture of this country which has influenced British society in so many ways. This book is consequently the outcome of the curiosity awakened through a continuing process of exchanging ideas – the result of my particular passion to assess what is similar and what is different.

As I wrote, it became evident that there were interconnections which do not become visible when one country's history is examined alone. For instance, ideas were transmitted internationally in the suffrage campaigns, peace movements and unions, along with birth control and social welfare organizing, in the period 1900–1930. Moreover, people, books, songs and films were going both ways across the Atlantic. Popular culture through the mass media of cinema and gramophone already linked the destinies of the two societies in the inter-war period. Bolton watched American soaps in the late 1930s and the British film industry was already creating a social identity of 'Britishness' for an American market. American investment, in electronics for instance, brought with it attitudes towards industrial organization in Britain. Women's lives have been shaped by these interacting changes in the design of the workplace, by new forms of communication and consumption.

Since the Second World War the dominant assumptions of American market capitalism and the radical resistance of social movements have both had an important influence in British society. Moral panics and conservative attitudes to social welfare have arrived from the US. But on the other hand, civil rights, black power, the women's movement, the gay movement and campaigns for environmental justice brought new ideas about rebellion to Britain. Taking the whole span of a century makes it possible to see how the interaction has been a two-way process, though the power of the American media is such that in more recent times Britain can seem to be on the receiving end of a one-way transmission. Historians being in somewhat less of a hurry than journalists are inclined to poke around for the underground diffusion of assumption.

The most intriguing puzzle is that here are two countries speaking the same language, yet pronouncing it very differently. Within each country, one vast and the other small, there are also diverse accents and distinct languages. Over the last 100 years there have been moments of intense connection and instances of utter incomprehension. There is a classic exam question, 'Compare and contrast': it is, of course, always easier said than done, especially because these are not homologous entities with synchronized impulsions. I have thus chosen an open-ended narrative in which there is space for what is distinct. But I hope that in spanning a century the overlaps and echoes become more evident and that this book will make it more possible to reflect on the remarkable changes and interchanges in the lives of British and American women in the last 100 years.

Chapter 1

1900–1914

BRITAIN

The New Woman

A new century demanded a new woman and she duly arrived, though opinion differed on how she was to be defined and what her freedom entailed. There was, for example, the rebellious young woman created in 1909 by H. G. Wells in his novel *Ann Veronica* who rejected the 'wrappered' life of the suburbs for one of sexual and intellectual independence in London. Denounced by the *Spectator* as 'this poisonous book'[1] and banned in libraries, *Ann Veronica* shocked, said Wells, because he had depicted a woman who 'wanted a particular man who excited her and she pursued him and got him. With gusto . . .'[2] His own well-publicized views on free love and his affair with Amber Reeves, who partly inspired the character of Ann Veronica, added to the scandal.

Wells's portrayal of the feminist Miss Miniver in the novel caricatured the suffrage movement, but in fact the militant agitation for the vote opened up a wider radical debate about women's psychological and sexual freedom. For example, independence was the watchword of the feminist journal the *Freewoman*, which, between 1911 and 1913, linked political rights with personal, economic and social change. Independence for some feminists meant sexual equality with men. Others saw it as detachment: men were pushed to the margins by the Swedish feminist Ellen Key, who advised women 'to regard men merely as a means to a child'[3] in her influential book *Love and Marriage*, which was translated into English in 1911.

It was not all talk. A rebellious minority set out to defy convention by opposing marriage in their own lives. They included anarchist

7

women like Rose Witcop, from the east London Jewish community, who lived in a free union with the anarchist Guy Aldred and the witty socialist feminist writer Rebecca West, who was to have a child with H. G. Wells. For some freedom meant rejecting not only marriage but also men. When the suffragette music-hall star Kitty Marion was in prison for militancy in the campaign for the vote, a fellow prisoner wrote to her, 'Thank goodness men are not the only pebbles on the beach to love, though they think they are.'[4] Small groups of women with 'advanced views' were to be found debating marriage and free love, adopting short hair and artistic styles of house decoration and clothing in provincial cities and small towns. Schoolteachers, clerical workers and skilled working-class women who were active in both the suffrage movement and socialism were likely to be part of this radical culture. Nor were the London suburbs all conformity. Ruth Slate and Eva Slawson's diaries and letters, later to be published as *Dear Girl*, provide a glimpse into a lower-middle-class culture which was politically and sexually inquiring. For example, Eva Slawson developed a passionate relationship with a working-class woman called Minna. This was a milieu in which radical Christianity, temperance groups, the Freewoman Circle and socialist speakers fostered criticism of conservatism of all kinds. External convention was disregarded for an inner moral sense – a theme which was to preoccupy the writer E. M. Forster in his portrayal of the Schlegel sisters in *Howards End*, 'new women' who found distinct solutions to the problem of how to balance the inward and outer pressures of conformity.

Less earnest rebels were shocking the pioneers of women's education. Women students at Queen Margaret Hall, Glasgow, demanded the right to make their own rules and entertain male visitors in 1902. Dorothy L. Sayers, well known later for her Lord Peter Wimsey detective stories, was spotted in Somerville, Oxford, in 1912, sporting 'a three-inch-wide scarlet riband round her head' and startling earrings, 'a scarlet and green parrot in a gilt cage pendant almost to each shoulder'.[5] Another dressy Oxford student who was rebuked for her clothes declared defiantly, 'I won't, I *won't*, I won't be a dowd!'[6]

Of course, they were not the first generation of new women. The very dons who seemed so stuffy had probably been 'new women' in their day, defying male prejudices which excluded women from the universities. The difference was that in the period 1900–1914 the personal aspiration for freedom was accompanied by a militant suffrage movement and widespread social upheaval. The spirit of rebellion reached deep into the conservative fastnesses of British life. In the northern spa town of Buxton, for instance, a young Vera Brittain, clad in 'white satin and pearls', was still 'gyrating to the strains of "Dreaming" and "The Vision of Salome"'[7] at the 1912 High Peak Hunt Ball. But as she circled the dance floor 'in the arms of physically boisterous and conversationally inept young men',[8] she was planning her escape from provincial young-ladyhood.

Politics

'Will the Liberal government give votes to working women?'[9] demanded Christabel Pankhurst and Annie Kenney at a Liberal Party meeting in the Manchester Free Hall in 1905. Theirs were the voices of the militant movement for the vote which was to reach beyond Lancashire and have an impact in many lands. Christabel Pankhurst came from a middle-class family which had a long history of campaigning for women's suffrage and social reform in Manchester. Her mother, Emmeline Pankhurst, had formed the Women's Social and Political Union (WSPU) in 1903. Annie Kenney was one of the Lancashire cotton workers, a group which had close links to both middle-class reform and labour politics from the late nineteenth century. Christabel, a dynamic young law student, already displayed a keen sense of how to publicize her politics. As they were hustled out of the hall, Christabel carefully and deliberately spat. They were duly charged with obstruction and assault. When they refused to pay their fines, they stayed several days in jail, to the embarrassment of the Liberal political élite. It was a sign of things to come; Christabel was to be a brilliant publicist for 'the Cause'.

'The Cause', however, had other advocates. Millicent Fawcett, veteran campaigner for the vote and leader of the much larger National Union of Women's Suffrage Societies (NUWSS), was inclined to regard the publicity Christabel Pankhurst attracted as something they could do without. In her autobiography, *What I Remember*, she remarked acidly, 'Instead of the withering contempt of silence the Anti-Suffrage

Spectacle and the Suffrage

Crowds would gather to watch the suffrage processions, which had a carnival atmosphere with their beautifully designed banners, the sashes in the purple, green and white of the Women's Social and Political Union, or the red and white of the National Union of Women's Suffrage Societies. In *The Spectacle of Women*, Lisa Tickner describes the women in their light summer dresses, straw hats and parasols, carrying irises and lilies, or proudly wearing black academic gowns, and the Men's Leagues, grey-coated, with writer Laurence Housman's banner in black and gold. On one suffrage march in April 1909, women dressed in the clothes of their trades, nurses and midwives in uniform, pottery workers in aprons or smocks, pit-brow women in shawls, poultry farmers carrying eggs, cooks with copper pans and bundles of herbs, demonstrating the range of women demanding the vote. Among them marched several prominent actresses, bearing the banner of the Actresses' Franchise League.

This was formed in 1908, drawing legendary actresses like Ellen Terry and Mrs Kendall, along with contemporary stars Violet Vanbrugh and Eva and Decima Moore, to its first meeting, where the actress and feminist campaigner Cicely Hamilton was among the speakers. The feminist actresses tutored women in public speaking, appeared in the dramatic pageants of the suffrage movement and acted in feminist plays. Ellen Terry's daughter Edy – her stage name was Ailsa Craig – was a key figure in putting on this political theatre. Not only the theatre but also popular entertainment was affected by feminism, when the popular music-hall artiste Kitty Marion joined the militants.

The suffrage movement was ingenious in expressing its political message visually: propaganda ranged from posters and postcards to inkstands and cups. Its iconography ranged from heroic figures like Joan of Arc to downtrodden women workers and reassuring domestic pictures of suffrage supporters making or cooking vegetarian dinners.

The anti-suffrage lobby responded with a set of hostile stereotypes: women in the suffrage movement were shrews, viragos, hysterics, unwomanly women who abandoned their children and lacked feminine allure. Their adversaries hinted at sexual frustration and masochistic gratification in caricatures of suffragettes. The battle for women's rights was not just about constitutional reform but about the images and symbols which shaped assumptions.

✳

papers came out day after day with columns of hysterical verbiage directed against our movement.'[10] These 'constitutionalists' in the NUWSS remained the majority active in the national network and on the mass demonstrations.

However, it was to be the militants – or 'the suffragettes', as the conservative paper the *Daily Mail* labelled them – who set the pace. They stormed the House of Commons, heckled cabinet ministers, broke windows and went to prison. The police were out of their depths in dealing with these insubordinate middle-class women who did not fit existing stereotypes of criminality. When a young middle-class woman, Victoria Liddiard, travelled from Bristol, deliberately positioned herself next to a policeman and threw a stone through the War Office window, she recalled, 'He couldn't believe that I'd done it.'[11] This determined lawbreaker was to become a lifelong campaigner for the ordination of women priests.

The ingenuity and daring of the suffragettes exploded gender stereotypes. In a few short years they were to challenge all the prevailing assumptions about womanhood. Even the Prime Minister's golf course was invaded. They also displayed great endurance. In 1909 Alice Paul, a young American social worker who was later to play a prominent part in the US feminist movement, climbed on to the roof of St Andrew's Hall, Glasgow, in an attempt to get into a cabinet minister's meeting. She stayed up there for a whole night in freezing rain before she was discovered.

In the same year Marion Wallace Dunlop began a hunger strike while in jail and the forced feeding of suffragette prisoners began. This

Suffrage militants released from Holloway Prison, north London.

was a brutal and humiliating procedure: the woman was held down, a gag was placed in her mouth and tubes were then inserted in her nose and throat. Not only was this gruesome ritual painful in itself, but it took place against the background of groans and cries as other victims were force-fed. The women barricaded themselves into their cells, so the crashing of crowbars, blocks and wedges echoed round the prison too. Kitty Marion described the extreme psychological response evoked by the pain and violation of forced feeding: 'I got up, dressed and smashed every bit of glass I could reach.'[12] When her tormentors returned that afternoon, she got on to the bed and started screaming with all her might.

Forced feeding provoked a public outcry and the government introduced the Prisoners (Temporary Discharge for Ill Health) Bill in 1913.

This was the notorious Cat and Mouse Act, which released prisoners weakened by hunger who were then rearrested when they recovered. The violence against property, however, continued to escalate and suffragettes evaded arrest by being smuggled into meetings in disguise or hidden in laundry baskets. In 1913 Emily Wilding Davison, who had already tried to kill herself to prevent forced feeding in jail, flung herself in front of the King's horse at the Derby.

Militancy as a tactic had contradictory effects. The bravery of the suffragettes won them admiration, not only from women but from men of all classes. Dockers formed part of Emmeline Pankhurst's bodyguard when she spoke in Glasgow in 1914 and Lord Lytton, brother of Lady Constance Lytton, whose health was permanently damaged by forced feeding, spoke in favour of the suffrage bills. The Men's Union for Political Enfranchisement was formed in 1909 to support the Women's Social and Political Union. However, militancy provoked considerable derision and hostility. The *Glasgow Evening Citizen* described the feminists' male supporters as 'poodles of the male sex, a contemptible Chase-me-Charlie breed'.[13] A correspondent in the *Derby Daily Express* in June 1914 advocated 'shaving the heads of every militant suffragette' and using 'the cat o' nine tails'.[14] A psychological explanation for women's demand for the right to vote was provided by a letter writer who opined that 'unmarried and childless women must have an outlet for their free energies'.[15]

'Suffragettes Who Have Never Been Kissed': anti-suffrage propaganda postcard, 1909.

The WSPU itself was affected by the militant tactics, for they strengthened a tendency already within the organization towards an authoritarian centralization. Christabel especially was extremely autocratic and demanded absolute obedience. Opposition of any kind led to ostracism and so there was a series of splits. Teresa Billington-Greig, a schoolteacher from Lancashire, was an early critic of the lack of democracy. As WSPU organizer in Scotland, she managed to establish a more responsive and open structure, but in 1907 she left to form the Women's Freedom League with Charlotte Despard, a socialist and supporter of the Irish nationalist Sinn Fein.

The final division came in 1913, when Charlotte Despard joined Sylvia Pankhurst and the Irish socialist James Connolly on the platform of the Albert Hall in London at a meeting called in protest against the lock-out of Dublin transport workers and the imprisonment of Irish trade union leader James Larkin. Christabel was furious at this link between suffrage and labour, and Sylvia, forced out of the WSPU in January 1914, made her base the East London Federation of the Suffragettes, with its working-class membership and links to the local labour movement.

The suffrage struggle created bitter conflicts which cut through all existing political allegiances. There were disagreements among socialists about whether to demand women's suffrage on the same terms as men, which would exclude most working-class women, or to adopt the wider policy of adult suffrage, which would include groups of working-class men who were still without the franchise. The Women's Liberal Federation was thwarted by the Liberal leadership's persistent rejection of their efforts to exert constitutional pressure for the vote. In Ireland supporters of Home Rule and the suffrage were faced with a dilemma when the Liberals under Asquith in 1910 promised Home Rule if the Irish nationalists would support the government in opposing women's suffrage.

There were differing theoretical perspectives too. Many liberal and socialist supporters of women's political rights saw this as an extension of individual rights; others based their case on an organic concept of the state and citizenship – a view endorsed by some social imperialists who called on women to serve the cause of Empire. For instance, Beatrice Webb, the Fabian socialist, finally came round to supporting votes for women not as a 'claim to rights or an abandonment of women's particular obligations, but a desire more effectively to fulfil their functions by shaping the control of state action'.[16] Arguments based on women's special qualities or circumstances coexisted with the claim to equality from the start. Moreover, some feminists were asserting that women were not just different from men, they were superior. Christabel Pankhurst, for instance, increasingly came to define the movement as a crusade against men, contrasting the purity of women with male depravity.

Women's suffrage had some Conservative supporters, such as Lady Betty Balfour, the Countess of Selborne and Lady Knightley, who were constitutional suffragists. In *The Tories and the People*, Martin Pugh points out that Conservative suffragists offered their party a way of embarrassing the Liberals and Labour by taking over the issue of votes for women. Indeed, the WSPU increasingly gambled on provoking the Tories to support women's suffrage to prevent disorder, with Christabel Pankhurst urging Tory support to prevent the women's movement going to the left. In contrast, Charlotte Despard and the Women's Freedom League sought to persuade both Liberal and Labour men to support poor women's particular claims on society. At a meeting with the Liberal leaders Asquith and Lloyd George in 1911, she said, 'I plead here for the weakest and most helpless women . . . the unmarried mother, the so-called illegitimate child, the widowed mother working night and day for her child.'[17] This conviction that the vote was necessary to secure social reforms like better pay, housing and education, along with school meals, nurseries and medical services, was shared by a group of Labour women which included Isabella Ford, a middle-class socialist organizer of trade unions for women, and Margaret and Rachel McMillan, campaigners for children. In 1912, they formed an alliance with the constitutional suffragists in the National Union of Women's Suffrage Societies with the help of its younger radical members, such as Catherine Marshall. Jill Liddington, the biographer of Selina Cooper, a working-class woman who became an organizer for the NUWSS in Lancashire, describes how she took the demand for the suffrage to factory gates, to mothers' meetings in northern chapels, to groups of the Women's Temperance Association and to trade unions. In 1912 Selina Cooper gained the backing of the miners and finally, in 1914, the Labour

Party voted for women's suffrage under pressure from the miners' union.

The suffrage movement raised issues of class and gender relationships in quite personal ways, as well as in the public political sphere. Not only did women of differing classes work together in the campaign but there was an ethos of common sacrifice which could defy class privilege. When Lady Constance Lytton was examined and released because she had a weak heart, rather than being force-fed with the other women, she cut her hair short, put on the clothes of a working-class woman and again threw a stone. Unprotected by her class position, she was unceremoniously force-fed; the subsequent heart attack left her right hand paralysed. At a more everyday level there was, however, a certain wariness and friction. Selina Cooper and a working-class supporter of the WSPU, Hannah Mitchell, were both very aware of the class differences between themselves and the middle-class leadership of suffrage groups. Even Sylvia Pankhurst, despite her determined links to the labour movement, retained some of the Pankhurst hauteur. Nonetheless, in the context of the British class structure the very existence of such cross-class collaboration was extraordinary. Jessie Stephen, a domestic servant who began her political training in Glasgow when she was twelve in labour women's groups, then joined the WSPU and later campaigned with Sylvia Pankhurst, recalled, 'We had a curious combination. You had very wealthy women, upper-class women, and the ordinary working class, but we got on well together.'[18]

The suffrage movement also probed deep into the intimate hierarchies of gender relations. In *Marriage as a Trade*, Cicely Hamilton scorned those women of the comfortable classes who were content with chivalry:

Personally this attitude . . . an attitude of voluntary abasement assumed in order that men may know the pleasure of condescension – is the only thing that ever makes me ashamed of being a woman; since it is the outward and visible expression of an inward servility that has eaten and destroyed a soul.[19]

There were very many women who did not agree. Indeed, though the feminist movement had a decisive influence on the politics and culture of the pre-war era, the majority of women joined organizations not to transform gender relations, or society as a whole, but to conserve women's sphere. The Tory women's organization, the Primrose League, had over half a million members and it too developed innovative social forms of mobilizing women across classes, stirring imperial sentiment with lantern shows and recitations of Rudyard Kipling during the Boer War. Also based on solidly conservative principles was the Mothers' Union, which had 400,000 members, and the Girls' Friendly Society, with 240,000. There was an Anti-Suffrage Campaign as well, which argued that women would lose their special influence if they claimed the right to the franchise. Ironically, however, its members did not escape accusations of an unwomanly preoccupation with public affairs. And when Britain's dependence on food and raw materials from abroad made tariff reform an issue from 1903, the womanly question of the 'Big Loaf' of free trade versus the 'Little Loaf' of tariff protection landed Conservative women in the Primrose League in the midst of national politics. They combined with the Liberal Unionist women in demanding that trade with the Empire be expanded.

Poverty and the conditions of motherhood troubled imperialists, Liberals and socialists alike – though for differing reasons. After the Boer War there was a panic that eugenic decline was reducing the British stock and putting the Empire in danger. Some Conservatives came to support social reform in order to compete with Germany. The Liberal Party was under pressure from reformers within its ranks and Labour was a new political force. Labour women's organizations like the Women's Co-operative Guild and the Women's Labour League were also pressing for action. From 1907 Liberal and Labour women on borough councils were promoting better schools, healthier housing, public baths and wash-houses, and improved maternity services. Local government served to extend a womanly sphere of responsibility into society.

The movement for better motherhood had several political meanings. Middle-class social investigators pointed to the need for education and more professional care in pregnancy. Working-class women's organizations sought changes which would provide material help to poor mothers and were also concerned about democratic involvement in policies and provision. A preoccupation with social motherhood could thus emphasize working-class women's duties as reproducers to society or develop into radical political demands for new social and economic rights. Echoing the ideas of the American feminist Charlotte Perkins

Gillman, whose novel *What Diantha Did* was being serialized in the socialist *Daily Herald*, Mabel Harding declared in 1912, 'Women are developing a social consciousness; they are becoming maternal in the grand sense of the word, seeking the best, not only for their own children, but for those of other women who are placed in less fortunate circumstances than themselves,' adding that 'motherhood in its wide sense' involved 'reaching out after all children' and a substantial pro-gramme of reform which included, 'pure food, a municipal milk supply, healthy schools, the raising of the school age, sound moral training, without any squeamish holding back knowledge of the facts of life that boys and girls should know, the abolition of sweated labour'.[20]

The reforms that were achieved did not meet the reformers' more radical hopes and were inclined to be stronger on regulation than on the redistribution of resources. In 1902 the training of midwives was introduced and the 1910 Midwives Act prevented those not certified from practising. The 1906 Education Act enabled local authorities to provide food for schoolchildren, and the medical inspection of schoolchildren followed in 1907, along with municipal milk schemes for babies. As a result of the 1908 Children's Act parents could be prosecuted for neglecting their children's health. The National Insurance Act of 1911 included a maternity benefit of 39s. for insured workers and established a system of health visitors. However, the Act did not cover sick women or recognize that women's domestic labour contributed to the family's livelihood. In his study of the state and the poor in twentieth-century Britain, *Poor Citizens*, David Vincent points out:

The regulations and the advice saw women only as mothers, and mothers only as dependants. There was no interest in the unmarried, and little sense that once they became wives their bodily and mental well-being was of importance in its own right, irrespective of their capacity to bear and raise children.[21]

Labour women's organizations did, however, begin to see the state as a legitimate provider of social services. Mrs Layton, for example, a midwife, took part in the Women's Co-operative Guild's Maternity Campaign, which, from 1912, lobbied the Liberal government to extend maternity and sickness benefit to poorer working-class women. The

Women's Co-operative Guild argued that this should be increased and paid for a longer period. They wanted more health visitors, women doctors and maternity hospitals, and pioneered demands for mothers' and babies' health centres, home helps for women who were ill and milk depots to secure the supply of uncontaminated milk.

A countervailing suspicion of external intrusion into domestic life persisted in working-class communities, for the workhouse system of poor relief had firmly fixed the idea that dependence on the state was necessarily demeaning, while generations of upper-class do-gooders had fostered a hatred of patronage and interference. Thus charitable schemes to reform the nutritional basis of diets, socialist women's proposals for co-operative housekeeping and demands for public services could all be viewed askance.

Despite this scepticism, campaigners for improved conditions for mothers and children established two important principles in the pre-war period. They showed that mothering was the concern of society and thus a responsibility to be partly shared through co-operative efforts and state resources being made available for women's welfare. For the liberal social reformer Eleanor Rathbone, this meant an allowance which would bring income to women and children. Margaret MacDonald of the Women's Labour League wanted housewives to develop policy on the home. For Labour women, social redistribution and democracy were linked. The Women's Co-operative Guild, for example, wanted more working-class women on local maternity committees and a Ministry of Health for Maternity and Infant Life staffed by women.

Work

Women's dependence on men in the family was reinforced by their low rates of pay. It was assumed from the start of their working lives that their position as wage earners was temporary. A study in Birmingham, for example, by E. Cadbury, M. Cecile Matheson and G. Shawn, *Women's Work and Wages: A Phase of Life in an Industrial City*, found that in 1901 the average wage of young women was only 10s. a week, 4s. less than they judged was necessary to keep healthy and respectable. In the woollen manufacturing region of Colne Valley in Yorkshire, wages for young girls began at 5s. and slowly rose to £1 at

The Arts and Crafts Movement and Women

Simplicity in design, the use of good materials and craft skill marked the Arts and Crafts movement, which had considerable influence in the early twentieth century. May Morris, daughter of William Morris, who inspired this aesthetic approach, started the Women's Guild in 1907. Initially women concentrated on 'feminine' crafts like fine embroidery, but they soon participated in the revival of craft metalwork, jewellery, enamelling, stained glass, hand-weaving, bookbinding and illustration.

Arts and Crafts' principles stressed that beauty was everyday. As Jessie Newbery, who incorporated needlework into artistic design at the Glasgow School of Art, put it in an article in *The Studio*, in 1897, 'I believe . . . that the design and decoration of a pepper pot is as important, in its degree, as the conception of a cathedral.'[22]

The Glasgow School of Art developed its own distinctive style. Though the designs of Charles Rennie Mackintosh are the best known, Glasgow produced several women designers and decorative artists besides Jessie Newbery. Frances MacDonald MacNair taught metalwork at the Glasgow School, and her sister Margaret MacDonald, who married Charles Rennie Mackintosh, produced the decorative work for the houses he designed. Ann Macbeth designed flowing 'aesthetic' fashions in the 1900s based on her teacher Jessie Newbery's clothes. By using cheaper materials, like linen and cotton, and combining them with detachable artistically embroidered collars and cuffs, she brought artistic dress to a new market of women on slender means. Ann Macbeth wanted to elevate home embroidery into an art and advocated teaching it to boys as well as girls at school. Her textbook *Educational Needlecraft*, written with Margaret Swanson in 1911, was influential not only in Britain but in Australia, New Zealand, Canada, India, South Africa, the West Indies and the United States.

The Arts and Crafts movement provided women with creative work by elevating traditional skills into an aspect of art. But women's position in the movement was an ambiguous one. In her study of women in the Arts and Crafts movement *Angel in the Studio*, Anthea Callen points out

Ann Macbeth in her embroidered collar: 'Artistic Dress for
Advanced Women of Slender Means', *c.* 1900.

that some leading male figures like Charles Ashbee were unsympathetic
to ideas of women's equality. In 'Threading the Beads: Women in
Art in Glasgow, 1870–1920', Liz Bird also observes that despite the
movement's intention of integrating arts and crafts, sexual divisions
remained: 'The decorative arts are female, they support the male arts of
architecture and art.'[23]

Nonetheless, arts and crafts were closely associated with the feminist
movement. Ann Macbeth regarded her work for the Women's Social
and Political Union as part of a wider commitment to art serving the
community. Mary Lowndes, who started a stained-glass firm, created
suffrage banners, drawing on stained-glass techniques and heraldic
imagery. Sylvia Pankhurst, herself a former art student, designed material
for WSPU propaganda – sashes, badges, jewellery and motoring scarves
– and when pageants were held in Edinburgh in 1907 and 1909, art
students at the Glasgow School produced the banners and costumes.

the beginning of the First World War. Moreover, the custom of tipping the money into their mothers' aprons left the young workers with only a penny for every shilling.

Even jobs open to the middle class – teaching, nursing and clerical work – were low-paid. Post office clerks were envied because they were civil servants with a seven–eight-hour day, sick leave, annual holidays and pension schemes, but women sorters got only £38 a year in the 1900s, and, because the civil service operated a marriage bar, sorters and clerks had to leave if they married. Equal pay was raised in unions representing clerks and teachers where women's work was clearly comparable to men's, only to be met with hostility from male teachers.

The better-paid professions were mainly barred to women. There were still only 553 women doctors in Britain by 1912; women were excluded from the upper ranks of the civil service, the law and account- ancy. Only a minority graduated from women's colleges at Oxford, Cambridge and London universities, but a growing demand for higher education from the middle classes contributed to new universities being established in towns like Reading. A few women graduates went on to academic posts in universities or teacher training colleges. Those whose families were able to pay fees of around £60 a year could join one of the university settlements, which provided a training in social work and were pioneering imaginative and humane approaches to nursery education and schools for children with disabilities. Some followed Beatrice Webb and Clementina Black into the expanding field of social investigation. Social service was not lucrative, but it provided an escape from the restrictions of the middle- and upper-class feminine world.

Some middle-class and a few of the better-educated working-class young women in London found their way into the new clerical jobs as 'typewriters' in the expanding financial sector. But most young women workers were far from being autonomous, Ann Veronica-style 'new women'. They existed in a network of interdependent familial relations which could be both supportive and restrictive. For them work might improve personal status in the family, but it was not about self-fulfilment and independence.

The trade union organizer Mary Macarthur summed up women workers' predicament: 'While women are badly paid because of their unorganized condition they may be unorganized mainly because they are badly paid.'[24] A draper's daughter from Glasgow, she was a member of the shop workers' union, before becoming president of the Federation of Women Workers in 1906. Formed after paper-bag makers in Edinburgh stayed out on strike for eight weeks, this new organization brought together several small societies which had been struggling to mobilize low-paid women. Mary Macarthur and Margaret Bondfield, another Fabian socialist from the shop workers' union, developed an evangelical style of trade unionism, making determined efforts to go out to unorganized women workers.

Low pay, irregular employment and domestic responsibilities made it uphill work to bring women workers into the organized movement, but nonetheless the numbers of women in trade unions increased between 1906 and 1914. The Federation grew from 2,000 to 20,000, while the overall membership, which included members of mixed unions, went up from 166,803 to 357,956. The efforts of organizers were helped by Lloyd George's 1911 Insurance Act, which, by allowing friendly societies and trade unions to administer health and employment insurance, created a practical incentive to join. The northern textile workers who campaigned for the vote continued to be the largest group of organized women workers. Smaller groups belonged to the Dundee Jute and Flax Workers and the National Union of Boot and Shoe Workers, as well as the organizations for teachers and clerks.

Large numbers of women, however, remained outside the trade unions. Domestic servants and shop workers had little freedom because they lived in, their personal lives were scrutinized by employers and they worked long hours. Home-workers, washerwomen, child-minders and small traders made contributions as working daughters and mothers which helped the working-class family budget, but they survived outside the formal economy. In occupations such as fishing and agriculture, women's unpaid labour was essential for survival but continued to be part of the family economy. Many factory workers were unorganized too, not only those in the smaller places which produced clothing and food, where work could be spasmodic and seasonal, but even in the vast Singer's sewing-machine plant at Kilbowie, Clydebank, in Scotland, where modern mass-production techniques had already been introduced by 1906.

From 1907 there was a wave of industrial rebellion against the consequences of mass production: speed-up and low wages. Ideas of workers' control and direct action at the workplace were being developed by left-wing socialists and syndicalists. Taking them at their word when Singer's sacked a woman for not working hard enough, the workforce went on strike; thousands of young men and women paraded with bands through the streets. Singer's broke the strike by conceding higher wages, and not employing the militants. New lessons of industrial organization were being learned by both sides.

By 1910 the rebellious spirit had affected low-paid unorganized women, whose livelihoods were precarious. Strikes erupted in London in 1910–14 among jam and pickle workers, rag pickers, bottle washers, laundry women, envelope, biscuit, cocoa and tin-box makers, and distillery and confectionery workers, who were earning between 5s. and 10s. a week. Outside the organized trade union movement, they were nonetheless part of communities familiar with resistance to the police and bailiffs. Mary Macarthur's policy was to try to unionize

Organizing the unorganized: women strikers in Millwall,
east London, early in 1914.

women workers into the Federation while they were in action, but events moved so quickly she was not always able to be on the spot. One strike she did not reach was that of the women in the Scots herring fishing trade, who travelled down the east coast to Great Yarmouth. They worked long hours for low pay, gutting and packing the fish, and slept crammed together in digs at night. In 1911 a woman put a red rag on a broom and went around the yards to get workers out on strike. This kind of spontaneous resistance was characteristic of women who were outside formal organizations.

There was an extensive debate about the causes of poverty in the pre-war period. Though the emphasis upon making women better managers of the family budget persisted, there was a growing realization among social investigators that the low income of working-class families was the real problem. A legal minimum wage was being discussed and the Fabian social investigator Clementina Black argued that this should be a living wage – enough to survive in decent conditions. An exhibition of the 'sweated industries' in London in 1906 demonstrated how women did sewing or made cigarettes at home for low pay and contributed to awareness of 'the sweating system', subcontracting of work to homes or small workshops. Fear of contamination – panic about the eugenic quality of motherhood – along with the growing conviction that better-paid workers were more efficient and productive, contributed to the anti-sweating campaign. In 1909 the Trades Boards Act set up a framework for fixing rates in trades like chain-making, box-making, lace-making and clothing. In 1910 Cradley Heath chain makers in the Midlands, who worked at home, became involved in a struggle for the rates fixed by the Trades Board, gaining support from trade unionists, socialists and feminists. State intervention in wage rates set a new precedent which initially raised hopes of ending 'sweated' pay.

Some middle-class campaigners against homework, along with some labour women, thought that married women should not work. In contrast, feminists, the Fabian women's group and women trade union organizers believed that work and earning a wage were crucial if women were to gain independence and confidence. 'Knowledge is power,' wrote Mary Macarthur in *The Woman Worker* in 1908. 'Organization is power. Knowledge and organization mean the opening of the cage door.'[25]

Attitudes to women's work were bound up with deep-rooted assumptions about women's place. But these attitudes were not uniform. Within the working class there were significant regional differences. In the Staffordshire Potteries, for instance, it was assumed that women continued to work when they had families. A woman who did not contribute to the family income was seen as lazy, and it was customary for men to help with cleaning and child-care. Moreover, economic change was drawing single women into paid employment. By 1911 nearly three-quarters of single women were in paid work. The effect of this shift was not simply material. It was accompanied by a consciousness in both the labour and the feminist movements that the organization of women meant breaking profound and interconnecting habits of subordination.

Daily Life

Cicely Hamilton observed in *Marriage as a Trade* that women's work in the home contributed to the acceptance of the sweated trades. Domestic toil was part of a culture which meant the woman 'learned to look upon herself . . . as a creature from whom much must be demanded and to whom little must be given'.[26] Low self-regard, however, affected women very differently, depending on their class. When the young upper-class Lady Violet Bonham-Carter asked her governess how she was going to spend her life, the answer was quick and decisive: 'Until you are eighteen you will do lessons.' 'And afterwards?' 'And afterwards you will do nothing.'[27]

The ideal of leisure was becoming feasible to a wider stratum lower down the social scale. Harley Granville-Barker, a playwright sympathetic to feminism, made a buyer in his play about an upper-class fashion house, *The Madras House* (1909), exclaim:

But it is the middle-class woman of England that is waiting for me. The woman who still sits at the parlour window of her provincial villa, pensively gazing through the laurel bushes . . . She must have her chance to dazzle and conquer that is every woman's birthright, be she a Duchess of Mayfair or a doctor's wife in Leicester. And remember, gentlemen, the middle-class women of England . . . think of them in bulk . . . they form one of the greatest money-spending machines the world has ever seen.[28]

In *The Edwardians: The Remaking of British Society*, Paul Thompson describes a society marked by ostentatious inequality: a rich family might consume in a single meal more than a charwoman and her family had to spend in two years. The patterns of consumption, moreover, were changing. In 1909 Gordon Selfridge brought the American-style department store to London. New luxury products for the wealthy, like hand-made motor cars and pioneer aeroplanes, were visible marks of privilege.

In contrast, the average working-class family was still living close to subsistence. Between 1909 and 1913 Maud Pember Reeves (mother of Amber), along with other members of the Fabian socialist women's group, studied the incomes and budgets of south London working-class families and wrote an influential account of what it was like to live on around a pound a week. They showed that one-third of a family's income went on wretched accommodation which was damp and overcrowded. Whole families crammed into one bed or sofa, the babies in banana crates for cots. Cooking healthy food was more or less impossible in these circumstances. Most women had only a frying pan, a burnt

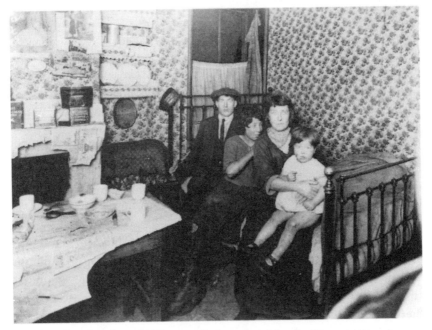

East London slum dwellers: unlikely material for the 'Imperial Race'.

saucepan and a kettle. Many families had no oven and few could afford the money for gas ovens fed by pennies in the slot meters, except on Sundays.

Diet varied by region. In *A Woman's Place*, Elizabeth Roberts notes that vegetables were cooked in Barrow and Lancaster, while in Preston, a mill town where married women worked from 6 a.m. to 5.30 p.m., convenience foods like fish and chips, pies and cakes were increasingly popular. But families had little to spare for the kind of mass-produced goods that were appearing in the United States. The multiple chain stores in Britain, like the Home and Colonial, still tended to be selling food – brightly labelled produce which brought imperial conquest into the kitchen.

'Doing nothing' was never an option, even among the better-off working-class families. Cleaning and washing involved a great deal of labour. Few artisans' houses had fitted baths and water had to be boiled in pots and kettles. Rugs had to be beaten and carpets brushed by hand; tea-leaves on the mat helped to absorb the dust. The lino or tiles inside had to be scrubbed, along with the steps outside, while washing clothes took all day. Mrs Murray of Derbyshire describes washday at the turn of the century:

First of all you sorted out your whites from your coloureds and put them all in to soak. Then you gave everything a good scrub with a brush on a washboard, especially the collars and cuffs. Then you boiled up the whites in the copper, poking them down all the time with a wooden stick and plenty of soap – pieces cut off a big block. After that you rinsed and blued them . . . to bring the whites up white. Then the coloureds had to be done, everything rinsed and put through the mangle. Then out on the line to dry. Then you had to clean out the copper and scrub it ready for next time.[29]

And this wasn't the end of it: there were collars, cuffs, tablecloths and curtains to be starched, not to mention all the ironing done with heavy irons heated on the stove.

For poor women it was not the emptiness of life which was the problem but an intricate domestic economy in which unpaid domestic labour was combined with low-paid activities. Relationships of mutual aid within both families and communities made an absolute division between employment and housework unreal. Ellen Ross describes one example in east London:

Mrs Barnes, whose husband provided her with a very scanty income, sold cooked sheep's heads and pigs' feet from a stall outside the Britannia Theatre in Hoxton, a business with which she had been helped by the local butcher. Her own economics included selling her rabbit skins and the remains of the sheep's heads to a nearby shop; her daughter sold rags and jam jars to ragmen. Mrs Barnes gave needy neighbours in Norfolk Gardens, Hoxton, free meals from her stall: 'When they were out of work and told her the tale, she couldn't refuse it.' On Saturday evenings after her week's selling was over, she . . . distributed her leftovers to those she knew needed the extra meal.[30]

Through such elaborate arrangements, in which the economic merged with the social, the poor achieved what seemed an impossible feat to middle-class investigators who chronicled their budgets – they survived. Credit was a crucial factor in the balancing of income and expenditure. Robert Roberts's parents kept a small corner shop in Salford, Lancashire. In *The Classic Slum*, he recounts how his mother would astutely appraise the humble applications for credit. Unable to buy in bulk, poor families would purchase goods prior to each meal. Even before children could earn, they were integrated into this domestic economy. Robert Roberts describes how they were kept busy going to and fro on errands, and regular customers would have their 'tick' book to record debts.

Girls experienced growing up very differently, depending on their class background. Novelist Naomi Mitchison's upper-class girlhood, for example, in a house full of servants, left her oblivious to tidying up: 'Dusters, soap, soda? These belonged to another world.'[31]

The exhaustion which resulted from frequent childbearing and poverty left little time in working-class families. Grace Foakes remembered how in some way her mother, an east London working-class woman, found space to care for her: 'I loved the times when I was poorly, because Mother would come and give me hot bread and milk sprinkled with sugar. I think the extra bit of loving helped me as much as the bread and milk.'[32] Kathleen Woodward's mother in a south London working-class home is portrayed more harshly in the autobiographical novel *Jipping Street*: 'She simply was not aware of anything beyond the needs of our bodies . . . At home it was always wintry.'[33]

Annie Davison was brought up in a very different family – cultured, socialist, working-class – in Belfast and Glasgow, and both her parents wanted a good education for their children. However, as she says in Jean McCrindle and Sheila Rowbotham's *Dutiful Daughters*, it was her father who could spare the time to discuss books and ideas.

Relationships and attitudes varied considerably within the working class. Annie Davison's socialist background provided her with a social and cultural world, from socialist Sunday School to the socialist Clarion scouts and the Clarion Players drama group. More typical was the courtship of the streets, the 'monkey parade', when young men and women eyed each other up and down, and outings to the music hall or the seaside. Vesta Tilley, who specialized in male impersonations, sang of the young men who spent the 15s. a week they earned on clothes to show off in a brief day of glory at the seaside: 'He's the seaside sultan, he's the monarch of the pier.'

Glamour and pleasure, however, remained brief moments before toil and family cares took over. The stern insistence on children handing over their wage packets and even the severity described by Kathleen Woodward were based on a realistic understanding of a precarious and harsh fate. Fear of death before the children grew up and of old age created vast financial institutions out of door-to-door collections in working-class areas. The pawn shop was a way of life among the poor. The workhouse still threatened, though the Liberals' Pensions Act in 1908 meant that men and women over seventy on incomes below £31 10s. a year could receive non-contributory pensions of between 1s. and 5s. a week. In her autobiographical account of rural life, *Lark Rise to Candleford*, Flora Thompson described how Oxfordshire pensioners collected their money from the post office in tears and brought flowers and fruit from their gardens to the girl who gave it to them over the counter.

Sex

There was fear of sex as well as of poverty. Newspaper reports document the tragic consequences: suicides of pregnant servants, corpses of abandoned babies and the 'bastardy-order cases', when desperate unmarried mothers took the fathers to court. The National Society for the Prevention of Cruelty to Children (NSPCC) exposed child sexual abuse and, along with the social purity organization the National Vigilance

Association, campaigned for the 1908 Punishment of Incest Act. Though incest was already a crime in Scotland, in England and Wales there was a reluctance to prosecute and cases were not reported in the courts. It was more common for parents to be prosecuted simply for neglect, like the widower father of eleven-year-old Emily Wilson. 'I don't like sleeping with him because he hurts me in bed,'[34] she told the NSPCC inspector in 1909. But the medical report recorded only soreness of the external genitals and Emily was sent to a children's home.

The National Vigilance Association was involved in rescue work with prostitutes and, along with various Christian and Jewish organizations, campaigned for a 'white slave traffic' bill. The suspects were foreign men – Germans, Jews (even though Jewish groups saw Jewish girls as the main victims), Indians and Chinese – who were accused of luring young middle-class women into sin and shipping them abroad into sexual slavery. Social purity combined sexual fears with resentment of economic competition, anti-alien sentiment, imperialist racism and fears of eugenic contamination. The Criminal Law Amendment Act was passed in 1912, with strong feminist support, in a period when the United States was also in the throes of a moral panic about the 'white slave trade'. Teresa Billington-Greig, who investigated supposed cases, was a scathing critic of feminist backing for a 'campaign of sedulously calculated sexual hysterics'.[35]

The British were inclined to associate sexual danger with other places. An American musical at the Shaftesbury Theatre in London, *In Dahomey*, was the talk of the town when it opened in 1903. A breakthrough for talented black performers Aida Overton Walker, Rhoda King, Birdie Williams and Ida Giges, it was very different from the patronizing black and white minstrel shows. *In Dahomey* brought the cakewalk to Edwardian England, upsetting the critics, who complained that it was 'a grotesque, savage and lustful heathen dance'.[36] The cakewalk – along with French novels and unsuitable German postcards – undermined the myth of reserved 'pukka' superiority which held the Empire together.

Anxiety about sexual disintegration interacted with concern about national economic and political vulnerability to create a widespread but unfounded belief that racial decline had set in during the 1900s. Eugenic propaganda was stimulated by the fact that the birth-rate was falling among the upper and middle classes, partly because of birth control, although among the poor large families remained common. Already in the early 1900s there was dissemination of knowledge of how to prevent births. Alice Vickery, a doctor who was a member of the Malthusian League, which campaigned for population control, had started giving contraceptive advice to working-class women. Knowledge of contraception and abortifacients was, moreover, evident in the letters from members of the Women's Co-operative Guild, published as *Maternity: Letters from Working Women*. But the regulation of fertility was still largely by word of mouth and many of the popular folk remedies could be very dangerous. Methods of abortion, for example, included scalding hot baths, gunpowder mixed with margarine, slippery elm and penny royal. Women's magazines such as *Home Chat*, *Women's World* and *Woman and Home* had begun to carry advertisements for pills to relieve 'female ailments', and in 1905 doctors started to report a tell-tale blue line on the lips, the sign of diachylon or lead-plaster poisoning. News of how to obtain such remedies circulated through the most respectable women's networks. One Sheffield woman heard of 'Mrs Seagrave's pills', which contained lead, 'from a lady she met at the Monday afternoon mothers' meeting in connection with her chapel'.[37] Pregnancy too was hazardous and, despite a slow improvement, infant mortality remained high. According to Grace Foakes in her account of life in London's East End, *My Part of the River*, when a new baby was born people would ask, 'Has it come to stay?'[38] Her own mother told her that a weak baby boy had not come to stay but was 'only lent to us for a little while'.

Ignorance and fear of the body and sexuality affected women of all classes. Menstruation was a psychological shock for Naomi Mitchison, and when another future writer and feminist, Vera Brittain, was accosted by a man in a train as a young girl, she was too ashamed to tell her parents. Secrecy was accompanied by much hypocrisy and censorship. When Harley Granville-Barker wrote of the death of a young middle-class woman who sought an abortion after a brief affair, the Lord Chamberlain banned the play, *Waste*, in 1906.

In contrast, the early writers on psychology like Havelock Ellis began to open up space for a 'scientific' discussion of sex. Ellis's non-judgemental case histories suggested a subversive continuum between 'normal' and 'abnormal' practices. He believed, however, that 'inversion' was inborn, a position adopted by some lesbian women, though it presented a view of female sexuality which lacked awareness of shifting sexual desires. The feminist movement in fact demonstrated how culture shaped personal feeling. It inspired passionate friendships between women, though not all were sexual or seen as 'inversion'. Very different perceptions of desire were already appearing within the movement before the First World War. While one strand in feminism emphasized spiritual transcendence and control over the body, finding fulfilment through a radicalized female culture, younger rebels round the *Freewoman* like Rebecca West and Stella Browne wanted equality in a mixed sphere, arguing impatiently that physical expression and defiant sexual courage were vital aspects of emancipation. In *Banishing the Beast*, Lucy Bland distinguishes three arenas of feminist debate: 'the campaign around sexual danger, the discussion of (heterosexual) pleasure, and the development of a new lesbian identity'.[39]

Popular attitudes to sex are extremely difficult to uncover. As Paul Ferris notes in *Sex and the British*:

Pleasure has to be glimpsed between the lines: 'Immoral relations before marriage are not unusual and are indulgently regarded' (Charles Booth, 1903, on the London poor), or, 'Girls do not seem to suffer in self-respect nor greatly in the esteem of others, if they yield themselves to the lad who is the sweetheart of the time' (James Devon, 1912, on the Glasgow poor).[40]

Divisions existed between the respectable and unrespectable working class, but here too there was considerable flexibility. Paul Thompson notes, for example, that in the Highlands of Scotland and rural Wales the country custom of 'bungling' – sharing a bed before marriage – survived. Paul Ferris records the case of Tabitha John: from a respectable working-class background in Llanelli, Wales, she had a boyfriend when she was under fifteen and went away with him and another couple in 1910 for a holiday in a village. They ended up in the same bed and married several years later. In contrast, Mr Vincent, a nonconformist and immigrant from a black Nova Scotia family who spoke Gaelic, living in Bute Town in the Cardiff docks, escorted his daughter to dances and waited outside to bring her safely home.

Music-hall idol Marie Lloyd.

The music-hall star Marie Lloyd expressed a great range of emotion for a popular audience that spanned differing classes. She veered from the romance of 'The boy I love sits up in the gallery' to the pathos of 'Outside the Cromwell Arms last Saturday night, I was one of the ruins that Cromwell knocked about a bit'. She played with ambiguity in 'She'd never had her ticket punched before' and was adept at negotiating contradictory demands from her public. When summoned to sing before a committee of reformers concerned about vice, she delivered her earthy repertoire with drawing-room decorum. Then, just as they were wondering what all the fuss was about, she sang 'Come into the garden, Maud',[41] much loved in respectable middle-class households, with saucy sexual innuendo.

Another Maud, this time the Canadian dancer Maud Allan, provoked a battle over sexual values by performing Salome's dance in chiffon veils and bare legs. When the National Vigilance Association tried to ban her act in 1908, protection from King Edward VII and Asquith saved her from censorship in London. Such upper-class tolerance, however, was both male-defined and based on discretion. Elinor Glyn's novel *Three Weeks* broke both taboos with its account of an older woman's desire for a younger man in upper-class society in 1907. Amidst the ensuing furore, an anonymous rhyme inquired:

> Would you like to sin
> With Elinor Glyn
> On a tiger-skin?
> Or would you prefer
> To err with her
> On some other fur?[42]

Young Nancy Cunard, daughter of the rich shipping magnate, found the book and read it aged eleven, provoking an outcry from her family. Reading *Three Weeks* was to be the first step towards a determined bohemian rebellion.

A more earnest bohemian from a middle-class Yorkshire background, Storm Jameson, arrived in shabby lodgings at London University just before the First World War. Sharing toasted muffins and sardines with the young men of the Eikonoklasts, a group of avant-garde students, she assumed that the new age was imminent. In her autobiography she captured the mood of the radical young intelligentsia, formed by labour unrest, feminist militancy and social and cultural rebellion:

Generations since ours have talked feverishly, but not with our confidence or our illusions. The difference between them and us is that we *knew* we were at the frontier of a new age . . . of social justice, freedom, perpetual peace. Our freedom intoxicated us; there was nothing we should not be able to attempt, no road not open to us, no barriers in the world of equals.[43]

THE UNITED STATES

The Awakening

Kate Chopin's novel *The Awakening*, the story of Edna Pontellier's adultery, scandalized St Louis society in 1899. In the book, Edna Pontellier's husband observes but cannot comprehend the inner transformation: 'He could see plainly that she was not herself. That is, he could not see that she was becoming herself and daily casting aside that fictitious self which we assume like a garment with which to appear before a world.'[44] The novel intimated a new sense of sexual and social identity.

This quest for self-realization was to bring the adventurous to Greenwich Village, New York's bohemian neighbourhood. The result was cultural and political combustion. There were feminists like the writer Crystal Eastman and the teacher Henrietta Rodman, whose bobbed hair, sandals and flowing gowns set the styles of the women who smoked and danced defiantly at a saloon known as the Working Girls' Club. Novelists Susan Glaspell and Neith Boyce could be found at Mabel Dodge's literary salon on Fifth Avenue, and the silent and contemplative Ida Rauh was first seen by her future husband, Crystal Eastman's brother Max, in the Village, dressed in a 'simple self-made unobtrusively becoming garment'.[45] Ida Rauh was to campaign for birth control and women's trade union rights, later acting at Cape Cod with the Provincetown Players, formed by Village radicals in 1915.

Max Eastman, a supporter of women's suffrage and, from 1909, a member of the Men's League for Women's Suffrage, which was linked with the British Women's Social and Political Union, took over the radical cultural magazine *The Masses* in 1913. He was one of a group of Village men, including writer Floyd Dell, who tried to challenge old habits of repression and control. *The Masses* discussed birth control, free love, divorce-law reform and prostitution, as well as economic emancipation and labour struggles. Committed to the external transformation of society, Village radicals debated the sexual theories of Sigmund Freud, Havelock Ellis and Edward Carpenter, and the philosophy of Friedrich Nietzsche and Henri Bergson, which defied established morality and asserted the will. They envisaged a psychological as well as a political awakening.

Not all the theories which excited Village residents were entirely new. The anarchist Emma Goldman, who published the magazine *Mother Earth* from 1906, had already been agitating for free love and birth control in the movement for years, while Charlotte Perkins Gilman, the influential socialist feminist thinker, had begun writing about women's economic dependence in the late nineteenth century and had a following in Britain as well as in the United States. Both had contact with the new rebels through the personal networks of New York's radical bohemia. Charlotte Perkins Gilman belonged to the Heterodoxy Club, which brought together radical women of all persuasions to discuss politics, art, philosophy and personal life. It was formed in 1912 by Marie Jenney Howe, a suffrage campaigner, and its members included Crystal Eastman, Henrietta Rodman and Ida Rauh, along with the turbulent anarcho-syndicalist organizer and speaker for the Industrial Workers of the World (IWW) Elizabeth Gurley Flynn. The common link was an interest in connecting psychological and social liberation. The Heterodoxy Club's debates began to outline a 'feminism' which extended beyond external rights to the personal transformation of gender relations, and the Club was to provide a space for a lesbian subculture.

The 'new woman' was not just a home-grown phenomenon. Members of the many immigrant groups in the United States kept in touch with advanced ideas from their respective countries. German immigrants pioneered nursery education with their kindergartens. Ellen Key's writing on feminism and motherhood was accessible to Swedes, while the Finns knew about the playwright, novelist and theorist Minna Cath. Radical ideas crossed the Atlantic via journals. Josephine Humpel Zeman, who started the first Bohemian feminist journal, *Zemske Listy* (*The Woman's Gazette*), in Chicago, was influenced by rationalist free thinkers from Bohemia. *Glos Polek* (*Voice of Polish Women*), the newspaper of the feminist and nationalist Polish Women's Alliance, was also produced in Chicago. It was enthusiastic about children's summer camps and conserving the environment, and carried articles on movements for women's emancipation in Turkey, Persia and China. There were debates about women's freedom in the Chinese-American radical nationalist press too. The execution of the Chinese militant nationalist Jiu Jin, who believed not only in opposing the imperialists but that male power had to be 'torn up by the roots',[46] was mourned in faraway America.

The 'new woman and the old man' had already become vaudeville jokes by the mid-1890s and at the turn of the century one performer, Earle Remington, introduced a routine in which she played a 'new woman' tramp. The warning was clear: an awful fate followed rebellion. But though vaudeville acts poked fun at reformers and working women alike, by 1912 there was a change of tune. The suffragette on stage upbraiding men was discovered to be popular with both women and men in the audience.

Vernon and Irene Castle: free style and fast movement
on the vaudeville stage.

Some aspects of the radical fringe entered the mainstream. Isadora Duncan's free style in dance had become a new craze. By 1914, when a popular dance star, the willowy Irene Castle, abandoned the 'unnatural lines of figures and gowns' and danced against 'fat, against sickness and against nervous troubles',[47] a new way of being women was in fashion. Freedom, it seemed, was good for you.

Politics

By the turn of the century the American movement for women's suffrage had established the National American Woman Suffrage Association (NAWSA), which was, as Barbara Woloch observes in *Women and the American Experience*, part of a wider middle-class 'nexus of associations – women's clubs, temperance societies, and charitable and civic organizations'.[48] One reason for their strength was the remarkable number of educated women in the United States. Barbara Woloch points out that by the 1890s American women already 'constituted one-third of college students, and over one-third of professional workers'.[49] NAWSA's leaders, Anna Howard Shaw and Carrie Chapman Catt, were two such women who had risen through the educational system to impressive academic and professional honours.

But NAWSA reached out beyond an élite. The focus was on gaining women's suffrage through state campaigns in the period 1896–1910. This meant that while the NAWSA leadership carefully cultivated respectability and avoided the wilder shores of feminism, the need to gain votes involved them in popular agitation. Yet despite the organizational skills of Carrie Chapman Catt, this strategy of winning the vote state by state did not prove successful. By 1910 it was still only Wyoming, Utah, Colorado and Idaho that had full women's suffrage. However, the suffrage movement had broadened as campaigners were caught up in the wider movement for social and moral reform in the 'progressive' 1900s.

By the 1900s a new generation of young college-educated women were forming local suffrage associations and propagandizing from door to door in poor neighbourhoods, as well as the richer suburbs. Florence Luscomb, for example, graduated from college in Boston and made her political debut in the Massachusetts Woman Suffrage Association on a soapbox in Dedham in 1904. A trolley tour to Boston's factory gates, crossroads and city centres followed. At Waltham they even persuaded a circus owner to hang a 'Votes for Women' banner on elephants.

News of the Women's Social and Political Union also began to reach the American activists. The daughter of the pioneer feminist Elizabeth

Ingenious propaganda.

Cady Stanton, Harriot Stanton Blatch, returned from Britain in 1907 filled with militant enthusiasm to form the Equality League of Self-Supporting Women in New York. The Equality League were quick to adopt imaginative ways of reaching the public, like sending 'sandwich girls' to advertise a 1908 rally in Coney Island, New York's centre of popular recreation. They also sought an alliance with the Women's Trade Union League, thus connecting political demands with the economic conditions of working women.

Ellen Carol DuBois notes that while the American suffragette movement was inspired by the WSPU, there were important differences: 'Not sharing, or forced to share, in the British emphasis on civil disobedience (mass arrests for suffrage activism did not occur in the United States until 1917), American militants focused instead on mastering the principles and enjoying the benefits of publicity.'[50] They used movies, commercial radio, telephones and advertising, and, learning from the labour movement, held outdoor meetings and translated their propaganda into Yiddish, Italian and many other languages to reach the immigrant working class. In Washington State in 1910, for example, suffrage supporters spoke at union meetings, state and county fairs, and adult education classes with the slogan 'Give the Women a Square Deal'.[51] They communicated through billboards, a monthly newsletter and plays, and even produced their own cookery book.

Alice Paul, who had also returned from Britain, joined NAWSA's congressional committee in 1913 with her friend Lucy Burns and revived the idea of gaining the suffrage through a federal amendment, applying the militant tactics of the WSPU. When they began to attack the Democratic Party and President Woodrow Wilson, however, the NAWSA hierarchy was embarrassed. The ensuing conflict led Alice Paul to form the National Woman's Party (NWP) with the socialist feminist Crystal Eastman in 1916.

As in Britain, the tensions in the American suffrage movement went deeper than tactics or political alliances. From the early 1890s the Southern states were legalizing segregation through the 'Jim Crow' laws. The NAWSA leadership, concerned about retaining the support of their white Southern members, rejected the attempts of black women suffrage supporters to get a national position against segregation. It was decided in 1903 that individual states should determine their own membership policies and segregation on suffrage marches was justified as expedient.

Black women continued to participate in the suffrage movement, but they also set up their own clubs, linking the demand for suffrage to the social, economic and cultural needs of black communities, in New York, Boston, St Louis, Los Angeles, Memphis, Charleston, New Orleans, Philadelphia and Tuskegee. They established state suffrage societies in New York, Delaware, Idaho, Montana, North Dakota, Texas and Maryland as well. These organizations became important bases for a wider self-help activism, while also providing policies and support for black politicians' campaigns. Black women were also centrally involved in the campaign against lynching, which had been started by the courageous journalist Ida B. Wells during the 1890s, and helped to set up the National Association for the Advancement of Colored People (NAACP) in 1909. It was thus never possible for black American women to focus on the suffrage in isolation or to accept a naïve view of sisterhood.

Conflict was not confined to NAWSA. Harriot Stanton Blatch's attempt to bring together women of different classes in the Equality League also ran into personal distrust and disagreement about how the vote was to be seen. One of the initiators of the popular campaigning approach adopted by the League, Maud Malone, resigned in 1908, complaining that the suffrage movement had been taken over by 'a well-dressed crowd'.[52]

While feminists like Alice Paul were firmly committed to the idea that women were no different to men and therefore should have equal rights, there was a significant strand in the women's movement that believed women had special qualities which they would bring to politics. As Sara Evans comments in Born for Liberty, 'Increasingly they drew on the politicized domesticity of the women's reform tradition. No longer focused primarily on women's just claim to equal rights as citizens, they argued that the state needed women precisely because of their difference.'[53]

The campaign for the suffrage developed in a period when the surveys of social investigators and the exposures of 'muck-raking' journalists were revealing poverty, crime and discontent amidst rapid urbanization. For socially conscious women teachers, librarians and social workers,

'Americanization' of the immigrant poor was an acceptably worthy cause which was at once womanly and independent. The idea of women's special role was thus connected to a wider movement of 'progressive' social reform. Jane Addams's pioneering social settlement in Chicago, Hull House, and Lillian Wald's Henry Street Community in New York, along with the National Consumers' League, which mobilized consumer pressure for reform, and the Women's Trade Union League, formed an astute lobby on matters of employment and welfare legislation. They were able to exert influence nationally, both through the Progressive Party, formed by Theodore Roosevelt in a split from the Republicans in 1912, and through the Democrats. Jane Addams, who was a prominent figure in the progressive movement, described this emphasis on women's specific contribution to social welfare as 'city housekeeping'.[54]

It was widely assumed by progressives that women's suffrage would be a moralizing force, bringing an awareness of women's and children's health needs, legitimizing state regulation of food, housing and sanitation, and exposing the conditions of the poor. Nevertheless, Jane Addams suggested that a certain wariness was in order, remarking wryly at a NAWSA conference in 1911, 'We have not wrecked the railroad nor corrupted the legislatures, nor done many unholy things that men have done, but then we must remember that we have not had the chance.'[55]

In fact, progressive maternalism had differing political emphases. At a local level, many white middle-class women put their efforts into reforming mothering by persuading immigrant mothers to change their diets, and reorganize their housekeeping and child-rearing. They organized baby conservation campaigns in Milwaukee, baby contests or derbies in Louisiana, Municipal House Cleaning Day in Pennsylvania, and corner gatherings of Italian and Russian women in Philadelphia. Such attempts to change personal practice could lead to broader social campaigns: for example, for pure milk supplies, for better sanitation in homes, including the provision of water, and for public laundries. The Pure Food and Drug Act of 1906 was a victory for the powerful network of women's clubs.

Many of these reformers were convinced that mothers should be at home, but there was some pressure to extend nursery provision. One model was the Helen Day Nursery in Chicago, set up in 1905, which had not only a flexible drop-in service during the day but an emergency night shelter. Women progressive reformers who served on school boards, along with teachers, supported better buildings, medical inspection, physical education and sex hygiene lessons. Cleveland teachers also pointed out that the children needed school lunches: 'Their pupils could not work on a diet of candy and pickles.'[56]

Among the more radical reformers was Julia Lathrop, a Hull House resident who, convinced that poverty was the real problem and familiar with international feminist debates on welfare, came to support Mothers' Pensions. She argued for state welfare, along with higher wages for both women and men. When patient lobbying by Jane Addams, Florence Kelley and Lillian Wald finally led Congress to set up the Children's Bureau in 1912, Julia Lathrop was appointed its head. She used her small budget to produce and distribute two pamphlets free of charge to mothers: 'Prenatal Care' in 1913 and 'Infant Care' the following year.

White and black welfare activists, as Linda Gordon shows in her history of single mothers and welfare, *Pitied But Not Entitled*, had differing emphases. While the impetus for reform among white middle-class women was often to protect mothers from work, black welfare activists were more likely to recognize that women needed to earn. The progressive coalitions had different political meanings depending on region. For example, in the South they could represent a white supremacist populism which was overtly hostile to black Americans' aspirations; agitation for compulsory education for white children, say, was based on fears of a black educated élite.

Black welfare activists, powerless in the South and with much less influence in the North on government and municipal policies than whites, were forced to rely mainly on self-help measures. The black women's clubs, the churches, the National Association of Colored Women (NACW) and black members of the Young Women's Christian Association (YWCA) provided networks of care for the elderly and nursery and educational groups. Also the Phillis Wheatley Settlement in Cleveland, the Russell Plantation and Calhoun Settlement in Alabama, and Victoria Earle Matthews's Little Rose Home in New York not only contributed to the social needs of black communities but fostered their own researchers and social activists. The approach of women like

Mary Church Terrell, president of the NACW and a founder of the NAACP, was 'lifting as we climb',[57] a motto which expressed not only the American dream of mobility but also a hard-won black culture of mutual aid.

Work

A young Jewish clothing worker, Clara Lemlich, made history on 22 November 1909 when she walked to the front of a strike meeting in New York's Cooper Union Hall called by the International Ladies' Garment Workers' Union (ILGWU) and passionately demanded a general strike in Yiddish. She was already well known among Russian Jews on the Lower East Side for organizing against the speed-ups and fines imposed on the young immigrant women in factories producing for the booming mass market created by department stores and mail-order houses. Clara Lemlich, who had been studying Marxist theory at the Rand School, an institute for workers started by the American Socialist Party, applied her lessons to the experience of the shirt-waist factories.

The unskilled labour force drawn to America by the opportunities created by new forms of production had previously seemed unorganizable because they were easily replaceable and ethnically divided. However, between 20,000 and 40,000 workers, including Italians and Jews, responded to her strike call, though the minority of black workers, who faced racist prejudice from some white workers, were used as scabs by the manufacturers. Without funds and repeatedly beaten and arrested on the picket lines, the strikers called on the Women's Trade Union League for help. When middle-class feminists and socialists joined the pickets, the strike received increasing publicity, and this intervention marked closer links between working women and the feminist movement.

The strikers were not successful in all their demands, but employers in the larger, more modern factories were prepared to negotiate with the ILGWU. Elizabeth Ewen observes that the unprecedented uprising had a deeper significance, for it 'lifted the work of immigrant women out of obscurity and into public consciousness'.[58] This awareness was accentuated in 1911 when a fire at the Triangle Shirt-waist Company

The New York shirt-waist makers' rebellion marks a new spirit among
young immigrant workers.

killed 146 people and injured many more. The employers had ignored
the strikers' demands for improved safety arrangements and kept their
800 workers locked inside the factory. The militant spirit of the rank
and file persisted in the subsequent wave of strikes in the garment industries of Rochester, Chicago, Philadelphia and Cleveland, in which
women demanded better pay and conditions and an end to the system
of subcontracting work out. Around 100,000 workers in the clothing
industry were to be drawn into disputes between 1905 and 1915. In
her study of women and working-class politics, *Common Sense and a
Little Fire*, Annelise Orleck notes that half the women working in the
clothing industry were unionized between 1909 and 1919, making them
a force to be reckoned with.

There was, however, conflict about how to organize. Mollie Schepps, one of the shirt-waisters influenced by the Women's Trade Union League (WTUL), reckoned suffrage would improve conditions. 'Equal say will enable women to get equal pay,'[59] she declared at a meeting in 1912. Industrial Workers of the World (IWW) agitator Elizabeth Gurley Flynn disagreed. Like the anarchist Emma Goldman and miners' organizer Mary 'Mother' Jones, she insisted that economic change in the workplace, not the vote, was the key to improving women's conditions and was scornful of the 'rich faddists for woman's suffrage'[60] who had supported the clothing workers.

The WTUL and the IWW had very different approaches to unionization, the former stressing an alliance based on gender across class lines and the latter stressing an absolute conflict between classes. However, both were prepared to adopt creative organizational tactics which spanned the workplace and the community. During the Chicago garment strike in 1911, the League persuaded landlords and lodging-house keepers to wait for payments, found accommodation for homeless strikers and fed 50,000 people a day. At Lawrence, a woollen textile centre in Massachusetts, Elizabeth Gurley Flynn was confronted by over twenty different nationalities to unite in the 1912 strike which shut down nearly every mill in the city. These included Lithuanians, Poles, Italians, Syrians and French. In *Radicals of the Worst Sort*, Ardis Cameron shows how the IWW was able to build on the personal networks which women had formed through contacts in shops, or while walking to work, discussing wage rates and prices, exchanging recipes or helping each other in hard times. These networks reached out to women in the community. They began to eat communally during the strike; some women attacked scabs with red pepper, while others humiliated the soldiers by taking scissors to the backs of their uniforms.

Despite the IWW emphasis on class solidarity, Elizabeth Gurley Flynn's own contact with radical middle-class women brought in supporters and reached out beyond Lawrence. For example, a young nurse active in the Socialist Party called Margaret Sanger escorted many Lawrence children to New York to stay with sympathetic families. Some 5,000 people turned out to greet them when they arrived at Grand Central Station. Another middle-class ally, the socialist Mary

The Photograph as Social Document

The photograph as social document was pioneered by Jacob Riis's portraits of immigrants and the urban poor in the late nineteenth century. A former police reporter, he took photographs to evoke pity and compassion. In 1904 Lewis Hine, a progressive teacher of sociology, also began to photograph immigrants arriving at Ellis Island, New York. He sought to counter hostile newspaper propaganda with images of bewilderment, reserve and dignity which drew on classical poses.

Changing images of labour became possible partly because new techniques enabled photographers to take pictures inside mills and sweatshops, but they were also inspired by the movement for social reform.

Arriving in the New World: Lewis Hines's photograph of a
young girl from Albania.

Lewis Hine's photographs documented the research of the six-volume Pittsburgh survey to which Elizabeth Beardsley Butler and Crystal Eastman contributed. His pictures of children and young workers in mills and mines for the National Child Labor Committee were used in their campaign meetings and reproduced in local newspapers as propaganda for legislation against child labour.

Conflicts between labour and capital assumed a new public visibility through newspaper photographs, which showed images of silk workers at Paterson, New Jersey, of children during the Lawrence strike and of the evicted miners and their families in their tent city at Ludlow, Colorado. Strike supporters began to see the impact of visual images. In a bitter dispute at Fulton Mills, Atlanta, labour journalist O. (Ola) Delight Smith adapted Hine's approach. An ex-telegraphist blacklisted for union militancy, she arrived in Atlanta to cover the strike as a reporter and ended up helping workers to organize. She used moving pictures, a hand-held camera and commercial photographers to make a visual record of defiant workers, company spies and arrogant company agents, mounting her photographs on cardboard and exhibiting them in shop windows. They not only gained public support but enabled strikers to look at their own actions and discover a collective identity. Some circulated as postcards.

The idea of producing postcards as a means of gaining support for strikes and campaigns was an innovation in propaganda made possible by the legalization of privately produced cards in 1898. Along with views and images of popular entertainers, postcards carried pro-labour messages. They also gave a glimpse of women's lives which would otherwise be invisible. While greetings cards in the 1900s presented Native American women in idealized, nostalgic poses, local photographers took pictures of Native American women's ordinary activities, shopping in the store or doing craftwork. These sometimes found their way beyond the community by becoming postcards. However, from around 1915 postcards too started to superimpose a view of 'traditional' life upon Native American women by drawing on nineteenth-century photographs. Along with greetings cards, the postcards were subsequently to become more romantic and stereotypical.

Heaton Vorse, remembered meeting Elizabeth Gurley Flynn for the first time at Lawrence, sitting on a 'mushroom stool at a quick-lunch restaurant'. She described the IWW leader as 'a very quiet person' off the platform, but as soon as she began speaking she stirred audiences 'with her Irish blue eyes, her face magnolia white and her cloud of black hair . . . it was as though a spurt of flame had gone through the audience'.[61]

Clothing and textile workers were not the only groups of women to organize. Women in the steam laundries of San Francisco unionized in 1900, rebelling against the enforced system of living in. By 1912 they had increased their wages by 30 per cent and initiated safety measures to protect themselves from the soda, ammonia and heat. Less-downtrodden women were mobilizing too. The telephone operators, from upper-working-class, often Irish-American backgrounds, were stylishly dressed high-school graduates. From 1907 they were demanding an eight-hour day, two-week vacations, standardized pay scales with automatic pay increases, improvements in their shift arrangements and clearer griev-ance procedures. The numbers of women clerks and saleswomen were growing too. In Chicago clerks managed to organize in 1904, though fluctuation in the economy caused them to lose members three years later. Saleswomen were on strike in 1912 in Lafayette, In-diana, and in Buffalo and New York in 1913. Even some teachers were becoming less distant from organized labour: women teachers marched with scrubwomen and candy makers on Chicago's Labor Day Parade in 1903.

However, as in Britain, many women were still working in areas where there were no unions: they looked after children, took in boarders, did washing. Those in small units and homeworkers were hard to organize because they were scattered and fragmented, often doing tasks which many others seeking work would be able to pick up quickly. In contrast to Britain, though, America remained a predominantly rural society. Rosalyn Baxandall and Linda Gordon point out in *America's Working Women* that until 1920 most Americans lived in the countryside or in small towns: 'Farm work was still the most common form of women's labor.'[62] Farm women's unpaid labour was crucial in the vast plains of the Midwest, as well as the Western frontier. In the poorer farms without piped water, gas or electricity, this meant seasonal fieldwork on top of housework. Among the stereotypical Wild West cowboys and gunfighters were a few famous cowgirls, such as Goldia Fields Malone, an early twentieth-century trick-rider, as well as a farmer. However, the day-to-day life of most Western women was more likely to be monotonous, isolated and bleak. The lawlessness of the West could sanction male violence and the cosy log cabins of Western mythology were hard work.

Hired work on farms was unpopular – the last resort of the desperate and those who were forced to the bottom of the hierarchy because of their race and ethnicity. Consequently many Mexicans and Chicanas, Japanese and African-Americans were among those working long hours in Western agriculture. Domestic service was an alternative for rural African-American women in the South, but the long hours, the lack of personal freedom, the uniforms which evoked servitude and the danger of sexual harassment made it equally unpopular. Black domestic servants headed up to the North, only to find that there too the employment on offer was extremely limited. Apart from the worst factory work, stemming tobacco or oyster-shucking, they had to enter domestic service again or do low-paid homework.

Jane Addams, Lillian Wald and Florence Kelley had pioneered investigative exposures of low wages, bad conditions and long hours through their work in social settlements and the Consumers' League. Young women investigators of labour conditions, like Crystal Eastman and Elizabeth Beardsley Butler, followed in their footsteps. Elizabeth Beardsley Butler's impressive *Women and the Trades*, for instance, is a vivid account of Pittsburgh in 1907–8. It includes this description of the 'stogy' industry:

I went into one cellar opposite Hill factory where two women and one man, all Negroes, were stripping in a room less than seven feet in height. The only source of air was a narrow door leading by a flight of steps up to the street. A tiny slit of a window at the far end was close-barred, and two-thirds of the cubic space in the room was occupied by bales of tobacco and cases of stripped stogy. Pools of muddy water stood on the earth floor, and the air was foul beyond endurance.[63]

The social investigators tramped up tenement steps in New York, finding Italian homeworkers finishing clothing, making artificial flowers or cleaning ostrich plumes, Syrians doing lace work or making kimonos and Jewish women producing straw hats and women's neck-wear. The latter were also to be seen selling fruit, fish or clothing on the streets, running candy stores, groceries, butcher's shops, cleaning and dyeing shops. These troubled middle-class reformers also found children tacking clothes, sewing on buttons and carrying bundles and boxes to contractors on the Lower East Side, and their accounts stimulated the demands of the National Child Labor Committee for protective legislation. In 1903 Marie Van Vorst revealed how, in the South, children were doing twelve-hour shifts in the textile mills. Women professionals also helped to provide scientific expertise for the progressives' campaigns against dangerous working conditions. For example, Alice Hamilton, Harvard Medical School's first female faculty member in 1911, strengthened the case for safety legislation by showing how poisonous materials like lead affected pregnant workers. It was not only social science and social medicine that were marked by the movement for social reform. Journalists exposed corruption and injustice, while artists and writers portrayed women workers and child labourers in a realistic way which aimed to touch people's consciences and change policies.

Some social reformers and women trade unionists began to turn towards the state to check exploitation in employment. Under pressure from Florence Kelley, a leading figure in the National Consumers' League, several states began to pass legislation to protect women and children, introducing a minimum standard of ventilation, adequate washing facilities, seats and mandatory rest periods. In Oregon, Florence Kelley mobilized support for a law which limited the hours of women laundry workers to ten. The National Consumers' League helped to prepare lawyer Louis Brandeis's brief in the case for protective legislation and in 1908 the Supreme Court upheld a statutory limit on the working day and the working week in the important *Muller* v. *Oregon* decision. This restricted employers' powers over their workers, but by asserting that women needed special protection the 'Brandeis brief' also undermined the case for equality at work. The Supreme Court decision was based on the preservation of motherhood and their offspring, not on any rights of women as workers.

The protection of womanhood had various interpretations. Mary

Phagan, a thirteen-year-old girl in the National Pencil Factory, Atlanta, who was found strangled in 1913, came to symbolize the greed of a heartless commercialism. Her Jewish superintendent, a Yankee, was accused and convicted of the murder on scanty evidence. He was lynched by a mob in 1915, and William Simmons transformed the populist protectors of the murdered girl, the Knights of Mary Phagan, into a revival of the Ku Klux Klan.

Daily Life

Progressive maternalist reformers were convinced that mothering and housework should be modernized: 'Science refuses to accept the old fatalistic cry, "The Lord gave, the Lord hath taken away, blessed be the name of the Lord," '[64] declared Julia Lathrop. There was a sustained effort to improve nursing and child-care by education. Impatient with folk customs, the reformers propagated 'American' medicine, child psychology, diets and hygiene. However, the detailed reports of the Children's Bureau were making it clear that education was not sufficient. Women took babies and small children to the beet fields of Michigan or to canning factories because the only alternative was to leave them at home. An alliance of radical progressives combined with more conservative organizations, the National Congress of Mothers, Parent-Teacher Associations and the General Federation of Women's Clubs, to create a powerful lobby for Mothers' Pensions. For radicals, these were to be the solution to poverty and dependence, while more conservative supporters believed that aid to the deserving poor would improve family life. The first state to introduce Mothers' Pensions was Illinois, in 1911, and in the next two years eighteen more granted state aid to poor mothers. Mothers' aid was not, however, a universal allowance: social workers assessed the applicants and it carried from the start the stigma of charity rather than resources which were claimed by right. Linda Gordon shows in *Pitied But Not Entitled* how it was to contribute to the creation of a two-track welfare system, one serving the insured male wage-earner and the other serving the vetted mother, who was defined as virtuous victim.

A more defiant assertion of womanhood was expressed in a recurring community resistance to big companies and trusts whose power extended beyond the workplace through their control over credit and distribution. Basic food prices and rent, crucial to the survival of the poor, caused women to mobilize in the streets. Their militancy was legitimated by their responsibilities as homemakers. In 1902, for example, when the price of kosher meat rose, Jewish Lower East Side housewives used neighbourhood networks to organize a boycott of New York butchers. As Mrs Levy, the wife of a garment worker, said, 'If *we women* make a strike, then it will be a strike.'[65] Rent strikes in 1904 and 1907–8 reproduced very similar forms of neighbourhood organization. Depression in 1907–8 resulted in widespread unemployment and families got into arrears; women armed with brooms and ashcans resisted eviction collectively. The tenement buildings in which they lived were crowded and uncomfortable. Eight or nine people would be crammed into two- or three-room apartments. Few had inside bathrooms. With only coal and wood in cold winters, the women struggled with the burst pipes when the ice thawed. Kerosene provided the lighting, while blocks of ice were the only form of refrigeration in the sweltering New York summers. There was, as Barbara Woloch observes, 'a sharp dividing line'[66] between the domestic circumstances of the urban and rural poor and the middle class. The newly built, comfortable apartment buildings in middle-class areas were equipped with central heating, electricity for light, telephones, refrigerators and gas for stoves.

Domestic reformers like Charlotte Perkins Gilman envisaged such apartments as the basis of a domestic revolution which would free educated women from housework. In her serial novel *What Diantha Did*, she imagined a cooked-food service arriving in containers carried by 'a light gasolene wagon'.[67] Collectivization of living arrangements and domestic services was not completely far-fetched. In *The Grand Domestic Revolution*, Dolores Hayden describes interest in co-operative housing schemes among workers, and some radical middle-class professionals set up communal houses. Alfred S. Heineman, for instance, designed an apartment hotel in Pasadena in 1913; he and his brother Arthur also built modest bungalows with connecting doors, so husbands and wives could live together with a degree of autonomy, while socializing with their neighbours. Several co-operative housekeeping schemes provided community dining clubs and cooked-food delivery services. Communal meals appeared during strikes and in the Midwest co-operative dairies provided water supplies and steam plants for laundry services.

The reorganization of daily life and consumption was not to develop on such communal or co-operative lines, though some projects persisted in certain areas. Instead it was Christine Frederick's and Lillian Gilbreth's vision of scientific management in the home which was to prevail. 'Home economics' came to mean not the development of new social forms but the middle-class housewife, promoted to executive, managing the new technology which surrounded her. By the 1900s the first electric washing machines were already being marketed. Domestic products were being promoted as symbols of the individual's chance to rise on the social ladder. For instance, the Vacuum Cleaner Company in 1906 proudly announced that its vacuums cleaned the White House. Humbler purchases too promised power and control. In 1900 a picture of a woman boxing appeared in an advertisement in *Everybody's Magazine*: DON'T HAVE TO TRAIN TO PREPARE FOR HOUSE-CLEANING. USE SAPOLIO. IT KNOCKS OUT ALL DIRT.[68]

Advertising was a million-dollar industry by 1910, selling mass-produced assembly-line clothes and the convenience canned food and brand-name cereals which were changing eating patterns. Advertising 'Shredded Whole Wheat', Colliers exhorted, 'If you are a worker in a shop, in the office or in the home you should eat a food that contains the phosphates and nitrates – the brain and muscle makers – prepared in a digestible form'; two Shredded Wheat biscuits were 'the ideal food for the desk man and all indoor workers'.[69]

Entrepreneurs applied their ingenuity not only in producing products and advertising them but in restructuring distribution and finding new outlets for consumption. The new type of city worker who required fast, healthy lunches might also shop in the A & P chain stores which were spreading to many towns. While on the Santa Fe railroad, the lunch counters and dining rooms set up by Fred Harvey transformed travel. The workplace speed-up, made possible by large-scale units and 'scientific management', was reaching into the daily life of big cities.

Entertainment was moving faster too. Baseball games had to be action-packed, vaudeville jokes came quicker, music was 'hot' and

Snacks with soda: the soda fountain, Rike's Department Store,
in Dayton, Ohio, 1912.

fashions were slick and ephemeral, like the images of desire appearing
at the 'flickers'. In New York young people would queue for the new
movie theatres, seeing shows several times over. They delighted in the
amusement halls, giggled in the 'Tunnel of Love', met in ice-cream
parlours, gazed at the windows of department stores, longing for the
smart labels. There were cabarets, music halls and vaudeville shows,
and cities like New York were dance-mad, doing the Grizzly Bear, the
Charlie Chaplin Wiggle and the Dip.

Sex

Entertainment meant big money from a market which now, because
of rising living standards and an expanding economy, included the
young working class with money to spare. 'Everybody's doin' it now'
announced Irving Berlin's song in 1911; the inference was that 'it' was
not just hunching to ragtime. The ebullient consumerism heralded a
pragmatically risqué culture. 'If you talk in your sleep, don't mention
my name', with its admonition, 'If you can't be good be careful', was

a party song in the 1900s and British music-hall performers Marie Lloyd, Vesta Tilley and the popular Vesta Victoria brought *double-entendre* songs over: 'You can do a lot of things at the seaside that you can't do in town.' Glamorous vaudeville singer Valeska Suratt's Parisian sheath gowns made audiences gasp. 'I don't wear petticoats,'[70] she announced to a reporter. When a Chicago woman went shopping in the new style, she had to be rescued from the crowd by the police. In 1908 Valeska Suratt and her partner, Billy Gould, introduced the Parisian Apache Dance, in which the jealous lover strangled his partner. Alternative Apaches proliferated – in one, with a gender twist, the prostitute knifes her pimp. The entertainment industry had discovered the delights of danger and followed it up with the Vampire Dance.

In *Male–Female Comedy Teams in American Vaudeville*, Shirley Staples describes how New York's young and fashionable élite were taking up the new dances in cabarets and nightclubs: 'Mingling with the men, who had always had a sporting life, were unchaperoned women of respectable backgrounds, now seen smoking and drinking, and showing their ankles and curves in dresses like those formerly worn only by

Enterprising early film heroine.

loose women.'[71] Slumming and taking in vaudeville shows had become fashionable by 1910 and the middle class took their cue from the rich. Married middle-class women were having smaller families and had more leisure time. Pleasure beckoned in big cities like New York. Along with the glitter of the department store, it was becoming respectable to go to cabarets, to *thés dansant* and tango teas. A new social space was opening for urban middle-class women. The cinema, besides projecting images of wilting heroines, was also attuned to changing aspirations among women. The 1907 film *Down with Women* showed a man who was convinced that women were inferior having his life saved by a woman doctor and being defended in court by a woman lawyer. From 1912 the popular film serials aimed at young working girls, such as *The Perils of Pauline* and *The Hazards of Helen*, presented assertive and resourceful heroines.

The fans of Pauline and Helen, however, earned such low wages in the clothing factories, shops and offices, lunch counters and amusement centres where they worked that they relied on 'gentleman friends'[72] for treats, clothes and sometimes to keep them. The men in turn expected sex: 'A girl has to be a sport to work in this job,'[73] declared a Portland waitress at an amusement centre. The ideal, of course, was to find a rich husband. In Arizona four 'Harvey' girls at Fred Harvey's El Tovar Hotel, Grand Canyon, achieved the dream of sexual mobility and married rich cattlemen. But low-paid glamorous jobs were more likely to raise expectations than to deliver millionaires.

Immigrant families' attempts to impose old-world restraints on daughters provoked resentment. Maimie Pinzer, a sales girl in Philadelphia, rebelled against the discipline of her Jewish family and became a prostitute. She was very successful until she became ill and lost an eye. By 1910 she had become a morphine addict and was living in poverty. Through the intervention of a reformer, Herbert Welsh, she began a remarkable correspondence with an upper-class Bostonian woman, Fanny Quincy Howe, and was herself later to help young prostitutes.

The Evangelical Alliance of the United States and Anthony Comstock, an inspector of the post office who was president of the Society for the Suppression of Vice, blamed immigrants and the rich for moral decay. Settlement workers like Jane Addams and Belle Moskowitz believed that the answer was for urban popular culture to be regulated and reformed. In 1908 a board was set up to censor movies, vaudeville routines were cleaned up and in 1912 drinking in cabarets was restricted by licences. Vice commissions investigated prostitution amidst a mounting panic about international rings luring innocent girls into the 'white slave traffic'. For evangelicals prostitution was caused by moral failing; but progressive and socialist campaigners argued it was linked to organized crime, corruption in local government and big business. From both perspectives sin was mainly associated with the city. Linda Gordon notes that single motherhood was regarded inaccurately as 'uniquely urban . . . the assumption that urban life produced social breakdown reverberated with an American tradition of romanticizing rural life'.[74] The single, immigrant working girl was consequently the focus for evangelical rescue and progressive improvement alike. This perception of a sexual crisis of control converged with class, race and ethnic prejudices. Emma Goldman pointed to the xenophobia evident in campaigns against the 'white slave traffic',[75] advocating instead contraception, women's right to economic independence and anarchism. The lower-class immigrant men who partnered middle-class women at the *thés dansant* were sexually suspect and race riots were triggered off in Atlanta in 1908 by rumours that black men had assaulted white women. The effort to reassert social control expressed a fear that hierarchies were being subverted. The Deep South rebelled against *In Dahomey*, the musical that was to be so popular in London, because it gave greater scope to black performers.

A crisis of authority between generations in the middle class troubled American commentators too. They complained of car-dating, the divorce rate, women's loss of femininity, the rebellion of children and the threat to the home. Journalists declared that it was 'Sex o'clock in America'.[76] Sex, of course, was nothing new. It was the shifting boundaries of behaviour which alarmed people. Christine Simmons notes that the borderline between 'good' and 'bad' women was becoming blurred. The reasons went deeper than a fashionable cultural defiance: 'By the 1910s young middle-class women's foothold in higher education, the labor force, and feminist and reform politics and institutions gave them an increasingly critical perspective on the old sexual order.'[77]

Prostitution

Prostitution was big business by the 1900s. It was also highly stratified. In San Francisco, while Mexican prostitutes charged $1 working from bare 'cribs' in run-down blocks, Jessie Hayman, a tall, fiery, redheaded madam, who ran an élite 'house', invested in property from her takings. Her rival Tessie Wall, a great wine drinker, collected antiques.

Not only the liquor trade but other local businesses had a vested interest in prostitution. Clothes were extremely important. Jessie Hayman advanced thousands of dollars against future earnings. Such purchases were not just for allure; they made rich women jealous. San Francisco prostitutes pioneered Paris fashions, which 'respectable' women copied. In Storyville, New Orleans, black prostitutes challenged the race divide as well. They bought some of their clothes from salesmen from the North, but they also openly paraded the streets, surveying shop windows with money to spend. The short skirts which were to become the mark of modern womanhood in the early twentieth century had their origins in the fashions of New Orleans prostitutes in the late nineteenth century.

Prostitutes were presented as the victims of male lust and commercial greed by reformers investigating vice, though there was some uncertainty about who was corrupting whom. In Butte, Montana, for example, when evangelical reformers mounted a frontal attack on 'the social evil', it was the men, not the women, whom they were protecting; they marched into the red-light district singing 'Where is My Wandering Boy Tonight?'[78] Long-term conversions evaded them. Gamblers and prostitutes packed the Casino Theater to hear about fire and brimstone for a week and then went back to business as usual. The view that women were the victims of foreign men was the theme of the vaudeville sketch 'The White Slaver' in 1908, in which an Italian discovers that a young girl, forced into prostitution, is his niece and stabs her enslaver.

Prostitutes certainly faced the real dangers of venereal disease and male violence, not only from their clients but also from their 'protectors', former wrestlers, prize-fighters, petty criminals, waiters, saloon-keepers or pawnbrokers who owned 'houses' or acted as pimps. However,

stereotypes of the victim of commercialism or the victim of male lust
did not tell the whole story. Not all prostitution was organized; the
boundaries between 'charity girls' who went 'all the way' for 'treats' and
the occasional prostitutes who supplemented low wages were flexible.
Nor were all prostitutes passive slaves to their pimps. Laura Evans kicked
her lover through a plate-glass window in Butte, Montana, for dancing
with another woman and Tessie Wall was to kill her ex-husband in 1917
after he divorced her. Prostitutes took collective action to defend their
interests too, forming a voting block in Denver and setting up the Dance
Hall Girls Protective Association in Cripple Creek, Colorado.

Defending gender borderlines in an article entitled 'Effeminate Men
and Masculine Women' in the *New York Medical Journal* in 1900, William
Lee Howard had fulminated against the new woman in higher education and political life: 'The female possessed of masculine ideas of independence, the virago who would sit in the public highways and lift
up her pseudo-virile voice . . . and that disgusting antisocial being, the
female sexual pervert, are simply different degrees of the same class
– degenerates.'[79]
Such 'new women' as Jane Addams and academics like M. Carey
Thomas and Vida Scudder were able to maintain a protected private
space and continued to live with their women companions while
remaining respected public figures. 'Boston marriages' in female colleges
and the romantic friendships of social settlement women remained
sexually ambiguous. The assumption that older middle-class women
did not experience lust persisted. 'Passing' among women lower down
the social scale disturbed gender boundaries more than same-sex friendship. Cora Anderson, a Native American woman who said in 1914 that
she had taken on the persona of Ralph Kerwinieo to protect her partner
and earn a living wage, was explicit about the power relations which
influenced her change of dress: 'It is still a man-made world, made by

men for men . . . Do you blame me for wanting to be a man, free to live life as a man in a man-made world? Do you blame me for hating to again resume a woman's clothes and just belong?'[80]

As in Britain, American sexual radicals distinguished themselves from nineteenth-century hypocrisy, pitting the new century against the old. In the process they too oversimplified nineteenth-century attitudes, ignoring an older tradition of sex radicalism as well as earlier less rigid gender boundaries around relations between women. Their battles were nonetheless of great significance. Women exercising choice about motherhood, defending unmarried mothers, assuming their right to economic and psychological independence and being frank about sexual pleasure were subversive causes.

A key issue was the right to knowledge. Commitment to disseminating information about sex brought sexual radicals into conflict with the guardians of virtue like Anthony Comstock, who, as inspector of the post office, policed the US mail for immoral literature. It was an extremely bitter fight. Ida Craddock, author of *Right Marital Living*, was pursued by Comstock and committed suicide in 1905. When birth-controller Margaret Sanger's column for the socialist magazine *The New York Call*, 'What Every Girl Should Know', was banned by the post office under the Comstock law in 1912, *The Call* responded by printing under the usual heading 'NOTHING by order of the Post Office'[81] in the blank space. The right to information about contraception was to become Margaret Sanger's life's work. Influenced by the ideas of workers' control among the syndicalists and socialists she met in New York, she coined the phrase 'birth control'[82] in her magazine *The Woman Rebel*.

While some rebelled, others dreamed. The young Jewish women in the clothing shops sang and, Houdini-like, fantasized about escape: 'All of us young people were sitting and dreaming in the shops. "Well, it's only for a season or two I'll be doing this, I'll be doing that." "I'll marry a man that will be able to take care of me." '[83] To both social reformers and sexual radicals this seemed to be an evasion. Yet, as Sarah Eisenstein points out in *Bread and Roses*, such aspirations could also be interpreted as a claim to a common womanhood with middle-class women, an aspiration for happiness rather than toil. At Lawrence the women marched singing the song 'Bread and Roses' and Rose Schneiderman, a cap maker born in Poland who worked with the Women's Trade Union League, recollected, 'We not only wanted labor laws and bread, we wanted roses too.'[84]

Chapter 2

THE FIRST WORLD WAR AND ITS AFTERMATH

BRITAIN

Choices

And there shone all April
In your eyes.[1]

The young man who wrote these lines to Vera Brittain in April 1914 was to die within eighteen months. When his uniform was returned, caked with the mud of a trench battlefield and stained with blood, Vera Brittain recalled in *Testament of Youth*, 'It was amid this heap of horror and decay that we found the black manuscript note-book containing his poems.'[2]

The innocence and delight of that last spring of peace in the countryside around Buxton had been irrevocably shattered. When Vera Brittain gave up her place at Oxford to join the Voluntary Aid Detachment (VAD) as a nurse in a London hospital, the desire to serve hardly seemed like a conscious choice; it was as if destiny had closed in around her. Such idealistic patriotism was to be sorely tested by the unnecessary discomfort and muddle of icy, ill-lit lodgings. Twenty young women shared one bathroom with a temperamental geyser from which 'tepid water trickled slowly into the bath'.[3] The VADs rose at 5.45 a.m. and walked to the hospital in all weathers, working from 7.30 a.m. to 8 p.m. As a result, they 'all acquired puffy hands, chapped faces, chilblains and swollen ankles'.[4]

After the chaperoned life of upper-middle-class Buxton society, she walked the streets of working-class London alone and nursed men in acute pain. When her father wanted her to come home, she replied:

Nothing – beyond sheer necessity – would induce me to stop doing what I am doing now, and I should never respect myself again if I allowed a few slight hardships to make me give up what is the finest work any girl can do now. I do not agree that my place is at home doing nothing, for I consider that the place now of anyone who is young and capable is where the work that is needed is to be done.[5]

The resolve to see life was legitimated by the commitment to serve. Her incipient feminism contributed to her desire to help the war effort. She was also made conscious of her privileged upbringing by the wartime encounters with men and women of other classes. Her patriotism contained a desire to go beyond the boundaries not only of her gender but also of her class. The reward was acceptance and connection. Travelling through France in May 1917, she records, 'We were much cheered by Tommies in a troop train that we passed, and cheered and waved to by the soldiers in the camps along both sides of the railways.'[6]

Alice Wheeldon, who lived not far from Buxton in Derby, had a very different war. She was a second-hand clothes dealer in her early fifties who had been a rank and file member of the Women's Social

Vera Brittain in VAD uniform.

and Political Union, selling newspapers and campaigning in the market-place. She was also a socialist, on the left of the Independent Labour Party (ILP). When war broke out that August, Alice Wheeldon's choice, in contrast to Vera Brittain, was one of decisive opposition. She and her daughter Hettie, a schoolteacher, were to join the No-Conscription Fellowship (NCF), an organization which helped young men who refused to fight. Started by ILP socialists Fenner and Lilla Brockway, the NCF included pacifists, like the former constitutional suffragist Catherine Marshall, as well as socialists like Alice and Hettie who believed that the war was sacrificing lives merely to safeguard profits.

Alice Wheeldon became part of an underground network who sheltered conscientious objectors on the run from the military authorities, who sought to intern them in camps. Towards the end of 1916 she was visited by a spy from the Ministry of Munitions intelligence unit who went under the name 'Alex Gordon'. There was an atmosphere of desperation and paranoia about high casualties and military defeats. State surveillance was widespread. Lloyd George was pushing hard for an increase in the production of munitions and determined to break the militant shop stewards' movement, which was not only pressing for 'workers' control' but making links with the peace movement. 'Alex Gordon' had already been trying to implicate left-wing shop stewards in his attempts to uncover saboteurs when he convinced Alice Wheeldon to write to her son-in-law Alf Mason, a chemist in Southampton, for poison. When the letters were intercepted, she and Hettie were arrested. Her defence was that the poison was intended for guard dogs at an internment camp for conscientious objectors; the prosecution said it was to assassinate Lloyd George with a poisoned dart while he played golf – along with King George and the Labour leader, Arthur Henderson, who was part of the wartime coalition.

The trial was a display of self-righteous patriotism conducted for the prosecution by F. E. Smith, the prominent right-wing lawyer and politician. He declared the Wheeldon family to be 'a gang of desperate persons poisoned by revolutionary doctrines and obsessed with an insensate and vile hatred of their own country'.[7] He also noted how Alice Wheeldon and her daughters used 'language of the most obscene and disgusting character'.[8] They were presented not only as politically deviant but as women who had transgressed the moral boundaries of gender.

Alice Wheeldon was jailed for conspiracy early in 1917. In the very different climate of the winter of 1918, she was freed in an amnesty, for by then Lloyd George wanted to regain his liberal credentials. But weakened by her hunger strikes in jail, she died in the influenza epidemic of February 1919.

The letters of the Wheeldon family and their friends, preserved as a result of this harsh and cynical invasion of the state into their lives, provide a glimpse into the lower-middle-class provincial milieu of radical opposition to the war. They are about everyday matters: mince pies, new blouses, periods. But they also convey a defiant culture: the women in this rebel network cut their hair short, read feminist, socialist and pacifist papers, and discussed Shaw's plays. They expressed a vehement revulsion against the hypocrisy of politicians and the carnage of militarism. There is a desperate isolation in the letters too. Alice Wheeldon was ostracized by neighbours, while Hettie lost her job as a schoolteacher. They had only a tattered network of left-wing feminists and socialists, who, like them, were war resisters. Alice wrote to one friend from her suffrage days, Lydia Robinson, that it was 'everybody who is a nobody' who had stayed loyal, 'the others don't want to know'.[9]

Politics

Among the 'somebodies' who had disowned the Wheeldons was Emmeline Pankhurst. From 1914 all the old alliances in the suffrage movement were overturned and the key issue became the response to the war. The leadership of the WSPU swung around to support the government, putting the militant campaign for votes for women after the claims of the soldiers. 'Could any woman face the possibility of the affairs of the country being settled by conscientious objectors, passive resisters and shirkers?'[10] asked Emmeline Pankhurst.

Her daughter Sylvia, however, took the same position as the Wheeldons – it was the capitalists' war. She spent the war years in opposition, often facing violent patriotic crowds at anti-war meetings, while still trying to improve the conditions of women in the east London working-class community. Other members of the WSPU such as Helen Crawfurd, an outstanding speaker in the Scottish suffragette movement, were also against the war, and the National Union of Women's Suffrage Societies (NUWSS) was similarly divided. Catherine Marshall, Helena Swanwick and Isabella Ford, for example, supported the pacifists, while other leading members like Eleanor Rathbone, Lady Frances Balfour and Millicent Fawcett maintained that women had to prove themselves by patriotic war work. It was the test which in Millicent Fawcett's words would prove them to be 'worthy of citizenship'.[11] Both sides could invoke concepts of womanliness in arguing their case. Supporters of the war stressed the right to serve as a basis for citizenship, extending the female sphere into patriotic duty. Feminist pacifists claimed that women were essentially opposed to militarism.

With Emmeline and Christabel Pankhurst allied with Lloyd George, Sylvia, rather uneasily, found herself working with the NUWSS rebels who had been in the constitutionalist suffrage camp. They, along with trade unionist Margaret Bondfield, were part of the British delegation to the international women's peace conference at the Hague in the spring of 1915. The conference, which was presided over by Jane Addams, hoped to mobilize women to put pressure on the politicians to end the war. But the British government refused them travel permits and only a few British women were to arrive at the founding meeting of the Women's International League for Peace and Freedom (WILPF). The Glasgow branch of the WILPF was formed by socialist feminists Helen Crawfurd and Agnes Dollan, who went on to hold a women's peace conference in June 1916. The No-Conscription Fellowship continued to work locally with war resisters, applying some of the tactics of the militant suffrage movement to the peace movement. In the summer of 1917, the Women's Peace Crusade (WPC) was formed, with Helen Crawfurd as honorary secretary. Groups spread across the country, campaigning in working-class communities. Women like the London ILPer and suffrage campaigner Florence Exten-Hann, the Glaswegian trade unionist and socialist feminist Jessie Stephen, and the radical suffragist Selina Cooper from Nelson ILP were part of this grass-roots anti-war movement which retained a strong commitment to democracy and social reform.

Neither the pacifist nor the anti-war stand was easy. The emotional strain of pitting oneself against a nation at war was considerable and the hardest part was that prejudice could be directed at others in the family.

For example, Minnie Baynton (later Vandome), the daughter of a well-known conscientious objector in Hackney, east London, nearly lost her scholarship to grammar school, until a Quaker headmistress at Laura Place grammar school in Clapton agreed to admit her.

War resisters, moreover, faced an overtly repressive state. The government's political use of its power to withhold passports was an example of the much tighter state control which restricted all opposition during wartime. The Irish socialist, feminist and pacifist Hanna Sheehy-Skeffington noted that while anti-war feminists were not allowed to travel, Emmeline Pankhurst was one of a 'regular army of lecturers' allowed to 'put her case for the war before American audiences', at the same time vilifying 'those nations that did not agree with her imperialist ambitions'.[12]

In Ireland the suffrage movement divided over the war and could not evade the bitter conflict between the unionists, who wanted to stay linked to Britain, and the nationalists, who wanted independence. For example, in Munster the Women's Franchise League voted in November 1914 to form an ambulance corps and banned the feminist paper *The Irish Citizen* for its anti-war views. Nationalists, including Mary MacSwiney, a teacher who was to play a leading part in Sinn Fein, resigned. The nationalist Irish Volunteers, however, were not in favour of women's suffrage and their women's wing, Cumann na mBan, despite its flamboyant and charismatic president, Countess Markievicz, was too loyal to the leadership for Hanna Sheehy-Skeffington's liking: 'an animated collecting box for men',[13] she called it. In contrast, the Irish Citizen Army, under the leadership of the socialist James Connolly, who was influenced by his time in the United States and the enthusiasm of his daughters for the vote, was committed to women's suffrage.

Connolly took a leading part in the Easter Rising of 1916 against British rule, and when the rebels captured the Dublin GPO, the republican proclamation which was read out promised women equal citizenship. Cumann na mBan members had defied the men and insisted on taking part in the rising and several Irish Citizen Army women played a prominent role. Countess Markievicz, who had joined the Citizen Army, commandeered vehicles for barricades and supervised first aid in full military uniform and her best hat with plumed feathers.

Countess Markievicz (Constance Georgine Gore-Booth)
in military uniform.

Like Connolly, she was sentenced to death after the defeat of the rebels, but later this was commuted to imprisonment.

The abortive rising resulted in hardened opposition to British rule. It also drew women into a more active role in the struggle for an independent Ireland. Hanna Sheehy-Skeffington did not support the Easter Rising, but her pacifist husband, Francis, had been killed by soldiers while he was trying to prevent looting. She too was to be imprisoned in May 1918 for opposing the attempt to introduce conscription in Ireland and joined nationalist women Maud Gonne and Constance Markievicz in jail in Britain. Not only was Cumann na mBan to change after the rising, but Irish feminists moved closer to the nationalists.

In England the experience of the war exposed the weaknesses in the idea of an alliance based on 'women's interests' apart from other political forces. The choices were not to be that simple. The demand for suffrage was shelved not only by those feminists who opposed the war but also by those who supported it. The anti-suffrage movement, to the consternation of one of its leading figures, Mrs Humphry Ward, was similarly in disarray by 1917, when moves for a suffrage reform package in Parliament brought up the issues again. Opponents of votes for women had feared that political rights would destroy the special sphere of womanly influence in the family. The war, however, had brought women into the male sphere and made the domestic front a matter of public concern. The women who took on supervisory war work began to see how a society was run; those who campaigned for better conditions at work and in communities became more confident and developed new demands for social provision. In the anti-war camp there were many, like Florence Exten-Hann, who came to an awareness of the need to democratize international as well as national politics, supporting an international peace force and a reduction in armaments.

Mobilization

In 1914 the radical pacifist suffragist Mary Sheepshanks declared that women must not simply bind 'the wounds that men have made', but 'use their brains to understand the causes of the European frenzy'.[14] But it was militarism rather than anti-militarism, nationalism rather than internationalism, which stirred most British women in 1914. In the early years of the war voluntary workers flocked to help the war effort on a charitable basis: 'Sister Susie sewing shirts for soldiers' was a popular refrain. Sister Susie rapidly became more adventurous.

Many upper- and middle-class women became nurses, like Vera Brittain, through the Voluntary Aid Detachment. These VADs nursed soldiers and also drove ambulances in the First Aid Nursing Yeomanry (FANY). FANY was a much-desired form of war service which tended to attract rich women, for driving skills, combined with the ability to pull strings, helped would-be ambulance drivers. Women volunteers also drove and maintained cars in the Mechanical Transport Company.

Raw young ladies were regarded with scepticism by professional nurses and by the army. When a young VAD managed to get transferred to the Ambulance Corps, the major to whom she reported teased her about her desire for adventure: 'I doubt if one half of you VADs and others are doing your bit just out of patriotism.'[15] But the risks were real enough. Some women volunteers were killed by bombs or diseases

Targeting the Kitchen

Food became a key issue as the war continued in Britain. At first voluntary groups tried to meet the food emergency. The National Food Economy League, the National Union of Women's Suffrage Societies' Patriotic Housekeeping Exhibition and the Food Reform Association propagandized with handbills, recipes and advice on nutrition, and *The Win the War Cookery Book* told housewives, 'The British fighting line shifts and extends now *you* are in it. The struggle is not only on land and sea; it is in *your* larder, *your* kitchen and *your* dining room. Every meal you serve is now literally a battle.'[16]

Mobilizing motherhood.

Ingenious wartime manufacturers linked partiotism and purchasing. For example, Lifebuoy soap would 'carry you to victory over Germs and Microbes of Disease . . . Enclose a Tablet in your next parcel to the Front. He will appreciate it,' while 'Tommy Atkins was still A1 and on the Active List thanks to Beecham's Pills.'[17] Nurses were told they should use Palmolive soap out of consideration for the wounded: 'They know that hard rough skins would irritate and often cause pain to the sufferers whom they have to tend and care for.'[18]

After 1915, with Germany's blockade causing shortages, the government targeted women as housewives. The emphasis on women's role in the home echoed the call to serve in war work. The kitchen assumed a new status as the key to victory: 'Eat Less and Save Shipping', 'Eat Less, Masticate More and Save a Pound of Bread per Person per Week.'[19] While the true patriot, according to the propaganda, was the type who ate asparagus and left potatoes to the poor.

✳

like typhus. Edith Cavell, the daughter of a Norfolk clergyman, was shot by the Germans in October 1915 because she assisted in the escape of Allied soldiers caught behind German lines.

Groups of women keen to 'do their bit' for the war began to get together on a voluntary basis, acquiring their own uniforms. These blurred gender distinctions and marked an aspiration for uniformity – with modifications: some FANY ambulance drivers, for instance, wore fur coats over theirs. The uniforms, which could be expensive, were in fact only superficially classless. For example, the khaki coat, skirt and felt hat with shoes and puttees worn by the Women's Volunteer Reserve to practise signalling cost £2 10s. Not surprisingly, it was middle- and upper-class women who were enthusiastic to join these uniformed volunteer groups. They met with a mixed reception. Dr Elsie Maud Inglis, one of the early women doctors and a feminist, was told by the military authorities to 'go home and sit still' when she first proposed an all-woman medical unit. She disobeyed and the Scottish Women's Hospital units came into being from July 1915. The Marchioness of Londonderry's Women's Legion had its own uniform and military-style hierarchy, but provided a reassuringly womanly service by cooking for the army. She had gained experience of such strategic intervention in her role as president of the New Ulster Women's Unionist Council during the militant right-wing resistance to Irish Home Rule before the war.

Some of these voluntary initiatives eventually became a recognized part of the war effort and were to be grafted on to the state. The Women's Police Patrols were first started by the National Union of Women Workers, a middle-class social welfare organization, to protect women and girls around military camps. They were employed by the Metropolitan Police under Mrs Theo Stanley and became part of the police force in 1917. Similarly the Women's Land Army had been preceded by a voluntary association, the Women's Land Service Corps. Though the Land Army was formed by the women's branch of the Board of Agriculture in 1917, it worked closely with the voluntary Women's Institute, founded by a former suffrage campaigner, Edith Rigby. The enthusiastic young women who joined the Land Army tended to be from non-manual occupations; some were university-educated. Farmers were doubtful if the Land Girls, who invariably lacked experience, could do farm work; some preferred to recruit old-age pensioners. The farmers' wives regarded the Land Army's overalls, breeches and leather leggings with disdain. *Punch* had great fun with Land Girl cartoons.

FARMER: Now let me see if you can milk that cow.
GIRL: (*by vocation barmaid and regarding the horns*) Which handle's for the milk and which for the cream?[20]

The Land Girls and the Women's Forestry Corps nonetheless became accepted figures in country life, with local legends growing around resourceful individuals, like the young woman who kicked a bull on the nose just as it was about to gore the man she was later to marry.

The women's services followed the Land Army. The Women's Army Auxiliary Corps (WAAC) and the Women's Royal Naval Service (WRNS) were founded in 1917 and the Women's Royal Air Force

(WRAF) in 1918. Robert Roberts remembered a difference in the social status of the women's forces: 'Class reared its head: the Women's Auxiliary Army Corps, we soon gathered, was for working-class females, whereas the "Wrens" and the "WRAF" catered for the nicer girls.'[21]

Women in the services could encounter hostility if they invaded male terrain. Mrs Stephens, for example, who was one of the first aircraft motorcyclists, found that the men initially refused to speak to her. Nonetheless, a remarkable transformation in women's lives had occurred. The exceptional circumstances of war had broken through assumptions about separate spheres, and pragmatically both women and men adapted to the unprecedented situation.

Work

The mobilization for war was to bring many women who had been employed as domestic servants, saleswomen, dressmakers and home-workers into regulated industrial work. In the first year, however, they tended to take over jobs left by men who had joined the services,

Doing a Man's Job:
woman operating railway signals.

delivering milk, driving wagons and window-cleaning. By 1915, in an effort to increase wartime production, attempts were made in earnest to recruit women into munitions, and the Munitions Act of June 1915 gave the government extensive powers over labour. In *Women and the Women's Movement*, Martin Pugh shows that substitution of women occurred mainly in the government-controlled workplaces. By October 1916 the number of women had increased by nearly 300 per cent in these, whereas in the uncontrolled workplaces the figure was only 36 per cent.

Women made and filled shells and cartridges, did labouring, cleaning, catering, driving and storeroom-keeping, worked in the optical instruments industry or became needlewomen and carpenters in the aircraft industry. They did not usually take over men's jobs in engineering, but tasks were broken down, which meant that unskilled workers could do parts of the men's jobs. The arrival of unskilled labour thus contributed to an American-style reorganization of production which was already under way. The introduction of scientific management techniques became more widespread in the war. Protective legislation was waived, so women worked at night. This was not always unpopular, as it meant they could do housework in the daytime, but they did complain about the length of their shifts: women workers had to stand sometimes for ten or twelve hours.

Munitions work was, of course, also dangerous. Agnes Foxwell, a middle-class volunteer who worked for six months as a supervisor at Woolwich, was dismissive about the dangers of 'trotyl' (TNT), claiming that a lotion distributed to the women counteracted the effect of TNT poisoning. The 'pale lemon colour and deep gold' of the workers' skins soon returned to their 'normal appearance'.[22] However, toxic jaundice could cause death; at least 349 cases of serious TNT poisoning were reported, and of these 109 people died. There was also the danger of explosions. An east London working-class woman, Dolly Scannell, recalled the terrible explosion at Woolwich Arsenal breaking the windows of her home in Poplar, east London. Women nevertheless sought munitions work, partly because the pay was higher, partly because the alternatives available were worse and partly because there was a strong feeling that it was the right thing to be doing for the war effort.

Scientific management in the munitions factories extended beyond the labour process to shape the culture of the workplace, with efficient canteens and uniform work wear. Agnes Foxwell describes how in retaliation against this regimentation, the women modified their gowns and how workshops developed their own fashions in caps, flowers, ribbons or laces. Even 'Auntie Ellis', the senior attendant, appeared in defiant bright scarlet laces: 'I'm wearin' the government's red tape,'[23] she declared.

Agnes Foxwell and other middle-class commentators stressed the camaraderie between classes at work. Previous contact had been so slight and remote that the interaction appeared remarkable. However, the social mixing was contained by the barriers which remained outside the workplace, in the women's hostels and during leisure hours. Working-class women, well aware of class distinctions, called lady volunteers 'Miows'[24] because of their accents.

The women were regarded with hostility by many male workers. Prejudice and dented craft pride mixed with fear for their jobs in the future if the 'dilutees' were to become permanent fixtures. Workers' control was partly about safeguarding craft workers' conditions, as was the insistence of the skilled engineers in the Amalgamated Society of Engineers that women be paid the same as men. However, in Sheffield in 1916 the militant shop stewards' movement consciously tried to link the skilled men with women and other unskilled workers, causing the police spies from the Ministry of Munitions Intelligence Unit to send in worried reports. The left-wing Sheffield shop stewards' leader J. T. Murphy recognized that the conflict between men and women was not confined to the workplace. In 1917 he wrote, 'We men and women of today have to pay the price of man's economic dominance over women which has existed for centuries. Content to treat women as subjects instead of equals, men are now faced with problems not to their liking.'[25]

The skilled male trade unionists' insistence on equal pay to protect the male rate was evaded by employers who paid lip service to the theory and then altered the work process. Mary Macarthur, who represented women on the Central Munitions Labour Supply Committee and the Health of Munitions Workers Committee, observed, 'Some simple adjustment was made to machinery – a twist drill, perhaps, was replaced by a flat cutter, an automatic stop was fitted to a lathe, and it was declared the work was not the same.'[26]

Nonetheless, equality between men and women workers really arrived on the agenda of labour relations as an aspiration not only among women organizers and campaigners like Mary Macarthur or Sylvia Pankhurst but among the rank and file. 'Same work – same money,'[27] demanded women transport workers in 1918. Towards the end of the war, women bus and train operators in Willesden, north-west London, stopped work when they were refused a 5s. bonus given to the men. Bus passengers who tried 'to chaff the girls' were warned 'that unless the principle of "equal pay for equal work" is conceded next week fresh trouble might be expected'.[28] They were joined by women from depots and garages in Hackney, Holloway, Archway and Acton, and the strike spread beyond London to Southend, Hastings, Bath, Bristol, Birmingham and South Wales. The government feared the spirit of rebellion would affect munitions and gave them the 5s. war bonus, but did not concede equal pay. The experience of regular employment and reasonable pay had enabled women workers to glimpse parity.

However, women workers continued to be regarded as special cases, and it was to be these protective attitudes to women as potential reproducers which contributed to some of the welfare gains in government-controlled factories. 'The workers of today are the mothers of tomorrow,'[29] said Lloyd George, and his concern about motherhood led to the introduction of protective clothing, seats, day nurseries, hostels and canteens. Woolwich Arsenal set up a model workplace nursery, with special children's bathrooms, toilets, chairs, rest rooms and playspaces. It also offered an allowance for mothers on night work for child-care.

Agnes Foxwell, like most other middle-class observers, saw these welfare gains as unqualified progress. Along with sports events, concerts or the pageant in which Woolwich Arsenal workers echoed suffrage imagery by appearing as Joan of Arc, they seemed to indicate harmonious work relationships. But the Standing Joint Committee of Women's Organizations, distrustful of the employers' control over hostels and canteens, were by 1917 pressing for greater democratic control by local authorities and trade unions. The role of trade unions thus extended beyond wages, to take up the social interests of workers during wartime

– an example of the contradictory impact of the state's entry into work and daily life.

The new relation between the state and industry was to bring some organizers, like Mary Macarthur, into close contact with government. Others, like Sylvia Pankhurst, tried to gain concessions from the wartime state while consciously resisting the coercive aspects of state intervention in industry and working-class neighbourhoods. Thus while some labour women became more pro-state during the war, others in the anti-war movement became increasingly anti-state.

Attitudes to the state crystallized most sharply in Ireland. In Dublin, women trade union leaders Helena Moloney, secretary of the Irish Women Workers' Union (IWWU), and Winifred Carney, Secretary of the Irish Women Textile Workers, had taken courageous action during the Easter Rising of 1916. Along with Louie Bennett, a pacifist and suffrage campaigner who took over the IWWU, such women could never forgive the execution of James Connolly by the British government. Feeling in Ireland was too bitter in 1917 for women labour organizers to work with the National Federation of Women Workers' English representative, who came over to try to raise the rates of munitions workers in Ireland. The lines of division were too stark and clear.

Daily Life

War invaded the humdrum everyday routines of survival. The German blockade meant that shopping queues got longer. Women were spending hours hunting for basic items, tempers rose and police were called in to control angry crowds. Dolly Scannell recalled how children would be mobilized by their mothers in the desperate effort to feed the family:

The older girls spent a lot of their time queuing at the shops for food. The rumour would spread, 'They've got potatoes down Chrisp Street' and they would be off like firemen sliding down poles. Hours later they would return like victors until Mother examined their buy and pronounced, 'Why, these are no bigger than peas. How am I to feed my hungry family?'[30]

The food crisis led to various alternative projects. For instance, the Food Reform Association set up its own shops and the Women's Labour

League, the sister organization of the Labour Party, started a communal kitchen on Westminster Bridge Road in London. The lack of servants caused by war work also inspired schemes for the social reorganization of domesticity. In 1916 in the feminist paper *The Common Cause*, Clementina Black proposed federated households to rationalize housework. *The Times* advertised another alternative for the rich in 1917: the Suction Cleaner Company's 'Electric Housemaid: Simply connect to electric lamp socket'.[31]

Matters which had previously been private, like the employment of servants and the choice of recipes, were suddenly affairs of state. A new government department of food under Lord Devonport was created in 1916. It exhorted loyal citizens to eat bean fritters and barley rissoles, but it also got involved in the distribution and consumption of food through the Local Food Committees and National Kitchens for Communal Cooking. Annie Swan, a middle-class volunteer who had been having difficulty at her local kitchen committee in Hertford convincing working-class women of the virtues of meat substitutes and boiled bones, was impressed by the Women's Labour League's Westminster Bridge kitchen's economies of scale through bulk purchasing. She spotted, however, that it was not the very poor who came with their baskets and buckets to take the food home. Back in Hertford, she set about convincing suspicious women that communal kitchens were not charity but a way of pooling resources. Her especial concern was to feed children.

Common needs brought about a certain convergence of activity among women regardless of politics. Sylvia Pankhurst, who had visited the community projects initiated by US social settlements and radical municipal experiments, established a cost-price restaurant, along with a co-operative workshop, in east London. Dinner cost 2d., or just 1d. for children, but those who could not afford that ate free. Around 400 people were served every day. Sylvia Pankhurst combined these projects with campaigns for state control of food prices. By 1915 she wanted the nationalization of food supply and distribution. The 1917 Russian Revolution encouraged her to demand the extension of these social and economic democratic rights. In 1918 her paper, *The Workers' Dreadnought*, called for free food distribution on the rates and the management of food production by workers' councils appointed by the

Trades Union Congress and local trades councils, with women making up half of each committee. Norah Smythe, a member of Sylvia Pankhurst's Workers' Socialist Federation, suggested in 1918 that people made homeless by air raids should follow the Russian example and take over empty houses. In her biography of Sylvia Pankhurst, Barbara Winslow shows how she tried to overcome the exclusion of many women from workplace councils with the idea of social soviets, which would enable housewives and other non-waged people to exert democratic control in local communities.

Working-class women who faced rising costs and whose personal existence was being endangered and disrupted by warfare responded by expressing a new sense of entitlement. In June 1915 the attempt to evict a Glasgow soldier's family was resisted by a crowd of angry neighbours, mostly women. This was to be the start of a rent strike organized by Agnes Dollan, Helen Crawfurd, Mary Barbour and Jessie Stephen through locally based 'close' committees, 'kitchen' meetings and mass pickets. Women picketed armed with pease meal and flour, and in street after street the notices went up: WE ARE NOT PAYING INCREASED RENT.[32] The Glasgow Women's Housing Association had support among the shipyard workers and there were some tentative links with shop stewards through the labour movement contacts of the women organizers. There was thus a danger that community rebellion would affect wartime production. As discontent spread to other towns, the government yielded to pressure and introduced the Rent Restriction Act in 1915.

Patriotic propaganda, communal self-help projects which reorganized shopping and eating, demands for state regulation of food and housing and militant forms of grass-roots direct action combined to transform what had been a personal area of life into a contested social terrain. A similar shift can be observed in attitudes and policies towards mothers and children. In the first year of the war a 10 per cent rise in the infant mortality rate and an increase in tuberculosis among women contributed to anxiety about motherhood and fertility which resembled the panic about racial decline in the Boer War. In 1914 a 50 per cent subsidy for expenditure by local government on maternity and infant welfare was made available by Herbert Samuel, president of the Local Government Board.

Awareness of the conditions of maternity was stimulated by infant and maternity welfare centres such as Sylvia Pankhurst's Mother's Arms, set up in an old pub called the Gunmakers' Arms. It included a baby clinic giving out milk and advice, along with a day nursery using Montessori play methods of education. Harrowing accounts of pregnancy and childbirth were published by the Women's Co-operative Guild in 1915. Their book, *Maternity: Letters from Working Women*, was all the more effective because it came from working-class women themselves and contributed to a campaign among labour women for municipal health centres, health education, home helps and health visitors. The formation of the Women's Institutes meanwhile brought maternalist concerns to women in rural areas.

Social imperialist fear about the national stock in wartime was another impetus for reform. Lord Plunkett, for instance, set up the Babies of the Empire Society. In some areas women's networks seized the maternalist moment and combined forces. When Selina Cooper spoke to Accrington Church Guild at the opening of its Maternity and Child Welfare Week in 1915, the Women's Imperial Health Society provided an exhibition of hygienic clothing for children. In 1917 the National Baby Week Council, with Lord Rhondda as chairman, Lloyd George as president and Waldorf Astor as vice-president, launched Baby Week with the slogan 'It is more dangerous to be a baby in England than to be a soldier.'[33] Selina Cooper, busy in the Women's Peace Crusade in Lancashire, found time to support Baby Week, though the minutes of Sylvia Pankhurst's Workers' Socialist Federation registered suspicion.

In 1918, when the Maternity and Child Welfare Act was passed, it seemed that local self-help projects were to be extended and that social responsibility for mothers and infants would result in a national network of services under democratic control. The act required local authorities to appoint committees for maternity and child welfare on which working women would be represented. It also allowed grants for home helps, lying-in homes, food for expectant mothers and children, crèches, day nurseries, convalescent homes and hospital treatment for children up to five years old.

Sex

Consciousness of society's responsibility for welfare could be a basis for challenging conservative sexual attitudes. An important breakthrough was the extension of separation allowances to women who were not formally married to soldiers. In 1917 Mrs Layton, the Women's Co-operative Guild delegate to the Local Government Board, was told that clerics felt respectable married women would be outraged if money was given to women living with men out of wedlock. Her response was, 'I explained that I represented the Women's Co-operative Guild . . . chiefly composed of respectable married women, and that the Guild entirely repudiated the statement that married women would be resentful.' She also asked the board pointedly to remember 'that every time a woman fell a man fell also'.[34] This argument for male responsibility was taken up by the Liberal National Council for the Unmarried Mother, in its demand for fathers to pay maintenance, along with the provision of accommodation to enable single women to work and keep their children. The more radical War Babies and Mothers League wanted the state to provide material help for unmarried mothers and an end to the cultural stigma of illegitimacy.

The war polarized attitudes towards the sexual and economic independence of women. Amidst disturbed reports of moral decline there were calls for various forms of intervention. Mary Allen, a former suffragette who was an early member of the Women's Police Service, maintained in *Women at the Crossroads* (1934) that separation allowances and wages had driven servants, caretakers, charwomen and munitions workers to drink, 'feverish excitements or extravagances'.[35] Panic about women drinking and fears of immorality led to the Women's Patrols, later to be the basis for women's entry into the police force. Organizations like the Young Women's Christian Association, the Church Army, the Girls' Friendly Society and the National Union of Women Workers tried to provide alternative forms of supervised leisure activities for young girls similar to those in US cities. They faced considerable competition. Angela Woollacott, in her study of the munitions workers, *On Her Their Lives Depend*, describes the popularity of American films in which romance combined with independence. A typical example was *The Eternal Grind*, in which Mary Pickford, the popular silent-film

Women and Popular Fiction

First World War popular fiction created a new kind of female heroine out of Voluntary Aid Detachment workers, munitions workers, the Land Army and ambulance drivers. Popular author Angela Brazil's schoolgirls longed to do their bit by nursing the wounded, driving a transport wagon or becoming a telephone operator. Magazines like *The Girls' Friend*, which aimed to reach working-class young women, advised them not to 'falter' but to keep 'to the call of duty'[36] and work for the war effort rather than getting married hastily. But working-class and middle-class readers alike preferred a mix of adventure and romance. *Beryl of the Biplane* by William le Queux was a 1917 novel about an intrepid 'air-woman' who got both. Beryl combined being an expert flyer, a clever counter-espionage agent and a 'uniformed chauffeuse' with petite fluffy femininity. Fellow airmen were amazed at the skills she demonstrated in fiancé Ronnie's powerful plane, while 'the way in which she manipulates the joystick often indeed astonishes Ronnie himself'.[37] When Ronnie slumps in the cockpit bleeding, Beryl successfully dives and banks to evade enemy attack, nursing him back to health to become, of course, his wife.

In 1916 *The Penny Pictorial* ran 'A Series of Romances Resulting from the Vast Changes in the Spheres of Women' by E. Almaz Stout. The formula was simple: male incredulity that a slip of a girl could drive a van or be a bank cashier, plucky heroine's heroic war work proves men wrong before finding romantic fulfilment – 'With a little moaning sob Molly fell forward into Henry Cardew's arms. But she was made of British fibre and she knew she must not faint or give way yet.'[38] The stuff of Britishness had female as well as male gender meanings.

✳

star, played a factory worker who saves her friend from ruin by getting her seducer, the boss's son, to marry her. Son number two, a socially conscious type, falls for the heroine, who then gets the boss to improve conditions for the workers.

The war disrupted established gender assumptions. The young women workers who formed their own football teams, went bicycling or dancing and flocked to theatres, music halls and cinemas were at once heroines of the war effort and dangerously autonomous. By 1917 the newspapers had begun berating them as 'flaunting flappers'.[39] The hostility was about class as well as gender. Male munitions workers' new motorcycles were viewed askance and these men were rumoured to be even hiring motor cars for nights out at the pantomime. But as Angela Woollacott remarks: 'While conspicuous spending in men workers signified a threat to the established hierarchy of social privilege, in women workers it was also considered portentous of uncontrolled sexuality.'[40] An exasperated Sylvia Pankhurst wrote in *The Home Front*, 'Alarmist morality-mongers conceived most monstrous visions of girls and women . . . plunging into excesses and burdening the country with swarms of illegitimate infants.'[41]

One visible symbol of preparation for the plunge was make-up. Evoking ritual cleansing, the romantic novelist Marie Corelli admonished women to wash the paint from their cheeks. Robert Roberts's father threw big sister Jenny's cosmetics on the fire, convinced that they marked the beginnings of immorality. But Jenny was earning good money: she 'stood unperturbed. "I either go on using it," she said, "or you can turn me out too." '[42]

Silk stockings were another mark of luxurious sin: munitions workers were said to be heading to theatres in taxis, clad in furs and silk stockings. Rumour mingled with reality. A Woolwich munitions worker, Lilian Bineham, recalled that there were indeed 'carryings-on . . . with the men away' and Elsie Slater from the Barnbow shell factory described how munitions workers would forget work and 'buzz on to York, with t' soldiers.'[43] These 'fast' ones were always, of course, other women. Robert Roberts considered that working-class women in Salford became 'more worldly-wise'[44] in the war. A pragmatic attitude towards sexuality enabled moral standards to stretch while still retaining a code of standards for self-protection. A south London waitress, for instance, remembered going out dancing a lot and meeting boys at the Elephant and Castle, but would not go out with soldiers: 'You've got to have a safeguard before you go intimate with men like that. If they turn rough, you've got no proof.'[45]

The consequences of an unwanted pregnancy resulted in such hardship that fear and sex continued to be never far apart. There were reports of the use of lead for abortions and of friends imprisoned for illegal abortion, although these were not, of course, peculiar to wartime. Illegitimacy rates per 1,000 live births *did* rise by 30 per cent during the war. However, because the birth-rate as a whole fell, fewer women actually had an illegitimate child than in 1911.

The outcry about women's sexuality was in fact part of a wider effort to secure social control. One aspect of moral regulation was an enforcement of work discipline. Mary Allen's policing of the munitions factories uncovered 'girls hiding away from their work in all sorts of places, or trying to escape from the shops on all manner of trivial pretexts'.[46] There was also concern to protect the troops from women, who were regarded as the source of sexual contamination, both metaphorically and literally. The army, accustomed to the colonies, where the Contagious Diseases Acts had continued to be enforced around garrisons, assumed that they should have similar powers to prevent soldiers from catching venereal disease. The army's approach was to provide 'clean' prostitutes and maintain a closed shop. Their proposal in 1914 that separation allowances be withdrawn from 'unworthy' wives and dependants of soldiers and sailors was rejected, but the wartime Defence of the Realm Act (DORA) was utilized to impose a curfew in Cardiff, and women were banned from pubs. In Sheffield women were not allowed to drink even in a hotel or restaurant after 6 p.m. Meanwhile, the army commander in Grantham had soldiers and police entering houses within a six-mile radius 'to see if the girls were in bed and see who was in the houses'.[47] *Votes for Women*, the paper of the United Suffragists, commented sardonically that the military authorities in Cardiff seemed not to realize that 'in protecting the troops from the women they have failed to protect the women from the troops'.[48] This confusion about who was protecting whom continued. The women police who had joined up to protect women were actually used to discipline them. In Grantham, as one glumly reported,

'We found that the women were getting large quantities of drink and were entertaining the men in their houses instead of being out on the streets.'[49]

The Women's Patrols that roamed parks, woods and dark alleys near army camps and depots met with a mixed reception from both working-class women and the police themselves. They pursued not only prostitutes but couples like a corporal and a woman clerk from Harrods, found having sexual intercourse in London's Hyde Park. He was fined and she was reprimanded. Lovemaking in parks was nothing new; the intervention of middle-class women in policing the sexual behaviour of working-class and lower-middle-class women did, however, mark a change in how personal behaviour was regarded. Discussion of sexuality shifted into the public arena.

There *were* real dangers behind the moral panic. A soldier tried to abduct Dolly Scannell as a child on Poplar Recreation Ground. She was rescued not by the Women's Patrols but by her sister and mother, who came running over the flowerbeds. After being examined by a doctor at the police station, she remembered going home, where her brother and father were having dinner: 'David looked at me as though I was a wicked girl. Father did not look at me at all.'[50]

The exceptional circumstances of war did have an effect on values, though not in the simple terms assumed by those who sought to police women's sexuality. A noticeable minority among the upper and middle class were questioning the sexual assumptions of their upbringing. The author of *WAAC: The Women's Story of the War* fell in love with a married man and her pre-war moral outlook went 'overboard',[51] though her friends who had not been at the front remained relatively unchanged. Birth-control information was being discussed more openly. Margaret Sanger visited Britain towards the end of 1914, meeting campaigners like Stella Browne, a Canadian member of the Malthusian League and a supporter of the *Freewoman*. Marie Stopes's *Married Love* was published in 1916 and, despite its flowery language, was a revelation to Naomi Mitchison, who, like many other young upper-class women, had been completely ignorant about sex when she married.

Tolerance towards the sexual casualties of war could appear in surprising places. The clergyman father of the young WAAC who wrote her story of the war was sympathetic to his daughter's experiences of wartime love and refused to condemn a nurse who bore his son's illegitimate child: 'It is not her fault,'[52] he said. Robert Roberts's father raised his head from the *News of the World* to damn 'trollops' when a henna-haired prostitute from Cardiff slipped into the shop, but his wife had a different attitude: ' "They've got to eat," my mother snapped, "like anyone else." '[53]

In 1936 the feminist Alison Neilans commented in Ray Strachey's *Our Freedom and Its Results* on a profound change in attitudes to the flesh during the war: 'The religious teaching that the body was the temple of the Holy Ghost could mean little or nothing to those who saw it mutilated and destroyed in millions by Christian nations engaged in war.'[54] Male combatant poets, all too aware that masculine bodies were vulnerable, wrote with a bitter edge about the women who could never understand their war and who kept men trapped in a militaristic masculinity. In 'Glory of Women', Siegfried Sassoon observed:

> You love us when we're heroes, home on leave,
> Or wounded in a mentionable place.
> You worship decorations; you believe
> That chivalry redeems the war's disgrace.[55]

In January 1918 unease and resentment about women's wartime assertiveness erupted in the bizarre case of 'The Cult of the Clitoris'.[56] This was the title of an article in *The Imperialist* (later *The Vigilante*) attacking, yet again, Maud Allan, who was to dance Salome at a private performance. The article appeared under the name of an MP, Pemberton Billing, but was written by Herbert Spencer, who was later to be certified as insane. It denounced diseased clitorises, homosexuals and spies in the Cabinet. Maud Allan sued for libel on the grounds that she was being accused of lesbianism. When she lost, a jubilant crowd carried Pemberton Billing shoulder-high. He was to go on to a successful parliamentary career. Lesbian sexuality entered popular public debate in this climate of paranoia and moralism – an indication of how narrow the boundary could be between the protection and control of female sexuality.

The Aftermath

Vera Brittain could feel only a dismayed detachment amidst the wild celebration of the London crowds when peace came in November 1918. In Yorkshire, Gwen Chambers, who had opposed the war, went for a walk on the moors to gather firewood. As she reached a wall 'a lark went up singing' on the other side: 'I put my head down on that wall and sobbed and sobbed. It was just something that this lark had, you know, that we'd done without for so long.'[57] Robert Roberts remembers how young people poured into dance halls in a kind of euphoria – and kept on dancing through 1919.

There was unemployment as the men came home and strong pressure on women to give up their wartime jobs. The *Daily Chronicle* interviewed a woman at the labour exchange who said she accepted she would never earn high wages again but was nonetheless happy the war was over. When asked what work she would do, she said she would take anything – except domestic service.

Though women returned to their old trades, they brought the experience of organizing with them. Dressmakers, milliners, laundry workers, hotel and restaurant workers, and even domestic servants rejoined the general labour unions and increased the membership of women's organizations. Women's trade union leaders were wooed by the coalition government, concerned to prevent industrial unrest. Margaret Bondfield and Mary Macarthur were both appointed to the Lord Chancellor's Women's Advisory Committee, and when the first meeting of the International Labour Organization was held in Washington, they were the two women members on the labour delegation of four from Britain.

Less tangible than the rise of the visible figures was a corresponding wariness among radical rank and file labour women. Melvina Walker, a working-class supporter of Sylvia Pankhurst, went to the first Labour Party Women's Conference and viewed the platform, which included the Fabian Beatrice Webb, with suspicion. She warned working-class women in *The Workers' Dreadnought*, 'Keep your eyes open, organize yourselves, don't be led away by people with "superior brains". We have something else. We have practical experiences.'[58]

Working-class women were indeed beginning to conceive how their communities might change. In October 1919, for example, Florence Farrow, a member of the Derby Women's Co-operative Guild, said that every mother should receive a pension for each child and milk should be municipally controlled to ensure that prices were kept down and that it was of good quality. There should be municipal baths, better housing, heating and lighting, with greater democratic control over energy. Teachers should be better paid as a step towards improving the education of working-class children and municipal cinemas should be set up to show children 'pictures which would bring the best out of them and give them a love of things beautiful'.[59] However, the hope of extensive, imaginative social reform rapidly receded, unemployment benefit was withdrawn at the end of 1919 and it was estimated that 100,000 women were among the unemployed.

Political reforms were, however, secured. In 1918 the Representation of the People Act had enfranchised all women over thirty who were on the local government register or were married to registered men. At the end of 1918, three weeks before the general election, women were allowed to stand for Parliament. Only one was elected: the Sinn Feiner Countess Markievicz, who was still in jail. In 1919 the Sex Disqualification (Removal) Act opened public offices and civil and judicial posts to women.

The confusing picture of advances and setbacks which characterized the period immediately after the war for women also affected women's organizations. Christabel and Emmeline Pankhurst's Women's Party called for support for nursing and expectant mothers, along with the cleansing of government departments of 'enemy blood'.[60] Mrs Fawcett's National Union was unsure whether to make egalitarian demands for access into the male sphere or focus on those based on women's special reproductive needs generated during the war.

In personal terms for some women the war was a catalyst which broke the pattern of their lives. Kathleen Woodward's contact with Mary Macarthur and the National Federation of Women Workers took her away from working-class life in London. She became a stewardess on a liner and a receptionist at a club, then a novelist. For some the war was a temporary break before returning to domesticity or casual jobs. Others, however, stayed put: Lucy Waugh, daughter of a Co-op Guild member from Walthamstow, entered the civil service as a typist in 1916 and continued to work there for twelve years. She was typical of a new kind of woman worker who was sufficiently educated to enter the civil service but whose family did not have enough money for her to apply to university.

Psychologically and culturally the end of the war opened completely new perspectives for Virginia Woolf. She wrote on 15 November 1918:

Instead of feeling all day and going home through dark streets that the whole people, willing or not, were concentrated on a single point, one feels now that the whole bunch has burst asunder and flown off with utmost vigour in different directions. We are once more a nation of individuals.[61]

But another woman writer, Katherine Mansfield, recoiled against the amnesia towards the war which pervaded literary circles by November 1919: 'I feel that in the *profoundest* sense nothing can be the same – that, as artists, we are traitors if we feel otherwise; we have to take it into account and find new expressions, new moulds for our new thoughts and feelings.'[62]

Women poets found it hard to express the consequences of what people came to call the Great War until a decade had passed. Sylvia Townsend Warner consciously sought new forms during the 1920s:

> I knew a time when Europe feasted well:
> bodies were munched in thousands, vintage blood
> so blithely flowed that even the dull mud
> grew greedy, and ate men; and lest the gust
> should flag, quick flesh no daintier taste than dust, spirit was
>   ransacked for whatever might
> sharpen a sauce to drive on appetite.[63]

THE UNITED STATES

Divided Loyalties

Anna Louise Strong, doctor in philosophy, campaigner for child welfare and Socialist Party member, appeared to be the epitome of radical progressivism. The First World War and the stormy class conflict of

Seattle, the shipping centre of the North-West, were to transform her life. In her autobiography, *I Change Worlds*, she described how she came to lose 'her America'.

She arrived in Seattle early in the war and was elected as the progressive candidate on the School Board. There were then several broad-based organizations opposing America's entry into the war and she threw herself into all of them enthusiastically. However, towards the end of 1916 the atmosphere changed as the country was drawn towards involvement. Anna Louise Strong found herself facing empty tables at the American Union Against Militarism: 'The respectable members were turning to war work. The presidents of the women's clubs were "swinging in behind the President".'[64] Only a handful of socialists, anarchists and Industrial Workers of the World – 'Wobblies' – remained. The IWW did not oppose the war as an organization but they refused to accept Woodrow Wilson's strike ban and were arrested in thousands. Anna Louise Strong defended an anarchist, Louise Olivereau, charged with sedition after distributing the Bible, Tolstoy, Lincoln and Thoreau to soldiers. This act of solidarity meant that Anna Louise Strong's former 'progressive' friends ostracized her. She did find new allies in the labour movement but never regained her faith in a democratic 'America'.

In contrast, Mary Church Terrell, the distinguished black lecturer and writer, opted for patriotic duty and applied for a clerical post in the War Department. She was first prevented from working with whites, then forbidden to use the same toilet. When she complained to the director of the bureau, she was told it was necessary because 'coloured people associate with thieves and harlots'.[65] In *Black Foremothers*, Dorothy Sterling describes how repeated humiliations finally forced Mary Church Terrell to give in her notice, writing in her diary, 'How I loathe these intolerable conditions.'[66] She did not, however, give up the struggle for the collective improvement of black Americans.

Neglected by women's organizations and discriminated against within trade unions, black women workers lacked the means of defending their position. Mary Church Terrell, along with Jeannette Carter and Julia F. Coleman, started the Women Wage Earners' Association in an attempt to develop self-organization. In September 1917 in Norfolk, Virginia, 600 women domestics, waitresses, nurses and tobacco stemmers in the association demanded higher wages and better conditions. The stemmers and domestics went on strike, joined by oyster shuckers, many of whom were husbands and brothers. Their claim was considered akin to sabotage. Plain-clothes police were brought in and wartime legislation invoked to arrest slackers.

Mary Church Terrell was active in black organizations, but her aim was integration and equality. Faced with the heading 'Race' when she applied for war work, she wrote 'American'.[67] She participated in the suffrage movement, joining the militant National Woman's Party (NWP) on their pickets of the White House. At the end of the war she was to be one of thirty American women, including Jane Addams and the first Congresswoman, Jeannette Rankin, who went to the International Congress of Women in Switzerland. Yet despite this commitment to integration, she found much ignorance and prejudice among white feminists. She experienced the contrary pulls of race and gender in a period when some of the space which had opened for a black élite was once more closing down.

Politics

The American suffrage movement had reached an impasse by 1914 in their campaign to win the vote through referenda campaigns state by state. Alice Paul was pressing for militant confrontational tactics in the Congressional Union and some younger women, impressed by the Women's Social and Political Union (WSPU) in Britain, wanted to fight for a federal amendment. The Congressional Union split from the National American Woman Suffrage Association (NAWSA) in February 1914 and conflict continued to fester between the two groups about tactics and wider questions of strategy.

Carrie Chapman Catt succeeded Anna Howard Shaw as president of NAWSA in 1915 and began organizing an impressive mass campaign. Suffrage supporters canvassed widely, holding thousands of meetings and giving out 3 million leaflets. They used imaginative forms of organizing which included street dances and bonfires, aiming to reach working-class voters in areas where new immigrants were arriving. Pragmatically Carrie Chapman Catt combined thorough organizing on a local basis with the campaign for a constitutional amendment. NAWSA's aim was to influence individual congress-

Taking the Wheel

American feminists adopted the motor car with enthusiasm. Olive Schultz's New York taxi service was sponsored by Harriot Stanton Blatch and operated from 1913 in front of the Women's Political Union on Forty-second Street. Olive Schultz herself was a symbol of new womanhood, a skilled mechanic, unafraid of night work, with a cap decorated in the purple, white and green colours of the suffrage movement. She was prepared for winter, driving with fur coats and woollen mittens for her passengers, as well as a warming device to heat the car.

In 1914 Crystal Eastman, Mary Beard and Inez Milholland inaugurated a programme backed by the Maxwell Motor Company to promote women's entry into automobile sales. Wilma Russey became the first woman to try to earn a living driving a cab in New York. She arrived in Broadway to work as a cab driver dressed in a leopard-skin hat and stole, brown skirt, high tan boots and long black gloves.

Making the motor car: early outdoor Ford assembly line.

Suffragists used cars in parades, open-air revivals and auto tours. On a trip from New York to Rochester in 1914, Jane Olcott transported firemen to a fire in Cortland, becoming an honorary member of the fire department there. By 1915 cross-country suffrage propaganda tours had begun. The motor car served both a practical and a symbolic purpose for feminists, demonstrating women's power and control. A 1919 story in *Motor Magazine* about the car and suffrage showed a picture of the veteran Anna Howard Shaw cranking her car. Women also took the wheel in Preparedness Day parades and volunteered to be ambulance drivers.

The woman driver combined masculine adventure with feminine glamour, but, as Virginia Scharft's *Taking the Wheel* shows, she remained a member of the élite. Henry Ford's breakthrough with the Model T was designed for the male breadwinner and family. Though a supporter of woman's suffrage, Henry Ford believed young ladies should marry and that a woman's place was on the Tin Lizzies' passenger seat.

✳

men to back suffrage and she adopted a time-honoured female approach, believing that even a rock gives way under the constant drip of water.

In contrast, Alice Paul saw demonstrations as a provocation. Resolved to challenge the Democratic Party, she formed the NWP in 1916 and went into opposition in California. When the NWP began a picket of the White House, Alice Paul was arrested and went on hunger strike for twenty-two days, gaining considerable sympathy for the militants, until the outbreak of war hardened attitudes against radical action of all kinds.

The differences between NAWSA and the NWP did not simply concern tactics. NAWSA shared the broad social aims of pre-war 'progressivism': protective legislation, equal pay, the restriction of child labour, municipal reform and pure-food regulation. There were certainly regional variations. For example, in Milwaukee, where the labour movement was a powerful force, a socialist, Meta Berger, struggled within NAWSA for a radical agenda of universal suffrage, special agitation among immigrant and working-class women and an alliance with local labour groups. But in general NAWSA's leaders regarded the vote as the key to a new era which, with women in government, would be organic and harmonious. However, Alice Paul and militant young women like Crystal Eastman, who was attracted to the NWP in New York, were meeting opposition head on, demanding a new kind of womanhood based on freedom and equality.

Opponents of women's suffrage, meanwhile, held to their own version of women's distinct characteristics. Instead of 'the muck and mire of partisan politics', declared one Florida congressman, the woman had her own 'proud estate as the queen of the American home'.[68] The argument that the public sphere was contaminated and that real fulfilment came from domesticity was accompanied by a view of the household as a miniature state in which female self-help kept order. 'Housewives, you do not need a ballot to clean out your sink spout. A handful of potash and some boiling water is quicker and cheaper,'[69] advised the Women's Anti-Suffrage Association of Massachusetts in their leaflet 'Household Hints'. Good cooking was the antidote to alcoholism; purifying your own icebox was better than pure-food laws.

The conflict between conservative and progressive versions of women's difference hinged on the boundaries between personal and public spheres. Instead of confining maternal values within the family, progressives argued that these were needed in government. In social reformer Lillian Wald's words, 'I believe that women have something to contribute to the government that men have not . . . They wish to take their share in the responsibility of society and to give back what has been given to them.'[70]

Both the creation of a new sphere for women's action and the invocation of womanly values were evident in the women's peace movement. On 29 August 1914, 1,500 women marched down New York's Fifth Avenue to the sound of muffled drums, marking the end of peace. Crystal Eastman called the first meeting of the Woman's Peace

Party of New York and the British feminist Emmeline Pethick-Lawrence urged American women to apply the lessons of the suffrage campaign to peace. Activity and militancy were needed.

Early in 1915 the Woman's Peace Party was established nationally, gaining the support of Jane Addams and Lillian Wald. It called the International Congress of Women at The Hague in April 1915, when American women joined the 1,000 representatives from twelve countries including Britain who sought to prevent war and gain the suffrage. Asserting a common bond as mothers, they formed the Women's International League for Peace and Freedom (WILPF), as a continuing force for motherly values in international relations.

The American women's peace movement combined several political strands. There was militant feminist separatism – men who tried to join a demonstration were told to organize a parade of their own – and a semi-mystical faith in nurturant motherhood. Angela Morgan, a poet and delegate to the conference at The Hague, praised the 'strongest cosmic force in the world'.[71] Crystal Eastman, in contrast, challenged the political mainstream as a socialist feminist. For example, she worked with the American Union Against Militarism (AUAM), which later developed into the Civil Liberties Bureau. In 1916 AUAM, along with trade unionists from the American Federation of Labor (AFL), met with Mexican labour unions when war seemed imminent between the two countries. President Woodrow Wilson appointed a commission and war was averted. Crystal Eastman thought this showed that it was possible to democratize international relations: 'We must make it known to everybody that people acting directly, not through their governments or diplomats or armies, stopped that war, and can stop all wars if enough of them will act together and act quickly.'[72] This vision of grass-roots intervention presented an alternative approach to international politics in which the key was democratic participation rather than the idea of essential female values.

The idea of American involvement in the war was far from popular in 1916. Resistance extended beyond the Greenwich Village radicals in Crystal Eastman's circle, who went into the New York branch of the Woman's Peace Party. Jane Addams and Lillian Wald were respected figures who carried considerable moral weight. In February 1916 Lillian Wald described to an ally in the AUAM, Reverend John Haynes

Holmes, from Manhattan's Church of the Messiah, how a group of Wall Street business magnates had cornered her at a reception:

They intimated that I was risking my reputation for wisely considered, constructive plans, though of course they did not say that quite as bluntly as it was a party . . . one of the gentlemen observed that conscription was good because the working men did not know how to obey in this country![73]

The election of 1916 forced a difficult choice upon feminist pacifists: Woodrow Wilson, the Democrat, was for peace but opposed to suffrage, while Charles Evans Hughes advocated women's suffrage and entry into the war. Crystal Eastman, Jane Addams and Lillian Wald backed Wilson, while the National Woman's Party and Alice Paul were for Hughes. Crystal Eastman's close friend the radical suffragist Inez Milholland, lecturing in the West, declared, 'We must say "Women First".'[74] Her death on this speaking tour at the age of just thirty made the political split even more painful. Differences were briefly buried at a memorial meeting for her which many strands of the feminist movement attended, but as the United States headed towards war in 1917 the divisions were to harden.

Support for peace had seemed an idealistic, empowering cause while the country was neutral. 'I am so on fire that I can pass the flames along,'[75] stated a supporter of the Boston Women's Trade Union League when she became involved in the peace movement in 1915. But it was a different matter after June 1917, when Woodrow Wilson declared that opponents of war were disloyal citizens. Crystal Eastman tried to persuade Jane Addams to call for mass meetings of mothers against the war, appealing to women's 'greater regard for life, both intellectually and emotionally'.[76] However, though opposed to conscription, Jane Addams and Lillian Wald administered registration programmes in their settlement houses. Jane Addams volunteered for Herbert Hoover's Food Administration and Lillian Wald chaired the Council of National Defense's Committee on Public Health and Child Welfare. It appeared that the warnings about loss of influence had made their point after all.

The New York Woman's Peace Party scorned the 'Sister Susie number'[77] in their newsletter, Four Lights. They denounced the atmosphere of aggression and violence which had emerged, including race riots in St Louis, where white women had joined the attack on black

Emma Goldman, unladylike anti-militarist and advocate of direct action,
speaking on birth control in Union Square, New York, 1916.

people. Hailing the Russian Revolution, *Four Lights* demanded liberty
of conscience for Americans against the war and Crystal Eastman argued
that the United States was in danger of autocracy. However, the
Espionage Act of 15 June 1917 made speaking, writing or organizing
against war an offence; the penalty could be up to twenty years in prison
and fines of up to $10,000. On 8 September 1917 the artist Boardman
Robinson drew a picture of a woman wearing black in the newsletter,
captioned 'You are the Widows of Democracy'.[78] The following month
the government forced *Four Lights* to close and the Woman's Peace
Party also ceased their agitation. Crystal Eastman said in 1918, 'Common
sense as well as loyalty and the habit of obedience to law counselled
this course.'[79]

War did bring new alignments – for example, Meta Berger sought
links with feminist militants in the NWP when her former allies in
NAWSA supported war – but the main effect of draconian wartime
legislation was to break up the women's networks which had created
bridges between radical left-wingers and respectable social liberals.

Socialists and anarchists who continued in opposition were severely persecuted; when Emma Goldman organized a No-Conscription League, the government arrested every young man attending the meeting, and it was not long before she herself was arrested. In court she appealed to the jury, saying that if America 'had entered the war to make the world safe for democracy', was it not necessary to 'make democracy safe in America'?[80] Her plea fell on deaf ears; she was imprisoned for two years and fined $10,000.

Mobilization

'What has "your" country ever done for you?'[81] asked Mary Marcy, appealing to class solidarity rather than womanly values in *The International Socialist Review* in 1917. Patriotism, however, proved a more powerful emotion. It was to inspire ideals of female heroism and reclaim the motherly sphere. When a passenger liner, the *Lusitania*, which was carrying munitions to Britain, was torpedoed in May 1915 and 1,000 passengers died, the Navy League used the tragedy to press for a larger navy so the United States could be prepared for war. A proposal by a Washington, D C, journalist, Elisabeth Ellicott Poe, for a Woman's Section was greeted sympathetically by the Navy League and this WSNL proceeded to contest the feminist pacifist appropriation of nurturant motherhood. Vylla Poe Wilson, for instance, declared, 'Woman has always been the conservator of home and life. It is only just that her voice, raised in a cry for preparedness to protect the lives and homes she has been the chief factor in building up, should be harkened unto.'[82] And Annie Cothren Graves maintained that American mothers knew that a strong navy was the best safeguard for their sons as well as for the country.

Supporters of women's special patriotic role established the National Service Schools in spring 1916. These quasi-military training camps for young women taught nursing and knitting socks and mufflers as well as telegraphy. The sense that they were helping their country and developing new skills enabled young middle-class women to find individual fulfilment and develop a collective *esprit de corps* through the camps.

Like the British anti-suffrage campaigners, the American patriots found themselves in an awkward position, defending a separate female sphere of domestic influence by taking public stands. They did, however, carefully avoid adopting a position against suffrage and were able to attract both supporters and opponents of votes for women. They were capable of asserting their autonomy: when the WSNL fell foul of factional fighting between the men in the navy and the Navy League in summer 1917, the women simply refused to be absorbed into the Red Cross and continued their knitting regardless of the military's administrative plans.

In Washington young Eleanor Roosevelt, whose husband, Franklin, backed Theodore Roosevelt's commitment to entering the war, heard Woodrow Wilson ask Congress to declare war in April 1917. She returned home, 'still half dazed by the sense of impending change'.[83] However, as a loyal Democrat she too began knitting, as well as entertaining troops and visiting sailors in hospitals and homes for the wounded and shell-shocked.

NAWSA had abandoned pacifism when war was declared and proceeded to denounce their opponents in the National Organization to Oppose Suffrage, claiming that this was a front for the liquor business's fears that votes for women meant prohibition. Carrie Chapman Catt invoked women's loyal contribution to the war effort as grist to the suffrage mill: how could President Wilson fight a war for democracy while depriving the patriotic middle-class women selling war bonds and working-class women doing the men's jobs in factories of the vote? In the short term it appeared that her approach had paid off. When Jeannette Rankin introduced a suffrage amendment into Congress on 10 January 1918, it got through by just one vote.

Work

Florence Luscomb spent 1914 and 1915 touring Boston's laundries recruiting working women for suffrage parades. The 'visual proof' that suffrage supporters were 'homemakers, mothers, daughters, teachers, working women – and not the unsexed freaks the antis declared they were',[84] had an undeniable effect upon the male voter.

The Women's Trade Union League provided a crucial link between the campaign for the franchise and working-class women. Not only had middle-class suffragists recognized the need to broaden their campaign, but working-class women were becoming active in the movement for the franchise because they wanted political power for labour reforms. In New York Mary Dreier, a prominent Republican suffragist, and Helen Marot, a Fabian socialist, worked with working-class women Leonora O'Reilly, Rose Schneiderman, Pauline Newman, Maggie Hinchey, Melinda Scott and Maud Swartz; while in Boston Julia O'Connor, one of the leaders of the telephone operators, was a successful student at the WTUL training school.

But the shift towards suffrage left the relationship of the WTUL to the American labour movement unresolved. Labour unions were not attuned to the particular problems faced by women organizers. On the other hand, the working-class women could encounter prejudice among suffrage campaigners. For example, in 1915 Harriot Stanton Blatch expressed resentment against immigrant men who could vote when she could not.

Conflict also occurred within the WTUL over policy. Mary Dreier was in favour of minimum-wage legislation for women in vulnerable areas like millinery, paper-box making, the flower and candy trades and retail. Helen Marot opposed protective legislation of all kinds and argued that they should concentrate on the larger factories. This approach, however, would have excluded many immigrant women and was fiercely opposed by Rose Schneiderman, whose Polish-Jewish origins made her conscious of immigrants' needs. The WTUL came to adopt a policy of protective legislation; women's social and biological disadvantages were to be supplemented by state intervention.

The outbreak of war did bring state intervention in industry, though for a much shorter period than in Britain, and some members of the WTUL were drawn into the new industrial bureaucracy. Mary Dreier became head of the New York State Women in Industry Committee for the Council of National Defense, and Melinda Scott worked on the National War Labor Bonds. But not all WTUL members were pro-war: Leonora O'Reilly and Julia O'Connor were active in the peace movement.

The war transformed the structure of production and laid the basis for new patterns of consumption. In the process any opposition was to be ruthlessly crushed. The Industrial Workers of the World never recovered from the onslaught of government repression during and immediately after the war. Even the intrepid Elizabeth Gurley Flynn, facing jail on a charge of inciting sabotage, wrote to Woodrow Wilson to plead for clemency. This attack on political rebels was part of a wider economic scenario in which employers went on the offensive to gain control over the workplace.

Industry was already being restructured when America entered the war. For example, the larger clothing factories had been regulated by the Board of Protocol Standards from 1913 and scientific management techniques introduced. Joint union–employer time-and-motion study teams recommended wages and standard procedures. The employers' drive for efficiency through scientific management affected women workers in contradictory ways. The system of regulation over the labour process reduced skilled workers' control on the job, but it also made semi-skilled women less vulnerable to sexual harassment by foremen and the small employers. On the other hand, though job techniques were made simpler, the work was not made easier. For instance, when the tasks of telephone operators were reduced to a manual of appropriate responses, the workforce was feminized – by 1917 it was 99 per cent female – but the pace intensified, leaving the women nervous and on edge. Headaches, backaches and eye strain were the result.

Scientific management's initiator, Frederick Winslow-Taylor, had in fact stipulated work breaks as part of the drive to increase production, and Lillian Gilbreth, an early adviser on the implementation of 'Tayloristic' management techniques, was particularly concerned about preventing fatigue. She advocated designing work processes and machinery for users, including workers with disabilities. Lillian Gilbreth was the human face of 'Taylorism', which was generally applied simply to increase productivity and remove power from shop-floor workers. Her critic, Helen Marot, pointed out that scientific management theorists ignored the 'creative impulse',[85] treating workers as automata, only able to respond to short-term stimuli. Helen Marot's *The Creative Impulse* was published in 1918, when American industry was seeking to emulate German production methods. Distrusting the authoritarian implications of these and lacking faith in the labour movement's readiness to transform the social conditions of work, hers was a lonely voice destined not to be heard.

When the United States entered the war, women did not immediately replace men. Male trade union resistance and a widespread scepticism about the need to call on women were common. As a well-known industrial engineer, Charles E. Knoeppel, advised, 'Get the lounge lizards and loafers first.'[86] However, before the Armistice almost 10 million women had entered paid employment. They went into steel and lumber mills and printing works. By 1918 they were handling baggage, repairing railway tracks, working as street-car conductors and delivering the post. Quite visibly women demonstrated that they could do work which had been regarded as essentially male. A few women also moved up business hierarchies, becoming tellers and managers in banks, for example. These, however, were the exceptions. The main tendency was for a shift to occur within the pattern of women's employment. As some women moved into male jobs, others entered the ones they had left, taking on menial tasks or entering offices. The wartime workforce was largely composed of women who had already been in paid work. For instance, the twelve women welders who were employed at the Mt Clare shops of the Baltimore and Ohio Railroad during the war were not new to industry; they included a former sewing machinist, a spooler and spinner from a cotton mill, a silk mill worker, a weaver, a button and a cigarette factory worker, a timekeeper, a telephone operator, a cashier, two munitions workers and a home dressmaker. Nor did the increases of women workers in manufacturing outlast the war. One trend which did last, though, was expansion in the communications industry: advertising, design and sales all became major areas of women's employment.

The wartime gender shift in employment took specific ethnic and racial forms. The secretary of the New Jersey Welfare League observed, 'Negro women are leaving the kitchen and laundry for the workshop and factory.'[87] It was true that as Hungarians, Italians and Jewish women moved into munition plants, black women left domestic service for manufacturing industry. But they had to take the worst jobs, frequently received less pay and were segregated in poor-quality washrooms, lunch rooms and lockers. The Southerners around President Wilson lobbied successfully to reinforce segregation in government work, as Mary Church Terrell discovered to her cost.

However, there were some kinds of resistance that could not be

Southern sawmill workers, 1918.

contained. Thousands of African-Americans from the South simply voted with their feet and headed north. Women, who had been forced to wash and clean for white families and could be coerced back to work with vagrancy laws or brute force in the rural South, followed their men or went alone to the Northern cities. Between 1916 and 1921 around half a million African-Americans migrated. Whether they were educated schoolteachers or semi-literate working women like the correspondent to a black weekly, the *Chicago Defender*, who wrote, 'I hope that you will healp [*sic*] me as I want to get out of this land of sufring [*sic*],'[88] they sought a better life.

Daily Life

The new arrivals brought their hopes to cities which bristled with enigmas. A middle-aged domestic worker wrote home to Alabama from Pittsburgh, 'Some places look like torment . . . & some places look like Paradise in this great city.'[89]

City life presented problems of housekeeping very different from those in the rural South. Newcomers struggled to adapt to doing their laundry and housework in congested households, burning wood and coal in an effort to save putting money into gas meters. Rents were high because black residents were contained within urban ghettos. As food had to be bought in small amounts, it was impossible for most families or single women to save through bulk-purchasing. 'They give you big money for what you do but they charge you big things for what you get,'[90] explained the Pittsburgh migrant to her friends in Alabama.

The National Industries Conference Board Survey estimated that between 1914 and 1920 there was a 104.5 per cent increase in the cost of living for wage-earning families and food prices rose even more steeply, by 199 per cent. Inflation affected the poor immigrant communities particularly as they too often shopped meal by meal, and ethnic food prices were even higher. Jewish women organized around consumption yet again early in 1917; kosher meat boycotts, protests and riots erupted in Cleveland, Chicago, Boston, Baltimore, Philadelphia, St Louis and New York. In New York women attacked pedlars, crying furiously, 'Give us bread.'[91] Maria Ganz, a participant, said prices had risen faster than wages and that the 'profiteer'[92] was to blame. The women declared themselves 'housewives of the City of New York, mothers and wives of workmen,' appealing directly to the president that they and their families were facing starvation 'in the midst of plenty'.[93] When they were accused of being German agents, Maria Ganz retorted that the charges were 'silly lies', asking, 'What do we women of the East Side know of European politics?'[94] The boycott was extended to other foods and after a few days the pressure proved effective and prices fell. The city's only response, however, was to restrict pedlars' licences to US citizens.

Foreign immigrants continued to arrive. They came with their families not only to the crowded city ghettos but also to mining settlements, like Christine Ellis's family from Croatia, who settled in Rathbun, Iowa. Single women were among the new wave of immigrants – half a million single women under thirty entered the States between 1912 and 1917. Some came to join husbands; others to meet them. Japanese men, for instance, found brides by exchanging photographs with families still in Japan. The picture-brides travelled to camps in the western United States, which provided labour for the railroads, mines, sugar-beet fields, salmon canneries, lumber camps and mills. Like other rural women, they drew water from wells and kindled wood for heat. Few rural homes had adequate plumbing in this period and women were often carrying water considerable distances.

It was, however, the condition of the urban immigrant which continued to cause social concern. Social work was beginning to acquire a new professional status in this period. The National Conference of Charities and Corrections was renamed the National Association of Social Work in 1917 and was to gain 4,000 members by 1921. The Massachusetts Society for the Prevention of Cruelty to Children was also becoming more professional and extending the scope of its activities from abuse to include neglect. Though social workers commented anxiously about children in black communities whose mothers were forced to work, holding the women responsible for the economic and social problems of the ghettos, their main endeavours were concentrated on white immigrants. Black women fell back on networks formed through church groups, penny-savers' clubs, kinship and friendship groups. They also received help from the middle-class black groups like the National League for the Protection of Colored Women and the National Association of Colored Women, who offered classes on nutrition, hygiene and household maintenance, and social clubs. Alongside the educated black middle class, there were a few outstanding black businesswomen committed to the black community. In Richmond, Virginia, Maggie Lena Walker's penny-savers' club, the Independent Order of Saint Luke, was growing into the first black bank. She saw financial association as a means of sustaining an alternative economic base of jobs and prosperity. Madame C. J. Walker had become the first black American woman millionaire through a mail-order beauty business. After the 1917 riot in East St Louis, she became involved in the National Association for the Advancement of Colored People's anti-lynching campaign.

African-American women shared a common experience of racial injustice despite class differences. But the gulf between white social workers and foreign immigrants was marked. The process of assimilation through the educational programmes and community projects, childcare centres and mothers' health centres was a complex matter of loss and gain. Americanization was assumed by the social workers who sought to bring their own standards of mothering to the immigrant poor to be automatically superior to the customs of the cultures from which the women came. Values and understandings were consequently denied and scorned by WASP social workers who had difficulty in distinguishing between parental irresponsibility, poverty and cultural differences. Despite their concern about the importance of motherhood, they frequently ended up institutionalizing children for want of a better remedy.

On the other hand, the case studies of the social workers revealed children left ill-clad in freezing apartments and children who were beaten and sexually abused. Sometimes immigrant mothers pressed the agencies for action; however inadequate, they were the only source of help. Linda Gordon cites the case of Mrs Amato, a poor Italian woman from Boston, suspected of negligence towards her large family, who complained of violence from her husband. Though he was convicted and imprisoned, he attacked her with an axe when he was released and beat the children so severely on the head that their 'eyes wabbled [sic]'.[95]

The intractable, enmeshed domestic tragedies they encountered convinced many progressive social workers of the need for Mothers' Pensions to be extended. By 1915 twenty-nine states provided these for 'children of reasonably efficient and deserving mothers who are without the support of the normal breadwinner'.[96] Another ten states had followed by 1919. However, the discourse of nurturant motherhood deposited single mothers between a rock and a hard place, hovering on a borderline between victim and sinner: like employed mothers, they were in danger of being censured as unfit. The embedded assumptions of the white middle-class investigators mattered because of their power over the meagre but vital sums of assistance which they could grant or deny. For example, only a small proportion of the Mothers' Pensions funds reached black mothers.

Educated middle-class mothers were facing dilemmas of their own as they tried to balance mothering with continuing intellectual work. In Greenwich Village in 1914 the teacher Henrietta Rodman conceived a plan for a Feminist Apartment House so mothers could combine a career and home life; kitchenless apartments, collective housekeeping and a roof-top nursery run on Montessori lines with food prepared in the basement and delivered by an electric service elevator were proposed. But lack of money and unwillingness among her middle-class feminist and socialist supporters, female and male, to do the domestic work caused the scheme to founder.

Far away from the circle of radical experimenters, Margaret Morse Nice was stranded in a bungalow in Norman, Oklahoma, with her husband and four children aged six months to eight years. Destined to become a distinguished ornithologist in the 1930s, in 1918 she was desperate: 'I was truly frustrated. I resented the implication that my husband and children had brains, and I had none. He taught; they studied; I did housework . . . I decided it would be better to be a bird.'[97] Birds, she noted, spent a short time caring for their young and then simply 'leave their houses for ever and take to camping for the rest of the year. No wonder they are happy.'[98] She recorded in her notebook for March 1919, 'Research is a passion with me.'[99]

Charlotte Perkins Gilman had imagined in her novel *Herland* (1915), the story of a collective co-operative society based around mothering, that women, as the 'Conscious Makers of People',[100] might hold the key to the evolution of a society based on unselfish, caring values. But such social maternalism was never able to take into account those women seeking freedom from the oppressive aspects of maternity.

Sex

Control over fertility was still a dangerous cause in the United States. In August 1914 two federal agents arrived at Margaret Sanger's home with an indictment for violating the Comstock law in her journal *The Woman Rebel*. She sat them down for several hours and convinced them of the need for birth control (the accompanying call in *The Woman Rebel* for rifles for the locked-out Colorado miners in Ludlow might have taken a little longer to communicate). Arraigned in the United States District Court for Southern New York, she fled to Montreal, boarding a ship heading for Europe under an assumed name. While on board she sent a cable authorizing the release of 100,000 copies of her pamphlet 'Family Limitation', which gave information about birth-control methods. She appealed for them to be distributed to 'poor working men and women who are over-burdened with large families' and made available to the 'thousands of women in the cotton states bearing twelve to sixteen children . . . women facing the torture of

The Vamp

Movie mogul William Fox, who began his career in the early nickel and dime cinemas, where the audience drew lots and won a chicken or $5 to pay the rent, created the 'vamp'. Theda Bara, whose real name was Theodosia Goodman, was the daughter of a Jewish tailor from Cincinnati. She was to be transmogrified by Fox into the child of a French artist and his Arabian mistress (Theda Bara is an anagram of Arab death) in the publicity campaign for her role as Cleopatra. She came to symbolize the vamp in 1915 when she starred in *A Fool There Was*, a film based on Rudyard Kipling's poem 'The Vampire'.

Her sultry allure was a European-style sexuality, markedly different from the clean-cut American girl-next-door style of Mary Pickford. The vamp was the 'other', the unknown and alien, invested with a dangerous power. Theda Bara went on to play many more menacing roles in, for example, *The Vixen*, *The Serpent* and *The She-Devil*. The formula was always the same: the vamp sets her trap for the man, only to be foiled by some external force. While the vamp could gain sexual ascendancy over her male victims, in the end she paid the price for transgressing gender stereotypes. When her sexual pull waned she faced rejection; the

The sexual pull of ethnic menace: Theda Bara.

domestic life of 'normal' women was denied to the vamp, who remained an outsider, exotic and apart.

Theda Bara's own career lasted only four years. To 1920s movie-goers, her style of sexuality seemed exaggerated and somewhat absurd. Nonetheless, a sex goddess had emerged from the new immigrant culture and had disturbed American society sufficiently to make its mark on the sexual fantasies of a generation. Forbidden and exotic sensuality joined Hollywood's profitable stock of human desires.

＊

abortion . . . mothers who lose their babies every year from poverty and neglect'.[101]

In Europe she researched the history and practice of birth control, meeting writers on sex psychology like Edward Carpenter and Havelock Ellis, with whom she had a love affair. She also made friends with anarchist and socialist advocates of birth control Rose Witcop, her companion Guy Aldred and Stella Browne. Havelock Ellis was, however, to convince her that the cause of sexual reform would be best served by separating it from the left.

Sanger's supporters in the United States tended to be linked to the Socialist Party, the Industrial Workers of the World or anarchist circles. In her absence a grass-roots agitation for birth control developed; supporters included Elizabeth Gurley Flynn, Emma Goldman and the socialist Kate Richards O'Hare. These left-wing allies connected control over fertility to workers' control and the right to knowledge. In September 1915 Margaret Sanger's estranged husband, William, was tried and convicted in a dramatic courtroom scene in which radicals shouted at the judge. When Margaret Sanger returned, crowds came to hear her speak on the right to birth control, and letters poured in from women telling of sexual unhappiness, exhaustion from constant childbearing, male violence and abuse.

Some of her radical supporters took direct action, setting up birth-

Margaret Sanger and her sister Ethel Bryne with supporters outside the Court
of Special Sessions in Brooklyn, New York, January 1917.

control clinics. With her sister Ethel Bryne, Margaret Sanger opened
the Brownsville clinic in Brooklyn in July 1916, giving immigrant
women information about cervical pessaries. Queues formed outside,
but among the women seeking advice was a policewoman. Margaret
Sanger, along with her sister and another clinic worker, was arrested.
Ethel Bryne's hunger strike in January 1917 led to a particularly brutal
force-feeding from which she did not recover for a long time. When
Margaret Sanger was released that March, she shifted her efforts towards
legislative reforms.

Though divisions within the left over the war and the Russian
Revolution, along with the wartime restrictions on radical organizing,
weakened the grass-roots movement for birth control, it was not the
end of the battles with the law. Despite Sanger's efforts to edge towards
respectability, the persecution of birth-control campaigners continued.
The socialist feminist journalist and agitator Agnes Smedley, for example,
was arrested in April 1918 because of her support for Indian nationalists
as well as birth control, bringing Margaret Sanger to her defence. In
prison Agnes Smedley met a young anarchist follower of Emma Gold-

man, Mollie Steimer, along with Kitty Marion, the British suffragette who was working with Margaret Sanger's birth-control organization. Kitty Marion had been in jail for giving a birth-control pamphlet to an agent of the Association for the Suppression of Vice. 'Kitty, Mollie Steimer, and I have wonderful meetings when we can dodge in some corner of the cell,' Agnes Smedley told Sanger in a letter, adding, 'Kitty is turning the place into a birth-control branch.'[102]

Kitty Marion knew how to agitate in prison from her suffragette days in Britain. She also retained her old music-hall flair: 'Kitty came clattering down the stone corridors every morning with the scrub pail in her hand. "Three cheers for birth control," she greeted the prisoners and matrons. And, "Three cheers for birth control," the prisoners answered back.'[103]

These radical campaigners for birth control were convinced that there was a connection between women's feelings of sexual helplessness and the political and economic system. The campaign was part of a wider challenge to social hierarchy and repression. As Margaret Anderson, the young lesbian editor of *The Little Review*, remarked, 'In 1916 Emma Goldman was sent to prison for advocating that women need not always keep their mouths shut and their wombs open.'[104] Birth control met a positive response from the Women's Association of Harlem in 1918, who chose it as a topic in their lecture series calling for black women to 'assume the reins of leadership in the political, social and economic life of their people'.[105] The birth-control agitation thus linked personal and political self-determination. Sexual radicals consequently were shifting an aspect of personal experience into the public sphere.

They were not alone. The American Social Hygiene Association, backed by John D. Rockefeller Jr, moved on to the offensive, warning that sex led to venereal disease, the 'epitome of all that is unclean, malignant and menacing'.[106] Their propaganda against 'The Enemy at Home' fulminated against VD, prostitutes and alcohol. Members of the association tried to close down brothels and taverns and secure the arrest of prostitutes, whom they held responsible for contaminating innocent members of the armed forces. In *Struggles for Justice*, Alan Dawley describes them as 'wrapping repression in the flag'.[107] Mrs John D. Rockefeller patronized the Committee on Protective Work for Girls, which patrolled dance halls and movie theatres, turning up the lights and stopping 'suggestive forms of dancing'.[108] The committee's guidelines were precise: 'Partners must be at least three inches apart, including heads. Hands must not be placed below the waist, nor above the shoulder, nor across the breast. Clasped hands must not be less than six inches from the body.'[109]

While the Social Hygiene Association advised continence and abstinence, and the Commission on Training Camp Activities did its bit to calm the libido by organizing sports events for the troops, the army handed out prophylactic kits to soldiers *sotto voce* and made early treatment of VD compulsory. When the American troops arrived in France, officials there were bewildered by the 'American Plan'[110] of continence and proposed medically certified prostitutes.

In Paris, meanwhile, Natalie Barney brought together American, French and British women writers who opposed the war in her Académie from 1917. It became the model for the famous international salons of the 1920s which created a visible space for lesbian women, but in the United States, apart from the Heterodoxy Club, sexuality between women remained a private matter even for very public women. Jane Addams, for example, had a close relationship with Mary Rozet Smith for many years. Lillian Wald also had an intimate inner circle which included Lavinia Dock, until they disagreed over Alice Paul's radical suffragism in 1915. Later a society woman, Mabel Hyde Kittredge, became a close companion.

The sex radicals sought to bring heterosexuality into the public arena of rational debate, while the social hygienists tried to demarcate vice and virtue in the commercial world of entertainment. Neither was entirely successful. The sex radicals assumed that human beings would be emotionally happier if sexual relations were frank, out in the open and modified by reason. This generous endeavour never quite came to terms with the very different idiom of sexuality emerging in popular culture. In the words of a 1916 song:

> You dare me, you scare me
> And I still like you more each day
> But you're the kind that will charm
> And then do harm
> You've got a dangerous way.[111]

Social purity, meanwhile, had to contend with the elusive impact of the image. Not only the movie moguls but advertisers had discovered that sex appeal was a seller. Soap, for example, was not just about cleanliness: 'You too can have the charm of "A Skin You Love to Touch",'[112] announced Woodbury Soap in the *Ladies' Home Journal* in 1918. Alan Dawley points out that though the atmosphere of 'wartime discipline' enabled the purity lobby to gain more power and secure prohibition in 1919, it was to be a 'pyrrhic victory', for 'the suppression of commercialized vice only led to the criminalized vice of bootleggers, gangsters, pimps and procurers in the Roaring Twenties'.[113]

The Aftermath

The United States Senate accepted the suffrage amendment in June 1919 and state after state ratified. On 26 August Harry Burns's mother sent a telegram to her twenty-four-year-old son: 'Don't forget to be a good boy and help Mrs Catt put the "Rat" in Ratification.'[114] Harry Burns duly cast the deciding vote and Tennessee, the thirty-sixth state, ratified. By November 1920 American women could vote; it was victory at last. It was, however, a victory based on a politics of compromise which left a bitter residue. In 1919, when the Northeastern Federation of Women's Clubs, an organization of African-Americans, applied to join the National American Woman Suffrage Association, they were told that as they did not have the Southern white vote their application could not be accepted.

Not only NAWSA but also the progressives round Jane Addams and Lillian Wald had resolved at all costs to stay within the mainstream of American politics; they too were prepared to make strategic compromises in order to achieve the vote and retain their influence for moderate social reform. Yet the price of their success was the disintegration of the women's networks which had crossed political boundaries.

A similar process could be observed in the Women's Trade Union League, which had also worked with the government during the war. As the WTUL leadership was drawn into the new official machinery of labour relations nationally and internationally, it became increasingly removed from grass-roots action. So when women workers were discarded from industry, the WTUL was hopelessly caught between the employers and labour unions hostile to women's employment. While they could protest, they were unable to defend women workers. For example, when the 'conductorettes' who wanted to keep their wartime employment won their case before the War Labor Board, the WTUL were unable to persuade the male trade union leadership to discipline a local who refused to accept the women in New York.

Ironically the WTUL's preoccupation with protecting women workers also contributed to job losses. Their victory in securing legislation preventing women under twenty-five working as telegraph messengers was extended in 1919 to female transit workers – to the fury of the women who were excluded from employment. These adverse effects of protection did cause some rethinking and in November 1919, at the First International Congress of Working Women in Washington, Margaret Dreier Robins made an important distinction. Rather than the protection of women in industry, which had been the male unions' approach, what was needed, she said, was 'the participation of women in plans to protect themselves'.[115]

The question which was to be increasingly forced upon the WTUL by events was which women were to have the power to plan and how were plans to be enforced? Mary Church Terrell was among a group of women who signed an appeal to the Congress from 'Representative Negro Women of the United States on behalf of Negro Women Laborers of the United States'.[116] But the particular needs of black women continued to be overlooked by the WTUL hierarchy.

The deciding factor in working women making gains was not simply a legislative framework but support from the grass-roots members of the unions. In Kansas City, for example, the men's insistence that women's guaranteed minimum wage be raised to equal the guaranteed rate for men was accepted by the War Labor Board, but on the whole the WTUL was not able to link state protection to trade union resistance.

The harmonious approach to labour relations pursued by the League was overtaken by the militant mood of workers in 1919. Strikes broke out all over the United States. In Seattle Anna Louise Strong was swept into the general strike which brought the city to a halt for several days in 1919. Workers freed from the wartime no-strike pledge demanded more pay, shorter hours and collective bargaining rights. Employers retaliated with a ferocious onslaught against labour. Not only leftists were denounced; even the Boston police, on strike for wage increases, were accused of Bolshevism. The telephonists, remembering how the police, who were from similar Irish-American backgrounds, had supported them, extended solidarity nonetheless.

These spontaneous rebellions of labour were led by the American Federation of Labor. Unlike the 'Wobblies', who had been compelled to turn themselves into a defence organization as their members were herded into jail, the AFL had emerged intact from the war. It was a conservative craft-based organization which excluded Asian and African-Americans. Though it represented many women workers, it retained the male craft workers' idyll of the male breadwinner and the wife at home. The extraordinary pressure of post-war labour militancy did force some change. The AFL slogan was 'Put Women in Second Line of Defense'.[117] Dana Frank describes in *Purchasing Power* how the Women's Card and Label League supported the union through boycotts and the promotion of the union label and shop card. However, she also points out that the involvement of women was only within the parameters of white 'American' trade unionism, for the boycotts frequently targeted non-union firms hiring Asian immigrant men and women.

Government denunciation of foreign-born radicals confirmed and fostered existing prejudices. The foreign born, anarchists, socialists, pacifists and radical feminists remained under attack as reds and Bolsheviks, regardless of their attitude to the Russian Revolution. Emma Goldman came out of prison in September 1919, having served two years for opposing conscription, but in December the anarchist speaker was seized and deported, along with 248 other immigrants, to Russia.

Agnes Smedley went to work for Margaret Sanger's *Birth Control Review* when she was released from prison, joining Kitty Marion in distributing birth-control literature in front of Macy's department store and continuing her defence of Indian nationalists threatened with deportation. The trade union protests against the Indians' deportation were mixed with xenophobia and racism. The Electrical Workers' local (branch) in Stockton, California, wrote demanding the 'deportations of all Hindus back to India',[118] a policy which would have delighted British intelligence agencies annoyed by the American sympathy for the anti-imperialist cause.

The Ku Klux Klan were gaining supporters hostile to foreign immigrants as well as blacks. Christine Ellis remembered how in Rathbun, Iowa, they promised people the houses of Croatian settlers, and went riding in the night to burn the fiery cross of hatred in front of the Catholic church and near the mine. Racism too was on the rise; black Americans were attacked and killed not only in East St Louis, but in Chicago, where the white men and women involved were given small sentences, while eleven black men were convicted of murder for defending themselves. Enraged by this racist injustice, Ida B. Wells, the campaigner against lynching and a suffrage activist, challenged Chicago's judiciary in the *Chicago Defender*.

In 1917 Emma Goldman had appealed to the 'kind of patriotism which loves America with open eyes', meaning 'love of the beauty of the land, the people who have produced her wealth and riches . . . the dreamers and the philosophers and the thinkers who are giving America liberty'.[119] In prison thousands of American radicals had been forced to reconsider this faith in the land of the free. Less explicit hopes of a better life were also fading. The black American poet Georgia Douglass Johnson wrote in 1918:

> I'm folding up my little dreams
> Within my heart tonight,
> And praying I may soon forget
> The torture of their sight.[120]

The dreams did not entirely die, but the radical vision of the early twentieth century was narrowed, fragmented and contained. Radicals, severed from liberals, were stranded on the margins. In Blanche Wiesen Cook's words, 'The Red Scare carved the heart out of American liberalism, and charted the course of twentieth-century politics.'[121]

These general political circumstances were to affect women's position as much as the campaigns for specific reforms. And as the dreams and hopes of transformation were stored away, they were assiduously recorded and filed by an ex-librarian, J. Edgar Hoover, tracking a spider's web of conspiracy which stretched out from leftists to include Jane Addams, Lillian Wald, Carrie Chapman Catt and even the young Eleanor Roosevelt, who had been so busy with her Red Cross canteens. In some circles liberal respectability cut no ice.

Chapter 3

THE 1920s

BRITAIN

Wild Young Things

Michael Arlen's novel *The Green Hat* was a best-seller in 1924. Its heroine, Iris Marsh, caught the mood of the times: 'You felt she had outlawed herself from somewhere, but where was that somewhere? You felt she was tremendously indifferent to whether she was outlawed or not.'[1]

Rumour connected Iris Marsh with Nancy Cunard, with whom Arlen had had an affair. She had graduated from her youthful reading of Elinor Glyn to become the author of a book of poems, *Outlaws*, in 1921. But it was her destiny to be celebrated less for what she did than for what she symbolized. The legend grew when *The Green Hat* became a play, and was performed on Broadway and then in London, with Tallulah Bankhead as Iris Marsh, in 1925. Though she resisted being the metaphor for an era, and actively pioneered recognition not only of the Dadaist and Surrealist avant-garde but of black artistes like Josephine Baker, her image as a 'wild young thing' of the 1920s persisted.

Writers were drawn to Nancy Cunard. Her elusiveness and detachment led a thwarted Aldous Huxley to work her into *Antic Hay* in 1923 and *Point Counter Point* in 1928. A friend, Mary Hutchinson, described her in 1924: 'She kept up perfectly her façade, behind which one seems to see a shadow moving – an independent, romantic, melancholy shadow which one can never approach. The façade was exquisite, made of gold leaf, lacquer, verdigris and ivory.'[2]

She was photographed in the same year by Man Ray in Paris with

Tristan Tzara, the Romanian creator of Dadaism. She wore a silver trouser suit, a mask and an old top hat of her father's.

The 1920s styles plucked specific male accoutrements out of context; appropriated and exaggerated, they were to be grafted on to a new culture of femininity. Ghosts of soldiers in khaki turned into the ubiquitous beige worn with flesh-coloured stockings. The boyish 'jumper' became fashionable in 1922. Hair was bobbed and then severely shingled in the Eton crop of the mid-1920s. Trousers, however, were still strictly for sport or for lounging on the beach. Even the fashionable lesbians in the intellectual avant-garde, Marguerite Radclyffe Hall, Romaine Brooks and Natalie Barney, wore skirts with their waistcoats, jackets, ties and monocles.

The 1920s 'young thing', wild or merely bright, was apparently always mobile; she danced, she gadded from cocktail party to club, she swam, she played tennis. Suzanne Lenglen, the French tennis player, shocked Wimbledon in 1920 by wearing a pleated skirt reaching mid-calf. Athleticism added to allure. Nor was it all show: 1920s women set records – they scaled Kilimanjaro and the Eiger, and swam the English Channel.

The restless young women of the 1920s were labelled 'flappers' by the newspapers again, and this time the name stuck. Though presented as an actuality, the 'flapper' was a half-truth that applied only to a minority. However, repetition has a way of substituting for reality and the media image generated a dutiful response from the voices of order and tradition. Barbara Cartland, the romantic novelist, was concerned that slim women would produce weak babies; while Dr Cecil Webb-Johnson warned discontented wives who read *Good Housekeeping* magazine in 1926 that the 'constant craving for change, for amusement, for excitement at any cost' led to 'the lined and weary face, the constant headaches, and . . . uncertainty and irritability of temper'.[3] The moral was clear: stay still and be content. At least it was less costly than the creams and potions advertised by *Good Housekeeping*.

Politics

Neither the flappers' styles nor *Good Housekeeping* were exactly the liberation for which the suffrage campaigners had fought so hard. But feminists could point to some legislative changes achieved over the decade. Women under thirty were finally allowed to vote after the passing of the 1928 Equal Franchise Act in the United Kingdom; and Irish women gained the franchise with the creation of the new Irish state in 1922. There were legislative improvements in married women's property rights and in the guardianship of children, while the 1923 Matrimonial Causes Act gave women equal grounds for divorce with men. Registration of midwives and maternity and nursing homes provided a check on maternity services. The lobby for moral reform, which included some feminists, achieved the Criminal Law Amendment Act of 1922, which raised the age of consent to sixteen, and the sale of alcohol to those under eighteen was banned the following year. A degree of economic support was also won. The 1923 Bastardy Act increased the maximum payments by fathers from 10s. to 20s. when an affiliation order was obtained. From January 1926 widows of insured men with children under fourteen and a half were granted a weekly pension of 10s. and children's allowances of 5s. for the first child and 3s. for subsequent children who were in full-time education. Insured women and the wives of insured men received old-age pensions of the same amount. These benefits were initiated by the Conservative government and then extended by Labour in 1929.

These were not, however, the extensive reforms which many feminists and labour women had envisaged. Moreover, very few women became candidates, with even fewer making it into the male bastion of Parliament. Agnes MacPhail had entered the Canadian House of Commons in 1918 and in the same year Countess Markievicz had been elected as a Sinn Fein candidate from Dublin to the British House of Commons. She was in prison for her part in the Easter Rising, so it was to be the American Nancy Astor who became the first woman MP in Britain, winning her husband Waldorf's Plymouth seat when he inherited a title. A maverick Conservative, she made her maiden speech in February 1920 in favour of the state regulation of alcohol. This had been imposed in Britain during the war and America had recently introduced Prohibition, but to many British Conservative MPs it was akin to Bolshevism. Never active in the suffrage movement, in 1920 Nancy Astor opposed the relaxation of the divorce laws which many feminists wanted. It was evident that women would not bring a

Imprudence in pearls: Nancy Astor, Conservative MP for Plymouth, the first woman to take her seat in the House of Commons, campaigning during the general election in 1923.

unified approach into the mainstream; they were divided on politics in general and on 'women's issues'.

The arrival, however, of the early women MPs did dent the masculine world of parliamentary practice and politics. No longer could its orientation to a single gender be taken for granted. Nancy Astor made history by being not only the first woman to take the oath but the first Member of Parliament who was allowed to wear a hat. Nor was it just appearances; she shifted the discourse of politics. When her ally on divorce, the right-wing Ulsterman Ronald McNeill, declared, 'Constancy was a virtue less characteristic of men than of women, but the attributes that attracted the opposite sex withered more readily in the female than in the male,' the elegant Viscountess exclaimed, 'Hear, hear,' adding, 'Women do fade quickly, but the thing that really holds men to women is not the physical charm. It attracts them, but it does not keep them.'[4] A Christian Scientist, Nancy Astor brought her own version of womanly moral reform to politics and introduced aspects of conservatism which were unfamiliar to the Commons.

She survived ridicule as a hypocrite when it was discovered that she had concealed her own divorce in the United States to protect Waldorf's political career. She was to pioneer a conservatism based on social reform, combining the role of aristocratic hostess at Cliveden with the defence of seamen and their families in her constituency, women's equal rights in the civil service, women in the police force and nursery schools.

Lady Astor stormed the male sphere with a mixture of American energy and grand-lady élan. 'Let yourself rip and wear all your pearls: prudence is not your game,'[5] advised her friend George Bernard Shaw in 1929. Wealth and privilege gave members of the upper class a certain leeway to exercise panache regardless of gender.

In contrast, the Liberal Margaret Wintringham, who took her husband's seat after he died, brought a more homely style to parliamentary politics in 1921. She had been active in the feminist organization the National Union of Societies for Equal Citizenship (NUSEC) and the Women's Institute. She identified with their broader, social housekeeping role, which she described as presenting homemaking 'in the light of a highly privileged, skilled and nationally important occupation'.[6]

Capable of mobilizing large numbers of women, the Women's Institutes were not confined to jam-making; they also took up the improvement of rural housing, village water supplies, electricity, rural telephones, bus services, the purification of milk for children and young mothers, the provision of midwives and infant welfare centres and education. Moral reform was an important aspect of this extended definition of housekeeping. They supported the women police as custodians of virtue and the censorship of the cinema, for example. There were, however, some barriers which could not be overcome by simply expanding the personal domestic sphere into politics. When 600 Women's Institutes affiliated to the League of Nations Union, they were accused of pacifism by the right-wing Navy League.

Ellen Wilkinson, the dynamic Labour member who was elected in 1924, adopted yet another strategy for operating in the predominantly male world of politics. A risk-taker, according to Martin Pugh in *Women and the Women's Movement in Britain* she occupied a boundary between the party loyalists like the Chief Woman Officer in the Labour Party, Australian Marion Phillips, Margaret Bondfield and Susan Lawrence, and the feminists, Helena Swanwick, Dora Russell, Dorothy Jewson and Frida Laski. She had served her political apprenticeship in the feminist and peace movements, and in the Communist Party. Her

Boundary woman: Ellen Wilkinson, Labour's first woman MP, leaving for the United States in 1926 to rally support for the miners' strike.

experience as a trade union representative from the Co-operative shops on the Trades Boards had taught her about low pay. A supporter of family allowances *and* trade union rights, she brought a tough recognition of gender and class into Labour politics. She was an MP who knew that Parliament was not the only face of the British state, for in 1920 she had been part of a Women's International League for Peace and Freedom (WILPF) delegation to Ireland to investigate reports of the cruelty of the British soldiers the Black and Tans. Giving evidence to the American Commission on Conditions in Ireland, headed by Jane Addams, she had described how 'The men come in the middle of the night, and the women are driven from their beds without any clothing other than a coat. They are run out in the middle of the night and the house is burned.'[7]

Personally too she was a boundary woman: an educated young woman from a working-class background, rooted in left politics, she also loved the theatre and the cinema, fashionable clothes and Elizabeth Arden cosmetics. She was a single woman without the protection of wealth or marriage and often tried to cram too much into her day. 'What I need is a wife,'[8] she once exclaimed.

These interpersonal boundaries of gender affected women's capacity to participate in the public sphere. Regardless of their politics, women MPs had to devise ways of finding a public/personal balance. Lady Astor had the support of Waldorf; Ellen Wilkinson relied on her sister Annie and never married. By the time she turned to serious love affairs, all the men she was attracted to were married already. There were certain hidden costs for an independent woman in politics; a younger generation was to observe these nuanced restraints on personal fulfilment and view emancipation in the public sphere more warily than the enthusiasts of the suffrage era.

The feminist organizations in Britain faced a difficult strategic dilemma during the 1920s. Were they to continue to agitate for the complete franchise or seek broader reforms? While the first course excited only a faithful few, the second revealed conflicting priorities. Lady Rhondda's feminist journal *Time and Tide* propagandized for reforms in the position of unmarried mothers and widows. It advocated changing the laws on child assault and protested against the unequal rights of guardianship of children, unequal pay for men and women teachers and inequality in the civil service. *Time and Tide*, which published writers like Helena Swanwick, Rebecca West, Vera Brittain, Winifred Holtby, Cicely Hamilton, Elizabeth Robins, Virginia Woolf and Rose Macaulay, occupied an important cultural as well as political space. The National Union of Societies for Equal Citizenship (formerly the National Union of Women's Suffrage Societies) focused on opening the professions and the civil service, gaining equal treatment on the honours list and an equal moral standard in divorce, solicitation and prostitution. Its members ranged from Liberals, such as Margaret Wintringham and Margery Corbett Ashby, to Conservatives, such as Lady Balfour, and mild socialists, such as Ethel Snowden.

Division occurred, however, in NUSEC not on party-political lines but over the approach to feminism. When Eleanor Rathbone took over as president in 1920, she challenged the dominant egalitarian assumptions. Instead of going for equal rights with men, she believed in demanding 'what we want as women, not because it is what men have got, but because it is what women need to fulfil the potentialities of their own natures and to adjust themselves to the circumstances of their own lives'.[9]

The emphasis on women's difference enabled feminists to make demands based on social needs rather than simply on equal opportunities with men. This approach had more relevance for women in traditional jobs and for women as wives and mothers. However, it presumed a distinct gendered nature and a unified set of womanly needs. Winifred Holtby challenged the idea of a 'woman's point of view'[10] in an article in *Time and Tide* in 1926 in which she argued that the human being took priority rather than gender difference. Human rights were thus the basis for one strand of feminism, while women's needs as women preoccupied the supporters of Eleanor Rathbone, who advocated cash payments for mothers as a solution to the economic dependence of women on men.

Labour women too tended to concentrate on demands based on an assumption of women's different needs. Their emphasis, however, was on the complementary relations of the sexes rather than on their antagonism. In *Labour Women*, Pamela Graves shows how their acceptance of a women's sphere was based on the reality of working-class women's lives, which were quite distinct from men's. Many grass-roots activist women came to politics through differing experiences in their families and through separate organizations like the Women's Co-operative Guild, which grew steadily through the 1920s to reach 66,566 members by 1930. Women in the labour movement did not assume a unity of interest between women of different classes. Instead they brought their own gendered class understanding into local politics, pressing for better housing, health and maternity welfare centres, municipal baths and libraries. A far-reaching vision of municipal politics can be seen in their debates and demands. They pressed for the local councils to provide basic services like electricity, for example, and noticed imaginative details in policy like the need for tea in parks. Their own childhood memories of humiliation by authorities in claiming poor relief and their knowledge of practical budgeting skills brought humanity and practicality on to local councils.

Labour women's organizations still retained a commitment not only to gaining access to the resources controlled by the state, but to the community-based democracy advocated by Sylvia Pankhurst. Even the Chief Woman Officer of the Labour Party, Marion Phillips, was convinced that working-class women could contribute to the design of housing provided by local councils. A desire to extend influence was also evident in the support from Labour women for birth control. This issue, along with child allowances, caused continuing conflict with the Labour leadership throughout the decade. By 1929, frustrated by their lack of influence upon the machinery of power within the party, a majority of women had become convinced that constitutional changes were needed in the Labour Party to give them a more distinct voice.

In *The Long Road to Greenham*, Jill Liddington shows how the politics of social motherhood was also being propagated by women's peace organizations, such as the Women's International League for Peace and Freedom and the International Women's Co-operative Guild, which was formed in 1921. They were critical of militarism in school textbooks and war films, they organized women's peace pilgrimages with Liberal women and held an anti-militaristic celebration of Armistice Day. Of course, 'womanly' qualities could be invoked for diverse causes. Conservative women threw themselves into Empire Day with equal fervour. Nor was it always self-evident what womanliness entailed.

Liberal politicians who had accepted the construct of a natural female disposition towards peace were flummoxed by angry working-class women during the peace negotiations after the First World War, demanding revenge for the death of their loved ones. Meanwhile, in 1924 in Ireland, P. S. O'Hegarty grumbled that the women of Dublin were the most implacable and hysterical participants in the civil war: 'The Suffragettes used to tell us that with women in political power there would be no more war. We know that with women in political power there would be no more peace.'[11]

Feminist certainties were being undermined on several fronts. In Ireland women in the nationalist movement were under pressure to subordinate gender to a wider political movement, and the bitterness caused by the civil war strained alliances between Catholics and Protestants as well as with English women. The idea of both a distinct female nature and a common condition of women was to dissolve during the decade. When Nancy Astor suggested that the women Members of Parliament form a Women's Party in 1929, the Labour women declined. The General Strike of 1926 and the miners' lock-out that followed had sharpened class feeling. Mary Agnes Hamilton said that Labour women saw 'sex equality' as 'only one element in our creed'.[12]

The links between socialist women and liberal feminists formed in the suffrage era were also to weaken in the 1920s. The understanding that the democratization of gender relations spanned personal as well as public experience was similarly overwhelmed. The submergence of what Stella Browne, the Canadian socialist feminist, called 'self-determination'[13] in a review of Margaret Sanger's *The New Motherhood* in 1922 was to be a loss not simply for the women's cause but for a radical, democratic political vision as a whole.

Work

Conflict about feminist strategy towards women's employment came to a head in the National Union of Societies for Equal Citizenship in 1927 over the question of protective legislation. When NUSEC agreed that the views of workers directly affected by protective legislation ought to be taken into consideration, the egalitarians, who wanted all barriers which prevented women entering work on the same terms as men to be removed, left to join the Open Door Council. The split followed several years of conflict between advocates of equal rights and Eleanor Rathbone's 'new feminists', who argued that women's interests were best served by recognizing gender difference. Not only liberal feminists but the socialists took different stands. Dora Russell argued for protective legislation to be extended to men, except for maternity provision, while another Independent Labour Party member, Dorothy Jewson, thought they should keep the existing protection for women and base future legislative protection on the nature of the job rather than on the sex of the worker. Selina Cooper was in a minority of labour women who opposed state regulation.

Trade union women, facing recession from 1920, and a decline in women's trade union membership, were inclined to see state protection as a last-ditch defence and abstract calls to equality as irrelevant. Equal pay was shelved for a focus on unemployment and low pay. In 1921 Lillian Thring, who had been active in the women's movement in Australia, as well as with Sylvia Pankhurst in east London, set up a journal for the unemployed called *Out of Work*, which carried reports of grass-roots groups of unemployed women forming in London, Lancashire and Yorkshire. In 1922 the Trades Union Congress (TUC) Women's Group held a conference on women's unemployment, demanding not only jobs and training but women's inclusion in unemployment insurance. Though state unemployment benefit had been extended by the coalition government in 1920, domestic servants, cleaners and home-workers were excluded.

Women's wage rates were forced down to the minimum fixed by the Trades Boards. Regulations over hours were ignored by employers, so women tended to get the worst of both worlds: low pay and long hours. Domestic service, which was extremely unpopular with the post-war generation, was an unwelcome alternative. If a post as a domestic servant was refused, women could lose their 'dole' money by being classified as not genuinely seeking work.

In 1922 unemployment led Lavinia Swainbeck from Newcastle to leave home, 'so there would be one less mouth to feed',[14] and become a domestic servant. Her description of her working conditions explains why this was such a desperate option. Her working day as an under-housemaid began at 6.30 a.m., cleaning the grate and laying a fire in the dining room. It ended at 7.30 p.m., when she turned down the beds, made up fires, emptied slops, filled the coal and wood containers and left morning trays set in the housemaid's pantry. On Sunday she attended church with the family and had to go to family prayers at 8 p.m.

There were campaigns throughout the 1920s for a minimum and a living wage, but they had little effect because unemployment and a decline in union membership weakened the labour movement as a whole. Women trade unionists felt the specific problems they faced as women were ignored by the male leadership and won the right to call their own conference to develop and exchange ideas in 1925. Not all women agreed with this separate gathering because they feared that their demands would be hived off from the TUC. However, it was not simply a matter of male indifference but of the types of work done by women. Low-paid industries like clothing and catering or jobs like domestic service and homework were either not well organized or outside the unionized sector altogether.

In 1926 the TUC called out workers in heavy industry after employers locked out the miners to force wages down. Relatively few women were included in the General Strike officially because they did not tend to be in these industries. Nonetheless, some women workers joined the General Strike spontaneously: Scottish textile workers and Rowntrees' confectionery workers in York, for example, stopped work. Women were also involved in support action in communities: in the South Wales mining areas they held mass pickets and attacked scabs, and in Hackney, east London, Lily Cook, now a pensioner, remembers being marched out of school as a pupil by the teachers to demonstrate.

The six-month miners' lock-out which followed the General Strike left mining families destitute. A Women's Committee for the Relief of Miners' Wives and Children was set up by labour movement women, including Marion Phillips, Susan Lawrence, Margaret Bondfield and Ellen Wilkinson. They organized fund-collecting and distributed food and clothing in the mining areas. Much of this was the poor giving to the poor. One supporter, Bessie Dickenson, a weaver, ended up by raffling 'all the stuff I'd collected for my bottom drawer and my umbrella as well'.[15]

In 1927 the Conservatives passed the Trades Disputes and Trade Union Act, which stopped sympathetic strikes, restricted the political levy to the Labour Party and prevented public service unions from affiliating to the TUC. As the public service unions were the base for the most articulate trade union women activists, this really affected women's impact upon the organized trade union movement, while the defeat of the General Strike broke the spirit of an already battered trade union movement. By 1930 trade union membership had been reduced to less than half its size in 1920.

Not surprisingly, survival came to seem more an individual than a collective matter. New kinds of light factory work were just beginning to open up for women in the south-east of England. Some were American-owned big companies or were influenced by American-style assembly-line production. Food production was one of the areas that was changing fast and Peek Frean's biscuit factory was considered a particularly desirable place to work by London school-leavers in the mid-1920s. Winnie Young was one of the lucky applicants; her uncle had put her name down in 1926 and she got a job. 'You were highly honoured,'[16] she recalled, when interviewed by Miriam Glucksmann for her book *Women Assemble*. The discipline imposed on the women was extremely strict but resentment focused not on management but on other workers. There was hostility, for instance, between older women, who had experience of wartime work, and the younger ones, who saw their jobs as temporary until they married.

It was clerical work, however, that really offered a path out of the manual working class. In London especially, there were plenty of opportunities for smartly dressed young women to move up the social scale. Dolly Scannell took advantage of them to improve her working conditions by going from office to office. However, subtle barriers remained. The mother of one middle-class suitor was suspicious of her east London address and inquired about the occupations of her brothers and sisters: 'When I told her I had nine she nearly collapsed.'[17]

Even the poorest women workers, without hope of social mobility, had their own personal survival strategies. Mrs Dunne, who was a canteen worker in the Liverpool docks, remembers one woman who hid 'a great many sausages under her aprons, looking very large indeed. The policeman wanted to know: "What have you got there?" "You'd better ask my husband about that!" she said.'[18] Turning difference to good effect, she got the sausages through the gates.

Daily Life

Real wages were rising from 1918 and the differences in pay between skilled and unskilled workers were being reduced. Working-class family size was going down and there was a degree of welfare. Moreover, the post-war generation had a stronger sense of social entitlement and remembered wartime promises of a land fit for heroes. Robert Roberts noted in Salford the emergence of a working class who were 'less sure perhaps of dogmatic moralities but more aware, better educated and growing more certain of its rights and needs'.[19]

Among these 'rights and needs' was a growing sense that life should be about more than bare survival. Alongside the older forms of working-class entertainment – markets, pubs, street singers and outings – modernity was mushrooming. Gramophones, wirelesses, dance halls, cinemas and clothes in the new American styles indicated that there was cash to spare – or at least the growth of credit. This kind of spending on leisure, however, was still predominantly confined to the brief period before young men acquired family responsibilities. Married women had less time and less access to cash than men, though individuals varied in how much they kept for themselves. Social custom regulated 'going out' and pubs remained largely male domains, though women were sometimes taken out to the nicer bars with pianos. Working-class women did go to the cinema, often with children in tow – sometimes smuggled through, like Mrs Dunne's sausages. But there were still those who simply never went out. In *A Woman's Place*, Elizabeth Roberts notes how upbringing and the discipline of family life made many working-class women habitually subordinate their own needs to those of their husbands and children. Rose Gamble grew up in a family of five in two rooms. They were all supported by her mother's charring. In *Chelsea Child*, she said of her mother, 'She had no vanities . . . [However] now and again a pretty pattern would catch her eye . . . on a scrap of cloth . . . or on a roll of lino standing outside the ironmonger's. "I'd like a frock of that," she would say.'[20] If times were not as hard as they had been, they were hard enough.

The family's livelihood was still largely determined by the male wage. If a father was a drinker or a gambler, if he deserted his wife, became unemployed or died, a woman could barely earn enough to keep a family. Norah Kirk, for example, was raised in a single-parent family in Nottingham; her father, a bigamist, deserted her mother, who was unable to support three children by taking in washing; when he failed to pay maintenance they had to go to the Poor Relief officers. In *Dutiful Daughters*, she recalled:

It was a big room . . . and you'd all be sitting in this room with forms, and in turn people stood before a bench of men and women. You used to have to go up to this bench with all these like JPs . . . and they'd ask you all sorts of questions . . . if a child went for the money with a written consent from the mother or father. They'd try to trap the children by asking different things.[21]

Claiming poor relief marked a family out for humiliation in the more prosperous working-class communities. However, in some depressed regions it was just part of daily life. Mary Malloy remembers how in Bootle, near Liverpool, going to 'the Parish in Marsh Lane' for food vouchers was not regarded as shameful, '. . . because everybody was poor and they were all the same. They just felt happy when they had something.'[22] The children had a piece of bread and a cup of cocoa before school; the real disgrace was having to ask for police clothes or for clogs.

Long-term unemployment was a major reason for poverty, not only in the north of the country but also in London, where it put considerable pressure on working-class boroughs with large numbers of claimants. In Poplar, east London, during the early 1920s the Labour council, led by George Lansbury, took the position that the richer boroughs should contribute. This became a major political battle in 1921, when councillors went to prison in an effort to change the law. Among those imprisoned were several labour women who had been active in the suffrage movement and taken part in local community struggles with Sylvia Pankhurst: Minnie Lansbury, Lansbury's daughter-in-law, Nellie Cressall, a laundry worker and mother of eight, who had served on the local Food Committee during the war, trade unionist Jennie Mackay, who had been involved in the school care committee and been a school manager, and Julia Scurr, active in the Irish movement and a Poor

Law Guardian. Susan Lawrence, the London County Councillor who defended the right of council charwomen to get equal pay, also went to jail. In other areas the same continuities can be observed: Jessie Stephen in Bermondsey, south-east London, Hannah Mitchell in Manchester, Selina Cooper in Nelson, Lancashire, were all socialists involved in the suffrage movement who shifted to campaigning around poor relief. Poor relief affected the whole family, but women's role in the household made it a gender issue.

Housing was another pressing need which groups like the Women's Co-operative Guild saw as having a special relevance for women. In 1924 the first Labour government was elected and subsidies were provided for local councils to build housing. As only the more prosperous working-class families could afford to rent these, overcrowding and insanitary homes continued to be a problem, not only in urban but also in rural areas. Increasingly aware of the housewife as an individual consumer, the Conservatives' approach was to encourage private house-building financed by building societies.

Social investigators who surveyed conditions in the depressed areas linked bad housing, along with drink and unemployment, to incest and domestic violence. The darker side of family life was rarely discussed publicly – the 1919 film *Broken Blossoms* was unusual in its treatment of male violence. But neighbours could exercise collective pressure. In 1924 Maud Wood's father was forced to leave the house, along with his mistress, by neighbours threatening a rent strike. She remembered it as 'the happiest day of my life'.[23] He had sexually abused her as a child and exercised a brutal authority. Such male power was not just economic: her mother supported the household by cleaning and door-to-door peddling.

Violence was not exclusively a male preserve. There were notorious local figures, such as the tough drinker with a lovely voice in Miles Platting, north Manchester, called Nancy Dickybird. The novelist Anthony Burgess remembers his stepmother, the landlady of the Golden Eagle, waiting for her, armed with a truncheon, knuckle-dusters and two loaded army revolvers. After being arrested many times, Nancy Dickybird was converted to the Salvation Army and switched to hymn-singing.

Nor were women always passive domestic victims. In their account of the Durham coalfield *Masters and Servants*, Huw Beynon and Terry Austrin record Vera Alsop's memories of her father-in-law coming home drunk and aggressive. Her mother-in-law 'got up on a chair and she took this tray of toffee. My father-in-law had a baldy head and every time he walked past her she hit him on top of the head with toffee.'[24] Another night after she had used rolls of paper, he woke up completely bemused: 'By, I don't know what's happened but my head's sore.'[25]

Violence was not restricted to the poor. In *A Childhood in Scotland*, Christian Miller describes the enclosed aristocratic world of her life in a castle. She was terrified of her cold and remote father, who beat his children. As they wept in their darkened bedrooms, her mother would play Chopin on the piano: 'This was her way of telling us that she was thinking of us. It would never have occurred to her to come personally to comfort us; that would have been tantamount to undermining my father's authority.'[26] The samples of the social investigators did not, however, extend to Scottish castles.

British social workers trained at the London School of Economics, or in the newer departments at Glasgow, Edinburgh, Leeds and Manchester, were attuned, as Kathleen Woodroofe notes in *From Charity to Social Work*, to 'practical assistance'[27] rather than the psychiatric or psychological approach of their counterparts in the United States. The original charitable impetus had been replaced by sociology, which taught them to consider 'low wages and labour laws'[28] rather than individual motivation.

The values of social housekeeping had been assimilated into educational policy by the 1920s. In 1926 the Board of Education declared in *The Education of the Adolescent*, 'On efficient care and management of the home depend the health, happiness and prosperity of the nation.'[29] The housewife was a key figure and better training in 'housecraft' would raise her status: 'Trained intelligence combined with technical skill would develop in her a sense of proportion and enable her to economize time; it would prevent her from sinking into the domestic drudge without leisure for the discharge of civic responsibilities and for social intercourse.'[30] The grandest of policies, however, could be somewhat different in practice. Dolly Scannell's housewifery classes at school taught how to cook for a poor family of six and plan household tasks. Promised a certificate, she decided, aged thirteen, she would show it to 'Mr Right', who would surely propose. But put in charge of the mashed potatoes, she failed the test by adding a whole packet of margarine.

Housekeeping as both craft and profession was being evangelically proclaimed by magazines like *Woman and Home* and *Good Housekeeping* in the 1920s. Novelist Rose Macaulay might tell readers in 1923, 'Let the house or flat go unkept. Let it go to the devil, and see what happens when it has gone there. At the worst, a house unkept cannot be so distressing as a life unlived.'[31] But this was heresy to readers, who were busy collecting hints about how to use carbonate of soda and line fancy sponge bags with old hot-water bottles.

Good Housekeeping provided not only household hints but a guide to beauty, carrying advertisements for Helena Rubinstein's products and telling you how to make your own cosmetics from garden herbs. Readers were also able to buy clothes by mail order, so women in remote country places could keep up with fashions. Such magazines carried an open invitation to the good life of the modern middle class. Know-how, culture and common sense combined with self-help and shopping to solve most problems in its pages. As the advertisement for the New Suburbia Gas Cooker put it: 'Come out of the kitchen. IT DOES ALL THE COOKING WHILE YOU SHOP OR PLAY.'[32]

The promise overtook reality, of course. The new consumer durables were expensive – washerwomen came much cheaper than the new washing machines, which were marketed at between £45 and £60. Moreover, running even a modest middle-class home was still time-consuming and arduous, while the emphasis on the craft skills of housewifery actually raised expectations of standards.

In 1922, Leonora Eyles, a journalist writing in the feminist journal *Time and Tide*, described a new social phenomenon, 'The Woman in the Little House'. Annie Britain, married to a respectable working man, was not desperately poor but was trapped in a tiny, jerry-built house in a new London suburb and stuck in a routine of washing, ironing, mending and child-care. Leonora Eyles advocated co-operative stores, kitchens and nurseries. Though the 'Co-op' did have extensive shops and services, which included milk delivery, and local councils set up co-operative laundries, this socialization of domestic work and child-care did not occur on the large scale that she envisaged.

Along with housecraft, 'mothercraft' was being propagated as a skill during the 1920s, but there was a sharp division in approach. Among the middle classes the modern theories of Dr Frederick Truby King were becoming popular. He advocated instilling internal discipline and a scientific approach to child-rearing. His follower Mabel Liddiard assured mothers in her *Mothercraft Manual* in 1928 that feeding at regular intervals and strict potty-training would result in 'self-control, obedience, the recognition of authority, and later, respect for elders'.[33] In contrast, the socialist nursery campaigner Margaret McMillan believed that small children needed stimulation and nurture.

The expansion of nurseries, envisaged after the war, never materialized, but she ran her own nursery in Deptford, south London. In a radio broadcast in 1927 she described the children's day. Children aged between two and five arrived at 8 a.m. and went to small shelters in a big garden, where they had a breakfast of brown bread and oatmeal porridge with milk. They spent their day amidst animals, with as much sun, light, colour, music and dancing as possible. The Deptford nursery cured them of rickets and anaemia and reduced the incidence of measles.

Maternal mortality continued to be extremely high throughout the decade, leading Ellen Wilkinson to declare in 1929, 'Marriage should be scheduled as a dangerous trade.'[34] Campaigners demanded the extension of maternity and child welfare, better health care, family allowances and birth control. However, danger in childbirth was not simply restricted to the poor. Rose Luttrell, married to a Wiltshire bank manager, lost her first baby when the GP did not realize that 'the baby's head was jammed against my spine'.[35] Like many middle-class women she chose a nursing home for her next three births. Incompetent GPs who used unhygienic instruments caused many unnecessary deaths. The maternal mortality rate in middle-class areas of Leeds was almost twice as high as in the working-class parts of the city, where most women relied on midwives. Middle-class private nursing homes also had a high mortality rate. In 1929 local authorities took over the dreaded Poor Law hospitals and began to improve maternity wards.

Better conditions for motherhood were relevant to both working-class and middle-class women, as the Independent Labour Party feminist

Health and Beauty

Health as the key to beauty was the message of the 1920s. Instead of the Victorian discipline of learning good posture, movement was the key. Margaret Morris, inspired by Isadora Duncan's free-expression dancing, pioneered movement to music as exercise. Actresses Elsa Lanchester and Phyllis Calvert were among the enthusiasts who donned flowing tunics to follow her regime. Margaret Morris also developed an interest in breathing exercises and had discovered yoga by the mid-1920s. She went on to adapt her exercises with physiotherapists and doctors for children with disabilities. Along with her belief in movement went theories of diet: she advocated fresh fruit, salads and vegetarianism and was an opponent of tea and coffee.

Health was a philosophical matter for Mary Bagot Stack from Ireland. Her theories of physical exercise drew on the Greeks and on Indian

Grace with vigour: Margaret Morris Dancers rehearse in Chelsea, south-west London.

yoga. The Bagot Stack Health School provided physical training which sought 'a rhythmic balance of body and spirit', which she said was particularly relevant to women as the 'race builders'.[36] The Women's League of Health and Beauty was to be the result.

Ballet was becoming increasingly popular as well. Dance schools opened by Marie Rambert and Ninette de Valois in the early 1920s were later to be the basis for the Ballet Rambert and the Royal Ballet.

1920s women were expected to be vigorous and graceful at the same time, and advertisers joined the bandwagon. One Grape-Nuts advertisement declared, 'Grandmother "went bathing" – girls like Molly go in to swim.'[37] Health, however, had its perils. Margaret Crawford Steffens warned the eager swimmers who read *Good Housekeeping* that they should apply cold cream before they went out into the sun and water. She also recommended a cleansing bath afterwards, especially for those readers who were likely to 'bathe near manufacturing plants or in harbours where the water is apt to be contaminated somewhat by the refuse from ships'.[38]

❋

Dorothy Jewson argued. Mothers and children had, she declared, 'a right to a SHARE OF THEIR OWN in the wealth of the community,' adding, 'Other services are concerned with the making of THINGS but motherhood with the making of human beings.'[39]

Though it was difficult to secure the social reforms for women which campaigners had imagined would follow from the suffrage, a consensus that the extension of social provision was desirable for women crystallized during the 1920s. Dissent came from the extreme libertarian right. An organization called the Mothers' Defence League shared the suspicion of the state expressed by writers Hilaire Belloc and G. K. Chesterton, but theirs were isolated voices.

Sex

The conviction that, in Dora Russell's words, 'there could be no true freedom for women without the emancipation of mothers'[40] inspired a campaign among Labour Party women for the right to contraceptive advice in the maternity and child-welfare centres funded by local authorities. In 1922 the suspension of a health visitor in Edmonton, north London, for giving birth-control information and the prosecution of the anarchist Rose Witcop and her companion Guy Aldred for publishing Margaret Sanger's *Family Limitation* focused public attention on birth control. When Marie Stopes was accused by the Catholic Dr Halliday Sutherland of 'exposing the poor to experiment'[41] in her clinic in Holloway, north London, which fitted women with the cervical cap, she sued for libel in a blaze of publicity and won on appeal in 1923. The middle class were using birth control by the 1920s, but the reformers who, following Marie Stopes, began opening clinics, wanted to reach the manual working class. Some, like Marie Stopes, were influenced by eugenic fears about the 'unfit' breeding. Others took the pragmatic view that birth control would prevent poverty and the dangerous abortions which contributed to the maternal death-rate. Dora Russell, Stella Browne and Rose Witcop, who were part of the radical wing of the birth-control movement, went further, connecting the right to birth control to a wider vision of social and economic democracy. Stella Browne declared in 1922 that it was crucial for 'woman's control of her own person and her own environment'.[42]

These socialist and anarchist women gained support not only from women who were anxious to limit their families but also from radicals committed to sexual liberation. For example, Harry Wicks describes in his autobiography, *Keeping My Head*, how birth control and free love were part of the Battersea socialist movement, along with opposition to vivisection and vaccination. When Stella Browne went to speak in Tredegar, South Wales, in 1923, she was greeted by a working-class audience of 900, eager to hear about sexual reform in Germany, France and Russia. Talking and doing, of course, were not always the same thing. Ruth Adler's Progressive Youth Circle in east London were discussing free love in the 1920s, along with other left-wing ideas. But she still crept into the Walworth Road clinic pretending she was about to be married because she was intimidated by the woman doctor: 'I couldn't tell her that I had wanted to sleep with a man before marriage.'[43]

Throughout the decade Labour women supporters of birth control challenged the Labour leaders and fought against the Catholic Labour lobby. Though the Labour Party conference in 1926 did pass a resolution in favour of birth-control advice in welfare centres, Catholic opposition proved too powerful and they turned their attention increasingly to getting the backing of the National Union of Societies for Equal Citizenship and the National Liberal Federation. In 1930 the Ministry of Health finally allowed advice for married women on medical grounds.

Abortion was an even more difficult issue to raise in the 1920s. While some abortionists operated for high fees, others like Elsie Friend, convicted in 1925, did it to help women who 'could not afford any more children'.[44] Not only did these illegal abortions sometimes result in death, but survivors could also suffer permanent damage to their health. Stella Browne was unusual in linking abortion to the demand for birth control. She insisted that without the right to abortion, women could not really have control over their fertility. This emphasis on reproductive rights as self-determination made her critical of attempts at social control. So while she supported Eleanor Rathbone's demand for family allowances, she rejected the suggestion in Rathbone's *The Disinherited Family* (1925) that the children of unmarried parents should be turned over to the Poor Law unless the parents married. Why, she asked, should children suffer if adults refused 'to turn a brief, though possibly worthwhile, illusion into a permanent incompatibility'?[45]

Though birth control was becoming more acceptable, not being married was generally regarded as a misfortune rather than a quest for autonomy in the respectable working class. Annie Davison, amidst Glasgow's intense socialist milieu, did consider a free union with her fiancé. But they decided that the risks of sexual rebellion were too grave and chose marriage. Courtship for most young working-class boys and girls on the 'monkey run' was still a matter of boisterous collective repartee. It was supplemented by visits to the cinema or to dance halls, but as many parents disapproved of dancing just getting out could involve considerable subterfuge and ingenuity. In *Leisure, Gender and Poverty*, Andrew Davies describes parents imposing a 'strict code of

'The Yellow Peril': racism and moral panic evinced in an early film still of 'dopegirls' from *The Dividend*.

behaviour' in Salford during the 1920s and 1930s – especially on girls; there were, nonetheless, fears of an 'alleged collapse of parental responsibility'.[46] Sex before marriage could mean that girls were branded as delinquents and the law reducing the age of consent contributed to this criminalization. In *Forbidden Britain* Steve Humphries and Pamela Gordon also note the racist panic about 'dope girls'[47] in London and Liverpool seduced by Chinese gangs. Annie Lai, a prostitute in Limehouse, was the substance behind the myth. She lived with Yuen Sing Lai, a gambler and opium dealer, until he was deported for killing a man with an iron bar in 1928. She ran his opium business and 'punk-apu'[48] gambling den until police closed it in 1930 and she was compelled to return to prostitution in order to support her children. As Maria Lin Wong points out in *Chinese Liverpudlians*, most relationships were not based on prostitution and drugs. Moreover, until the First World War opium-based medicines such as Godfrey's Cordial had been widely available.

Attitudes towards women's illicit heterosexual desire outside the confines of the upper classes and the intelligentsia could also still be extremely punitive. In 1923, for example, Edith Thompson was hanged, aged twenty-nine and possibly pregnant, after her twenty-year-old lover, Freddy Bywaters, a seaman, attacked and killed her husband, Percy. There was no evidence that Edith Thompson had helped to murder her husband and evidence that she had planned the attack was slight. She was portrayed, however, as an evil adultress who had led a younger man into crime. The case touched a nerve, partly because the Thompsons were a typical upwardly mobile couple who were heading towards social respectability. Percy was a clerk who had taken elocution lessons to lose his London accent and Edith, a milliner from a working-class background, was bright and intelligent. She dressed smartly, learned French and did amateur dramatics with Percy. They moved out to the suburbs in 1920, buying a house for £250 in Ilford. Their marriage, however, was not happy. Percy, a ponderous, possessive man, drank and was occasionally violent; in contrast, Freddy, who was their lodger, liked the romantic thrillers which Edith read and shared her

Edith Thompson with her lover, Freddy (left), and the husband he murdered, Percy Thompson (right).

143

Lesbian Style

Sexuality between women became part of a public discourse when Marguerite Radclyffe Hall's *The Well of Loneliness* was prosecuted in 1928. Radclyffe Hall, who had come to accept the view that lesbianism was congenital, produced a novel about the love between women ambulance drivers which contained very little actual sex. Compton MacKenzie's skit on a lesbian community, *Extraordinary Women*, published in the same year, was far more explicit. It was not so much sex as the advocacy of open relations between women which was offensive to the authorities. E. M. Forster and Virginia Woolf were both prepared to testify for the book, but the judge refused to call them. *The Well of Loneliness* was forfeited and not published again for twenty-one years in Britain. Nonetheless, the publicity which surrounded the novel contributed to the emergence of a specific kind of lesbian identity.

Radclyffe Hall with Una, Lady Troubridge.

Marguerite Radclyffe Hall and Una Troubridge were both from upper-class families and Radclyffe Hall's inheritance gave them freedom to live together in style as lovers. In *Cutting a Dash*, Katrina Rolley demonstrates how they contributed personally to the creation of an image of the lesbian. In the early 1920s this coincided with modern styles for short hair; Radclyffe Hall adopted an Eton crop a few years before it became fashionable. Their smartly tailored skirts and jackets – even breeches for Cruft's dog show – had an elegant air. Towards the end of the decade, when longer hair came back into fashion, the masculinity of Radclyffe Hall's outfits were no longer acceptable as modern style and marked out a distinct identity.

Both women saw themselves in terms of Ellis's psychological category congenital inverts; while Radclyffe Hall assumed a masculine role, Una Troubridge adopted increasingly feminine clothes. Masculine cross-dressing, which had initially been a gesture of autonomy, came to be the image of the lesbian which prevailed over the decadent sophisticates in Natalie Barney's salon, caricatured by Djuna Barnes in *Ladies Almanac* in 1928, or the shifting parameters of gender in Virginia Woolf's *Orlando*, published the same year.

love of dancing. Though their lovemaking was snatched and secretive, in a deserted railway carriage and in Wanstead Park, she had her first orgasm with her lover. Their intimacy was recorded in her letters to Freddy while he was at sea. Edith Thompson's romantic sensuality ended tragically in an execution which brought several witnesses, including the prison governor, to oppose capital punishment. A petition, signed by over 1 million people for a reprieve, was turned down. Her case illustrates the repressive attitudes which survived the glitter of the decade.

Dora Russell's *The Right to be Happy* appeared in 1927. An appeal against guilt and repression, it combined the egalitarian feminist demand for 'the right to do any man's work'[49] with a commitment to a new culture. She tried to break stereotypical versions of gender difference: 'Men have pushed on to us all the reticence and virtue, we in turn push on to them all the brutality and vice.'[50] The optimistic spirit of the book was in defiance of the times in Britain, but it received a good reception in America. While lecturing in the United States, however, she was refused permission to speak to a mixed audience of male and female students on the sexual reforms proposed by the World League for Sex Reform, and she came to the conclusion that 'in England you might say what you liked on these topics as long as you DID nothing, whereas in America you might DO as you wished provided you did not speak of it'.[51]

By the end of the 1920s there was a mood of doubt. Women who had been sure about the solutions only a few years before were no longer so certain. Leonora Eyles, for example, who had gone through a divorce, reflected on the contradiction between her feminist principles of independence and the actuality of her marriage. Writing in *Good Housekeeping* in 1928, she said, 'I prided myself on making no demands whatever upon him, thinking that thus we should have perfect equality. The result was that in the end he came to hate me.'[52]

A Room of One's Own, Virginia Woolf's classic which was published the following year, was going against the grain. It was, however, more restricted in aspiration than the radical plans of social change which had inspired many feminists at the beginning of the decade. The demand for £500 a year and a room of one's own was aimed at a minority of the educated middle class. Nor was the cultural transformation which would enable 'Shakespeare's sister' to be born going to happen in a hurry; the time scale was 'a century or so'.[53] It was an intimation of emancipation as a long haul – much longer than had been imagined a decade before. In her autobiography, *The Tamarisk Tree*, Dora Russell wrote that the impact of the American financial crash of 1929 was not only economic: 'There are periods in human history, when, without apparent reason, at first imperceptibly, the movement in one direction goes into reverse, the change occurs not only in the economics and politics of the time, but even in the motivation of human lives.'[54]

THE UNITED STATES

Playing along the Danger Line

High society in Montgomery, Alabama, turned out as usual for the annual masked ball, 'Les Mystérieuses', in 1921. That year an especially daring dancer held the floor dressed in a brief grass skirt. With every eye upon her, she lifted her skirt over her head and gave a final provocative wiggle: 'A murmur went over the auditorium in a wave of excitement and everybody was whispering "That's Zelda!" . . .'[55]

Zelda Fitzgerald, a new-style rebel Southern belle, was presented by her novelist husband, Scott Fitzgerald, as the personification of the 1920s flapper, 'flirting, kissing, viewing life lightly, saying damn without a blush, playing along the danger line in an immature way – a sort of mental baby vamp'.[56] Though she appeared to be playing the part with zest, the two partners were to remember this period in their lives very differently. He said in the early 1930s, 'We were about the most envied couple . . . in America,' to which she replied, 'I guess so. We were awfully good showmen.'[57]

After more than a decade of emotional battling, his drinking and her mental illness, Scott Fitzgerald told his wife, 'I would like you to think of my interests. That is your primary concern, because I am the one to steer the course, the pilot,' and when she asked him what he wanted her to do, he responded emphatically, 'I want you to stop writing fiction.'[58] Zelda Fitzgerald, who had wanted to be 'mistress of her own fate' by being light-hearted and unconventional, had rejected the dreary option of the 'emancipation' of an older generation because she thought that all it brought was 'a career that calls for hard work, intellectual pessimism and loneliness'.[59] She was to discover in her turn that love, freedom and fulfilment were elusive bedfellows.

The 1920s flapper frantically dancing and experimenting with sex was partly a chimera created by the media. The new independent woman appears lighting up Lucky Strike cigarettes or triumphantly riding the waves in a Coca-Cola advertisement of 1923. Adverts like these were actually a response to the personal rebellion and consumer power which had emerged in the preceding decade, when flapper habits

Keeping slim with Lucky Strike, 1929.

had upset moralists. The media of the 1920s was, however, able to transmit flapper styles on a mass scale. But it was not simply a matter of image and style, for behind all the razzmatazz a genuine sense of confusion existed about how to be a modern woman. In 1922 Freda Kirchwey defined herself as a 'left-wing feminist and internationalist'.[60] But this could not resolve inward uncertainties. In *Our Changing Morality* in 1924, she observed how the modern woman found, 'The old rules fail to work; bewildering inconsistencies confront her . . . Slowly, clumsily she is trying to construct a way out to a new sort of certainty in life.'[61]

This restless quest for identity was most intense among the white upper-middle-class educated young women, many of whom turned to psychoanalysis for enlightenment. However, sexual rebellion and the aspiration for personal autonomy had a wider influence. 'Las Pelonas', 'the Bobbed-haired Girls', feature in a verse from a *corrido* in the Los Angeles Mexican community in the 1920s. The 'flappers' stroll out for a good time in their straw hats after the harvesting and cotton-picking is done. Families divided over bobbed hair and bathing suits. An older Mexicano remembers telling his daughter, 'You can bathe at home. I will educate you . . . but [I will] not buy a bathing suit. You can wait till I am dead and buy it then.'[62]

The sexual dynamics of rebellion had, however, different social meanings. Young black women intellectuals, for instance, encountered a complex series of restraints upon a purely sexual personal search for autonomy. Respectability and education were vital in their struggle for freedom. Hazel Carby points out that novelists like Jessie Fauset 'faced a very real contradiction . . . if they acknowledged their sexuality and sensuality', for this simply got them branded in racist terms as 'primitive and exotic creatures'.[63]

Bessie and Sadie Delany were always conscious that they were being watched and judged by whites as representatives of the young black intelligentsia. When they moved to Harlem they were surrounded by the ferment of the Harlem renaissance. However, Sadie commented in *Having Our Say*, 'Being good girls, Bessie and I did not venture too far into the jazz scene. After all, we were Bishop Delany's daughters.'[64] Bessie, however, did throw herself into the debates about race, politics and culture. Rejecting the moderate Booker T. Washington, 'a smoother of the waters', for the more militant strategy of W. E. B. DuBois, she marched in so many protests 'it's a wonder I didn't wear out my feet'.[65] Like other educated black women, she recollects, 'I was torn between two issues – colored and women's rights. But it seemed to me that no matter how much I had to put up with as a woman, the bigger problem was being colored.'[66] Nonetheless, the day women got the right to vote in 1920 was one of the happiest days of her life.

Politics

In 1920 Crystal Eastman believed that with the suffrage won, the next question on the agenda would be 'how to arrange the world so that women can be human beings, with a chance to exercise their infinitely varied gifts in infinitely varied ways instead of being destined by the accident of their sex to one field of activity – housework and child-raising'.[67] She understood feminism to be not only about access to political and legislative power, or social and economic improvements, but an extension of democracy in the fullest sense to include social equality and individual self-expression. However, there were divergent interpretations of feminism and many were much narrower than Crystal Eastman's generous vision. The 1920s brought feminist social reform issues on to a mainstream agenda; yet it was a more restricted definition of feminism that would prevail.

The National Woman's Party called a conference in 1921 to consider strategic directions for feminism after the suffrage. Several approaches were already evident. Florence Kelley from the National Consumers' League put the emphasis on protective labour and social legislation. Black women pointed out that in practice they were still unable to vote in the South, that physical intimidation and lynching affected black women as well as men. There was a strong peace and internationalist lobby which focused on women's contribution to foreign affairs. Alice Paul from the NWP, however, was adamant that all these were merely diversions from the 'pure feminist program',[68] which ought to be concentrating on removing laws which restricted women's freedom and equality. These disagreements were to pull women in contrary ways later in the decade, though in the early 1920s the League of Women Voters, along with the Women's Joint Congressional Committee, constituted a powerful bloc which Republican and Democratic politicians could not ignore.

The Eighteenth Amendment, prohibiting alcohol from being made or sold in the United States, came into effect in 1920. It was regarded as a victory not only by sections of the patriotic right but also by many women reformers who saw alcohol as a cause of poverty and violence. Other issues which women progressives had raised – equal pay, an eight-hour day, abolition of child labour, services for maternity and infant health, employment boards, a minimum wage, along with the prevention of lynching – seemed at last to be on the political agenda. Women were acquiring a new visibility in public life, not only in the Children's Bureau but in other government bodies. In 1920 Congress set up the Women's Bureau in the Department of Labor. All the energy and accumulated experience of the suffrage campaign and local struggles for basic community services and improvements at work seemed to be finding a wider sphere of policy creation and implementation.

The Sheppard-Towner bill for maternity and infant health education was passed by Congress in 1921. It made funds available for educational services to teach women about nutrition, sanitation and caring for children. Legislation followed in forty-one states, making Sheppard-Towner funds available for health conferences, home visits by public health nurses and a range of other services.

The infant and maternal mortality rate in the United States was even higher than in Europe and the response, especially in remote rural areas, was enthusiastic. For example, in 1924 200 women attended a meeting in an isolated part of Mississippi, riding in on horseback or walking several miles with small children. The improvement of mothering was linked to the banning of child labour and attempts to extend the minimum-wage legislation, which from 1912 had enabled boards to be set up state by state to fix the wages of the low-paid.

The social reforms achieved by the women's lobby in the early 1920s through state legislation were, however, circumscribed and from the mid-1920s to be whittled away. Sheppard-Towner did not provide for health care because of opposition from the medical profession. Moreover, it had a differential impact; though beneficial to poor rural whites, it had much less effect upon black, Hispanic and Native American communities. In 1929 the final blow came when funds were withdrawn. Also the child-labour amendment of 1924 was ratified by only six states between 1924 and 1930 and minimum-wage legislation was threatened when the Supreme Court claimed it violated the Fourteenth Amendment's guarantee against unreasonable infringement of freedom of contract.

Prohibition was a divisive issue in the 1920s. Social reformers were caught between their desire to protect the working class from drink and their defence of free choice. This Wet–Dry conflict cut through the liberal women's networks. In 1928, for instance, a wet Democratic presidential candidate, Al Smith, was supported by Eleanor Roosevelt, but Jane Addams refused to back him because she stood by the Eighteenth Amendment banning alcohol. Prohibition increasingly became a conservative cause, expressing the small towns' suspicion of big-city decadence.

Right-wing Republicans were on the attack too against the remains of the progressive lobby, which was becoming increasingly isolated and defensive. In 1921 Republican Vice-President Calvin Coolidge declared women's colleges to be hotbeds of radicalism, harbouring Bolsheviks, and Brigadier General Amos A. Fries was to issue a spider's-web chart from the Chemical Warfare Section of the war department detailing the subversive character of women's and church groups. The Daughters of the American Revolution, originally among those accused, did a swift turn-around and by 1924 were denouncing the Women's Trade Union League and government Women's Bureaux for trying to Bolshevize the United States by destroying the family.

The extreme right took on the causes of social purity and the protection of women, giving them very different meanings from the progressive women social reformers. In spring 1922, for example, the *Denver Post* reported that the car of Canadian evangelist Aimee Semple McPherson had been hijacked by four white-robed Klansmen, who had kidnapped her and a woman journalist. The Ku Klux Klan had arrived in Denver the year before and marched through the streets removing movie posters which they found offensive. In the early 1920s they ran for office in the town and became a powerful influence in the local Republican party. The Klansmen led the blindfolded women into

Women supporters of the Ku Klux Klan parade in
Binghamton, New York.

a room, reciting their creed: 'One God, one country, one flag, the supremacy of the white race, chivalry toward women, purity and cleanness among men'.[69] Sister Aimee promised them her prayers as long as they 'stood for righteousness' and 'defended the defenceless'[70] – a proviso which was open to a wide interpretation. The Klan committed to 100 per cent Americanism, was hostile to Catholics, Jews and foreign immigrants, as well as to blacks. It was recruiting women to its ladies' auxiliaries with its promise of safeguarding female purity and was fast becoming a menacing force in local politics in the North as well as in the South.

The direct political challenge from the right was accompanied by a more insidious cultural stereotyping of feminists and maternalist progressives alike. A conservative psychological assault was gaining popularity. It played on fears of spinsterhood and mannish lesbians, analysing a political commitment to feminism as maladjustment, neurosis or immaturity. Internal pressures were also diminishing white middle-class women's social and political engagement. It was not easy for women accustomed to the heady activism of the suffrage and municipal 'city housekeeping' campaigns to switch to strategic lobbying in Washington. There was a certain weariness as well. Ruth Pickering, who had been a member of the Heterodoxy Club and written on labour struggles, declared in 1927, 'I have traded in my sense of exhilarating defiance (shall we call it feminism?) for an assurance of free unimpeded self-expression (or shall we call that feminism?). In other words I have grown up.'[71] She had shifted towards writing on dance, jazz and modern art for *The Nation* and *The New Republic* with a sense of release. There were also generations with differing political and cultural experiences. A psychologist, Lorine Pruette, divided American women in 1927 into three categories: an older group who had struggled hard to get into positions of influence; a slightly younger group who were less bitter but still concerned about independence; and the new generation of girls who were 'frankly amazed at all the feminist pother and likely to be bored when the subject comes up'.[72] *Harper's* magazine in the same year was dismissive: 'Feminism has become a term of opprobrium to the modern young woman.'[73] Dismissed on the one hand as infantile regression, feminists were also scorned as old-fashioned, unattractive and out of touch.

Divisions among women's groupings further weakened the loose coalition campaigning for social reforms. When the National Woman's Party introduced the Equal Rights Amendment into Congress in 1923, Florence Kelley and Jane Addams feared the insistence on absolute equality would endanger the laws protecting women from working long hours, at night or in dangerous trades. The conflict polarized and any common ground, like the proposal that protective laws should be extended to cover male workers, was submerged. Crystal Eastman's socialist feminist combination of demands – equality for women wage earners, social resources for housewives and mothers, a change in the sexual division of labour in employment and in the home, the transformation of household tasks through the reorganization of domestic life and the introduction of technology – seemed a pipe dream. Instead, both the campaigners for equality and the believers in protection accepted the existing basis of social relations as a given. The idea that changing women's circumstances involved shifting the wider structures of society was forced into retreat.

Though this was a powerful trend clearly visible at the centre of national politics, it was not the only development in the decade. It is overly simple to characterize the 1920s as the era of a purely individual personal rebellion among women. Ex-suffrage campaigners did not lose the habit of organizing because it proved hard to secure legislative change. They went instead into a range of voluntary organizations: the Women's Christian Temperance Union, the American Association of University Women, the National Federation of Business and Professional Women's Clubs, the National Parent-Teacher Association, the National Council of Jewish Women. The Women's Trade Union League, the National Consumers' League and the Women's International League for Peace and Freedom still organized, even though their influence had waned.

Moreover, at a local level women were taking public positions. For example, in Chicago Mary McDowell became Commissioner for Public Welfare in 1923. Mary Margaret Bartelme became the first woman judge in Illinois in the same year and was especially involved through her experience in the Juvenile Court with the problems of young women, establishing three girls' homes and raising money for fostering. In 1924 Seattle got a woman mayor, Bertha Knight Landes, a prohibitionist and supporter of municipal reform. Such women were gaining knowledge of both social policy and how to draw up legislation. So while they were blocked in their attempts to change society from the centre, many social reforms were being achieved locally by piecemeal burrowing from within.

Black women, who had never exercised any influence upon national politics at the centre, were extremely active in the 1920s in a whole range of movements. Mary Talbert led the Anti-Lynching Crusade from 1922 and the Federation of Colored Women's Clubs pressed for legislation. Local black women's clubs and church groups educated women to campaign for social welfare. Jamaican-born Amy Jacques Garvey, in Marcus Garvey's United Negro Improvement Association (UNIA), linked the cultural role of the 'New Negro Woman' to the struggles of the black urban working class and to Third World women in her column, 'Our Women and What They Think',[74] in the journal of the Garveyites, *The Negro World*, until she and Marcus Garvey had to leave for Jamaica in 1927. The UNIA did not seek integration but emphasized Pan-Africanism and autonomous black organization and culture. Just as it aimed to reverse racial stereotypes and give them positive meanings, the Garveyite movement gave women a differentiated role – though this was not always accepted quietly by Garvey's female supporters.

Religious organizations, like the 1920 Commission on Inter-Racial Co-operation of the Women's Council of the Methodist Episcopal Church, were beginning to open up a forum for debate between black and white women in the South. The Young Women's Christian Association (YWCA) appointed a joint committee of black and white women to study race problems in 1922. There was also some local liaising: for instance, the Co-operative Women's League in Baltimore worked with white women's civic leagues on campaigns for better health and sanitation services and for education.

Education is another indicator which belies the frivolous flapper image of the era. The growing numbers of women attending colleges and the expansion of courses through groups like the YWCA and the League of Women Voters meant that the new women of the 1920s were much better qualified than their mothers. Most of them aspired to combine careers with marriage and a family. The number of female graduates tripled in the decade, while those gaining doctorates nearly quadrupled. The number of women professionals also rose by 50 per cent – twice as fast as the increase in the female workforce. However, three out of four of these educated young graduates entered the 'women's' professions – libraries, social work, teaching. Only a few found their way into jobs as journalists, editors, lawyers, doctors, professors, scientists or civil servants, or went into business. The expansion in education did not alter the gendered structure of employment. A significant minority of African-American women, such as the poet and librarian Anne Spencer, were also part of this new generation of intellectuals. A consciousness of racial injustice infused their education: when Clara Jones was leaving home to become a student her grandfather, a former slave, reminded her, 'You're going to get your education and it's not yours – you're doing it for your people.'[75]

Education with a social purpose was also the inspiration for innovatory adult-learning projects such as the Bryn Mawr Summer School for Women Workers, which started in 1921. Its founder, M. Carey Thomas, had been influenced by British experiments, the Workers' Education Association and National Labour Colleges. However, she linked gender explicitly to class, hoping 'that equal opportunity for the manual workers of the world might be hastened by utilizing, before it had time to grow less, the deep sex sympathy that women now feel for one another'.[76] Carey Thomas was from a wealthy Quaker family and had been active in the peace and feminist movements. She combined a commitment to equality with a conviction that women had a special role. Her life illustrates how the values of the pre-war progressives were able to persist in the 1920s, nurtured by bonds of love and friendship between women in the midst of the 'Roaring Twenties', with its emphasis upon the heterosexual flapper.

Work

The bitter ideological battle over protection which had divided the feminists who argued for equality from social reformers who wanted the state to shield women from harsh conditions made a balanced assessment of the actual effects of legislation to protect women workers difficult. It also eroded any middle ground for compromise. Reformers who backed protective legislation encountered considerable opposition from employers and defended their position increasingly on the grounds that women were a special case, rather than seeking to extend the laws to include male workers. The maternalist arguments about women's gender difference merged with a pragmatic recognition that, given the lack of trade union organization among women, protective legislation constituted a last-ditch defence.

The National Consumers' League (NCL) and the Women's Trade Union League insisted that most working-class women were for protective legislation, citing a 1927 NCL survey in New York which showed that four out of five working women favoured a law limiting their labour to forty-eight hours a week. They also claimed that legislation did not have a discriminatory effect.

Protective legislation did safeguard a basic minimum in the industries where women predominated, though the emphasis upon women's difference also contributed to the view that women were a distinct section of the labour market. In *Out to Work*, Alice Kessler-Harris points out that the real problems with the emphasis on difference were the areas where only a few women were employed. Biology could be used as a social justification for exclusion as well as protection.

New kinds of employment were opening up in banking, real estate, retail sales, administrative and clerical work; offices were beginning to be mechanized and scientific management techniques were being applied to the new typing pools. The numbers of 'white collar' women were growing. There was also an expansion in glamorous but unorganized jobs which were part of the growing leisure industry – everything from bowling alleys to the ultimate dream of the cinema. Not only would-be stars made money from films. Settlement worker and leading Democrat Belle Moskowitz became a successful businesswoman making public relations films. There continued to be a few rags to riches stories in the black community: Lillian Harris Dean in New York's Harlem, for instance. She had migrated to New York in 1901 from Mississippi, bought an old baby carriage and a large washbasin and started selling pig's feet. 'Pig Foot Mary', as she was called, was investing in real estate by the 1920s. Completely uneducated, she was an astute and extremely tough businesswoman. When tenants or agents fell behind with their rent, her response was, 'Send it and send it damn quick.'[77]

Singers

The success of blues singers like Ma Rainey, Bessie Smith, Ida Cox, Clara Smith, Alberta Hunter and Ethel Waters enabled them to occupy what Hazel Carby describes as a 'privileged space'[78] among African-Americans. Aware of the problems faced by black women in both the North and the South, through their artistry they transcended the 'boundaries of the home', taking their 'sensuality and sexuality out of the private into the public sphere'.[79] Some songs, like Ma Rainey's 'Back Water Blues', about the destruction of floods in Mississippi, expressed collective experiences of black Americans, but a more typical theme was the personal dynamics of sexuality. It was the period of mass migration from rural poverty to the city. The railroad took men away and left women alone, but it also held out a promise of freedom for young single women.

Segregation meant that the 'privileged space' of blues singers like Bessie Smith was always ambivalent. She gave special white-only performances, yet had to confront Ku Klux Klansmen trying to destroy her show tent. She was to die as a result of a car accident in 1937, turned away from a hospital in Mississippi because she was black. Singers like Alberta Hunter, who adopted a more mellow style, were able to make the transition from blues to popular entertainment when styles changed. In 1928 she played Queenie in *Showboat* with Paul Robeson in London; the Prince of Wales liked her voice and Noël Coward wrote 'Travel Along' for her. During the 1930s she became a radio star, but she too eventually went out of fashion and worked for many years as a nurse before she was rediscovered in her eighties.

The blues interacted with vaudeville, where white performers Mae West, Fanny Brice and Eva Tanguay made their names in the 1920s. Blues singers performed in musical revues, as well as clubs and speakeasies. As musical fashion changed in the 1930s some blues singers, like Ethel Waters and Hattie McDaniel, went into Hollywood films, though as Hazel Carby points out, this was again 'subordinate space',[80] as they were acting black maids to white women sexual symbols like Mae West.

The 1920s saw intense interaction between different styles of popular music. Record companies discovered the raw hillbilly music of the Appalachians, which in its turn had already assimilated influences from black popular culture. Jacqueline Dowd Hall notes how Appalachian music had combined British and Irish folk songs with the Afro-American banjo as the railroads were being built: 'Such cultural interchanges multiplied during the 1920s as rural tradition met the upheavals of industrial life.'[81]

Mobility, the radio and militant resistance fostered an explosion of creativity in which women songwriters and singers participated. Ella Mae Wiggins in the textile area and Aunt Molly Jackson and Sarah Ogan Gunning in the mining towns sang about the social and personal problems women faced in Appalachia. The new industries attracted young women who defied a destiny of constant sorrow. Two sisters, Ethel and M. C. Ashworth, aged eighteen and seventeen respectively, who were arrested in the Elizabethan strike, had come from Virginia to work in the rayon plant, 'hollering and singing [in a] Ford touring car'[82] – not quite the workers Henry Ford had had in mind when he marketed his Model T. Modern mass culture did not always make for docility.

✳

In general, however, African-American women continued to face racist discrimination and segregation. This affected their conditions in jobs and also determined their occupational prospects. Forced to take the worst types of employment in Northern industries, like meat-packing or steam laundries, they were concentrated in jobs where organization rarely existed. Despairing of the white-dominated trade unions, Nannie Burroughs formed the National Association of Wage Earners in 1920 to publicize the needs of black women working as domestic servants. Other minority working-class women also faced barriers because of gender and ethnicity. Mexican women, for example, were mainly doing the unorganized low-paid work in textiles, laundries and bakeries, while Japanese women in small family businesses or domestic service were even more remote from the trade unions. Even educated, mainly white, middle-class graduates experienced gender segregation in employment; young women in banking, for example, found they could advance only to a certain level.

However, the 1920s saw a significant change in the composition of the labour force, with married women becoming more likely to enter paid employment. Alice Kessler-Harris notes that:

In 1920 less than 2 million of the 8 million wage-earning women were married. By 1930, more than 3 million of the 10 million women who worked for wages were living with husbands – the proportion of married women had jumped from 22.8 per cent to 28.8 per cent of the female workforce – an increase of more than 25 per cent.[83]

The American Federation of Labor, resisting employers' attempts to break the unions, took a defensive position, arguing against married women working and advocating higher pay for male workers – the family wage. More positive approaches took on the reorganization of work and time. Psychologist Lorine Pruette, for instance, broached the idea of part-time jobs for married women. In 1925 another advocate of a better balance between employment and housework, Ethel Puffer Howes, established Smith College Institute for the Co-ordination of Women's Interests, to develop alternative forms of employment and co-operative housekeeping.

The aspiration for free time and a better life was not restricted to middle-class wage earners: a New York woman worker's response to a survey conducted by the National Consumers' League was, 'I want more time to live.'[84] Even in Appalachia, where the textile industry recruited from among the farming community, the new generation rejected their mothers' lives of unpaid labour on the farms, of low-paid home-work and taking in lodgers. Several strikes for higher wages and better conditions involved women in the late 1920s and early 1930s. In 1929 in Gastonia, North Carolina, Ella Mae Wiggins, a mill worker and song-writer, was murdered during a bitter and violent strike in which six women were killed while picketing. These strikes broke through the racial divisions between workers to draw black and white women into industrial unions, marking the real beginnings of the better-known development of industrial unionism in mass production from the mid-1930s.

Though they were struggling as workers alongside men, these working-class Appalachians also protested against problems they faced as women. Ella Mae Wiggins sang of the working mother who had to leave her children for the factory and then did not have enough money to buy them food and clothing. And Bessie Edens, in 1929 a striker from Elizabethton in the Appalachian south, wrote in an essay for the Bryn Mawr Southern Summer School:

Women have always worked harder than men and always had to look up to the man and feel that they were weaker and inferior . . . If we women would not be so submissive and take everything for granted, if we would awake and stand up for our rights, this would be a better place to live in, at least it would be better for the women.[85]

This collective assertion of rights as women in the working class, with its intimation of wider social change, was neither a claim for special protection nor an assertion of individual equal rights. Class, like race, affected how gender needs were articulated.

Daily Life

A barrage of propaganda from advertisers presented American women with a vision of personal freedom through buying the new domestic products that were coming on to the market. *Life* magazine in 1923 featured 'A Modern Witch' in an apron and short skirt flying astride a vacuum cleaner up to the heavens. In *The Great American Housewife*, Annegret S. Ogden notes how sales boomed: by 1928 two-thirds of American houses were wired for electricity and the home-appliances market rose faster than the population. Between 1923 and 1928, when the market began to falter before the stock-market crash of 1929, sales of vacuum cleaners went from 3,850,000 to 6,828,000. There were similar increases for other goods: irons from 7,000,000 to 15,200,000; refrigerators from 27,000 to 755,000; washing machines from 2,915,000 to 5,000,000. Radios were arriving in working-class as well as middle-class houses. This consumer boom was partly based on rising incomes, but also on credit.

Sport

On 6 August 1926, nineteen-year-old Gertrude Ederle broke both male and female records when she swam the English Channel in 14 hours 31 minutes. Greeted in New York with the tickertape welcome reserved for celebrities, she had confounded sceptics who thought women could never compete athletically with men, beating the male record by two hours. There were other record-setters in the 1920s: Glenna Collett became the first woman to break 80 for eighteen holes in golf, Floretta McCrutcheon defeated bowling champion Jimmy Smith and Hazel Wightman won US titles in tennis. This was the era of the star, and sportswomen were becoming household names.

Doughty pioneers had braved the male sports bastions before the war but in the 1920s sportswomen made an indisputable impact. They were evident not only in swimming, tennis, ice-skating and golf, but also in softball and basketball, and symbolically 'Women as Athletes' appeared as a heading in the *Reader's Guide to Periodical Literature* in 1922.

In 1920 American women entered the Olympics for the first time and two years later the National Amateur and Athletic Federation (NAAF) was founded. NAAF was committed to boys and girls being on an 'equal footing with the same standards, the same program and the same regulations'.[86] However, suspicion that women were not able to compete equally made Girl Scouts' president Mrs Herbert Hoover, who led the Women's Division of the NAAF, contest the egalitarian approach. Arguments for a separate and different sphere for sportswomen ranged from their physical weakness, through fears that sport would make women unfeminine, to a distrust of male competitive values and the commercialization of sport.

A changing cultural image of femininity during the 1920s began to subvert the old idea that athleticism was desexing women. Top tennis star Helen Wills, for example, was praised in 1926 for 'the wonderful womanhood that uses sports to enhance its womanly charm instead of to affect [*sic*] an artificial masculinity'.[87] Commercial backers also discovered that charm was a crowd-puller. Colonel Melvorne McCombs,

Nothing is certain: 1920s androgyny confusing the beach censors at
Long Beach, 1926.

Ready for take-off: Elizabeth Robinson,
winner of the gold medal in the 100-metre run
at the 1928 Olympics.

an insurance company's basketball coach, observed that a press controversy in Dallas over players' shorts increased the regular attendance at
the basketball game from 150 to 5,000. The skimpy fashions of the 1920s
put a new emphasis on athletic bodies and narrowed the gap between
health and glamour. Gertrude Ederle retired from competitive sports to
become an adviser on fashion in 1926.

However, the opponents of women in sport did not give up easily.
In 1928 a petition protesting against the newly added female track and
field competition in the Olympics claimed that women had no part to
play. The organizers compromised by dropping the women's 800-metre
race.

✳

It was not only *things* that were being marketed but a way of life that
was ostensibly open to talent. The smart young writer Dorothy Parker
mocked the idyll when her husband tried to persuade her to move out
of New York to Hartford:

> We'd build a little bungalow
> If you and I were one,
> And carefully we'd plan it so
> We'd get the morning sun.
> I'd rise each day at rosy dawn
> And bustle gaily down;
> In evenings cool, you'd spray the lawn
> When you came back from town.[88]

Access to consumer goods was, of course, uneven and unequal. Ruth
Alice Allen's survey of Texas women working in cotton production in
1928–30 noted how one woman 'took her ironing ten miles into town
to use an electric iron'.[89] Moreover, modern expertise and labour-saving
devices in the home did not necessarily mean idleness; domestic standards
rose and laundry and baking, which had tended to be done outside the
home, were reverting back to the housewife. All that shopping for bar-

gains took time; beauty too became hard work, as more and more products appeared on the market with Helena Rubinstein, Elizabeth Arden and A'lelia Walker contributing to the expansion of the cosmetics industry, which was to reach $141 million by 1925. American women were enthusiastically embracing consumer culture.

Ironically just as the bubble burst, consumption was acquiring its own theorists. Helen and Robert Lynd, in their famous study *Middletown* (1929), posited the view that it had replaced fulfilment in work, and Paul H. Nystrom, a marketing professor at Columbia University, argued in *Economic Principles of Consumption* (1929) that 'Consumption supplies an avenue through which to carry out one's desires for self-realization,' suggesting, 'Through consumption more directly than in any other way the individual determines and develops his social position and escapes from feelings of loneliness.[90]

Christine Frederick, who wrote *Selling Mrs Consumer* in 1929, applied this approach to the middle-class American housewife, encompassing social consumption as well as individual purchasing. She celebrated the fact that women were asserting themselves by demands 'for more kinds of food, more leisure, more athletics and sports, more education, more travel, more art, more entertainment, more music, more civic improvement, better landscaping and city planning, more literature, more social graces, more social freedom and more cosmopolitan polish and smartness'.[91]

Alongside the private consumer boom, city housekeeping was not completely defunct in the 1920s, though it was becoming more professionalized through the growth of social work. Middle-class reformers still sought to Americanize through welfare projects which brought the values of modernity along with practical help. The Chicago Women's Club, for instance, were busy expanding the use of the public schools by creating adult classes and setting up a model nursery. Their experimental Infant Welfare Station not only provided clinic care but aimed to increase democratic participation by involving mothers. They also supported the Civic Music Association, which provided free or inexpensive concerts in neighbourhood parks. Church groups and settlements continued to provide advice and assistance. In the 1920s Stewart House in Gary, Indiana, for example, offered help on employment, health and legal problems. The Methodist minister's wife, Leila Delaney, ran the baby clinic and mothers' club, while the minister's sister looked after the day nursery.

Both white and black women in the labour movement were also developing social forms of consumer power. The American Federation of Labor supported workers' co-operative laundries, food co-operatives and co-operative stores. In her study of consumer organizing in Seattle, *Purchasing Power*, Dana Frank shows how Seattle labour women created their own Co-operative Club on the model of the British Women's Co-operative Guild, providing a social and educational base for working-class housewives. Seattle women also set up a Women's Exchange, through which they sold dry goods, their own sewing and old clothes. In 1921 the West Seattle Co-operative Club started a day-care centre and filled up a 'hope chest' by sewing and donating clothing, sheets and pillowcases for poorer women. Another expression of social consumer power was the boycott: the Seattle Card and Labor League mobilized the wives of white trade unionists to boycott stores which did not allow unions in the early 1920s. They also supported women trade unionists in strikes in this period.

A similar connection between the interests of women in the community and workers was made by the Colored Women's Economic Council when they organized wives and relatives of black Pullman porters in several cities in the mid-1920s. In 1927 Mattie Mae Halford assured the Brotherhood of Sleeping Car Porters that they 'need never despair as long as the women stand ready and willing to lend assistance'.[92]

American labour women did not have political organizations through which they could put pressure on the state to provide social resources like British Labour Party women were doing in this period. However, poor mothers who sought assistance on behalf of their children from the Mothers' Pensions administered by the Children's Bureau can be seen expressing a sense of entitlement on their children's behalf. 'I am so sore that I had such little ed[u]cation not to [k]no[w] that my children had a right to help and go thrue school,' wrote Mrs M. S. from Minnesota in 1927.[93]

Mothers' Pensions never became in practice the rightful reward for maternal service to state and society which the early progressive maternalists and feminists had envisaged. The stigma of charity surrounded them and the investigative process was harsh, humiliating and discriminatory. Assumptions about who were deserving recipients bristled with ethnic and racial prejudices. African-Americans continued to be less likely to receive pensions than whites, and even among whites, those born in the United States, Ireland or Germany were likely to be more privileged than others. By the late 1920s the maternalist feminist case for motherhood endowment, which had always gone against the grain of self-help, was losing conviction.

Middle-class feminism had also shifted emphasis by the late 1920s to focus on equal opportunities for professional women. By the late 1920s the association of feminism with change in poor women's daily lives in communities or at work had become tenuous.

Sex

Self-help found an ally in self-expression during the 1920s. The commercial images of glamour assumed a new visibility: 'Miss America', for instance, was created in 1921 to prolong the tourist season in Atlantic City. Fashion contributed to the fantasy of mobility. Paul Nystrom described the clothes of the 1920s as suggesting the possibility of jumping 'out of oneself'.[94] The movies communicated transitory identities; riches

Atlantic City beauty contestants, 1923.

and romance, it seemed, could be attained by the poorest Cinderella. Nor was it all illusion. People did move in the 1920s American social hierarchy. Stuart and Elizabeth Ewen note of the department store:

A new way of understanding oneself in relation to society was emerging. Linked to matters of personal decoration, it broke from a past in which *who you were* in society was a matter of social and economic class . . . Social identity, according to the schema, was there on the racks, to be bought.[95]

The message of mobility exercised a powerful influence regardless of social and economic circumstances. The sociologist Emory Bogardus, writing on Mexican immigration to the United States, noted that girls were running away from the strict supervision of their homes. One Mexican mother blamed American values, 'this terrible freedom in the United States.'[96] Japanese Associations in this period issued photographs and wrote asking other Japanese communities to treat runaway brides as outcasts.

The individual promise of freedom could be appropriated for collective defiance too: on trial for picketing in Elizabethton, Appalachian agitator Texas Bill faced her accusers in 1929 wearing a fashionable black picture hat and black coat. But it was more usually associated with the go-getting enterprise of the 'gold-digger' who contrived to beat men at their own game by ingenious subterfuge. 'It doesn't pay to go straight,' declared a sixteen-year-old taxi dancer in Chicago in 1926. 'The girl who goes crooked gets all she wants.'[97] She convinced the men she met dancing that she would like to go out but had to work. She got the money she would earn in a night, plus a little extra and a meal from them, then escaped by saying she was going to use the telephone or the rest room: 'Of course I can only work that a few times but there's one born every minute.'[98]

Higher up the social scale young college women, who were now routinely petting, were playing with sexual arousal in situations of physical intimacy which would have been scandalous in their mothers' generation. One study of college youths found 92 per cent of coeds petted and a third eventually had sexual intercourse, though usually with a fiancé. It was a flirtation with freedom: the trick was to arouse desire and then either duck out or get a husband.

The autonomous existence of the 1920s office girl in the city meant that sin was an option rather than being the way of life of the fallen woman. In *The Job*, Sinclair Lewis's Una Golden falls for Walter Babson, a restless dissatisfied post-war young man who did not know 'what he wanted, but he wanted something stronger than himself'. Meanwhile, Una reflected on the subway, 'I never thought a nice girl could be in love with a man who is bad, and I s'pose Walter is bad. Kind of. But maybe he'll become good.'[99]

Reforming the Walters of the world might constitute a challenge but it was not one that drew the Southerner Margaret Mitchell (later to write *Gone With the Wind*). She told a friend in 1926 that a *mix* of the bad and the good was essential for morale: 'I think a man who makes improper proposals is a positive necessity in a girl's life – just as much of a necessity as a man whose intentions are honourable and who believes you the personification of all ignorance and innocence.'[100]

In 1924 in her poem 'Ballade at Thirty-five' Dorothy Parker explicitly rejected the cover of an *ingénue* and, following her 'natural bents', gained wisdom from 'the sum of experiments'. Wisdom, however, did not necessarily bring sexual happiness and fulfilment; she glances off from sensual and emotional commitment: 'I loved them until they loved me.'[101]

The emphasis upon the flapper has obscured other kinds of 1920s 'new women' who continued to combine personal and public quests for emancipation. The desire was still there for intimacy and an active life. Many women who played a key role as educationalists, social investigators and administrators continued to live in 'Boston marriages' with other women: M. Carey Thomas's close companionship with Mary Garrett was just one example. Eleanor Roosevelt gravitated towards these women's networks within the Democratic Party's milieu. Her friends Marion Dickerman and Nancy Cook lived in a feminist co-operative in New York and Esther Everett Lape lived with Elizabeth Fisher Read. Stylish and unconventional, they are described by Blanche Wiesen Cook as:

Dedicated to public affairs, they were also devoted to each other. They sought to maintain a balanced and artful life, and lived in a world of elegance and daring. It was a world that they created; there were no blueprints or traditions. They answered to nobody, and to no established order.[102]

Other worlds of personal expression were being created in 1920s America. Commenting on the 'Harlem Rush', the unrespectable street and speakeasy culture, in his biography of Billie Holiday, Donald Clarke writes. 'While African-Americans had been kept in the dark about their own culture and pressured to make their "culture" conform to the white, they carried on creating it where nobody was looking.'[103]

The creativity of those pushed to the margins exercised a continuing influence on the white mainstream through entertainment and was to echo through the popular media around the world. Black women blues singers were exploring autonomy, sex and power in their own way. Bessie Smith's 'Young Woman's Blues' declares 'I ain't gonna marry, ain't gonna settle down'.[104] Ma Rainey's 'Prove It on Me Blues' sings of friends who 'must've been women, cause I don't like no men'.[105] Ida Cox was clear about the kind of man she wanted. 'One-minute papas' were told not to apply:

> I've always heard that haste makes waste
> So I believe in taking my time
> The highest mountain can't be raced
> It's something you must slowly climb.[106]

It was a theme that Mae West took over in her bawdy song 'A Guy What Takes His Time' in the early 1930s. Mae West, who had made her career sending up the red-hot-momma image in vaudeville, was one of the first white foghorns who combined elements of black and white popular culture in the new mass-entertainment market. In her 1928 film *Diamond Lil*, set in the 1890s, an era which suited her unfashionable hourglass figure, Lil, greatly desired by male admirers, stays in control. When one enthuses about 'your hands, your lips, your hair, your magnificent shoulder', Lil quips, 'What're you doin' honey? Making love or takin' an inventory?'[107] She falls, of course, for the man who is not available – the Salvation Army officer trying to convert her – and delivers her most famous one-liner, 'Come up and see me some time', making the censors unhappy by adding, 'You can be had.'[108]

Mae West was an unlikely sex symbol in an era when *ingénues*, good sports, 'constant nymphs', the kittenish Clara Bow or Mary Pickford's girl next door prevailed. Mae West represented the other side of innocence, and by laughing at lust she contained the lure of the bad, which was a powerful undercurrent in flapper sexuality. Humour was a way of sidling over into a position as a commentator from the wings. It enabled her to be a woman and an observer of sexual power plays. The black blues singers, in contrast, did not manoeuvre themselves, but were placed on the margins by white culture. They too sang of sex and power, but without the jokes. Hazel Carby notes how the blues present 'sexual preference as a contradictory struggle of social relations', expressing a protest 'against the objectification of female sexuality within a patriarchal order' while trying 'to reclaim women's bodies as the sexual and sensuous subjects of women's song'.[109]

Reflecting on Trixie Perry, on trial with Texas Bill in Elizabethton in 1929, Nettie Reece made a comparable reclamation; she remembered her fellow striker with respect in an interview given more than fifty years later. Trixie Perry, who appeared in court wrapped in the American flag, had been married briefly but then gone on to have children by several men. Nettie Reece observed, 'Trixie was not a woman who sold her body . . . She just had a big desire for sex . . . And when she had a cause to fight for, she'd fight.'[110] She was careful to add that Trixie worked hard after the strike as a restaurant cook, that her six children did well and 'never throwed [their mother] aside'.[111] Flappers, after all, were not the only women bidding for freedom.

Chapter 4

THE 1930s

BRITAIN

The Personal and the Political

The overt demands for women's emancipation in terms of political and economic change go into retreat during the 1930s. This was not because women's problems were resolved. The anxious single women who hovered in tea-rooms knew that ageing would undoubtedly bring impoverishment, while those in suburban villas between the wars were buying things and absorbing household hints with a nagging sense that something was missing; indeed, the term 'suburban neurosis' came into vogue at this time. But there was no political expression for such discontent. Instead, the personal conflicts of femininity were to be aired in the cultural space of novels or in women's magazines. For example, Mary Borden, discussing 'Financial Independence for Wives' in *Good Housekeeping*, wrote of the 'chaos of illogical notions, contradictory longings and confused images'[1] of contemporary femininity in 1933. Habits of dependence and possessiveness, how to balance conflicting claims of work and children, or love and freedom, were all of intense concern to modern middle-class women, while working-class readers of stories in *My Weekly* and *Weekly Welcome* could toy with romantic freedom, consoled by the values of the home. The gender nerves of the 1930s were attuned to personal sensibility rather than to public campaigning.

The social and cultural changes of the inter-war years were raising new issues which did not fit the public feminist reference points. Also the attempt to live and bring up children according to radical principles had proved more difficult than initially envisaged. Leonora Eyles, by

1937 in her mid-forties, was overwhelmed by a feeling of failure: 'If I had my time to go over again I should not attempt so much,'[2] she confessed in *Good Housekeeping*. It was not simply her age; the faith that changes could be made in the pattern of personal existence by demands in the public sphere had wavered.

From 1931 Virginia Woolf collected thousands of extracts from newspapers and biographies in an effort to understand the culture of the era. She cut out quotes and facts about women, men, sexuality, sport, religion, education, politics and social mores. When she produced her essay *Three Guineas* in 1938, the sense that a crucial realm of understanding was being buried led her to assert that 'the public and the private worlds are inseparably connected'; she believed that the 'private figure' was as important as the 'public world' and that if either was disregarded, 'Both houses will be ruined . . . the material and the spiritual'.[3]

The effort of integration was assailed by the external facts of economic recession and the rise of Fascism; the second Labour government of 1929 was defeated in 1931 and Ramsay MacDonald joined the national government. Chris, the heroine of the trilogy by Lewis Grassic Gibbon, *The Scots Quair*, climbed up to her son Ewan's back room. He was studying the strata of Scotland's ice age and as he told her about his book she realized:

And the thing is happening again – all over the world the Ice is coming, not the Ice-time that ended the Golden Age, but the Ice of want and fear and fright, its glacier peaks on the sky by night, and men looked out bewildered to see it, cold and dank, and a dark wind blew, and there was neither direction, salvation, nothing but the storming black lour of the clouds as the frosts and the fog of this winter came.[4]

Hitler took power in Germany and Sir Oswald Mosley left the Labour Party and organized the British Fascists. By the mid-1930s there was an atmosphere of violence and fear; unemployment, anti-Semitism and distrust of politicians and the police led to a polarization in which support for the extreme right grew along with membership of the Communist Party. Such dramatic external events eclipsed the nuances of cultural change occurring in gender relations. It seemed that personal concerns were being devoured by the extremity of events. This

coincided with the growing scepticism among women who had campaigned for feminism that a way could be found to translate the dilemmas
of personal life into the public sphere.

Politics

Unemployment and the response to Fascism dominate the politics of
the 1930s. At the beginning of the decade the divisions in the Labour
Party weakened opposition. It was to be the former trade union leader
Margaret Bondfield who, as Minister of Labour, modified National
Insurance so that a married woman who was made unemployed was
subject to more severe terms in order to qualify for benefit than a single
woman or man. Margaret Bondfield maintained that her 1931 Anomalies
Act was an attempt to prevent fraudulent claims. The effect was devastating: it disqualified 180,000 married women who had paid their contributions. Some redoubtable voices were raised in opposition: Rebecca
West, Lady Astor, Emmeline Pethick-Lawrence and Selina Cooper
spoke at a meeting in Central Hall, Westminster, in 1933.

However, it was the National Government's Means Test in 1931
which really threatened the survival strategies of working-class families
by investigating the whole household. It presented an issue which
affected men and women alike and labour women united with men.
They were increasingly inclined to identify class rather than gender
as the main cause of women's wrongs – responsible for barriers in
employment opportunities, the high rate of maternal deaths, the mal-
nutrition of children and the rise in food prices. This was not simply
because of the change in objective circumstances, but because the
Communist Party now tended to set the terms in which gender was
seen in relation to class. In the early 1930s the Communists' emphasis
was on equality as workers; from the middle of the decade the line
shifted to stress the needs of mothers. Women who had been active in
earlier feminist campaigns had either been demoralized by infighting
and defeat or been dispersed by the shifts in political alliances. Selina
Cooper continued to battle for the unemployed, inclining, like many
people on the left, to the Communists; Dora Russell was absorbed in
running her free school rather than in Labour Party conferences. The
decline of the Independent Labour Party broke the institutional link

between feminism and labour. Instead of the democratic left, it was increasingly Tory women rebels – Mavis Tate, Irene Ward, Thelma Cazalet, Lady Astor and the Duchess of Atholl – who were prepared to defy their party's orthodoxies on issues which affected women. This in turn affected the manner in which 'feminism' was defined.

The rise of Fascism in Germany, along with the outbreak of the Spanish Civil War in 1936, when the Republicans were challenged by the right under Franco, strengthened the emphasis in the left upon a unity of interest between men and women. Women marched with men on the huge demonstrations against the Fascists in east London, and, like men, disagreed about tactics. Bertha Sokoloff, a young Communist recruit, was part of a militant left youth culture, selling the party youth paper, *The Challenge*, listening to dance bands on the radio, eager to be part of the mass confrontations against the Fascists in the streets of the East End. In contrast, Edith Ramsay, a Christian social worker, identified with the more cautious Labour Party, the Jewish Board of Deputies and the settlement workers at Toynbee Hall.

Big marches were not the only manifestation of conflict. There was everyday harassment of Jews. In one incident the Fascists stoned the windows of a Stepney laundry class to prevent Jewish girls from attending; they were forced to escape by a side gate, while Edith Ramsay walked through the silent, hostile crowd. Jewish refugees were admitted if they could find sponsorship. Elli Adler, aged thirteen and a half, came to work as an au pair. Rita Altman got a domestic visa and managed to train as a hairdresser. She has suppressed the memory of Germany: 'I suppose it's survival, isn't it, or amnesia.'[5] Ironically, they escaped the Holocaust to encounter not only anti-Semitism in Britain but prejudice because they were from Germany or Austria.

Fascism aroused a broad humanitarian opposition among feminists. One young Jewish scholarship girl had a high school headmistress who addressed school assemblies on the evils of anti-Semitism. Years later Asphodel remembered her teacher with affection: 'She was a liberal educationalist who really believed in education for women.'[6] Well-known feminists – Vera Brittain, Winifred Holtby, Lady Rhondda, Monica Whateley and Ellen Wilkinson – protested against the persecution of women who opposed Fascism in a pamphlet, 'Women Behind Bars', in 1935. Eleanor Rathbone, Virginia Woolf, Violet

Spanish Civil War

The outbreak of civil war in Spain in 1936 after the elected popular-front Republican government was challenged by the Nationalists, led by General Franco, resulted in the arrival of many volunteers. A minority went to support Franco, but the majority went to fight the threat of Fascism and to defend democracy. Among them were women from Britain, as well as from many other countries, including the United States, Australia, Canada, New Zealand and South Africa. Some were Communists, socialists or anarchists, while others travelled to Spain out of a less defined belief that democracy everywhere would be threatened by a Fascist victory.

A British artist and sculptor, Felicia Browne, was killed fighting in the Republican militia, but most women were involved as nurses, secretaries, translators, administrators, writers and observers. Jessica Mitford, Nancy Cunard and Sylvia Townsend Warner were among the writers. Observers included Ellen Wilkinson, who challenged the policy of non-intervention and told the Commons when she returned from a women's delegation, 'The British people will pay, and pay heavily, for what their government has done to poor little Spain.'[7] The leader of the women's delegation to Spain was the Conservative Duchess of Atholl, the first Scottish woman MP, who chaired the National Joint Committee for Spanish Relief, which united Spanish aid organizations.

Women volunteers accomplished extraordinary feats, operating pioneer field hospitals with inadequate equipment and escorting children across the Pyrenees. Leah Manning from Spanish Medical Aid and Edith Pye from the Society of Friends went to Bilbao in 1937 to bring back 4,000 Basque refugee children to Britain.

The experience of Spain, the tragedy witnessed, was recorded by both writers and the medical and administrative workers, many of whom recognized that Spain had a wider significance. Defeat of the Republicans augured a grim future in Europe. Shiela Grant Duff, who became, aged twenty-one, the first British woman to work as a foreign correspondent, wrote, 'To my generation the Spanish Civil War appeared as one of the great battles of human history and its mythic quality moved us all.'[8]

✳

Bonham-Carter and Margery Corbett Ashby were other prominent women who stood against Fascism, regardless of differing political affiliations. Though they denounced the gender implications of Nazism, their rejection was based also on a general revulsion towards the political policies of Hitler. Feminism did not, however, guarantee automatic anti-Fascist inoculation: Mary Richardson, the militant suffragist, joined the Mosleyites.

Conservative women were uneasy about the whole issue, which skewed the points on their political compass. With a few notable exceptions, they oscillated between patriotic dismay at Chamberlain's foreign policy, anti-Bolshevism and sympathy for the Nazis. The real passion, however, at the grass roots of the party in 1939 focused not on political violence but on the fear of sexual danger. When the Conservative government proposed to abolish flogging, Mrs Churches, a mother of ten children from the West Midlands, addressed the Conservative conference 'as a mother to protect the honour of our children', reassuring her listeners that she was not speaking 'of our sons'.[9] The threat came from other men, 'all sorts of imported labour . . . and believe me some of them are not at all "desirable" – you know the class of men concerned. I should not like to touch them with a pitchfork.'[10]

To the right of the Tory Party were the women who actually joined the British Union of Fascists (BUF), which formed a women's section in 1933. Women too wore black shirts, canvassed for BUF candidates and, despite initial opposition, addressed BUF meetings. Olive Hawks, for example, was described in *Blackshirt* as holding a 'friendly and interested'[11] meeting of farmers' wives at Whitstable, while Doreen Bell had some success in Leeds at a factory-gates women's meeting.

Women blackshirts salute Fascist leader Sir Oswald Mosley,
east London, 1936.

Several BUF women, including some titled ladies, were selected as
council and prospective parliamentary candidates. Special social activities developed for women, which ranged from jumble sales to jujitsu
and eurhythmic exercises. Martin Durham shows there was confusion
about Fascist policy towards women: some members of the BUF
believed that Fascism was compatible with feminism, arguing for equal
pay, while others saw it as protecting women from the harsh male
world. As war drew closer, Fascist women opposed British involvement:
Anne Brock Griggs, for instance, described it as 'a politicians' war . . .
backed by Jewish money'.[12]

The women's peace organizations were caught in a difficult dilemma,
their pacifism put to the test by the threat of Fascism. The Women's
International League for Peace and Freedom became increasingly isolated and though the Women's Co-operative Guild reached a membership of 87,246 in 1939, it divided over the war and never recovered its

former strength. Prominent feminists also split. Vera Brittain could not renounce the pacifist position she had taken between the wars, but Ellen Wilkinson, Dora Russell and Eleanor Rathbone decided that Fascism was too great a threat and supported rearmament. So too did Edith Summerskill, a feminist doctor, politicized through her work on maternal and child welfare, who was elected as a Labour MP in 1938.

Applying anthropology to the study of ordinary Britons, Charles Madge and Tom Harrison found a mood of general confusion in their Mass-Observation surveys. Women leaned towards appeasement, constituting 'the conservative, peace-at-any-price and pro-Chamberlain element',[13] at least until their husbands came home, when they changed their minds. On the eve of war against Fascism, Mass-Observation noted perplexed despair and fear, along with a minority strand of anti-Semitism.

Work

By 1933 women's trade union membership had fallen to 728,388, a reduction of 46 per cent since 1920. Male membership in unions in the same period went down by 48 per cent. Along with this long-term decline in organizational power went the fear of unemployment, which affected manual and clerical workers alike. Even in London office workers had lost the confidence that they could find another post; instead, they tried hard to look as if they were working hard and hid the wedding rings which would have brought instant dismissal, as many firms operated a marriage bar.

Unemployment among women was made invisible by the marriage bar and by the tendency of women not to register because they could not claim unemployment benefit. The government was never particularly concerned about women and most of the training schemes were for men. One private scheme publicized on a Paramount newsreel brought a few 'attractive'[14] young women from South Wales to train as models at the Lucy Clayton agency in London. Kate Reynolds from County Durham was among those who were resettled under the Land Settlement Scheme on a smallholding in Andover. She and her husband had to work from dawn to dusk: 'It was our livelihood and we made the best of it.'[15]

Others protested. The organization of unemployed women drew on the work done during the 1920s by Communists and socialists. The first women's contingent from Yorkshire and Lancashire went on the National Unemployed Workers' Movement march in 1930. One Blackburn weaver, Maggie Nelson, covered the whole 250 miles with a forty-pound pack on her back. As they walked they sang – 'Who Were You With Last Night?' mingled with the 'Internationale'. There were disputes with local Labour as well as Conservative Councils over accommodation, which could be the workhouse, or worse. Mary Docherty, a Communist domestic servant and miner's daughter, who went to meet the Scottish Hunger March in Edinburgh in 1933, remembered how the authorities forced them to sleep on the pavements. When cuts were made in benefits in 1934, women in Wales took militant action. The dole office was stormed in Merthyr, and in Rhondda they marched to protest to the Prince of Wales, who was visiting

Maggie Nelson leading 1934 Hunger March: the Means Test hit women as workers and as mothers.

Cardiff, and were stopped at Pontypridd after breaking through three police cordons. It remained hard for the unemployed to convey the desperation they felt to the rest of the country. Ellen Wilkinson's famous march from Jarrow in 1936 with 200 unemployed workers was important in changing the public's view of the unemployed and forcing the Labour Party's involvement.

Unemployment varied greatly depending on the region, and the response in areas where there were more jobs – parts of London and the South-East – was by no means automatically sympathetic. People from the depressed North and the Celtic fringe, especially from Wales, were stereotyped as dirty and breeding like rabbits; they were blamed for taking people's jobs and cutting wage rates. Londoners looked down on the Welsh and Irish girls who were brought in as domestic servants. Unemployment also had a differing impact on men and women depending on local employment patterns. In Dundee the shipyard workers were sacked but women were still able to earn in the jute trade. The men who stayed at home were called 'kettle boilers'.[16] In Londonderry in Northern Ireland, women continued to work in textiles, clothing and the linen trade, but there was not much work for men and it became known as 'petticoat city'.[17] The slump hit the staple traditional industries worst where men predominated, though in cotton-manufacturing women were more likely to lose their jobs than men.

Despite unemployment there were still women workers who were determined to fight for union recognition and better conditions. Gertie Roche started work at Montague Burton's huge Leeds clothing factory in the early 1930s. She found herself in four rooms, each of which held 2,000 people. The canteen was like a football pitch and the place was seething with union activity.

We were having strikes every other week at that time, strikes in order to unionize the place, protesting against harsh instructions that were coming in to us, and people just refused to be bullied and treated in this way. The experience of seeing how other people reacted within that factory was an education. I became very vociferous against any attempt to reduce our wages or increase our workload and I very quickly became a shop stewardess and a member of the factory committee.[18]

The skilled male workers were still the best organized but women were taking over the organization of the union in the clothing factories in Leeds.

It was not easy to get the Trades Union Congress (TUC) to take on women's issues. One delegate in the mid-1930s described it as 'like asking for bread and getting a stone'.[19] There was, however, awareness of the need to recruit women. Scotland led the way in building up women's trade union membership by starting special short trade union schools in the early 1930s. These were followed by attempts to find imaginative ways of presenting the case for trade unions. In 1934 in London, women put on a five-day Pageant of Labour with over 1,000 performers. In 1937, in an effort to be up to the minute, the TUC even issued a leaflet with a picture of a young woman in a two-piece swimsuit, promising potential recruits that trade unionism resulted in health and beauty.

Women trade unionists did manage to get the TUC to back their demand for council nurseries and to reach out to unorganized workers with 'A Domestic Servants' Charter' and 'A Nurses' Charter', which demanded shorter hours. They also continued to argue for equal pay, an issue which revealed how under the apparent unity old hostilities still smouldered. The General Secretary of the Union of Post Office Workers wrote in the annual report of the union in response to a proposal for equal pay in 1935, 'Division, segregation, de-amalgamation, redundancy and most of our present ills are traceable to the policy of employing less men and more women.'[20]

Equal pay was not simply an economic issue; the political implications of denying women equality at work were being made apparent by the Fascists and the argument was being fought out in the trade union movement. One speaker at the Post Office Workers' conference in 1935 was cheered for saying Mussolini and Hitler had the right idea and that 'no country could afford to despise its male population'.[21] Eleanor Stewart, a member of the Transport and General Workers' Union, explicitly opposed Nazi ideas that the woman's place was in the home at the 1935 Scottish TUC Conference of Unions Enrolling Women. When the attempt was made to introduce a marriage bar for shop workers, men as well as women in the Union of Shop Distributive and Allied Workers protested. One member declared the proposal contained 'the first seeds of Fascism'.[22] But the marriage bar was a reality for many women in teaching and in the civil service in Britain. Even at the London County Council (LCC), which had a reputation as an enlightened employer, a referendum of members of the Staff Association in 1935 showed that men still supported the rule which said women had to leave when they got married. The danger of the struggle for equality going into reverse was all too evident in Britain, as well as in the Irish Free State, where legislation in the late 1930s explicitly prevented women working in an effort to provide jobs for men, despite outcry from leaders of women trade unionists Louie Bennett and Helen Chevenix.

Equality, even when it was won, could be a lonely business; professional women were in a minority and made to feel it. When Emmerson Price became the first woman architectural assistant at the LCC in 1934, she was banished to a room under the roof of County Hall to renovate old workhouses and fever hospitals, away from the rest of the team. Moved eventually to the design section, she was confronted by a boss who complained, 'I have had some of the greatest idiots, fools and drunkards in this office and now for my sins I am to be landed with a woman!'[23]

The trade unions, divided over equal pay and equal opportunities, were also slow to recognize that a new kind of woman worker was emerging in the light industry expanding in the South-East. Though assembly-line production was still only operating on a small scale, it relied heavily on female workers. Many were young and single, but some had families to support and the new factories did not always impose a marriage bar. Modern companies producing food, domestic goods, gramophones and radios were employing women at rates which were higher than could be earned in domestic service, waitressing or small clothing workshops. The introduction of a moving conveyor-belt assembly line forced workers to speed up and discipline could be strict. At the EMI factory at Hayes near London (known locally as 'The Gram', because it was an offshoot of the Gramophone Company, the American-based multinational), work started at 7.33 a.m. prompt. You were locked out until lunchtime if you arrived late. On the other hand, EMI welcomed married women as 'bread and butter'[24] workers who would be less likely to organize, and firms used corporate strategies to retain workers' loyalty. Hoover, for example, had a resident doctor, its own fire brigade, a canteen and a laundry for overalls. The main attraction, though, was the money. Edith Boyd, from depressed South Shields, escaped from domestic service in Hampstead to Hoover's Perivale factory, which made vacuum cleaners. She told Miriam Glucksmann, 'I got more money each week and the first thing I did was to buy a bicycle on hire purchase.'[25]

The new industrial workers might have been conscious of being a privileged élite but they did not prove entirely docile. There were several spontaneous rebellions among women who were not unionized. Resentment of speed-up imposed by rate-fixers and time-study men was a source of conflict. At Lucas, a motor components firm in Birmingham, Jessie McCullough turned round, saw she was being timed and realized it was in order to increase the speed of the line as she was a fast worker: 'Well, I had a talk with the girls about it and in the end . . . we all refused.'[26] Some 10,000 women refused to work and Lucas backed down to prevent unionization. Jessie McCullough, however, was to be blacklisted throughout the Birmingham area.

The close of the decade brought improvements not because of gains in terms of equal rights but because new chances of employment had been established and low-paid women workers were included in the 1938 act which introduced legal holidays of one week with pay. In *Women and Trade Unions*, Sheila Lewenhak notes a spirit of impatience among the young, who 'took for granted all the things for which the post-First World War women militants had had to strive so hard, and then went on to ask for more concessions'.[27] However, equal pay and equal insurance rights returned to the agenda in 1939, when the National Union of Clerks produced the 'Industrial Women's Charter'. Accepted by the TUC, it was overtaken by events. In September 1939 war was to sweep many more women into production, with, however, little control over conditions.

Daily Life

In *The Condition of Britain*, published for the Left Book Club in 1937, the socialists G. D. H. and Margaret Cole inquired whether there were still two nations within the country, 'confronting each other for the most part with mutual disapproval and lack of understanding, and incapable of living together on terms of common humanity'.[28]

It was certainly the case that social division was stark. In 1938 a majority of the population, 88 per cent, had incomes of less than £250 a year or £5 a week. Of these 31 per cent earned only £2 10s. Seebohm Rowntree's survey in York in 1936 had found nearly 18 per cent of the population studied below the poverty line, while a similar study in Bristol the following year revealed 19.3 per cent living without many basics. Meanwhile, the top 2,000 families' incomes averaged £43,500 a year.

Ostensibly the world of such 'society' women remained intact. Ladies still took two hours to get up and dress, spending the morning reading letters and giving cook instructions before going out shopping. Lunch parties, tea, bridge, dinner, the theatre – they somehow filled their days. An army of nannies paraded their offspring through the parks and contained them in nurseries. Children would be seen for about an hour at breakfast or nursery tea. A new generation was being programmed to repeat the procedure. In *Hons and Rebels*, Jessica Mitford described how the girls in her upper-class family were educated in English, French, simple arithmetic and taught sufficient cookery and household management to run a large house while being 'trained, by precept and example, in the normal virtues, which included chastity, thrift, kindness to animals, considerateness to servants and common sense'.[29]

The system did not, of course, always work. The outer world was impinging on the enclosed bubble of privilege. When older sister Unity joined the British Union of Fascists after meeting Oswald Mosley,

Nannies at a society wedding waiting for a glimpse of the bride.

Jessica took out a subscription to the *Daily Worker*. By 1935 'it was becoming rather apparent . . . that not all of us were turning out quite according to plan'.[30] Jessica escaped a conventional upper-class destiny by running away to Spain with her rebellious cousin Esmond Romilly.

It was still customary for all young women in 'society' to do the season, which, besides being presented at court, involved much flower-arranging and window-shopping, along with lunch parties with other debutantes. There were balls, Ascot, Cowes yacht week, the Chelsea Flower Show and film premières, the aim of the whole exhausting process being to find a husband, but here too dissidents could be found. Vivien Mosley, who did not share her father's politics, held her coming-out ball in 1938 in a ramshackle house in Regent's Park owned by none other than Maud Allan, whom she vaguely recalled had made it into society as 'a predecessor of Isadora Duncan'.[31] Vivien Mosley also remembered a group of young people who used to talk politics and ideas through the dances 'tottering down from the upper floors and all the old dowagers having an absolute fit'.[32] These 'Liberal girls'[33] of the 1930s included Laura Bonham-Carter, who married Jo Grimond, the Liberal Party leader, and Shiela Grant Duff. Bored by the 'coming out' rituals, she was drawn towards left-wing intellectual friends at Oxford, like Douglas Jay. When she was presented at court, dressed in ostrich 'feathers and trains', he appeared in mackintosh and tennis shoes and jumped into the Rolls-Royce; the chauffeur and footman, 'perfectly trained',[34] did not even turn their heads. Along with a minority of other rebels like Jessica Mitford, she was to make her escape with relief into 'the real world'.[35]

The 'real world' was increasingly taking its toll on women's health and the maternal death-rate continued to rise until 1936. When the British Medical Association published a minimum diet for health in 1933, consisting mainly of bread and potatoes, the National Unemployed Workers' Movement showed that it was beyond the reach of unemployed families, and Communist women leaders campaigned for milk and school meals, along with improved conditions of maternity. In 1933 several women's organizations, including the National Union of Societies for Equal Citizenship, the Women's National Liberal Federation and the Women's Co-operative Guild, established the Women's

Health Committee, which surveyed 1,250 working-class mothers' conditions. Along with the continuing dangers of child-bearing, they detailed anaemia, constipation, bad teeth, rheumatism, gynaecological ailments, varicose veins, phlebitis, neuralgia, backaches and breast abscesses. Their investigations revealed women like Mrs K. in Durham, who got up at 3 a.m. to see men off to work and went to bed at 11 p.m. Women who kept families of seven on unemployment benefit and the pay of teenagers, without gas, electricity or a bath, had no time to be ill, even though their doctors advised rest and less work. Leisure was akin to Utopia. A country woman from Essex with six children at school told Margery Spring Rice, the author of the influential book which drew on the survey, *Working-class Wives*, 'I really think mothers should have a holiday once a year . . .'[36] She had had only ten days' rest in sixteen years.

There were hints of sexual anxieties in the reports of overcrowding. A woman surveyed in Marylebone, London, said in the early 1930s that she did not

. . . think it decent for us all in one room with two well-built girls and a boy 10 sleeping besides them. My nerves are getting so bad with the worry of bringing them up decent. My doctor said I must get more rest, but it is impossible to rest at night.[37]

The Depression never affected the middle-class conscience as acutely as the poverty of the Edwardian era, but it did bring sections of the intelligentsia to a greater awareness of social issues. Along with the popular Penguins and Left Book Club editions, there was an interest in social reportage in theatre and on the radio. The pioneer broadcaster Hilda Matheson saw radio as a mediator between experts and the citizen, and the BBC talks department covered social topics like unemployment. In Manchester Olive Shapley was recording the experiences of miners' wives during the late 1930s in a new kind of broadcasting, which, like Mass-Observation's surveys, let people speak for themselves.

The Depression affected the working class in different ways. The more prosperous were listening to gramophones and radios, going to funfairs and the cinema, and buying ready-made bread, tinned soup, baked beans, custard powder, blancmange, jelly mixes and Sunday treats of tinned salmon and peaches. Food prices fell, leaving the employed relatively better off. In her study *Women Assemble*, Miriam Glucksmann

British Films

If royalty had not existed the British film industry during the 1930s would have had to invent it. In 1933 *The Private Life of Henry VIII* was a great hit and it was followed by Anna Neagle in *Nell Gwyn*, who had an honorary regal status not appreciated in the US, where it was censored. But it was the death of King George V and the abdication of Edward VIII in the anxious year of 1936 that made historical films about British royals the rage. *Tudor Rose* told the tragic story of Lady Jane Grey, the 'Nine Days' Queen'. More queens were to follow. Flora Robson, as Elizabeth I, delivered her Tilbury speech in *Fire Over England* in 1936 and Anna Neagle played Victoria in *Victoria the Great* the following year. Made at the request of the Duke of Windsor, it was packed with patriotism. Mass-Observation found it was top of Bolton's most popular films; *Stella Dallas* came second.

Flora Robson as Elizabeth I in
Fire Over England.

When not being queenly, British stars spent a lot of time being ladylike. Anna Neagle was ladylike; Margaret Lockwood was plucky and ladylike, tracking down spies in *The Lady Vanishes* (1938); and Jessie Matthews was ladylike and a good chum in *The Good Companions* (1933), based on the novel by J. B. Priestley. Wendy Hiller acted the cockney flowergirl who is turned into a lady by Professor Higgins in *Pygmalion* (1938). The exception was Gracie Fields, who could not be ladylike. She appeared in *Sing As We Go*, a film about the closure of a mill in 1934, rushing around a Blackpool funfair. With a screenplay by J. B. Priestley, the theme song came to symbolize British working-class grit and endurance in the Depression and it made Gracie Fields a star. However, as Graham Greene pointed out, her films were characterized by 'a sympathy for the working class and an ability to appeal to the best of circles'.[38] Northern cinema-goers might see her as 'Our Gracie', but by 1938 she was 'national treasure' and signed by Fox 'for the highest salary ever paid to a human being'.[39] Sadly the Lancashire humour got lost in Hollywood.

Women's roles as queens, ladies and chums of various classes were, like Britannia on the penny, emblematic. British audiences were presented with metaphors of national unity who happened to be female rather than with possible femininities. Historical dramas fostered a definition of English identity which was to be part of the popular patriotism of the war years. Comedy lightened the image. If royal dramas personified the nation, working-class humour broadened the social base by keeping everybody's chins up. For the women in the audience, they promised inclusion in the shared privilege of Englishness for keeping everything together through queenliness or pluck.

✳

found families in the South-East had abandoned the old flat irons which had to be heated on the stove for electric irons by 1939. New housing estates had electricity, although this was not always reliable – the supply at Hayes got overloaded and blew up, and an association had to be formed to collect money to get the Electricity Board to come and rewire the houses. Despite mishaps like these, working-class families were renting electric cookers from local electricity showrooms and by 1938 68 per cent of families owned a gas cooker. Washing powder, Rinso and Oxydel, was replacing soap and the Acme wringer had reached working-class homes. In comparison to the United States though, the spread of consumer goods was still restricted. By the end of the 1930s only 6 per cent of electrified homes owned any electrical appliances and the vacuum cleaners made by women like Edith Boyd at Hoover were mainly bought by the middle class (working-class women mopped the lino and used a carpet sweeper on rugs), while washing machines were restricted to an élite 4 per cent of UK households.

The Conservatives, made sensitive to the 'homemaker' by women's organizations such as the Women's Institute, made a canny bid for the housewives' votes between the wars, reducing duties on food, improving the distribution of Empire food, providing subsidies for agriculture, extending the electricity system and encouraging the building of cheap houses. Home-ownership promised the suburban lifestyle of the middle class, while convenience foods offered leisure and individual choice. Jean MacGibbon, a middle-class member of the Barnes Communist Party, driven by middle-class guilt to the local Women's Co-operative Guild, sat singing 'Jerusalem' beneath the insignia of the rainbow in a municipal housing estate and longed for the courage to refute 'the assertion that Co-op biscuits were best'.[40] The truth was that Huntley and Palmer's were better.

Married to a publisher, Jean MacGibbon was part of the progressive section of the middle class that was shifting leftwards politically and socially. When she became pregnant, she bought a Harrods pram and phoned the Truby King Mothercraft Training Centre in Highgate, north London: '"I believe you run a six-week course in looking after babies. Can I send my maid along?" "Why don't you come yourself?" was the restrained reply.'[41]

If taking mothering seriously was part of a commitment to modern enlightenment and planning, so was exercise. Mary Bagot Stack's League of Health and Beauty got permission from George Lansbury, the Commissioner of Works under Labour, to do their first public display in Hyde Park. Her *Building the Body Beautiful* (1931) was a call to action. The *Sunday Referee* described it as 'admirably adapted to the needs of, let us say, the ordinary young woman who must work for her living and who can only utilize her leisure in health-giving and beautifying exercise'.[42] By 1933 there were 60,000 of them, busily keeping fit in satin shorts. For less athletic aspirants to the life force, there was Barbara Cartland's 1935 'can do' advice book, *Touch the Stars: A Clue to Happiness*, which told you how to stay optimistic regardless of the Depression through romantic love.

Many simply made do with the radio, the new municipal swimming pools or the cinemas. In its 1937 study of cinema-going in Bolton, Mass-Observation found girls and young women who went twelve times a week. They divided between fans of *Stella Dallas*, who wanted realistic dramas, to the romantics, who sought forgetfulness. This kind of 1930s popular culture presented a world where virtue was rewarded. Beatrice Hamer, thirteen, of Bolton enjoyed the film *San Francisco*, in which a city was destroyed 'through its vice and wickedness'.[43] Even better, 'a bad man retrieved his character through a good woman'.[44] In her analysis of working-class women's magazine fiction during the 1930s, Bridget Fowler notes that good and evil were clearly demarcated. The male villains were frequently employed in the leisure industry as sensuous jazz musicians, dance-band players or hairdressers. This deviant masculinity of modern times disturbed reliance on the customary and the known.

The boundaries could not always be maintained. 'Below the decencies and conventions of everyday life, there lies a vast reservoir of strange things,'[45] says the psychologist in Agatha Christie's *Appointment With Death* (1938), expressing a wariness about appearances characteristic of her novels, which tended to be set in the Home Counties, middle-class suburbs and genteel guest houses, the 'new' England where it was no longer clear who is who and what is what. In *Forever England*, Alison Light describes the quiet conservatism of middle England keeping itself to itself with an uneasy feeling that evil might well be moving in next door.

'Stay young and beautiful if you want to be loved,' went the song. This was serious advice, and it was being heeded by women of all classes. Make-up, now respectable, was big business. Helena Rubinstein declared the democratization of glamour with her cosmetics. Besides her products there were also those of Elizabeth Arden, Revlon and Yardley, the latter with sculpted boxes in the shape of their emblem, the bee; lower down the social scale came Ponds, Boots and, cheapest of all, Woolworths. In Salford Friday night was called 'Amami night' after a popular shampoo. The girls washed their hair while the boys went drinking. The profits of the cosmetics firms were boosted by the cinema's images of glamour, which could be culled and appropriated by women of all classes – factory workers, shop girls and debs went to the same films. Styles were quickly copied on the High Street. As Sally Alexander says, high heels and 'the tilt of the hat gave the illusion of wealth'.[46]

However, the glamour achieved by young working girls was often based on home-made hard work. Sally Alexander found from her interviews with working-class London women that the sewing machine bought on hire purchase was a crucial asset: 'Often inherited from mother or mother-in-law', it enabled 'the mantle of glamour' to be passed 'from the aristocrat and courtesan to the shop, office, or factory girl via the film star.'[47] As for the beauty products, there was also a material restraint which Rubinstein's claim ignored: prices. *Vogue* magazine advertised hair remover at 13s. 6d. for the de luxe size when the social investigator Seebohm Rowntree estimated that basic food for two adults and three children cost 17s. 10d. a week. Elizabeth Wilson observes that 'the democracy of beauty'[48] proved, moreover, to be frequently elusive, because the cheap make-up working-class women could afford did not produce film-star looks. Playwright John Osborne remembers his working-class mother's Woolworths 'knicker-bocker glory of rouge which . . . looked like a mixture of blackcurrant juice and brick dust'.[49]

The marks of class have a way of moving: as some distinctions melted, others became more pronounced. As working girls attained aspects of the veneer, the upper class found invisible weapons of privilege. Smell, for example, communicated class and smell took time. The only anti-perspirant was Odo-ro-no, which took twenty minutes to dry and lasted a week. The debs accordingly instituted Odo-ro-no night, banishing BO to the shop girls and typists. Gender identities were class-specific: they were shaped not only by a common popular culture but by particular social encounters. When the debs gathered for informal get-togethers, they exchanged information which appeared to be of no consequence – hairdressers and cosmetics mingled with incidents of the night before. But as Ann Schuster recalls, 'It was all part of trying to learn how to be sophisticated – that was what we all wanted to be. Sophistication was the ultimate: knowing how to put on a veneer.'[50] Sophistication was barely attained when the fear of ageing began. *Vogue* advertised a product called Luxuria, which promised to defeat wrinkles. The social definition of old age for women still came early. A group of single working women formed the Over Thirty Association in 1935 against discrimination in employment; it took a decade for it to be renamed the Over Forties Club.

Sex

Between the wars women's resolve not to have large families was turning into population statistics. Methods are difficult to verify, but it would appear that many couples continued to use coitus interruptus rather than contraception. Despite the Ministry of Health ruling allowing birth-control advice to be given in welfare centres, knowledge of contraception and sex was still hard to come by for the young and unmarried. Peggy Wood, from a middle-class Protestant family in Northern Ireland, remembers her mother leaving 'sort of ooey-gooey books around'.[51] One of the London working-class women interviewed by Sally Alexander said, in contrast, 'We learned the dirty way.'[52]

'The dirty way' had its dark side. Suppressed memories of childhood abuse surface in oral interviews years later. Not only fathers and male relations but other adult men, including apparently respectable figures, could be molesters. One woman from Paddington, west London, remembered the vicar of her local parish church regularly trying to put his hand up her skirt. It also had a smutty hilarity. In 1937 Mass-Observation researchers in Blackpool – the working-class seaside mecca – stood solemnly outside the 'Fun House', where puffs of air blew up women's skirts as they went in. One observer, a Labour Party activist married to an Oxford don, was propositioned by several men, including a middle-aged man in a bowler hat, who asked with northern directness, 'Will yer come to bed with me, love? 'Ave you done it before?'[53]

The practicalities of courtship were not conducive to sexual fulfilment. In Mass-Observation's Worktown – in reality Bolton – illicit sex took place in the back streets. The London middle class headed in motor cars to country lanes, to the distress of Mrs Bramwell Booth, the widow of the founder of the Salvation Army, who complained of 'brothels on wheels'[54] in Barnet and Potters Bar. Pregnancy outside marriage was still a disaster. Peggy Wood said, 'You have to realize that in my kind of set-up, pregnancy was not something you dared risk. I mean, I – I had in mind that if I ever did get pregnant, suicide would be the only practical way out.'[55]

The Abortion Law Reform Association (ALRA) was formed in 1936 by birth-control campaigners Stella Browne, Dora Russell, Frida Laski and Joan Malleson. An estimated 500 women were dying each year from abortions and ALRA's supporters argued that legalized abortion would end the deaths, suffering and fear caused by unwanted pregnancies. Some ALRA members advocated abortion for eugenic reasons, but Stella Browne persisted in demands for the right of every woman to control her fertility. The Birkett Committee was set up to investigate maternal mortality and abortion, calling on a wide range of organizations to see if abortion was increasing. When ALRA gave evidence in 1937, Joan Malleson argued diplomatically that legal abortion would increase family happiness. But Stella Browne, still the rebel, broke the taboo which made the case for abortion only permissible on behalf of the unfortunate others. When asked how she could know that abortion need not be harmful, she replied, 'I have . . . the knowledge in my own person that, if abortion was necessarily fatal or injurious, I should not be here before you'.[56] The subjective voice in the campaign for abortion was not to be heard again until the early 1970s.

The sexual radicalism which connected personal happiness with social change had become marginalized by the late 1930s. It was still customary in Battersea, south London, for new recruits to the Communist Party to be introduced to the local birth-control centre, but this was not part of public politics any longer. If the political battle had been lost, a cultural shift had nonetheless occurred. Mass-Observation found some forthright commentators in 1939. Kate, a stenographer married to Sid, declared, 'Sid and I haven't got any repressions left. I don't think. Not when we're alone, anyway. We share our dirty jokes.'[57] It would seem that those images of glamour were getting to young men too. 'I'm afraid,' an engineer on HMS *Maidstone* confessed, 'the thought of Ginger Rogers with a tin opener excites my interest much more than Mrs Chamberlain surrounded by roast duck.'[58]

In October 1938 *Picture Post* was launched with two cover girls leaping through the air. Photo-journalism introduced a respectable sexuality, seen through the masculine lens of a radicalized social photography. This spirit of candour was still not what Stella Browne had called in the 1920s a 'sexual vocabulary'[59] for female desire. Nor did it reach everywhere. On reflection, Peggy Wood acknowledged the unnecessary agony of her Northern Ireland upbringing, but insisted, 'we had just as much excitement out of sex'.[60] Reserve had its pros and cons too. Vera Brittain, who recoiled from the public lesbian identity of *The Well of Loneliness*, challenged the modern suspicion 'of affection between women'[61] when she published her memoir of Winifred Holtby, *Testament of Friendship*, in 1940. Yet if the new frankness about sex cloaked many layers of ambiguity, a resolute desire to comprehend all aspects of sexual feeling was part of a commitment to being self-conscious women. In *Testament of Friendship*, Vera Brittain recorded Winifred Holtby's observation on Virginia Woolf's writing: 'There are the

The first *Picture Post* cover in 1938 heralds new hope for a better Britain.

moments of revelation which compensate for the chaos, the discomfort, the toil of living. The crown of life is understanding . . . These are the moments in which all the disorder of life assumes a pattern; we see; we understand; and immediately the intolerable burden becomes tolerable.'[62] It was an insight which had been hard won, salvaged out of disappointments.

THE UNITED STATES

Suppression and Engagement

In 1937 Helen Keller, blind and deaf from infancy, mourned the death of her teacher Anne Sullivan in a journal in which personal loss mingled with political dread of Fascism. 'Teacher' had awakened her from a 'dark silence without language or purpose or faith'.[63] Anne Sullivan had held her hand under a pump of running water and repeatedly written W-A-T-E-R on her palm. Now there was no greeting from her teacher, and all the radical hopes Helen Keller had cherished seemed to be overwhelmed by the 'disheartening retrogression apparent in civilization everywhere'.[64] External forces carried the threat of the 'dark silence'[65] engulfing all humanity.

Yet even though the Great Depression and the rise of Fascism set the political agenda so decisively during the 1930s, new ways of participating in mainstream politics were to be devised by women concerned about reform. Franklin D. Roosevelt's election as President in 1932 gave America an unusual First Lady, the apparent epitome of the responsible wife, mother and grandmother who could still engage with public life, bringing reforms into the mainstream. 'Get into the game and stay in it,' she advised women; 'throwing mud from the outside won't help. Building up from the inside will.'[66]

Eleanor Roosevelt shared the progressive politics of the 1920s 'new women' who were her close friends, but she also knew her husband's political world from the inside. Her idealism was set in tough pragmatic roots. She believed women could bring special spiritual contributions to politics, yet advised them to leave their 'womanly personalities at home'.[67] Her biographer Blanche Wiesen Cook shows, however, that the balance Eleanor Roosevelt maintained between her public, extremely visible role and her own personal needs was an exercise in tremendous self-control. A perceptive journalist, Lorena Hickok, saw through the public façade when she was covering the election campaign in 1932. She noted that Eleanor Roosevelt was curiously 'withdrawn – shut up inside herself'; there was also something she could not 'define or understand', and as the journalists drove away, she observed, 'That woman is unhappy about something.'[68]

Lorena Hickok, who became a close friend and companion, was to learn more over the years of the personal unhappiness behind the front of the Roosevelt marriage. However, the strain was not generally evident. The First Lady of the New Deal turned outwards in unprecedented ways, journeying thousands of miles, writing a popular newspaper column and talking on the radio. One cartoon showed miners in the depth of the earth looking round and exclaiming, 'Here comes Mrs Roosevelt.'[69]

Politics

Franklin D. Roosevelt's New Deal drew on the progressives' social vision and adapted forms of state intervention developed during the First World War. It aimed for economic recovery through boosting purchasing power. As Rosalyn Baxandall and Linda Gordon point out, it had 'mixed effects on women'[70] in terms of both employment and welfare provision. The National Industrial Recovery Act of 1933 fixed minimum-wage guidelines and maximum hours for men and women workers. Though declared unconstitutional by the Supreme Court in 1935, this was replaced with the Fair Standards Act of 1938, which again confirmed maximum-hours and minimum-wage standards. These regulations were important for women, who were concentrated in low-paid jobs, though the minimum rates were lower for women than for men. The works programmes of the New Deal focused on the male unemployed. The New Deal administration aimed to get men's jobs back and saw the employment of the male breadwinner as the answer for poor families.

The Social Security Act of 1935 provided a minimum level of support for the old, people with disabilities and the poor. It included Aid to Dependent Children (ADC), extending the aid paid to widows to a broader group of women in families where the men had deserted or were mentally or physically incapable of working. Though it was vigorously denounced as a socialist measure by Roosevelt's opponents, this was an extremely limited form of welfare, and white administrators, especially in the South, restricted payments even to black families who were eligible. ADC, moreover, carried a stigma, for mothers who received payment were likely to be seen as inadequate. In *Pitied But Not Entitled*, Linda Gordon demonstrates how New Deal welfare reinforced the two-track system established at the beginning of the century. Widows of insured men became eligible for insurance money in 1939. In *The Wages of Motherhood*, Gwendolyn Mink comments, 'With the worthy widows of deserving male wage earners now channelled through social insurance, ADC reformers began to fix their gaze on the family "broken" by wage-earning motherhood, "illegitimacy" and race discrimination.'[71]

The New Deal enabled women's networks to surface as individuals gained influential positions. The consensus was social reform and welfare, not equal-rights feminism. Grace Abbott, who had gained considerable administrative experience in the Children's Bureau during the 1920s, managed to revive the health programmes which had been abandoned in 1929. The Children's Bureau also set up services for homeless and neglected children. Ellen Sullivan Woodward, who was appointed Director of Women's Work in the Federal Emergency Relief Administration, sought to offset the gender bias in unemployment relief, creating training programmes for women bookbinders, mattress makers and seamstresses, as well as household workers and domestic servants. Alert to racial as well as gender discrimination, she stressed the need for the New Deal to reach black women. Mary McLeod Bethune, who was appointed Director of the Division of Negro Affairs, had a background of activism in the black women's clubs movement. Along with Juanita J. Saddler, she brought a combined awareness of race and gender into the politics of the New Deal.

The appointment of former Hull House resident Frances Perkins as Secretary of Labor, Nellie Tayloe Ross as first woman Director of the Mint and Florence Allen as the first woman on the United States Circuit

First Lady Eleanor Roosevelt with Mary McLeod Bethune, Director of
Negro Activities, and Aubrey Williams, Director of the
National Youth Administration on Problems of the Negro and Negro
Youth, Washington, DC, 1937.

Court of Appeals demonstrated women's capacity to take on a general
responsibility for policy, administration and judicial affairs, though they
were not particularly concerned about reforms for women. Eleanor
Roosevelt worked in the Democratic Party with her friend Molly
Dewson, a social worker and campaigner for minimum wages for
women, and also developed the power of the Women's Division.

Native American women never became part of these influential
women's networks, but the New Deal affected their lives through the
Indian Reorganization Act (IRA) or 'Indian New Deal'. Its impact
was contradictory. The IRA set up new tribal constitutions which
gave women formal political rights. In some places this meant women
were represented for the first time. The snag was that the IRA's
attempt to protect land rights strengthened the position of male-headed
households, which in tribes like the Iroquois actually weakened women's
economic status. Alice Lee Jemison, of Seneca and Cherokee descent,
opposed the Bureau of Indian Affairs as a threat to Iroquois sovereignty.

The New Deal policy of encouraging instead of suppressing Indian culture did help to develop traditional craftwork, though the danger in the enthusiasm for tradition was that the reservations could segregate rather than nurture. The Indian New Deal did, however, provide some training for Native American women as domestic workers and seamstresses. It also led to new opportunities for an educated minority. For example, Gladys Tantaquidgeon, a Mohegan, studied Algonquian Indian culture as an anthropologist and then became a community worker for the Bureau of Indian Affairs, specializing in Indian arts and crafts. The New Deal stimulated interest in folklore, anthropology and history, as well as creating jobs.

During the 1930s the insistent pressure of black women finally led white women in Southern religious organizations to take a stand against lynching. In 1930 Jessie Daniel Ames from Texas, a member of the League of Women Voters who had been a suffragist and had campaigned for the Sheppard-Towner Act for equal pay, Mothers' Pensions and child welfare, as well as prison reform, labour laws and peace, set up the Association of Southern Women for the Prevention of Lynching. This brought white women in the Methodist Woman's Missionary Council, an organization with 250,000 members, and the National Council of Jewish Women to investigate accusations of rape, exert pressure for law enforcement against lynching and oppose racism in their own homes.

Eleanor Roosevelt gave moral authority to the struggle against racism. When the conservative Daughters of the American Revolution (DAR) tried to prevent black opera singer Marian Anderson from appearing in Constitution Hall, Washington, she resigned from DAR. Marian Anderson saw the headline on a San Francisco newsstand: MRS ROOSE-VELT TAKES STAND.[72] While symbolic public gestures like these did not end racism, they were important as visible signs against prejudice, though Franklin D. Roosevelt continued to compromise between the views of his wife and her liberal friends, his need for black support and his old loyalties to the white Southerners in the Democratic Party.

While the New Deal was initiated as a top-down affair, the social problems of the Depression, unemployment and homelessness led to various grass-roots community movements which were able to put pressure on the Roosevelt administration. Dorothy Day, a left-wing journalist who had converted to Catholicism, set up a House of Hospitality during the winter of 1933–4 on New York's Lower East Side to shelter the poor and homeless. Inspired by the French Catholic Workers' Movement, it encouraged a new kind of social activism. There were forty similar refuges in different parts of the country by 1940.

The American Socialist Party was in decline but the Communists were to gain support during the 1930s. They were influential in the Unemployed Councils of the USA, which included a high proportion of women. Formed as a national organization in 1930 with one-third of the 1,320 delegates women, the Unemployed Councils mobilized the unemployed to demand more cash and relief in kind and helped families resist eviction by moving furniture and belongings back into the houses emptied by eviction notices. They supported women workers' claims for equal insurance, opposed the dismissal of married women workers and campaigned for medical care for homeless, unemployed women and hospital care for those who were pregnant. Thus while gender equality was seen as less pressing than class injustice, the Communist Party provided an organization which endorsed equal relations between men and women and was a focus for those who wanted more radical changes than the New Deal offered.

In the second half of the decade, the party was a key element in the broad-based anti-Fascist resistance which attracted women of very different backgrounds. Among the women who went to Spain during the Civil War were writers Martha Gellhorn, Lillian Hellman and Dorothy Parker. Dorothy Parker was also the founder of the Hollywood Anti-Nazi League in 1937 and chaired the Women's Committee of the American Committee to Aid Spanish Democracy. Reflecting on her time in Spain, she dropped her cynical stance to state simply, 'I became a member of the human race.'[73] Despite the Republicans' defeat, she believed 'what they stood for, what they have given others to take and hold and carry along – that does not vanish from the earth'.[74] Salaria Kea, a black American nurse who had organized against racial segregation at the Harlem Hospital School of Nursing and helped set up a hospital for Ethiopia when it was invaded by the Italians in 1935, joined the American medical unit for Spain in March 1937 and was warmly welcomed by black Americans fighting for the Republicans.

Even though feminist organizations were at a low ebb, anti-Fascism

American nurse Salaria Kea on her way to Spain with the
Abraham Lincoln brigade.

contributed to a redefined spirit of internationalism. An awareness of women's democratic rights, along with a politicization of culture, was being expressed in movements against colonialism. An awakening sense of identity and dignity among Caribbean intellectuals, among them the feminist poet Una Marson, for example, interacted with African-American debates. In the Hispanic community in New York a Puerto Rican schoolteacher and journalist, Josefina C. Silva de Cintron, led the Union de Mujeres Americanas and the League of Spanish-speaking Democrats. Her monthly journal, *Revista de Artes Yhetras*, founded in 1933, propagated Spanish language and Latin-American culture, while also featuring feminist writers like Julia de Burgos.

Issues of culture and identity were being raised also through the work of anthropologists like Ruth Benedict, Margaret Mead and Zora Neale Hurston. In differing ways their work validated alternative values to Western male-dominated capitalism. Ruth Benedict's *Patterns of Culture* (1934) included not only positive accounts of Native American culture but a study of a matrilineal society which rejected violence and gave women considerable authority in the family. Margaret Mead's work on New Guinea questioned prevailing American assumptions about gender roles, while Zora Neale Hurston's research into rural black folklore subverted the materialism of American society. Women participated in the politics of the New Deal, but they can also be seen questioning the mainstream culture in ways which had significant political implications.

Work

The Depression reawakened antagonism to married women working. When the Lynds returned to Muncie in the mid-1930s they were told in no uncertain terms that 'men should behave like men and women like women'.[75] In 1936 a Gallup Poll revealed that 82 per cent of the population thought wives should not work if their husbands had jobs and a majority were in favour of legal restrictions.

As Jacqueline Jones points out in *Labor of Love, Labor of Sorrow*, the debate about married women working during the New Deal incorrectly assumed this was 'a new and startling development'.[76] The polls erased the experience of black American women and disregarded the circumstances of Mexican women in the canneries of Los Angeles or the San Joaquin valley cotton fields, humping 100-pound sacks of cotton on their shoulders. It was poverty rather than choice that led many women to work, and indeed forced whole families to labour. Juanita Loveless's father had been a railroad worker in rural Texas before the Depression. Compelled to pick cotton when he lost his job, she remembered how the men would be collected along with their children from the farms. She was hired by the day at the age of seven — it kept them from 'starving to death' in 'the real tough Depression days'.[77]

Throughout the 1920s the trend had been for more women to enter paid work, including married women. Sherna Berger Gluck notes that by 1930 one in nine married women were wage earners — mostly from the 42 per cent of families living at or below subsistence. By the end of the 1930s nearly 15.5 per cent of all married women were in paid jobs; the husbands of over a third of these were earning less than $600 a year — barely half the median income in 1939.

Opportunities for middle-class women declined during the Depression. Along with legal restrictions on married women in some states, there was informal discrimination and it was harder to get work in teaching, libraries, social work and book-keeping. Many were forced to take less skilled forms of clerical employment, which continued to expand among white women. By 1940 a third of all white women had clerical jobs. Only 1.3 per cent of black women were in this kind of white-collar work, though a few Chinese women were beginning to inch their way into the job market. Because the New Deal was successful in keeping up the demand for services, beauty parlours, waitressing and the telephone companies continued to provide jobs for women. More exotic was the film industry. Not only actresses but writers like Lillian Hellman and Dorothy Parker were busy in Hollywood.

Despite hard times there were some individual success stories. Lorena Hickok was typical of a tough new breed of women in the media, determined to make it in a man's world. Neysa McMein made her name designing the covers of magazines like *McCalls* and the *Saturday Evening Post*, while Helen Hokinson was a popular cartoonist. Journalist Dorothy Thompson became a household name, second only to Eleanor

Roosevelt. American women continued to hit the news. Mildred Ella (Babe) Didrikson Zaharias excelled as a sportswoman first in basketball, then in athletics; her feats simply could not be ignored. However, despite her performance in the 1932 Olympics, where she won the javelin and hurdles and took second place in the high jump, there was no established structure for Olympic women athletes. To support her family, the Olympic star worked in vaudeville until her marriage to wrestler George Zaharias enabled her to build a career in amateur golf. Another extraordinary star of the 1930s was Amelia Earhart, who flew solo across the Atlantic in 1932, crossed the Pacific in 1935 and mysteriously vanished on a round-the-world trip in 1937.

Pearl Buck, writing at the end of the 1930s, thought that women's interest in work and a profession had never been lower. However, this was only part of the truth. It rather depended where you looked. In her study *Feminism in the Labor Movement*, Nancy Gabin notes that female membership in unions increased during the 1930s from 265,000 to 800,000. From the mid-1930s both skilled and unskilled workers in the mass-production industries were taking advantage of the right to unionize secured by the National Labor Relations Act in 1936. Union leaders in the United Auto Workers and the Congress of Industrial Organizations did not set out to recruit women, but they were swept up in the mass union drives and militant sit-down strikes. Patricia Wiseman, for example, had worked at Flint, Michigan, during the sit-down strike, and during a 1937 sit-down at Bohn Aluminum in Detroit, she refused to help prepare food with the women. Taking her place with the men on the picket, she told them, 'You're getting $15 a week more than I am for the same number of hours and I'll be damned if I don't work as hard as you do!'[78]

When the work was divided into men and women's jobs, women workers generally accepted lower rates in the new plants as they were still higher than they could earn elsewhere. However, at Philco's, a large radio manufacturer in Philadelphia, jobs were reclassified in 1938 and 1,500 women found themselves working in areas which had formerly been seen as men's. The workforce, many of whom were overqualified for assembly-line work, began to question job inequality. The slogan 'Same work, same pay'[79] could be heard at Philco.

The Folk

Folk arts of all kinds flourished in the 1930s – the other side of the machine age's functionalist design. Quilting was revived as a home craft among white and black women. The Women's Bureau in the New Deal encouraged craftworks as a source of employment. Craft centres set up for Southern Mountain women by the Tennessee Valley Associated Co-operatives produced bedspreads, pottery, metalwork, leatherwork and woodwork, as well as rug-hooking, toy-making and quilting. The Women's Bureau helped with marketing, encouraging groups like the Young Women's Christian Association to pay better rates than the sweated wages of home-workers.

Native American crafts like basket-making were developed. Lucy Parker Telles applied traditional skills learned from the Miwok and Paiute people to making a prize-winning giant basket, thirty-six inches

Manufacturing folk: Seminole woman using a
Singer sewing machine.

in diameter and twenty inches high. Pablita Velarde, a Tewa Indian painter from Santa Clara Pueblo, New Mexico, was encouraged to paint from experience by her teacher, Dorothy Dunn, at the Santa Fe Indian School, run by the Board of Indian Affairs. In 1933 she was chosen to work with artist Olive Rush on Works Progress Administration (WPA) murals for Chicago's 'Century of Progress World Fair'. She was to be employed on other WPA arts projects and became an arts and crafts teacher at the Santa Clara Day School.

Scholarly interest in folklore and anthropology contributed to a new appreciation of traditional popular art of all kinds, including music. Folk-singer Aunt Molly Jackson was recorded by collector Alan Lomax singing of witchcraft and miners' struggles in the Appalachians. However, celebration could also isolate and confine. Brought to New York by left literary propagandists, Aunt Molly Jackson found herself regarded as quaint, of interest as a folk heroine but cut off from her roots in Kentucky. She sang of the loneliness of urban poverty, an old woman in New York waiting for the gas and electricity to be turned on.

> My heart it is a breaking, it's Christmas Eve night
> I'm in the slums on the East Side without any light.
> I've no gas or electric to make myself a cup of tea
> Oh tell me, fellow workers, how can this be?[80]

✳

The United Auto Workers did formally support equal pay for women workers. However, Nancy Gabin says they pushed the demand only as a defensive measure when management threatened to replace men with women. Trade union men retained old ideas about women's place. Nonetheless, equal pay was on the agenda of a powerful workers' union and, as Ruth Milkman observes in her essay 'Gender and Trade

Unionism', 'The ideal of equality opened up new possibilities for women in organized labour.'[81]

In 1939 the socialist Mary Heaton Vorse wrote a book, *Labor's New Millions*, in which she argued for a new trade unionism which did not 'stop at the formal lodge meeting' but saw 'the union as a way of life involving the whole community'.[82] A practical expression of this social vision was the growth of the 'Ladies Auxiliaries', which linked the wives of strikers to union struggles. In the mid-1930s the Minneapolis Truckers' Auxiliary and the Flint Women's Emergency Brigade played crucial roles in the dramatic events of the Minneapolis General Strike and the Flint sit-down. Auxiliaries also helped to create an alternative social and personal world of labour. In Strutwear, Minneapolis, for instance, a hosiery workers' auxiliary formed in 1938 planned social events – dances, picnics, parties, a diamond ball and bowling teams – as well as organizing classes on labour history and economics. Social occasions, such as a birthday party for a black member in an Italian home, helped to break down divisions and prejudice. Groups excluded from the labour movement through racism – Chinese women garment workers, Southern black and white women tobacco workers – were also joining trade unions in the late 1930s, while new organizations were appearing among laundry workers and domestics. The New Deal provided a framework for a broader vision of trade unionism which produced a fierce counter-offensive from employers.

Daily Life

Even in the boom years of the 1920s sections of the American working class had known unemployment, especially in mining and textiles. After the 1929 slump, however, unemployment became so widespread that it broke up the normal patterns of daily life in many industrial towns and rural areas. In the early 1930s there were food and rent riots in several cities, including Chicago in 1931, where black women were among a crowd attacked by police during mass resistance against rent payment. It was evident that neither the left nor the right had convincing solutions for the crisis. Consequently the desperate hope that Roosevelt's election would signal a way out went deeper than the normal response to politicians. It was to be expressed in thousands of poignant personal letters to Franklin and Eleanor Roosevelt. Mrs H. E. C. from Troy, New York, for instance, sent her ring and a ring of her mother's as security to Eleanor Roosevelt in 1935. In return she asked her to send baby clothes and diapers: 'It is very hard to face bearing a baby we cannot afford to have and the fact that it is due to arrive soon, and still there is no money for the hospital or clothing, does not make it any easier.'[83]

Reality never lived up to these hopes. New Deal administrators could be at best patronizing and at worst hostile to the unemployed. A strong feeling remained that poverty was akin to failure. Even in the Democratic Party there was opposition to welfare provision. Mrs N. J. S. from Fayetteville, West Virginia, wrote to tell Eleanor Roosevelt in 1936, 'Personally I have found that the more you give the lower classes the more they want.'[84]

Gender as well as class bias persisted. New Deal policies focused on the unemployed male breadwinner and the dependent family. While the plight of mothers with babies and young children was indeed desperate, women were also affected in other ways. For example, low-paid women who headed households often combined several forms of economic activity in order to support their families by doing home-work, going out cleaning, taking in lodgers, setting up bakeries, restaurants or beauty parlours in their homes. One East St Louis black woman who worked as a meat trimmer all day, as well as looking after a lodger and three children, told a government investigator, 'I don't hardly see myself how I make out.'[85] Too much work and low pay could be problems, as well as unemployment.

Destitution also affected a growing number of single women. By 1932 2 million women were unemployed; homeless young women roamed the streets, sleeping rough in railway stations or behind the heating ducts in subway bathrooms. They were the invisible unemployed. 'It's one of the great mysteries of the city where women go when they are out of work and hungry,'[86] wrote Meridel LeSueur. Eleanor Roosevelt lobbied for special provision for the young unemployed women which would provide 'healthful employment and useful instructions amid wholesome surroundings'.[87] The result was the

Depression America: Maryland farming family, 1937.

She-She-She camps, set up in 1933. But the provision for women was always less than for men.

Many young women decided to take a chance and head to the city. Stella Nowicki, for instance, had left home, a farm with no electricity or toilets, aged seventeen, for Chicago 'because there was not enough money to feed the family in 1933 during the Depression'.[88] She was to become active as a Communist labour organizer. Juanita Loveless, in contrast, was taken by her mother in an old car to a camp in Oklahoma, where they lived in a shack and she peddled bootleg whiskey in the honky-tonk beer bars. Found by a woman police officer, she was sent off to become a domestic servant. Families split up under the pressure of the Depression, though economic necessity could also make the family a means of survival. Jessie Lopez de la Cruz, who was to become a farm workers' organizer, was brought up by her grand-mother when her mother died of cancer in a farm workers' camp in California. She picked mushrooms and mustard greens on the hillsides while her brothers killed rabbits and sold tripe with garlic (*menudo*). The schoolteacher gave her leftover food to take home from school dinners.

The New Deal fostered values which took the edge off the harsh competitive ethic and validated social and cultural initiatives. African-Americans' tradition of collective self-help inspired several practical schemes which contained a broader vision. For example, in the Alpha Kappa Alpha's Mississippi Health Project, members of a black sorority took health care to sharecroppers by turning their cars into mobile health vans for several weeks every summer from 1935 to 1942. Each year they immunized over 15,000 children, and supplied dentistry and treatment for malaria and VD for thousands of poor adults. Efforts to develop economic alternatives by directing black purchasing power continued in the black community. The Housewives' League of Detroit, formed in 1930, pledged themselves to buy from black businesses. The Young Negroes Co-operative League in New York bought goods collectively to save money and also took on consumer education. Ella Baker, who had recently graduated, was employed under the New Deal to teach about the co-operative implications of buying power. In Chicago the League ran co-operative restaurants and were involved in co-operative housing projects.

Interest in creating social spaces in the built environment revived. In Chicago, for example, enthusiasm for public housing could draw on the knowledge of trained women professionals like architect Mary Long Whitmore and Elizabeth Wood, a housing administrator. Some of the Utopianism of the radical wing of municipal housekeeping could at last be put into effect; playgrounds and green spaces became a reality. The murals funded by New Deal arts projects created a community art which enabled women artists like Louise Nevelson, Lee Krasner, Isabel Bishop and Alice Neal to gain commissions.

Many artists and writers regarded their work as part of a wider social project, creating what William Stott has described as 'documentary expression'.[89] One of the most creative photographers of the era, Dorothea Lange, followed the migrant poor, immortalizing the despair of the Depression in her picture of the destitute wife and children of a pea-picker in 'Migrant Mother', taken in California in 1936. Marion Post Wolcott also photographed the rural poor, and in 1935 Margaret Bourke-White travelled in the South with writer Erskine Caldwell to produce the book *You Have Seen Their Faces* in 1937. The title echoed *Can You Hear Their Voices?*, a play produced by Hallie Flanagan at the

Cinema

'Some day my prince will come,' goes the song in Walt Disney's *Snow White and the Seven Dwarfs* (1938). However, women in 1930s Hollywood movies were not only cast as waiting. Joan Crawford's screen occupations included shop girl in *Our Blushing Brides* (1930), cub reporter in *Dance Fools Dance* (1931), café entertainer in *Laughing Sinners* (1931), paper-box factory worker in *Possessed* (1932), stenographer in *Grand Hotel* (1932), prostitute in *Rain* (1932), housemaid in *Sadie McKee* (1934) and cabaret singer in *The Bride Wore Red* (1937). Needless to say, she went up in the world by marrying or becoming the mistress of a rich man in most of these roles, but 1930s heroines were frequently gainfully employed in the meantime.

Films enabled women to aspire to a better life in fantasy. For example, in *Possessed* Joan Crawford gazes into the windows of a passing train on a hot summer night on her way home from the box factory to see a different world of iced cocktails and evening dresses. As the train stops, a man hands her champagne – an entry into the other life of the rich and glamorous. In response to his question about what she wants from life, she says, 'Me.' When she gets home she is impatient with her boyfriend's criticism because she is slightly drunk on the champagne: 'You don't own me. Nobody does. My life belongs to me.'[90] She leaves for New York and Clark Gable.

The messages of films directed at women were ambivalent; the yearning for freedom tangles with longing to be possessed, not only by men but by motherhood. In *A Woman Rebels* (1936), Katharine Hepburn has a child with a married man, sets up a feminist journal, refuses to marry a devoted suitor – 'I need no one . . . I'll go on by myself'[91] – and devotes herself to caring for the child. There is a kind of bargain to be struck with liberty. Maternal sacrifice is also the theme of *Blonde Venus* (1932), in which Marlene Dietrich combines wifely devotion to her sick husband with cross-gender allure in an affair with Cary Grant. Forced out to work, she dons a gorilla outfit for her cabaret routine. 1930s women had to make their choices in tight corners. As well as lifting the audience out of humdrum reality, they also presented awful warnings. You could leave the cinema relieved that your life was not racked by intensity and disaster.

There were nonetheless several possibilities presented to white women viewers. The scope for African-American women was much narrower. In the role of black maid, their destiny was to provide security for white heroines by their resourcefulness. Hattie McDaniel is the notable exception, managing to transcend the restricted stereotype by talking back. In *Gone With the Wind* (1938), based on the novel by Margaret Mitchell which had sold an unprecedented 8 million copies since its publication in 1936, Hattie McDaniel made another record by becoming the first black actress to win an Oscar. She said of her role as 'Mammy': 'I tried to make her a living, breathing character . . . to glorify Negro womanhood; not the modern, streamlined type of Negro woman who attends teas and concerts in ermine and mink, but the type of Negro of the period which gave us Harriet Tubman, Sojourner Truth and Charity Still.'[92] It was left to low-budget alternative black film groups to present a wider range of roles for black women.

✳

Vassar Experimental Theater in 1931. In 1935 Hallie Flanagan became national director of the Federal Theater Project, one of the four arts projects set up by the Works Progress Administration. It too provided jobs, reached working-class audiences, and was lively and experimental. Between 1935 and 1939, when it was closed, 30 million people attended its productions.

Both ideologically and practically there were strong pressures towards collectivity, to being part of a 'group', an inclination caught by Mary McCarthy in her novel about young women during the 1930s, *The Group*. There was, however, also a quite different current. The bohemian avant-garde's emphasis on pleasurable self-expression was diverted into a consumer culture based on the individual household; modern house decor, a motor car and foreign travel became the aspirations of the middle class.

This freedom-as-lifestyle was checked by the Depression, which saw a revival of the self-help ethic. Advertisers in the early 1930s adopted a pragmatic attitude, showing Mum making do, and many housewives did revert to canning, baking, growing their own vegetables and darning old clothes. Fear haunted even those who were not destitute. Weeping widows losing their homes for lack of a policy were featured in the life insurance advertisements. The popular radio serial *Stella Dallas* (on which the film was based) portrayed a lower middle-class divorcée coping through sacrifice.

However, the New Deal was successful in stimulating consumer demand and the market which developed in the 1930s was not restricted to the middle class. The notion of basic necessity had been socially redefined; despite the Depression, most urban Americans had electricity or gas by the mid-1930s. In Cleveland, for instance, the Federal Real Property Inventory found that 98 per cent of homes had electric lights, 98 per cent cooked with gas or electricity, 96 per cent had plumbing and a toilet, and 89 per cent had hot and cold running water. This meant that everyday domestic goods were in demand on a mass scale. When the mass-production industries picked up in the late 1930s, retailers like the A&P were geared to mass consumption and the new consumers included workers in the new industries with money to spend.

An American popular identity took shape during the 1930s through the mass media, which increasingly aimed at women as well as men. 'Blondie', the popular cartoon strip, began in 1930 as a flapper, but she and her husband, Dagwood Bumstead, evolved into everyday Depression folk. Comic strips, confession-style women's magazines,

Blondie in her militant flapper days.

Dance till you drop: 1934 dance marathon, Washington, DC.

daytime radio serial soap operas and the movie weepies focused on personal drama with women in mind. Gracie Allen and George Burns's *Burns and Allen* radio show had accumulated 45 million listeners by 1940, laughing away at Gracie's dizzy femininity.

The sense that economic forces were beyond control, the mix of hard times and a consumer culture, resulted in an oscillation between living for the moment and fear for the future, between thrift and an impulse to gamble on luck. Families gathered round the radio to listen to comedy shows, boardgames like Monopoly became the rage, dance marathons delighted the young and in the cinema Walt Disney presented realms of disorder, through which, as Warren I. Susman points out in *Culture as History*, Mickey Mouse, the Seven Dwarfs and Co. somehow find hidden threads to serenity and happiness.

Even those for whom the promise seemed remote could still dream. Fanny Christina Hill, a black domestic servant from Texas, looked at the wedding presents of a white middle-class young woman and vowed she would have the same things herself. It took her a long time but slowly she acquired 'a crocheted bedspread, an Afghan like she had, and a tablecloth. Then I bought the silver.'[93]

In the short term, there was, of course, always window-shopping. In *The Standard of Living*, Dorothy Parker described two young steno-graphers, Annabel and Midge, stalking their dreams down Fifth Avenue on a Saturday afternoon. One earned $18 50c. a week and the other $16, but they were free to imagine a legacy of $1 million and copy the styles of the movie stars:

Annabel and Midge did, and completely, all that young office workers are besought not to do. They painted their lips and their nails, they darkened their lashes and lightened their hair, and scent seemed to shimmer from them. They wore thin, bright dresses, tight over their breasts and high on their legs, and tilted slippers, fancifully strapped. They looked conspicuous and cheap and charming.[94]

Sex

Behind the glamorous front of the siren-styles of the Depression were real economic restraints. Even sophisticated city-dwellers like Annabel and Midge still lived at home and gave half their salaries to their parents, and they were among an élite of working girls. Margaret Sabo was a more desperate case: she put an advertisement in the *Bridgeport Post* when she was nineteen, '$1,800 Buys Me for a Wife.'[95] Her father, a factory worker, had lost his job and this was the only way she could pay off the family's debts. Meanwhile, for Mexican cannery workers there was little time for dreams or romance. Love was timed by the fruit and vegetables they processed in the cannery: 'We met in spinach, fell in love in peaches and married in tomatoes.'[96]

In the early 1930s couples were wary of marriage and it was only after 1934 that marriage rates were to recover. Women were also having fewer children. Meridel LeSueur described the fear of young women in the Depression: 'I don't want to marry. I don't want any children. So they all say. No children. No marriage.'[97] Women were buying jellies, suppositories and douches on a mass scale. Contraceptives were big business, though Margaret Sanger's preferred method, the diaphragm, was still restricted mainly to the middle class and constituted a tiny 1 per cent of a $350-million-a-year industry. The demand for knowledge of birth control was spreading; one working-class woman walked five miles on a cold winter's day to get advice from Margaret Sanger's clinic in Maine. Mill-workers in Paterson, New Jersey, who were members of a Working Women's Council, organized a birth-control clinic. Rural women too wanted birth control. An Ohio farmer's wife wrote, 'It spoils married life to be worried all the time about having more babies.'[98]

Margaret Sanger had moved very far from her early emphasis on women's right to sexual self-determination. A more respectable, professional approach had come into vogue in the 1920s. She could make little impact on Roosevelt's New Deal, despite sympathy from Eleanor Roosevelt, because the President wanted to placate Catholic voters. However, 'planned parenthood' was gradually becoming part of social policy. In 1936, for example, the Illinois Birth Control League was finally accepted by the Illinois State Welfare Association; Catholic opposition had been overcome.

Concepts of individual rights over reproduction and arguments for population control by the state coexisted uneasily from the late 1930s. Birth control never lost its eugenic edge as a means of controlling the black birth-rate and in 1937 the same ideas were applied to Puerto Rico. It was to be eugenic fears which really caused a breakthrough in the South too. In 1937 North Carolina offered birth control through its public health programme and other predominantly Protestant Southern states followed. Black leaders challenged the racist element in population control, but there was also pressure in black communities for birth control to prevent unhappiness and hardship. In Baltimore, for instance, the black community's campaign led to the creation of the Northwest Health Center in 1938, sponsored by black ministers, social workers, teachers, housewives and labour leaders.

The concern for respectability made birth-controllers reluctant to take up the issue of abortion. But middle-class women paid abortionists, who operated by bribing the police in many cities, and among the rural and urban poor the 'folk' methods of pills, knitting needles, nails and pencils persisted. It seemed by the late 1930s that sexual attitudes had become somewhat more liberal. *The Ladies' Home Journal* discovered that 70 per cent of American women believed in birth control, while 69 per cent agreed with divorce.

Underneath the rationality, however, there were hints of strain. Meridel LeSueur described the stresses of gender among young unemployed couples: 'He cannot provide. If he propagates he cannot take care of his young. The means are not in his hands.'[99]

'Manliness' was socially bound up with the power to earn. Without the capacity for control over life which came from work, the existing terms of masculinity were threatened. While the Depression undermined the material situation of the male breadwinner, an exaggerated form of maleness was culturally celebrated both in the New Deal's manly-worker images and in popular culture, where tough-guy crime fiction, John Wayne-style cowboys and Superman concealed unstated anxieties. The mid-1930s also saw a sex-crime panic as newspapers featured stories of 'psychopaths' and commissions investigated sexual crime. The incidence of violent sexual crime was not in reality on the increase, but there was a powerful perception of danger from drifters, rootless unemployed men and homosexuals – outsiders who were not part of either family or society.

Anxiety about disintegration in the everyday fabric of existence contributed to a self-consciousness about culture which was to influence not only anthropologists but also popular psychologists and a neo-Freudian school of psychoanalysis which had a profound intellectual influence. Karen Horney's study of anxiety, *The Neurotic Personality of Our Time* (1937), saw neuroses as both caused by the contradictions within specific cultures and as patterning the culture in the attempt to find escape routes.

Ambiguities about gender identity switched between a conservative Utopianism of happy-ever-after conformity and a fascination with breaking the patterns of conventions. This was the era in which women overwhelmingly declared that they desired motherhood and fashion celebrated the ultra-feminine allure of the siren. It was also the decade in which Gertrude Stein's *Autobiography of Alice B. Toklas* became a best-seller and a Broadway hit. A novel by the German writer Christa Winsloe became *Mädchen in Uniform* (1931), one of the first films about lesbianism shown in the United States. And meanwhile Eleanor Roosevelt, ostensibly the personification of modern enlightened marriage, lived the ambiguities of the 1930s with her husband's infidelities and her own passionate friendship with Lorena Hickok.

It was beginning to be possible to express an ambivalence in attitudes to fulfilment and desire. Women who took the 1920s freedoms for granted felt no need for overt rebellion. Margaret Bourke-White did not want to marry again after an initial unhappy experience, but explained that she was not against marriage. The dilemmas of educated women went deeper than ritual rejections of convention. The life she had 'carved out' as a photographer meant that she wanted 'to complicate my living as little as possible. The very source of my life for me, I believed, was to maintain in the midst of rushing events an inner tranquillity.'[100] In order to throw herself into her work, recording the intensities of human experience, she needed 'an inner serenity as a kind of balance' and this was impossible if, every time she had to leave, she was torn apart by 'fear of hurting someone'.[101] Margaret Bourke-White was in an unusual position, but she expressed a wider experience of the personal complexities which were beginning to emerge from the politics of emancipation: 'People seem to take it for granted that a woman chooses between marriage and a career as though she were a stone statue on the country courthouse, weighing one against the other in the balance of her hand. I am sure this is seldom so.'[102]

Chapter 5

THE SECOND WORLD WAR AND ITS AFTERMATH

BRITAIN

'Doing Our Bit'

'Behold Worrals, she's emerged to do her bit in this war,' declared the *Girls' Own Paper* in October 1940, adding that their new heroine had 'a genuine love for planes' and was 'ready to take all personal risks in the service of her country. She's made up her mind that there'll always be an England.'[1]

The *Girls' Own Paper*, produced by the Religious Tract Society, had been rather slow on the anti-Fascist front. It had barely stopped congratulating German girls in the Hitler Youth Organization for selfless dedication to handicrafts and physical education when war broke out. Initially it advised readers to get on with their schoolwork and take up knitting, but after France fell and the British were evacuated from Dunkirk in 1940, the paper decided that enough was enough and took an editorial stand: 'We've all been shaken out of our ruts and we have all got to show what we are made of today as never before.'[2]

Worrals, like her fellow character Biggles, was created by Captain W. E. Johns, who was a keen supporter of aspirant women flyers. Unlike real-life WAAFs, his heroine and her blonde companion Betty Lowell ('Frecks') fought Germans and wore the coveted wings. Though Worrals had an admirer, handsome Spitfire pilot Bill Ashton, her utter devotion to her country's cause left little space for personal sentiment. When Bill finally manages to say, 'You know, kid, you mean an awful lot to me. If anything happened to you, I should never forgive myself,' Worrals replies sternly, 'Be yourself. You'll laugh at all this nonsense in the morning.'³ Even after the war Worrals was still hunting German spies. Mary Cadogan remarks that the Worrals stories 'put across . . . the virtues of courage, teamwork, loyalty to cause and country and the value of friendship'.⁴ It was a version of womanhood as heroic service and personal denial which was to live on in the post-war period and become a crucial linchpin of social cohesion.

While Worrals was aimed at twelve-year-olds, glamorous Jane, a comic-strip figure in the *Daily Mirror*, was intended for an older working-class readership. Jane had first appeared in 1932 but her real era was the war, when she became the forces' pin-up. Jane and her little dog Fritz were constantly getting into scrapes, but always muddled through. She worked as a colonel's driver, a secret agent, a N A A F I canteen worker and a Land Girl, recruiting men to the army, thwarting German spies, capturing German parachutists and uncovering traitors. Extremely accident-prone, when not in uniform Jane was clad in lacy underwear which she was inclined to shed escaping from bulls or amorous villains. When Jane stripped, morale soared. Christabel Leighton-Porter, the

Jane, the *Daily Mirror*'s morale booster.

model for Jane, remembered with amazement the popularity of the comic-strip character, who was painted on tanks and lorries and tattooed on to chests: 'She became more than just a comic figure who lost her dress in the slightest breeze.'[5]

Jane had her own suitor, Georgie Porgey. In the early years of the war she had some problems containing his advances, but things tended to settle down a bit as time went by, with Georgie Porgey becoming quite handy at rescuing her. He had a long wait – like Worrals, Jane was still busy with various assignments after the war and could not take time off to marry him. Jane might be blonde and have a dizzy manner, but, again like Worrals, she represented a femininity in which personal inclination was subordinated to public duty. This wartime ideal was persistent: Cliff Parker notes that it was not until 1959 that Jane 'finally sailed away into the sunset with Georgie'.[6] By then her mix of earnest endeavour and saucy suggestion was outdated.

Politics

It did begin to look as if Lady Astor's idea of a cross-party female consensus might crystallize in response to women's wartime predicament. In January 1940, twenty-one women's groups came together at a conference called by the old suffrage organization the Women's Freedom League. Margery Corbett Ashby was concerned that voluntary work was contributing to unemployment and critical of the lack of women in responsible positions. A member of the egalitarian feminist Six Point Group, Dorothy Evans, wanted to know why foster mothers only received an allowance for looking after children, arguing that they too were doing national service and should be paid. Throughout the war, assemblies called Women's Parliaments kept up the pressure for reforms, ranging from increases in the separation allowances which were paid to servicemen's families to a demand which came from the Glasgow Women's Parliament in 1942 for 'cheap laundry and repair facilities'[7] to be set up by the state.

However, when it came to state policy, women were not at all powerful. There were only twelve women MPs in Parliament when the coalition government was formed in May 1940; these included the Conservatives Lady Astor, Irene Ward, Mavis Tate, Thelma Cazalet-

Keir, the Liberal Megan Lloyd George and Eleanor Rathbone, who was an Independent. Among the Labour members were Edith Summerskill, Agnes Hardie and Jennie Adamson. The small band of women MPs used the lady members' room known as 'The Boudoir'[8] as a base for working out common policies, though Ellen Wilkinson had a government post and some informal influence through her affair with Herbert Morrison, and tended to keep her distance. At the centre of power in the War Cabinet there were no women at all. Pressure from prominent feminists and MPs led to the creation by the Minister for Labour, Ernest Bevin, of the cross-party Woman Power Committee, which included Edith Summerskill. Their relation with the coalition government and with Bevin in particular was uneasy and sometimes openly acrimonious.

In *Women Workers in the Second World War*, Penny Summerfield has analysed a schizophrenia in state policy during the war: women were needed at work and yet their position in the home had to be safeguarded. Nonplussed by the problem of mobilizing women, the Ministry of

Sixteen-year-olds from Southwark, south London, registering for war work at their local Labour Exchange, January 1944.

Labour eventually appointed a Women's Consultative Committee, which supported the introduction of National Service for single women aged twenty–thirty in December 1941. There were exemptions for women with children under fourteen and women running households with even one adult, including those who had domestic servants. The Women's Consultative Committee tried to steer between the protection of mothers and housewives which, from differing perspectives, was the aim of the 'new feminists', most of the Conservatives and many of the Labour women and the egalitarian feminists.

Mavis Tate, Thelma Cazalet-Keir and Edith Summerskill were prominent members of the lobby for equal pay, mounting a protest when equal pay was not included in the National Service Number 2 Act and securing equal compensation for female civilians injured in bombing raids. Equal pay for women teachers was part of R. A. Butler's 1944 Education Bill. However, Ernest Bevin threatened to resign and Winston Churchill insisted on a vote of confidence in the government if it was left in. With such heavy male ministerial guns pointing at them, the equal-pay campaigners were forced to put up with a Royal Commission.

Ellen Wilkinson, along with many rank and file Labour women, was suspicious of Woman Power's egalitarian strategy as advancing only the claims of professional middle-class women. Instead, Labour women campaigned for forms of social consumption which would take the pressure off working-class women – socialized milk supplies, rent control and council housing – and were preoccupied with the everyday problems of working-class evacuees. Despite these differences in emphasis, the war did bring a revival of interest in the woman question, because many aspects of life which had been regarded as individual assumed a social significance and became the business of government officials and policy-makers. As the novelist Elizabeth Bowen put it, 'Life is being lived temporarily on a public stage.'[9]

Mobilization

The military and industrial mobilization of women was half-hearted during the so-called Phoney War from September 1939 to May 1940, but at the end of May the British Expeditionary Force had to scramble out of Dunkirk. Invasion seemed imminent; the Blitz and the Battle of Britain followed. The need to mobilize the whole country was evident. In March 1941 all women aged between nineteen and forty had to register at employment exchanges so that the Ministry of Labour could direct them to essential work. Conscription in December 1941 brought women for the first time into compulsory wartime service. The Second World War, even more than the First, impinged on women of all classes.

However, as in the First World War, a social hierarchy had already been established by the voluntary organizations: the Auxiliary Territorial Service (ATS), founded by members of the Women's Army Auxiliary Corps (WAACs) from the First World War in 1938, the Women's Voluntary Service (WVS) and the Women's Land Army. All these were headed by upper-class women. An élite group of civilians, the Air Transport Auxiliary (ATA), which included famous pilots like Pauline Gower and Amy Johnson, ferried planes. When the women's forces were created, the middle class tended to find their way into the Women's Auxiliary Air Force (WAAF) and the Women's Royal Naval Service (WRNS). As Gail Braybon and Penny Summerfield say, the ATS was a 'Cinderella service',[10] despite its controversial glamorous recruitment poster. It was to receive a lift when Princess Elizabeth appeared in ATS uniform. The special cap designed for her was copied by milliners and worn by Celia Johnson in the film *Brief Encounter* (1945). Other 'Cinderellas' were the civil defence services, the Auxiliary Fire Service and Air Raid Precaution, along with the Women's Timber Corps and the Land Army volunteers. The Land Girls' song expressed their frustration:

> When this silly war is over
> Oh how happy I shall be
> When I get my civvy clothes on
> No more Land Army for me.
> No more digging up potatoes
> No more threshing out the corn
> We will make that bossy foreman
> Regret the day that he was born.[11]

The final straw came when they were put behind the Boy Scouts in a

The Kitchen Front

Wartime shortages made food a matter of state policy and women of course had a key role. 'Thanks to government planning the foods that will feed you and your family to the pitch of fighting fitness are right at your hand,'[12] declared the Ministry of Food in its 'Food Facts'. Women were told, 'To release ships and seamen on the fighting fronts you, on the "Kitchen Front", have the job of using these foods to the greatest advantage.'[13]

Marguerite Patten, a home economist, found herself no longer giving demonstrations of gourmet dishes for the electrical industry. Instead she worked for the local authority in Lincoln, travelling around to villages in the evenings to demonstrate wartime recipes. In one local hall the only appliance was an old oil cooker, which the caretaker cleaned when the demonstration started: 'The cooker produced fumes and smoke like

Economic planning: Mrs Whitham, mother
of sixteen, with her ration books, 1945.

a London peasouper fog and the audience and I spent the session gasping for breath with tears running down our cheeks.'[14]

In 1942 she joined the Ministry of Food and ran a food advice stall in Cambridge's market square. Later, as a home economist with the Food Advice Division, she spoke in hospitals and welfare clinics and even set up a counter in department stores. Home economists became evangelical, travelling in mobile vans and touring caravans, and the BBC had its *Kitchen Front* broadcasts.

The wartime diet stressed soups and fresh vegetables – potatoes featured prominently. Fresh salted cod from Iceland and white haricot beans provided crucial protein. Corned-beef hash and rissoles substituted for 'real' meat. These were in fact quite nutritious, though dull and extremely labour-intensive. There was much bottling and preserving – the Women's Institute got its jam-making image from the wartime endeavour to use fruit carefully. Cake-making required considerable ingenuity. Dried eggs became available from America in 1941, but there were actually eggless sponges and 'queen cakes'. Nella Last, who cooked for the Women's Voluntary Service canteen in Barrow, recorded one successful cake made in November 1941, with dripping skimmed off beef bones, two eggs preserved in her water-glass bucket and the peel of two oranges stewed with prunes.

Nutrition was a scientific field which really came into its own during the war. Among the scientists working on vitamins were Dorothy Hodgkin and Honor Fell, in charge of the Strangeways Laboratory in Cambridge. Lesley Hall describes how they both ran their laboratories in a 'homely', democratic manner: staff at Strangeways used to meet in a 'familial'[15] style and Honor Fell prepared tea for guests herself.

✳

victory parade at the end of the war. The Land Army simply rebelled and forced a flummoxed army to let them march behind the ATS.

If the extent to which women from different classes really mixed in the forces was quite limited, there could nonetheless be a broad range of encounters within the same class. One veteran WAAF officer remembered a Cambridge student, an elementary school teacher, an art student, two Harrods shop assistants, an eighteen-year-old society debutante and 'an amusing collar-and-tie type who'd created records on the motorcycle'.[16] A small minority of women in the services were black. Officially the British welcomed black volunteers from the Caribbean, but racism was pervasive towards both them and black women from Britain. A West Indian member of the ATS was refused a new issue of shoes with the remark 'At home you don't wear shoes anyway'[17] and when Amelia E. King, from an east London black family, volunteered for the Women's Land Army she was turned down by the Essex County Committee because she was black.

American women volunteers, keen to get into the war before the US formed women's services, came to Britain. Pauline Gower, as head of the women's section of the ATA, invited the American flyer Jacqueline Cochran to find women pilots. Among them was Emily Chapin, a secretary and spare-time pilot who managed to cross the Atlantic despite German U-boats. Nineteen-year-old Maria Elizabeth Ferguson was less fortunate: on her way over to join up after the bombing of Pearl Harbor, her ship, the *Avila Star*, was torpedoed and she spent twenty-one days in an open boat nursing twenty-seven male survivors. She received the British Empire Medal for 'magnificent'[18] courage.

It was not all heroism and glory. A Southerner, Mary Lee Settle, was grabbed and flung in the mud by her fellow WAAFs one day: 'That'll teach the fuckin' toffy-nose . . . You think we're a dirty lot, with your baths and your bare body. Oo wants to look at it? A ten-bob tart's wot you are.'[19] Thus initiated, she learned to swear, to keep her vest on and to wash less. British weather came as a shock. Eve Sugden from Virginia could not believe that people would visit Morecambe, on the northern Atlantic coast, 'voluntarily in peacetime for fun'.[20]

In retrospect it was the everyday discomforts that women remembered: running up and down Morecambe front in January, shirts open at the neck and stockings rolled down, army soup that tasted like dishwater in camps on freezing moors, maggots in landladies' sandwiches while in the Timber Corps and the humiliation of the Free from Infection or Scabies parade, which a former WAAF described as looking for 'bugs, scabies and babies'.[21]

Nevertheless somehow the raw recruits were transformed, turning into fighter controllers and plotters guiding pilots in by radio, facing bombers in barrage balloons, working in the ack-ack batteries and radar units, and operating anti-aircraft searchlights. Some became nurses in mobile field hospitals, like Iris Ogilvie, a tiny Welsh woman who landed with the troops on a Normandy beach during the D-Day operation in 1944. Those working in civil defence coped with unexploded bombs, dressed wounds by the flickering light of hurricane lamps and calmed the distress of bombed-out families. Some were to be honoured for outstanding acts of bravery. Four women got the George Cross – the civilian equivalent of the Victoria Cross – including a WAAF, Corporal Joan Daphne Mary Pearson, who shielded an RAF pilot from a 120-pound bomb which exploded nearby and saved his life. Still, when Mass-Observation interviewed a group of WAAFs in 1941 about their post-war plans, they said they would like to stay on as it gave them the chance to travel, but accepted that their time in the forces would be temporary. The exceptional nature of wartime meant that women's extraordinary actions were part of the suspension of normal life; they did not necessarily affect how women were regarded in the long term.

Conscription had quite different meanings for women themselves. For some it seemed an intolerable invasion of personal autonomy – half-way between prison and boarding school; for others it was the luxury of being told to drink a pint of milk a day. A character in Elizabeth Bowen's novel *The Heat of the Day* (1949) expressed horror at state intervention in daily life: 'A Mobile Woman dared not look sideways these days – you might find yourself in Wolverhampton (a friend of hers had) or at the bottom of a mine, or in the ATS with some bitch blowing a bugle at you till you got up in the morning.'[22] However, for the young and unattached, especially for those from families where there were few alternatives, the forces could bring freedom. Jean Mormont, from a north London working-class family of eighteen, described the ATS as 'a chance to get away, like, see the world. It was a jolly good life . . . you got so much freedom in there

. . . I wasn't used to it . . . We used to have dances and all sorts . . . and then, well, they used to move you all over the place.'[23]

Work

The women who volunteered or were drafted into war work met a mixed reception. Midlands factory workers regarded glamorous London shopgirls with awe, incredulity and apprehension. Some men seemed to deny that the women were really there, like Mrs Grossman's elusive trainer, who was meant to be showing her how to repair air-craft at De Havilland's: 'You could never find him. He treated me all right, but he used to think I couldn't do it. He didn't think any of the girls could, but we outshone some of the men.'[24] There was overt hostility as well. Gail Braybon and Penny Summerfield record one incident in a Birmingham factory when the men on the night shift deliberately loosened the nuts on the lathe to slow the women on the day shift down – sabotage which could have caused an accident.

Resistance to women workers in factories was a mix of prejudice and fear of gender difference, combined with anxiety that women workers would erode trade union rights. There was pressure to raise production, the special legislative protections for women were abandoned, workers were doing twelve, sometimes even eighteen hours at work, and unions were not able to call strikes. On the other hand, women's membership of trade unions increased dramatically. The Amalgamated Engineering Union (AEU) and the Electrical Trades Union (ETU) finally allowed women to join. Denise Riley notes that in contrast to the '5 or 6 per cent' at the start of the war, 'the peak point of unionization and female employment in 1943 saw some 23 per cent of employed women unionized'.[25] Women trade unionists gained rest breaks, factory doctors, canteens and better toilets. New female welfare officers, nicknamed by the press 'Bevin's belles', appeared in the wartime factories in an attempt to curb the rise in accidents and improve health and conditions. Toxic jaundice and dermatitis were less common than they had been in the First World War because of more precautions, but there were other hazards. Maria Tardos, a Cypriot immigrant who was sewing on gas-sensitive pads, found that the tips of her fingers were being melted by chemicals.

Eleanor Roosevelt visits Women's Voluntary Service exhibition recruiting women for part-time war work, Bristol, 1942.

Eleanor Roosevelt did a fact-finding tour of factories in Britain during 1942 and was impressed by the mobilization of women workers. But she observed that the 'age-old fight for equal pay is still going on'.[26] Women rarely got the rate for the job, but their pay was invariably higher than it had been in pre-war employment and they were more likely to compare their wage packets with one another than with the male rate. One exception was a strike for equal pay at the Rolls-Royce aero-engine plant at Hillington, near Glasgow, in 1943 when the women broke the law and walked out.

Though the pay and companionship were positive aspects of wartime work, the long hours discouraged women with families. The government used many inducements to recruit women, ranging from appeals on the BBC and in women's magazines to lorry parades of young women demonstrating their new skills in filing, riveting and drilling components. The most practical innovation, and one which was to leave its mark on the pattern of women's employment after the war, was the introduction of part-time work. One woman who had been a housewife for fifteen years told Mass-Observation that after being 'a cabbage . . . you feel you've got out of the cage and you're free'.[27]

The absence of the men and the exceptional circumstances of the war years also brought a new social awareness among women writers. Writers as far apart as Virginia Woolf and Barbara Cartland recorded wartime life. Novelist Mollie Panter-Downes sent a regular letter from London to the *New Yorker*. Women reported the horrific consequences of war as journalists and photographers. Iris Morley, for example, was one of the first British correspondents to send news of the concentration camps. Early in 1945 she was an observer at a camp in Estonia shortly after the Germans left. The surrealist photographer Lee Miller, an American who had worked with Man Ray, caught the tragic irony of the Blitz. The war, combined with the state's interest in communication, encouraged the social documentary. At the BBC, Hilda Matheson worked on a government-backed propaganda project, *Britain in Pictures*,

'Revenge on Culture' or 'Fallen Angel' from *Grim Glory* by Lee Miller,
London, 1940.

with Dorothy Wellesley. Several women artists – Laura Knight, Evelyn Dunbar and Ethel Gabain – did realistic paintings and drawings of women's war work for the Ministry of Information Artists' Advisory Committee, while Lee Miller's *Fallen Angel* (1940) – a female statue lying amidst tombstones with a cut across the neck – symbolized total war.

Even male-dominated professions began to change: the Institution of Mechanical Engineers admitted its first woman member in 1944 and Dr Janet Vaughan, a haematologist, was the Medical Officer in charge of the North-West London Blood Supply Depot, leading a group of scientists employed by the Medical Research Council. The numbers of women employed as dentists, solicitors, barristers, accountants and architects increased. Professional women were most likely to say that they wanted to continue working after the war. Not surprisingly, though, women doing hard, physical, boring work in factories were liable to see leaving their job at the end of the war as a release. Wartime surveys into women's attitudes to work thus produced conflicting responses and did not probe very deeply into the actual contexts in which women balanced home and work. They also disregarded the fact that women had worked before the war and that not all families were supported by male breadwinners. Caroline Haslett, who was President of the Women's Engineering Society, spoke out on behalf of skilled women workers, but many women simply assumed that their position as workers was temporary. In the Midlands factories they sang:

End of the shift at the gasworks, 1941.

I'm only a wartime working girl.
The machine room makes me deaf.
I have no prospects after the war
And my young man is in the RAF.
K is for Kitty calling P for Prue
Bomb Doors Open
Over to you![28]

Daily Life

While the government was appealing to women to help the war effort it displayed a curious insouciance about how houses were to be cleaned and children cared for. It was all very well for the upper-class Women's Voluntary Service to admonish others to leave beds unmade and meals uncooked – they had servants after all. Child-care was an insuperable obstacle to taking on paid work, yet the government was slow to provide nurseries. John Costello notes that by

the beginning of 1941 only fourteen government-sponsored nurseries had been set up and a survey of a typical industrial town in Lancashire revealed that of 241 mothers of pre-school children interviewed, only thirty-six were at work, because of the lack of cheap child-care facilities for their infants.[29]

Initially the Ministry of Labour favoured child-minding on a voluntary basis, but it became clear that this was failing by autumn 1941. Ernest Bevin, at the Ministry of Labour, became convinced that child-care must be provided and the number of factory-based nurseries did begin to increase. However, opposition came from the Ministry of Health, which continued to favour self-help and neighbourhood mutual aid. The medical profession was divided; some Medical Officers of Health thought that nurseries would teach children 'regular habits',[30] but the Medical Women's Federation pointed to the danger of infections, and the British Medical Journal, using American research on children in hospital, argued in 1942 that 'the biological unity of mother and little child cannot be disregarded with impunity'.[31] By 1944 it was backing its warnings of delinquency and a prolonged Age of Resistance with the psychological theories developed by Melanie Klein about the innate psychic aggression of the infant, and referring to work by D. W.

Winnicott and John Bowlby: 'In the years from two to five the battle between love and primitive impulse is at its height . . . Destructive impulses let loose in war may serve to fan the flame of aggression natural to the nursery age.'[32]

The labour movement was in favour of day nurseries funded by local authorities and women demonstrated for these, stopping traffic by wheeling their children in prams decorated with the slogan 'We Want War Work, We Want Nurseries.' A combination of pressures produced 1,500 day nurseries providing 71,806 places at a cost of 1s. a day by the autumn of 1944. But these still served only a quarter of all the children under five with mothers doing war work. The rest had to rely on child-minders; if there was no one in their family or friendship network, children had to be boarded with strangers. This was not always the kindly mutual aid envisaged by the Ministry of Health. Clara Moore, for instance, arrived at the farm where her children were staying to find the two-year-old tied down in the cot.

The patterns of daily life were severely disrupted during wartime. After war was declared in 1939 1½ million mothers and children were evacuated into the countryside. Novelist Naomi Mitchison, who lived in the hall at the fishing village of Carradale in Scotland, welcomed her evacuees, but others found themselves billeted in homes where they were resented and felt socially uncomfortable. Families left the cities and settled in requisitioned holiday camps, wooden seaside chalets and caravans. The air raids meant people spent the night in shelters or huddled in fields outside cities; water and power supplies broke down and those who lost their homes became destitute migrants. In September 1940 Barbara Nixon, an air-raid warden, described the exhausted east Londoners covered with dust, drifting 'miserably westwards',[33] carrying bundles or pushing perambulators. She records that a middle-class woman on the 38 bus complained and that people tried to exclude them from West End shelters: 'The newspapers told the country that London could take it. But locally there were sour comments on what journalists knew about it.'[34]

'My Darling Sweetheart' wrote Winnie Roberts, 'you must forgive me the tone of my letter yesterday as my nerves are just on edge. We endured a terrible night last night and the sirens have gone since I have started these few lines.'[35] The letter was never to be finished. It was

Wartime Songs

'We never stopped singing,' is how Mickie Hulton Storie remembers her time in the Auxiliary Territorial Service. 'We knew all the words. That played a very big part in our lives . . . We could lose ourselves.'[36] *Music While You Work* played in the factories and the dance bands were at the palais at night.

A plumber's daughter from East Ham, east London, called Vera Lynn became known as 'The Forces' Sweetheart'. She caught the wartime mood with songs like 'We'll Meet Again' and 'The White Cliffs of Dover'. The military authorities were initially alarmed by the popularity of her songs. In her memoir, *Vocal Refrain*, she writes:

What the boys were supposed to need was more martial stuff, a view that completely overlooked the experience of the previous world war, which as it grew grimmer, produced steadily more wistful songs. As I saw it, I was reminding the boys of what they were really fighting for, the precious personal things, rather than ideologies and theories.[37]

More popular even than Bing Crosby, her songs like 'Faithful for Ever' and 'There's a Boy Coming Home on Leave' expressed an ideal of constant and faithful love. Anne Shelton, a singer with Ted Heath's dance band, had a hit with 'That Lovely Weekend', which hinted at pleasure that was less permanent, the intense brief encounter of wartime: 'Those two days in heaven you helped me spend'.

The wistful songs kept coming – 'I'll Walk Alone', 'Silver Wings in the Moonlight', 'Paper Doll' and, of course, Irving Berlin's 'White Christmas', which crossed the Atlantic in 1942. But the song that really defied national boundaries was the German 'Lili Marlene'. Recorded by Vera Lynn, Bing Crosby and Marlene Dietrich, 'Lili of the Lamplight' became a romantic legend.

A German soldier-poet originally wrote the words about two girls, a greengrocer's daughter called Betty (Lili) and a nurse, Marlene. When the Swedish cabaret singer Lale Andersen recorded it in German, she received a million fan letters from German soldiers. Goebbels distrusted the song because he feared it might undermine morale; in fact it became popular with soldiers on both sides. Lale Andersen was arrested when she tried to flee from the Nazis to join her Jewish boyfriend in Zurich. Goebbels let her live after the BBC announced that she had died – to prove that the British told lies. The record she called her 'fateful song'[38] had saved her life.

✳

found in the rubble of the bombed house in Liverpool where Winnie Roberts died with her baby daughter, Maureen.

War brought not only tragedy but grim inconvenience. Peggy Wood, a middle-class woman from Northern Ireland whose fiancé was in the forces, said in *Dutiful Daughters* that she found the deadly boredom the worst: 'If you want my image of the war, it was from eleven o'clock till one o'clock in the morning on a station platform waiting for a train that never came.'[39] Some 10,000 women ordnance workers at Chorley, Lancashire, were in bleak internment-style huts surrounded by barbed wire when Billy Butlin, founder of the famous holiday camps, arrived, sent by the Ministry of Supply to raise morale. He organized dances, amateur theatricals and gave the huts a coat of paint.

Ironically the rationed wartime diet and enforced exercise improved the health of some working-class people who had been living in poverty during the Depression. Canteen food may not have been *haute cuisine* but it supplemented the ration books. However, everyday living was complicated by queues and shortages in shops. Food and clothes rationing led some people to turn to the black market, but among others a spirit of ingenuity and squirrel-like hoarding appeared. Old woollens were unpicked, clothes redesigned at home, string and paper recycled and toys handed on. Bikes, silk stockings and nylons (which arrived from America in 1942) became precious commodities. At Vickers' engineering factory in Newcastle upon Tyne, Sadie MacDougal remembers that, with rationing, for a pair of stockings it was three coupons – out of twenty, what had you left? So that's why we got our legs painted. Got a straight line up the back, like a pair of fully fashioned stockings, only in paint. We used to sweet-heart some of the boys from the drawing office who could draw nice straight lines and put the dots on.[40]

Incredibly, people adapted. C. M. Beith's grandmother 'was afraid of nothing and certainly not of Germans . . . "If the bomb's got my name on it," she'd say, "I'd as soon have a cup of tea first."'[41] Eileen Haligan's Liverpool family developed air-raid rituals. When the siren went they would rush for the coal cellar. It was her job to wind up the record player for the singsong to Vera Lynn: 'Between air raids my dad and uncles would have a quick whip-round and go down to the pub for a swift half and a half-dozen bottles of Guinness for my mum and aunties, and packets of crisps for us kids.'[42]

The cinema was as popular as ever. Along with films about working-class life such as *Love on the Dole* (1940) or Hollywood's *How Green Was My Valley* (1942), audiences laughed at George Formby and Old Mother Riley. Film critic C. A. Lejeune noted too that, from the invasion of the Netherlands to the battle of the Pacific, 'the sturdy British citizen'[43] waited in line to watch what happened to Scarlett O'Hara; *Gone With the Wind* ran and ran. Why?, she wondered, and then answered her own question: 'There is little harmony and content in our own souls . . . A mind that is heavy and disturbed does not want to reach very high or delve very deep. It wants to be distracted by many and even little things. Great emotion at such a time is painful and dangerous.'[44]

Bombs or no bombs, people were dance-mad. This was the era of swing, and besides singers like Vera Lynn, big bands like Glenn Miller's, Benny Goodman's and Tommy Dorsey's were all the rage. The BBC made Victor Sylvester, the Geraldo Orchestra, Ted Heath and Joe Loss popular. Foxtrots and slow-waltzing revived to romantic tunes like 'You Made Me Love You'; less sedate was the 'Black Out Stroll', a version of the Lambeth Walk, and of course the Hokey-cokey. In London at the Paramount on Tottenham Court Road and at Hammersmith Palais there were swing contests and jitterbug marathons – just like the ones that had been popular in the United States during the 1930s. When the GIs came over they would feel at home.

Sex

'Oversexed, overpaid and over here,' was a myth put about by the traitor Lord Haw-Haw in the broadcasts he made to undermine morale, according to one Birmingham teenager: 'It was just the case that the British women and the American GIs were in the same place at the same time – it was rather pleasant really.'[45]

Another British woman remembered the Americans as 'cheeky compared to . . . Mr Frigidaire Englishman', adding that it was a boost to the ego to be 'greeted with "Hello, Duchess" (and you were treated like one) or "Hi, Beautiful"'.[46]

The generosity of the Americans with chocolates, cigarettes and nylons became proverbial – one GI bride was wooed more prosaically with bacon because her husband knew the cook on the base. Earning around £750 a year, the American private was a rich man compared to his British equivalent, who got less than £100. There was a certain bewilderment on both sides in the encounter between the two cultures.

'It was rather pleasant, really': American troops meet British women members of the Auxiliary Fire Service, 1942.

In an effort to smooth the way, NAAFI canteen workers were told by the military authorities that Americans thought the British were stand-offish and that they should not snub them when addressed with terms like 'Hiya, Baby!' as such phrases were a 'normal conversational opening' in the United States and should be interpreted as 'Lovely day, isn't it?'[47]

The GIs in their turn were extremely puzzled by the British custom of making love standing up, fully clothed, in dark side streets or parks – there was a common belief that you could not become pregnant upright. The problems came about because of the Americans' upfront persistent courting methods and refusal to take 'no' for an answer, which led to complaints of sexual molestation. Margaret Mead was sent over to apply her knowledge as an anthropologist to the clash in sexual attitudes. She concluded that British girls had little experience of the dating and flirting to which Americans were accustomed from their school days. But the Americans were not doing all the pursuing; they were themselves being hunted by some British women, including freelance prostitutes the Piccadilly Warriors, who made a beeline for lonely GIs. Regardless of cultural incomprehension, many lasting romances blossomed too and 20,000 British women were to apply to become GI brides after the war. Others waited for men who never returned: Dawn Yardy, for example, was engaged to Stewart Koger, a Choctaw Indian corporal, who died in the Normandy invasion.

The most serious conflict occurred between the GIs themselves, because British women went out with black American troops. Fights started between white and black GIs when a black sailor kissed a white girl at the station in Manchester in 1944. British hotels responded by banning all black men, including West Indians resident in Britain. In September 1945, when black American troops were to leave for home, women lined their camp, singing, 'Don't fence me in'.[48] The local police were called to defend the men but, declining the protection, they broke out of camp and the military police had to be called. Barbara Cartland, who was working as a WAAF moral adviser, was adamant that it was 'the white women who ran after the black troops not vice versa'.[49]

Sex came out into the open during the war as something to joke about: 'She'll be wearing khaki issue when she comes', 'Up with the lark, to bed with a Wren.' But it also became public in ways which fostered old fears and prejudices. Propaganda about VD generated terror and the persistent rumours of sexual promiscuity in the women's forces maintained the double standard of morality by blaming the women. In 1941 Edith Summerskill and Violet Markham investigated these accusations by touring 123 military camps and interviewing thousands of servicewomen; their resulting report dismissed charges of immorality. In fact, VD and illegitimacy rates were lower in the Auxiliary Territorial Service than among comparable groups of civilians in 1942. The pervasive double standard towards male and female sexuality also meant the women had to deal with unwanted sexual advances which could sometimes become violent assaults in a cultural climate which was indulgent towards the men and severe on the women. Even pin-ups like Clark Gable, Tyrone Power and Erroll Flynn were banned by ATS officers, while the scantily clad female pin-ups were accepted in the male forces.

Life in the women's forces resulted in a wider recognition of lesbian sexuality. Jean Mormont expressed a live-and-let-live attitude because of her time in the ATS:

I never knew what a lesbian was and I met some girls in there and it used to puzzle me, I couldn't make it out – you know, till I was told, like, you know, by the other girls, what it was about. I thought to myself, well, you're learning all the time . . . good job me mother don't know . . . they used to lay on the bed cuddling one another . . . You know, after a while you just don't take any notice. It's their way of life, and that's it. They don't interfere with you, or they don't try it on me. I didn't mind.[50]

If women were caught, however, they were dismissed. One young working-class ATS member, Joan Stewart, was mystified to hear that two girls were 'about to be thrown out of the army because "they had been found in bed together"'.[51] Sharing beds had been a feature of her childhood because of overcrowding: 'To me a single bed was paradise.'[52]

The war did affect sexual attitudes. Encounters had a random intensity and wartime circumstances made for flux. Men proposed sex sooner, but they also proposed more often. If death was arbitrary, so was life. John Costello quotes one housewife as saying, 'We were not really immoral, there was a war on.'[53] The numbers of illegitimate births rose;

in 1945 they were 9.1 per cent of total births, double the rate before the war. However, Martin Pugh points out that the figures are somewhat misleading: around one-third of mothers conceived 'out of wedlock'[54] during the 1930s, but most of them married later. Because the war delayed marriages, the figures were inflated.

The popular perception of the unmarried mother was a delinquent teenager, but, as John Costello shows, 'The highest recorded rate of illegitimate births was *not* among teenage girls but among women between twenty and thirty.'[55] The moral panic about teenage girls was about social control as much as about sex. In the first three years of the war there was a 100 per cent increase in girls 'in need of care and attention'.[56] One east London magistrate blamed 'jungle rhythms . . . and slushy movies'.[57] Other explanations were the absence of fathers, working mothers, evacuation and, of course, GIs. In 1942 Herbert Morrison was concerned about 'the procreation of half-caste children' and rumours that British wives and daughters were being 'debauched by American coloured troops'.[58] Meanwhile, a Home Office study concluded in 1943: 'To girls brought up on the cinema who copied the dress, hairstyles, and manners of Hollywood stars, the sudden influx of Americans speaking like the films who actually lived in the magic country and who had plenty of money at once went to the girls' heads.'[59]

There was outrage when 'the Radio Doctor', Charles Hill, interviewed a group of teenagers about sex and one girl broke into the discussion to declare, 'Sexual intercourse before marriage would be wrong if it's just anyone. If it's the chap you're going to marry that's different. It isn't quite right but it isn't exactly wrong.'[60] Such reflections were a sign of things to come.

The Post-war Era

A desire for social justice and a sense of hope permeated British society as the war was ending. In 1944 in *The Journey Home Report*, Mass-Observation noted that these aspirations for change were tinged with fear that there would be a return to the poverty of the 1930s. A cartoon by Zec in the *Daily Mirror* on 5 June 1945 showed a potbellied man in a top hat promising 'Better homes' and 'full employment' in 'Slum Street', while a working-class mother points him out to her young son, saying, in the words of a popular comedian, Tommy Handley, 'It's That Man Again.'[61]

Mrs Jean Hanson wrote to the paper on the same day, expressing a common sentiment:

I am a married woman with a family of three. I shall vote Labour because I believe it will be best for my family. We shall never cease to thank and praise Mr Churchill for seeing us through the dark years of the war, but neither we nor our children can exist on gratitude.[62]

Naomi Mitchison heard the news of Labour's victory in Kettering, Northamptonshire, where her husband, Dick Mitchison, had just defeated the Conservative John Profumo. Back in Carradale, she tempered her delight on 31 July 1945 in the diary she kept for Mass-Observation with the comment, 'I'm afraid this isn't exactly socialism in our time yet.'[63] Still, a broad faith that a better society was in the making was widespread. The Women's Institute adopted the hymn 'Jerusalem' as its anthem, while Betty Harrison, a Communist trade unionist in the tobacco industry, recalled that left-wingers in the labour movement 'had such feelings of a new beginning – almost a new world in 1945 when Labour was elected'.[64]

Some dreams were more modest. Zelma Katin, who had been a bus conductress, mainly looked forward to a rest, writing in her book, *Clippie*, in 1944, 'I want to lie in bed until eight o'clock, to eat a meal slowly, to sweep the floors when they are dirty, to sit in front of the fire, to walk on the hills, to go shopping of an afternoon, to gossip at odd minutes.'[65]

There was a powerful longing for personal life and space to do everything which had been impossible during the war, including going on holiday. The baby boom of 1946–8 and the continuation of the wartime trend to marry young took some women happily out of the labour force. But there were those who wanted to carry on: for example, Barbara Davies, who had been a weaver in Mytholmroyd, West Yorkshire, before the war and had moved to Armstrong Whitworth's aircraft factory in Coventry. Like many women who had experienced the pay and conditions of wartime employment, she did not want to return to the northern textile factories. But she remembered the union representative finding the women 'quite an embarrassment'.[66]

There were shortages of labour in some industries so the move into paid employment was not completely reversed. The cotton, rayon and nylon industries were keen to recruit women, and there were vacancies in the Women's Land Army, in nursing, midwifery and teaching. The numbers of clerical and administrative workers continued to grow and the light-engineering factories in the South-East employed more women. By 1948 there were actually 350,000 more insured women workers than there had been in 1939.

The demand for labour led to some old regulations and restrictions being waived. Women doctors tended to continue in their professions regardless of whether they were married or not. Marguerite Morgan, a mother of three small children in Coventry, was recruited as a primary school teacher by her son's desperate headmistress, who had more than ninety children to educate and only one seventeen-year-old assistant. She was later to train as a teacher. However, prominent figures in science and business or public corporations were rarely female. Among the exceptions were Dorothy Hodgkin, who worked on penicillin and vitamin B_{12} and was made a Fellow of the Royal Society in 1946, and Pauline Gower, the aviatrix from the Air Transport Auxiliary, who became the first woman to serve on the board of a state airline, the British Overseas Airways Corporation, before her early death giving birth to twins in 1947.

The campaign for equal pay was renewed with cross-party support, propagandizing not only with leaflets and meetings but with the film *To be a Woman* (1949), made by one of the few women film-makers, Jill Craigie. Pressure from parliamentary feminists resulted in the 1944 Royal Commission on Equal Pay being set up. Among those who gave evidence was Joan Robinson, the left Keynesian economist, who observed that women's earnings were likely to be lower than men's anyway because of childbirth and child-care. She said there was no 'economic justification for adding artificial handicaps to the natural one' and warned the Commission that 'cheap labour tends to be wasted like salt on the side of a dinner plate'.[67] However, this was an aspect of Keynesian economics which did not prove acceptable to the majority on the Commission, who decided that women were of an inferior value to employers because of lower efficiency. Minority dissenters were Janet Vaughan, Dame Anne Loughlin and Miss Lucy Nettleford. In 1945 women in the civil service and local government did receive equal pay in some grades, but the Labour government's pay freeze in 1948 prevented its extension in the public sector. So though the post-war demand for labour brought women back into the workforce, most of them were offered only low-paid jobs. Thus when the demand for women's labour was at its highest in 1948, women's wages fell from 53 to 45 per cent of the men's rates.

When Geoffrey Thomas conducted a survey in 1947 of 2,807 women, he found that the majority did not feel they could do paid work if it interfered with their domestic lives. He concluded that appeals to married women to ease the labour shortage were not going to be successful unless some 'practical steps were taken to deal with the problems that face them'.[68] Once again the dilemma about woman's role was being raised. Was she to be regarded as a producer or a reproducer? Was she a citizen mother or simply a human being who happened to be female? The trade unionist Ethel Chipchase, from the Railway Clerks, argued against the grain in 1947 that housewives as well as women in paid work should have the choice of a nursery place, but the Ministry of Labour saw nurseries simply as an adjunct of production, and by the late 1940s trade union women had narrowed the terms of their defence to these economic grounds. The government's determination to make local authorities pay for nurseries resulted in cuts despite demonstrations and an occupation in a Yorkshire nursery. Similar contradictions were evident in other areas of state policy: the National Insurance Act of 1946, for example, assumed that married women in paid employment were necessarily dependants; if they chose to pay contributions they received lower benefit. Despite the Women's Co-operative Guild's efforts to assert that unpaid mothers and homemakers were productive workers, they were insured only through their husbands, not in their own right.

The Women's Co-operative Guild argued for community-based reforms to meet the needs of mothers. Their demands included the continuation of wartime nurseries until better replacements could be built, more maternity and child-welfare clinics, a national maternity service, family allowances, pensions for married women and better public housing. They had not lost the Utopian vision of the inter-war years; a resolution at the Congress in 1946 called for electric washing machines to be provided for all new houses for families, with the cost included in the rent.

Labour women like Ellen Wilkinson and Jennie Lee (elected again as an MP in 1945 and married to the formidable Minister of Health Nye Bevan) were inclined to see general improvements in housing, education and health as the best means of tackling women's problems. Pressure for improved family welfare came from an influential middle-class lobby who advocated nurseries and after-school play centres on the grounds that they would educate mothers and children. Holidays paid for by social services for poor families, family tickets on trains, family holiday camps, and rest homes for tired housewives were being proposed. Ideas of transforming domestic architecture, communal restaurants and laundries were revived and washing machines on hire purchase were suggested. The conviction that the family was the key to a better society survived the war. In Denise Riley's words, 'Family health was a building block in the edifice of national health, spiritual and physical.'[69]

William Beveridge, whose plan for welfare systematized and extended wartime reforms, shared this concern about the well-being of the family. He also recognized the importance of domestic activity in the economy. He said that married women were 'occupied on work which is vital but unpaid, without which their husbands could not do their paid work and without which the nation could not continue'.[70] His welfare system, which aimed to provide security and alleviate poverty, had its origins in a cross-party consensus for reconstruction which had coalesced during the war. The coalition government passed the Family Allowances Act just before Labour took power in 1945 and established a 5s. allowance for every child after the first. This was not a large sum and was regarded with some suspicion by male workers as a bribe to increase the birth-rate: 'The wife said she wasn't going to have a baby for five bob a week.'[71] It was also seen as a way of preventing inflationary wage claims and gained some Conservative support on this basis. Eleanor Rathbone continued to argue that family allowances should enable the woman to be independent, but this was not how they were seen in the Beveridge plan. He personally believed that benefits should be paid only to divorced and separated wives if they were the innocent parties and he did not provide for unsupported mothers. He set a special maternity benefit at 50 per cent higher than unemployment and disability benefit to offset the lower rates paid to women; this was introduced in 1948 but reduced in 1953. His conviction that 'in the next thirty years housewives as mothers have vital work to do in ensuring the adequate continuance of the British race and of the British ideal in the world'[72] gave priority to women as reproducers within an organic view of the family. Despite the gain of family allowances and maternity benefit, the structure of the welfare state was based on the assumption of women's dependence on the man in the family rather than on women's rights as individuals.

It also retained many of the old structures of authority and deference. Margaret Powell, a former domestic servant, describes in her autobiography, *Climbing the Stairs*, how the National Health Service, introduced by Bevan in 1948, improved conditions for patients, but observes:

There was only one thing that was exactly the same and I suppose always will be and that is that neither nurses, house surgeons nor the visiting specialists would ever answer any questions about your condition. In fact they never stayed long enough by your bed for you to get the question out.[73]

The socialist commonwealth, cobbled together by Labour amidst post-war scarcity, established the values of collectivity, responsibility and security – no mean feat in the context of what had gone before. Direct democracy, still advocated by thinkers like G. D. H. Cole, was pushed to the sidelines, to erupt under the pressure of circumstance with varying political repercussions. Lillian Thring, the former campaigner for the unemployed, supported homeless squatters in Ashington in Essex, for instance. Food shortages and queues continued even though the government abolished purchase tax on household goods in 1946 and reduced the prices of basic foods through subsidies. The right-wing Housewives' League campaigned against Labour over food and fuel shortages and lack of consumer choice – a cause the Conservative Party espoused with enthusiasm. Continuity with the 1930s is evident, despite the war and the changes introduced by Labour; the new Britain of Beveridge was also one of booming building societies and the return of the Ideal Homes Exhibition.

Though the divorce rate soared after the war and illegitimacy peaked, the sexual disintegration which some moralists feared did not occur. Barbara Cartland, having switched to counselling men who had returned from the war to find their wives pregnant by another man, advocated pragmatism and adjustment: 'At first they swore that as soon as it was born it would have to be adopted, then sometimes they would say, half-shamefaced at their generosity, "The poor little devil can't help itself, and after all, it's one of hers, isn't it?"'[74]

The introduction of social welfare coincided with anxiety about the disruption of family life caused by the war. The 'problem family', first noted as an explicit social category in the 1930s, had been confirmed by the studies of evacuees, when working-class children's conditions had become more visible to middle-class investigators. The Eugenics Education Society took the conservative position that inadequate mothering was a result of inherited low intelligence. A more liberal attitude was that of the Women's Group on Public Welfare, who argued the need to educate mothers in their report *The Neglected Child and His Family* in 1948. Jane Lewis describes how psychology was influencing social workers and laying the basis for attitudes which were to become predominant during the 1950s: 'The cause of family failure was thus still conceptualized at the individual level, not as moral failure leading to pauperism, as in the nineteenth century, but as personal failure to achieve mature personalities and relationships.'[75]

The psychological defence of the rights of children, and the emphasis on affectionate care and personal interaction which replaced the regimented theories of child-rearing, were being popularized in Dr Benjamin Spock's *Baby and Child Care*, published in Britain in 1947. Also crossing the Atlantic were theories which stressed the importance of the mother in early childhood. These were to increase the emphasis on the responsibility of mothers in the family, and as the nurseries closed this came to mean the mother as full-time carer.

There were a defiant few who were not pro-natally inclined. The women sleuths in Nancy Spain's detective story *Poison for Teacher* (1949), set in a girls' school, Radcliff Hall, disliked children and regarded schoolgirls as a potentially sinister force. Nancy Spain, who had been a Wren, resolved shortly after the war 'that I didn't want to meet *anyone* who would make me put on a skirt'.[76]

'Do you do as you like?' enquired problem pupil Julia Bracewood-Smith of sleuth Miriam Birdseye.
'Er – yes,' said Miriam. 'Yes, I do.'[77]

248

After a decade of doing one's bit, the inclination to do as one liked appeared all the more enticing. It was glimpsed on the flickering screen in the plush, exotic cinemas which transported the viewer from austerity to Hollywood, and in Dior's famous long-skirted New Look – which, as Lou Taylor points out in Juliet Ash and Elizabeth Wilson's *Chic Thrills*, was not so new but an adaptation of the narrow waists and full skirts produced by French couturiers for the wives and mistresses of the occupying Germans. Longings for individuality, for rest, for leisure, for baby-sitting, for glamour, adventure and Ideal Homes were evident in the late 1940s. The 1950s had already begun.

THE UNITED STATES

Wartime Image

A cover girl with a difference appeared on the front of the *Saturday Evening Post* in May 1943 – Rosie the Riveter. Norman Rockwell's picture of Rosie presents a confident, broad-shouldered figure with muscular arms, eating her lunch. Rosie, the woman war worker, has her goggles on her brow, her nose in the air, a large phallic riveting tool on her lap and a copy of Hitler's *Mein Kampf* beneath her feet. The backdrop is the Stars and Stripes. Melissa Dubakis compares the 'monumentality and power' in the design to 'Michelangelo's andro-gynous figures'.[78] The image differs from the monumental style of the 'manly'[79] art of the 1930s because there are touches of frivolity – ROSIE written on the lunch box and the line of merit buttons across her breast.

Rosie's face conveys a multiplicity of meanings: 'I'm a cat's whiskers war worker', 'I am not amused', 'I am not sexually available' are all there on the surface. But Rosie's Irish pink-cheeked country-girl look has an expression of spiritual dedication which is in contrast to her earthy, sensual being. Rosie is both of the people and yet made excep-tional through sacrifice; a quasi-religious symbol, she transcends gender. However, Melissa Dubakis suggests that this is temporary; the riveting tool lies in her lap like the infant in Michelangelo's *Pietà*. The hint is

Rosie the Riveter by Norman
Rockwell.

there that Rosie's tryst with production could be ended with the return
of normal life.

Other less complex Rosie images also juxtaposed the power to do
hard and heavy work with a reassuring femininity. The 'We Can Do
It' poster produced by the War Production Co-ordinating Committee
again has a woman with muscular arms clenching her fist, but this manly
gesture is belied by the glamour of her make-up. The recruitment
poster for the US Crop Corps, CALL TO FARMS, showed a slender,
willowy young woman giving a V-sign for Victory, dressed in a figure-
hugging boiler suit and driving an enormous tractor.

'Rosie the Riveter' found her way into several songs which became
popular on the radio. Rosie, whose boyfriend Charlie was in the
Marines, could be relied upon to keep 'a sharp look-out for sabotage/
Sitting up there on the fuselage'. She featured in a Broadway play and
women war workers were glamorized in films like *Meet the People*
(1944), in which Lucille Ball played a defence plant worker, and *Since
You Went Away* (1944), which presented Claudette Colbert as a welder.
Even 'Stella Dallas' took a defence job.

Women's difference was deliberately enhanced in the new definition of female identity. Translated into a male sphere of machinery and military accoutrements, glamour distinguished wartime women and the temporary sacrifice of service to country covered the underlying maternal dedication of self. Propaganda did, however, shift gender norms by defining female virtue through public activity. Working-class women appeared in a new visual idiom of power and skill, no longer simply the helpless victims of exploitation portrayed in the photography of the progressive era. This was the white working-class woman ennobled as patriot – there was no black metaphor equivalent to Rosie. But individual images of black women as welders and air-craft mechanics made an appearance in the documentary photography and newsreels which flourished during the war.

The photographers from the Army's First Motion Picture Unit were known as 'shutterbugs' and contrived, when they could, to combine commercial work with patriotic duty. David Conover, an army corporal, told one attractive young war worker at Radiophone Co. in Los Angeles who posed happily for the delighted shutterbugs that she should become a model. An excited Norma Jeane, who was folding parachutes for the minimum wage of $20 for a sixty-hour week, wrote to her mother, telling her that he had said 'I photographed well and that he wants to take more'.[80] And so he did – the first pictures of the future Marilyn Monroe as a model.

Politics

For the first time in her life, Juanita Loveless was in demand. She had moved to California and got a job at Kreager Oil Company when America entered the Second World War in 1941. 'Newspapers, just splashed everywhere: "Help Wanted", "Help Wanted", "Jobs", "Jobs", "Jobs",' she recalled. 'Propaganda on every radio station: "If you're an American citizen, come to gate so-and-so . . ."'[81]

The Roosevelt administration moved from the New Deal of the 1930s into a popular social patriotism. With the country geared to war, Roosevelt sought to persuade Americans that freedom, prosperity and security could be achieved only through sacrifice. Ostensibly this was an appeal to all American citizens. Nonetheless, despite the need for women to be mobilized in the war effort, there was the predictable ambivalence about gender roles in state policy. The desperate need for labour set one agenda. After women who were already employed shifted into defence work, high-school graduates were targeted. Patriotism combined with glamour was the message from the government and the media. However, by 1943, even with the disabled, high-school students and businessmen doing their four-hour victory shifts, it had become clear that the demand for labour was not being met. Accordingly, determined attempts were made to persuade the Mrs Stay-at-Homes to take on full-time jobs. As a result, by 1944 one in three women defence workers had previously been a full-time homemaker and around 2,770,000 mothers of 4,460,000 children were in paid employment, many of them combining full-time work with domestic responsibilities.

The shift into the paid labour force was made despite the opposition of the majority of married men, who did not want their wives in defence work, and also in the face of considerable lack of enthusiasm among

Jessie Ward, Natalie Donaldson, Vera Campbell, Verneal Austin and Glendora Moore, leaving for army training at Fort Des Moines, Iowa, 1942.

many women, who thought they could best help the war effort by doing what they were already doing. Not surprisingly, mothers of young children were particularly reluctant. The demand for labour, combined with the fact that many mothers needed the wages, did, however, bring significant numbers of women into paid employment. The problem of child-care was thus brought out into the open as a public issue. At first the government tried, with varying degrees of success, to get local communities to arrange child-care. Lack of provision resulted in a high level of absenteeism and latchkey children, causing sociologists to warn of a post-war generation of juvenile delinquents. Eventually, in 1943, federal funds were made available through the Lanham Act. Nonetheless, the majority of women had to make private arrangements.

A major difficulty was the division among policy-makers over child-care. General Louis McSherry at the War Production Board stated that 'adequate facilities for the care of children of working mothers'[82] were a priority, but the Children's Bureau argued that a mother should see the home and children as her first responsibility. Their concern to protect women meant that they lost control over nursery provision, while wartime public day-care acquired a 'relief image'[83] which strengthened popular prejudice against it. The model child-care centre at the Kaiser shipbuilding company on the north-west coast showed what could be done. Parents could leave the children as they went to work in the yards and collect them at the end of the shift. This flexible nursery was, moreover, run by child-care workers who believed in the benefits of interaction between young children. A crucial element was cost, since replacing women's unpaid labour adequately was expensive. Karen Skold describes the ingenious system of funding: the cost 'was absorbed by the Maritime Commission when it purchased the ships'.[84] However, by mid-1944 child-care centres served only around 140,000 children and, as in Britain, private arrangements were still the norm.

The demand for equality was given a boost as the National War Labor Board authorized employers to put women's rates up to allow equal pay 'for work of comparable quantity or quality on the same or similar operations'. But it did not alter the female rates and firms varied considerably in the extent to which they complied. In 1943 the General Federation of Women's Clubs, the National Association of Women Lawyers and the National Federation of Business and Professional

Women's Clubs introduced a new version of the Equal Rights Amendment (ERA) to Congress: 'Equality of rights under the law shall not be denied or abridged by the United States or any state on account of sex.'[85]

The old battle was resumed between those who argued that women required special protections and those, like Alma Lutz, who asked, 'Are women an integral part of a democratic government or are they a class apart, unfit for the rights and freedom that apply to them?'[86] Though the ERA was to founder in the House Judiciary Committee, it had received a much broader range of support and was no longer a demand confined to the National Women's Party. One advocate was the artist Georgia O'Keeffe, who wrote to Eleanor Roosevelt, 'I wish you could be with us in this fight – you could be a real help to this change that must come.'[87] For her the ERA was connected to 'the idea of true democracy – to my country – and to the world eventually – that all men and women stand equal under the sky'; it was also about changing 'the girl child's idea of her place in the world'.[88]

Fear that the war would indeed change women's expectations was voiced when Congresswoman Edith Nourse Rogers, who had served in France as a civilian auxiliary in the First World War, introduced a bill to establish the Women's Auxiliary Army Corps (WAAC). One Senator asked, 'Who will then do the cooking, the washing, the mending, the humble homely tasks to which every woman has devoted herself. Think of the humiliation! What has become of the manhood of America?'[89]

Women mobilized by the Women's League of Defense and other voluntary groups were pressing President Roosevelt to take action, but nostalgia for a world where girls were girls and boys were boys was shared by many Americans. As one GI put it, if women entered the military, 'we would throw away our own self-respect – our right to pledge in earnestness to "Love, Honor, and Protect" the girls we want to marry'.[90]

The WAAC bill was defeated by a narrow margin in 1942, but Jacqueline Cochran, back from providing American women recruits for the British, formed the WASPs (Women's Auxiliary Service Pilots) with Nancy Harkness Love, a pilot who had ferried planes for both the British and the Canadians. The navy bill also got through with Eleanor

Roosevelt's help and WAVES (Women Appointed for Voluntary Emergency Service) was created. 'They'll be sending us dogs next,'[91] grumbled a recalcitrant Marine on hearing that there was to be a Women's Reserve for the Marines. But women Marines there were, along with Coast Guards (SPARS), and finally the army got its WAACs, headed by Oveta Culp Hobby, a newspaper executive lawyer and mother of two. Nicknamed 'Doughgirl Generalissimo' by the press, her skill in cutting through red tape soon 'earned her the accolade Spark Plugs,'[92] according to John Costello.

Her first battle was with army chiefs over the design of the uniform. They wanted the women to be clearly differentiated from the soldiers; on the other hand, they would make no concessions to feminine

Delivery pilots, 1943.

frippery. Oveta Culp Hobby got the WAACs into army colours, but the uniform was an unsatisfactory compromise. Meanwhile, the WAVES had commissioned a New York fashion house which made clothes for the Duchess of Windsor and Hollywood stars to create theirs. The distinction persisted and, as in Britain, navy women acquired a superior status to those in the army.

Mobilization

'You have taken off silk and put on khaki,' Director Hobby told the new recruits to the WAAC, 'all for essentially the same reason – you have a debt and a date. A debt to democracy, a date with destiny.'[93]

The WAACs, who, like their British counterparts, had impressed their military trainers with their capacity to drill, were initially mainly college-educated. They joined out of a mixture of motives, among which the desire to escape from unhappy homes and boring jobs and to find adventure was more common than patriotism. Disillusionment with military discipline and spartan conditions was soon to lead many to wonder whether taking off silk had been such a good idea after all. Those who stuck it out sang:

> Hats and shoes and skirts don't fit,
> Your girdle bunches when you sit,
> Come on, rookie, you can't quit.
> Just heave a sigh, and be GI.[94]

However, large numbers voted with their feet and went AWOL, until the WAAC became the WAC, the Women's Army Corps, and so subject to military discipline. In contrast to Britain, conscription of women was rejected as politically impossible and instead an advertising campaign was launched to glamorize the women's forces. When this was a disastrous failure, the educational requirements for recruits were lowered and the press seized on cases of prostitutes, alcoholics and a would-be WAC who thought that she was the Duchess of Windsor. Director Hobby made sure that the original educational standards were reimposed.

An unintended consequence of the need to attract women into the forces was that the latter became protected spaces for lesbianism. The authorities tolerated lesbian relationships because they did not affect military discipline and because male officers found it difficult to see sex between women as real sex. The main concern was to avoid scandal. Racism, however, remained entrenched in the military as a whole. The 4,000 African-American women who served in the WAC were invariably doing kitchen work and were unlikely to be sent overseas. They were kept in segregated barracks, mess halls and recreation places. The fifty-six black nurses in the Army Nurse Corps were initially allowed to look after only black patients. WAVES remained white until Roosevelt instructed the admittance of black women in 1944; less than 100 were affected, though, because the war had nearly ended. A few Japanese-Americans and Native Americans joined the WAC, among them Grace Thorpe, a member of the Sauk-Fox tribe, who went to New Guinea and was selected as one of General MacArthur's staff members at his headquarters in Japan.

While some generals saw women simply as clerical workers, others, like Eisenhower, who had been impressed with women in the British services, were prepared to innovate. He introduced women auxiliaries in his campaign headquarters while Commander-in-Chief of the Allied landings in North Africa. WACs also served in Sicily and Italy, and worked with British women in the D-Day preparations. They proved themselves to be particularly skilled as photo-interpreters and, along with army nurses, faced bombing and the danger of diseases.

The generals might have come round, but many of their officers remained unconvinced. The director of WAVES, Captain Mildred MacAffee, observed, 'The military services are so conspicuously a man's world that the appearance of women therein was startling . . . The surprise of men at the accomplishment of women was not flattering, but it was fun.'[95]

Farmers, especially in the Midwest, where, unlike the South, it was not customary to employ black, Hispanic and Asian women, were equally sceptical about the Women's Land Army, founded by Florence L. Hall. They were reluctant to trust women – and strange women at that – with expensive machinery. Farmers' wives proposed that Land Army volunteers should do their housework so that they could drive the tractors and much of the extra labour eventually was to be provided by family members. One South Dakota woman who was putting in fourteen- and fifteen-hour days grumbled that, 'if it wasn't for all this home-front work . . . I too could apply for an outside defense job and earn big money'.[96]

Work

'War is hell,' Mark Leff remarks, 'but for millions of Americans on the booming home front World War II was also a hell of a war . . . The politics set in motion by a peculiar blend of profits and patriotism, of sacrifice and unprecedented prosperity, gave a distinctive cast to American wartime life.'[97]

The war presented women with opportunities to earn higher wages and to learn new skills. They became welders, electricians and ship-fitters. These were the Rosies who captured the popular imagination, like the rigger in the Portland, Oregon, shipyard who did the wiring up the fifty-foot masts of the Liberty ships. The historian Anne Firor Scott describes a very different consequence of war: the absence of the men created openings for young educated women in higher education. She enrolled in a Masters programme at Northwestern University in 1942 and then went to Washington as an intern in the National Institute of Public Affairs, a Rockefeller-funded scheme to bring young people into government. Her diary recorded a permanent feeling of guilt because she was finding fulfilment when others were making sacrifices. She was not alone. The number of women doing degrees in medicine and law doubled and increasing numbers of women went into engineering. Teachers and social workers moved out of the women's professions and into banks, insurance, businesses and administration. Lower down the social scale, there was a huge expansion of clerical employment. However, in *A Generation of Vipers* (1942), Philip Wylie lambasted career women and dominating mothers, and even in white-collar areas women were frequently paid less than men and gender still meant restricted job opportunities.

Work in the wartime defence industries did not automatically become available to African-Americans; only after marches and protests did firms start accepting black workers. Fanny Christina Hill, for instance, got a job at North American Aviation in Los Angeles in 1943 after the Negro Victory Committee had marched on the local employment office. Pressure from the United Auto Workers' Union and the local civil rights group meant there was a higher proportion of black workers in this plant than in others. Even so, she says that the employers 'did everything they could to keep you separated. They did not like for a Negro and a white person to get together and talk.'[98] Black women did, however, finally break into manufacturing industries as a result of the war.

Another group that contributed to the growing numbers in industry was older married women. They had already been moving into waged work during the Depression and the war merely accelerated the trend. Most women in defence work had already been employed, but even so Glenda Riley notes an increase of slightly more than 50 per cent of female workers between 1940 and 1945.

A new confidence in themselves as workers developed among women in wartime, despite male fears that standards would fall. As in Britain, there was a growth in unionization. Sara Evans writes, 'The number of organized women grew between 1940 and 1944 from 800,000 to 3 million and the female proportion of organized labor from 11 to 23 percent.'[99] There was also a dramatic increase in the number of women holding union jobs, while Elizabeth Faue notes a gender shift in trade union consciousness. The Congress of Industrial Organizations-affiliated United Electrical Workers' Union (UE) wooed women with an appeal to solidarity, sexuality and consumption. Betty Union, for example, needs a wage adjustment so she can dress well:

> The cost of stockings – WOW!
> The cost of clothes! WHY, HECK!
> If we don't get wage adjustments,
> I'm going to look a wreck.[100]

The idea of solidarity extended into daily life. Buying power became part of the trade union ethic; the appeal was not only to women as mothers or housewives. Trade unionism became sexy: 'Peggy O'Connor, thrifty and wise, wears union hosiery, has many guys.'[101]

American workers caught a glimpse of equality. Juanita Loveless testifies to an inchoate unorganized class consciousness towards the end of the war, when it became evident that there were people getting rich

without making the same sacrifices as the war workers had. 'The rumblings began with that – and the discontent. It raced through the plant, through the bowling alleys, through all the places where the young people got together.'[102]

Some divisions were challenged. Vicki L. Ruiz describes how the United Cannery, Agricultural, Packing and Allied Workers of America, a democratic union, managed to unite Mexicans, blacks and Anglos. A few trade union women were developing the idea of equal rights as a result of their wartime experience. The Women's Bureau in the United Automobile Workers' Union (UAW), formed in 1942 and headed by Lillian Hatcher, a black auto worker, was to play an important role in the struggle for equal rights after the war. Ruth Young, a leading organizer in the UE invoked Roosevelt's promise of freedom from want, in claiming the right to work for every man and woman who wished to do so. Women in the UE also questioned the historical division of labour which defined some jobs as male and others as female. The UAW Women's Bureau, at its conference in April 1945, discussed the need for job evaluation to analyse skills and experience so that different types of work could be compared. This approach to equal rights for women in the workplace was later to become known as comparable worth.

Very different messages were coming from the advertising industry, mobilized by Roosevelt to sell the war. The War Advertising Council co-ordinated private firms who were able to keep their brand names before the public while acquiring patriotic kudos. For example, the Eureka Company praised women war workers while saying that, when peace came, 'like you, Mrs America, Eureka will put aside its uniform and return to the ways of peace . . . building household appliances'.[103] The general message was a call to sacrifice in order to defend the 'American Way of Life', with the promise of abundance for consumers and no labour conflict after the war. Sacrifice had a particular gender twist; 'It's the *least* I can do for you, son,'[104] says the Munsingwear plant-worker mum to a young boy in a company advertisement.

Companies were preparing for peace before the war had ended. Westinghouse issued its 'Home Laundering Guide' in 1944, even though it did not have any automatic washing machines to sell: 'Some day soon . . . you'll be free from the drudgery of washday. Come "V" Day . . . the hard work of washing will be done for you . . . automatically in the new Westinghouse Laundromat.'[105]

Mrs Consumer was a key component in the free enterprise system.

Daily Life

The war did not impinge on daily life as it did in Britain. Two-thirds of American women remained at home, and unless a member of the family, a close friend or sweetheart was in the services, the war was a remote affair. Some did voluntary work – gardening, canning, collecting tin cans and selling war bonds – but for the majority war was part of the news, marked by a new character in a radio serial like the popular *Fibber McGee and Molly*. As Anne Firor Scott noted in her diary in 1941, 'private lives go on despite public disaster'.[106]

Wartime circumstances did, however, affect popular assumptions and indirectly contributed to new patterns of daily life. 'Can women in war industry be good mothers?' asked psychiatrist Dr Leslie Hohman in 1942, and went on to advocate a 'schedule' of household tasks and shared child-care between partners so that both parents could spend engaged time with their children in 'companionship'.[107] Suddenly women's time was of social significance. Though British restaurants were set up providing meals at 23c., there were more entrepreneurial innovations. One Detroit food company devised a menu of prepared food selling macaroni and cheese, spaghetti, chilli con carne, cod fish-balls, chicken à la king, chicken pies, potato salad and creamed spinach. Dorothy Roosevelt, who was responsible for women's problems on the Detroit War Production Board, was enthusiastic, saying in 1944, 'Through such a set-up we figure we could save a woman three hours a day – a minimum for shopping and preparing and cooking food.'[108] The early 1940s also saw the first frozen prepared food: Birds Eye produced baked beans and a Boston firm prepared the ubiquitous chicken à la king. By 1945 the W. L. Maxson Corporation had produced the first complete frozen dinners – they were bought up by the army for their planes. This new food technology emerged rapidly alongside a starkly contrasting domestic backwardness. In 1941 a third of all households were still cooking with wood or coal and many women were still relying on an outside source of water.

There was a wartime housing shortage in the areas where you could get high-paid war work. Young single women and black Southerners flocked into the Northern cities seeking jobs. Landladies preferred men to women, whom they regarded as 'more bother', and there was discrimination against blacks. Rents soared and inflation ate up the high wages. Urban riots broke out in Harlem, Detroit and twenty-five other cities in the summer of 1943 over jobs and housing. Fanny Christina Hill's solution was to room with her sister and another girl: 'We were accustomed to shacking up with each other. We had to live like that because that was the only way to survive . . . In the kitchen everybody had a little place . . . You had a spot in the icebox; one shelf was yours.'[109] She adapted to rationing: 'It taught me there's a lot of things you can get along without. I liked cornbread a lot, and we had to use Cream of Wheat, grits, to make cornbread. I found out I liked that just as well.'[110] Eventually she was to buy her own house with her sister because the landlady tried to raise the rent.

Some of the black Southern migrants moved into the housing left by Japanese-Americans, who were forced into relocation camps. Mrs Itsu Akiyama, from the Hood River Japanese community in Oregon, remembered how, when they were told they had six days to sell all their belongings before departure, 'There was a shortage of suitcases in Hood River, so we had to order them by mail.'[111] Mrs Misuyo Naka-mura's long-haired Scottie dog ran after the pick-up for a mile as they headed down the highway to the railway station, where they were herded on to the trains like 'cattle and swine'[112] for the long journey to the barbed-wired camp 1,000 miles away in the desert. Some 10,000 people lived in tar-paper barracks patrolled by guards. Private space had been appropri-ated and time hung heavy. Mrs Itsu Akiyama crocheted a large bedspread and tablecloth, but 'put it in a trunk because I had nowhere to display it'.[113] She struggled with the words of 'Should auld acquaintance be forgot' in a class. In another camp Teiko Tomita wrote poetry:

> Within the iron stockade
> Always composing poems
> From the sorrows of war
> A little consolation.[114]

Young Nisei – the generation brought up in the United States – faced a painful choice. They were eventually allowed to leave the camps to study or join the military. A hundred Nisei women became WACs, but they felt like deserters; the cost of wider opportunities resulted in a break with their families and communities. Many internees never recovered from the experience of the camps and retreated into a despairing stoicism they called '*Shikata-ganai*' (It is beyond control; it cannot be helped so accept it as it is).[115] The war imposed drastic changes upon Japanese-Americans; public disaster really did devour private life.

Sex

'Any funny business on the job, it'll be you who goes out like a light,'[116] warned Katherine Archibald's foreman at the Moore Dry Dock Company in Oakland. She was there studying the effect of war on women, blacks and chicanos and could refute at first hand the glamorous propaganda of the advertisers: 'Women guards stalked vigilantly through the warehouses, the workshops and the rest rooms looking for a coy curl unconfined by a bandanna, the bejeweled hand and the revealing sweater.'[117]

The women workers themselves policed dress style; though the clerical workers wore tight sweaters, short skirts or elegant black dresses, fashion did not go down well on the shop floor. Katherine Archibald observed ironically, 'Like soldiers infiltrating enemy lines, women in the shipyards had to be camouflaged lest the difference in sex be unduly noted and emphasized.'[118] Not only gender but class was at issue: among the industrial workers no one was going to pull rank and gain an unfair sexual advantage.

Dinah Shore's 1940 hit 'Yes, My Darling Daughter' had advised virtue as the best strategy. However, this assumed eager suitors. By 1943 *Good Housekeeping* was warning, 'Somebody's After Your Man'.

Pin-ups and Super-girls

The Second World War pin-ups had their origins in the French 'naughty postcards' popular with Allied troops in the First World War – 'Better than cheesecake,'[119] declared a New York editor. By the 1940s, the pin-ups had assumed stylized poses. Betty Grable, her million-dollar legs in shorts and high heels, with cleavage showing, was the classic. This was no Rosie but an image of femininity which, in John Costello's words, was 'untouched by war, work or ambition'.[120]

When Betty Grable got married, Darryl Zanuck of Twentieth Century Fox feared she would lose her position as number one pin-up, but instead GIs wrote to her husband asking for a wedding photo. The pin-up provided comfort and a nostalgia for peacetime normality, as well as the erotic suggestion of a sexuality just out of reach. The pictures were for dreaming – one showed a smiling woman having a bath in a soldier's helmet.

In contrast to the wholesome American-pie style of Betty Grable, Rita Hayworth and Jane Russell smouldered an impossible invitation to possess and presented a glamorous power with which women could identify. With looks like that, you could surely get any man.

The allure of the wartime pin-up is in the tension between what is acceptable in the external moral code and what is unconscious and desired. The images both played with the yearning to return to life as normal and touched the profound rupture in social convention caused by war.

If the pin-up was about arousal, when the servicemen decorated their tanks and planes they created icons of the male orgasm. These were representations of sexual power which mixed pornography with the comic-strip super-girls surfacing from the early 1940s. Wonder Woman, for example, first appeared in *All Star Comic* in December 1941. She was devised by psychologist William Moulton Marston as an alternative to the tough-guy heroes in comics. She can fight, but like Batman and Superman, she can also reform. As a member of the Justice League of America, she was to monitor the American way of life and protect it against the enemy within and without during the Cold War. Mary Cadogan describes her as both 'the most voluptuous of sex objects' and

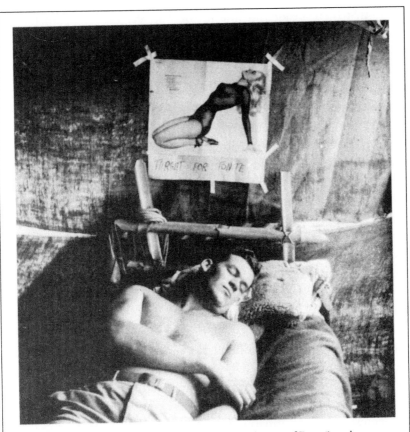

Dreaming in Darwin: Flying Captain R. N. Skipper of B-24 Squadron
takes a nap while stationed in Australia, 1943.

also 'multi-faceted and always evolving', contriving at the same time to
be Amazonian and all-American.[121] Miss 'Black' Fury also made her first
appearance in 1941 as a newspaper comic strip, illustrated by a woman,
Tarpe Mills. Like Wonder Woman, she is a fearless redresser of wrong;
indeed, Miss Fury was so dedicated to democracy that she would wield
the lash, whips and branding irons in its defence.

Now that men 'headed up the list of war scarcities'[122] women were doing the hunting – even the hijacking. Women were warned how to spot 'man-stealers'[123] in the guise of the Vamp, the Pal, Big Sad Eyes and the Button-Twister. Before the war women college students had been in a sought-after minority; now the ratio was reversed. *Esquire* magazine published a cartoon with a fainting coed and a dangling phone, captioned, 'Someone called her for a date'.[124] One consequence was a change in dating patterns. Young women college students who a few years earlier would have been part of the dating roundabout which defined popularity began to see 'going steady' as the ideal. And 'going steady' raised the sexual stakes. 'How far to go?' – a question that was to preoccupy sex advice manuals and columnists for the next two decades – came out into the open. The prevailing refrain was, 'Reprice your line. Limit the supply of yourself. Make yourself scarce and watch your value go up.'[125] This message from a teen advice column in 1942 echoed what had been said in the 1930s and was to be repeated up to the 1960s.

However, the assumption that women were able or willing to be the sexual restrainers was coming under pressure during wartime. An American committee which investigated VD among British service women recommended contraceptive advice for the WAACs, causing Director Hobby to assert that 'taboos and punitive measures' were the best deterrent; sex information would 'reflect an attitude towards sexual promiscuity that, whatever the practice, is not held by the majority of Americans. The army ... is no place to propagandize new social attitudes.'[126]

Rumours about the sexuality of women in the services abounded. The American public, like Katherine Archibald's foreman, apparently held women to be solely responsible for sex. Congresswoman Edith Nourse Rogers, on the other hand, was convinced the stories were Nazi plots, and Military Intelligence and the FBI were called in to investigate. They solemnly reported that the scandalmongers were military personnel, especially soldiers who had 'trouble getting dates', officers' wives and other quite ordinary folk, most of them with 'completely American backgrounds'.[127] Nonetheless, by September 1943 the army had changed its tune; WACs were not to be treated as 'inmates of some well-chaperoned young ladies' seminary'[128] any more but as army personnel. By 1945, they were getting sex advice which was very similar to the men's. The army had been forced to rubber-stamp 'new social attitudes' despite itself.

Pragmatism about priorities was applied to lesbian relations as well. When Eisenhower tried to get rid of lesbians in Sergeant Johnnie Phelps's battalion, she pointed out that they had had 'no illegal pregnancies, no cases of venereal disease',[129] that he had awarded good-service commendations and that it would mean losing all the file clerks, section heads, most of the commanders, with her own name at the top of the list. She says his response was brief: 'Forget the order.'[130] Lillian Faderman points out that the tolerance was 'because the military especially needed women who wanted to do work that was traditionally masculine'.[131]

The military were mainly concerned to prevent scandal. An inquiry was instituted at Fort Oglethorpe when the mother of a twenty-year-old WAC complained that she was being corrupted. The young WAC appeared unabashed by the army officers and frankly acknowledged that her experience was pleasurable: 'Well, while we were laying on the bed . . . she pulled my skirt off. She was kissing me and then she got down in front of the bed on her knees and started kissing me in the privates. Is that what you want, sir?'[132] An army psychiatrist pronounced, 'It is a sort of mutual masturbation, if you ask me.'[133] A few resignations and transfers followed and the file was buried.

The war brought into being a popular and visible lesbian culture which was no longer simply confined to artistic chic. When Mildred from upstate New York went harvesting with the Land Army she saw two women behaving amorously and another woman told her, 'It's called lesbianism. There's really nothing wrong with it.'[134] This was a revelation: 'For the first time I had a name for myself.'[135] Witnesses at Fort Oglethorpe reported codes and signals being used to identify sexual preference. This new sense of personal identity was accompanied by the development of a social milieu of clubs and hangouts. Lesbians were gathering at places like the If Club in Los Angeles and Monas in San Francisco. Rusty Brown, a civilian welder for the navy, remembers that butch and femme roles were strictly observed in these clubs; two butches did not dance together: 'Who was going to lead? We would both be dominant.'[136]

Lesbian and homosexual culture was not completely contained within the club scene, however. Juanita Loveless recalls hanging around with friends in Los Angeles, going to the bowling alleys, the movies and tea dances: 'Straight people became very friendly with homosexual people, more so the women.'[137] When some of her friends gave her *The Well of Loneliness*, she realized that they were 'different', but her memory of the war years was that 'we accepted people then'.[138] The emergence of a public space for working-class lesbians found an echo in mainstream fashion. Whereas Dietrich or Garbo wearing slacks had made headlines during the 1930s, Lillian Faderman notes that 'women who worked in war factory jobs during the early 1940s were actually obliged to wear pants [which were to] become a permanent part of American women's wardrobe'.[139] The *Minneapolis Tribune* had been worried in 1942 that WACs and WAVES and women welders would not want to tend the babies when 'the boys come marching home',[140] but the press in general found another gender shift even more perplexing. They had only just got over the teenage 'Victory girls' who sought casual sex with servicemen when a new female youth phenomenon appeared – the bobby-soxer. Some 30,000 of them rioted about a skinny 4F-classified young crooner called Frank Sinatra in 1944. Psychologists were mystified by the attraction of this new genus of masculinity.

The Aftermath

When the men came marching home, most Americans assumed that women were going to return to being housewives. Indeed, a substantial number of people thought women with husbands who could afford to support them should not be allowed to work. Most women workers, however, said they wanted to continue in paid employment and, having experienced well-paid jobs and learned new skills, resisted going back into 'women's work' in laundries or domestic service. Lola Weixel recalled that welding 'was a special thing. At the end of the day I always felt I accomplished something. There was something to be seen.'[141] For some, continuing paid work was a necessity: for example, Juanita Loveless, who was separated from her husband, took her small baby in a basket to the restaurant where she got a job as a waitress. Others really welcomed a temporary rest after struggling to care for children and work in wartime jobs.

The fan and the crooner: Frank Sinatra makes the
cover of *Movie Fan* magazine.

There were few organized protests. Women war workers had no
organization through which they could voice discontent collectively
and union support was patchy and variable. They did register their
preferences, however. The United States Employment Service had

nearly twice as many applications from women as men for semi-skilled and skilled jobs in manufacturing in 1946. At the 1946 United Auto Workers' Union convention women members challenged the classification of work by gender and the custom of dividing seniority lists into male and female, which had enabled firms to shed women workers. The UAW was to put up more of a fight on seniority rights than the United Electrical Workers' Union, but ultimately the post-war position of women in industry was decided not by the unions but by management's hiring policies. Ruth Milkman shows that in the electrical industry women were to be rehired in large numbers for lower-paid jobs; this was not the case in the auto industry, which reverted to its predominantly male workforce.

By 1950 women constituted 28.8 per cent of the labour force – only slightly below the percentage in wartime. They had simply shifted to lower-paid work in factories or to light-manufacturing or were absorbed by the growth in service and clerical employment. So the pre-war trend for married women to work was reasserted, but the effort to break down the division between male and female jobs was to prove much harder. This was true not only for the manual working class but also for professional women, as male competition and special educational provision for the returning GIs meant that their chances of rising were much smaller than they had been during the war. Women in technical and scientific employment faced similar obstacles.

The campaign for equality was no longer restricted to professional women's organizations, for the Women's Bureau became a permanent feature of the UAW Fair Practices and Anti-Discrimination Department. The UE News carried articles and interviews with women workers about workplace and domestic issues (some of them written by a young labour radical, Betty Goldstein, later to become well known as Betty Friedan). There was a rebellious spirit among rank and file workers, who responded to inflation with the largest strike wave in US history between 1945 and 1947. African-Americans who had helped to win the war against Fascism and for democracy were also in a confident mood and determined to fight racism at home. The arguments for equal opportunities were being made in terms of both race and gender. For instance, Ebony magazine, which started in 1945, advocated individual betterment but saw this as backing black women's employment. There was a strong feeling that, at least for the middle class in the North, opportunities were opening up. Even in the South, the fact that big capital would invest only if it could rely on law and order seemed to augur well for integration. Lena Horne, the singer and civil rights campaigner, was quoted in *Ebony* in 1945 as saying, 'This may be the first generation in the history of our race where Negro families will have something to leave their children.'[142]

The old opponents of equality, however, were also stirring. The war had hardly finished before the Red Menace was being rediscovered. America was soon in conflict with the Soviet Union's foreign policy for hegemony. A series of spy cases contributed to a change in attitude towards Communists within the US. In 1946 J. Edgar Hoover claimed that reds had penetrated the media and education; there were reports that the Ku Klux Klan were reorganizing and Joe McCarthy was elected as Senator for Wisconsin, along with a group of extreme right-wing Republicans.

By 1947 a conservative political and social climate had come to prevail. McCarthy, a blustering, opportunistic bully who had a gift for popularizing the politics of the extreme right, brought them from the margins to centre-stage in the period 1947–54. McCarthyism was an atmosphere of witch-hunt and terror rather than a coherent doctrine. Thousands of radicals were pursued and hundreds jailed in these anti-Communist purges, and among the casualties were the clerical workers' unions, in which women were particularly active and, in 1949, the UE, with its positive attitude to women recruits and support for pay equity.

McCarthyism also served as a means of dismantling the institutions and culture of the New Deal and blocking the move towards a welfare state. One of McCarthy's first successes was preventing extensive public housing being created by the Democratic leader, Harry Truman. Lining up with the powerful real-estate lobby, he denounced public housing as the breeding ground of Communism and said it caused broken homes, juvenile delinquency and divorce. A drinker, gambler and womanizer, Joe McCarthy was not exactly the moral right. Nonetheless, the McCarthyite era saw an assertion of repressive gender relations and extreme homophobia.

It was not just a matter of the growing power of McCarthy as an individual, but also the popular response he was able to manipulate and

Eleanor Roosevelt and the UN

Shortly after the death of her husband, Eleanor Roosevelt was telephoned by the new president, Harry Truman, and asked to be the American delegate at the first United Nations Assembly, which was to be held in London. Her first reaction was that she had no experience of foreign affairs. However, she was persuaded and set off on the *Queen Elizabeth* with the rest of the American delegation. She spent the voyage diligently reading the briefing material and, on reaching London, declined Lady Astor's invitation to visit Cliveden with the other delegates. She was welcomed by old friends like Lady Stella Reading, head of the Women's Voluntary Services.

Assigned to the committee which, because it dealt with humanitarian matters, was seen as relatively uncontroversial, she nonplussed the male delegates, who were intently engaged in a debate about procedure, by asking if she could bring her knitting. If the preliminary sessions were frustrating, she had plenty to do outside the Assembly, counselling GI brides, lunching with the Royal Family – 'nice people but so far removed from life'[143] – and, under pressure from former suffrage leader Lady Pethick-Lawrence, holding a meeting in her office to discuss how to get better representation for women in the UN. She was dubious about special women's groups, but observation of the male delegates convinced her that women could do as well – perhaps even better. 'I'm so glad I never *feel* important,' she remarked. 'It does complicate life.'[144]

Her committee, far from being low-key, became the site of a major row with the Soviet delegate, Vishinsky, over the rights of political refugees to asylum. He argued that such rights would enable Nazis to escape, while she pointed out that without them Spanish Republicans might have to return to Franco's Fascist regime. She won and, writing home, remarked how she had earned Dulles's back-handed compliment, 'When you were appointed I thought it terrible and now I think your work here has been fine,' concluding, 'So, against odds, the women inch forward – but I'm rather old to be carrying on this fight.'[145]

In January 1947 she made a crucial contribution to the debate on how human rights should be defined. In contrast to the socialists and social democrats, who tended to emphasize the collective at the expense of the individual, Eleanor Roosevelt insisted, 'It is not that you set the individual apart from society but that you recognize in any society that the individual must have rights that are guarded.'[146] The Americans were not enthusiastic about the economic and social rights which were supported by the Communists and by British socialists, but she managed to persuade them to accept this wider definition of rights in the draft. The format followed the American Declaration of Independence and an unexpected stumbling block occurred when the Indian delegate Hansa Mehta protested at the use of 'men' instead of 'people'.[147] Eleanor Roosevelt tried to persuade her that American women had never felt excluded by the word 'men', but Hansa Mehta was not convinced.[148]

The intransigence of the Soviets and the shift to the right which was occurring in the United States contributed to a decline in enthusiasm for the UN in the American media. Eleanor herself was coming under attack: the right-wing columnist Westbrook Pegler called her 'a coddler of Communists'[149] living on the tax-payer's money. In December 1948, however, the Declaration was accepted by the UN and, even though not a legally binding document, it was to become a reference point for international customary law.

'The first step has been taken,'[150] Eleanor Roosevelt wrote to Helen Keller.

the willingness of the Republicans to go along with his accusations for political gain, which made resistance difficult. In the Democratic Party too the alliances of the New Deal era had disintegrated. The liberal candidate Henry Wallace was defeated by Harry Truman in 1948 and Truman reacted defensively to red-baiting and to McCarthy. Old bogeys about the enemy within were revived with a vengeance when the Soviet Union exploded the atom bomb. In 1948 the leadership of the Communist Party was jailed. Among them was Claudia Jones, a Communist writer of Caribbean origin, accused of seeking to 'overthrow the government by force and violence'.[151] This onslaught from the right created an atmosphere of fear and isolated American leftists.

The absence of any effective political opposition to the right, from either the left or the centre, made ideology, culture and daily life assume a particular significance. Women's role became a metaphor for a broader contest about social values. In the media debate about whether or not women should have jobs it was really the desired shape of American society as a whole that was at issue. The emphasis on women's essential difference from men struck a deep chord in post-war America; after the long years of Depression and war, there was a profound yearning for an ideal of 'normal' life. When *Fortune* magazine polled its readers in 1949, 46 per cent declared that a college education should prepare women for marriage and the family; only 10 per cent thought this should also apply to men. An extreme example of hostility to a wider sphere for women which used psychological jargon to upbraid feminists as subversive neurotics was *The Modern Woman: The Lost Sex* by Marynia Farnham and Ferdinand Lundberg. Serialized in *The Ladies' Home Journal* in 1947, their diatribe had one positive result: it led Simone de Beauvoir to write her classic, *The Second Sex*. However, as Joanne Meyerowitz points out in 'Beyond the Feminine Mystique', their extreme case against women's emancipation was far from being the consensus. Farnham and Lundberg were fighting from a position on the extreme right of the spectrum.

Cultural attitudes to gender remained a contested area during the 1940s. Joanne Meyerowitz shows that media values were contradictory; while domesticity and femininity were being stressed, so was individual success in careers. Indeed, in this period when it seemed that private virtues ruled supreme, readers of *The Woman's Home Companion* in 1947 and 1949 elected as their most admired women Eleanor Roosevelt, Helen Keller, Sister Elizabeth Kenny (the Australian medical researcher who had developed heat treatment for polio, adopted in the United States in the early 1940s) and Clare Boothe Luce (conservative author and congresswoman).

Moreover, the ideology of domesticity never really took hold among black American women. Claudia Jones observed caustically in 1949 that it made no sense to talk about 'the Negro woman's place' being at home when 'Negro women are in other people's kitchens.'[152] *Ebony* did make the point that becoming a 'Mom'[153] was better than being Mammy and working for whites, but on the whole it celebrated black women's achievements in fields that had previously been closed to them: for example, law, medicine, engineering, pharmacy and businesses like estate agency.

Young black women were eagerly entering colleges in a period when many white women were either not continuing their education after high school or dropping out of their college courses. Mary McLeod Bethune wrote in 1947 of 'the great harvest that is now coming to the Negro womanhood'[154] and Paula Giddings hows that this moment of hope contributed to an extraordinary cultural renaissance. For example, Gwendolyn Brooks won the Pulitzer Prize in 1949 for her second volume of poetry, *Annie Allen*, while Ann Petry became a best-selling novelist with *The Street*. Pearl Primus, a Trinidadian dancer who had studied anthropology at Columbia, choreographed her own compositions, *Like Strange Fruit* and *Shendc*, in 1947, mixing contemporary racial issues with African dance. Black women excelled as musical performers in several fields. The concert singer Carol Brice was the first African-American to win the prestigious Naumberg Award. Along with Dorothy Maynor and Lillian Evanti, she followed Marian Anderson to fame in classical music. A new sophistication and complex artistry were being expressed by Billie Holiday, Ella Fitzgerald, Sarah Vaughan and Lena Horne in jazz and by Mahalia Jackson in gospel music. When a new record label, Atlantic, issued Ruth Brown's 'So Long/It's Raining' as rhythm and blues in 1949, the race music of urban blacks, discovered by whites during the war, found a female star who was to establish a new musical idiom for women rock singers.

The feminine mystique of the post-war era was only part of the story.

Moreover, the rush to buy was not simply because women were inveigled by firms who had lost their defence contracts, but because people had held back during the Depression and the war. Farm women, for instance, finally got their irons and in some cases washing machines, as a reward for long hours of labour on the wartime farms. The basic hardship which remained was all the more resented because there was a strong feeling that ordinary Americans were entitled to a better life now the war was over. Inflation caused mass protests in 1946. Anne Stein, who had organized farm workers in the 1930s and was a member of the Women's Trade Union League, was involved in action against meat-packing companies over prices and a milk strike in Washington. There was also a desperate housing shortage which forced millions of people to share accommodation with families and friends or live in trolley cars or abandoned huts. One couple set up a home in a department-store window in order to bring attention to homelessness.

Consequently, when William Levitt bought up some potato fields on Long Island and applied Henry Ford's mass-production techniques to housebuilding he was on to a winner. People queued up for days to buy a $7,990 house; one pregnant woman had to be rushed to hospital from the line. William Levitt set up a coffee and soup stall – a $1,000 profit per house meant he could afford to sustain potential buyers. Modelled on a Cape Cod style, the identical houses came with a Bendix washing machine, a built-in electric stove, a refrigerator and an eight-inch television set, paid for in instalments. Life in Levittown, however, was not quite the bland suburban idyll. Matilde Albert, an early settler in 1947, recollected:

There were no telephones, no shops. In the blizzard of 1947 the only telephone booth blew down. There was no grass, no trees, just mounds of dirt, and snow covered it all . . . We ran out of oil. I was stranded and couldn't even drive . . . but everyone was most helpful; everyone helped everyone else.[155]

The women of Levittown were putting a lot of work into their own homes and families, but they were doing much else besides. As Rosalyn Baxandall and Elizabeth Ewen remark:

A unique aspect of early Levittown was that everything had to be built from scratch, with women playing a leading role in forming a system of public education from nursery school through high school and a large public library.

Suburban women were often thought of as engaging in endless kaffeklatches, gabbing about trivia. In reality they were building a world for themselves, their children, and their community.[156]

Black families had difficulties moving into these suburban neighbour-hoods. Even if they were not barred outright, they could face considerable prejudice. When Fanny Christina Hill and her husband finally bought a house on a white street, a fiery cross appeared on the lawn of one of the few other black residents. Only when her husband shot a snake were they accepted, because he had a gun and could use it. The reason for taking such risks was graphically described by Ann Petry in *The Street*, in which a black working mother, having found a place to live with her son, worries because 'there was no one to look out for him after school'.[157] In the poor neighbourhood there was danger from traffic, gangs of big boys and, most insidious, an urban street culture which could trap and destroy. Finding him trying to earn money by shining shoes, she slaps him in rage and despair. It was a severity rooted in both fear and love:

If he's shining shoes at eight, he will be cleaning windows at sixteen and running an elevator at twenty-one and go on doing that for the rest of his life. And you're afraid that this street will keep him from finishing at high school; that it may do worse than that and get him into some kind of trouble that will land him in a reform school because you can't be home to look out for him because you have to work.[158]

Many Americans had held back from marriage during the Depression and the war years. This, combined with relief that the men were back safely and a panic about being left on the shelf, resulted in a marriage rate in 1946 of 16.4 per thousand people. It was the highest rate in any record-keeping country, apart from Hungary, in the twentieth century and those marrying were young as well, including college students. The returning servicemen were looking for women with whom they could settle down, and young women were keen to get husbands rather than go out with several dates. Underneath the yearning for security, however, there were tensions and anxieties. The GIs who had seen war bristled uncomfortably with young college women or war workers who seemed unaware of what they had been through, while there was resentment on the women's part of the foreign brides who came back with some of the servicemen.

By the late 1940s certain social protections were wearing thin. It was as if a price had to be extracted for the relaxation in sexual mores during the war, leaving a harshly punitive attitude in the space left by chivalry. An extreme example of blaming the victim occurred at the University of Michigan in 1947, when a male student attacked and raped a nineteen-year-old coed he was driving home: he was charged with assault but the university suspended both students. In *The Modern Woman: The Lost Sex*, Marynia Farnham and Ferdinand Lundberg had bemoaned the demise of the forceful bridegroom in the same year: 'We live today in the era of the apologetic bridegroom, successor to the sturdier rapist of a bygone day.'[159] Farnham and Lundberg dismissed the idea of rape in marriage as simply something imagined by the bride.

Mainstream sex advice, in contrast, promoted marriage as a more equal partnership which, through planned parenthood and mutual pleasure, would strengthen family life. At the New York Clinical Research Bureau, for example, the successful counsellors Lena Levine and Abraham Stone held group therapy sessions for men and women and were surprised at the relief expressed by people in discovering that their anxieties were not completely individual. The men were worried because of failure to maintain erections and the women blamed them-selves for their own lack of sexual satisfaction. Linda Gordon points out that while Levine and Stone's approach was to stabilize rather than to reform, they did recognize that the sexual problems they encountered were not simply personal.

That sexual attitudes were socially defined became evident when the wartime tolerance of homosexuality and lesbianism in the forces changed abruptly with peace. 'Queer' ships brought homosexuals and lesbians to the nearest port and left them there; gay communities sprang up in cities like New York and San Francisco and a club culture strengthened the sense of identity which had begun to crystallize during the war. This was just one of the changes in personal life which were to have a political impact in the future.

Jacqueline Jones describes the Second World War and the post-war decade as 'seedtime years for the modern civil rights and women's liberation movement'.[160] Despite the political conservatism of the McCarthy era, there were longer-term processes at work within society which were to bring new kinds of radical movements into being. The

New Deal's legacy was not completely destroyed and a few links were maintained with older traditions of radicalism. Voices like Elizabeth Gurley Flynn's, defying Farnham and Lundberg in the Communist press, or Antoinette Konikow's column in the Trotskyist paper *The Militant*, insisting on women's right to control their bodies, reached only small groups of people but somehow these ideas persisted. As national director of the National Association for the Advancement of Colored People, Ella Josephine Baker brought her grass-roots organizing experience in the co-operative movement of the 1930s into the NAACP from 1943 to 1946 and then involved parents in campaigns against segregation in schools. Community activism thus persisted despite the lack of any political co-ordination, while some of the personal, moral concerns about human life which were to lead to the peace movement are described by Anne Firor Scott. She and her housemates formed a Ten Years to Live Club at the end of the war, because they thought the planet would have been blown up by then.

There was, however, one particular date with destiny in 1949 which was to have consequences nobody could have foretold. A conservative starlet, Nancy Davis, disturbed to see her name on a list protesting about convictions against Hollywood writers for refusing to disclose their political beliefs to the House of Un-American Activities Committee, contrived to wangle dinner with the president of the Screen Actors' Guild. Ronald Reagan, who was informing for the FBI, was able to reassure her that this was because she had a namesake, the wife of a liberal Democrat. Nancy, however, had long-term plans: 'I knew that being his wife was the role I wanted most.'[161]

Chapter 6

THE 1950s

BRITAIN

Becoming a Woman

'One is not born, but rather becomes, a woman,'[1] wrote Simone de Beauvoir in *The Second Sex*, which was published in English in 1953. This emphasis upon the process of 'becoming' challenged the view that a 'changeless essence' of femininity determined women's destiny. Her phrase resonated with a new generation ready to accept that one's womanhood was of one's own making.

This 'production of a feminine self',[2] to use Jackie Stacey's words, was not just an idea. It was turned into a material reality by the mass market which was emerging in the post-war years. To the young, for whom mundane matters of manufacturing outlets held little interest, it seemed that the Atlantic simply narrowed of its own mysterious accord and that bits of Hollywood – that elusive, precious veneer of glamour – came floating over, to land, like a cargo of treasure, on British shores. It was not just clothes; becoming a woman was indeed being shaped by the expansion of consumer choice, but identification involved an active search for an ethos too. In *Star Gazing*, Jackie Stacey describes how British women were attracted to the 'glamour, excitement and sexuality'[3] of Hollywood. Film stars were models of femininity to be assimilated. Patricia Ogden recalled how she cut her hair 'DA style'[4] and bought clothes like Doris Day. Jane Wyman's tulip hair followed, until she changed her 'image'[5] again and bought a suit like one worn by Marilyn Monroe in *Niagara*. Through the cinema women could enter a great span of possible worlds – wealth, glamour and romance beckoned, along with freedom. Films served as a means of transcending the humdrum. One particularly dedicated escapee, Veronica Millen, saw *Calamity Jane* eighty-eight times, forty-five of them in one fortnight. Her sisters, who were Elvis fans, thought she was 'mad going silly on a woman'.[6]

The 1950s appeared to be the epitome of the conventional decade, yet paradoxically it generated resourceful rebels. Jean McCrindle, a student at St Andrews University in Scotland, looking around for alternative ways of becoming, settled on a motley crew: Florence Nightingale, 'Mother' Jones, Beatrice Webb, the Brontës, Vera Brittain, Alva Myrdal, Margaret Mead, Doris Lessing and, of course, Simone de Beauvoir. Alison Hennegan, a few years younger, was meanwhile fascinated by Nancy Spain, the writer and broadcaster on the popular TV quiz programme *What's My Line?*, 'in well-cut tweed jackets, good shirts with elegant cuff-links and dashing cravats',[7] flirting with gruff fellow panellist Gilbert Harding, a closet homosexual.

Considerable ingenuity was required to find contrary sexual role models in the 1950s. In a Dumfries grammar school in Scotland, budding feminist Alison Fell oscillated between wanting to be either a ballerina or Biggles and Dan Dare (the spaceman in the boys' comic *Eagle*). Later it was to be a tussle between Lana Turner, Marilyn Monroe and Audrey Hepburn, or war heroes and heroines like Douglas Bader and Odette, for the Second World War still stalked the popular imagination. Eventually she settled for the 'Bad Girl Look',[8] inspired by the French existentialist singer Juliette Greco, and of course, following Brigitte Bardot, 'she learns how to pout'.[9] Another future feminist writer, Carolyn Steedman, recalls playing at being Annie Oakley in the Midlands, dressed in a brown gingham dress, a cowboy hat and carrying a rifle.

A generation of cultural contortionists were being prepared to fly planes, explore outer space, tunnel their way out of POW camps and pull the fastest gun in the Wild West, while looking yielding and cute in high heels, nylons with straight seams, pencil skirts and tight cardigans buttoned down the back. And so it was that amidst the pastel shades and the thick-pile carpets of 1950s new prosperity, heroic aspirations, images of adventure, sacrifice for a noble cause, courage and daring somehow crept into the production of a feminine self. Dam-busters, wooden horses and tunnels became symbols of a less tangible escape from a fixed feminine destiny. The repercussions of experience are

Girls' Fiction

The books being read by girls during the 1950s were remarkable for their continuity. Rupert Bear was still popular; so were *What Katy Did*, *Anne of Green Gables* and *Swallows and Amazons*. Edith Nesbit, Elinor M. Brent-Dyer's *Chalet School* books and Elsie Oxenham's *Abbey Girls* were being read, as were, from a more recent past, Biggles and Worrals. Along with country dances and the maypole, they contributed to the aura of being connected to an historically unspecific 'tradition'.

There were, however, a few modernizing modifications. Rosemary Auchmuty points out how, from the late 1930s, Elsie Oxenham's schoolgirl heroines were less likely to have intense romantic friendships with one another in between the energetic folk-dancing. Moreover, in place of brusque references to heterosexuality which appeared in the 1920s editions, such as, 'Being in love's a fearful disease. I hope I never catch it,' by the 1950s Joan, in *Tomboys at the Abbey* (1957), was imagining that 'love was a feeling for which one would give up everything and be glad to do it'.[10]

The tomboys, however, did survive. Even Enid Blyton's *Famous Five* books, which present a secure world of class and race privilege, had boyish Georgina. There were some intrepid girls in the comics too. *School Friend*, which, along with *Girls' Crystal*, *Bunty* and *Girl*, was extremely popular, featured Betty Roland and Joan Derwent on a quiet country holiday with their chum Peggy West in 1954. At school they would go into action in 'robe and hood to battle against tyranny'[11] and sure enough a mystery comes along which requires climbing out of windows, down knotted robes and scaling towers up the ivy.

Girl expanded on the tomboy theme to include a range of adventurous jobs and historical heroines. *Girl Annual: No. 7* carried an article by Naomi Mitchison, 'Air Nurse', set in the Highlands of Scotland, and a true-life story of Policewoman Shirley tripping up a thief as he tried to grab Lady Corkerdale's jewels at a charity ball. There were Emmeline and Christabel Pankhurst (no signs of Sylvia) and Helen Keller, 'an ambassadress of peace and goodwill between nations and a bringer of hope and comfort to all the physically handicapped'.[12]

Girls crossed over into boys' fiction of course, reading the equivalent comic to *Girl, Eagle,* and listening avidly to Dan Dare on Radio Luxembourg. None of this was exactly preparation for a quiet life in the suburbs. Even Alison Uttley's Little Grey Rabbit lived in an odd family grouping with Hare and Squirrel, braved Brown Owl and got involved with eccentric fippgures like the Wandering Hedgehog.

Girl sleuths Wendy and Jinx in the glossy upmarket comic, 1956.

unpredictable, for the routes of the imagination are not charted. Thus Ronald Searle created his playful schoolgirl horrors at St Trinian's to erase memories of the real horrors of having been in a Japanese POW camp. No soft, yielding femininity held back the girls of St Trinian's; they personified anarchic possibilities for the younger teens negotiating the snares of becoming.

Politics

'Rights for women, so far as my generation is concerned, is a dead issue,' declared writer and broadcaster Marghanita Laski. 'I was born too late for the battle. Older and nobler women struggled that I might be free, and did their work so well that I've never bothered about being bound.'[13]

Older feminists, like Edith Summerskill, Margery Corbett Ashby and Thelma Cazalet-Keir, were becoming isolated figures. Thelma Cazalet-Keir, defeated in the 1945 general election, never got accepted again as a parliamentary candidate in a safe Tory seat: 'I was forced to the conclusion that the only effective qualification would be a change of sex.'[14]

On the whole, women involved in public life, regardless of their political views, wanted to be accepted for individual competence rather than as representatives of their sex. Special treatment was regarded as patronizing and demeaning. Jennie Lee's 'most distasteful task' in 1957 was allowing herself to be nominated for the Women's Section of the Labour Party's NEC: 'I considered it an anachronism.'[15] Women Labour MPs like Shirley Williams, Judith Hart and Barbara Castle, as well as the Conservative Mervyn Pike, concentrated on areas seen as male, like colonial affairs, defence and the economy. They aimed to be MPs, not women MPs.

There were still very few women in Parliament. Between 1945 and 1959 twenty-nine women were elected for Labour, fifteen for the Conservatives and one for the Liberals. The problem was not simply overt discrimination. Jennie Lee observed, 'The tug of domestic ties can be a greater barrier to women entering Parliament than the prejudice of selection conferences.'[16] There was still an assumption that women in public life would not be mothers. A quiet resolve to change this can

Young Tory candidate
Margaret Roberts with Kent
greengrocer.

be detected among several younger women during the course of the
decade, but it was seen as a matter for personal arrangement not public
protest. Women who managed to combine having families with a
political career needed supportive men in their lives – husbands or
fathers, and preferably both. It also helped to be reasonably well off. With
this combination, thirty-two-year-old Margaret Thatcher managed to
be elected as a Conservative MP when she was the mother of five-year-
old twins – no mean feat in 1958. But even she had been rejected for
several constituencies and had taken up a career as a lawyer before
winning Finchley. Martin Pugh remarks 'She clearly resented advice
to the effect that she should go home, have her babies and postpone
politics.'[17]

A handful of women MPs continued to raise issues in Parliament
which related specifically to women. On the Labour side, apart from
Edith Summerskill, there was Eirene White trying to liberalize the
divorce laws, while the Conservative Joan Vickers tried to get obligatory
deductions from husbands' wages for deserted wives. Lack of support
within Parliament made links to non-party pressure groups extremely
important. The Equal Pay Campaign Committee backed Irene Ward

(Conservative) and Douglas Houghton (Labour) in their efforts to put pressure on the government. The London County Council Staff Association achieved a breakthrough when the LCC granted equal pay in 1952 to all women in grades where both men and women were employed. In 1955 women civil servants also gained equal pay. Teachers followed in 1956, along with workers in the National Health Service and the gas and electricity boards. The public sector and nationalized industries led the way; women trade unionists in private industry were still not able to secure equal pay, though in 1957 the new European Economic Community's Treaty of Rome held out a faint hope, with its acceptance of equal pay.

Many of the old divisions about what kinds of reform best suited women's interests persisted. The Labour women's organization, for example, did not support Eirene White's efforts towards more liberal divorce laws and Esther Hodge, an egalitarian feminist, describes a fierce row at the British Federation of University Women in July 1954 when the demand for protective legislation was raised, even though it was aimed at ensuring that the legislation applied equally to men and women.

The divisions which seemed most important, though, were about politics in general, not about women's issues. Although British Communists did not experience a McCarthy witch-hunt on the American scale, the atmosphere of persecution did affect them. Campaigning for the Rosenbergs, who, accused of spying, were facing the death penalty in America in 1953, Anna in Doris Lessing's *The Golden Notebook* described the British as 'tight, suspicious, frightened'[18] during the Cold War. The Communist Party split in 1956 after Khrushchev's revelations about Stalinism and the Soviet invasion of Hungary. Dorothy Thompson, who had been a member of the Communist Party Historians' Group and active in left politics in Yorkshire, was among the intellectuals who resigned and formed the new left journal *The Reasoner*. The creation of the new left groups marked not just a new political structure but a desire for an alternative kind of radical politics. Among the working-class women who took part was the Leeds clothing worker Gertie Roche, who had been the Communist Party women's organizer in Yorkshire during the early 1950s. A thinker and activist formed by the CP and the industrial struggles of the 1930s, she was appalled by the evidence of trials and atrocities and the invasion of Hungary.

Labour women dwelt in a more pragmatic world of political compromise. But among them too the key issues were not about women's conditions but about the general differences between the right and the left within the Labour Party. For example, Alice Bacon in Yorkshire, Bessie Braddock in Liverpool and Jean Mann in Scotland were aligned with the right and Barbara Castle and Judith Hart with the left. Also on the Labour left was the MP for Camden, Lena Jaeger. This north London borough was involved in a furore in 1957 when the Council gave all the staff a holiday on May Day and flew the red flag from the town hall.

Rank and file Conservative women tended to define their public political role in terms of their responsibility for the moral ordering of society. They took womanly matters into the arena of male politics and showed a revival of the rebellious spirit which had led them to revolt over law and order during the late 1930s. In 1958 Tory women at their conference defended corporal punishment, demanded stiffer penalties for crime and more police, and advocated flogging for adult offenders and birching for young offenders. They argued that these harsh measures were needed to protect young girls and older people. Gender was thus invoked by the right-wing rank and file when it was hardly evident in the rest of the political spectrum. Young working-class men, depicted as 'louts' or 'toughs',[19] were regarded as out of control. In *Iron Ladies*, Beatrix Campbell sums this up as 'a highly *sexualized* discourse in which the causes of crime were clearly felt to lie in a disturbance of proper sexual difference. Louts were the legacy left to society by working wives, broken marriages and television programmes full of "sex, savagery, blood and thunder".'[20]

Though this right-wing emphasis on women as victims who needed protection continued to have an emotive appeal (it was adapted by the Fascists in the late 1950s to become the protection of white women from black men), mainstream Conservatism was steering towards the centre. Beatrix Campbell shows how, from the early 1950s, the party was prompting a consensual image of 'the wife as a woman *with rights*'[21] – the Conservative women's conference in 1955 took them at their word and demanded the reform of married women's tax. The women's page of the Conservative Party monthly, *Onward*, featured successful wives like the elegant Conservative councillor Lady Isobel Barnett of *What's My Line?* TV fame. The new image of the Conservative woman was one of elegance and discriminating consumer choice – the social world of *House and Garden*.

The Conservative consumer wife came to be associated with freedom of choice and abundance, whereas Labour was stuck with the 1940s' image of austerity and bureaucratic planning – in the 1951 election the Housewives' League protested against price rises under Labour. However, the majority of women had voted Labour in 1945 and while middle-class women moved to the right, in 1950 working-class women were still supporting the Labour Party more than men were. The Labour MP Jean Mann maintained in *Woman in Parliament* (1962) that the Conservatives were able to appeal to working-class women during the 1950s because of their recognition of the housewife. But labour women retained their own interpretation of consumer issues; for example, the Women's Co-operative Guild was still able to mobilize on a mass scale against the decontrol of food by the Conservatives in the early 1950s, which led to higher prices.

The membership of the Women's Co-operative Guild tended to be ageing, but they proved more responsive than party political structures to the moral concern about peace which was to inspire the Campaign for Nuclear Disarmament (CND). In 1950 there had been a call at the guild's Sheffield Congress to divert research for military purposes to industrial development, and in 1954 they had begun to agitate against nuclear bomb tests, emphasizing the dangers to mothers and children. Vera Leff, a member of the Golders Green Women's Co-operative Guild, the National Assembly of Women and the Communist Party, along with a group of other Guildswomen, called a local meeting in 1955 about the effects of radiation on unborn children. Early in 1957 a Nagasaki schoolteacher, Kikue Ihara, told a meeting of Guildswomen how her city had been devastated and appealed to them as 'good mothers of Britain'[22] to prevent nuclear war. The group showed the film *The Children of Hiroshima* and made contacts with other opponents of nuclear weapons, among them Gertrude Fishwick, a former suffragette in the Labour Party and the Anglican Pacifist Fellowship, Arthur Goss, a Quaker, and a Labour doctor, Sheila Jones.

From these small beginnings, the National Council for the Abolition of Nuclear Weapon Tests was formed in 1957, after the H-bomb tests at Christian Island and the Labour Party's refusal to support banning the bomb unilaterally. Jill Liddington points out that at least two-thirds of its support came from women. The new movement assimilated a range of influences. Women demonstrated in May 1957, dressed in black sashes, emulating the 1956 anti-apartheid protests against the treason trials of Ruth First and other members of the African National Congress, and the feminists Vera Brittain and Edith Summerskill were among the speakers at the first women's anti-nuclear demonstration. Peggy Duff, an impressive organizer from the Labour left, became secretary of the new organization and went on to play a key role in CND.

Launched in January 1958, CND quickly showed that it was able to reach a new political constituency which included the middle class. A typical rank-and-filer was Margaret Widgery, a Methodist, who joined Maidenhead CND when she and her husband were building their own house and their children were small. Impressed by the Quakers in the war, she recalls becoming a 'CNDer' because of 'a strong feeling

CND supporters marching into
London from Aldermaston, 1959.

for peace'.[23] CND was also able to draw in prominent writers like Iris Murdoch, Jacquetta Hawkes and Rose Macaulay, and actresses Peggy Ashcroft, Constance Cummings and Mary Ure. Rose Macaulay joked about the 'stage army of the good',[24] but it always mixed the respectable with the anarchic: the intrepid direct-actionist Pat Arrowsmith, for instance, was among those to come into conflict with Peggy Duff.

While women played an important role in the movement, the initial emphasis on mothers' special relationship to peace did not appeal to the younger generation of CNDers. Instead, CND was to become a new kind of social movement. Although it had strong roots in the old left, its commitment to the extension of direct democracy into daily life and personal behaviour meant it broke with the idea that the end justifies the means. Along with the new left groups which were springing up in several towns, it contributed to a rediscovery of a libertarian radicalism which appealed to a new generation. CND represented an alternative lifestyle as well as a political cause. Being against the bomb meant brown rice and sandals. Gender was not usually at issue, though in 1958 in *Women in Bondage* V. M. Hughes argued against a 'man-centred'[25] view of life and was concerned that the H-bomb threatened animals and plants as well as people. While at the end of the decade the Tory Party had the air of some kind of immutable essence of government, this new left on the radical fringe was to prove socially and politically tenacious.

Work

When Elizabeth Harrison came to Crook, near Durham, from India, she thought women who worked in factories were 'rough people'; working in a dress factory changed her mind: 'There was a saying that if you worked in the factory you were either among the needy or the greedy. Most of us were needy.'[26] She was a part-timer on the housewives' or twilight shift, which had been started in November 1950 to recruit women. Firms had been forced to adapt to women's situation in the home by the demand for labour and the declining numbers of unmarried women available for work. As more married women were going out to work, there was a marked shift in the age composition of women workers. Whereas in 1931 half the women in the workforce were under twenty-five, by 1951, when the Conservatives took power, only a third of them were.

Attitudes to women's employment when children were young varied regionally. A 1959 study on shift work in Yorkshire, an area with a long tradition of women working, found that women with pre-school children were in favour of it. However, in Scotland Barbara Thompson and Angela Finlayson found that Aberdeen women were less ready to accept shifts. Some husbands also opposed their wives working. Nonetheless, a survey of 253 Aberdeen women who had their first baby between 1950 and 1953 showed that 35 per cent were working five years later. The wives of unskilled and semi-skilled men were most likely to be employed – money was undoubtedly the main factor. But many women also liked to work because of the company. One said that she was 'fed-up and could climb the walls – being shut in at home all day'.[27]

There were problems, however, in the pattern of part-time work. It tended to be low-paid and part-timers who worked less than thirty hours a week were not entitled to benefits. As male trade unionists were inclined to declare that part-timers should not be there, rather than organizing them, their rates stayed down. Like homework, which unions in the boot and shoe, hosiery and clothing trades were complaining was on the increase again, part-time work provided employers with a cheap, flexible labour force and kept women in low-paid occupations. Despite equal pay in the public sector, women's pay declined in relation to men's over the decade.

Unskilled and semi-skilled manufacturing jobs in cotton textiles and the potteries, where women had been organized, were declining because of foreign competition or mechanization. The growth areas in women's employment were distribution and light industry in the Midlands and the South-East, where women had been 10 per cent of the workforce in 1939 and by 1951 constituted 22 per cent, and the clerical and administrative sector, which had expanded with the welfare state. Labour shortages in the health service led to the recruitment of nurses and midwives from the West Indies and Ireland. Ann Rossiter points out that by 1951, 22.4 per cent of Irish-born women were in the professional occupational category, mainly as nurses and midwives.

There was also a demand for more teachers, though the numbers of women going into higher education were still relatively low. In the 1920s only 27 per cent of undergraduates were female and the figure hardly changed until the late 1950s, when a slight rise occurred. Arguments against an academic education for girls were based on the idea that it would be wasted when they married and had children. Lady Simon in Manchester was among a small group of professional women who were lobbying for expansion. The Crowther Report in 1959 was a compromise, distinguishing between the intellectually 'less able girls'[28] and the rest. Getting into the latter category meant exemption from education for motherhood – a stimulus to those with little fondness for domesticity to stay on and apply for higher education. Swots were apparently not expected to breed!

There were emotive pressures within popular culture which set fulfilled femininity against external intellectual interests and demanding employment. Monica Dickens, the successful writer of humorous novels, warned career women in *Woman's Own* in 1956 that they could be endangering the love of their children. She portrayed shallow ambition on one side and the deeper virtues of homely intimacy on the other. A good mummy was not the 'efficient career woman who pops in and out of the house at intervals, knows a lot of stimulating people, and can talk about everything, except trivial, day-to-day matters that are the breath of family life'.[29]

The mother-centred psychology, stressing warmth and direct, overt affection, which had begun as an alternative approach to the rigid discipline of prevailing child-care, had acquired a conservative twist by the 1950s. Ironically, it was to feed anxieties and feelings of inadequacy among women with children whether they worked or not. Psychoanalytic emphasis on the importance of the mother's relationship to the child had begun to be popularized by Donald Winnicott's broadcasts in the 1940s. Influenced by Melanie Klein, Winnicott pointed out the importance to toddlers of external transitional objects, which they infused with, in Janet Sayers's words, their 'internal sense of being at one with the mother'.[30] Sayers shows how Winnicott's version of Klein dropped the pessimistic view of childhood emotions like anger and envy, which she had developed in the grim years of the 1930s, in favour of an emphasis upon harmonious union with the mother. The mother was thus immensely responsible and immensely to blame if she reared misfits, oddballs or trouble-makers. Klein herself regarded this 'idealized image of mothering' as an 'anxiety-motivated flight'.[31]

There were cultural forces at work outside the internal wrangles within psychoanalytic theory which made Winnicott's mother-centred approach more acceptable than Klein's emphasis on the existence of infantile rage or Freud's stress on tension between the individual and society. Winnicott's work seemed to be confirmed by John Bowlby's influential report in 1951 for the World Health Organization, *Maternal Care and Mental Health*. This not only stressed the child's need for a 'warm, intimate and continuous relationship with his mother'[32] but stated that working mothers were one of the causes of mental illness. Bowlby's theories touched both anxiety about women's role and fear of juvenile delinquency. As Martin Pugh says, he was over-generalizing from the often unhappy experiences of wartime evacuation, or from those of children in the impersonal care of institutions, and did not consider the impact of absent career-minded fathers at all. Unfortunately, any separation from the mother was equated with deprivation. Bowlby's report became a popular Penguin book, *Child Care and the Growth of Love* (1953), and in 1958 he produced a pamphlet which, in response to the question 'Can I Leave My Baby?', told women that, although brief periods of care by fathers, grannies or neighbours were permissible in emergencies, or while visiting their own mothers, the 'exacting job [of motherhood] is scamped at one's peril'.[33]

It was well-nigh impossible amidst all this to argue that good nurseries and after-school care would enable women to make the choice about how to earn a living and look after children in less troubled circumstances. Even so, the child psychologists did not convince everybody. Stef Pixner's mother, a single parent in the Communist Party who worked as a typist, dismissed with scorn 'new ideas suggesting that broken homes and working mothers turn latchkey children into juvenile delinquents', although she worried nonetheless and 'hedged'[34] them round with rules.

A forthright defender of working mothers was Margaret Thatcher, who wrote in 1954:

What is the effect on the family when the mother goes out to work each day? If she has a powerful and dominant personality her personal influence is there the whole time . . . From my own experience I feel there is much to be said for being away from the family for part of the day. When looking after them without a break, it is sometimes difficult not to get a little impatient . . . whereas, having been out, every moment spent with them is a pleasure to anticipate.[35]

Conservatism had its inconsistencies. The British upper classes had, of course, relied on nannies and boarding schools for generations without any social panic about mother deprivation. On the other hand, mother-centred arguments struck a deep chord in the Labour Party. Jennie Lee paid her respects to the full-time wife and mother, like her own, but defined a type, in which she included herself, who was 'not suited to a life confined to the home, however much we love a good home in the background . . . It would have made matters worse, not better, if I had given up my political work.'[36]

Types like Jennie Lee found their defenders in the sociologists Alva Myrdal and Viola Klein. The authors of *Women's Two Roles*, they were resigned to a long siege, saying in 1956, 'The emancipation of women is slow and it is a process prolific of internal conflicts.'[37] Their book was mainly concerned with educated middle-class women, not working-class mothers, and their case for combining work and home was cautious and moderate. It did not involve men doing work in the home, for instance – an idea which was being presented in the United States in the same period. *Women's Two Roles* took a modernizing, no-nonsense stance: the state needed women's labour, and efficient organization of the home as the children grew older would make employment and motherhood compatible. The authors were brusque about personal doubts. Stay-at-home housewives were being deluded and encouraged 'to indulge in an irrational self-pity'.[38] As for mother-centred psychoanalytic theory, they observed testily, 'Between the Scylla of "rejection" and the Charybdis of "over-protection" the education of the child steers an uncertain course. It is probably best for parents not to meditate over-much on these dangers lest their natural confidence be destroyed by self-consciousness.'[39]

Daily Life

Queen Elizabeth II, who ascended the throne in 1952, was the first British ruler to be crowned Head of the Commonwealth. For the Coronation on 2 June 1953, the young Queen chose a dress designed by Norman Hartnell. Woven and embroidered in jewels on the dress were a maple for Canada, a lotus flower for India, wheat, jute and cotton for Pakistan, the protea of South Africa, a Welsh leek, Scotland's thistles, the Tudor rose, the fern of New Zealand, the wattle of Australia and Ireland's shamrock. Hartnell had an extra shamrock embroidered in the skirt for luck without her knowing.

An Australian, Thelma Holland, a director of Cyclax, was responsible for the make-up and had to work hard to convince the Queen that she should wear a new crimson lipstick rather than her usual pale pink because of the lights in Westminster Abbey. The Queen was reported to be calm as the gold state coach left Buckingham Palace. When asked if she was all right, she described how her horse, the Derby favourite Aureole, had behaved in training that morning. Her

New meanings for monarchy, 1953.

personal preference would no doubt have been to stay with Aureole, but instead she promised to serve her country and the Commonwealth, and her subjects became, in Liz Heron's words, 'the first post-imperial generation'.[40]

In the *Sociological Review* in December 1953, Michael Young and an American sociologist, Edward Shils, celebrated the Coronation as a 'great act of national communion' in which the Queen and her family were joined to 'one great national family', adding, 'Devotion to the Royal Family . . . does mean in a very direct way devotion to one's own family, because the values embodied in each are the same.'[41]

To mark the Coronation, the children of Portsmouth were issued with a book by Richard Dimbleby, the television announcer, in which the youthful Princess Elizabeth was quoted telling the Mothers' Union in October 1949, 'Some of the very principles on which the family, and therefore the health of the nation, is founded are in danger. We live in an age of growing self-indulgence and of falling moral standards.'[42] Writing in the new left collection of essays *Out of Apathy* (1960), the historian E. P. Thompson commented on 'the regression of our time': tradition was being recast and reset as 'junk jewellery' through the stabilizing 'state ritual of monarchy'.[43]

Crowds waited patiently in the rain to see the Coronation procession; children's cardboard periscopes dissolved and Wrens stuffed chocolate bars from the crowd in their dripping hats. State ritual was a gift to TV manufacturers; 10 million people sat round black and white televisions that day. Elizabeth Wilson watched endless 'heraldic animals made of plaster' jerking by on the television: 'How does she go to the lavatory, we wondered, as Richard Dimbleby intoned.'[44] Liz Heron, meanwhile, was walking over the hills of west Scotland with her friend Ann, making up stories of revenge against enemies: 'Foremost among them are the Queen and the class bully. The Queen because she is rich and English, and the English are all our enemies because of Bruce and Bannockburn, and Bonnie Prince Charlie and Mary Queen of Scots.'[45] Stef Pixner was eight and saw signs of things looking up. Sweets had recently come off the ration and she was able to buy gobstoppers, liquorice sticks, honeycomb and sherbet: 'It's 1953. Year of the Coronation and the climbing of Mount Everest . . . We get given a silk handkerchief with Buckingham Palace on it, a silver spoon and a tin of chocolates.'[46]

Mary Grieve's optimism expanded beyond gobstoppers. She worked on the popular magazine *Woman*, which combined enthusiasm for consumer goods with enthusiasm for the family and the monarchy. She writes, 'A whole new world of commodities flowed in on the flood-tide of the 1950s. Younger women had never known such joys, few older women had been able to afford them pre-war.'[47] She was strategically placed to observe the flood-tide. Popular women's magazines were reaching a vast market – five out of six women read one magazine a week, many saw more than one. And, says Mary Grieve, 'The women's magazines, with their close understanding of women . . . and their printing techniques, carried this new life straight into the homes and hearts of millions.'[48] A significant factor was, of course, the advertising revenue they received.

There was an ambience of improvement and stolid optimism. Thousands tramped round the Ideal Homes Exhibition for inspiration. Houses were improved with Formica surfaces, new cleaning products like Flash came on to the market, frozen peas replaced the soggy ones in tins, there were tins of mandarin oranges for treats and plastic cups arrived. Pressure cookers cooked faster, making alarming sounds; the middle classes bought washing machines and refrigerators. More and more people sat glued to their new television sets, watching a family supposedly just like themselves, *The Groves*, or laughing at American shows like *Burns and Allen* and *I Love Lucy*. Big families were in vogue, though the birth-rate had settled back to its 1930s level. Sociologists thought the family was coming on very well indeed. Fathers were reported to be more home-centred – watching television, playing with the children more and busying themselves with DIY.

The details of daily life and relationships were, of course, never straightforward. The picture of the 1950s as a decade of harmonious modernity and security obliterates the cracks and bumps behind the wallpaper. Britain was still an unequal society – though one in which inequality was not admitted. Moreover, modernity appeared in differing guises, ranging from the idealism of the 1951 Festival of Britain to the penitential tower blocks built on the cheap as part of the Conservatives' housing policy. Michael Young and Edward Shils hailed the 'assimila-

The World of The Tatler *in the 1956 Season*

The political and social tumult of the times caused only the faintest ripples in the upper-class magazine *The Tatler*. The young women who were following the season read about an orderly, hermetic realm of hunt balls and charity balls, point-to-points and horse-races, the boat race and polo matches. Comments on royalty were rare and politely impersonal: 'The pheasant shooting around Sandringham has been good this season,'[49] announced *The Tatler* on 11 January. Pictures of women with children tended to include family portraits as pointers of distinguished lineages reaching back over the centuries, though the young photographer Antony Armstrong-Jones had begun to detach his subjects against backgrounds of lace and silk to evoke a timeless modernity.

The British upper classes in this period seemed to acquire physical characteristics different from those of people of other classes, and, indeed, of the European smart set, who occasionally made it into the magazines. They were marked out by having shed all obvious traces of sexuality; nor were there many signs of the influence of Bowlby and Winnicott. On 7 March Jennifer, on a BOAC strato-cruiser bound for Jamaica with the Marquess and Marchioness of Normanby, told the readers of *The Tatler*, 'The Normanbys are to be congratulated on the way they are bringing up their enchanting little family. Everyone was full of admiration for the way the children behaved – they were so good that one hardly knew they were on board.'[50] In this world, children were still expected to be seen and not heard. They appear as toddlers in family portraits and in party clothes, or, in the case of a grumpy-looking Emma Rothschild, on a skiing trip.

The outside world entered through the ballet and skating – enthusiasms shared with the middle classes. Dame Ninette de Valois, who founded Sadler's Wells Ballet, and Dame Margot Fonteyn were both featured in *The Tatler*. There was some anxiety about the musical *The Pyjama Game*, which was felt to be too realistic, but it was Elizabeth Bowen's book reviews which informed *Tatler* readers of the other world. Reviewing Frank Tilsley's novel *Criminal in the Family*, about the Greensmiths, who

THE LIMERICK HUNT BALL was held at Adare Manor, Co. Limerick, by kind permission of the Earl and Countess of Dunraven. It is the first time that a hunt ball has been held at Adare Manor for thirty years. *Above*: Lady Dunraven, the hostess, with Captain Peter McCall

Major Richard Dill with Lady Zinnia Denison, daughter of the 4th Earl of Londesborough, who came over from Newport, I.o.W.

Mr. Simon Hornby, one of the Dunraven house party and Lady Caroline Wyndham-Quin, daughter of the Earl of Dunraven

Rituals of privilege: Limerick Hunt Ball featured in *The Tatler*, 1956.

A CENTURY OF WOMEN

lived on a council estate on the outskirts of a Midlands industrial town, she inquired, 'Have you and I, reading the newspapers, not wondered what does become of the "good home", the steady obscure family, of some young criminal suddenly in the limelight?'[51] Sydney, the adored third son, goes wrong, over-mothered by the welfare state. His actual mum is an 'ageing incorrigible dream-girl' who is 'pouchy under her strident make-up'[52] (the lower classes are still not getting their make-up right). Elizabeth Bowen gave Colin Wilson's *The Outsider* a sympathetic review in June, commenting, 'If the Outsider dominates the present-day scene, may this not be because we live in an age in which it becomes difficult to grow up?'[53] As small boys of seven in *The Tatler* looked like elderly gentlemen, it is not clear what her readership would have made of this.

Another voice from outside, Elspeth Grant, covered the cinema. In July she reviewed *My Teenage Daughter*, starring Sylvia Sims and Anna Neagle: 'Scores of scruffy-looking seventeen-year-olds obviously with troglodyte tendencies, jammed together in a smoke-filled cellar where they writhe, rock and roll dementedly to the primitive tumult of a small but aggressive band'.[54] When the teenage daughter (Sylvia Sims) takes up with 'a repellent young wastrel', begins wearing sweaters and gets into trouble with the law, her magazine-editress mother (Anna Neagle) is rebuked by a magistrate 'for neglecting her duties towards the child'.[55] In Elspeth Grant's opinion the magistrate was unfair to Anna Neagle: 'My goodness – nobody could have worried more about the girl.'[56]

The signs of change are there, though. While the duffel coat was still a garment intended for point-to-points, Leslie Caron and Dorothy Tutin were presenting alternative styles of femininity, there were advertisements for a book on Sappho, for Coca-Cola and for Tampax, and an article about gender ambiguity in boy–girl roles played by Margaret Leighton and Vivien Leigh in Shakespeare. And 'it', discovered in America during the First World War, finally reached the English upper classes in the person of Jayne Mansfield. By February 1957 Elspeth Grant was praising her in *The Girl Can't Help It*: 'Prowed like a pouter pigeon, waisted like a wasp, and with a stern as firmly rounded as a Thanksgiving Day pumpkin', Miss Mansfield was said to make other women 'seem as sexless as a roll of linoleum'.[57]

tion of the working class into the moral consensus of British society',[58] but in material terms working-class families assimilated on the bottom rungs of the ladder of opportunity. Catherina Barnes, interviewed in *Dutiful Daughters*, was one of the lucky ones who got a council house on the outskirts of Carlisle. It seemed 'like a palace', even though the walls were so thin 'you could hear the neighbours changing their mind'[59] and the shops were a mile and a half away. She had to push her three young children in the big pram because she could not leave them with anyone. Her husband's wages as a railway cleaner did not pay the rent, so she took in sewing until she found work as a nurse in a psychiatric hospital, which meant getting up at 5.15 a.m. and rushing back by 2.30 for the children. Class assimilation and not scamping on motherhood were harder to live through than might appear from surveys.

For some too there was no question of assimilation. The 1950s were about surviving for Daisy Noakes in Sussex, whose husband, a former agricultural worker, was disabled. For many working-class women like her, it was not a matter of commodities flooding into their lives but the continuing existence of the welfare state which made the difference. Daisy Noakes knew that in the past it would have been the workhouse: 'The social security really did help families like ours . . . I managed with what I was allowed, but had to count every penny before spending it and I can honestly say I never had a debt.'[60]

But the young ones, as Liz Heron notes, were shedding deference and growing up with an optimistic confidence in social entitlement. With the malt supplement and the free school milk on the welfare state came a 'sense of a future that would get better and better, as if history was on our side'.[61] They were not, however, shielded from all social tensions. Ursula Huws, with a Welsh father and an English mother, watched Welsh valleys being flooded for England and heard 'hard new English words'[62] like snack bar and juke box entering the Welsh language. In Liz Heron's Scotland, Catholics and Protestants were battling it out still and 'Ireland was everywhere around us, a protective blanket of second-hand memories and martyred history and bitter victimology'.[63] Gail Lewis, with a black father and a white mother, living in Kilburn, north-west London, learned very young that there were no-go areas in her street for a black child. The house was firebombed at the time of the Notting Hill riots of 1958. West Indian immigrants, who from 1952 were barred from the United States, were settling in growing numbers in Britain, and there were also a small number of Africans, mainly students.

Ron Ramdin notes that the riots marked the demise of the Commonwealth ideal, with its multiracial front. But along with the recognition that Britain had a 'colour problem' came various interracial clubs and a strengthening of existing black organizations. Two women were prominent in these early groups: Amy Ashwood Garvey (the widow of Marcus Garvey) ran a hostel and club in North Kensington and was president of the Association for the Advancement of Coloured People, while Claudia Jones's *West Indian Gazette*, started in March 1958, provided a voice and helped to define an identity for West Indians in Britain. The first issue of the paper declared that they were 'a community with its own special wants and problems'.[64] It was to organize the first Caribbean Carnival in Notting Hill in 1959, take up women's rights and make common cause with Asian immigrants, who also experienced racism.

The culture of consensus and adjustment generated its opposite. Myrdal and Klein noted that professional and business women 'were afflicted by doubts of their essential femininity', while housewives worried whether they were 'neglecting hidden talents'; they did not 'yet feel "at home" in both worlds'.[65] Angry Young Men, of course, were the noisy and noticeable protesters, but Liz Heron points out that young, educationally mobile women were also affected by a powerful 'sense of not belonging'.[66] The rites of tradition cloaked rapid industrial and technological changes and large-scale environmental and social restructuring. Working-class people were moving to get better jobs or being relocated as slums were cleared or roads built, and some of their children were transplanted into the grammar schools, which forced a separation from their families and class as the price of social mobility.

Communications and 'style' were being transformed too. While the mass fashion promoted in the women's magazines cultivated an etiquette for the aspiring, called 'fashion sense', with clothes made out of the new synthetic wonder materials, some young girls looked at their mothers and said, 'How dull.' Groups began to mark themselves out by their clothes. Tricia Dempsey in Lambeth, south London, got a 'Teddy-girl two-piece costume, it was a finger-tip drape, cut of the coat'; this cost £13 13s. – a major investment which took her 'six months to pay for'.[67] Then there was a flat beret with a 'big hat pin with a pearl on it, and string pearls all tied up and that horrible pan-stick make-up, thick brown and great big, thick lips, cerise pink . . .'[68] In Sheila Francis's Welsh village the clothes had to be assembled from jumble sales and donned sneakily at the bus stop. Stef Pixner, however, who had observed the bohemian fashions in Hampstead and was dreaming of playing in a skiffle group, acquired a duffel coat and colourless nail varnish and was all set to go on the Aldermaston march. Aged fourteen, she had decided, 'Life isn't all jam and honey.'[69]

Sex

Unsuitable sex has a mysterious way of emanating from somewhere else. While in North America it had been associated with exotic European women, in Britain during the 1950s it was regarded as imported from France, Italy or the United States. As if the GIs and Hollywood were not enough, Gussie Moran shocked (or delighted) Wimbledon in a short tennis skirt in 1950. Then there was sleaze – Hank Janson's pulp fiction with lurid covers and titles like *Broads Don't Scare Easy* and magazines called *Razzle* or *Silk Stocking Stories* troubled the censors.

The anthropologist Geoffrey Gorer found the English to be a chaste lot on the whole in the early 1950s. In *Exploring English Character* (1955), half of his sample had not had any sexual relationship before or after marriage except with their spouse. Moreover, there was a dislike of people making a fuss about sex. Mass-Observation found only a third of the people they questioned thought a good sex life was essential to happiness. Sex, it was felt, should not be made the 'be all and end all of life',[70] and was definitely not something that people went on about in public.

Sexuality, thus held at bay, dwelt in half-submerged ribaldry, tantalizing allure and a transcendent romanticism, with a nasty side of hypocrisy and prurience. In her novel *Down Among the Women*, Fay Weldon captures the ducking and diving which was the reality behind the moral front: 'Marriage to the unmarried male is a trap, and sex the bait, which by stealth and cunning may yet be won.'[71] For women, the trick was to be sexy without looking as if you were trying. The women's magazines devoted considerable space to this intangible matter of allure. Barbara Schreier describes how an American image of femininity in the 1950s oscillated between the 'dutiful homemaker' and the 'tempting siren', with women expected to 'shift effortlessly' between the two simply by 'a change of clothes'.[72] Angela Partington shows how this translated into English dress style as a mix of 'glamour' and 'restraint'.[73] One of the elaborate distinctions of class which marked out the common from the respectable was the extent to which sexuality was obvious. Allure relied on a muted mystery, not an overt come-on.

By the late 1950s there were beginning to be some changes. In *Dutiful Daughters*, Christine Buchan remembers how a 'sexy cousin'[74] in Aberdeen bought a book when she was fifteen called *How to Attract Men*. She also began to curl her eyelashes. Her working-class Scottish father 'had a fit', not only about the book but 'all this stuff about raising your eyelashes up and down'.[75] Parents shocked easily in the 1950s.

Music expressed the changing mood. One day, tuning in to the crackling commercial station Radio Luxembourg from her Welsh village, Sheila Francis heard a new sound: 'Elvis Presley sang "Heartbreak Hotel", and the songs we'd known before became ghosts from another era.'[76] If 'Smoke Gets in Your Eyes', 'You Give Me Fever' and 'Unchained Melody' had intimated a world of mysterious, diffused passion which broke the boundaries of the mundane, rock'n'roll blasted out a naked sexuality.

With hindsight it is easy to observe that the two sexes were not being reared for mutual comprehension. Geoffrey Gorer found that when he asked the men what qualities they most desired in a wife, the majority emphasized good housekeeping. The women, however, said that their ideal husband should be 'understanding'.[77] While there was a barrage of information hitting women about housecraft, less attention was being paid to turning out understanding, romantic men. Young men in the 1950s were still doing their National Service in a male culture which David Morgan describes as putting 'a taboo on tenderness'.[78] According to Jeffrey Weeks, after Guy Burgess and Donald Maclean defected to the Soviet Union, 'an air of paranoia'[79] developed about homosexuality in the early 1950s.

There were quite contrary messages about what constituted desirable masculinity. Was it the DIY Dad with his trowel or the square-jawed war heroes Hollywood was exporting in the first half of the decade? As elusive as allure were 'the "real" men', who, Jean McCrindle says, 'seemed to be men who had fought in the war'.[80] In *The Golden Notebook*, Doris Lessing recorded how they appeared to be vanishing, and by 1959, when Melanie McFadyean's father left her mother, real men had passed into the realm of fairy stories:

I always wondered what he meant when he talked about 'real' men. He said they didn't wear overcoats or pullovers. They didn't drink tea or feel the cold. For a long time I believed him. I supposed they were like him. They'd love me and take me out, treat me and thrill me when they chose and then go to their other lives which were nothing to do with me.[81]

Sensitive tough guys like Montgomery Clift and James Dean began to appear in American films, but they found it far too demanding combining contradictory poles of masculinity to be understanding. They were so mixed up, they needed understanding themselves. So did the Angry Young Men – the fictional anti-heroes in John Osborne's play *Look Back in Anger* (1956) and John Braine's novel *Room at the Top* (1957). Their cult of hard masculinity expressed the dislocation of men caught between classes. The Angry genre, however, broke through an unstated bulwark of class privilege in its rejection of deference, and the work of playwrights like Arnold Wesker, Shelagh Delaney and later David Mercer provided voices for a search for new kinds of personal relations which had political and cultural implications.

The mid-1950s were a crucial turning point, in terms not only of politics but of social perceptions. Doubts about the prevailing attitudes to sexuality, gathering beneath the surface, began to seep through the fabric of assumption. An early sign of suppressed unease was the troubled response in 1955 to the hanging of Ruth Ellis. In her autobiography, *Left, Left, Left*, Peggy Duff, who was involved in the campaign against the death penalty, describes crowds rushing to see the execution notice outside Holloway prison. The young and beautiful nightclub hostess had murdered her lover after a miscarriage because he had been unfaithful. Ruth Ellis belonged to the upper stratum of women who dwelt in the twilight of respectability.

The Stepney prostitutes logged by researcher Rosalind Wilkinson were decidedly beyond the pale. She looked for 'problems' but found people – they told her about truanting from schools, dreams of adventure and ideal husbands, and made observations about sex and politics. One said she enjoyed prostitution but another told her, 'You don't know the things they do and the things they want. Be all right walking down the street, talk to you ever so nice, but when they get alone with us women, well some of them are like rats in holes.'[82] The women feared the Home Office wanted to clear them off the streets for the Festival of Britain. One told the sociologist, 'It's no good making reforms if you don't understand the people you are making them for.'[83]

Indeed, when reform came after the Wolfenden Report a few years later in 1959, it was more concerned that prostitution should not be visible than with the women's interests, and street prostitutes were tidied away to operate as call girls. Nonetheless, Wolfenden's insistence that the law should prevent public affronts to decency, rather than presume to regulate private behaviour, opened up a crack in the front of hypocritical respectability. As Jeffrey Weeks says, it was an admission that shifts had occurred in post-war society: 'The Report recognized the argument that homosexuality might be a threat to the family, but so, it was suggested, were adultery and divorce, and these were not illegal.'[84]

In *Abortion in England*, Barbara Brookes shows how throughout the 1950s several organizations were pressing for the legalization of abortion. The Abortion Law Reform Association continued its campaigning, the National Association for Child Welfare supported abortion for the 'mentally deficient'[85] in 1952, and in 1954 the Women's Co-operative Guild voted for reform. Mrs Amy Griffiths stated, 'What we want is freedom for a woman to make her own choice, whatever the reason and whether she is married or not.'[86] A survey conducted by the *Sunday Mirror* in 1956 found that 51.9 per cent of the 2,000 people they surveyed favoured abortion on request and a further 23.4 per cent accepted it on health grounds. By the late 1950s the subject was out in the open on radio and television. The case was mainly argued in terms of the social injustice and medical danger of back-street abortions, but in 1958, in *Women in Bondage*, V. M. Hughes passionately defended the right to birth control and abortion on the grounds that men had no right 'to dictate to women what shall happen to their bodies'.[87]

In 1956 D. H. Lawrence's *Lady Chatterley* was filmed in French and was among the books being smuggled in from Olympia Press in Paris. Allen Lane at Penguin Books decided to take a gamble on the change of attitude and publish an unexpurgated edition. So ironically Lawrence, who hated emancipated women and inveighed against the pleasures of the clitoris, was to become the symbol of sexual freedom during the 1960 trial.

Sleaze was going upmarket by the late 1950s. The battlelines were clear cut. Judges denounced the book *Don't Mourn Me, Toots*, while homosexuality, fetishistic fantasy, sexy gamekeepers and outsiders were aligned with sleaze. It was not only a matter of being 'agin' the authorities. There was, in Elizabeth Wilson's words, 'the search for authenticity . . . truth to feelings, truth to one's individuality'.[88] In Shelagh Delaney's play *A Taste of Honey*, performed at Joan Littlewood's pioneering Theatre Workshop in working-class Stratford, east London, in 1958, homosexuality, single-motherhood and race were all dealt with sympathetically. One of the characters, Jo, says, 'I don't know much about love. I've never been familiar with it.'[89] In 1960, E. P. Thompson, writing as an older new left socialist considering the meaning of the cultural rebellion of the young, commented, 'They had opted for honesty . . . But when the last illusion has been shed, feeling arises from a logic beyond either illusion or belief.'[90]

The age of apathy thus found its protesters. And the protesters found the Aldermaston march, which began to acquire a reputation for being sexy as well as defiant. Sleeping bags on a school floor and Slough in the rain are not obvious stimuli to eroticism, but desire is unexpected in its manifestations and though the marching young appeared to have shed the romanticism of a few years before, their sensible duffel coats concealed yearnings which were not entirely restricted to the larger purpose of banning the bomb. However, the nudge-nudge of sleaze and the mystery of sex were dissolving into a joke. In the radio comedy *The Goon Show*, mounting sexual innuendo and male braggadocio were deflated by a pathetic little male voice asking, 'What's it like?'

THE UNITED STATES

Femininity

Two women came to symbolize 1950s American femininity: Marilyn Monroe and Doris Day. Though apparently polar opposites, both presented versions of the natural. In his biography of Marilyn Monroe, Donald Spoto points out that she represented, 'the post-war ideal of the American girl, soft, transparently needy, worshipful of men, naïve, offering sex without demands'.[91] However as 'a woman with a strong sense of her body's power',[92] her sexuality was always unpredictable, untamed and thus suggested an independence which could not be controlled.

Marilyn Monroe was uneasy as an archetype, constantly trying to transcend the public figure of Marilyn Monroe and oscillating between vulnerability and self-assertion in her personal relationships. She alternated between using her power as a great star and denying it, fleeing

Marilyn Monroe: mix of desire and confusion.

Hollywood for New York and jeans while studying the Method in Lee Strasberg's Actors' Studio. The FBI started keeping a file on her in 1955 because of her relationship with playwright Arthur Miller, and J. Edgar Hoover ordered that every attempt she made to leave the country be monitored. This was not the normal stuff of sex symbols.

If Marilyn Monroe was, in Donald Spoto's words, an 'amalgam of desire and confusion',[93] Doris Day's image apparently contained no complications whatsoever. This really was an all-American beauty as wholesome as cornflakes, with antiseptic good-sport looks. Her pert, fresh, freckled face was always happy; unmarked by experience, it still had character. This was an idiom of femininity which suited suburban and would-be suburban women. Her body was an attainable size 12 and her pastel sweaters, slim skirts and shorty pyjamas were ideal mass-fashion prototypes.

Judith Crist, writing in the New York *Herald Tribune* in 1965, when Doris Day was no longer in fashion, suggested that she had struck the same chord as 'Blondie Dagwood':

We red-blooded American movie-goers like our stars to stick to comic-strip mores or clichés, with bumbling males appreciating the premium we put on virginity and wifely virtue and coming to heel at the proper pay-off time. We want our stars cutesy and ersatz sexy, properly ranch-housed and domesticated, if female, and properly frisky but ultimately domesticated, if male.[94]

Yet even at the height of the cultural conservatism of the 1950s, this quintessential American woman was by no means a passive symbol. From *I'll See You in My Dreams* (1951), where she played a pushy wife who manages to run her immigrant husband's career without him knowing, through the tomboy in *Calamity Jane* (1953) to the woman who claims Rock Hudson for matrimony in *Pillow Talk* (1959), she was resourceful and not at all the victim. The message was that while sex and love could be dangerous, women could exert power by channelling allure and keeping it within contained limits. She played some darker roles too – in *Love Me or Leave Me* (1955), for example, in which she was raped by her lover. In 'Nice Girls Do', Judith Williamson points out that, 'The desire for a reassuring picture of "the girl-next-door", with an unthreatening sexuality, was clearly strong enough . . . to produce a particular, selective viewing of Day's films.'[95]

If Marilyn Monroe was publicized as untamed nature, Doris Day was promoted as a healthy, cleansing force. Of course, both versions of nature were contrived. Marilyn Monroe, always anxious about her looks, faced the camera carefully prepared and Doris Day's sporty outdoor styles were always Hollywood smart.

An important difference was their relationship towards their public image. Doris Day, who compared herself with Betty Grable and Shirley Temple, simply disappeared behind her screen self. Despite two marriages and a son, she came over as the screen virgin who sought the conventional 1950s life. In contrast, Marilyn Monroe publicly displayed the two selves of star and woman. When she divorced Joe DiMaggio, she declared, 'To tell the truth, our marriage was a sort of crazy, difficult friendship with sexual privileges. Later I learned that's what marriages often are.'[96]

She actively tried to change her screen roles. In *Diamonds are a Girl's Best Friend* (1953), when the father of her wealthy boyfriend says, 'I thought you were dumb,' she got a line inserted, 'I can be smart when it's important, but most men don't like it.'[97] The title-song became her theme tune as the not-so-dumb-blonde. She sang it, along with 'Do It Again', to the troops in Korea, wearing a tight-fitting lavender dress despite the snow. After her last performance in Korea, she added, 'I felt I belonged. For the first time in my life, I had the feeling that people seeing me were accepting me and liking me. This is what I've always wanted, I guess.'[98]

The unpredictability in the version of natural femininity which was part of Marilyn Monroe's appeal means the image keeps moving; she is never the same. Her elusiveness is perhaps the key to her continuing fascination – she outlasted the decade as sexual myth. Doris Day remains fixed, in her chinchilla muff, 'the girl every guy should marry . . . true blue, understanding, direct, honest, and even a little sexy'.[99]

Politics

Sylvia Plath's novel *The Bell Jar* (1963) opens on a hot, airless July day in New York in 1953 when the only news was the execution of Julius and Ethel Rosenberg, charged with spying for the Soviet Union. Young Esther Greenwood is sickened by the 'goggle-eyed headlines staring up at me on every street corner and at the fusty, peanut-smelling mouth of every subway'.[100]

The oppressive atmosphere of repression and fear which had begun in the late 1940s intensified after Joe McCarthy lashed out at Communist sympathizers in government jobs at a speech to the Republican Women's Club of Wheeling, West Virginia. As Sally Belfrage says in her memoir of the 1950s, *Un-American Activities*, ' "McCarthyism" didn't begin or end with the senator; he was only, in the early fifties, its loudest mouth.'[101] But McCarthy did wield considerable power until 1954, when he cast his net too wide in attempts to smear the US army and in the process alienated the Republican leader, President Eisenhower. But his popularity empowered extreme right-wing groups, as well as right-wing Republicans like Richard Nixon.

Communist Party members and the foreign-born were obvious targets. Elizabeth Gurley Flynn was among the Communist leaders tried under the Smith Act in 1952 for conspiring to advocate the violent overthrow of the government; she was to be imprisoned, aged sixty-five, in 1955 after a long trial. The young Dorothy Healey, branded 'The Red Queen of LA' and 'Hard and Bitter as Nails' by the press, was given a prison sentence of five years and fined $10,000 by the court. Left-wing writing and ideas had turned into criminality. Claudia Jones, unable to persist with legal appeals against deportation when she became ill after her release from prison, had to leave the United States for Britain in 1956.

Having created the Communists as bogeys, it became a matter of guilt by association. For example, the Mexican actress Rosaura Reveultas was one of many arrested and deported for subversive activities in 1953. She had played the female lead in *Salt of the Earth*, a film about a miners' strike in New Mexico, produced and directed by members of the blacklisted Hollywood Ten. Sally Belfrage's mother, Molly Castles, lost her job at *McCalls* magazine after the FBI called, and was deported to Britain because she refused to testify against her ex-husband, Cedric Belfrage, the editor of *The National Guardian*.

McCarthy's notorious inaccuracy added to the climate of arbitrary terror which affected not only the suspects but also their families. The paranoia extended to engulf more and more people. Mary McLeod Bethune went to express the anxieties of black leaders to Eleanor

Roosevelt in 1951. Roosevelt, outraged by Richard Nixon's red-baiting tactics against the Democrat Helen Gahagan Douglas, was herself attacked by her old opponent Westbrook Pegler in 1953: 'The time has come to snatch this wily old conspirator before Joe McCarthy's committee and chew her out,'[102] he wrote. Needless to say, McCarthy never attempted to chew the formidable former First Lady.

It was to be a Republican congresswoman, Margaret Chase Smith, who first challenged the witch-hunting atmosphere of the McCarthy trials. In June 1950 she said the Senate was being debased by 'calumny, fear, ignorance, bigotry and smear', adding that a Republican victory through such tactics 'would be a lasting defeat for the American people'.[103] Hers was a lonely voice and years later she told Harry Truman's daughter, Margaret, 'To be honest with you, I was a little doubtful if I would be able to carry through on it. That was how nervous I was about it.'[104] She had good reason to be nervous, for McCarthy was being treated with deference by leading members of her own party and was extremely popular with the electorate. Even when the witch-hunt atmosphere was finally checked in the mid-1950s and McCarthy had lost his position of power and was an ill and broken man towards the end of the decade, the extreme right did not abandon their anti-Communist crusade. One of McCarthy's former researchers, Phyllis Schlafly, set up the Cardinal Mindszenty Foundation with her husband, Fred, in 1958 with a view to educating the world about the dangers of Communism.

McCarthyism was never simply about politics; there was a tremendous emphasis upon social conformity and an ideal of the family. These connections between the right and conservative approaches to gender were not entirely new. The Ku Klux Klan had articulated a view of gender relations based on the protection of white women during the 1920s, while in the 1940s Gerald L. K. Smith's America First movement, which was dominated numerically by women, had mixed anti-Semitism and racism with an insistence that women should stay at home and serve their husbands. In the 1950s, liberal academic women were again accused of being left-wing sympathizers, and there were virulent attacks on homosexuals and lesbians. Psychiatry and social science were utilized to give authority to repressive definitions of normal behaviour.

If uppity unmarried women were viewed with suspicion, women as a category, however, were invoked by politicians like Eisenhower. In the 1952 presidential contest he came up with a modern-day version of the old idea of women as moral cleansers of the political sphere, appealing to them as 'guardians of government morality'.[105] This concept of a special relationship to politics did have a resonance, for it promised respect and power behind the scenes. Women themselves, though, did not have the public visibility of the Roosevelt era. While a few notable women like Edith Nourse Rogers, Oveta Culp Hobby, India Edwards, Gladys H. Knowles and Clare Boothe Luce were prominent as individuals in the political parties, women lacked any organized collective voice for their interests as women. Despite the popularity of theories of women's difference, there was a strong feeling that the days of special claims were over, the assumption being that as women were equal these were no longer necessary. The Women's Division in the Democratic Party was abolished in 1952 and the Republicans altered their party structure along similar lines.

The organizations which had had their roots in those distant, hopeful days of progressivism were on the wane. The Women's Trade Union League finally disbanded in 1950 and the National Consumers' League was barely active. Along with the League of Women Voters, it had been losing members in the post-war era. The Women's International League for Peace and Freedom had become marginal during the Second World War, but survived to oppose the Korean war in the early 1950s. The National Woman's Party, though its membership was much reduced and ageing, continued to be exclusively preoccupied with securing the passage of the Equal Rights Amendment. Congress rejected the ERA in 1950; Katharine St George tried again in 1953 and the amendment reappeared in 1954, 1956 and 1957. Despite lack of support in Congress, the ERA did provide a focus for a loose network of women's organizations which acted as a lobby, and in 1953 Eleanor Roosevelt allied herself with the National Federation of Business and Professional Women (BPW), changing her position on equal rights. Verta Taylor says that the professional women's groups which clustered around the National Woman's Party in the 1950s 'directed little effort toward expanding the base of support for women's rights';[106] instead they maintained existing organizations, surviving when the political odds were against them. Rather than assuming the utter demise of all forms of organized feminism, she comments, 'The term "élite-sustained" seems appropriate for describing the stage of the movement in this period.'[107]

'What Has Happened to the Feminist Movement?' asked Arnold W. Green and Eleanor Melnick in 1950. They went on to caricature the 'old-fashioned, separatist, militant feminist' movement, which they contrasted with the 'shoulder-to-shoulder stand with American men' taken by contemporary women.[108] The dismissal of 'feminism' was, however, accompanied by pragmatic writing which continued to raise questions about being a woman. Pearl Buck, Dorothy Thompson, Mirra Komarovsky, Margaret Mead and crime writer Dorothy L. Sayers reached large readerships in a language of common sense which did not appear to be political. Somehow dissidence was communicated. A young coed, Kate Millett, arrived at the University of Minnesota in 1952 and began questioning whether women all wanted to have children. 'You ought to see a therapist,'[109] her classmates told her.

The formation of the Daughters of Bilitis (DOB) in 1955 by a San Francisco lesbian couple, Del Martin and Phyllis Lyon, provided an alternative cultural base for lesbian women uncomfortable in the butch/ femme milieu of the bars. They took their name from Pierre Louÿs's song cycle dedicated to women of the future. Barbara Gittings was just beginning to explore her sexual orientation in 1956 when she found fifteen women in a living room discussing a new periodical, *The Ladder*. She was to form the first East Coast chapter of DOB in 1958. She told Jonathan Katz, 'We didn't have any clear sense of what we were going to do' – what seemed important was simply 'lesbians . . . getting together' and 'sheer survival of the group'.[110] The DOB group was small and cut off from working-class bar culture, but the FBI and the CIA infiltrated them. Lillian Faderman writes, 'The FBI file on DOB stated, as though the mere fact in itself were evidence of the organization's subversiveness, "The purpose of [DOB] is to educate the public to accept the Lesbian homosexual into society."'[111] The right was quicker to understand the implications of sexual politics than the pioneers themselves.

It was to be the Civil Rights movement, however, which decisively broke through the conservative climate and inspired the radical social movements of the 1960s; in the words of singer and activist Bernice

Reagon, civil rights was 'the centering borning essence'.[112] In 1954, after years of trying to bring up cases against the 'Jim Crow' system of segregation, the National Association for the Advancement of Colored People won an important case when the Supreme Court ruled that segregated education violated the Fourteenth Amendment of the Constitution. Pauli Murray, who had been active in community and labour politics under the New Deal and then trained as a lawyer during the 1940s, helped to win this judgement. Drawing on social science data, she showed that the social, economic and psychological impact of a segregated system made a mockery of the promise of equality.

There had been a long unsuccessful struggle to desegregate the buses before Rosa Parks refused to give up her seat in Montgomery, Alabama, on 1 December 1955. Rosa Parks was an NAACP member and a Methodist, a seamstress who had attended the integrated Highlanders Folk School in Tennessee and was friendly with one of its founders, a

Contesting segregated space in Norfolk, Virginia, 1956.

fellow member of the NAACP, Virginia Durr. Jo Ann Robinson, a college teacher and member of the Baptist Church and Women's Political Council, a black professional organization, produced a leaflet calling for a boycott and, when Rosa Parks was convicted, the black population of Montgomery refused to board the buses. Over 10,000 people gathered at a church that night to hear a young preacher, Martin Luther King, speak of the power of non-violence.

The circumstances in which these ideas were to be tried out were dangerous and terrifying. High school student Elizabeth Eckford was faced by an angry white mob and the bayonets of the National Guard when she tried to enter an all-white school in Little Rock on 2 September 1957. She told civil rights organizer Daisy Bates:

They glared at me with a mean look and I was very frightened and didn't know what to do. I turned around and the crowd came toward me. They moved closer and closer. Somebody started yelling, 'Lynch her! Lynch her!' I tried to see a friendly face somewhere in the mob – someone who maybe would help. I looked into the face of an old woman and it seemed a kind face, but when I looked at her again, she spat on me. They came closer, shouting, 'No nigger bitch is going to get in our school. Get out of here!' I turned back

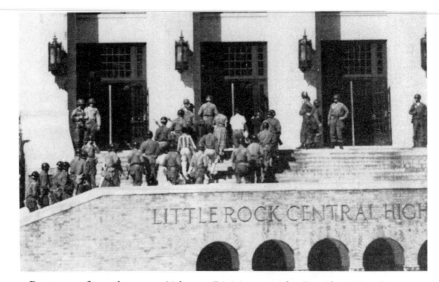

Paratroops from the 101st Airborne Division, sent by President Eisenhower, escort nine black students into school, 25 September 1957.

to the guards but their faces told me I wouldn't get any help from them. Then I looked down the block and saw a bench at the bus stop. I thought, 'If I can only get there I will be safe.'[113]

She was surrounded by the shouting crowd but with help from a white man and a white woman got on a bus to safety. The photo of her sitting in front of the school, alone amidst a white mob, was to flash around the world – an undeniable testament to the principle of equal civil rights.

In 1957, when Ella Baker went to work for the Southern Christian Leadership Conference, a regional coalition led by Martin Luther King, she brought ideas about decentralization and democratic organization developed through years of community work. As Barbara Ransby says, 'Ella Baker's message was simply that "strong people don't need strong leaders".'[114] The confidence generated by the struggle for civil rights and its emphasis on participatory democracy led to a more general sense of social entitlement. Linda Gordon observes:

As part of a ground swell of civil rights agitation in the 1950s, black women began asserting that the right to receive welfare was one they were entitled to as citizens, just like the right to vote. The success of this claim not only increased the AFDC [Aid to Families with Dependent Children] rolls, but also increased the proportion of blacks among AFDC recipients.[115]

She shows that this claim to social citizenship was 'one of the many ways in which "the sixties" began in the 1950s'.[116]

While politics at the centre was both conservative and male-dominated, community groups were emerging in Northern cities. In New York, for instance, tenants' federations, dismantled in the early 1950s after state rent controls were introduced and McCarthyism had hounded out Communist leaders, were replaced by borough-wide organizations. These were led by working-class women who were also conspicuous in the Save Our Homes movements in neighbourhoods threatened by developers. In Los Angeles the threat of urban renewal and the eviction of the poor mobilized the Mexican community against property developers.

Among middle-class women too, self-help organizing linked women in the family to wider neighbourhood networks. Sara Evans notes the involvement of women through church groups, Parent-Teacher

Associations, the Young Women's Christian Association and the League of Women Voters: 'The fifties mother maintained the home as a bulwark of social stability rather than a training ground for future citizens. She also joined in a wide range of community activities as an extension of this domestic vision.'[117]

In the new suburbs women helped set up churches, schools, parks and libraries and new forms of organizing were becoming evident. For instance, the Christian Family Movement, a white middle-class Catholic organization established in 1949, adopted a small group structure and aimed itself at married couples concerned not only with 'the betterment of their own family situations but also with the life of families everywhere'.[118] In 1956 the first all-female La Leche group met and discussed an article on breast-feeding which had appeared in *Reader's Digest*. Started by Mary Ann Cahill, these groups, which gathered in members' living rooms, were ideally suited to home-based women. The leagues grew to include non-Catholic women and encouraged mothers to trust their own feelings and experiences in opposition to the scientific approach to mothering. Members were strengthened by personal rapport: Mary Jane Brizzolara reminisced, 'to go to the first meeting and discover a whole room full of women who had the same feelings and the same values – it was great'.[119]

The idea that women were different from men in their approach to politics and society not only exerted a powerful conservative influence but was given radical meanings. For example, an appeal to women's closeness to nature was made by Rachel Carson, a writer on nature studies alarmed by the environmental dangers of pesticides like DDT, when she lectured to the women journalists' national gathering in 1954. She said that their roles as 'housewives and mothers' gave them an added understanding of the threat of a 'perilously artificial world'.[120] Vera Norwood comments:

Few understood that in making a popular connection between middle-class 1950s domesticity and the natural web of life ecologists dubbed earth's household, Carson had given her female audience a powerful argument for taking their concerns for the safety of their own homes, and their expansive feeling of responsibility for the homes of other animals, into public arenas controlled by professional men.[121]

By the mid-1950s, awareness was growing too about the long-term effects of the atomic bomb. In 1955 twenty-five Japanese women who had been terribly disfigured by the bombing of Hiroshima came to the United States at the invitation of a Quaker group and received plastic surgery. The visit was extensively covered by the press and the women appeared on the popular TV programme *This is Your Life*. Reports of cancer as a result of radiation were coming out and women's peace activism revived in opposition to the threat of atomic warfare. Women's Strike for Peace expressed a motherly anxiety about strontium-90 in milk, bringing them into conflict with the military and American Cold War foreign policy. They formed chapters in all the major cities, organized marches and lobbied their representatives. This was an extremely respectable middle-class movement, morally convinced that it was women's mission and duty to prevent a nuclear war.

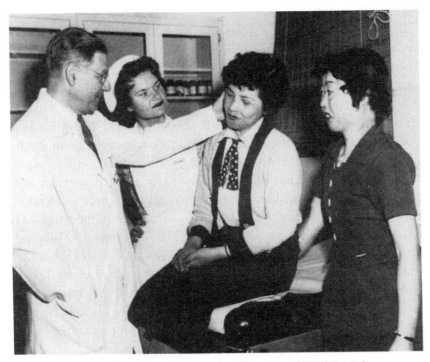

New faces from America: Toyoko Minowa and Michiko Sako, victims of the Hiroshima bomb, with their plastic surgeon and a nurse at Mount Sinai Hospital, 1955.

The emphasis on women's difference and their closeness to nature thus had various political meanings: it justified their removal from the public sphere, yet it could provide a route back into politics which contained a creative critique of the existing structures of political life.

Work

Glenda Riley notes a paradox of the 1950s: 'While business leaders, politicians and social commentators insisted that women return to the home, women themselves were moving into the job market in huge numbers.'[122] She shows that female employment grew at a rate four times faster than men's: in 1950 women were 29 per cent of the total workforce; by 1960 this had reached nearly 35 per cent. Among black women the rates of participation in paid employment continued to be high: over 40 per cent of black mothers with small children worked outside the home.

There were still many women who worked out of desperate need, for whom the idea of choosing between home and career was Utopian. Though more black women were moving into white-collar jobs, including sales, from which they had previously been barred, many were still domestic servants. Puerto Rican women, who had migrated to the United States in large numbers after the Second World War, were also stuck on the bottom rungs of the labour market, many of them in the low-paid garment industry in New York. And, like black women, their labour force participation was high: 39 per cent in 1950, compared to 28 per cent for Anglo women. Unskilled manufacturing work, including clothing, was to decline over the 1950s and 1960s, intensifying the economic problems of low-paid workers. The only alternative for poor black and Puerto Rican women was to take low-paid service work like waitressing, catering or jobs in hospitals. Many remained unorganized, race combining with class and gender to confine them to a subordinate section of the labour market in which neither the ideology of the suburban homemaker nor a liberal emphasis on women's employment as a means of individual advancement made much sense.

An ethic of social service to the poor whom they served could make workers in hospitals reluctant to adopt conventional forms of trade union action. But the Civil Rights movement brought a new awareness of discrimination among black and Hispanic women workers, enabling, for example, the health workers' Local 1199 to organize in New York in the late 1950s. When ancillary workers at six voluntary hospitals went on strike in 1959, the Spanish language newspaper *El Diaro* hailed it as '*la cruzada*'.[123] The *New York Times*, commenting on the women picketing, said, 'They feel for the first time that they "belong", and this groping for human dignity through group recognition is more important than more cash.'[124] The cash was undoubtedly more important than the journalist could imagine, but it was true that this was no ordinary strike. Local 1199 was to revive traditions of social unionism with strong community links among that 'other America' excluded from the prosperity that was being enjoyed by the mainstream.

Working mothers were accused of neglecting their families and told that children who felt abandoned could become the juvenile delinquents of tomorrow. This tendency to blame all social ills on women was contested by Joyce Cowley in *The Militant*, the paper of the Trotskyist Socialist Workers' Party, in 1955. Emphasizing that women worked because they needed the money, she also challenged the correlation between women's employment and children's neglect. She quoted a Wayne University study of delinquency in Detroit which indicated that children of working mothers were actually less likely to become delinquent.

A new trend, however, was for white women with husbands in the higher income groups to work in order to supplement the family income. Cultural assumptions were slow to adjust. A lawyer, Reka Hoff, responded in 1956 to the hostility towards career women by asking why it was that they were constantly forced to justify themselves: 'If unmarried, their career is designated a "substitute" for marriage; if married, their career is designated a "substitute" for motherhood; if a mother, their career brands them as selfish and neglectful.'[125] Women were caught between contradictory admonitions; warned against being over-solicitous, smothering moms, they were made to feel guilty if they were not at home.

A few voices were to be heard arguing that if social structures did not fit women's situation they needed changing. For instance, in 1952 in a pamphlet 'UE Fights for Women Workers' Betty Friedan noted the contrast between the treatment of women in manufacturing jobs and

Women and Abstract Expressionism

When Lee Krasner was a student, her teacher, the Cubist Hans Hofmann, praised her work with the words, 'This is so good you would not know it was done by a woman.' She remarked wryly many years later, 'He thought he was paying me the highest compliment.'[126]

The fragmented aspiration of Lee Krasner's *City Verticals*, 1953
(© ARS, NY and DACS, London 1997).

Discouraged by their teachers from linking art with their experience as women, 1950s women artists were in reality treated differently as women by the art establishment. To be labelled as a woman artist provoked condescension – but the alternative was the likelihood of being dismissed altogether.

Lee Krasner, who was sympathetic to Trotskyism in the early 1940s, was an Abstractionist before her husband, Jackson Pollock, became celebrated for his action painting in the late 1940s, but despite a long career and exceptional work, she was to be overshadowed by him in the public arena. Both Pollock and Krasner came out of the radical cultural milieu of the New Deal and there were, as Peter Wollen notes in *Raiding the Icebox*, ironies in the 'convulsive'[127] Pollock becoming the emblem of high American art in the Cold War era. In contrast, Lee Krasner was not to be recognized as a significant Abstract Expressionist artist until she was over seventy, and her major retrospective at New York's Museum of Modern Art was held only a year before her death.

Helen Frankenthaler, who was also an Abstract Expressionist, developed a unique technique of staining colour, yet she too was slow to gain recognition. Only when Kenneth Noland and Morris Lewis adopted her technique was she to be acclaimed as an innovator. Helen Frankenthaler, who explicitly resisted the idea that gender affects artistic expression, was ironically to be labelled feminine because of her choice of colour.

Abstract Expressionism appeared to transcend gender categories and both Lee Krasner and Elaine de Kooning deliberately signed their works with their initials, wiping out all traces of gender. Whitney Chadwick points out, however, that, 'All of the artists involved with Abstract Expressionism identified the process of generating images with nature.'[128] The abstraction of 'nature' concealed both the gender differences in women's and men's relations to 'nature' and the fact that it is not a given but partly a historical and social concept. It was thus peculiarly difficult for the women artists to cast off confining ideas of female difference, while criticizing the actuality of specific differences. In retrospect Lee Krasner said of her relationship to Abstract Expressionism, 'It is quite clear that I didn't fit into it, although I never felt that I didn't. I was not accepted, let me put it that way.'[129]

After Jackson Pollock's death, Whitney Chadwick notes that Lee Krasner 'developed a unique idiom. Deliberately choosing colours with "feminine" connotations, she used them in ways that negated their traditional connotations'.[130] Perhaps this tension is one reason why her work can be seen to swing, in Barbara Rose's words, 'back and forth from the abstract to the figurative, the geometric to the organic'.[131] Keeping moving, after all, is a means of avoiding being pinned down as essentially female, while keeping open the option of not being obliterated by a universalism that denies one's distinctness. Lee Krasner herself commented, 'All my work keeps going like a pendulum . . . For me I suppose that change is the only constant.'[132]

✳

the glossy image of women as consumers, and Mirra Komarovsky criticized the prevalent assumption that women were somehow naturally destined for pure domesticity. Her *Women in the Modern World*, published in 1953, proposed changes in the organization of employment and more social provision of maternity leave, day-care and laundry services. She believed that the role of men was socially mutable too: they no longer needed to be the bread-winning patriarch; earning and homemaking could be divided between both partners.

In practice, however, the structure of society continued to be posited on the clear-cut division of labour which assumed women were full-time in the home. This was a supposition, of course, which had never fitted the reality of many poor women, particularly black women; in the 1950s, though, the gap between assumption and actuality was being experienced by more and more white middle-class women as well. They were compelled to adapt to a cultural schizophrenia in which economic pressures pulled one way and prevailing attitudes the other. An uneasy compromise was struck: women's work was seen as helping out, a secondary income rather than a career. In *Homeward Bound: American Families in the Cold War Era,* Elaine Tyler May shows how the home-based consumption of the 1950s could be justified as contributing to the good of the family and thus, in a roundabout way, helped to make women's paid work acceptable. But such ambivalence contributed to a feeling of unease among middle-class and upper-working-class women; whatever option they took could always be seen as failure.

Yet throughout the 1950s achieving women continued to be praised in popular magazines like the *Reader's Digest, The Woman's Home Companion, Negro Digest* and *Ebony.* Joanne Meyerowitz argues, 'The stories affirmed long-lived bourgeois platitudes about hard work, freedom and upward mobility. In the postwar era, these platitudes gained new currency in the Cold War attempts to distinguish the autonomous individuals of the "free world" from the suppressed masses under communism'; they validated 'nondomestic behavior for women, a significant counterpoint to the "feminine mystique" . . . An ethos of individual achievement subtly subverted domestic ideals.'[133]

Among those celebrated were individuals who triumphed over disability or illness. Joanne Meyerowitz notes, 'Helen Keller was virtually sanctified in the mass culture.'[134] Babe Didrikson, who had become a champion golfer, was an inspiration when she continued playing despite having cancer. Black leader Mary McLeod Bethune was also among those acclaimed as one of the world's greatest living women. Historical heroines ranged from Phillis Wheatley, the first American black woman poet, to cowgirl Annie Oakley.

Conflicting versions of women's role clashed head on in the debates about girls' education. Was it worthwhile for girls to go into higher education if their real destiny was motherhood? Should they be given a different kind of education which would equip them for domesticity? A contrary point of view stressed the need for womanpower – the optimum utilization of human resources in competition with the Soviet Union. In fact, women did continue to move into colleges, though the opportunities described by Anne Firor Scott during the Second World War had gone and men returning from the services had entered higher education in large numbers. The percentage of all women aged twenty-three receiving first degrees was to rise steadily from 6.2 in 1946 to 10 in 1955; however, they were more likely to be

in teachers' colleges or liberal arts colleges. The barriers remained in
the male-dominated academic fields such as science, where part-time
employment cut women with children, however talented, out of the
career structure.

An ingenious accommodation was devised by a few achievers.
Women were to be found turning womanly experience into careers.
In the Federal Civil Defense Administration, for example, Jean Wood
Fuller and Katharine Graham Howard were made responsible for involving women in civil defence. Jean Wood Fuller, who criticized
attempts by women's organizations like the American Association of
University Women to get a ban on atomic tests, appealed to women
as housewives and mothers to apply their domestic skills to survival.
One of the most publicized campaigns was for the home bomb shelter, known as Grandma's Pantry: 'Is Your Pantry Ready in Event
of Emergency?' asked the brochure, concluding, 'With a well-stocked
pantry you can be just as self-sufficient as Grandma was.'[135] American
housewives were advised, 'Add a first aid kit, flashlight and a portable
radio to this supply, and you will have taken the first important step in
family preparedness.'[136]

1950s Home Sweet Home in
the family fallout shelter.

In the business world too it was a woman, Ruth Handler, who, in 1955, hit upon the idea of advertising toys directly to children on television, and in 1959 invented Barbie Doll – the epitome of childlike sexuality – which made a fortune for her firm, Mattel Toys.

Daily Life

In the early 1950s the atomic bomb was to become internalized; part of the anxious psyche, it was the subject of pop songs, films and nightmares. For the schoolchildren who wore identity dog tags and did A-bomb drill, the bomb had replaced Walt Disney's Big Bad Wolf as the symbol of unspoken fears.

There were several indicators that something was seriously wrong. The first lobotomy was performed in 1956 on a sixty-three-year-old woman; some surgeons saw it as the solution to the mad housewife syndrome. The consumption of tranquillizers rocketed. Alcoholism and divorce were also rising, and so were the numbers of women claiming Aid to Families with Dependent Children.

Yet, ostensibly, white middle-class women were enjoying the good life, shared to a lesser extent by the black middle-class and the better-off working class. As one black settler in the Long Island suburb of Roosevelt put it, 'I was fortunate . . . I was able to live the typical suburban type of life, a house, a dog, two kids, a pool in the backyard. I didn't have to work.'[137] The daily life of housewives and mothers appeared to be easier thanks to modern conveniences; even farm women in the new generation no longer spent time bottling, as they could freeze food. 'The Susie Homemakers' in the suburbs could escape from the harsh, competitive world of business and the grey conformity of organization man. The suburbs promised a life away from the decadence and danger of the city – a world of green lawns, Bermuda pink interiors and a tamed nature.

Women at home were encouraged to see themselves as the creators of positive alternatives to corporate and bureaucratic mores. Mothering too was being redefined; Dr Spock's child-centred approach was taking over from the disciplined theories of the earlier baby experts. The ideas of the British campaigner for natural childbirth Grantly Dick-Read were gaining advocates and La Leche League, in propa-

Lesbian Culture

It was the 1950s, with its emphasis on heterosexual family life, which paradoxically was to see the early homosexual and lesbian organizations. The pioneering Daughters of Bilitis focused on education, integration and legal reform and did not initially refer to themselves as lesbians, using instead terms such as the variant or simply the homosexual. However, by 1959 there were signs of gender tension: at the male organization's Mattachine convention in Denver, DOB founder Del Martin insisted, 'Lesbians are not satisfied to be auxiliary members or second-class homosexuals.'[138]

There were also class differences among lesbian women. Lillian Faderman observes that despite heterosexual stereotypes of the lesbian, 'It is not accurate to speak of a "lesbian subculture" since there were various lesbian subcultures in the 1950s and '60s, dependent especially on class and age.'[139]

The Ladder and DOB's magazine *Vice Versa* appealed to middle-class lesbians who were careful about dressing conventionally – acceptably feminine, but not too feminine. At the summer resort of Cherry Grove, wealthy lesbians favoured the chic styles of the Parisian Natalie Barney circle. They viewed butch dress askance and by the late 1950s were moving out as butch/femme women began to arrive. An early issue of *The Ladder* also grumbled, 'The kids in fly front pants and with butch haircuts are the worst publicity that we can get.'[140]

The Well of Loneliness still influenced styles in the bars, and butch and femme roles were actually becoming more pronounced during the 1950s. Being part of an embattled community contributed to the pressure to conform to conventions which were being produced within the subculture. Butches were getting tougher than they had been in the 1940s. The danger of attack had increased and police raids on bars meant not only jail and a charge of disorderly conduct but sexual humiliation by the police.

Yet a social gulf made it difficult to connect the resentment generated by persecution with the embryonic organizations. Donna, an American Indian woman, remembers:

Some gay men I knew took me to a One [homophile organization] meeting in LA. I liked it, but it wasn't for women at my level. I was working in a plastics factory. I couldn't think about political movements. Neither could the other women I knew. We did a lot of drinking because the poorer you are the easier it is to take if you're half-loaded. At the bar where I hung out a lot of women would come after work. We'd work all day with nothing to show for it, and we felt we might as well buy a beer where we could be around company of our own kind.[141]

Despite the gulf between the young working-class bar culture and older middle-class and upper-class lesbians, Lillian Faderman describes how, in the adverse climate of the 1950s, without a history of conscious political organization, lesbian women were finding, 'ways to exist and be nurtured in an environment that they had to build outside of the larger world that they knew disclaimed them'.[142]

gandizing for breast-feeding, presented an alternative model of female success through harmony with one's body. In the process, they asserted the power of women's experiential knowledge. Lynn Y. Weiner observes, 'Emphasizing the experience and wisdom of mothers rather than the expertise of doctors, the league by the mid-1950s anticipated later feminist calls for a woman's health movement by questioning the medicalization of birth and infant care and challenging the influence of "experts" on changing definitions of motherhood.'[143]

However, while motherhood was being invested with a new meaning as self-fulfilment through a return to nature, by the late 1950s the fertility rates of both white and black women were beginning to move down again. Robert L. Daniel comments:

Despite its reputation for dedication to family and children, the fifties did not sustain the intensity of the late forties. The post-war rush to the altar was over by 1950 . . . In reality the 1950s marked the end of the post-war trend of a rising level of family formation and of increasing fertility rates.[144]

Nonetheless, the sphere of personal experience was being validated not only by groups like La Leche, who were at variance with the consumer culture, but within popular culture as well. Elaine Tyler May notes a shift in popular novels: in the mid-1940s entrepreneurial values were being praised, but by the mid-1950s success for men as well as women was defined through the family. Fatherhood, certainly for the white middle class, was being presented as a vocation. Similarly popular television soaps focused on fathers in the family – their jobs were by the way. Only Ricky Ricardo in *I Love Lucy* shows signs of a career, and as he is a bandleader, he is outside the middle-class norm. There was uncertainty, then, not only about where women were meant to be but also about the proper place for men.

This lurking anxiety gave the suburbs a sinister edge. In her 1987 novel *The Night*, Alice McDermott captures the unease:

They were bedroom communities, incubators, where the stop signs and traffic lights and soothing repetition of similar homes all helped to convey a sense of order and security and smug predictability. And yet it seems to me now that those of us who lived there then lived nevertheless with a vague and persistent notion, a premonition of doom.[145]

Doom came in the shape of teenage rebellion. Before suburban parents had even collected all the goods they were planning for the home, their daughters, who had seemed happy enough only a short while ago with their hula hoops, were heading off in pursuit of rebels without a cause, donning black sweaters to sit at the feet of beat poets or joining the students campaigning for civil rights. Ironically, though, the rebels adapted classic 1950s concepts to attack their parents. Parents were blamed for not understanding their offspring, while the beats' rejection of materialism and celebration of immediate experience rejigged invocations of nature in the maternalist and domestic ethos from which they had sought to escape.

In *Young, White and Miserable: Growing Up Female in the Fifties*, Wini Breines writes:

Disaffected teenage girls longed for something significant in their lives. 'Authentic', 'genuine', 'real' were words they used (or implied) repeatedly. They felt that somehow being white, female and sheltered precluded the experience of meaningfulness. The sense that the culture was rife with hypocrisy, everyone keeping up appearances in one form or another, generated a yearning for genuine feeling. So did the smallness of their lives.[146]

Youthful rebels rejected the family, the suburbs and the criteria of consumer success held out to earnest achievers. Instead they identified with an idealization of the philosophical drifter – the outsider. Outsiders were, of course, male culture heroes; the girls were simply allowed to tag along.

Clare Boothe Luce saw doom coming when *The Blackboard Jungle*, with its rock 'n' roll background music, was chosen for entry in the Venice Film Festival while she was ambassador to Italy in the mid-1950s. After she denounced its 'degenerate'[147] portrayal of juvenile delinquency, it was replaced with *Interrupted Melody*. Unbeknown to her, she had an ally in Elizabeth Gurley Flynn, who, in 1956, was writing from her prison cell complaining about a pop song called 'Dungaree Doll'. Neither, however, was on the winning side. Youth culture and rock music were providing a mass market which was extending way beyond the R&B label. When Ruth Brown was asked by *Rolling Stone* magazine in 1990 at what point rhythm and blues became rock 'n' roll, she replied, 'When the white kids started to dance to it.'[148]

Rock 'n' roll was the kind of subversion McCarthyism could not deal with. On the other hand, in the crossover from black to white markets a significant metamorphosis occurred. In *She's a Rebel*, Gillian Gaar tells how Willie Mae Thornton (Big Mama) sang 'Hound Dog' 'with a lazy blues drawl that has [her] bawling at her errant suitor that his days are numbered; she sees through his smooth-talking jive and even his wagging tail can't entice her any more'.[149] Big Mama recorded 'Hound Dog' in 1953, three years before Elvis Presley, whose version shifted its gender meaning and exploded into a vast white market. She was later to claim she received only one royalty cheque of $500. It was a pattern to be repeated many times in the music industry. Cultural rebellion is one thing; material and social change takes a little more effort.

Sex

The hydrogen bomb dropped on Bikini Island in the South Pacific went down with a photograph of Rita Hayworth, and the island was to give its name to the skimpy two-piece swimsuits worn by bombshell bathing beauties. As sex was so evidently explosive, it seemed to require clearly defined conventions in order to impose upon it some patterns of predictability. Going steady was a well-established ritual by 1950 and during the decade it was to start younger and younger. Common at fifteen, it could be found even among twelve-year-olds. Customs varied from place to place: couples might exchange a ring, an ID bracelet or a Puppy Love anklet inscribed with 'Going Steady' on one side and 'Ready, Willing 'n' Waiting' on the other. 'Going Steady' was not meant to last for ever.

The codification of eroticism was elaborated in the sex advice manuals. In *From Front Porch to Back Seat*, Beth Bailey quotes one marriage text which explained:

In necking, stimulation is from the 'neck up' and the 'main' areas of sexual stimulation remain covered by clothing. The neck, lips and ears are 'utilized extensively as sexual objects'. Petting, on the other hand, 'includes literally every caress known to married couples but does not include complete sexual intercourse'.[150]

The purpose of all this instruction was to demonstrate how to arouse desire without going all the way. Sally Belfrage's friend Debbi was an adept at this tricky balancing act:

In Debbi's stories she is always the innocent victim who wins out. 'So he's takin' me out in his Pop's new De Soto, and we're moochin' around, and he goes, So howsaboutit, kiddo, ya wanna brew? and I go, Not me, Daddy-o, I'm drivin', so he goes Izzatso, get you since when, you can't drive, and I go, Ya wanna bet? So he gets me on his *lap*, right? and I'm having conniptions, li'l ole me at the wheel and what can I do? I'm drivin', what a panic, and all of a sudden I get this *feelin'*, you know? Like I'm sittin' on somethin'? and I go, Crikey, either this car is bumpy as all get out or you got a extra beer bottle in your pocket. And then I realize! I coulda *died*, swear to *God*! Story of my life. Wasn't that just George?'[151]

The sexual conventions of the 1950s gave the appearance of freedom because previously forbidden forms of behaviour were incorporated into an explicit and acceptable way of courting. But in doing so they marked out boundaries. Alice Walker, the daughter of black sharecroppers in rural Georgia, was one of those who were on the outside looking in:

I gazed longingly through the window of the corner drugstore where white youngsters sat on stools in air-conditioned comfort and drank Cokes and nibbled ice-cream cones. Black people could come in and buy, but what they bought they couldn't eat inside . . . I was an exile in my own town and grew to despise its white citizens almost as much as I loved the Georgia countryside.[152]

The power and danger linked to sex could give young white heterosexual women who fitted the stereotype confidence, but it excluded misfits and women outside the prevailing WASP culture. Danger also had its nasty side, for the definition of perversion was increasingly clear-cut. Judy Grahn describes the purge in the military in 1950, when lesbians were tricked into incriminating others and then dismissed as undesirables: 'Everything I touched was spoiled.'[153]

The McCarthyite witch-hunt invaded the personal sphere of sexual relationships, but neither the left nor the Civil Liberties Union recognized homosexuality or lesbianism as public political issues. They were treated as a kind of sickness which psychoanalysts busily set about curing. One lesbian woman went into analysis with insomnia and her analyst cheerfully notched up a cure when she began an affair with a married man, even though she was still not able to get to sleep. Self-hatred brought some lesbians to seek cures themselves – at considerable expense of course.

Guilt and self-hatred were not confined to lesbians and permeated many conformist heterosexual relationships too. Maria Kimball's marriage was apparently happy, yet she added a troubled note in her contribution to a study of marriage conducted by E. Lowell Kelly. Viewing the sexual practices of the 1940s in the light of the 1950s, she wondered whether 'mistress patterns' had been created: 'It was stupid of me not to anticipate that his oft-expressed philosophy of the desirability of sexual freedom indicated that he would be prone to infidelity.'[154]

In *Young, White and Miserable*, Wini Breines describes the 1950s as a
'culture of containment'.[155] Codes of personal sexual behaviour and
psychoanalytic theories were affected, along with the prevailing assumptions in social science. Sexual containment was to be integrated into
state policy; Margaret Sanger called it approvingly 'national security
through birth control'.[156] From the 1950s, population policies, which
had been initially applied to Puerto Rico and Haiti in 1939, were to
be more widely exported through US foreign policy as a solution to
poverty in the Third World. Population control was presented not as
a complement to the redistribution of wealth, but as an alternative
which would prevent the rise of Communism. When the first human
trials of oral contraceptives were conducted in Puerto Rico and Haiti,
the researchers, financed by Margaret Sanger's friend Katherine McCormick, justified the tests by the extreme poverty of the woman guinea
pigs – 'The gratitude of those selected was pitiful,'[157] noted the
researchers. The 'population bomb' philosophy was then to be reapplied
to the black and Puerto Rican poor in the United States.

Sexual anxiety fed into and was reshaped by a huge market. There
was, of course, nothing new about consumption as a means of achieving
a sense of personal well-being. But with padded bras for twelve-year-
olds and a 39-D bra as a mark of status, it was to reach new levels and
involve heavy expenditure for parents. This was by no means frivolous
consumption. Young women were assured that a sexy red dress for a
dance could be the vital key to marriage. Investment in sexual allure
led back to the home again.

It all added up to very big business indeed. In 1956 *Life* magazine
reported that American women were spending $1.3 billion on cosmetics
and toiletries, $660 million on 'beauty treatments', $400 million on
soap and 'electric devices' and $65 million on reducing their weight.[158]
The total ($2,425 million) was twice the total defence budget of Italy.
Stuart and Elizabeth Ewen show how the 'channels of desire' were
being materially and culturally restructured during the 1950s. Cinema
and television were presenting increasingly standardized images of
beauty (nearly all of which were white) and these in turn were being
marketed through a mass fashion industry. For example, one Bronx
manufacturer had a turnover of $80 million by the mid-1950s, based
on selling chic, inexpensive clothes like the shirt-waister dress popular

with office girls, film stars and society women. The Ewens comment, 'For people nurtured by denial and living in a world increasingly defined by the principles of appearance and display, mass fashion served as a powerful lens of expectation. The democracy of images came together, promising to fill the thirsty wells of hope, of long-standing desires . . .'[159]

This marketing of desire, however, was never completely controllable. The democracy of images presented the possibility of every young woman (who was white) achieving the external show of allure and thus a form of power which could break through boundaries of social class or sexual convention. The persistent psychologizing and the sex-advice manuals were also eliminating what Margaret Mead described as 'a guaranteed reticence'.[160] Dr Alfred Kinsey's sociological studies of sexual behaviour surveyed intimacy in a solemn, somewhat owlish manner. However, his *Sexual Behavior in the Human Female*, published in 1953, caused outrage by reporting that by 1950 more than half the women in the country were not virgins when they married. With the gap between what was said and what was done thus exposed, people were inclined to invoke his statistics rather than individual moral standards of sexual behaviour. Kinsey also publicized the well-kept secret of the clitoris – he was greatly preoccupied with measuring them. All the matter-of-fact stuff about nerve endings – even if it over-simplified erotic sensation – was an abrasive materialist antidote to the unphysiological psychologizing about female sexuality.

The gushy enthusiasm in the sex-advice books about the pleasures of the honeymoon bed could backfire too. Some inquiring young women like the singer Cher decided to investigate: 'I wanted to find out what it was all about so I just did it, all at once, with the little Italian guy next door I was madly in love with. When we'd finished, I said, "Is this it?" He said, "Yeah" and I said, "Well, you can go home." '[161] If the moral advisers of the 1950s underestimated the curiosity that they aroused in the young, their oversell of romantic marriage-oriented sex also served to sow the seeds of doubt. Wini Breines cites one middle-class girl who, led to expect that 'stout-hearted young men' would come courting, ready 'to cherish and protect us', was disillusioned to discover a grimmer reality: 'No one in those romantic movies ever had to go to the VD clinic or get an abortion.'[162]

The rebellious minority were to jettison the values of the white middle class *in toto* as rank hypocrisy. The search for authenticity in beat culture was a release for young women; it promised a more meaningful intensity than the standards of mass fashion and the restrictions of dating conventions. Carolyn Cassady began a relationship with her husband's close friend Jack Kerouac: 'Butterflies bursting from cocoons had nothing on me. Now I was part of all they did; I felt like the sun of their solar system, all revolved around me.'[163] It was necessarily a fragile power, without the bulwarks which conventions supplied. And time was to reveal that even the beat subculture, which appeared to have no rules, had them after all, buried in implicit assumptions which the men still defined.

For young Americans outside the white middle class, the juxtaposition of mass culture and their parents' values could be disturbing and discordant. In *The Woman Warrior*, Maxine Hong Kingston describes how she watched Betty Grable in *Oh You Beautiful Doll* and subverted her mother's attempt to marry her off to a FOB – Fresh Off the Boat. When young men, new to America, were invited to look her over, she dropped dishes and spilled soup on them. While her mother was assuring them that her daughter could sew and sweep,

I raised dust swirls sweeping around and under the FOB's chair – very bad luck because spirits live inside the broom. I put on my shoes with the open flaps and flapped about like a Wino Ghost. From then on, I wore those shoes to parties, whenever the mothers gathered to talk marriages.[164]

She was to escape from the FOBs by going to university, but her mother did not give up: ' "Though you can't see it," my mother said, "a red string around your ankle ties you to the person you'll marry. He's already been born and he's on the other side of the string." '[165]

The anxiety of parents about their children recurs generation by generation, but the 1950s saw a veritable social panic about that new creature 'the teenager'. The energy that went into asserting as norms notions of tradition which were, in fact, relatively new constructs was matched by the energy that went into defying them. The main brunt of all this angst was taken by the mothers, who were held responsible for the kids turning so mysteriously into rebels.

Amidst all this, Betty Friedan was labouring away with an article for

McCalls about her class reunion. 'What do you wish you had done differently?'[166] she asked this group of educated middle-class women. Their answers revealed the 'problem that had no name',[167] which she was later to write into *The Feminine Mystique*.

It was the black playwright Lorraine Hansberry, however, who, with remarkable prescience, glimpsed another cultural and social paradigm. She wrote to *The Ladder* in 1957, calling on women to dissect and analyse 'male-dominated culture':

Otherwise . . . the woman intellectual is likely to find herself trying to draw conclusions . . . based on acceptance of a social moral superstructure which has never admitted to the equality of women and is therefore immoral itself. As per marriage, as per sexual practices, as per the rearing of children, etc. In this kind of work there may be women to emerge who will be able to formulate a possible concept that homosexual persecution and condemnation has at its roots not only social ignorance, but a philosophically active anti-feminist dogma. But that is but a kernel of a speculative embryonic idea improperly introduced here.[168]

As the little girls sat engrossed in TV programmes like the *Queen-for-a-Day* show, which rewarded the 'most pathetic' woman with such desirable gifts as enough Rice-a-Roni for a year, the 'embryonic idea' was hardly evident. Nonetheless, it was to be questions like these, raised by women who were on the outside looking in, which were to touch the inward contradictions being lived by those within the culture of containment. The effect was indeed to be explosive.

Chapter 7

THE 1960s

BRITAIN

The Ferment

Novelist Angela Carter was in no doubt about the 1960s: 'I grew up in the fifties – that is, I was twenty in 1960, and by God, I *deserved* what happened later on. It was tough in the fifties. Girls wore white gloves.'[1] Clement Attlee and the 1944 Education Act were responsible: 'All that free milk and orange juice and cod-liver oil made us big and strong and glossy-eyed and cocky, and we simply took what was due to us whilst reserving the right to ask questions.'[2] The diet somehow got into the *Zeitgeist* – 'there was a yeastiness in the air'.[3]

And the yeast rose through the culture before it reached politics. It was there in the novels which explored how to be women, from Doris Lessing's lust and autonomy to Edna O'Brien's romance and abandonment. Margaret Drabble and Penelope Mortimer wrote of the discomforts of housewives and mothers before the emergence of a woman's movement and, in 1962, Naomi Mitchison broke into the male preserve of science fiction with *Memoirs of a Spacewoman*, a novel about sex and communication with alien life forms.

The sense of flux, of being on the edge of transformation was there in the music. Actress Julie Christie particularly remembered the Doors, Jimi Hendrix and Janis Joplin: 'It was free . . . potent – it excited me and still somehow personifies the time of excitement and breakthrough and danger.'[4] During the early 1960s Terri Quaye, herself a singer and drummer, used to hang around in Dobells, the famous London record shop, to hear the latest American jazz imports. Noting the 'unstiffening of the English ear', she says that 'the accelerating Caribbean influx and with them Blue Beat' contributed.[5] So did the music of the American urban ghetto.

Rhythm and blues inspired the rock bands which were sprouting as if from nowhere in the northern cities. A generation of young women went pounding towards this British sound head on. At lunch hour in a Liverpool Catholic grammar school:

Busy chrysalises elbowed each other in the toilets, abandoning and adapting tell-tale evidence of high school morality, rolling skirts at the waistband to within a whisper of indecency, the more dextrous skilfully dabbing long Bambi lashes on upper lids and short, thick lower lashes under lower lids. Then pan-sticked and panda-eyed, the transformation complete, we swarmed down Mount Pleasant, aware that we were at the hub of something exciting and new.[6]

These were the days of the Beatles and the Cavern, when stars were to be met in your friend's street. It didn't last, of course; they went away – sometimes to America.

It was never quite as open as it seemed either. Terri Quaye remarked in retrospect:

Apparently all hell was breaking loose, but it made little difference to the black community. The release from society's constraints only applied to the young whites, and as with most phenomena those enjoying it would find it hard to believe that it was of little consequence to those only permitted to be onlookers.[7]

The initiators of the ferment were men and a hip élite quickly formed in the music business. Nonetheless, amidst the druggy status-seeking of the late 1960s, there was a passionate desire to meld Utopia with everyday living. This counter-culture opened up possibilities for women as well as men. Julie Christie sums up the dream of the decade: 'love of everybody . . . the feeling that you were part of the human race and that we are all much of a muchness'.[8]

As all customary boundaries dissolved, the young kept their eyes wide open and their ears flapping in the wind.

Politics

Not everyone's ears were flapping, of course. 'I have never understood the ferment of the sixties I hear so much about,'[9] stated Barbara Castle in 1988. 1960s popular culture might be turning inside out, but she was too busy making policies realities as a Cabinet member in Harold Wilson's 1964 Labour government to bother much about ferments. This was her chance to act on her belief that, 'It is hard for anyone, male or female, to fulfil themselves if they are poor, ill-housed, ill-educated and struggling with ill-health.'[10] Her approach consequently was to tackle women's needs as part of general social issues. Labour did not make a complete break with Tory policy, for they too had been clearing slums and building hospitals in the early 1960s. But the ethos of Labour as the modern, caring party and the plans for expansion in social provision did mark a difference.

'I was overjoyed': Barbara Castle, the new
Cabinet Minister for Overseas Development, leaves
Number 10 Downing Street on 17 October 1964.

Barbara Castle did not see equality simply in terms of opportunities to rise to high positions. She was convinced that more important was the chance for women:

to find out what they are, what they want to be and whether they are given the backing of society to lead the lives they want to lead. Real equality must go down to the mundane things, like how do I get enough to live on, do I or do I not have children, who will help me to bring them up.[11]

Harold Wilson was willing to work with and promote women: Jennie Lee, Shirley Williams, Judith Hart and Margaret Herbison were all prominent in his government. He was also prepared to land them in the hot seat. Barbara Castle moved from Overseas Development to Transport and finally to Industry – a stormy position in the late 1960s because Labour was trying to convince unions to accept wage restraint. But it was introducing the breathalyzer in 1968 that made her realize that 'the sex war was not dead'; darts teams wrote, threatening, 'We'll get you yet, you old cow.'[12]

The Labour government was not loved by 1968, and not only on account of the breathalyzer. From 1967 welfare gains were being whittled away. A charge was put on NHS prescriptions in 1967 and free milk for secondary school children was ended. Margaret Herbison resigned in protest against welfare cuts. The sociologist Peter Townsend pointed out that in real terms Labour in office had not in fact narrowed the gap between the poor and the better-off. Unable to control profits, the government was regulating incomes to make the economy more productive and, in the process, trying to curb trade union freedom. It took the strike of the Ford's sewing machinists, combined with the threat of Labour women MPs voting against the government, to enable Barbara Castle to insist in 1968 that equal pay should be phased in through incomes legislation.

The spate of sex legislation was to be Labour's most radical legacy. Much of this was introduced by back-benchers and passed on free votes, with MPs following their consciences. Parliament was responding to changing social attitudes rather than initiating permissive policies, though Labour's Roy Jenkins exerted some influence. The Sexual Offenders Act of 1967 legalized homosexuality between consenting adults and in the same year the Medical Termination of Pregnancy Act, introduced by the Liberal David Steel, legalized abortion if two doctors certified that it was needed on medical or psychological grounds. The Family Planning Act enabled local authorities to provide advisory services on birth control. Reform of the law relating to divorce was achieved in 1969: a divorce could now be obtained on the grounds that a marriage had completely broken down after a separation of two years if the couple both wanted to part or five years if only one party sought divorce. The Matrimonial Property Act secured the wife an equal share in family assets. Censorship was also abolished in the theatre in 1968.

The new-image women in the Conservative Party led by the corporate modernizer Edward Heath went along with some of these reforms. Sara Morrison was given the job of shifting the Tory women's organization away from social panics about law and order towards local participation in voluntary bodies and acceptance of moderate change. She identified with the tradition of Tory social reform initiated by Disraeli and supported equal opportunities. But most active Tory women were not in the professions or business; they were housewives and were accustomed to a Toryism which respected them as homemakers. They wanted security, not opportunities. Instead of being congratulated, they felt increasingly marginalized within the party and under siege from the alarming eruptions which surrounded them in society. Joan Hall from Keighley finally rebelled and questioned the leadership at the 1968 Conservative conference. There was no longer any clear distinction between socialists and Conservatives, she complained. Who was going to champion 'the law-abiding tax-payers and rate-payers'[13] who were not among the demonstrators? It was, however, a thankless task trying to mobilize a constituency which, in its own mild way, was being affected by la dolce vita of Tupperware parties, coffee mornings, eating out and foreign holidays. Tory women voters' hairstyles softened during the decade, their skirts moved slowly up the leg, and some of their children were the demonstrators, which made them quietly uncomfortable about the police.

The scandal in 1963 of Tory minister John Profumo's affair with Christine Keeler, and revelations about spies and diplomats having sex with the same women, had made it difficult for the Conservative Party to take the moral high ground. Instead, Mary Whitehouse, a right-wing secondary school teacher, worried because Marriage Guidance counsellors were being brought into schools to discuss sex education and upset about the BBC, which she believed had fallen prey to 'the exponents of the New Morality',[14] produced a women's manifesto. Speaking in the name of the woman in the street in defence of 'established morality',[15] she said she felt censored. In fact, Mary Whitehouse was accustomed to organization, having been a member of the religious right-wing Moral Rearmament movement. A skilful grass-roots campaigner, she created the Clean Up TV campaign and later the National Viewers' and Listeners' Association.

In 1968 Enoch Powell's racist 'Rivers of Blood' speech expressed hostilities against black immigrants which had previously been voiced publicly only by extreme right-wing groups. He defeated the Tory leadership on immigration with his appeal to defend England. This exclusionary interpretation of the nation from an MP and a well-known public figure brought fear into the life of Sona Osman, whose father was from Pakistan. She was aged eight and living in a two-bedroomed flat in Brixton, south London, when racism and imperialism invaded her childhood. Her teacher had told her to bring in something from her weekend for the school noticeboard and she chose a photo from the *News of the World* of NHS doctors and cleaners. She wrote an essay considering what would happen to all 'the poor sick English people'[16] if Enoch Powell got his way and immigrants were sent home.

In *The Iron Ladies*, Beatrix Campbell says, 'The concept of the Conservative nation, housed many meanings – from sexuality, the family and the state, to the soul of the cities and the colour of skin.'[17] Fears of a loss of identity, the collapse of fatherly authority in the family and selfish working mothers breeding delinquent youths converged in a demand for the protection of the family, women and children – by which was meant, of course, white families and white women and children. In Beatrix Campbell's words again, 'Women became the metaphor for loss of control – they were the victims of strangers.'[18]

Another gendered metaphor had appeared momentarily on the left as the extra-parliamentary peace movement grew in the early 1960s. In November 1961, pram-pushing mothers led 400 marchers to the Soviet Embassy with a letter to the Russian leader Khrushchev:

Up to now women have not had much to say in politics; but ... we can't just go on cooking food for our families when we know it is being contaminated with radioactive poisons. We know that women all over the world, especially those who have or hope to have children, feel as we do.[19]

But in general women participated in CND as concerned individuals with differing political perspectives. David Widgery has recounted how 'Pat Arrowsmith's kayak bobbed between the parked nuclear submarines'[20] at Holy Loch in Scotland. The anarchist Leila Berg remembered CND as a 'joyous' movement in which people were 'ungagging themselves, and their boldness was creative and imaginative'.[21] It was not always so joyous for Peggy Duff, sandwiched between the Labour right and anarchists chanting 'Stuff Duff'.[22]

Peggy Duff, Secretary of CND: organizer of
the Aldermaston marches against nuclear weapons, she took on
accommodation, first aid, anarchists and the Labour Party.

By 1963 the arguments about the Committee of One Hundred's non-violent direct-action tactics were straining CND's broad-church politics. Peggy Duff stood with her loud-hailer bellowing, 'This way for lunch, marchers,'[23] as the Aldermaston march approached Reading. About 1,000 Spies for Peace ignored her and vanished into the woods to reveal a secret Regional Seat of Government to preserve top people in the event of a nuclear attack. She spent the night patrolling the marquee full of weary CNDers in their sleeping bags to stop the Fascists cutting the ropes. Somehow she kept her sense of humour, recognizing that a bridge had to be kept open between the old left and this radical newcomer to politics, so impatient of paternalism (or maternalism) and insistent on political self-reliance. As CND crumbled in the mid-1960s, she formed closer links with the American peace movement and became active in the campaign against the Vietnam War. The bomb, she decided, was 'a symptom, not a cause'; the underlying 'threat to peace lay in the hegemonies of the super-powers, and especially of the United States'.[24]

The impact of CND as a social movement persisted, however, despite fragmentation. The anti-authoritarianism of direct action went into community politics, campaigns around prisoners' rights, protests about the draconian treatment of the homeless in hostels and libertarian education. Bomb culture also affected the emerging counter-culture of poetry, raves and underground magazines. Home was becoming an existential moment, while the family was presented as the site of authoritarian repression in the psychiatric rebellion of David Cooper and R. D. Laing. Cultural rejection of establishment values flipped meanings round. Mum, maligned in the 1950s for neglecting offspring, was turned into the villain once more for failing to comprehend 1960s mind-blown youth. (Laing's mother was appalled when 'fuck' appeared in one of his books.)

R. D. Laing's questioning of the inhuman treatment of mental patients he had observed during the 1950s led him to a more general critique of oppression in everyday relationships. He gave child-centred psychology a new twist with his exploration of the way parents and children related in families. By 1967 he was asking why individuals accepted repression and authority from the state. The rejection of habits of obedience and the need to change consciousness were themes of the

Dialectics of Liberation conference at the Roundhouse in north London that year. For a week the speakers, who included David Cooper and R. D. Laing, linked psychological colonialism with imperialism. They were, however, all men and Stokely Carmichael, who brought the political ideas of black power from the United States, scornfully dismissed a white woman who tried to speak from the floor. The resulting clash of loyalty was remembered as a turning point by several women who were later to join the Women's Liberation movement.

Angela Carter described the late 1960s as 'like living on a demolition site'.[25] After the Tet offensive in 1968, the anti-Vietnam War marches got angrier and more violent, declaring solidarity with the Vietcong. In 1968 the May Events in France inspired hope of an alliance between students and young workers. Students occupied their universities, demanding a more democratic relationship between students and teachers and challenging the authoritarian knowledge factory, which, they claimed, was geared to business and military interests and was churning them out to be cogs in the capitalist system. Amidst startling upheavals and occupations of colleges, young women dreamed of being guerrilla fighters but were sent to make the tea for budding revolutionaries and required to type the anti-authoritarian leaflets. Not surprisingly, they began to ask questions. Rebellion reached the schools. The student newspaper *Black Dwarf* reported that Folkestone schoolgirls of thirteen were being kept under 'parental house arrest'[26] for reading Leila Berg's Penguin Book about the libertarian comprehensive school, Risinghill, arguing about the Vietnam War and joining the Schools Action Union.

Meanwhile, over in Belfast the young Catholic intelligentsia were watching American civil rights activists on television and seeing some inescapable connections. Mary Kay Mullen was among the students who went on the historic 1968 march for Catholic civil rights from Belfast to Derry. She had just arrived as a mathematics student at Queen's University, Belfast, and the place was buzzing with ideas, but 'men did not consider me or my women friends capable and equal'.[27] She and the other women distributing leaflets did feel resentment, but 'few women (apart from Bernadette) spoke up and although at times I longed to express my opinion, I was too scared and inarticulate to speak out.'[28] The marchers were ambushed violently by Ian Paisley's supporters

Bernadette Devlin, Irish independent republican, was elected MP for Mid-Ulster at the age of twenty-one in a 1969 by-election.

before they got to Derry. Frances Molloy was knocked to the ground and kicked, escaping only when a man intervened: 'Can't you see she's only a wain?'[29] At home with her mother, she watched 'this wee student girl outa Cookstown be the name of Bernadette Devlin . . . talking rings roun' the big important people of the day'[30] on television. Bernadette Devlin was to become an MP in 1969, flummoxing the British press with her revolutionary socialist politics and her miniskirts.

Ideas about Women's Liberation began to travel internationally and news of the American movement combined with a range of discontents. Mothers with young children meeting in a south London 1 o'clock Club were inspired by Juliet Mitchell, author of a pioneering article on women's oppression, 'The Longest Revolution', to set up a women's group. The Hull Equal Rights Group was also formed in 1968 to support a safety campaign after men were killed on a trawler. It was led by Lil Bilocca, a Hull fisherman's wife, who faced opposition from fishermen as well as the owners. After sewing machinists at Ford's Dagenham plant went on strike in the summer of 1968 for the right to be graded as skilled, the National Joint Action Campaign for Women's Equal Rights (NJACWER) was established by trade unionists.

Arguments for rights, claims within society as it was, were converging with the idea of liberation which came from a new left vision of social transformation. Not just a transfer of political power or economic ownership but the democratization of all relationships in society and an end to personal as well as public inequalities seemed possible in the late 1960s.

In January 1969 *Black Dwarf* announced the 'Year of the Militant Woman'. Women's Liberation groups did indeed spring up in many parts of the country. In London they grouped into a loose federation, the London Women's Liberation Workshop, and began producing a newsletter, *Harpies Bizarre*, later renamed *Shrew*. Stickers attacking the sexism of swimwear adverts, 'This Exploits Women', were stuck on the posters in the London Underground; the Ideal Homes Exhibition and the Miss World beauty contests were picketed: 'Mis-Fit. Mis-Conception. Mis-Placed.'[31] The 'misfits' discovered some allies and a history. Labour Party member and former suffragette Jessie Stephen spoke at the first public meeting held in Bristol; clothing worker Gertie Roche supported the younger women in Leeds Women's Liberation, and Audrey Wise, an official in the Union of Shop Distributive and Allied Workers, was a link between labour and liberation. NJACWER and small left Trotskyist groups encouraged interaction and the first national conference had its origins at a radical history gathering at the Oxford trade union college, Ruskin, in autumn 1969. The new movement combined a sense of being unique and of coming out of nowhere with a desire for roots. Ideas seemed to be rushing through the air to be grabbed; it was as if the whole world was bursting at the seams and everything was about to change.

Work

In the early 1960s there were few obvious signs that by the end of the decade women trade unionists would be questioning not only pay but the whole position of women. The clues were there, however, in the statistics, which showed that in 1961 women made up a third of the workforce and that more than half of them were married women. They were there buried in the economic and sociological monographs too. T. E. Chester was telling readers of the *District Bank Review* in 1962 that it was 'a forlorn hope' to imagine that jobs were to be filled by 'a reserve army of devoted spinsters';[32] married women were going to be the means of expansion.

As families became smaller it was more feasible for women to go out to work for longer, but fitting paid work around one's family raised problems. A few writers were questioning the types of employment available. Elizabeth Gundrey was also wondering about the lack of pension rights for temporary workers and Nancy Seear about lack of training, which could make the jobs of unskilled women vulnerable to technological change.

From the early 1960s, the National Union of Tailor and Garment Workers and USDAW were pushing for equal opportunities, and a small band of women, including Audrey Wise and Christine Page of USDAW, kept returning each year to the fray. Nurseries were also being discussed, along with the campaign for cervical-cancer screening, which was supported by a wide range of women's organizations, including the Women's Institute and the National Assembly of Women, and in 1965 Mrs Fenwick from Dundee raised the question of birth control at the TUC conference.

In summer 1968 the historic strike of Ford's sewing machinists put equality on the agenda. They struck for the right to be included in a higher paid grade which was all male, thus challenging Ford's grading system. Rose Boland, who emerged as spokeswoman, pointed out in an interview in the Trotskyist *Socialist Worker* that the definition of skill was gender-biased: 'When we go to the Ford Company, we have to pass a test on three machines. If we don't pass that test, then we don't get a job. So why shouldn't they recognize us as skilled workers?'[33]

The Ford sewing machinists did not win their demand to be graded equally but they did get a rise. Their strike was politically sensitive, as Labour was trying to impose an incomes policy, and symbolized a new spirit. As Audrey Wise remarked, 'Everybody thought of cars as being about the track, about engines, and metal, and here you had women working with soft materials, sewing, and they could stop a huge car factory . . . Women are not used to feeling powerful, so it had a very great effect on them.'[34]

The strike was an indication of wider grievances. Why, asked Mrs H. Sloane at the 1968 TUC conference, were women excluded from the industrial training boards set up by Labour? Women like her had had enough with just ' "sitting next to Nellie" to learn the job'.[35] Miss J. O'Connell, declaring that she was tired of asking the men for support, said women were being condemned to 'industrial apartheid'.[36] James Connolly had been right that women were indeed 'the slaves of slaves' and, echoing Martin Luther King, she told Congress, 'We want more than the promise of a dream.'[37]

This spirit of militancy was aroused partly by the hope that the government was really committed to reforms for the low-paid, as well as exasperation at the set-backs. Labour's redistributive claims for incomes policy crystallized a recognition of injustice in the division of wealth in society. Daisy Nolan, a post office worker who was an active campaigner in the NJACWER, challenged Labour in 1969: 'To put it crudely, they are saying that if women get equal pay, then the government would rather see the money come out of the pockets of the higher-paid workers than out of the profits of the unearned income of the shareholders.'[38]

Other rank and file trade union women were following the example of the Ford's sewing machinists. Some 200 women at Lucas's Acton factory struck for equal pay and grading rights in December 1969. Bus conductresses, who had been on the NJACWER march in the summer, led by Kath Fincham, were opposing the introduction of one-man buses, demanding equal fringe benefits (they had won equal pay at the end of the First World War) and battling with men in the Transport and General Workers' Union, who were trying to prevent women becoming drivers.

There were early warning signals that the economy was changing. The government contributed to the growth of casualized labour when it allowed contract cleaning in civil service buildings from 1968, ignoring the TUC demand for a centralized direct cleaning force. There was evidence that homework, especially in the London clothing industry, with its quick-turnover boutique trade, was on the increase. Economic restructuring meant that a new electronics industry was developing, with unorganized women workers, while in depressed regions women on low wages were the only family earners. Daisy Nolan noted that Londonderry, in Northern Ireland, was known as the 'maiden's city'.[39]

Reflecting on women's failure to rise in industry in a report in 1968,

Nancy Seear blamed the attitudes of employers, male trade unionists, women's low expectations and women bosses who blocked other women. She believed that, in a male world, 'sexually unsuccessful women' enjoyed having 'scarcity value'.[40] However, two spectacular 1960s success stories were Mary Quant and Margery Hurst, who, by responding to a flexible market, were running firms with international interests. Mary Quant became a tycoon through a mix of art-school bohemianism and shrewd business sense. Her 1950s Chelsea boutique had expanded into the American market by 1962, with Jean Shrimpton modelling her clothes. Mary Quant, who was awarded the Order of the British Empire in 1965, combined the traditional skill of a couturier with the very modern ability to market a look. Margery Hurst was another successful businesswoman who had started small. By 1965 her Brook Street Bureau had become the largest secretarial agency in the world. It had all begun when her husband left her with a three-week-old baby and she had found that she could not earn enough from typing.

Dorothy Hodgkin receives the 1964 Nobel Prize for Chemistry in the presence of Princess Christina, Queen Louise, King Gustaf Adolf and Princess Sibylla.

She started the agency alone, drawing on her only work experience, as a welfare officer in the Women's Auxiliary Territorial Services during the war, to run it.

A spectacular individual achievement was the Nobel Prize won by Dorothy Crowfoot Hodgkin in 1964 for her work as a crystallographer on the molecular structure of Vitamin B_{12} and penicillin. Dorothy Hodgkin, a working mother (and grandmother), challenged by example the case for directing girls' education away from academic success towards family and domestic responsibilities. Social changes too were pulling young women into higher education. New opportunities of relatively well-paid work for educated women were developing in the state sector. Teachers and social workers were still doing the caring and nurturing which was seen as feminine, but they were also professional workers, often active trade unionists and earning enough to make them independent. It was this confident and growing stratum, radicalized during the 1960s, that was to become active in the new Women's Liberation movement.

Daily Life

Sociological pessimism about family disintegration was being replaced with a new optimism by the mid-1960s. The decline of the father's authority and the growth of more democratic and equal relationships were cheerfully interpreted as improvements. Welfare services were commonly regarded as a means of strengthening this kind of family life by enabling working-class parents to spend more time with their children. Instead of enforcing order, the role of the modern family was to be a unit of consumption and, in the words of sociologist Hannah Gavron, to give 'more recognition to the individual as a self-sufficient independent person.'[41]

This basic tenet of nineteenth-century liberalism, appropriated by 1950s conservatism, turned out to be one of the most subversive aspirations of the 1960s. Hannah Gavron's book *The Captive Wife* (1966) was one of several influential sociological studies which challenged the earlier orthodoxy that working mothers damaged their children. She put the emphasis instead upon the damage to mothers caused by isolation in the home. Deprivation was redefined to mean the lack of a social environment for children, thus questioning theories about the need for the constant presence of the biological mother. Women, she observed, straddled a contradiction. Society still responded to them 'for what they are rather than what they do', but this conflicted with 'socializing processes' in the family and the school which 'stimulate some degree of orientation towards achievement'.[42]

Impressed by American community organizations like Parent-Teacher Associations, she noted that equivalents were less common in Britain, but mentioned the Pre-schools Playgroups Association and the Campaign for the Advancement of State Education. (By the end of the decade, there was also to be Gingerbread, representing single parents, and the Housewives' Register.) 'The community,' argued Hannah Gavron, should 'include young children "in"',[43] with places for pushchairs on public transport, play spaces for children in big shops and museums, while nurseries and health centres could employ mothers who should be able to take their own children with them to work. Her common-sense approach disguised the radical implications of questioning both the built environment and social attitudes to care: 'Instead of children being excluded they should be . . . catered for.'[44]

The conflict that Hannah Gavron saw between the position of the housewife and the expectations of the post-war generation of young educated women was made more acute because the workload of middle-class housewives in both Britain and the United States was steadily increasing, though the social value of domesticity was in doubt. Suzanne Gail's personal account of herself as a housewife in the mid-1960s, published in the *New Left Review*, expressed the contradiction forcibly:

Can you imagine what would happen to a man who was suddenly uprooted from a job in which he placed the meaning of his life, and delegated to a mindless task in performing which he was also cut off fairly completely from the people who shared his interests? I think most of the men I know would disintegrate completely. The maternal 'instinct' is a comfortable male myth; a woman can only give freely if she is in a position where she does not feel deprived herself.[45]

Awareness of the lack of an independent existence was widespread by the late 1960s. One middle-class Guildford housewife said, 'When I'm in the bath it's the only time I'm myself,' while a working-class woman

Clothes

The youth market ensured that ideas and art transmogrified into clothes at top speed, a process which was greatly helped by the art schools, packed with the ingenious young themselves. Nature and modernity, which had both influenced artistic circles in the 1950s, were to slug it out on the boutique racks during the 1960s. First came the Bardot-influenced naturalism. This did not mean no make-up but just, as Elizabeth Wilson says in *Adorned in Dreams*, paler make-up, along with lots of denim and short (and getting shorter) PVC macs. CND set its own styles – old Levi's shrunk and sewn up tight down the inner leg, black sweaters and donkey jackets in 1962–3. For more formal occasions there was the shift dress, made famous by Jean Shrimpton. By 1964 Mary Quant was marketing the ultimate in the natural – make-up called Starkers (advertised by a girl who was naked except for her long hair) – and was considering topless dresses. Toplessness never caught on, but the 1950s foundation garments were being relegated to the middle-aged. Roll-ons were being dumped by the early 1960s and by the mid-1960s the suspender belt was looking tacky. Shorter skirts made tights a necessity.

Increasingly it was the boutiques selling relatively inexpensive clothes that set the styles, but in 1964 high fashion hit back. Courrèges' 1964 Paris collection regained the initiative with his space-age designs and both the miniskirt and the trouser suit, which were to become mass-production staples, had their origins in Paris. Elizabeth Wilson shows how several influences converged in the mid-1960s. Courrèges' futurism 'adapted the sartorial and visual clichés of science-fiction comics',[46] which had already passed into art. Pop artists were playing with the iconography of comic books, echoing those orgasmic wonder women that had decorated Second World War planes and weapons. Bridget Riley's op art was also quickly turned into hard-edged, zigzagging designs for clothes. Continuing a tradition of incorporating the styles created by the *demi-monde*, the fashion world marketed Christine Keeler's long black leather boots; kinky was really something to be at Biba's boutique. A trace of St Trinian's can be found too in Mary Quant's 'classless young woman', whom Elizabeth Wilson likens to the 'Madcap of the Upper Fifth'.[47]

Alexandra Pringle, then a schoolgirl, watched the young women on Chelsea's King's Road: 'They wore big floppy hats, skinny-ribbed sweaters, keyhole dresses, wide hipster belts and, I believed, paper knickers. They had white-lipsticked lips and thick black eyeliner, hair cut at alarming angles, op-art earrings and ankle-length white boots . . . They had confidence and, it seemed, no parents.'[48] Up in Liverpool, still at their Catholic grammar school, Moureen Nolan and Roma Singleton were busy copying Biba styles and crocheting (a revived skill previously confined to elderly ladies): 'It was a good idea, if crocheting a dress, to get the more intricate and dense flower patterns

The era of the boutique:
shopping in Chelsea's King's Road, 1969.

over the boobs, particularly if one was going bra-less.'[49] (No bra was a fashion before it was created by the media as a symbol of Women's Lib.)

Barbara Hulanicki's shop Biba, originally a mail-order firm selling cheap clothes to young mod girls, opened in Kensington and was responsible for the big felt hat in 1966. It also popularized feather boas and crêpe and satin materials, which in turn stimulated hunts through second-hand shops and cupboards for old fur coats, men's round-collared shirts and tablecloths with fringes which could be draped into outfits.

By the summer of 1969 modernity had faded, along with Harold Wilson's new scientific revolution, while the natural denims had shifted to hippie authenticity (cotton material and Indian styles). But late-1960s styles also played with opposing themes: as well as the authentic anti-commercial strand, many British hippies were urban and into decorative, romantic retro-chic. This, as Elizabeth Wilson observes, turned into the pastiche which contributed to 1970s camp. Both strands of anti-fashion were to transmogrify as fashion. Laura Ashley, who opened her first shop in 1968, quickly began to market what had been an anti-fashion authentic aesthetic. In the early 1970s she was to open a Laura Ashley in Paris. The responsiveness of small shops and designers to the ideas coming from the wearers of clothes had paid off. Invention was clearly not confined to the élite of high fashion any more.

✳

from Jamaica, living in east London, reflected, 'We women are just shells for the men.'[50] That mothers were held in low esteem was evident in this pyramid of social status produced by East End hairdressing day-release students in the late 1960s:

The Queen
pop singers (various grades)
employers
principal of college
vice-principal of college
teachers
hairdressing students
black people
mothers.[51]

One reason for mothers falling behind during the 'Swinging Sixties' was that consumption had become such an important element of status among the young. Elizabeth Wilson records that, 'By the second half of the 1960s nearly 50 per cent of all outerwear was being purchased by the age group 15–19.'[52] Young women were especially likely to spend on clothes and cosmetics. Styles remained class-bound, but there was a much larger convergence, especially in the youth culture of big cities. Mary Quant hailed this as a classlessness:

Once only the rich, the establishment set the fashion. Now it is the inexpensive little dress seen on the girls in the High Street. These girls are alive . . . looking, listening, ready to try anything new . . . They represent the whole new spirit that is present-day Britain – a classless spirit that has grown up out of the Second World War.[53]

The Liverpool young really felt that they *were* the new spirit. In the words of a 1960s Catholic working-class schoolgirl:

Young people suddenly had an important voice; they were being listened to, followed even. And Liverpool youth was at the front of this heady cultural thrust. It didn't matter any more that my scouse accent was raw and unrefined, there were people all over the country envying and trying to imitate the guttural tones that singled me out as a Liverpudlian.[54]

Even the Queen Mother and Princess Margaret were seen tapping their feet and clapping at the Beatles during the Royal Command

Performance in 1963. Princess Margaret was the swinging royal, meeting Antony Armstrong-Jones's friends around trendy *Queen* magazine. The food critic from *Queen*, Quentin Crewe, introduced her to Cleo Laine, the black singer from Southall. The 1960s were socially fluid and deference was definitely on the wane.

This did not, however, mean that they were truly classless. Not only did inequality persist, as Ken Loach's 1966 television film about a homeless single mother, *Cathy Come Home*, graphically demonstrated, but class affected how people related to one another and how they felt about themselves. Norah Kirk, for example, finally made it to the middle-class suburb of her dreams, only to find herself cut off from the wider networks of mutual aid which had existed in the Nottingham working-class area of the Meadows: 'Here you hardly see them . . . to say good morning to.'[55] Irene McIntosh, from a working-class background in Fife, Scotland, was part of the expansion in teachers' training. Along with many working-class young women, she did not consider university, but was steered towards a vocational education. In fact, she found the college 'a walkover'[56] but hated the authoritarian atmosphere and wished later that she had done a degree. Her husband was middle class and though she liked her in-laws, her own parents 'never felt at ease with his parents'.[57] Barbara Marsh, who came to Britain in 1962 from Jamaica, observed the intricate barriers of both class and race in England. She worked in Midlands factories, doing light-engineering work first, and then got a cleaning job in London when she started a family. Office people 'would come in the office and see you and never say "Good morning" to you because you were the cleaner . . . they think they are nice and you are only the cleaner'.[58] When it came to race, there was little pretence even of equality. As Terri Quaye says, 'The Swinging Sixties for the majority of London's black community meant Rachmanism' – Rachman, the slum landlord, provided accommodation, but at a price – and 'racism was accelerating', for 'there were now too many of us to be invisible'.[59]

Even for those who appeared to have an automatic entrée into the tinsel society, there were barriers. Michelene Wandor, Cambridge graduate, mother of two, married to a successful American publisher, arrived at the all-night rave at the Roundhouse to launch *IT*, the new underground magazine, in 1966. She looked around at 'the nubile, still just teenage teenagers with their post-jail-bait image. She had long hair and a short skirt but she didn't fit in. She was a mum.'[60] Michelene Wandor summed up the decade:

> the sixties was a time when many people went to pot
> except for me.
> I did not
> during the sixties
> I yearned
> a lot.[61]

Sex

When Penguin Books published *Lady Chatterley's Lover* in 1960 they knew they risked prosecution. The trial, in 1961, marked out a new boundary in public discussion of sexuality. Penguin's victory meant that sleaze had had its day, though the ethos of the 1950s lingered on. The 1959 Street Offences Act had not only moved prostitutes off the streets; it had, as Carol Smart observes, led to court decisions which 'extended police jurisdiction over prostitutes into their own homes'[62] by making it illegal to solicit from your doorway or windows. In practice the police were less inclined to prosecute, but the penalties were harsher when they did.

In 1963 it was a call girl in the upper echelons of the vice business who embarrassed the establishment. John Profumo, a Tory MP, lied to the House of Commons about his relations with Christine Keeler, who also had a Soviet diplomat as a client. Christine Keeler's trade was part of the dissolute 1950s rather than the rebel 1960s, but she and Mandy Rice-Davies had the insouciant cheek of the new era, with no trace of the fallen *femme fatale*. As Nigel Fountain points out, when 'middle-aged mobs shouted abuse at her . . . she sped away in large cars . . . it seemed less outraged morality they were proclaiming than outrage at being left behind in the 1950s'.[63] It seemed in 1963 as if everyone who was not outraged was laughing at Tory hypocrisy – including some of the more mischievous Tories. Sara Maitland's upper-class father in Scotland taught her to recite for liberal Conservative friends,

There was a young girl called Christine
Who shattered the Party machine;
It isn't too rude
To lie in the nude
But to lie in the House is obscene.[64]

More earnestly, in 1963 John Robinson, the Bishop of Woolwich, interpreted Christianity as being about love rather than external morality, and a group of Quakers maintained that love included homosexuals. The Marriage Guidance Council too had loosened up on the facts of life. They now thought sex was OK as long as there was a loving relationship (marriage preferred). The pill was generally welcomed; evidence of its side-effects was ignored. By the mid-1960s those still arguing that knowledge of contraceptives encouraged promiscuity were fighting a rearguard action.

The good news, however, took time to get around. In 1956 Norman Dennis et al.'s study of a Yorkshire mining community, *Coal is Our Life*, reported a discussion between two women about contraception in which one feared it would offend her husband. Information was still being picked up by word of mouth. Fiona McFarlane from Glasgow, married to a factory worker, records in Jean McCrindle and Sheila Rowbotham's *Dutiful Daughters* that she knew nothing about contraceptives until she overheard two women talking about the pill and went to the doctor, who put her on it. In the early 1960s information was particularly difficult to obtain for the young and unmarried. Even at the end of the decade, when the pill had had an impact in Britain, in Southern Ireland contraceptives were still illegal and had to be smuggled in. In Ireland it remained daring to speak out in public in the North as well as the South about sex and contraception.

In the early 1960s in Britain abortion was illegal, though more and more doctors were interpreting the proviso 'at risk' liberally. Alongside the NHS a semi-legal medical practice had developed for women who could pay, making it blatantly obvious that there was one law for the rich and another for the poor. The abortions performed within the NHS on mothers who had been given the drug thalidomide, which caused deformities, also blurred the line between medical and social reasons for terminating a pregnancy. The Abortion Law Reform Association renewed its campaign for legislation and there were several attempts to get private members' bills through before David Steel's bill was passed in 1967 (it did not apply to Northern Ireland). Abortion-law reformers varied in their approaches. Some retained eugenic concerns, but these were now being vigorously contested. In 1965 Lord Silkin, for instance, maintained that 'inadequate'[65] women should receive abortions, to the fury of Lady Wootton, a Fabian socialist and feminist, who wrote to warn him of the implications: 'I have known too many Tory doctors who really think that the 'lower classes' ought not to be allowed to reproduce themselves, though, of course, they would not put it like that.'[66] The liberal Christian John Robinson argued that the decision to have an abortion should be the woman's, and not mediated by a judge or doctor. But the 1967 act did not give women the right to decide. Two doctors had to agree that the mother's life was at risk, or that her physical or mental health would suffer. Legal abortion was a victory for ALRA, but they were, as Barbara Brookes remarks in *Abortion in England*, caught out by their own emphasis upon health grounds, which handed control to the medical profession. The legalization of abortion was swiftly followed by the formation of the Society for the Protection of the Unborn Child (SPUC), which asserted the right to life of the foetus. It had strong backing from the Catholic Church. The liberalization of legislation relating to sex also provoked fears among some of the older feminists that the relaxation of repression would make women more vulnerable. Lady Summerskill managed to delay the Divorce Bill in 1969, calling it a 'Casanova's Charter'.[67]

In 1966 in 'The Longest Revolution', Juliet Mitchell had pointed to the historic significance of widespread and reliable contraception. Child-bearing had become 'an option' and the possibility was there for making motherhood 'totally voluntary'; a complete disassociation of 'sexual from reproductive experience' meant 'the mode of reproduction could potentially be transformed'.[68] However, Geoffrey Gorer's 1973 study, *Sex and Marriage in England Today*, revealed that despite people's perception of the pill's impact during the 1960s, 63 per cent of women still did not have sex before marriage. There was pressure to be sexy, but equally there was pressure to get married.

Most immediately noticeable were the changes in the visual images

Icons

1960s ideals of beauty were attainable. It was not just that clothes could be bought, but the elaborate glamour of the Hollywood stars was replaced by less complicated styles. Film star Julie Christie and singer Marianne Faithfull had natural healthy good looks which followed the Bardot style of long blonde hair, but without her sultry seduction. They bobbed like daffodils amidst the decadence. Models Jean Shrimpton and then Twiggy (Lesley Hornby) introduced the waif. It was as if the Little Match Girl

Cockney glamour and the Liverpool Sound crossed the Atlantic: Twiggy in 1967 shirt dress.

had grown up and was mighty surprised to find herself a big earner. Even if you were not quite beautiful, you could still be attractive, like the perky girls in the music business – Cilla Black, Sandie Shaw and Dusty Springfield. Independent-minded and sassy-looking, these were girls next door who were now working in the big city. Descendants of Doris Day, they had adapted to an era when virginity was no longer either feasible or fashionable.

1960s icons were youthful; it was *definitely* not the decade of the older woman. Beauty was straightforward. Nobody was spending time on seduction any more and the *femme fatale* was *passé*, although she did make a bit of a comeback in 1966 when the underground paper *IT* put a picture of Theda Bara on their launch issue by mistake (they had been looking for the original 'It' girl, Clara Bow, and muddled them up). The Theda Bara vamp and the Faye Dunaway 1930s gangster look from the film *Bonnie and Clyde* popularized kohl and berets.

When the music eventually died, the symbols of the 1960s were as puzzled as anyone else about who exactly had been swinging. 'I was on the outside looking in,' wrote Julie Christie in 1988. 'I was always on the fringes of people whom I perceived as really being in the epicentre of the vortex.'[69] Louise Ferrier appeared in *Oz* at the end of 1969 looking like the male hippie dream, but from inside the dream things were more prosaic: 'I used to get totally paranoid smoking dope,' she told Nigel Fountain in 1988, adding that she and Richard Neville might have looked 'like an ideal exciting couple' but the reality was different.[70]

✳

of femininity. Sex was becoming more overt: women were ready and raunchy, aggressive and yet yielding in 1960s advertisements. Male fantasies came out from under wraps and pleasure beckoned. Images of femininity were communicating blatantly opposing messages of freedom and subordination. The hippie underground exploded in psychedelic erotica, making the schizophrenia more acute. Young women confronted forms of feminine representation which were sexually reductionist while signalling infinite expansion of one's consciousness. Moreover, these images were dissolving and reforming in constant flux before one's eyes.

Such contradictory sexual messages could hardly fail to be unsettling, and with the male-defined permissiveness of the 1960s went a contrary awakening of expectation. As Julie Christie says of her character in the film *Darling*, 'Here was a woman who didn't want to get married, didn't want to have children like those other kitchen-sink heroines; no, Darling wanted to have *everything*.'[71] Punishment, which had always accompanied such female sexual assertion in popular culture, began to look ridiculous. One young 1960s woman, Jane, remembered the pill as meaning, 'Sex was not a big risk any more and nor were men.'[72] Even after she stopped taking the pill, she retained the confidence it had brought: 'I was allowed to have what I liked and did not have to be frightened of sex because it could trap me into things. I didn't have to be punished.'[73]

The sense of relief, the desire to talk openly about what had previously been said in private among close friends, was evident in Nell Dunn's 1967 interviews, *Talking to Women*. Women were beginning to articulate what they wanted from sex. Mary Quant proclaimed in 1969 that the pill had put women 'in charge . . . She's standing there defiantly with her legs apart, saying, "I'm very sexy, I feel provocative, but you're going to have a job to get me. You've got to excite me." '[74]

Several snags emerged. Young men had, after all, not been prepared by their 1950s upbringings for the new Quant-style woman. They could find it quite literally difficult to rise to the challenge of women in charge. Moreover, while it was true that being able to pull a man was good for the ego, the Quant approach did not attend to who was in charge after he came, or take into account that women (also brought up on 1950s doctrines that it was the nice girls who didn't who got their

men) were often not at all sure if they wanted the onerous responsibility of taking control. Marianne Faithfull describes these convolutions
in the power relations of gender in her autobiography, *Faithfull*, suggesting that Mick Jagger's bisexuality made him actually *more* emphatic
about women being distinct from men. This, along with his 'obsession
with appearances', contributed to his insistence on 'female props'.[75]
He was not unique. The hippie counter-culture encouraged self-
expression and the dissolution of barriers, but in the process it erected
other implicit divisions. Natural woman was inventive in bed but she
still did the housework and was somebody's chick.

It was not to prove so easy to cast off the punitive attitudes towards
sexual freedom simply by willing them to dissolve. Elizabeth Wilson
argues that 'the opening out of sexuality . . . was . . . the inverse of the
tight-arsed fifties . . . a kind of emotional diarrhoea'.[76] There was a
powerful strand of self-destructiveness in 1960s alternative culture.
Marianne Faithfull, who was herself caught within this negativity,
reflects how, as Mick Jagger saw her simply as an extension of himself,
to hurt herself was to hurt him: 'I wanted to destroy my face. A
systematic cold-blooded self-desecration.'[77]

Sexual behaviour varied greatly. At one extreme there were the
groupies, described by Angela Carter as 'collecting fucks from pop
singers in a manner that a less physically energetic age might have
collected autographs'.[78] More like religious devotees than hedonists, in
between they made the tea and cleaned up the joint ends. But in the
same period Gina Adamou, part of Islington's Greek-Cypriot community, was banned from walking through Chapel Market with her
sister because a young man 'sort of commented'.[79] Her parents found
her a husband when she was seventeen and a half. It happened that they
were happy together, 'but the iffy thing of it is, it's a gamble'.[80] Most
young women were between the two extremes. Irene McIntosh, for
example, got married, had children, started a brief affair, then thought
better of it. The 1960s were about testing the water as much as about
decadence.

A questioning of sexual power relations was becoming evident
beyond the counter-culture as more young women found themselves
confronting conflicts in sexual assumptions. For instance, a group of
East Enders training to be typists and hairdressers commented:

'Why is it always naked women on the tube, why aren't there naked men?' 'The Pope must be bent. He doesn't like women, does he? He's against the pill.' 'I'd like to take boys out in a car late at night in the rain and push them out in the road and make them walk home.' 'Every boy in this place is a raving sex maniac, and yet they say they want to marry a virgin.'[81]

As Leila Berg says, the decade ended as it had begun, with a trial. This time it was a bear, cartoon character Rupert Bear, rather than a gamekeeper who was causing trouble. Australian Richard Neville and the two other editors of the underground magazine *Oz* were accused, with a fourteen-year-old 'accomplice',[82] of conspiring to corrupt public morals and possessing, publishing and spreading obscenity. School-children producing their own issue of *Oz* had given the innocent cartoon bear from the conservative newspaper the *Daily Express* a large penis and allowed him to have sex with the American cartoon figure Honeybunch. Educationalist Leila Berg donned a modest mauve dress and was a witness for the defence. The trial lasted six weeks and ended with the editors going to prison. Marsha Rowe, who had come from Australia to work on *Oz*, reflected later that she had not realized 'the importance of Rupert Bear in the British pyschE'.[83]

Richard Neville, who had started *Oz*, was coming under pressure from women like her in the underground press about the depiction of desire. The Gay Liberation Front had just been formed and was also contesting the heterosexual assumptions which pervaded the 1960s vision of liberation. Sex, by 1969, was a political not a private issue. Elizabeth Wilson, who had first 'gingerly descended the steps of the Gateways Club in 1960 to the strains of . . . "Only the Lonely",'[84] ten years later was being banned by the bouncer for distributing Gay Liberation leaflets.

THE UNITED STATES

The Ferment

'In 1960, the problem that has no name burst like a boil through the image of the happy American housewife,'[85] wrote Betty Friedan in *The Feminine Mystique* (1963). Her book turned all those old prejudices against working mothers around: they emerged as the sane ones. It was the stay-at-homes who were turning to drink, tranquillizers and bowling alleys (which provided nurseries): 'Said the manager of Albuquerque's Bowl-a-Drome: "Where else can a woman compete after she gets married? They need competition just like the men do . . . It sure beats going home to do the dishes." '[86]

The Feminine Mystique was the work of an experienced journalist and it made an emotive case which needed to be stated. There was real substance to the thwarted unhappiness that Friedan uncovered and her book was to have a formative effect on 1960s radicalism. On the other hand, Betty Friedan missed the nuances of suburban middle-class life which did not fit so neatly into the case she was making; she thus crystallized an experience which was only part of the truth and did not bother with contrary material. There were plenty of women who were extremely busy and active outside the home even though they were not in paid employment, while others preferred time at home when the children were young and paid work as they grew older. The assumption in *The Feminine Mystique* was that if women could only get paid employment, they would feel better. But this passed over the problems of women who were already combining jobs and mothering and ignored the fact that many jobs – even middle-class jobs – were not particularly creative.

The Feminine Mystique did not consider the wider changes that were needed by poor women and it generalized from models of white femininity. Paula Giddings points out that the bored dependence and lack of alternative ways of being women 'seemed to come from another planet'[87] to most African-American women. Not only was paid work more customary; examples of women who were courageous and independent abounded both locally and in American society. These were, after all, the years of the Civil Rights movement. Even as *The Feminine*

Mystique was being published in 1963, Charlayne Hunter-Gault became the first woman to graduate from the University of Georgia.

Daniel Horowitz has demonstrated how the omissions of *The Feminine Mystique* obliterated the awareness of social and economic inequality present in Betty Friedan's writing in the 1940s and early 1950s. This example of self-censorship is one indication of a more subtle kind of silencing which was to be the legacy of the McCarthy era. Class injustice became unmentionable. Yet the social commitment of the 1940s *did* survive, albeit transplanted into the milieu of middle-class radicalism. He comments:

Friedan did not write *The Feminine Mystique* simply because she was an unhappy housewife. Nor was Friedan alone. Gerda Lerner, Bella Abzug, Eleanor Flexner, and Milton Meltzer are among those active in the labor movement in the 1940s who would emerge as people who helped shape post-1963 feminism.[88]

The pressures to conform to stereotypes of femininity were real enough, but mixed messages about desirable womanhood continued during the 1960s. And, as Susan Douglas points out in *Where the Girls Are*, not 'all women bought into' the consumerist feminine mystique:

By 1963, women like my mother were in an untenable position. They worked all the time yet their work inside and outside the house was taken for granted and poorly valued. To even approach the level of material comfort that *Leave It To Beaver* and *Father Knows Best* suggested that everyone had, millions of families needed mom in the workforce.[89]

She imagines such moms 'fuming and fantasizing about jail break' in laundry rooms and kitchens or watching Samantha in *Bewitched*, a popular TV sitcom which started in 1964: Samantha looked like any attractive suburban housewife but, by 'twitching her nose', she was able to exert 'power beyond the kitchen or the living room'.[90]

The daughters of course were planning their own jail breaks, as Susan Douglas puts it, 'blasting Beatles records'[91] in bedrooms. Another site of subversion (as in Liverpool) was the 'girls' bathroom', remembered as a 'red hot spot' in Susan Seidelman's documentary film *Confessions of a Suburban Girl*.[92] Beatlemania reached North America late in 1963, just after the assassination of President Kennedy. Not only did they

With a little help from witchcraft: Samantha (left, played by Liz Montgomery), with her mother, Endora (played by Agnes Moorehead), and husband, Darren (played by Dick York) in the popular TV series *Bewitched*.

dent the square-jawed version of masculinity, they also touched a nerve of gender identity among their young women fans. Teenage girls loved particular Beatles, but they also actually wanted to be Beatles themselves. This was one way of *not* being like your mother. Betty Friedan sombrely reports another option. One seventeen-year-old she interviewed dreaded becoming like her mother so much that she had 'retreated into the beatnik vacuum'.[93]

In fact, the beatnik life, and later the hippie subculture, could be hard work for women. Diane di Prima, pioneer beat poet and novelist, migrated from New York in 1968 with several babies, various dogs and fourteen grown-ups. Upon arrival in San Francisco they either took to their beds or busied themselves 'organizing be-ins, delivering free food, selling or manufacturing illegal chemicals, publishing anarchist manifestos, designing political broadsides, creating light shows for rock concerts, feeding stray guitarists, or making beaded earrings or candle glasses out of colored pebbles'.[94] None of these activities resulted in much disposable income; consequently she paid the rent by sending 'gobs of words . . . off to New York' which would come back with 'MORE SEX' scrawled across the top page in her editor's 'inimitable hand'.[95]

The hard grind in the beatnik or hippie vacuum was actually another problem looking for a name – one that Betty Friedan missed. Alix Kates Shulman, ex-prom queen and future feminist, communicates this contradictory experience in her novel *Burning Questions*, in which a pioneer 1950s Greenwich Village beatnik turns into a 1960s radical young mother. She marches to Washington in the mass demonstration of 1963, joins Women Strike for Peace (a group of middle-class mothers whose protests defied the remnants of McCarthyism in the early 1960s) and Dr Spock in the 1966 demonstration to the Pentagon. She becomes active in the Parent-Teacher Association, feels 'a shiver of lust' for her bearded left-wing baby-sitter, begins an affair, joins one of the first Women's Liberation groups in New York and falls in love with a woman.[96] Change came quickly in the 1960s.

Women's Liberationists like her shared the 'can do' message of *The Feminine Mystique*. Betty Friedan had been influenced by Abraham Maslow's human potential psychology, but a similar assumption of infinite possibility pervaded popular culture. Joanne Meyerowitz argues that Friedan's success with the book was because it was both new and not new: 'It reworked themes already rooted in the mass culture.'[97] 'The feminine mystique' was not just named in 1963, it became a household phrase. As so often happens, the naming of a grievance was surfacing just as the situation was changing.

Politics

As the new decade began, Eleanor Roosevelt was still America's 'Most Admired Woman'. In her mid-seventies, she was trying to keep a low profile politically, despite pressure to back a candidate to lead the Democratic Party. Nonetheless, she inclined towards the liberal Adlai Stevenson rather than the ambitious young John F. Kennedy. She had noted his evasive stances on McCarthy, disliked his father's advocacy of non-intervention against the Nazis and was wary of the Catholic political lobby, partly because of old battles with right-wingers like Cardinal Spellman and partly because the values of the Protestant élite from which she came had a residual influence upon her.

Pragmatic as ever, when Kennedy was chosen in 1960, she nonetheless invited him to her cottage, Val-Kill, at Hyde Park. William Walton went with him for moral support and recalled that Kennedy left 'absolutely smitten'.[98] When he was inaugurated, Kennedy asked her to be at his side, but she preferred to sit in the open, wrapped in a mink and a blanket, and listened as he called to a new generation: 'Let us begin anew . . . ask not what your country can do for you – ask what you can do for your country.'[99] The great renewal was to be a mixed bag. Before Kennedy's assassination in 1963 and the presidency of Lyndon Johnson, the US was to threaten to invade Cuba in 1961 and become more involved in Vietnam. It was the Civil Rights movement which, by exposing Southern racism, really raised hopes of a new beginning.

Most people in 1960 were not focusing on women's rights, but Eleanor Roosevelt was an exception. She was quick to spot an absence in Kennedy's call to begin anew: only nine of his first 240 appointments were women. She sent a three-page list to the White House with the names of women capable of top administrative posts. In fact, Kennedy made only ten senior appointments of women to positions in the executive and judiciary which required Senate approval and he never had a woman in his Cabinet. He did, however, agree, at her prompting, to the Commission on the Status of Women in 1961. Eleanor Roosevelt became too ill to continue chairing the Commission and died from tuberculosis of the bone marrow in 1962.

The Commission's report in 1963 marked a watershed between the 1950s mystique of femininity and the liberal and radical egalitarianism which was to follow in the 1960s. It opposed sex discrimination in government employment and demanded 'equal pay for comparable work',[100] equal widows' benefits from social security and paid maternity leave. However, it dithered on whether education should prepare girls for motherhood or lift women's 'aspirations beyond stubbornly persistent assumptions about "women's roles" and "women's interests" and result in choices that have inner authenticity'.[101] And though

Eleanor Roosevelt had changed her mind on the Equal Rights Amendment, which egalitarian feminists still wanted, Esther Peterson, who headed the Commission and was Assistant Secretary of Labor and Director of the Women's Bureau, feared the ERA would threaten protective legislation. The Commission argued instead that the latter should be extended to men. It did endorse some flexibility in regulations on carrying weights and accepted homework for clerical, editorial and part-time research workers, though industrial homework was still opposed. Instead of the ERA, Esther Peterson wanted 'specific bills for specific ills'[102] and an Equal Pay Bill was introduced by Edith Green, becoming law in June 1963. It was to be for equal work; the more extensive proposal of comparability was rejected on the grounds that it was not practicable.

Women's rights were to be included in the 1964 Civil Rights Act by a strange twist of political fate. The National Woman's Party, still led by the indefatigable Alice Paul, complained that the bill did not protect white Christian women of United States origin and they secured the support of a conservative opponent of civil rights, Howard W. Smith. He always insisted that he was sincere in his commitment to what came to be called the sex amendment, though he told reporters at the time, 'You grasp any snickersnee you can get hold of.'[103] It began to look as if the old conflict between race and sex had been reopened. Many liberals feared that the sex amendment would make the bill ridiculous, but Pauli Murray, the prominent black attorney, supported it, pointing out that black women too were affected by sex discrimination. In fact, the conservative bid to block the bill misfired. Male ribaldry convinced women representatives (apart from Edith Green, who insisted racial oppression should have priority); Martha Griffiths declared that if there had been any necessity to point out that women were a second-class sex, the male laughter would have proved it.

All over the country pressure was kept up to ensure that legislation turned into reality. The Commissions on the Status of Women between 1963 and 1967 pushed for equal pay, minimum wage legislation and an end to discrimination in jury service, in marriage and in property rights. They also campaigned for local community services and better child-support provision. An institutional framework was thus established for women active in government, education and trade unions to network. An important consequence was the formation of the National Organization for Women (NOW). Betty Friedan, Pauli Murray and Dorothy Haener from the Union of Automobile Workers called a meeting in Betty Friedan's hotel room at the Washington Hilton during the Commission's 1966 conference. The women who crammed in and grumbled began NOW as a ginger group with twenty-eight members.

The Civil Rights Act was followed by the 1965 Voting Rights Act and a ban on discrimination in housing in 1968. Racism in the South was not to be ended by legislation, but these were nonetheless major advances. They made it illegal to turn black people away from lunch counters, education and transport were integrated, and for the first time Southern blacks were able to register and elect black representatives. Black people in the South had gained these laws at considerable cost.

Kathryn Clarenbach, chair of the National Organization for Women, with NOW President Betty Friedan in Washington, DC, in 1967 at the second conference: Clarenbach's connection to the Wisconsin Commission on Women and the Department of Labor's Women's Bureau brought an organizational strength that was matched by Friedan's skills as a media publicist.

They had been clubbed, goaded with electrically charged cattle prods, beaten, tear-gassed and murdered by whites determined to deny them basic civil rights. In Birmingham, Alabama, whites bombed a church in 1963 and four black girls aged between eleven and fourteen were killed.

Black women played a vital part in the Civil Rights movement. Ella Baker, who was working for the Young Women's Christian Association, had encouraged students who were sitting in at lunch counters to link up and they formed the Student Non-Violent Co-ordinating Committee (SNCC) in 1960. Her ideas of 'group-centered leadership' had an important influence on the politics of SNCC, though she did not believe in absolute non-violence when attacked. Ruby Doris Smith was one of many black students who dropped out of college to join SNCC. In 1962, aged seventeen, she experienced jail and injury, braving the danger of the freedom rides and demonstrations to emerge as a political leader while she was still in her early twenties.

Black women were often the ones who took the risk of sheltering SNCC campaigners, as well as canvassing, demonstrating and attending mass meetings. Fannie Lou Hamer, twentieth child of a sharecropper and married to a sharecropper in Mississippi, 'put her hand up as high as I could get it'[104] when SNCC members came on a voter-registration drive. She knew she risked death, but it seemed as if whites in the South had been trying to kill her 'a little bit at a time ever since I could remember'.[105] In the summer of 1964, 63,000 black voters were registered in Mississippi.

Until the Freedom Summer of 1964, when many whites started to come down to help the movement in the South, the civil rights struggle was mainly black. But the media coverage galvanized the young, including many 'red diaper' babies who decided to act on the principles their parents had been forced to conceal in the McCarthy era. The Civil Rights movement did not affect only students. Some older middle-class white women, especially teachers, were also taking the ideas into church groups, Parent-Teacher Associations, the Young Women's Christian Association and the League of Women Voters. One woman who went to an Ethical Culture Group because they had child-care, ended up working with a Southern black community: 'I had wanted to do something. This was the very first step.'[106] Another such woman, Viola Liuzzo from Detroit, was to be assassinated in Alabama during the historic Selma to Montgomery march of 1965.

The arrival of large numbers of young white women led to some tense sexual dynamics in SNCC in 1964–5. The white women could feel judged as racist if they said no to male sexual advances, but then found that they were not treated as political equals if they said yes. Black women who were part of the leadership, like Ruby Doris Smith, were more likely to be treated as equals in a public political context, but the men often looked for sex with white women. In November 1964 Casey Hayden and Mary King wrote a position paper anonymously, challenging the 'assumption of male superiority', which they said was 'as widespread and deep-rooted and every much as crippling to the woman as the assumptions of white superiority are to the Negro'.[107] Very few people took this seriously in the atmosphere of intense violence and danger, and Stokely Carmichael, a leading member of SNCC joked, 'The only position for women in SNCC is prone.'[108]

By 1965 there was a shift in consciousness in SNCC away from non-violent, decentralized organizing to a growing sense of the need for an autonomous black movement, which Ruby Doris Smith Robinson came to support. Several forces thus converged to marginalize white women like Casey Hayden and Mary King, who were not only concerned about women's position but wanted a less centralized structure. Moreover, it was becoming obvious that while many white people in the North were morally shocked by Southern racism, they were reluctant to admit African-Americans to jobs and housing. Civil rights, as Ella Baker had said in 1960, were 'bigger than a hamburger'.[109] The symbolically important struggle around public space and the pressure for law reform were revealing the extent of economic and social inequality, not only in the South but in the North. Many young radicals, politicized by the Freedom Summer, turned their attention to poverty in the Northern cities. Civil rights thus influenced the radical student movement in the North, which was having its own arguments about structure and aims. And it was within the Students for a Democratic Society (SDS) that the conflict over sex oppression was to be fought out with considerable bitterness. As Sara Evans remarks, 'The fullest expression of conscious feminism ricocheted off the fury of black power and landed with explosive force in the Northern white student left.'[110] The battlelines of consciousness were complicated. When women walked out of an SDS conference in Illinois in protest in December 1965, Sara Evans records that the 'only man to defend their action was a black man from SNCC'.[111] The chapters of SDS were to become one of the recruiting grounds for the early Women's Liberation groups, which began to form from 1967.

Johnnie Tillmon, a poor black mother of six in Watts, was quick to see that civil rights were about social entitlement. She began to organize other women receiving Aid to Families with Dependent Children (AFDC) around welfare rights in 1963. Social investigators had rediscovered America's poor in the early 1960s, though the solution was often still assumed to be educating the poor to take advantage of opportunities. Kennedy's 1962 Public Amendments to the Social Security Act enabled states to expand job-training and casework services to people on welfare and President Johnson's Economic Opportunities Act of 1965, continuing the ethos of domestic reform, set up programmes for a War Against Poverty. By 1965 AFDC was the largest public assistance programme. Grants varied greatly from state to state, for ideas of the deserving and undeserving poor lived on and continued to be marked by racial prejudice. White women were still more likely to be allowed the special-needs payments than black women.

Poverty campaigners grew more militant and many groups who came to help were themselves changed by the experience. For example, in Brooklyn liberal Catholic nuns who started doing individual casework with children and their families came to the conclusion that poverty was a social question requiring collective action. In 1967 George Wiley founded the National Welfare Rights Organization (NWRO), which by 1968 had 10,000 members. Martin Luther King met Johnnie Tillmon and other leading members of NWRO, Etta Horn and Beulah Saunders, when he launched the Poor People's Campaign just before his assassination in 1968. He imagined an alliance of all the groups locked out from America. Though this never materialized, welfare needs brought black and white poor people together in a common movement. As Linda Gordon comments:

In the 1960s a welfare-rights movement forced the courts to restrict the arbitrary power of states to invade recipients' privacy and cut off benefits summarily. Even more important, this activism created a more dignified image of the work of poor single mothers, reminding the public that mothering was not only work, but socially useful work.[112]

Welfare activists did have an impact, despite the alarmed opposition of local élites, who opposed the federally sponsored Community Action Program. The expanding economy helped as well. In 1962 the US government calculated that 23 per cent of the population were living in poverty. By 1973 this had been reduced to 11 per cent. However, the distribution of wealth did not alter significantly despite this radical phase of American politics. Indeed, it was the poorer tax payers who really financed welfare for the very poor. By 1975 the bottom one-fifth were to be paying twice as much tax as they had done ten years earlier. Meanwhile, the richest one-tenth paid 16 per cent less.

By the late 1960s the mood of welfare activists had become angry as funding was cut and community groups were being subject to controls. The relentless Vietnam War was becoming increasingly unpopular, among the soldiers as well, many of whom were from poor black families. Black Power fists began to appear on their helmets. Black Power came to be denoted by shoot-outs, but the Panthers had a social and economic programme and their ideas of community self-help drew on a long tradition of African-American self-determination. An early advocate of black power, Ruth Turner Perot, argued in 1967 for black consumer power, co-operatives and businesses, along with black arts and history. She invoked the 'power of self-knowledge'[113] together with mutual aid.

Other groups began to take direct action. In November 1969 Grace Thorpe (the former WAC at General MacArthur's headquarters) was one of a group of Native Americans to occupy Alcatraz Island in San Francisco Bay, saying they wanted to depollute the Bay area and make the island a centre for Native American Studies for Ecology. Young chicanos and chicanas too were walking out of school, protesting at the racist curriculum and teaching. These movements of the excluded did not ask to join America as it was, but asserted their right to redefine their own lives. In response, President Nixon was to step up internal surveillance on activists in the new social movements from 1968 and there were violent clashes with the police on anti-war demos. It did indeed seem that the Vietnam War had been brought home and that America was at war with itself.

Rebellion extended beyond those who were 'locked out', involving, in Herbert Marcuse's phrase, a 'great refusal' among some of the privileged. This was true not only of the student movement and the anti-Vietnam War protesters but also of the radical Women's Liberation groups from 1967. They rejected both the claim for equal rights within the system made by N O W and the maternalist approach of groups like Women Strike for Peace and the Jeannette Rankin Brigade, which stressed women's special relationship to politics as nurturers. Naomi Weisstein, who helped to form a group in Chicago in 1967 which included Shulamith Firestone and Jo Freeman, remembered, 'We weren't fighting for the unhappy privilege of competing in the American jungle. We wanted to change it, to create a Peaceable Kingdom.'[114] They were not driven by 'the passion for the possible',[115] which Toni Carabillo says inspired N O W, but by a vision of transformation which, in Naomi Weisstein's words, took 'ecstasy as our guide'.[116]

The small consciousness-raising groups (a term coined by Kathie Sarachild, who had been in the 1964 Freedom Summer) created a context in which women could draw on their own experiences and interpret them together, rather than invoking theoretical knowledge. They talked about how they would like to live and rear children, about illegal abortions and rape. Rosalyn Baxandall, a red diaper baby in one of the early New York radical feminist groups, was already a radical activist but had 'never talked to people at that level'.[117] Femininity was not something to be taken for granted any more. Everything became political – going out without eyeliner, for instance, which Naomi Weisstein describes as 'like wearing a big Day-Glo sandwich sign saying HATE ME, I NO LONGER CARE WHETHER I'M PRETTY'.[118]

The absence of eyeliner was not so noticeable to the world, but when former child star Robin Morgan, along with Kathie Sarachild, Carol Hanisch, Alix Kates Shulman and other radical women from New York, Boston, Detroit, Florida and New Jersey, crowned a sheep in Atlantic City in September 1968 in protest against the Miss America contest, Women's Liberation became national news. They dumped

Taking a break during a Women's Liberation protest against the Miss America
Pageant at Atlantic City, 1968.

'instruments of torture to women'[119] – high-heeled shoes, bras, girdles,
Playboy, Cosmopolitan and *The Ladies' Home Journal* – into a Freedom
Trash Can and were mythologized as bra-burners.

Disagreements developed as fast as the movement itself grew. Was
the aim to reach all women or declare a lock-out among the liberated
by separating from those who remained contaminated by cosmetics and
nuclear families? Was the enemy capitalism or was it men? Were the
origins of oppression social or psychological? And once the personal
was political – what did you do about it? At an early meeting on
Thanksgiving Day 1968, women from thirty groups in the US and
Canada argued fiercely in the plenaries and talked about sexuality in a
workshop organized by Anne Koedt and Ti-Grace Atkinson far into
the night. The discussion focused on Anne Koedt's 'The Myth of the
Vaginal Orgasm'. All ' "normal" concepts of sex'[120] were to be discarded
– the clitoris and celibacy were in. A new consensus dismissed vaginal

379

stimulation as false consciousness, though Shulamith Firestone's view that pregnancy was inevitably oppressive met with more opposition. As Alice Echols points out, 'The breaking down of old prescriptions sometimes engendered the creation of new ones.'[121]

By 1969, the radicalism of the new women's groups was beginning to have an effect on NOW, especially in New York. New York feminists spoke out about the personal suffering of illegal abortions and defended a doctor who was on trial for performing an abortion. Under pressure, Betty Friedan changed her position to back abortion as 'A Woman's Civil Right'.[122]

The women who emerged as visible media figures in a movement that so abhorred leaders were not always the ones who were important in keeping groups together or running projects. Work with welfare mothers in Baltimore, with women trade unionists in Seattle or with tenants in Boston was less newsworthy but as characteristic of the early movement as the dramatic Yippie-style interventions. The challenge was being taken into all kinds of institutions too: Mary Daly revealed the male bias in Christianity, radical nuns formed a coalition, women at San Diego State University, Old Westbury and Cornell set up early women's studies courses.

In June 1969 the New York police raided a gay bar, the Stonewall Inn, in Greenwich Village. Lillian Faderman records how, instead of 'scampering off', gay men, drag queens and a few butch lesbians fought back, remarking, 'It is unlikely that a gay and lesbian riot could have occurred at any previous time in history.'[123] Gay activists identified in solidarity with this working-class protest. The class separation between a working-class bar culture and middle-class protesters began to diminish and a distinctive lesbian consciousness began to emerge among women who were often college-educated but not always of middle-class origin.

Late-1960s America thus saw a remarkable process of politicization which reached deep into the culture. Vicki Crawford's observation of Mississippi's Civil Rights groups holds true for the other social movements as well: 'The beliefs that ultimately inspire the mobilization of thousands (and millions) have often been tested and retested in obscure and out-of-the-way places by individuals who may never write manifestos, lead demonstrations, call press conferences, or stand up before TV cameras.'[124]

Radical ideas affected women far away from centres of activism under the pressure of circumstance and example: an Appalachian mother began to move to the left when her son was sent to Vietnam, while a Catholic Nixon supporter declared she thought black people were 'right to want to lead themselves'.[125]

Politicization did, of course, work both ways, producing reaction as well as radicalism. Phyllis Schlafly's bid to become president of the National Federation of Republican Women was defeated by liberal Republican women in 1967. But women did support the extreme right. Jacqueline Jones points to the 'anonymous women who sprayed insecticide at Selma marchers'[126] and the grim white registrars who prevented blacks from registering. Nor was it only the left who were politicizing daily life. The John Birch Society played on fears of sex education in school and Ronald Reagan campaigned successfully in California in the mid-1960s by denouncing student orgies. The right too saw the personal as political in this hurricane of a decade.

Work

The Civil Rights movement meant that equality gained legitimation, but what this actually meant for women was not at all clear. Various meanings jostled against one another and sometimes overlapped. Was it extending equal protection to men at work? Was it equal opportunities? Did this involve equalizing housework and child-care between both sexes, and also providing community services to help parents? Or would equality come only with that elusive beloved community in which all relationships were going to be transformed – a chiliastic vision that had flitted from civil rights to the student movement, touched welfare-rights organizing, resurfaced in some strands of the radical women's groups and lurked as a shadowy presence seeking substance in new kinds of workplace organizations.

The differences in approach partly depended on the varying options, and these in turn were greatly affected by class, by race and ethnicity, by age, disability, whether you had children and where you lived. A growing number of professional women were frustrated by the lack of acknowledgement and advancement in their career opportunities. Young educated mothers wanted to return to better-paid work. Women

I'll Sing If I Want to

Lesley Gore had her first hit, 'It's My Party', in 1963, the year of *The Feminine Mystique*, and this was followed by 'You Don't Own Me'. Despite the independence of her songs, she recalled, 'Even though I was a big-seller, they only cared about males. That was always clear to me. They just thought it was easier to sell males. It really got to me after a while.'[127]

Think of 1960s music and it is the famous male groups who come to mind making the transatlantic interconnection. But the women were there all along and their music was crossing back and forth too. Petula Clark, for instance, had a hit in the US with 'Downtown' in 1965. Lulu, Cilla Black, Sandie Shaw, Dusty Springfield and Marianne Faithfull came over as part of the British invasion of the mid-1960s. They, in turn, had been influenced by American music – Doris Day, combined with Motown and folk. Also, Dusty Springfield, Lulu and Cilla Black 'owed an obvious debt to the girl group era',[128] as Gillian Gaar shows.

The Shirelles had been the first all-female group to reach the top of the US single charts in 1961, asking 'Will You Still Love Me Tomorrow?'. As Susan Douglas notes in *Where the Girls Are*, this was an ideological breakthrough in the context of 1950s female pop music. Here were teenage girls voicing a dilemma which was still *sotto voce* in the culture: 'Should the girl believe everything she'd heard about going all the way and boys losing respect for girls who did?'[129] or should she believe what he said as he held her in his arms? Here was a completely traditional female topic of love – but with a difference: 'It was about female longing and desire, including sexual desire.'[130]

The girl groups not only created an idiom in which desire could be expressed, they also observed boys' looks and behaviour in musical girl talk. Rebel heroes like the Shangri-Las' 'Leader of the Pack' and references to sexual violence and female self-abnegation, along with an assertion of independence and a delight in having fun, were new to women's pop music. The girl groups themselves tended to look ultra-girly in their frilly dresses, but the Shangri-Las broke with this too when they wore hipster trousers, shirts and go-go boots to sing of the motorbike gang leader's death.

Controlled by the music business, girl groups did not last long and rarely saw the money they made. Black girl groups also did not get the television bookings. The appearance of the Supremes on *The Ed Sullivan Show* marked a breakthrough. On the whole, women were singers rather than musicians – notable exceptions were Goldie and the Gingerbreads, who were more popular in Britain than in the US.

The formidable individual women singers who did emerge during the 1960s extended the scope of women in popular music despite the racism and sexism in the entertainment world. Diana Ross paid tribute to Martin Luther King at the Royal Command Performance in London in 1968, and Aretha Franklin gave Otis Redding's song 'Respect' new gender and race meanings in 1967. Both women combined glamour as popular singers with a political assertion of black rights in the manner pioneered by Lena Horne, Billie Holiday and Ella Fitzgerald in jazz. In

The Supremes: stars of Motown.

contrast, the two outstanding white women stars, Joan Baez and Janis Joplin, both broke conventional rules about appearance. *Time* magazine grumbled in 1962 that though Baez was 'palpably nubile',[131] despite her lack of lipstick and disregard for rollers, there was little sex in her singing. In contrast, at the end of the decade, the non-glamorous Janis Joplin's raunchy sexuality was regarded as too sexy. It seemed that women singers just could not win.

Ellen Willis points out that all the women singers faced a dilemma: the masks they could adopt on stage were 'men's fantasies',[132] not their own. Thus Janis Joplin broke with stereotypes and launched another one: 'Joplin's revolt against conventional femininity was brave and imaginative, but it also dovetailed with a stereotype – the ballsy, one-of-the-guys chick who is a needy, vulnerable cream puff underneath.'[133]

She sang about lust and she sang about extremes which were part of the self-destructive side of the counter-culture. As Ellen Willis notes, the male counter-culture defined liberation for women as sex, which in Joplin's singing 'became charged with a secret energy of an as yet suppressed larger rebellion'.[134] Sexuality, rutting in masochism and defiance, takes on a certain desperation in Joplin's voice: 'Freedom's just another word for nothing left to lose.'

Women were able to expand the range of subjects they could sing about as mainstream performers; negotiating sexual identities was to prove more tricky.

✳

supporting families needed work and could not get by on women's wages. As more and more educated middle-class women came on to the labour market, they were inclined to compare themselves with men. They had after all been told that they were equal and that their work resembled that of their male colleagues. But for many working-class women equality with a man just meant hard work – an option which was all too familiar. As Donna Redmond, a single Appalachian mother who had migrated to Atlanta, Georgia, in order to earn enough to support her children, put it, 'I don't want to compete with a man. I don't *have* to compete with a man. I *know* I can do it.'[135]

Economic expansion and the demand for women's labour contributed to a new confidence and to new frustrations. There were contradictory expectations about work and family life, and an evident gap between consumer images of housewives and the real women rushing between two lives. By 1960 one in five women with children under six and nearly 38 per cent of those whose children were over sixteen had paid jobs. During the 1960s 7.8 million women joined the labour force, 5.2 million of whom went into clerical work. While the service sector – especially clerical work, teaching, sales, nursing, cleaning – was the expanding area, there was a slight shift to male jobs: craft workers, mechanics, repairers, construction workers and blue-collar supervisors. One incentive is likely to have been pay. Women's average earnings during the 1950s had actually fallen in relation to men's. In 1960 women earned just under 60 per cent of the male rate; in 1950 it had been 65 per cent. Yet many women were supporting families. Equal-pay legislation in 1963 was an important breakthrough, but it did not solve low pay in jobs which were classed as female.

Women in the professions were still concentrated in elementary and secondary education, nursing and libraries; on the whole they were not working as doctors or lawyers or college professors. But the great expansion in higher education started to bring more women into college posts, and this was to make the right to gain access to male professional zones a key issue for a new wave of middle-class liberal feminists. Some exceptionally gifted women were becoming visible in the scientific and technological fields, which had been so male. For example, Gertrude Elion discovered Imuram, a drug which helped to prevent the rejection of kidney transplants in 1962, and also contributed to the treatment of viruses and cancer. In 1963 Maria Goeppert-Mayer became the first American woman to win a Nobel Prize for physics because of her contribution to the shell structure of atomic nuclei, making her the second woman to gain this award (the first was Marie Curie in 1903). In 1964 another physicist, Chinese born Chien-Shiung Wu, was the first woman to win the National Academy of Science's Comstock Prize. Computer pioneer Grace Murray Hopper had been forced to retire from the navy in 1966 aged sixty, but she was recalled during the Vietnam War to reorganize their computers. Ann Moore came up with some more basic technology by creating the Snugli child carrier: she had been part of President Kennedy's Peace Corps in 1961 and noticed how West African women carried their babies.

Brilliance, inventiveness and audacity got a minority through the system, but there were tremendous prejudices to overcome. Jerrie M. Cobb, for example, was the first woman to qualify as an astronaut in 1961, yet was told by NASA that women could take less physical stress than men. The same was true in public life. Aileen Clarke Hernandez, appointed to serve on the Equal Opportunities Commission (EOC) set up by President Johnson to carry out Title VII of the Civil Rights Act, found herself confronted by a 'sea of male faces and derision about sex discrimination'.[136] As a black woman committed to equal rights, she was exasperated by the prevailing assumption that black civil rights related only to men. The Commission even booked a meeting in a private male club that excluded women, as if she simply was not there. Title VII was a joke for the media. Were men going to be employed as *Playboy* bunnies was what the *Wall Street Journal* wanted to know in 1965.

Not surprisingly all kinds of moderate and reasonable women grew angry. Aileen Clarke Hernandez gave up on the EOC and joined NOW. As the EOC shillyshallied about action on discriminatory help-wanted ads, Pauli Murray, who had researched constitutional law exhaustively in developing Title VII, began to think another march on Washington was needed 'to secure equal opportunities for all'.[137] She saw equal opportunities as involving social reforms such as maternity leave and nurseries. Betty Friedan contacted her and she was to become one of the founders of NOW. Ti-Grace Atkinson had been a Republican, but went on a picket of the *New York Times* to protest about the discriminatory help-wanted ads in the mid-1960s and was puzzled to be called a lesbian. She too joined NOW and was to become a radical feminist in the late 1960s.

Women's lives, however, were not only being affected by gender inequality. Vast structural economic changes were occurring in this period. The mechanization of agriculture in Puerto Rico and Mexico had forced people off the land, while the modernization of Southern cotton production meant African-Americans could no longer work in agriculture. The Appalachian coal industry had also gone into decline during the 1950s. The authors of *Who Built America?* show that millions of Americans, 'especially minorities and women', were 'doomed ... to a "secondary labour market" characterized by low-paying, insecure, non-union jobs'.[138] Women from this 'other America', as Michael Harrington called the poor in the working class, would play an important role in the new kinds of workers' organizing which were beginning to break away from the corporate unionism of the 1950s.

Cesar Chavez's National Farm Workers' Association came to symbolize this new labour movement. It began small, with Cesar Chavez, Helen Chavez and Dolores Huerta. A teacher who was doing voluntary Catholic charity work, Dolores Huerta came from a farm-working background and, though she had never handled contracts, she learned about them in one and a half weeks. She had six children and was pregnant with a seventh (she was to have eleven) when she began organizing. Helen Chavez ran the credit union and Jessie Lopez de la Cruz became the first woman organizer in the fields. Dolores Huerta said that the power touched by the farm-workers was about more than employment rights: 'Poor people's movements have always had whole families on the line, ready to move at a moment's notice, with more courage, because that's all we have. It's a class not an ethnic thing.'[139]

The link between work and community was also present in Local 1199's historic New York hospital workers' strike, which involved many women, in 1962. Black and Puerto Rican community leaders gave their support and the strike led to Governor Nelson Rockefeller granting collective-bargaining recognition to hospitals. In 1968 the union was to win a $100 minimum wage. Local 1199B was launched in 1968, when women hospital workers in Charleston, South Carolina, went on strike for 113 days, gaining an increase and establishing a credit union. They attributed their victory to 'a winning combination of 1199 union power and soul power'.[140]

Occasionally 'the other America' contrived their own ways of doing things. In North Georgia women workers in the Levi-Strauss, Blue Ridge jeans plant decided to go it alone in 1967 after a bitter wildcat strike in which Levi-Strauss used scab labour. Supported by unionized men in the Copper Company, the strikers set up their own factory, McCaysville Industries, in Fannin County, which did not force speed-ups and allowed time off for sickness and breaks. At McCaysville, children could come after school, or husbands drop in for a chat. 'Country music floats through the building,' wrote Kathy Kahn, herself a singer, and 'everyone in the factory is treated equally.'[141]

Daily Life

The 1960s began with reassuring signs of continuity. Down at the Texas State Fair in 1961 the crowd round the fall-out shelter section was bigger than that at the prize cattle exhibition. Americans were going to be well protected from the enemy without. Margaret Moore, a nutritionist, was there with handy hints: 'Pickles will help ease thirst and canned vegetables are an extra source of liquid.'[142] Sensible families could continue to consume underground when the bomb dropped. *Time* magazine ran a cover story that year, 'The Sheltered Life', listing all the fall-out goods you could buy. Not only had a new market definitely arrived; it was reassuring to know that family values were going to survive the bomb.

Jackie Kennedy's arrival in the White House, when her husband defeated Nixon in 1960, ought to have been equally reassuring. But somehow this glamorous young mother who seemed to be constantly skiing or horseriding made the 1950s-style maternalism look old-fashioned and dowdy. Then along came some rather odd TV programmes. Advocates of family values saw their own reflection starting to get wacky in the popular *Flintstones* series: 'Own Your Own Cave and Be Secure'. Worse was to follow in 1964 and 1965 with first *The Munsters* and then *The Addams Family*. In *Where the Girls Are*, Susan Douglas remarks, 'The antithesis of Donna Read, these mums did not bake chocolate chip cookies or take the PTA seriously. They were more likely to be making frog-eyeball stew or teaching the kids how to tie hangman's knots and build toy guillotines.'[143]

Edginess around middle-class mothering was accompanied by a veritable outcry about mothers on welfare – particularly black mothers on welfare. Daniel Moynihan's 1965 report, 'The Negro Family: The Case for National Action', focused on the high proportion of single female-headed households among the poorer black working class. Moynihan's primary concern, the creation of black male employment, was of much less interest to the press than the fertility rate of young black women. Instead of considering what the women who were bringing up families alone really needed to solve the accumulative problems of urban poverty, the media put them on trial. They were accused of sexual irresponsibility and welfare parasitism and of being responsible for crime and a crisis of masculinity.

Like all moral panics, the onslaught was based on exaggeration and several social problems were conflated in the search for a vulnerable and convenient scapegoat. Jacqueline Jones points out that one reason the figures for teenage illegitimacy went up so dramatically in this period was that older married black women were having fewer children. The increase was proportional: the actual figures were not that much different from what they had been in the 1950s. The attack on black welfare mothers turned into opposition to welfare spending – a consequence that Moynihan deplored. Paula Giddings observes that the real problem with Moynihan was his sexism, for he unrealistically envisaged the labour market being restructured so that black men could take over black women's jobs.

In the moral panic which followed his report, white people's stereotypes came back with a vengeance: the criminal black male and the sexual black woman were conjured up once more. The group with fewest economic resources was being blamed for problems created by economic interests over which it had no control. Pauli Murray opposed the negative approach of the Moynihan report with a positive set of proposals for black women's liberation:

adequate income maintenance and the elimination of poverty, repeal or reform of abortion laws, a national system of child-care centers, extension of labor standards to workers who were excluded, cash maternity benefits as part of a system of social insurance and the removal of all sex barriers to educational and employment opportunities.[144]

But this did not make sensational copy and it would have hit the pockets of the middle class.

The assumption that America was a land of infinite opportunity encouraged the view that the poor must have failed personally. Conservatives branded poverty as premeditated failure: welfare mothers were lazy scroungers. The reverse, in fact, was more likely to be the truth. In 1967 the *New York Times* reported a White House study which had found that 'Only 1 per cent on welfare lists are able to work.'[145] AFDC grants were a derisory $40.95 a month per person in the late 1960s, and you had to be desperate to face the bureaucracy of welfare. As one member of the National Welfare Rights organization executive said, 'You don't get anything for nothing. They make it hard as dirt.'[146] The numbers of people getting assistance for children related, not surprisingly, to the unemployment figures. In 1968 William K. Tabb showed the total that year was $2.8 billion for 6.1 million individuals in poor families, while those receiving assistance because they were old, blind or disabled – 2.8 million people – was $2.6 billion: 'The hue and cry over "welfare" payments to reward mothers for having so many children hardly corresponds to the importance of this item in the total budget.'[147]

Welfare mothers were stereotyped as black and living in the inner city, but the poor were, of course, white as well. For instance, Shirley Dalton, a member of a Pentecostal Church in Dellslow, West Virginia, went on welfare rather than see her seven children go hungry because of 'false pride'[148] when her husband was made unemployed. For her too, welfare-rights organizing was about pride and entitlement. She told Kathy Kahn, 'Someday us poor is going to overrule. You got to shine a little light to let people know who you are.'[149] The female poor could be middle class too. For example, in the early 1960s when her husband left her, a middle-class woman, Betty, was stranded in Levittown and forced on to welfare. She was reported by neighbours when she began another relationship – a victim of what Winifred Bell, writing in 1968 in the journal *Social Work*, described as 'welfare witch-hunts'.[150]

The rich had their own kind of family problems, especially if there were teenagers in the family. Nancy and Ronald Reagan were horrified when they visited daughter Patti at boarding school on Thanksgiving vacation in 1965. Patti Reagan remembered, 'I was going through my Julie Christie–Beatle period. My hair was parted *way* over on one side, hanging in my face. I had on thick black eye make-up and white lipstick, and my skirt was so short and tight I could hardly walk.'[151] Patti never understood why she was 'in this family'; her teenage ambition was 'to go join the circus'.[152]

And Patti was one of many. Teenagers uncertain of who they were anxiously did the quizzes in *Seventeen*, *Glamor*, *Teen* or *Mademoiselle* to discover their fragrance type and resolve their identity problem. There were all kinds of ways 'to be' on offer. Among these 'selves' were the young vulgarians, with heavy black eyeliner and back-brushed hair or beehives piled up on the top of their heads. There were blonde beach-girl beauties in scanty bikinis who dated beach-boy surfers and featured in Gloria Steinem's *The Beach Book* in 1963. There were the perky girls like Goldie Hawn, doing the Twist, the Mashed Potato, the Watusi and the Locomotion with what Jane and Michael Stern describe as 'anything-is-possible energy'.[153] American middle-class parents adjusted to the frenzy, only to discover that their daughters, chameleon-like, were turning into intense, soulful protesters with long, straight, Joan Baez-style hair and donning the blue denim of Southern sharecroppers. Stuart and Elizabeth Ewen comment, 'Denim provided an anti-fashion, an anti-uniform.'[154]

If white girls adopted the styles of outsiders, bohemians, drifters and workers, black girls' styles became more and more glamorous. The girl groups of the early 1960s were carefully groomed by 'charm' experts and Susan Douglas notes that the rise of Diana Ross and the Supremes created a way of being 'sexy yet respectable'[155] that white girls wanted to emulate.

Both fashion and anti-fashion, of course, were part of a vast expanding market; as one 1963 headline put it, 'Teens Grow as Top Target for Many Products'.[156] Advertisements played on fear and created pressure to conform, but a shift in aspiration had become evident. Helen Gurley Brown's *Sex and the Single Girl* was a best-seller in 1962, not because it told you how to get married but because it told you how to have a good time with men. It was followed by a cookery book, *The Saucepan*

Barbie Dolls

Barbie, Mattel Toys' popular creation, was responsive to the spirit of the age. She abandoned her 1950s ponytail for the perky bulb cut in 1961. By 1964 this had become the flip cut. She and her boyfriend, Ken, were into the latest dances and *Barbie Magazine* invited its readers to 'Join Barbie and Ken at a Twist Party'.[157]

Mattel Toys kept Barbie's image middle-of-the-road trendy in the Jackie Kennedy style during the mid-1960s, but her small cousin Francie was on the scene by 1966 to represent the youth avant-garde. Flat-chested, with long, straight hair, Francie was a Beatles fan who wore patterned tights and micro miniskirts. She was followed in 1967 by Twiggy, who, just like the real Twiggy, had a 31-23-33 figure and short blonde hair. There was a fashion time-lag, however, for she wore a swinging London 1965 bright blue, yellow and green minidress with matching yellow boots. Ken disappeared in 1967 (gone underground?) and resurfaced in 1969 with an entirely new smart hippie look: shiny white trousers and a Nehru jacket.

Barbie turned her back on the wild days of the 1960s with her 1970 maxi-mini outfit: Lurex miniskirt, topped by maxi-coat, worn with high-heeled boots. As Jane and Michael Stern remark in *Sixties People*, 'The perky days were over. High fashion was back in style.'[158]

✳

and the Single Girl, which in 1965, according to Jane and Michael Stern, had 'all the ingredients for that light-hearted leap from filing cabinet to flambé'.[159] 1960s young women's interest in pleasure, quick meals and glamorous jobs had stimulated a new kind of 'how to' literature.

A similar faith that sexual identity was malleable influenced the new feminism. In a paper for the American Academy of Arts and Sciences conference in October 1963, Alice Rossi said, 'By sex equality I mean a socially androgynous conception of the roles of men and women . . . This assumes the traditional conceptions of masculine and feminine are inappropriate to the kind of world we can live in in the second half of the twentieth century.'[160] The young radicals who formed the early women's groups also believed that you made your own way of being women and that this involved a new way of being men. They were, as Susan Douglas puts it, determined 'to ride full tilt'[161] against the contradictions. Theirs was a confidence and security unique among women in large numbers in any period in history.

There were, however, many women like Donna Redmond, working-class, married at fifteen and divorced with two children. She was not impressed with the androgynous future: 'If a woman doesn't have the right to look like a woman then she doesn't have any rights. If a working woman wants curls in her hair, damn sure let her have curls.'[162] Indeed, if your face was your fortune and you had not much else going for you, androgyny was a dubious blessing. Instead, you might as well get your 'double-knit Acron polyester perma-press' shorts and ponchos in 'white modacrylic pile on a polyester back' from the catalogues and long to look like Miss America.[163]

As the decade ended the lines of rebellion were more muddled than they had seemed in those early years of civil rights and Beatlemania. The cult murder of Sharon Tate and four friends in the Bel-Air district of Los Angeles by the Family, led by Charles Manson, exposed the sinister aspect of the counter-culture's fascination with extremes of experience and dissolving boundaries. In 1969 in Miami teenagers, supported by celebrities like Anita Bryant, rallied for decency and gave three-minute speeches about God, parents and patriotism.

Sex

When the pill became available in 1961, *Reader's Digest* prophesied 'one vast, all-pervading sexological spree'.[164] The following year *Lady Chatterley's Lover* was joined on the best-seller list by *Sex and the Single Girl*. Gloria Steinem's September 1962 *Esquire* article, 'The Moral Disarmament of Betty Coed', confirmed that more and more college girls regarded premarital sex as a personal matter and wanted to go on the pill. When Gael Greene interviewed hundreds of students for *Sex and the College Girl* (1964), she found a similar mood. Exasperated at the hypocrisy of the moral code in which she had been reared, one Radcliffe student told her, 'The truth is nice girls do.'[165]

The advice to young women had become blatantly contradictory. Journalist Ann Landers continued to warn that no one would marry you if you lost your virginity, but in early 1960s films like *Splendor in the Grass* (1961) and *Love With the Proper Stranger* (1963), the heroines' problem was sexual repression. In Susan Seidelman's 1994 documentary film *Confessions of a Suburban Girl*, the women remember being good girls and wanting to be bad girls. But the real bad girls on the edge of their suburban lives were the tough Italian girls who guarded their pitch fiercely.

Between contradictory messages, young women in the first half of the 1960s were caught between polarities and forced into uneasy compromises. (Going to bed with your boyfriend was all right as long as you kept your swimsuit on.) Meanwhile, popular media sex advice was getting odder and odder: 'Brush him lightly all over with face-blusher brush . . . Take his temperature . . . Make a sandwich out of him and two pillows . . . Frolic in a man's chest hairs,'[166] and for avid readers of comic books with a taste for vigorous S&M, 'Pow! Bam! Splat – Girls who like to get punched'.[167]

William Howell Masters and Virginia Johnson's *Human Sexual Response* was published in 1966. In Lynne Segal's words:

They comprehensively recorded the bodily contractions, secretions, pulse rates and tissue color changes occurring during more than 10,000 male and female orgasms, produced in the laboratory by 694 white, middle-class heterosexual men and women, building upon Kinsey's surveys to provide a new paradigm for Western studies of sexuality.[168]

Masters and Johnson's scientific investigations emphasized the importance of sexual satisfaction as a means of reducing the rising divorce rate and they put forward a model of equality in which women's orgasms were the mark of successful sex as well as men's. Their work was known popularly for their stress on the clitoris and was to be taken up by feminists because it offered an alternative approach to female sexuality. Lynne Segal observes that their scientific medical stance, however, missed the complexity of human feelings accompanying the physiological signs of arousal, a reductionism which passed into the sex therapy movement which they inspired.

Pessimism about the possibility of human interaction was evident elsewhere in the culture. Susan Douglas evokes the go-go girls who 'pranced and shimmied in their cages' behind pop singers: 'Autonomous yet objectified, free to dance by herself on her own terms, yet highly choreographed in her own little prison, seemingly indifferent to others yet trapped in a voyeuristic gaze.'[169]

Confusion about sex was not only apparent in teenage culture but had hit the bastions of the suburban middle class too. Moral certainties which had compelled secrecy or repression in the 1950s were in disarray. In *Wives*, one woman describes how after several affairs in the 1950s she fell for a younger man. She broke off the relationship when his wife tried to commit suicide, but in the late 1960s they resumed: 'Well, life is short and there's nothing like good sex.'[170] Another woman in Richmond had been approached by someone she knew to swap partners. Her husband had said no, though she added that they did not care what other people did. Despite the new tolerance, 'It sure is strange at the PTA meetings. It's hard to concentrate when she's talking about new sand for the kindergarten sand box.'[171] However, guilt experienced in an earlier era could also produce antagonism to the new permissive attitudes. Harriet, married to a salesman, felt bad about an affair with a married man when she was twenty. She was 'furious about this sex education stuff in school. It ought to come from the home.'[172] If her mother had been able to talk to her about sex, she believed she would not have entered into the affair.

Sex education in schools was accompanied by the acceptance of birth control. Despite the continuing opposition of the Catholic Church, conservative as well as radical voices advocated contraception. For example, by the end of the decade the Committee to Check the Population Explosion was linking the birth-rate to crime and drug addiction, asking, 'How many people do you want in your country?'[173] Population control was their solution to urban discontent. By the early 1960s a shift could be detected on abortion. As in Britain, it was affected by the tenacious fight of Frances Oldham Kelsey to get the drug that caused nerve damage and deformities in embryos, thalidomide, banned. In a much-publicized case, TV celebrity Sherry Finkbine went to Sweden for an abortion in 1962 because she had taken thalidomide. Though there was outrage among opponents of abortion, the case for abortion was seen in a new light. By 1966 one survey showed that 65 per cent of the population were in favour of a liberalization of the laws. In 1967 Colorado became the first state to legalize abortion for rape, incest, or when a mother's physical or mental health was in danger or if the child was likely to be born with severe mental or physical disabilities. The right wing and the Catholic Church were troubled by the changes. The Catholic Church began to organize Right to Life groups from 1965, hiring a firm, Spencer-Roberts, to set them up in California in 1966.

The relaxation in attitudes to heterosexuality were accompanied by more tolerant attitudes to homosexuality. During the early 1960s clergy in some Protestant churches responded to Daughters of Bilitis and Mattachine campaigning with educational programmes. By 1966 tolerance was overtaken by the positive assertion of the slogan 'Gay is Good', and lesbian and gay male student groups emerged in Columbia, Cornell, NYU and Stanford the following year. Alma Routsong, who, under the pseudonym Isabel Miller, wrote *Patience and Sarah*, based on the true story of two women living together in the 1820s, described a new cultural openness. She was using herself in her work, 'not disguising, which I had always done before, trying to find heterosexual equivalents'.[174]

Towards the end of the 1960s it seemed possible to break through sexual taboos. The expression of what had been forbidden or unspoken brought a tremendous sense of relief and power. Reflecting on her marriage, Alma Routsong remarked, 'You have to flatter him . . . by your own inferiority . . . While you love men, and need their love, need their approval, there are certain adaptations you have to make that are crippling to you.'[175]

Others, like Donna Redmond, saw sex differently:

Hell it's part of being a woman to make her man feel like a big man. And that doesn't mean you're his slave . . . If you're in there just for your own satisfaction, you may as well forget it. Well, if I'm gonna sleep with a guy, I'm gonna let him know I'm the best damn woman he's had in a long time and he's gonna want to come back. And if I'm really interested in a man, I want him to feel like he's the king. It makes me gratified to know I'm woman enough to do it.[176]

The dilemmas about sex and power did not go away, but women who lived through this period saw the conventional frameworks of assumption being turned inside out – for better or worse. As one contributor to Susan Seidelman's *Confessions of a Suburban Girl* remembered, 'All of a sudden all the rules changed.'[177]

Chapter 8

THE 1970S

BRITAIN

One Foot on the Mountain

'How better to enter a new territory but together? How could the strange landscape be mapped singly when no apprenticeship had been served?'[1] Playwright April de Angelis captures the powerful Utopian impulse in the early Women's Liberation groups, where personal memories were mined and 'discovered as political through sharing, identifying, recognizing, naming'.[2] It seemed as if politics and culture had melted into one and creativity had transcended all known boundaries.

The pull of the movement called into question existing relationships. Novelist and poet Alison Fell declared in 'Love Song – the beginning of the end of the affair',

> But I am the woman with
> one foot on the mountain,
> my tread turns earth
> and my stumblings are moving me beyond you.[3]

The resolve to break through restraints, defy the taboos around femininity and become new women was fierce and undeniable. The collective culture of the new movement was springing from individual desires for personal transformation which went deeper than any ideology. It involved a psychological break with all that had gone before.

Women's Liberation inspired poetry, plays, novels, paintings, sculpture and films in which subjectivity acquired new social meanings, and these in turn flowed into political demands. The closeness of art and politics was made apparent in the visual rituals of demonstrations.

Sculptor Val Charlton modelled a giant shoe out of papier mâché, and the old woman who had so many children she did not know what to do took to the streets demanding nurseries and free contraception.

But humour could not prevent a culture of complaint and protest from wearing thin as time passed and the world went on just the same – or pretty much the same. There was, moreover, a great distance between the discontents of daily life and images of alternative Utopian possibilities, whether these symbolized some imagined loss of power, like the massive Earth Mother goddesses painted by Monica Sjoo and exhibited at feminist conferences, or the existential vagabond in Nelly Kaplan's film *La Fiancée du Pirate* (1969). Much admired by feminist film-makers, here was a whore who did not repent and was not punished. Nelly Kaplan said the important thing was to 'keep away the sentiment of guilt . . . The road is open, she can choose, she is free, she will fight to keep her freedom.'[4]

Real women, however, still worried away, and guilt, overtly banished, craftily found its way back through the crevices of the psyche. As the confidence in the possibility of change faltered in the late 1970s, the Utopian urge to break the patterns of culture turned inward and anger took over – anger against men and anger against other women. 'Women who live with men,' wrote Sheila Shulman in 'Hard Words or Why Lesbians Have to be Philosophers', 'have never discovered/ that insurance is a racket.'[5]

Feminists in the 1970s faced a tension which has afflicted many radical movements, oscillating between making a separate culture and demanding access to the mainstream. In 1979 art historian Griselda Pollock sought a third way, acknowledging what was distinct about being a woman yet engaging with 'the main currents and institutions of contemporary art practice'.[6] Women were not completely apart from male-dominated culture, though 'they have occupied and spoken from a different place within it'.[7] Angela Carter tackled the same dilemma as a novelist in her allegory *Passion of New Eve* (1977), where a woman is born from a man's body, while Laura Mulvey's film with Peter Wollen, *Riddles of the Sphinx* (1977), explored the psychological and social dilemmas of mothering. Entry into male-defined culture involved a denial of what was specifically female, yet it was precisely the passionate nature of the bond which created an obstacle to women

Wendy Taylor and *Brick Knot*, Hayward Gallery, London, 1978.

transforming the external social world. The recognition of such complexities could be paralysing. The press photograph of Wendy Taylor's massive sculpture *Brick Knot*, exhibited at the Hayward in 1978, showed her caught inside it. The image was more than just a publicity gimmick. In the course of the decade the confident conviction that women were moving towards an alternative culture had been replaced by a realization of the immensity of what had been undertaken and a keen awareness of the snares.

It was not simply a matter of feminists consciously seeking a new culture. They were caught within wider changes which had brought the movement into being. And these shifts in the structure and perceptions of the everyday were not affecting gender alone. In Angela Carter's short story *Reflections* (1974), an 'ageless hermaphrodite knits a web that keeps the worlds inside and outside the mirror separate and all hell breaks out when s/he drops a stitch.'[8] Doris Lessing, who kept her distance from the emerging movement for women's liberation, had moved away from her earlier preoccupation with what it meant to be a woman. She was, however, extremely concerned about what happened when the inside and outside worlds collided. Her novels in the 1970s ruthlessly mapped a culture in disintegration until, in *Shikasta* (1979), she took off into 'a new world': 'It is by now commonplace to say that novelists everywhere are breaking the bonds of the realistic novel because what we all see around us becomes daily wilder, more fantastic, incredible.'[9]

Women had no sooner put one foot on the mountain than what had seemed like perfectly solid ground began to dissolve under their feet.

Politics

Ruskin, Oxford's trade union college, was awash with women on the last weekend in February 1970. Some 400 arrived with sleeping bags; there were about sixty children and forty men, some of whom looked after the crèche. Ruskin's hall was too small and the conference had to decamp to the austere Oxford Union, which had only recently bestirred itself to admit female students. But even this forbidding place could not quell the buzz and hum. There were talks about equal rights at work, about housework, about fathers sharing child-care, and women and crime, as well as historical ones about women's resistance in crowd action and in French revolutionary movements. In between, clusters of young women in the ragged fur coats and with the long, straight hair of the 1960s generation could be seen talking intensely about everything under the sun. A completely new kind of movement had broken to the surface. However, apprehension, excitement and relief were the predominant emotions at the time, rather than any notion of the future. One of the organizers, a former actress and trade union student at Ruskin, Sally Alexander, remembered a collective joy: 'We'd done it . . . It felt like the culmination of something. It didn't feel like the absolute beginning.'[10]

Out on the streets of Oxford, Saturday shoppers, interviewed by film-makers about their views on Women's Liberation, were merely bemused or amused. The intensities of the first few hundred were still remote eccentricities. However, the following November the movement became national news when Women's Liberation demonstrators invaded the Miss World contest with bags of flour, tomatoes and stink bombs, chanting 'We're not beautiful, we're not ugly, we're angry.'[11] The protest took on a more sinister meaning because a bomb was planted by a small group called the Angry Brigade in the BBC van outside.

Bombing the spectacle gained few supporters, but it was a symptom of a wider turmoil in British society which contributed to the development of the Women's Liberation movement. The demands accepted by the early women's conferences – equal pay, equal education and opportunity, twenty-four-hour nurseries, free contraception and abortion on demand – never expressed the actual range of its politics. Indeed, like the French students of 1968, there were those who distrusted demands because it was thought that capitalism would be all too eager to co-opt radicalism by granting reforms.

On International Women's Day in March 1971, the first Women's Liberation demonstration wended its way through London's West End. Cheerful despite a blizzard, the 500 had become thousands, and they sang 'Stay young and beautiful if you want to be loved' with gleeful irony. The small groups really mushroomed after this march. By spring 1971 they were busy campaigning for more nurseries, free contraception and abortion on demand, making contact with local schools, unsupported mothers' groups, Claimants' Unions, tenants' groups and

Sally Alexander (left) holding the banner at the head of the first Women's
Liberation demonstration in Britain, March 1971.

women shop stewards. Some had set up co-operative playgroups; others embarked on sex education for teenagers; one group tried re-writing fairy stories and several produced local magazines. Many of the women who joined had been active in movements against the Vietnam War and were soon to be caught up in the militant resistance to Edward Heath's attempts to curb the unions and protest against British intervention in Northern Ireland. The interconnection between women's lives and politics seemed undeniable.

This was particularly true in Northern Ireland. The first groups tended to be university-based but keen to extend their membership by going outwards. They set out to discover the actual circumstances of women's lives in the North and understand how these differed from those of women in Britain and in the South. Margaret Ward recalled that partition meant 'most of us had little awareness of how women across the border lived or how very different were the restrictions they faced'.[12] Their demands for legal rights had a more radical significance than in Britain because of the different relationship historically of the British state to Ireland and because Catholic civil rights had brought a violent response from Protestant organizations.

In the early 1970s the working-class Catholic community had become rapidly disenchanted with the British army, who had supposedly arrived to protect them. Old bitternesses revived and when men were taken away to internment camps nationalist women, forced to cope on their own, began to organize, while Protestant women likewise formed a women's section of the United Defence Association. In contrast, Margaret Waugh in the South believed women could be the harbingers of a different kind of politics. She made contact with Mary Robinson, then a senator in Southern Ireland, and they began a campaign for women to become active in all political parties. Then in May 1971 forty women from the new Women's Liberation movement in the South took the train to Belfast and returned with contraceptives, still illegal in Catholic Ireland. These fragile early links were to be sustained between Irish women in the North and the South, though the conflict between Republicans, Unionists and the British army was to put serious strains on the women's movement in the North.

The early 1970s were tumultuous enough in Britain. Edward Heath's attempts to restrict workers' rights through the Industrial Relations Act in 1971 led to demonstrations and strikes, which included a growing number of women workers. The Tories fulminated against welfare 'scroungers' and reduced subsidies on medical prescriptions, dental treatment, council housing and school milk. Welfare was seen by many people as an entitlement and the Tory commitment to selective benefits was regarded as going back to the bad old days of the humiliating means tests of the Depression. Sir Keith Joseph's family income supplement, the first direct subsidy to the poor since the early nineteenth century, seemed a poor alternative to increasing the universal family benefit.

The up-and-coming politician Margaret Thatcher acquired her 'Milk Snatcher' reputation when free school milk was cut. Her biographer Hugo Young maintains that this was not entirely fair, since Labour had already cut secondary school milk and it was really the scheme of her predecessor at the Department of Education and Science, Iain Macleod. Ironically, sheer diligence and tenacity meant that Margaret Thatcher actually managed to expand her budget until 1973. However, she made quite sure that the Conservatives' Green Paper on anti-discrimination, introduced in response to the Liberal peer Nancy Seear's bill in the House of Lords, excluded education and training.

Though in retrospect their policies seem relatively moderate in comparison with those of the 1980s and 1990s, the Conservatives managed to broaden the opposition against them. In a Britain which expected progressive improvements in both income and welfare, they faced a movement of resistance which spanned not only trade unionists but substantial sections of the liberal and radical middle class, who were, moreover, convinced that society could get *better.*

The Women's Liberation movement shared this optimism about social change. The small groups not only had consciousness-raising sessions but also campaigned in markets and council estates for family allowances, abortion and free contraception, and joined trade union women on picket lines. By 1974 there was a broad coalition which included the National Council for Civil Liberties, the National Joint Council of Working Women's Organizations, along with Women in Media and the Women's Lobby from Women's Liberation pressing for anti-discrimination legislation. At the Edinburgh Women's Liberation conference that autumn, two new demands were accepted: for legal and financial independence and for an end to discrimination against lesbians, along with 'the right of all women to a self-defined sexuality'.[13] There were, however, signs of tension between radical feminists who aimed to create a separate female place and socialist feminists who believed in autonomous alternatives, such as women's centres, *and* in working within existing institutions, such as the health service and the unions.

Labour was in power from 1974, creating a political context in which it was possible for pressure groups on anti-discrimination and social policy to have an impact. They passed the Sex Discrimination Act, and the Equal Pay Act came into force in 1975. The 1975 Social Security Pensions Act ensured that women out of employment because of 'home responsibilities' would retain full pension rights. The Employment Protection Act (1975) made paid maternity leave a statutory right, made dismissal on grounds of pregnancy unfair and required employers to give mothers their jobs back within twenty-nine weeks of childbirth. Labour also created the Equal Opportunities Commission (EOC), influenced by the American example.

There were, however, exemptions and loopholes in the new laws. Equal pay, for example, related only to work where no material difference existed between male and female employees. Part-time workers were not included in the maternity provisions and making individual claims against discrimination was a cumbersome and lengthy process. The EOC itself was a cautious institution. By the late 1970s the *Guardian* described it as a 'rather wet lady-like body too concerned with holding its skirts down against the rude winds to have a go at entrenched masculine strongholds'.[14] Joni Lovenduski and Vicky Randall point out in the EOC's defence, 'This was a new body of law and a new agency in an area of civil rights, which had very little British legal tradition behind it.'[15] In the United States civil rights had also involved a tremendous social movement around race and the demand for women's equality was backed by the National Organization for Women. No equivalent existed in Britain. The Women's Liberation movement was lukewarm about equal opportunities, which were regarded as limited and reformist; women trade unionists wanted protective legislation to be extended to men, not abolished, and Labour women were inclined to see social provision as more relevant than legislative equality.

The social gains of welfare had been whittled away by inflation and there were new problems, like the increasing numbers of one-parent families. As part of its overhaul of welfare policy, Labour introduced a non-contributory invalidity pension in 1975 and an invalid care allowance in 1976. They did not bring in the one-parent family maintenance allowance recommended by the Finer Committee in 1974. Instead they extended the family income supplement and combined family allowances and child tax allowances in child benefits in 1979. Women benefited from these and other forms of social provision – domestic services, home helps, meals on wheels, day-care centres, nurseries, community hospitals.

This social wage was widely regarded as minimal redistributive justice. However, 1975–6 was to be a turning point. After the sterling crisis and the IMF loan in 1976, Labour introduced welfare cuts and wage restraint. This onslaught on working-class living standards combined with an ideological recasting of those who were dependent on welfare. The denunciation of scroungers in the popular press, present as an undercurrent since 1968, gathered momentum. Claimants were increasingly defined as non-citizens, despite evidence that fraud constituted only 3p in every £100 accurately paid in 1977 and that millions in benefits went unclaimed by people who were entitled to them.

While the poor were being scapegoated for economic crisis, the Queen's Silver Jubilee in 1977 became a ceremonial invocation of the family as a symbol of social harmony. James Callaghan, Labour's new leader from 1976, beamed avuncularly through the patriotic populism, maintaining that Labour should do more for families. However, Margaret Thatcher, who had become the leader of the Conservatives in 1975, declared 'We are the party of the family.'[16] She meant by this less direct tax, not more welfare, which, she argued, undermined the family's ability to stand on its own feet.

In contrast, in *Family Policy* (1970), Margaret Wynn had argued the need to have a long-term commitment to 'the transfer of resources to investment in future generations'.[17] This never happened; people with children in fact lost out economically during the decade. Moreover, as Lady Howe, who chaired the EOC, remarked in 1978, along with the rise of single parents, a change had appeared in the structure of two-parent families:

The traditional single-role family, where the wife stayed at home and the husband went to work, is disappearing. As a society, we are right to worry about what is happening to women as they struggle to carry the double burden of their traditional duties and their role as workers.[18]

Commentators were disturbed too because divorce rates had gone up dramatically. However, as Melanie Phillips noted in *New Society* in 1978, 'At the centre of the pressure on the family . . . stands the change in women's expectations and the reluctance of society to acknowledge that change.'[19]

The Women's Liberation movement had arisen from these contradictory pressures and responded with campaigns which connected social and economic rights with personal self-determination, demanding free contraception (granted in 1974) and abortion, and mounting extensive local struggles for greater control over maternity and health care. Women's groups also highlighted issues of sexual coercion by challenging images in the media, creating in the process new forms of defence and resistance. From the early 1970s, Women's Aid Centres, for example, were providing a refuge for women dependent on violent partners, and revealing the extent of a previously hidden suffering. The National Women's Aid Federation was formed in 1975 and by 1977 there were 200 refuges in the United Kingdom. The first Rape Crisis Centre was opened in London in 1976 and women in other towns followed suit. In 1977 the first 'Take Back the Night' demonstration was held in Edinburgh. It reflected the fear many women had of walking alone in cities. But it also indicated a growing tendency among some strands of feminism in Britain, as in the United States, to regard violence as the key to male–female relations. The 1978 Women's Liberation conference divided so acrimoniously on the question of inherent masculine violence that no one was ever prepared to call another one. This was an indication of the ethos of desperate confrontation which marked the politics of the late 1970s.

Feminists participated in a mass occupation of a proposed nuclear reactor site at Torness in Scotland in 1978. The Organization of Women of Asian and African Descent (OWAAD), the first black women's organization, formed in 1978, mobilized against the immigration laws and particularly against the humiliating virginity tests imposed on

Women's Theatre

Early Women's Liberation demonstrations drew on 1960s agit-prop street actions and on hippie happenings. Ritual was being radicalized and feminists in Britain, as in the United States, were quick to adapt the idiom, making burlesque out of femininity. The Electronic-Nipple Show arrived on the Miss World demonstration in 1970 and the newly formed Women's Street Theatre Group performed Bryony Lavery's *Sugar and Spice* on the 1971 International Women's Day march, parading with giant sanitary towels. One of the participants, Buzz Goodbody, was to become the first woman director at the Royal Shakespeare Company and the group evolved into the Women's Theatre Group, which, like other radical theatre groups, believed in working collectively. Their plays dealt with such topics as women's fantasies and included *Out on the Costa del Trico*, about the equal-pay strike of 1976. Michelene Wandor and Dinah Brooke's *Sink Songs* (1975) focused on domestic subordination. The convergence of personal life and politics in the Women's Liberation movement brought new themes into women's theatre. In 1976 actress Miriam Margolyes performed Jill Posener's lesbian character Ginny in *Any Woman Can* at the Institute of Contemporary Arts in London. When the play toured Scotland with Gay Sweatshop, church groups got performances banned, but students rushed around to find the cast alternative venues. The content of the plays was extending beyond propaganda by the mid-1970s. Monstrous Regiment's first two plays, *Scum* by Claire Luckham (about women in a laundry during the Paris Commune of 1870) and Caryl Churchill's *Vinegar Tom* (about witchcraft), were both historical; though influenced by the women's movement, they were not overtly didactic.

By 1977, when Ann McFerran did an interview in *Time Out* with a group of women playwrights, there were interesting divergences in approach. Michelene Wandor said her writing and her commitment to the women's movement were inseparable; she wanted to change not only 'the position of women . . . but society as well'.[20] Caryl Churchill had initially thought of herself 'as a writer before I thought of myself as

Women's Theatre Group performance of
Out on the Costa del Trico, the play that publicized the
1976 Trico strike for equal pay.

a woman',[21] but her perceptions of women's predicament had led her to a feminist perspective. She remarked that this was quite different from 'a feminist using writing to advance that position'.[22] In contrast, Mary O'Malley, Irish author of *Once a Catholic*, was emphatic: 'I'm not a feminist (although according to my dad we're descended from a famous woman pirate).'[23] She saw class as a more important division than gender.

By the late 1970s women's theatre had reached the mainstream, but alternative groups were experimenting with form as well as content. For instance, *Dockwallopers* abandoned scripts for improvisation. The result, like Mike Leigh's *Abigail's Party* (later to become a film), was a naturalism which sometimes went out the other side and turned into surreal humour. They performed *Gin Trap*, about middle-aged Midlands women going to singles clubs, and *Blisters*, about a ballroom-dancing competition at a Butlin's holiday camp. Theirs was not an heroic proletariat in struggle, but one desperately clinging to the edges of a crumbling society.

Throughout the decade an important impulse had been the expression of a private female sensibility through the public arena of the stage. Running counterpoint was an awareness that, as Cherry Potter put it in 1977, the general 'philosophical problems' remained 'the male preserve' in drama.[24] Caryl Churchill's 1979 play at London's Royal Court Theatre, *Cloud Nine*, took on this challenge, showing how imperialism and patriarchy continued to shape British identity through cross-race and cross-gender casting. True to the spirit of the late 1970s, it was a dramatized analysis of social structure and was much more preoccupied with commenting on the restraints on human consciousness than sounding an optimistic call to revolt.

✳

women coming to join men. Afro-Caribbean and Asian women in the inner cities were also being drawn into resistance against police and racist violence. Southall Black Sisters for instance, formed in 1979, after a demonstration against a National Front meeting in Southall at which a young white teacher, Blair Peach, was killed. In 1978 the London-based Women and Ireland group was campaigning against strip-searching and a women's committee formed to make people in Britain aware of violence against Irish women by soldiers, though in both Northern and Southern Ireland feminist groups were deeply divided over the armed struggle.

The mood among workers in Britain had become bitter and pessimistic by 1977, when mass pickets assembled outside a photographic processing laboratory, Grunwick's, Dollis Hill, north-west London,

Jayaben Desai, leader of the 1976–7 strike at Grunwick's
processing laboratories in north-west London: the year-long strike marked
a new, harsher industrial climate, as management rejected
arbitration, and also made visible the conditions of the low-paid,
mainly Asian, female workforce.

where a group of mainly Asian women were on strike for the right to
unionize. Audrey Wise, by then a Labour MP, was among those arrested.
In the 1978–9 'Winter of Discontent' low-paid public-sector workers
rose in rebellion against the Labour Party's attempt to keep wages down.
Among them were women ancillary workers in hospitals, school-meals
workers and home helps. Their protest was met with a storm of abuse
from the popular press and led Margaret Thatcher to wonder, 'What
sort of a society is this which breeds such callousness?'[25]

Barbara Castle still thought that Labour could have gone against the
gale if they had stressed 'the sort of society in which we believed'; Jim
Callaghan's approach, however, was the conservative 'steady as she
goes'.[26] It was to be Margaret Thatcher who presented an alternative
vision of society, extolling self-help, thrift and individual endeavour
against the bureaucratic inertia of the state – and, of course, the scroungers. From 1979, when she led the Tories back into power, taxing the
rich was to be no longer social redistribution but the politics of envy.
She set about dismantling the claim to social entitlement of the needy
and the idea that equality was a desirable goal.

The party of the family did cut direct taxes. But Geoffrey Howe's
1979 budget enabled the richest 7 per cent to get 34 per cent of the
total. The poorest 10 per cent gained only 2 per cent of the tax cuts.
Child benefit for single parents was increased by 50p, but the poorest
who were on supplementary benefit had it docked from their benefit.
Moreover, value added tax (V A T) was almost doubled; indirect taxation
was substituted for direct taxes in order to give concessions to the rich.
Margaret Thatcher had discovered a new source of wealth – the poor.
They might not have much, but there were a lot of them.

Other long-term Thatcherite proclivities were evident in the first
year: an attention to detail, active intervention in every department, a
capacity to exert a charismatic charm upon those she favoured and a
tendency to arouse intense antagonism among her opponents. She was
inclined to exert authority with greater emphasis than male leaders –
no doubt a habit she acquired on her long march through the Conservative Party to the top – and possessed the outsider's sharp eye for
resentment simmering among underlings. Her visits to government
departments were apt to upset the top brass and delight the cleaners.
She courted back-benchers and had a gut understanding of the resent-

ment of right-wing Tory women, ridiculed under Heath's ascendancy as 'the dinosaurs in twin sets'.[27] The grocer's daughter who acquired the queenly use of 'we' and a posh voice created herself in that imaginative space dear to Conservative Party women, where class and gender were transcended by an effort of will. But Britain's first woman prime minister was not one to dwell amidst the women. Barbara Castle, one of her shrewdest critics, spotted a 'combination men fear most: a brain as good as most of theirs plus a mastery of the arts of femininity'.[28]

Thus armed, Margaret Thatcher set about ousting liberal Conservatism's claim to be the modernizing wing of the party. The new right ideas espoused by her mentor Sir Keith Joseph moved from the dotty margins to centre-stage. As Hilary Wainwright points out, the free-market economic theories of Frederick Hayek presented the right with 'a moral . . . crusade'.[29] The welfare state and trade unionism were henceforward to be associated with an era of shiftlessness and rot. 'We stood for a new beginning, not more of the same,'[30] she was to declare in *The Downing Street Years*. The phrase echoed the promise of the Reaganite right in the United States.

Work

In the first half of the 1970s the numbers of women in paid work increased steadily by around 120,000 each year. Despite marked regional variations, it looked as if the growing numbers of women workers meant the end of separate labour markets. When the Equal Pay Act of 1970 came into force on 1 January 1976, it seemed that women really were going to become equal economic citizens, and women's pay did indeed slowly rise from 65.4 per cent of men's in 1970 to 75.7 per cent in 1977. However, by 1978 it had already started to decline.

There were several reasons for the restricted impact of the act on women's pay. Equality legislation was evaded in a variety of ways. When the London School of Economics monitored twenty-six organizations between 1974 and 1977, they found that employers, sometimes with male trade union support, had changed the content of men's and women's jobs and introduced new grading systems. However, the majority of women were not doing jobs which could be compared with men's. In 1971 84 per cent of working women were concentrated in jobs where women predominated and the 1980 Women and Employment Survey found 63 per cent still in jobs only done by women, which of course tended to be low-paid. Access to better-paid ones remained restricted. By 1978 women still constituted just 1 per cent of bank managers, 2 per cent of chartered accountants and university professors and 5 per cent of architects.

Old attitudes died hard too. In 1972 the *Sunday Times* could pronounce, 'Among women in business are quite a few who work only because they have been forced to, because they have no man to live off.'[31] The 'Swinging Sixties' had left sexual stereotypes intact. 'If you want to be a super secretary instead of just an ordinary adequate one, never turn your back on your boss as you leave his office,'[32] Rhona Churchill told readers of the *Daily Mail* in 1970.

Nonetheless, changes did occur during the 1970s which could not be reversed. David Vincent pinpoints one: 'Where work had once taken place between school and motherhood, now motherhood occurred in an interval between school and work.'[33] The attempts in the late 1970s by the Conservative Patrick Jenkin to bring back censorious attitudes to working mothers fell on stony ground. It was increasingly assumed that women *had* to work. Also while equality legislation did not in itself provide the solutions, its existence did legitimate action. Women's claims were encouraged by a feeling that justice was on their side. Throughout the decade manual and clerical workers, often new to trade union membership, stood on the picket line in strikes for equal pay or protests against low pay and demanded the right to unionize. Women in low-paid service work, like cleaners, attempted to improve conditions and low-paid public-sector workers began to rebel against their role as carers on the cheap in the welfare state.

During the 1970s economic disputes were taking on wider political and social meanings, and women were contributing to the innovatory forms of industrial action which occurred. In 1970 Gertie Roche found herself swept into the leadership of an unprecedented mass uprising among Leeds clothing workers in which women workers played a key role in rejecting the negotiated increase allowed them through the Wages Councils as too low. Women went *en masse* from factory to factory calling others out on strike. Challenging officials in the union, as well as employers, they elected grass-roots workers' committees. Not simply money but the desire for more say in their economic destinies were important in this and in subsequent disputes.

In the first half of the 1970s, there were a large number of strikes for equal pay, against low pay and the right to join the union among women in manufacturing industry. Because joining a union could be a more difficult step for women, they approached membership often in a more evangelical way. By 1975 they made up 26.8 per cent of trade union membership. The unions still remained male-dominated and hierarchical, however, and the minority of women who gained posts could find themselves isolated. Nevertheless, the combination of legislation and feminist influence, especially in the white-collar unions, was bringing demands for the extension of equal pay to include work of equal value and for a much broader view of equality and control. Sexist language and behaviour and the hidden forms of discrimination experienced by women in a male-dominated movement were being fought out at branch level and in the TUC.

Race emerged as an important issue in the trade union movement and Afro-Caribbean and Asian women were a new and dynamic force. In 1974 Asian women at Imperial Typewriters in Leicester walked out because the pace of work was increased beyond endurance, defying racial prejudice from employers, trade unionists and workmates. Jayaben Desai emerged as the leader of the historic strike at Grunwick's in 1976–7, in which the determination of the Asian workforce to unionize became an incontestable symbol of a changing British labour movement. Though the strike involved clashes with her own union, Jayaben Desai, who was familiar with the teachings of Gandhi, was in no doubt about trade unionism as a principle. She described how she had been influenced by watching others strike on television:

I realized that the workers are the people who give their blood for the management and that they should have good conditions, good pay and should be well fed. The trade unions are the best thing here – they are not so powerful in other countries. They are a nice power and we should keep them on.[34]

The growing confidence of women workers developed at the same time as the women's movement and, just as they saw other trade unionists on the TV, they heard about 'Women's Lib' in the media. Sometimes the connections were more direct, as when feminists arrived on the picket lines as supporters. Songs, books, magazines, theatre and films from the women's movement helped publicize disputes. The Working Women's Charter campaigned in the trade unions and local trade union research groups gave practical help. Women trade unionists' campaigns for social issues like nurseries were strengthened by feminist involvement in unions, and issues like male violence and abortion were brought on to union agendas. In 1978 the TUC organized a march of 100,000 for abortion rights. It was their first ever demonstration on a non-workplace issue and it was the result of several years' grass-roots campaigning by feminists. Links between workers and users of public services were also established with help from feminists in the occupation of the Elizabeth Garrett Anderson hospital in 1975–6 and the Hounslow Community hospital in 1977. When the TUC endorsed a ten-point charter, 'Equality for Women within Trade Unions', in 1979, it was accepted that equality meant not simply equal opportunities but special provision for women workers in order to build up confidence and take account of child-care. The charter was the basis for expanding educational courses for women and monitoring women's role in unions.

However, one set of problems had hardly begun to be recognized when a new set presented themselves. Between 1970 and 1979 manufacturing jobs declined overall by 17 per cent. London lost many jobs as companies moved out or closed down. Unemployment in the UK in 1977 reached a peak of 1.6 million and was particularly high among women workers by the late 1970s. Ruth Cavendish noticed the change within a short seven-month period in London. In 1982 in *Women on the Line*, she described how in 1977 getting a factory job was straightforward but by 1978 the labour market was much tighter. She noted too that most of the women in the worst jobs were black or Asian, and they knew as much about women's subordination as any feminist. She worried that an increasingly inward-looking women's movement could offer little in the way of practical strategic help to these low-paid women workers.

Average real wages fell by 8 per cent between 1975 and 1977. Differentials between the low-paid and higher-paid workers also narrowed – which helps to explain why women's rates rose in relation to men's. Not only equal pay but the Labour government's commitment to the social contract fostered ideas that wages were a matter of social justice rather than scarcity on the labour market and union bargaining power. It was to be the low-paid in the public sector who finally exploded in frustrated anger against union officials and Labour's pay restraints.

Women workers had lived through an extraordinary decade of occupations and equality legislation – plans and alternative plans. Many women workers had experienced workers' participation and tried to democratize conditions in their home lives as well as at work. They had held out in strikes and lost weeks of wages, and sometimes the friendship of their neighbours, in order to establish the basic right to organize. Women with little previous activity in the trade union movement had become involved in co-operative work-ins, where skills were shared and marriages put at risk. And women who had come to a country they had known only through colonial myth had found themselves hurtled into violent clashes between labour and police. Yet in 1979 38 per cent of workers had earnings below the decency threshold, and, of course, many of these workers were women. The Conservative government in its first year in office reduced the power of the Wages Councils to regulate the earnings of workers in low-paid industries.

However, in the same period, there were signs that young professionals were moving up. The arrival of *Cosmopolitan* magazine in Britain in 1972 had first shown that this new market existed. When a rival, *Company*, was launched in 1978 the hope was that 400,000 of them were going to become new readers. 'We just want to show women that everything is possible,'[35] said its editor, Maggie Goodman. Thus even as some forms of hierarchy between women seemed to be dissolving, new forms of social division started to appear.

Daily Life

The industrial upheavals of the 1970s upset routines of daily life and scattered reports began to appear of working-class housewives, unable to look after their families in the customary way, taking direct action. During the 1972 miners' strike, women in the Midlands mining areas forced food shops and fish and chip shops to lower prices and began to buy food collectively. During workplace occupations of the Triumph

Women in the 1972 miners' strike showing support for
the men: Dennis Skinner, Labour MP for Bolsover, joins their protest at the
Coal Board offices in London.

factory at Meriden in 1976 and the Wildt Bromley factory in Leicester
in 1977, wives' support groups formed.

There was resistance too against the impact of industry on communities. In 1971 Swansea women blocked the entrance of a factory
which had been blackening the canal with industrial waste. Carbon
fall-out turned washing black, drove wildlife from the area and was
damaging health. 'Twenty years ago we just accepted our lot,' one woman told Beata Lipman, a journalist from the *Observer*. 'We wouldn't
have thought about protesting. But things have changed and we just
won't stand for it any longer.'[36] The danger of asbestosis led Women
Against the Dust to form in 1976. They were angry because their husband's work placed the whole family at risk. In *Spare Rib* Amrit Wilson
reported a member saying, 'The law puts people away for murder while
others get rich on death.'[37]

Not simply class deference but the old ethos of whispers, charity and
sexual contempt which had surrounded single mothers was also being

418

challenged. The Claimants' Union was formed in 1970 in response to rising unemployment. It aimed to help the unemployed to help themselves through collective action and it included single mothers. Gingerbread, an organization for single parents, was started in the same year by Tess Fothergill. She wanted it to be a ginger group for 'bread', but it tended to become a mutual aid group for baby-sitting and collective shopping and eating.

The formation of these groups was part of a wider rediscovery of poverty. In 1970 the Child Poverty Action Group showed that 3 million children were growing up in poverty. Sonia Jackson reported the case of Bridget Jones, a former secretary who, having been left with three young children by her husband, had applied to a tribunal because she could not support them on social security of £12 6s. The judge rejected her appeal, saying she had 'luxuries'[38] – a washing machine and a television. Poverty was not restricted to single mothers. Susan Matthews had been delighted to move from their caravan to a council flat with her husband and daughter, Jenny. But the £5 rent out of his £13 a week as a paint salesman meant they had problems buying clothes, could never go out and could barely afford small treats. Eleanor Connor, who was supervising a new project on Liverpool estates, the Playmobile – a corporation bus which had become a travelling playgroup – found, 'There's a tremendous lot of discontent from people who thought they were coming to Utopia when they moved in; it's got a very restless, unsettled atmosphere.'[39]

Though Labour and Conservatives disagreed about universal or selective welfare, the prevailing consensus in the early 1970s was that social provision needed to extend to meet new needs. Grass-roots community activists, among them women radicalized by the women's movement, were discovering the extent of the problems missed by the welfare state. Influenced by the American new left, they began by taking direct action. By the mid-1970s, however, they were turning towards local authorities for resources. Housing co-ops, community nurseries and women's centres became bases for ideas and experiments in participatory democracy and pressure points for the redistribution of social resources. By the late 1970s the women's movement had left its mark on the health service, nurseries, social work and local government.

The impulse to reform public provision was accompanied by a

growing unease about the personal from the early 1970s. Disturbing facts about family life were coming out into the open. The popular press discovered 'the battered baby syndrome' and in 1970 the *Sun* revealed, 'An astonishing number of wives . . . accept violence as part of the normal relationship between a man and a women.'[40] Criminologists E. Gibson and S. Klein showed that 58 per cent of women killed between 1967 and 1971 were murdered by a husband or lover. Rebecca and Russell Dobash, analysing 3,020 cases of violence in two Scottish cities in 1974, found that 39 per cent occurred between men, but that 26 per cent were attacks on wives. They believed that by explaining this domestic violence 'we will gain important insights into the contemporary family'.[41]

The comforting, secure idyll of the 1950s family no longer appeared to fit. The scepticism about family values in Ken Loach's film *Family Life* (1970) was influenced by the radical psychiatry of the 1960s and its depiction of the family as psychologically claustrophobic touched a nerve among the young working class. The family was also under fire because as more women with children took paid work outside the home, the unfair distribution of household tasks became increasingly apparent. 1960s sociologists of the family, preoccupied with the family as a unit of consumption, had failed to notice that it was also a place of work. Ann Oakley contested their assumptions about symmetrical relationships by documenting the division of labour in the home in *The Sociology of Housework* (1974). In the mid-1970s Jane Lewis records that 'husbands performed less than one-quarter of all domestic work and less than 10 per cent of routine domestic work'.[42] Change came in the second half of the 1970s, but was mainly among partners where women worked full-time; those who worked part-time, including women with young children, were still doing most of the work at home. One way of coping was to get children to help. Sue Sharpe's interviews with Ealing schoolgirls in the early 1970s recorded their complaints. Among them was Harwinder, an Asian girl:

At home it's all a rush because our parents are always at work so we have to do all the work and everything. I do mainly all the housework so I feel pretty tired. My mum tells my brother to do chores but he won't even pick his own dishes up. He says, 'No. My dad doesn't do anything, so why should I?'[43]

The most dramatic change was the number of mothers of under-fives taking paid jobs. Between 1971 and 1976 the proportion of children under five who spent time apart from their mothers rose from one child in six to one in four. Margaret Thatcher's target as Education Secretary in 1972 was 15 per cent full-time education for three- and four-year-olds, part-time education for 35 per cent of three-year-olds, and 75 per cent of four-year-olds by 1982. These targets were never met, even though they were relatively modest by European standards – in France in the same period 97 per cent of four-year-olds had nursery schooling. The demand remained acute. Margaret Bone found in 1977 that as many as two-thirds of mothers of pre-school-age children wanted some child-care.

The old Conservative reflex of blaming the victim was becoming less popular in the first part of the 1970s. Sir Keith Joseph's declaration in 1974 that poor mothers were breeding too many unfit children backfired and he found himself regarded as a reactionary embarrassment. The moderate Conservatism of Sue McCowan was more in touch with the times. In 1975 she pointed out that 'latchkey children, truancy and juvenile crimes were grave problems', but maintained diplomatically that women could stay 'feminine' while becoming more involved in the world outside the family.[44]

A shift occurred in psychological theories about the upbringing of children. The assumption that children needed the continuous presence of a mother had given way to an acceptance that young children could relate to several caring adults as long as they felt secure and familiar with them. The idea that fathers should be more involved with child-care was also gaining popularity. By the late 1970s the taboo against fathers being present during childbirth was being challenged by many young couples.

Moreover, child-care campaigners did not just want more of the same. The ad-hoc pattern of provision of pre-school playgroups, child-minders and state nurseries led to creative pressure from carers and parents for innovation. Child-minders formed their own association. Local Under Fives groups co-ordinated child-minders, nursery workers and parents to lobby the local authorities and campaigned on a wide range of issues: toy libraries, funding for democratically run community nurseries, safer crossings on roads. During the 1970s most

Rebel Dress

The fashion trade heaved a sigh of relief: it was the early 1970s and glamour was back. The fashion columnists were saying that it was decisively so. Maxi-skirts were in the shops and the mass market was getting into gear. Not everyone was happy, of course. Hosiery manufacturers noted with dismay that the long skirts hid laddered tights. They took some comfort from the brief craze for hotpants and produced coloured tights for warmer winter wear.

Back in the boutiques, however, all was not well. Prices were going up and they were frantically competing for a shrinking market. Unemployment, industrial unrest and the three-day week were not good for business. Desperate owners decked sales girls out in new styles. Their problems were not just economic. Mass fashion had lost its capacity to provide a simple thread through popular cultural trends. The result, says Elizabeth Wilson in her study of fashion, *Adorned in Dreams*, was 'a kind of overkill of style'.[45]

Not only women but men took to yellow satin flares. Glam rock, popularized by Marc Bolan and David Bowie, mixed urban hippie camp with Las Vegas and men's clothes went over the top. To the tune of 'Sorrow' (1973), boys adopted feminine signals of allure and, even more perplexing, girls appeared in outfits which made them look like Bowie doubles. It was not at all clear who was who. Mass fashion seemed to have lost its grip. Little consolation was to be found either from the austere, hard-edged styles of young working-class West Indians. Rude-boy braces, shirts and jeans were adopted by girls and boys alike. By the end of the 1970s they got a new lease of life through Two-tone music and were being adopted by whites as well as blacks.

Key sections of the youngish white middle-class market, meanwhile, were simply bunking off. Trendy twenty-somethings were into dissident fashion: army surplus overalls and bomber jackets. They were raiding second-hand shops, buying cheap flowery blouses to wear with jeans and combining 1940s-print frocks with hacking jackets. Mass imports of ethnic styles added long Indian skirts, mirrored kaftans and Mexican ponchos. The Women's Liberation dress code by 1976 had become somewhat schizophrenic: Kickers and bib-and-braces overalls alternated with long floral dresses, suggestive of imminent natural childbirth. Laura Ashley was successful in marketing this new look, which incorporated earth mother hippie nostalgia with an idyll of English

The first issue of *Spare Rib*, June 1972: this popular feminist glossy helped to form a subculture in which naturalism in dress styles combined with thrift shop chic.

country life. Her dresses, however, were simple to copy and hippie entre-preneurs began to do just that in the provinces, cutting her prices by a third.

In *Street Style*, Ted Polhemus describes 1976 as the year 'the age of Aquarius was indefinitely on hold'; a new generation was growing up 'in the shadow of the hippie's ever-optimistic, Utopian dream.'[46] Peace, love and breadfruit were developing a paunch and beginning to look like a bad joke when, during that very hot summer of 1976, curious and diverse styles of dress were to be found at Louise's, a lesbian club in London's Soho. Inspired by fetishism and the tacky, they wore PVC and rubber from Malcolm McLaren and Vivienne Westwood's shop SEX or the kinky glamour-wear firm She 'n' Me. They mixed string vests, army surplus and sexy lingerie. A few wore bin-liners with Doc Marten boots, ripped T-shirts, dog collars, safety pins and tight drain-pipes. The emergence of a new deviant subculture was watched by Louise, a figure from an earlier bohemian era, who sat elegantly drink-ing champagne at the back of the club. Though precursors of punk styles can be found in New York's clubland and in Patti Smith's black leather gear, punk as an attitude struck a particular chord in late 1970s Britain. Its delight in artifice and incongruity, its nihilism – 'There is no future' – and its angry rejection of Utopia, expressed the mood of the era. The punk penchant for styles scavenged from inner-city skips prefigured postmodernism's fascination for a bit of this and a bit of that. When punks turned underwear into outerwear, they confronted the public world with its secret fantasies. While the media went wild, the fashion industry gulped at the vista of Armageddon – then rapidly put string vests and jump suits with zips into production.

✳

big cities spawned a network of community nurseries, food co-ops, squatters' groups, housing co-ops and communes, tenants' organizations, law centres and Claimants' Unions, as well as Women's Aid Centres and Rape Crisis Centres. Out of the mix of radical self-help and demands for more control over welfare came a dynamic and responsive vision of social well-being which began to question top-down planning.

Feminists began to take these ideas simmering away at the grass roots on to the agenda of national politics through pressure groups like the National Council for Civil Liberties (NCCL) and the Child Poverty Action Group. Patricia Hewitt (General Secretary of the NCCL in 1974, aged twenty-six), Tess Gill, Jane Cousins, Anna Coote and Ruth Lister were among those lobbying the Labour government. The struggle to defend the abortion laws against anti-abortion private members' bills too had brought feminist activists closer to Labour MPs like Renee Short, Jo Richardson and, of course, Audrey Wise, whose support in the House of Commons was vital in defeating the bills. The campaigns against domestic violence also had some immediate influence on legislation: for instance, the 1976 Domestic Violence and Matrimonial Proceedings Act made it easier to get an injunction restraining violent partners and making arrest possible. Applications rose from 339 in 1972 to 3,000 in 1976 and the Housing (Homeless Persons) Act of 1977 obliged local authorities to provide accommodation. Community-based politics, with its emphasis on direct democratic control, thus presented policy demands to Labour through grass-roots mobilization in society.

However, by the Queen's Jubilee of 1977 the radical street parties had been replaced by Union Jack hats and bunting. Democratic community was drowned by a wave of popular patriotic nostalgia for an England that time forgot. A new generation of rebels was more likely to be drawn to the nihilistic defiance of the Sex Pistols' irreverent 'God Save the Queen' – banned on the BBC – than sombre debates on alternative economic and social policies. Radical social commentators held out little hope for the future. Jim Allen's television play *The Spongers*, which was screened in January 1978, described how a single mother in a northern town was driven to kill herself and her children through debts, the effect of cuts and uncomprehending social services. It expressed a cynicism about Labour which had become widespread on the left. She was in a Labour area and her oppressors were welfare state social workers.

LABOUR ISN'T WORKING was the famous slogan devised by Saatchi and Saatchi for the Conservatives. Margaret Thatcher was elected Prime Minister in 1979 with the promise that she would take a new broom to Britain. Inflation and inefficiency were to be swept away, along with idlers, strikers and scroungers. She too was critical of the bureaucratic welfare state, not because she wanted it to be democratized, but because she wanted to reverse the growth of public services – and indeed nursery provision was quickly cut. In contrast to the pessimism and increasing defensiveness of the left, the right had a positive vision of the future they wanted to create. And they found a broad social base which extended beyond the traditional Tory voters. A *New Society* survey in 1979 found that active trade unionists, the poor and the highly educated felt pessimistic about the future, the poor being particularly worried about crime. In contrast, the group which had voted Tory, those with some education but not highly educated, were optimistic and believed most fervently in an ethic of self-reliance. Utopia had lurched dramatically to the right and Hayek's neo-liberal economics had transmogrified into British housewifery and a new common sense.

Sex

Sex, by the early 1970s, had become a cause. Enthusiastic crusaders like Ken Tynan, Richard Neville and Germaine Greer were campaigning for it to be out in the open, an all-pervasive element of daily life. No boundaries, no taboos, no deviants, no hostages to guilt and repression; more sex, better sex, different sex was on the agenda. Sex, like society, was expected to change. There were those who believed that nakedness, in public view, accompanied by facts, cleared up sexual hang-ups – an optimistic rationalism endorsed visually in Tony Garnett's film *The Body* (1970). There were advocates of therapy influenced by Wilhelm Reich who linked mind and body in their cure for neurosis. There were members of Gay Liberation, formed in 1970, who affirmed Gay is Good, and announced that Coming Out was to be the basis for a new collective movement. And there were defiant individualists like Germaine Greer, who believed that the uncensored expression of fantasy was a necessary starting point for what she called in *Oz* 'Pussy Power' or later 'Cuntpower' – the retrieval of women's capacity for imaginative invention.[47] She saw the expression of female erotic desire as the subversive force which would dissolve 'patriarchy'. Holding no truck with reformers, she wrote in *Suck*, the magazine she helped edit, 'Our cause is sexual liberation.'[48] She was soon to resign, denouncing her fellow editors as 'counter-revolutionary'.[49] They had all agreed to be photographed in the nude, but had published only her picture.

Among the reformists who reached a wider public than the iconoclastic and short-lived *Suck* was Jane Firbank, the twenty-eight-year-old deputy editor of *Forum*, a magazine which sought to take the guilt and fear out of sex. She told journalist Linda Blandford in 1972, 'I think I'm fairly sexually liberated . . . and . . . one of the things I'm liberated from is neurotically going to bed with people I don't really want to go to bed with . . . I was so overwhelmed that someone wanted me it never occurred to me to say no.'[50]

The majority of *Forum*'s large readership in 1972 were women, and Anna Raeburn, then twenty-seven, ran the Adviser Service. She was dealing with 'frightened . . . horrifyingly guilty' people and could empathize: 'I always had a very high sex drive and I eventually made myself feel like a whore. I thought if you even talked about sex you had to be a whore, a doctor or a lesbian.'[51]

She was to go on to write a column in the feminist magazine *Spare Rib*, and replaced legendary agony aunt Evelyn Home on the mass circulation *Woman*. Her approach on the phone in 'Open Line' on Capital Radio was forthright. When Janis rang in to say her husband was not satisfying her, Anna Raeburn said, 'You have to get a hold of him and say, "Look, this is nothing against you or your manhood, but our relationship is not satisfying me."' It transpired that the husband was a premature ejaculator: 'Is he worried by it?' 'No, it doesn't seem to bother him.'[52] The man was clearly incorrigible. When Anna Raeburn recommended that he be given 'The squeeze technique' in *Understanding Sexual Response* from the Family Planning Association Book Centre, Janis said he would not read it. An impasse had been reached: Janis did not want to leave the premature ejaculator, but Anna Raeburn thought his resistance to improvement was 'putting himself into a power position'. The threat of Janis leaving 'might bring him to his senses. On the other hand, of course, you run the risk that you might never see him again. But quite frankly, if you're as bored as you say you are [Janis had turned to drugs] I don't think that's any great loss. Somebody has got to break the circle.'[53]

Full-frontal heterosexual sex in the 1970s stepped out of the porn shops into media parlance, including women's magazines. *Cosmopolitan* showed there was a big market for a magazine with a frank but light-hearted attitude towards sex: 'I was a Sleep-around Girl', 'Can Adultery Save Your Marriage?' and 'Who Me? VD?' were typical early titles. In 1973 Elinor Goodman warned in the *Financial Times* that advertisers were tempted by the 'spending power' of the young and warned that 'the old "knit your own royal family" concept' would no longer do.[54]

Some voices of patriarchal authority had, however, survived the 'Swinging Sixties'. During the *Oz* defendants' appeal over Rupert Bear, Lord Chief Justice Widgery, ploughing through the small ads, was disturbed to find in a plug for *Suck*: 'a salaciously written account of the joys from the female aspect of an act of oral sexual intercourse . . . and . . . no suggestion anywhere which would imply that this was a wrong thing to do or in any way induce people not to do it'.[55]

When *Oz* magazine was finally cleared in 1972, Mary Whitehouse's National Viewers' and Listeners' Association launched a Petition for Public Decency. She had recently been to battle over Ken Tynan's sex show *Oh! Calcutta*, a cause in which she had been supported by the Dowager Lady Birdwood, a supporter of moral rearmament. Mary Whitehouse and her supporters objected to sex being broadcast to all and sundry as a violation of the private sanctity of the family. They saw the sexual revolutionaries, reformers and the porn business as part and parcel of the same canker spreading irresponsibility and causing social disintegration. Sir Keith Joseph told right-wing Conservatives 'to take inspiration from that remarkable woman,'[56] but she made sure that her allies extended beyond the right. When the Festival of Light held a big rally in Trafalgar Square in 1971, the Right Reverend Trevor Huddleston was among its supporters.

A Catholic and former Labour politician, Lord Longford, produced the Longford Report in 1972, seeking to reform the nation's morals by defining obscenity as material 'which outrages contemporary standards of decency or humanity accepted by the public at large'. The report received a lot of publicity, but had no immediate impact. Pornography in the first half of the 1970s became more overt and sales were booming. Psychologists were arguing that it had no evil effects and, indeed, by giving 'relief' could prevent evil. Juries were increasingly seeing it as a fact of life and were reluctant to convict.

Lord Longford had asked the London Women's Liberation Workshop for their support and this most decentralized of organizations had tortuously rejected the offer in a letter explaining their view that pornography was a symptom of oppressive sexual and social relationships, not the cause. Wary of legal censorship, feminists in the early 1970s were inclined to contest images they saw as insulting rather than turn to the state. Film-maker Laura Mulvey, for example, wrote, 'The time has come for us to take over the show and exhibit our own fears and desires.'[57]

The problem was, of course, how? Sexual attitudes were embedded in existing culture and alternatives came from what was there already. The cheery any-woman-can approach to sex which was characteristic of early 1970s Women's Liberation sex advice was, as Lynne Segal shows in *Straight Sex*, partly a modification of behaviourism. Continuity is evident too with 1950s and 1960s faith in authenticity and frankness.

Art critic John Berger's influential *Ways of Seeing* had distinguished between 'the nude', the cultural creation of the male gaze, and nakedness, which revealed the self. In this spirit the Women's Liberation movement was committed to extending knowledge about the body and being frank about female physiology. Influenced by American feminism, self-examination groups formed to share knowledge of the clitoris and examine the cervix. When a film for TV, *Sex in Our Time*, featured one of these in a programme entitled 'Women, Sex and Identity', the series was dumped. There was evidently more than one way of defining obscenity.

The Catholic Church mobilized opposition to abortion in the early 1970s and played an important role in the Society for the Protection of the Unborn Child, which held large demonstrations in Liverpool and Manchester in 1972 and 1973. While some opponents of abortion believed that it was wrong under all circumstances, others, like Labour MP James White, who introduced an anti-abortion bill in 1975, thought that access to abortion should be restricted. Supporters of SPUC argued that greed, American money, Fascist ideology and the 'permissive élite' were luring pregnant women into abortions. SPUC itself was always well financed and able to mobilize thousands on its demonstrations. It aimed at the mainstream middle of the road. Phyllis Bowman, the founder of SPUC, was embarrassed when an ultra-right-wing group, the National Assembly, in which Lady Jane Birdwood was a prominent figure, supported them in the autumn of 1975 as part of their policy of opposing the 'equalization' of the British and 'Alien' populations: 'Some of us are very left wing,' she protested. 'For example, I am.'[58] Conservative voices in SPUC maintained that women needed more protection, but some opponents of abortion advocated better social provision for poor mothers, schoolgirls and mothers with handicapped children. The anti-abortion group LIFE provided short-life housing, but this did little towards the continuing costs and long-term responsibility involved in having a child.

Campaigns for free birth control, for sex information and for abortion put the women's movement in the sexual freedom camp. Women's Liberation campaigners for abortion stressed women's right to choose and opposed the power of the Church, the state or the medical profession to determine women's fertility. They said that every child should be a wanted child. Abortion was connected with the need for more control over all aspects of daily life. For instance, a black feminist, Emma Lewis, said that the struggle for abortion rights was also about resisting the system of racist pressures, money and profits. However, the case for abortion was rarely associated with women's right to sexual pleasure. Surrounded by people going on about sex in the mass media, the women's movement was downplaying sex from the mid-1970s – the period when resistance to SPUC began in earnest. It was left to MP Renee Short to connect abortion with sex, while addressing the Labour Women's Conference, a gathering which no one in 1976 would have suspected of belonging to the 'permissive élite'. Sexual freedom in the women's movement during this period was implicitly assumed to mean women having more control in sexual relations, being frank about fantasies and sexual problems, being more active in bed and more autonomous. However, there was considerable suspicion of the *Cosmopolitan* approach as a commercialized rip-off which over-simplified and individualized women's liberation.

Moreover, the move out of the Gay Liberation movement into Women's Liberation from 1974 had resulted in a challenge from lesbian women to the assumptions of the heterosexual majority that sex meant sex with men. Lesbians were by no means an homogeneous entity politically or sexually. In *Sweet Freedom*, Anna Coote and Beatrix Campbell pointed out that in reality the women's movement included lesbian women who 'continued to have sexual relations with women and not with men – because they desire women, because they have managed to find a supportive social milieu, because they don't desire men (even dislike or hate them), because they feel that only thus can they express their sexuality'.[59]

However, in the late 1970s a group called the Leeds Revolutionary Feminists were arguing that men should be avoided not because of sexual preference but as a political duty. Having defined men as a group as the symbol of social and sexual evil, all men were regarded as potential rapists and heterosexual women were branded as collaborators. In 1979 the group maintained that the only acceptable alternative was 'political lesbianism'.[60] This pessimistic approach was influenced by similar strands in the North American movement, but it was also partly based on the grim evidence of the Women's Aid and Rape Crisis Centres and found confirmation in instances of blatant male bias in the legal system, as well as in personal experiences. Indeed, one of the reasons political lesbianism was not effectively challenged was that it was an extreme statement of a perspective that had wider support. All the Northern Ireland women's groups joined a campaign to free Noreen Winchester, who was imprisoned for killing her father, who had repeatedly raped her and her sister. Mr Justice Slynn's release of a guardsman who had violently raped a seventeen-year-old on the grounds that the rapist 'allowed his enthusiasm for sex'[61] to get the better of him outraged British feminists in 1977. In the late 1970s a series of murders in West Yorkshire caused terror among local women until 'the Ripper', Peter Sutcliffe, was finally arrested.

The dismissive response of the police and media to the death of the prostitutes among his victims was also noticed by feminists, who pointed to the need to challenge the division between 'good' women who deserved protection and sexual outcasts. Influenced by their equivalents in the United States, prostitutes' groups were themselves campaigning in the late 1970s for decriminalization of their working conditions – for example, the legalization of advertisements – along with protection against violence, extortion and intimidation by existing laws. They had the support of various groups, including the National Council for Civil Liberties and the National Association of Probation Officers. Feminists, however, were divided between those who argued in favour of decriminalization and those who condemned the prostitutes for providing men with sexual services.

The shift within feminism reflected a wider rejection of the 1960s permissive moment. Escort agencies were prosecuted in 1976 and this was followed by clamp-downs on hotels in London. The vice squad in Manchester was reactivated by a zealous chief constable, James Anderton, in raids of obscene publications in 1977. A group called the Responsible Society was propagandizing against the liberal sex education of the Family Planning Association in schools. Meanwhile, Mary Whitehouse was successfully reviving the blasphemy laws against *Gay News*, pursuing the *Little Red School Book* and making strenuous efforts to stop the 'propaganda of disbelief, doubt and dirt' in the media. She was no longer being dismissed as a bad joke but had become, in Ray Gosling's words, 'established and seemingly effective'[62] by 1976. In 1978 William Whitelaw, deputy leader of the Conservative Party, told her National Viewers' and Listeners' Association, 'We have a duty to conserve the moral standards on which our society has been based.'[63] As Paul Ferris remarks, 'The days of sexual reform by legislation were over ... Margaret Thatcher's Conservatives arrived in 1979 with a moralistic agenda tucked away behind the main business of economic reform.'[64]

Yet the fuss about sex and sin disguised the profound changes in ordinary behaviour and attitudes which had occurred. As Jeffrey Weeks points out, 'Between 1970 and 1979 the divorce rate trebled for those under twenty-five, and doubled for those over twenty-five. In Britain, at the end of the 1970s, there was one divorce for every three marriages.'[65]

Britons continued to marry enthusiastically, but increasing numbers of young people were living together. Having a child without being married was no longer scandalous; as Jill Turner said in *New Society* in 1978, the one-parent families had arrived. *Spare Rib* offered adverts for vibrators, along with advice on lesbian mothers' custody rights.

Daughters told bemused parents about their lesbianism; Holloway prison was said to be tolerating lesbian relationships. It looked like moral decay to some, but to large swathes of the population a pragmatic approach to sexual morality had become a new common sense. Angela Neustatter and Gina Newson quote one young woman who decided to have an abortion: 'We looked at everything and came up with the conclusion it wouldn't have anything to come into the world to. I was at college, Rob was on a government training scheme, there was no room at either of our houses and we were obviously penniless.'[66]

Such pragmatism proved more resilient than the Utopian vision of a 'public imagery for women's desires'[67] which Linda Nochlin, a feminist art critic, had conceived in 1972. 'Women's desires' remained decidedly murky. It was not at all clear if these were simply the flip-side of men's or a quite different kettle of fish. Toni Holt, over from the United States in 1974 looking for British men to pose for *Playgirl*, claimed she was after 'men who have charisma, not just technically perfect men',[68] a quest which suggested that women had more demanding criteria for pin-ups than men. Romantic novelist and well-known desire expert Barbara Cartland, meanwhile, was producing between 6,000 and 7,000 words a day extolling women's difference and sales were booming. She warned that women were all turning themselves into Liliths and Eves and losing men's respect. It was time to bring back the redeeming Virgin Woman, who could guide and inspire men. The antidote to 'porn, the kitchen sink and women's lib' was to restore a wonderful past of glamour, extravagance and 'class', which would 'usher in a new Romantic Age'.[69]

In 1977, Barbara Cartland's sixteen-year-old step-granddaughter Diana Spencer was introduced by her sister Sarah to Prince Charles on a ploughed field near Nobottle Wood. She was wearing jeans and wellies and the Prince of Wales found her 'very jolly'.[70] It did not appear to be quite up to the *Love and Linda* standard of rapture, nor was young Diana particularly attached to either stepmother Raine or step-grandmother Barbara. She did, however, like reading romantic fiction and glamorous soaps were her favourites on TV.

THE UNITED STATES

I am Woman

Helen Reddy's 1972 song 'I am Woman' became a hit after women who heard her singing it on TV rang radio stations asking resistant disc jockeys to play it. The critics hated it. 'For a lot of men, thinking about the women's movement makes them grab their groins,' she reflected. 'What can I say? I didn't say that we were going to cut their dicks off or anything, you know.'[71] When she received the Grammy award for Best Contemporary Female Pop Vocal Performance for 'I am Woman' she thanked God, 'because She makes everything possible', which resulted in angry letters denouncing her: 'You skinny, blasphemous bitch.'[72] But Helen Reddy's song not only got into the mainstream US charts; it was adopted by the United Nations as the theme song for International Women's Year in 1975. Like the ideas of Women's Liberation, it travelled all over the world.

The mood of defiant optimism seemed infectious. Even Republican Nixon supporter and honky-tonk woman, country singer Loretta Lynn, was fantasizing about freedom, swinging on the chandelier in 'Hey, Loretta' and upsetting good ol' boys in Nashville by singing about the pill.

Women's Liberation did more than affect mainstream popular music; it inspired alternatives. In the early 1970s there was the Chicago Women's Liberation Rock Band with Naomi Weisstein on Rounder Records and Meredith Tax's reworking of an old folk song, 'There was a Young Woman Who Swallowed a Lie', on Virgo Rising: The Once and Future Woman. A revival of interest in music from mining and textile communities inspired Hazel Dickens, Alice Gerrard and Kathy Kahn to revive traditional songs and write new ones about the women of the Appalachians. The first women's label, Olivia Records, was formed in the mid-1970s by a group of women which included former members of the lesbian Washington, DC, militant feminist collective the Furies. Olivia Records issued Cris Williamson's *The Changer and the Changed* (1975) and this folksy collection sold over a quarter of a million copies, even though it was restricted to alternative radio shows because it contained a song about loving a woman.

One of the musicians on *The Changer and the Changed*, June Mill-
ington, said she thought 'that women's music was the feminine principle
becoming manifest, because it was time for it to manifest'.[73] Similarly
Judy Chicago, frustrated as a woman artist within the male-dominated
art world, decided in 1970 that she had 'to help develop a community
that was relevant to me and other women artists'.[74] Working with her
friend Miriam Schapiro, and influenced by Barbara Hepworth, Georgia
O'Keeffe and Lee Bontecou, she searched for a hidden female imagery
behind 'the façade of formalized art concerns' which was 'a metaphor
for the female self'.[75] When they showed the vagina-like flower forms
at the 1971 Rap Weekend in Fresno, women wept, hugging them in
passionate recognition.

But the discovery of a female culture was to be fraught with disputed
definitions and contesting claims to speak for a new vision of woman-
hood. For a start, not everyone saw themselves as flowery vaginas.
There were easy-riders looking for a walk on the wild side – 'Sweet
Betsy the Dyke', for example, sung by Les B. Friends to the tune of
'Sweet Betsy from Pike'.

> Oh do you remember Sweet Betsy the Dyke
> Who came from New Jersey on her motorbike,
> She rode across country with her lover Anne,
> And said to all women, 'YOU KNOW THAT YOU CAN!'
> So leave all your men folk and come on with us.
> If you don't have a cycle, we'll charter a bus . . .

Moreover, women artists were not focusing on gender alone. Social
documentary photographers like Reesa Tansey, who worked with
Mexican American farm workers, and Georgeen Comerford, who
took photos of hospital workers, were part of a revival in labour photography which was visually portraying inequalities of class, race and
ethnicity as well as gender. When Faith Ringgold, a socially committed black woman artist, won the Creative Artists Public Service Program award, she decided to use the money to do a mural
for the Women's House of Detention on Riker's Island. When
she asked the inmates what they would like to see, they told her
to paint a long road leading out of jail, 'the rehabilitation of all
prisoners, all races of people holding hands with God in the middle.'[76]

She presented *For the Women's House* to the women inmates in 1972.

Black women, confronting the interconnections of racial and gender subordination, looked back into the past for cultural inspiration and understanding. The search to express the destructive consequences of racism, along with black women's defiance and capacity to survive, resulted in several notable works of fiction: for example, Toni Morrison's novel *Sula* was published in 1975 and *The Song of Solomon* in 1978. In an interview in 1973, Alice Walker connected this discovery of a past with the possibility of a different future: black struggles in the 1960s meant, 'We have made a new place to move.'[77]

The focus on difference brought awareness of differences within difference. Anita Valerio, part chicana and part American Indian wept in the 'sweat' ceremony for the past of colonization and subjugation, yet knew very well that her lesbianism 'was a barrier between myself and my people'.[78] By the end of the decade 'I am Woman' was becoming a statement that required innumerable parentheses. Instead of searching for an essential female self, some women artists began to hold up mirrors to mirrors, finding bizarre reflections. Cindy Sherman, who described herself as 'the girl friend' – an outsider looking in at the male art world – used her own image in the *Untitled Film Still* (1977), a series of photographs influenced by her interest in film noir and psychodrama, to demonstrate absurdity in 'the fakeness of role-playing'.[79] Art critic Wendy Slatkin described her self-portraits as a wider statement about autobiography – 'a patchwork quilt of constantly fluctuating unfixed personae'.[80]

Politics

In 1970, 50,000 women marched down Fifth Avenue in New York to commemorate the fiftieth anniversary of the Nineteenth Amendment, which had given women the vote, and over 100,000 women supported the Women's Strike for Equality across the country. New members flocked into the National Organization for Women (NOW) or joined one of the small Women's Liberation groups spreading across America. These, along with child-care groups, tenants' groups, welfare rights and union caucuses, which included many women of colour, were raising women's issues in every aspect of society.

The new movement was soon to make a remarkable impact on political legislation. In the words of Representative Bella Abzug, 'We put sex discrimination provisions into everything. There was no opposition.'[81] At the beginning of the 1970s it seemed that at last the tide was going in the direction of equality. The Labor Department issued all federal contractors with affirmative action guidelines in 1970 and the following year a US House subcommittee began hearings on the Equal Rights Amendment – the first since 1948. The ERA was passed in 1972 by the Senate and sent to the states for ratification. The Equal Employment Opportunity Act in the same year made it possible to take legal actions through federal courts in order to enforce Title VII of the Civil Rights Act. The Education Amendments introduced by Representative Edith Green were passed by Congress banning sex discrimination in educational institutions. They affected not only academic posts but college sports teams. In 1972 also a US District Court in Pennsylvania decided that a foetus is not a 'person' and thus that the Fourteenth Amendment and the Civil Rights Act could not be used against abortion. Then in 1973 the Supreme Court ruled that Jane Roe had been denied a medically safe abortion and that this abridged her personal privacy, guarded by the Constitution's Fourth Amendment – a legal basis for abortion very different from that in Britain.

Support for women's rights extended through the political spectrum in ways that were inconceivable in Britain. Bella Abzug, Betty Friedan and Representative Shirley Chisholm formed the National Women's Political Caucus to make women more visible in politics in 1971. A year later not only had there been significant increases in the proportions of women at national party conventions but Shirley Chisholm had become the first black woman to campaign for presidential nomination. The two issues of ERA and abortion cut across party political divisions. By 1974 even the Republican President's wife, Betty Ford, was for ERA and the legalization of abortion. Liberal feminism's influence reached out to the population lobby, to social welfare organizations and to the older women's networks; the American Association of University Women, the Young Women's Christian Association and the League of Women Voters took up the ideas of autonomy and rights.

The radical grass-roots Women's Liberation groups were more wary of seeking political power. In the early 1970s they were involved in work around abortion and contraception, women's health and the care of mothers and children in clinics. Groups made contact with high school girls and established links with hospital workers, telephone operators and other working women. They set up child-care projects, self-defence classes and women's centres, along with several publications providing advice on housing and legal rights. In 1970, Bread and Roses, a socialist feminist co-ordinating network in Cambridge, Massachusetts, stated, 'Only an autonomous women's movement can stage a successful fight against male supremacy . . . the success of that fight demands radical social change, and the defeat of other forms of institutionalized human suffering, like racism and class oppression.'[82]

A broad commitment to social change and opposition to all forms of inequality were common in early 1970s Women's Liberation, along with a general commitment to levelling and democracy. The belief that the personal was political meant making efforts to overcome inequalities between women, and hierarchy was resisted fiercely. The suspicion of stars was not simply ideological anarchism; the recent experiences of

A member of the Third World
Women's Alliance at a New
York Women's Liberation rally
in August 1970.

the black and student movement had provided ample evidence of the damage the media could do by creating leaders. However, in *Daring to be Bad*, a study of New York radical feminism between 1967 and 1975, Alice Echols shows that the anxiety about leadership had negative consequences too. Not only did it result in painful recriminations but it also sometimes gave rise to extreme forms of vanguardism and 'draconian rules to ensure egalitarianism'.[83]

There was anxiety about exclusion as well as hierarchies. For instance, reporting on co-operative nurseries, Rosalyn Baxandall noted the lack of black and Puerto Rican mothers involved in their New York Liberation Nursery: 'The objection seemed to be that our nursery was non-institutional; dirty and sloppy, and emphasis was placed on free play rather than structured learning.'[84] Distance from some of the structures of Women's Liberation groups did not, however, mean lack of support for the aims. Paula Giddings quotes a Louis Harris–Virginia Slims poll of 1972 which showed that 62 per cent of black women favoured 'efforts to strengthen or change women's status in society', compared with 45 per cent of white women; 67 per cent of black women' expressed 'sympathy with efforts of Women's Liberation groups' compared with only 35 per cent of white women.[85] Despite Black Panther suspicion of the white Women's Liberation movement, women like Kathleen Cleaver were challenging male arrogance and egotism in the early 1970s. Some black women worked within NOW and the Women's Liberation groups, but others, feeling the need for autonomy, established the National Black Feminist Organization (NBFO) in 1973. In 1974 the Combahee River Collective in Boston took the position that 'racial, sexual, heterosexual, and class oppression' were 'interlocking'; it was the 'synthesis' which 'creates the conditions for our lives'.[86]

Activist gay women were also demanding equality in confrontations which were to influence the political mainstream. Groups like the Alice B. Toklas Democratic Club helped gain support from Democratic candidates for equal rights for homosexuals. Some of the small lesbian groups sought a rigorous political purity. Charlotte Bunch, who was a member of a militant group called the Furies, reflected, 'We had a sense that we were against the world and that we had to believe in ourselves.'[87] The belief that the personal was political could stiffen into prescriptive prohibitions about the personal details of behaviour. As June Arnold put it in *The Cook and the Carpenter* in 1973, 'The two things we are trying to do – set up a counter-culture and make a revolution – it's hard to do both things at the same time.'[88]

Nonetheless, the turmoil of the early 1970s was a period of extraordinary political creativity. The struggle for abortion was just one aspect of the wider politics of the body which surfaced from the discussions of consciousness-raising groups. The politicization of personal life introduced issues of sexual harassment, rape and domestic violence to the public agenda. 'Sexual politics', to use the phrase coined by Kate Millett in her influential 1970 book, challenged relationships of inequality within the family, envisaging differing forms of living together and bringing up children.

Not only did personal politics transform the scope of politics, it politicized the expression of imaginative resistance. Culture and politics combined as feminists took guerrilla action against exhibitions in museums which excluded women or brought the desire for a new scholarship into radical protests. In 1971 Sarah Eisenstein, a young feminist historian who marched with a thousand other women to the Pentagon in protest against the Vietnam War, stood on the steps of the Pentagon and linked women's resistance to imperialism to a wider history of resistance; the women who died in the Triangle Shirt-waist fire, the Wobblie women, women suffrage campaigners, witches and women in the Paris commune. 'We are women whose history has been stolen,'[89] she told the demonstrators. A new generation of the radical intelligentsia was demanding that knowledge be linked to experience and that learning engage with life. Women's studies arose from this passionate sense of intellectual commitment and women's history was among the new areas of inquiry which opened up. Everything from theology to architecture was thrown into question.

The need for cultural combat was confirmed by the derision and ridicule with which the media greeted the Women's Liberation movement. Journalist Susan Brownmiller remembered how male editors would instruct women covering feminist events, 'Get the bra burning and the karate up front.'[90] She took part in the feminist sit-in at *The Ladies' Home Journal* in 1970. The new feminists were undaunted by the power of the media, countering with alternative papers and by forcing the mainstream to carry articles by sympathetic women writers. The hostile coverage they received could misfire. As Susan Douglas points out, the media men made the mistake of assuming 'that feminists, like the pods in *Invasion of the Body Snatchers*, cannibalized perfectly happy women and turned them into inhuman aliens'.[91] When Gloria Steinem started *Ms.*, she revealed that the pods and their allies constituted a significant market. By 1973 *Ms.* had a subscription list of 200,000.

The advocates of women's rights and women's liberation did, however, have some determined opponents even in these early confident years. The Catholic Church launched a major campaign after *Roe* v. *Wade* legalized abortion in 1973. Some extreme Protestant and Jewish groups also challenged abortion rights, bringing these old religious opponents into an uneasy alliance. Those hostile to abortion were not all politically right-wing on issues such as welfare or nurseries. However, when Phyllis Schlafly turned her attention from opposing Nixon from the right to organizing against the ERA, a co-ordinated right-wing resistance coalesced. In a period when the demonization of Communists was losing its sting, sexuality and gender issues began to be a crucial area of political combat. By 1973 she had formed a coalition which included the Daughters of the American Revolution, the National Council of Catholic Women and the Conservative Cause, as well as groups like Women Who Want to be Women.

Rosalind Rosenberg notes how Phyllis Schlafly combined this organizational lobbying with forms of flexible political mobilization that resembled those used by feminists and the new left: 'Schlafly believed in the same highly decentralized, grass-roots organizing that radical feminists had relied on in spreading consciousness-raising across the country. Bowling clubs, church groups, neighbourhood block associations formed the divisions in her well-organized army; she was the general.'[92] She had three great advantages over her opponents: she was not embarrassed to lead, or to collect cash, and she occupied a space they had vacated – 'Mom and apple pie'.[93] The new right was thus able to argue that the feminists dismissed the value of mothers, the security of older homemakers, the rights of the unborn and the job protection of women workers, and were just not 'real women'.

Women were active and visible in a wide range of radical movements:

Gloria Steinem, editor of *Ms.*, speaking in Washington, DC, in 1977.

student protests, opposition to the war in Vietnam, the Weather underground and the black movement. The 1972 acquittal of Angela Davis,
philosophy student and Communist, on charges of murder, kidnapping
and conspiracy because of her friendship with a black prisoner, marked
a changing mood among juries, who were not prepared to be swayed
by anti-Communist prejudice any longer. The American Indian Movement (AIM) used direct action in protests against the historic injustice of
white colonization, occupying Wounded Knee in 1973. A grandmother,
Gladys Bissonette, was among the negotiators, and AIM organizer
Anna Mae Aquash took part in the invasion, as well as in the occupation
of the Bureau of Indian Affairs in Washington, DC. The FBI ransacked
her house and threatened to take away her children, and in 1976 she
was found dead, killed by a bullet in the back of her head. The FBI
blamed AIM, who said the FBI were responsible for the murder.

The authors of *Who Built America?* show how the legacy of the 1960s
persisted into the 1970s in rebellions which shared 'a sense of democratic
empowerment'.[94] In 1973, for example, women at Brookside, Harlan

County, went on the picket line in support of miners on strike for union democracy. Armed with broomsticks and walking sticks, they lay down in front of cars. When the police arrested them, the miners' wives took their children to jail and the photographs of women and children behind bars made national news. The Brookside women themselves made the connection between defiance of gun thugs and police and a new-found respect from their men at home. Confrontations over racial and class injustice were thus raising their own questions about gender politics. As Johnnie Tillmon, a member of the National Welfare Rights Organization (NWRO), wrote in 1972, 'For a lot of middle-class women in this country, Women's Liberation is a matter of concern. For women on welfare it's a matter of survival.'[95]

By 1974, however, the NWRO had collapsed. Its demise was symbolic of a wider strategic crisis during the mid-1970s in the movements for democratic empowerment which had their origins in civil rights. As the dreams of transforming American society faded, the political commitment to changing relationships in the family was superseded by NOW's more pragmatic issue-based politics. While NOW concentrated its efforts on getting the ERA ratified, locally many feminists became completely immersed in particular projects: counselling programmes, centres, health care. The 1970s also saw a dramatic increase in the numbers of women in higher education, not only in two-year colleges and part-time courses but in the longer academic four-year institutions, where women students, 46 per cent at the beginning of the decade, actually outnumbered men by 1980. The creation of thousands of women's studies courses had a significant impact on academic teaching and also inspired new forms of trade union education.

These changes made it possible for many American women to live more independently. It began to seem that freedom was a simple matter of individual choice. In 1975 novelist Erica Jong defined the feminist as 'a woman who assumes self-dependence as a basic condition of her life'.[96] Assertions about self-dependence were viewed askance by some women who were dependent on men as housewives and mothers. In 1981 journalist Barbara Ehrenreich reflected that, 'The economic stresses of the seventies split women into two camps: those who went *out* to fight for some measure of economic security (either out of necessity or choice, though the distinction is not always a meaningful one), and those who stayed at home to hold on to what they had.'[97]

Phyllis Schlafly gave a political voice to those holding on to a home-based femininity, arguing in 1977 in *The Power of the Positive Woman* that, in contrast to the Women's Liberationist's negativity about herself:

The Positive Woman starts with the assumption that the world is her oyster. She rejoices in the creative capability within her body and the power potential of her mind and spirit. She understands that men and women are different, and that those very differences provide the key to her success as a person and fulfillment as a woman.[98]

It was an old argument, but Phyllis Schlafly was able to attach the 'can do' confidence which had been the strength of radical feminism to a revamped conservative justification of women's essential difference from men. Positive Woman was the upbeat one, not the 'dog-in-the-manger'[99] Women's Liberation type.

By the late 1970s the political and social context had changed; gays and lesbians were bearing the brunt in an anti-gay backlash. Anita Bryant, the Christian fundamentalist singer, led a successful campaign in 1977 to repeal an anti-discrimination ordinance in the Florida public schools by arguing that homosexuals were corrupting the young. Violent attacks also began on abortion clinics in the late 1970s, while in 1979 the Pro-Family movement shifted from being a grass-roots coalition to challenging liberal feminism and the gay movement over policy. The Family Protection Act was drafted with Connie Marshner through a right-wing think tank, the Free Congress Research and Education Foundation. The moral right was well organized and well financed. In *From Margin to Mainstream*, Susan M. Hartmann notes, 'The diffuse opposition to feminist goals, which had existed since passage of the ERA, developed into a powerful and highly organized movement. That movement not only demonstrated its force in stalling ratification of the ERA, but it mobilized opposition to nearly every measure of concern to feminists.'[100]

By the late 1970s the conviction that Women's Liberation held clear answers to a better society had gone. Cultural feminists and eco-feminists were arguing that women had their own values and were suspicious of demands for equal rights with men. It was evident that the economic problems faced by poor women were getting worse not better. Black, Asian-American and chicana feminists continued to insist on the importance of these everyday material issues. Alma Garcia mentions the farm workers' movement, welfare rights, undocumented workers and prison rights as concerns of chicana feminists which 'were seen as far removed from the demands of the white feminist movement'.[101]

Some women, however, were on their way up. Diann DeWeese Smith in Chicago switched from organizing rape support groups and help for abused women at the Young Women's Christian Association to networking leading business and professional women. She collected bank vice-presidents, university presidents and law firm partners in the Chicago Network, Inc. in 1978. 'I suppose I'm just like an old firehorse when it comes to organizing: I smell women organizing, I go!'[102] she said. A member of the Chicago Network, Colleen Dishon, remarked, 'The beauty of networks is that all options are open. They can go anywhere.'[103]

Work

'You've come a long way, baby,' declared the Virginia Slims advertisement smugly. Alternative networks among business, managerial and professional women mushroomed during the 1970s to offset the male advantage of 'old boy' contacting, and with them went books and magazines which picked up on the self-affirming message in feminism and applied it to individual enterprise. There were, for instance, the Good Old Girls of Minneapolis and CAN, an acronym for Career Advancement Network. They did not serve only young or college-educated women. NOW member Tish Sommers had publicized the hardship of divorced or widowed older women who had been mothers and homemakers and by 1978 centres had opened in sixteen states. In 1978 the Displaced Homemakers' Network was formed, linking divorced women with the labour market and encouraging them to reapply homemaking skills as entrepreneurs. Leilani Lovern, for example, a divorced mother of three who had worked as a bus driver before becoming unemployed, became the owner of Magic Mop, a home-cleaning business in Baltimore, helped by the Maryland Center for Displaced Homemakers.

Women's business and professional self-help networks were accompanied by the legislative and policy work of such groups as the Women's Lobby, the Women's Rights Project of the American Civil Liberties Union, policy centres and various legal projects. The alliances between newer feminist organizations like NOW and the traditional organizations, among them the National Council of Jewish Women, brought together lobbying skills, while vital support came from women within the legislative system. Despite differing political views, such women as Martha Griffiths, Bella Abzug, Shirley Chisholm, Edith Green, Geri Joseph, Gladys O'Donnell and Patsy Mink all worked on women's equality legislation. Affirmative action was extremely effective in increasing the percentages of professional and managerial women. Even the military were not exempt. The National Coalition for Women in Defense, formed in 1977, pushed for entry to non-traditional assignments and legal pressure from the Women's Rights Project forced the military to stop dismissing pregnant servicewomen.

Achievers were appearing in places that might have surprised the Virginia Slims advertising team. In a challenge to job segregation, New York NOW brought a lawsuit against the New York City Waterfront Commission and got temporary work permits for more than 100 women dock workers in 1979. As women entered male jobs, they brought broader issues of gender to the fore. For example, firefighter Linda Eaton asked to nurse her baby at work in her time off. Not only did the firechief refuse, but Iowa City officials threatened disciplinary action if she breast-fed in the firestation. NOW took up her case of sex discrimination at work in 1979.

Race and ethnicity continued to place women at a disadvantage. Karen Reed, a single mother of American Indian descent, managed to get herself off welfare by becoming a gill-netter, fishing for salmon in Puget Sound, Washington State. Women without men had gone fishing in the past, so her own family accepted her fishing. But gill-netting meant that she faced prejudice in the mid-1970s from the multi-million-dollar white sports fishing industry as an Indian and as a woman. Loan applications were laborious and she was denied financial backing. Minority women with high qualifications could also be forced to take less skilled jobs or work for less pay. Nonetheless, they made real, if uneven, gains. A minority of American Indian women were moving into managerial, professional and technical employment, though many were still in low-paid food service or cleaning work. Many more black women were becoming administrators, insurance agents and bank officials, as well as doing clerical jobs. Robert L. Daniel records that the proportion of black women workers doing white-collar jobs rose from 37.9 per cent to 49.3 per cent between 1972 and 1980. Japanese-American women were moving into jobs formerly held by white men in engineering, management and administration and as sales representatives in the financial sector. In contrast, working-class Puerto Rican women, still overwhelmingly concentrated in New York City, not only lost factory jobs but also faced cuts in clerical work because of technological innovation and the movement of firms out of the city. As middle-class women from racial and ethnic minorities edged up the social scale, the class differences which divided them were becoming more evident. Class remained outside the remit of equal opportunities.

The issue of discrimination at work was becoming more acute because increasing numbers of women were the sole breadwinner and access to men's jobs was particularly vital for working-class women who were supporting children alone. Even in two-parent families ill-health or the structural unemployment which was affecting many industries could force dependence on the female wage-earner.

However, the emphasis on equal rights was only part of the solution. Barbara Garson, who toured 'Charlie Chaplin'[104] factories in the 1970s, discovered women on the assembly line at the Helena Rubinstein factory were in favour of the division of male and female work because it gave them some protection by preventing men with higher seniority ratings from bidding for their jobs. Equality could rebound. At AT&T affirmative action plans in 1972 put 16,300 men in traditionally female jobs and only 9,400 women in male ones. This was followed by a mass elimination of lower-level clerical and supervisory posts.

Affirmative action also failed to take into account the low-paid jobs where women made up the majority of the workforce in the clerical and service sectors and in the clothing industry. An alternative strategy was for women to push for the re-evaluation of skills. But when nurses in Denver claimed their work was undervalued, a US District Court judge ruled against them, saying comparable worth was 'pregnant with the possibility of disrupting the entire economic system of the United States'.[105]

While the demand for gender equality challenged the injustice which kept women's pay stuck at 60 per cent of the average man's and raised expectations of what could be possible, it did not engage with the social and economic reasons for the poverty and unemployment which were being faced by American workers of both sexes as firms began to restructure and move production to cheaper sources of labour. Many women were not simply operating as individual economic units but were connected to a family economy, and their livelihoods cannot be assessed only in terms of their own employment. From 1973 there was a downward pressure on male wages which particularly affected black families. Black male working-class men, moreover, were more likely to be unemployed than whites from 1972 and there was high unemployment among black teenage girls. Consequently the apparent gain of the black women who were moving away from domestic service and into the white-collar sector could be restricted in reality by financial responsibility for the family, even when children had grown up.

The shift from manufacturing to service and clerical employment within the economy as a whole increased the numbers of women workers and the trend for more married women to enter paid employment continued. But getting one of these jobs did not necessarily mean Friedan-style fulfilment. 'If they're gonna give me a robot's job to do,' Ellen, a filing clerk at the Fair Plan Insurance Company, told Barbara Garson, 'I'm gonna do it like a robot.'[106] By the late 1970s Barbara Garson noted the arrival of some 'versatile little machines' which might have been utilized to make work more interesting but which in fact 'permitted a form of electronic supervision that exceeded anything conceivable in the old-fashioned factory'.[107]

Yet if the picture of women's working conditions was one of a mixture of gain and loss, the radical spirit of the decade inspired a will for change. Ruth Milkman remarks that 'almost all the growth in labor organization membership was comprised of women workers'.[108] The unlikely, the vulnerable and the genteel alike shared a hope in change. Women jockeys, artists, prostitutes and tennis players organized with enthusiasm. Strikes erupted among downtrodden sections of the workforce who had seemed unorganizable. For instance, in 1972 Mexican-American women at Farah Manufacturing Company went on strike for the right to be represented by a union. Proximity to the border made organization in El Paso difficult and the women had put up with intimidation and sexual harassment because they needed the work. They travelled all over the United States organizing a boycott, helped by unions, churches, students and women's groups. In 1974 Willie Farah was forced to reinstate the strikers and recognize the union. By the late 1970s it was losing support, but a sense of pride remained. As one striker put it, 'I don't believe in burning your bra, but I do believe in our having our rights . . . it has changed a lot of things for me.'[109] Another struggle which challenged the subordination of race and gender occurred in 1975, when Navajo women electronics workers, sacked for trying to unionize, occupied their plant with the help of the American Indian Movement.

There were several disputes too over women's equality. One strike among white suburban women bank workers in Willmar, Minnesota, for example, lasted from 1977 to 1979 – the longest bank strike in US history. They wanted equal pay, a promotional ladder and an affirmative action plan. They gained women's movement and trade union support, with sympathizers withdrawing their bank deposits. On the other hand, in the 1970s trade union women also expressed distrust of the women's movement. Cathy Tuley, an activist in the Service Employees' International Union told an interviewer in the mid-1970s that she felt Gloria Steinem was 'fighting for women like herself, professional women, and that she's not thinking of women in the whole sense, just part of them. So I don't consider myself part of her movement.'[110] Ruth Milkman observes that despite the distrust of the 'individualistic thrust' which was the dominant public image of 'corporate feminism', a distinctive new consciousness was developing during the 1970s among young working women – 'trade union feminism'.[111]

New organizational forms can be seen among women workers in the 1970s linking class and gender. For instance, women coalminers trained by the Coal Employment Project in Oak Ridge, Tennessee, networked with women in Wyoming, New Mexico, West Virginia and Illinois to put pressure on coal companies to employ women. In San Francisco in 1971 two women with a long history as union activists,

Women and Sport

In 1970 top women tennis players, including Billie-Jean King, Rosemary Casals, Nancy Richey Gunter and Julie Heldman from the United States and Ann Jones from Britain, rebelled against the custom of paying women less prize money by simply refusing to play. A cigarette firm provided them with $170,000 for a fourteen-week women-only circuit which was a resounding success. They brought signs demanding Women's Liberation to Wimbledon in 1971, outraging the British media. Despite sneers about 'Women's Lob', journalists had to admit the skill of the women players in 'shot-making tactics' and their crowd-pulling popularity, and BBC commentator Larry Hodgson conceded that they had proved their worth 'game, set and match'.[112] During the 1970s

Sport and sisterhood: Martina Navratilova and
Chris Evert, Wimbledon, 1978.

women's tennis became very big business indeed and the sponsorship money rose accordingly.

Athletic feminism was also emphasizing gender equality and challenging sex segregation in Little League baseball and high school athletics. While feminists invoked Title IX, the National Collegiate Athletic Association, an organization of university presidents, mobilized against campaigns for a share in college budgets for women. They saw disaster ahead – the destruction of the college football teams!

Women began to take up unfeminine sports. The *New York Times* reported that whereas there had been a few hundred women weight-lifting in 1974, by 1976 there were 10,000. Olympic runner Francie Kraker delighted in the physical pleasure of running – the sense of harmony, ease and power in movement. She said in 1973 that she felt sorry for 'girls with their fleshy bodies done up in cute clothes for the benefit of their men. I feel sorry for them because I know they don't have any idea of what it's like to get out there and move the way most guys do sometime in their life.'[113]

But Willye White from Mississippi saw it as more problematic. An outstanding athlete who in 1972, aged thirty-two, had won her seventeenth US title in the long jump, clearing 20 feet 6¼ inches, she said in 1975:

As an athlete you take on certain masculine qualities on the field. Off the field you have to be feminine . . . A female athlete is always two different people. A male athlete can be the same all the time. He doesn't have to defend his masculinity. On the track I walk very stiffly but on the street I make sure that everything is moving.[114]

On 12 March 1972 the state of Mississippi held Willye B. White Day in her honour and the black woman who had picked cotton drove through Greenwood, her home town, in a Buick, to be greeted by the mayor and cheered by the townspeople. As she entered the library, where her grandfather had worked as a gardener, the walls were covered with her photograph. Sportswomen's victories in the 1970s were about more than prize money or an increased proportion of the budget; they were turning prejudice into respect.

Jean Maddox and Joyce Maupin, founded Union W A G E – an acronym for Women's Alliance to Gain Equality – which publicized conditions in the Silicon Valley electronics industry, as well as among Third World electronics workers. The innovative United Farm Workers' Union elected Dolores Huerta as their vice-president in 1970. Along with the feminist movement, they were the inspiration for two innovative women's organizations among clerical workers formed in 1974: Nine-to-Five in Boston and Women Employed in Chicago. From the early 1970s gay workers were organizing too. Barbara Gittings formed a gay caucus in the American Library Association and David Waldron and Carolyn Innes co-founded the Gay Nurses' Alliance. In 1974 the Coalition of Labor Union Women (CLUW) was founded by a group of trade union officials, some of whom had been early activists in NOW. Two women with considerable experience in the unions, Olga Mader and Dorothy Haener, were among the initiators of CLUW, which sought to put pressure on the American Federation of Labor–Congress of Industrial Organizations. While Nine-to-Five wanted to develop new organizational forms within the unions, Ruth Milkman observed that, in contrast, CLUW 'takes the existing structure of the labor movement as given, and directs itself towards increasing the status and power within that structure on its own terms'.[115]

In general, however, trade union feminism broadened the activities and concerns of labour. One important contribution was a new approach to education. Barbara Mayer Wertheimer, the labour historian, described the feminist labour programmes as 'action-oriented education for change'.[116] Along with courses came books, art, music and films. Two notable examples were *Union Maids* and *With Babies and Banners*, both about women's participation in union struggles in the past.

Not simply methods of organizing but relationships, conditions and indeed the very meaning and purposes of work were being questioned by working women. From the mid-1970s awareness of sexual harassment led to groups like the Working Women's Institute in New York or the Coalition Against Sexual Harassment in Minneapolis providing counselling and legal advice. Women also played an impressive role in raising safety issues in offices, factories and among farmworkers. Karen Silkwood became active in the Oil, Chemical and Atomic Workers'

Union at Kerr-McGee's plutonium-processing plant in Oklahoma when she found that the workforce were being exposed to radioactive hazards. She died in a mysterious car accident after being harassed for many months by company personnel. NOW kept up pressure for an inquiry and, in 1979, Kerr-McGee Corp. was found liable for her plutonium contamination and forced to pay the family $10.5 million. Her story was to be the basis of a popular film with Meryl Streep.

Like their counterparts in Britain, working women in the United States can be seen extending the definition of workplace control to include sexuality and the body. Sex workers began to organize when COYOTE was formed in San Francisco by former prostitute Margo St James. It was followed by PONY in New York, Dolphin in Hawaii, KITTY in Kansas, and many more. All these groups aimed to enable prostitutes to determine their own needs. Rejecting state-regulated brothels, they were arguing for decriminalization of their work. In 1979 a National Task Force on Prostitution was set up which put forward prostitutes' demands for rights.

The effort to gain more control over the conditions of livelihood also involved struggles with the state over natural resources. Among those who mobilized were Margaret Carlson, a Yurok leader, and Joyce Croy, a Hoopa leader, both active in resistance over fishing rights in the Puget Sound in 1978. Joyce Croy told Terri Suess from the Washington feminist newspaper *Northwest Passage*, 'I've been waiting a long time for this and it finally happened.'[117] It was a sentiment that many other working women who were standing up for their rights in America could have echoed.

Daily Life

Even in the era of radical rebellion and liberal equal opportunities, the dilemma of how to balance the conflicting claims of work and home continued to tear women apart. Lillian Rubin, a white working-class mother interviewed in the early 1970s, described living the split: 'You're either at work feeling like you should be home with your sick child, or you're at home feeling like you should be at work.'[118] Couples tussled over this 'work—not work'[119] question. Many working-class men had an ideal of a wife at home, but the economy of the household increasingly required two incomes.

Who did the housework became a real conflict as more and more women took on paid employment. At the end of the decade a study by the Project on Human Sexual Development at Harvard showed that while many men now *thought* they should help with housework and child-care, even when women had a full-time job less than 3 per cent of fathers did most of the household tasks and only 12 per cent shared them equally. Lillian Rubin's research showed too that it was not simply domestic work that rankled but the bargains struck over free time and whose leisure interests took priority.

Unease and protest were propelled by the extraordinary changes occurring in the family. Glenda Riley sums these up:

By 1980, only 15 per cent of American families were composed of a father who worked and a mother who stayed at home to care for the children, a figure that had stood at over 70 percent in the early 1950s. With the assistance of the birth-control pill, the average family size fell to 1.6 children. At the same time, roughly 50 percent of marriages ended in divorce, and 23 percent of adults chose to live in single-person households.[120]

The result was that the family as an assumed model and the family in real life were diverging dramatically. This had mixed consequences for women. The humiliation of divorce and illegitimacy which had caused earlier generations so much suffering no longer had the same cultural force. Marriage and heterosexuality were not the only options which could be openly lived. Single motherhood became more visible and unashamed. Earlier generations had been forced into unwanted abortions or made to give up their babies against their will. Some had been pressurized into unhappy marriages or had faced the social disgrace of being unmarried mothers. However, the options were still restricted. Not only was life on welfare demoralizing and grim; there was also a general tendency for divorced women and their families to suffer because their standard of living tended to decline.

The feminist writer Ellen Willis suggested in the late 1970s that 'the family'[121] needed to be stretched into alternative forms to meet the changing situation. In contrast, pro-family advocates dismissed the oppressive aspects of women's lives in the family in the past and concentrated on the negative and disintegratory contemporary elements. Part of their conservatism was a nostalgic yearning for a more caring and communal society. But there was a punitive resentment and a terrible fear of disorder which focused on those they regarded as deviant. The family consequently became a metaphor for an ideal of America, a constructed model of a lost innocence.

The conservative Utopia of the new right sought harmony by a harsher regulation of radical rebels and the subordinated other America. Return to a world where the state was kept at bay meant reversing the claims to social entitlement and the very idea that society at large was responsible for individual citizens which had been present in Christian social action, in social liberalism, in progressives' campaigns and in the New Deal. By one of those strange twists of politics, however, the state was brought back in through the back door. The family – invested with both private authority, the father, and private care, the mother – was to be safeguarded by the state and local government. These were somehow to ensure that wives and mothers were financially protected, that women were protected at work, that pornography was banned, that abortion was made illegal and that sex education upheld the moral views of the Christian right. Ironically, the degree of state intervention necessary to defend the ideal family would have been considerable.

The ideological offensive mounted by the new right made it extremely hard to consider the actual advantages and disadvantages in differing ways of bringing up children or to acknowledge that there were no easy answers. In the late 1960s Carol Stack, a white anthropologist, went to study a poor black community near Chicago which she called 'the Flats', showing in her 1974 book *All Our Kin* that '"the household" and its group composition was not a meaningful unit to isolate for analysis of family life',[122] because individuals could well sleep in one household, eat in another and contribute economically to yet another. Statistical surveys of the household missed a whole range of kin-based ties and economic and social exchanges. Such extended networks among poor black families provided a great deal of support to women. On the other hand, Carol Stack showed how they also restricted individual options. For instance, older women relatives could feel threatened by a younger woman forming a permanent new relationship with a man, because of both loss of earnings and the threat to their

Phyllis Schlafly campaigning against the Equal Rights Amendment in the rotunda of the Illinois State Capitol, 1978.

involvement with children. Another problem could be lack of personal space, because of overcrowding, which was particularly resented by teenage girls, who were more at home than their brothers.

The right-wing preoccupation with the morality of the family also dismissed the practical problems of livelihood which affected personal relationships in real families. As Johnnie Tillmon put it in 1972, 'Welfare's like a traffic accident. It can happen to anybody, but especially it happens to women.'[123] She challenged 'that old lie that AFDC mothers keep on having kids just to get a bigger welfare check'.[124] The grants were barely enough for food and clothing.

The numbers of poor mothers claiming welfare between 1970 and 1973 rose dramatically. However, Teresa Amott shows how a reversal of the gains made by welfare organizing can be detected from 1973. This trend continued throughout the 1970s and 1980s:

Since 1973, the number of people on AFDC has remained constant at roughly 10.7 million. At the same time, the number of those potentially eligible – predominantly people living in poor single-mother families – grew substantially. In 1973, nearly 85 percent of children living in poor families collected welfare (AFDC); by 1986, less than 60 percent received benefits.[125]

The reasons were not simply ideological. The oil crisis hit the United States in 1973. Concerned to protect profits while making the US economy internationally competitive, *Business Week* acknowledged in 1974, 'It will be a hard pill for many Americans to swallow – the idea of doing with less so that big business can have more.'[126] Some Americans, the most vulnerable, were to be given harder pills than others. However, in 1974 the oil crisis looked like a blip; a solid ethos of assumed prosperity still surrounded the middle class and the unionized working class. Life, it appeared, was destined to improve. Middle-class kitchens were replete with gadgets and household products. The scale of private consumption was far ahead of that in Britain and patterns of everyday life differed too. In the US private purchasing was much more important in defining living standards, while Americans expected much less of public services than the British.

Self-help networks, consumer protests, community organizing and environmental campaigns, did, however, continue to present an alternative perspective of mutuality. Collective solutions to social ills still seemed possible. For instance, the Sisterhood of Black Single Mothers, started in Brooklyn in 1974 by half a dozen women who wanted to share their experiences, paired single mothers in their twenties and thirties with adolescent mothers to help find housing, jobs and baby-sitters. By the end of the decade they had grown to 256 members and extended into the Bronx and Westchester, intervening in local politics and doing educational work. Comparable networks were formed among rural women: for example, Transition Resources in Orangeburg, South Carolina, which helped rural women to find jobs through an individual 'buddy'. The Boston Women's Health Book Collective, which produced *Our Bodies, Ourselves* in 1970, inspired women's health networks nationwide that asserted women's control over their bodies. Many feminists were enthusiastic about natural childbirth and suspicious of medical technology in births. Breast-feeding was back in favour among middle-class mothers. La Leche was still thriving – 4,000 attended its conference in 1979 – and INFACT, Infant Formula Action Television, boycotted products of the Nestlé Company to stop baby milk being marketed to Third World women. There was also action around domestic and sexual violence. NOW member Del Martin's *Battered Wives* (1976) was the first major report on domestic violence in America, but news of the British shelters had already crossed the Atlantic and shelters and networks were springing up all over the country. In Nevada the Sparks network established a shelter in 1977 and organized an underground support system to help women evade men who were pursuing them.

Protests occurred over prices, housing and the environment. Along with a group of friends, Jan Schakowsky demonstrated about meat prices in Chicago in 1972; this spread into a nationwide meat boycott. She said her inspiration was Gloria Steinem and *Ms.* magazine. Rent strikes and resistance to evictions in San Francisco's Chinese community were led by Mrs Chang Jok Lee of the Ping Yuen Residents' Improvement Association. Chinese women also opposed the urban renewal in Boston encroaching on Chinatown, and campaigned for community control and education in Los Angeles, along with better housing in New York.

Concern about the effect of chemicals in the water in Tennessee upon her children led Nell Grantham to become involved in a residents' environmentalist coalition. In South Dakota Women of All Red

Nations, a women's organization connected to the American Indian Movement, became worried about the high rate of miscarriages and birth defects on the reservation and investigated sewage and pesticide spraying, finding radioactive waste. Lois Gibbs's individual protest helped to make other women aware of hazardous chemical waste in Niagara Falls, New York State, in 1978, when she connected her son's serious ill-health with toxic waste. They formed the Love Canal Homeowners' Association. Very different kinds of women thus began to take public action on environmental issues because of their personal concerns as mothers.

Though the idea of control over everyday social problems continued to have an impact, as the decade wore on the assertion of individual autonomy was on the ascendant, becoming a search for external images, lifestyles and role models as well as a psychological and sometimes spiritual quest. To be fat or to be thin; to wear bell-bottoms or dress middle-aged; to look like Jane Fonda or the stars of Grand Ol' Opry; to love a man or love a woman. It was a decade of choices. It was also a decade of confusion. One thirty-two-year-old mother of two told Lillian Rubin, 'I wish I could be dependent on him like he says. But how can you depend on someone who does the things he does.'[127]

Sex

Beverly was thirty-two in the early 1970s, and married to an accountant in Memphis. They had five children. Her mother had been an alcoholic and had 'had a lot of men in and out . . . There were a lot of uncles in the family . . . I set out to be a prude.'[128] Having married a man she met in high school, she became bitter because he had been unfaithful and was bored in the relationship. Recently she had begun to have dreams about his death.

We make love about four times a week . . . I never have to initiate sex. He usually falls asleep in the chair . . . He won't go to bed, so I go upstairs, and he wakes up later during the night – oh, at three or four o'clock. For sex. It's not usually too good, to be polite about it. He'll roll me over; he already has an erection. He inserts himself and I almost get awake. He has his ejaculation, withdraws, and then he goes to sleep. You don't fight with a man like that. You just don't talk about it.[129]

Media Models

'Television . . . does not provide human models for a bright thirteen-year-old girl who would like to grow up to be something other than an ecstatic floor waxer,'[130] grumbled Caroline Bird in a 1971 *TV Guide*. The anti-ecstatic floor-waxer tendency had become a significant force among viewers in the early 1970s: 75 per cent in a 1972 survey of 120,000 people in the magazine *Redbook* agreed that 'the media degrades women by portraying them as mindless dolls'.[131]

The media adapted by either simply missing women out – in the male road or buddy movies – or ingenious adaptation. A new kind of sitcom, *Maude*, assimilated the assertive mood of the early 1970s and made it funny. Played by Bea Arthur, Maude was described by *Time* as having 'the voice of a diesel truck in second gear'.[132] She liked a political argument, stood up to men and decided, when discovering that she was pregnant, aged forty-seven, to have an abortion. This really was a new style of sitcom, but though Maude defied conventions, she also was a joke herself, so the show had it both ways.

Mary Tyler Moore, on the other hand, was younger and did not have to act the battleaxe. She was an independent woman in a good job as a TV producer. *The Mary Tyler Moore Show* aimed at an audience of modern young women and was followed by *Rhoda* and *Phyllis*. All three dramatized the lives of women who were not traditional suburban wives. But they had a difficult balancing act being supportive and humane in a cut-throat world. In Susan Douglas's words, 'Old contradictions never die; they just get new outfits.'[133]

Black women were allowed to be forceful, but this usually meant a stereotype of the matriarch; the alternative was to be sultry and exotic – an image adopted by Hollywood. One variation, Teresa Graves's role as the woman cop in *Get Christie Love*, tried combining the two; she was given the unlikely line, 'You're under arrest, sugah.'[134]

The women cop series were succeeded by action films like *The Bionic Woman*, *Wonder Woman* and *Charlie's Angels* in 1976. Some 23 million households watched Farrah, Jaclyn and Kate each week and the programme was particularly popular with college graduates, women as well as men. They were glamorous, efficient and directed by a man you never saw. Television had found a way of reconciling the tension between active and passive representations of women. The Angels, looking like *Playboy* pin-ups playing Joan of Arc in bell-bottoms, showed neither mercy nor favour. As the women got tougher, instead of individual 'bad' women being punished, a generalized violence

Not the clinging type: Wonder Woman personified glamorous autonomy.

lurked around the new autonomous heroines, though butch lesbians remained caricatures of evil.

By the end of the decade, *Dallas* was playing ingeniously on the audiences' fascination with sexual combats. Its heroines were contrasts. Reasonable Pam, the liberal individualist, is refuted by Sue Ellen's profound pessimism about reforming Ewing men: 'You have two choices. You can either get out or you can play by the rules.'[135] Conservatism and radical feminism merge in Sue Ellen's analysis of male–female relationships: 'In a couple of years they'll look at you in the same way – as property. And you'd better be wrapped up in a pretty little package.'[136]

Popular culture grasped the ambiguities that politics bypassed. In Susan Douglas's words:

Watching the cat fights, we could see, enacted before our eyes, our own daily, never-ending struggles between that portion of our psyches still tethered to pre-feminism and the other portion firmly hitched to feminism. What did it mean to be a woman and, in the wake of the women's movement, what kind of a woman should we be?[137]

✳

In Seattle, Cecile, active in the Episcopal Church and Cub Scouts and married to a man in insurance, said they had become more experimental in their lovemaking. But Lillian, twenty-nine, living in Cambridge, had found it impossible to adapt to her husband's attempt to change the pattern of their sexual relationship:

Our love affair began in a very set way, plain, straightforward, male superior. This is the way it went, and this is the way he treated me. And after a point he said that he wanted it another way, and it didn't take. I'm not afraid of the difference, I enjoy the difference, but it's him.[138]

She had begun a secret affair with a man with whom sex was 'very mutual and easy'.[139]

Confusion about how to be a woman had reached the WASP

bedroom by the early 1970s in no uncertain terms. Alice Gerrard caught the discomfort and unease of women who faced a world spun round in 'Custom-made Woman Blues'. The woman who had 'tried to be the kind of woman you wanted me to be', found she could not 'keep a hold' of her man: 'And now you say you're tired of me and all of those things I thought you wanted me to be.'[140]

Sexual expectations were in collision. Many of the working-class women interviewed by Lillian Rubin in 1972 regarded sex as a duty, a reward for virtue or an insurance policy: 'He can find someone to give it to him, so I figure I better do it.'[141] The men wanted oral sex, which most of the women saw as revolting. The women found it hard to say what they wanted: 'I don't like to think he might think I was being aggressive, so I don't usually make any suggestions.'[142] One man objected because his wife didn't ask in a 'nice, feminine way'.[143] Another wished that his wife would take the initiative. One woman complained, 'He keeps trying to get me to read those books, but what difference would it make? I don't know who those people are. There's a lot of people do things; it doesn't mean I have to do them.'[144]

Those books were not only being read by her husband. Suddenly sex was being openly discussed in the media. Best-selling sex manuals like Dr David Reuben's *Any Woman Can* (1971) and Alex Comfort's *The Joy of Sex* (1972) and *More Joy of Sex* (1974) urged couples to pursue pleasure. In *Open Marriage* (1972), Nena and George O'Neill suggested that partners 'needed room to grow' and said that 'outside sexual experiences' could be 'rewarding' as long as they were in 'the context of a meaningful relationship'.[145] Barbara Seaman, an editor on *Family Circle*, published *Free and Female: The Sex Life of the Contemporary Woman* in 1972, which warned women that sexual frustration could be bad for your health, bringing on cramps and headaches. The sex manuals conveyed with their confident air that pleasure could be achieved and they were modified by some feminists to present a new model of an autonomous, active female sexuality. Alix Kates Shulman described this approach as 'Think clitoris'.[146]

One consequence of thinking clitoris could be the conclusion that men were simply not worth the bother. As the saying went, 'A woman without a man is like a fish without a bicycle.' Lesbianism was more than a sexual preference for many women in the early 1970s; it represented a way of finding sexual pleasure without being subordinate. A member of NOW, married to a Presbyterian minister for twenty-five years, mother of five children, was transformed by going to a women's consciousness-raising group:

I realized . . . that I didn't have to be a good little girl anymore. What I wanted was an equal relationship, but I doubted it would be possible with a male – not any of the men I knew. They were trained as I had been trained, to have certain expectations about men's privileges and women's duties, and they had no reason to give it up. I did. I knew with a woman we could both just start from scratch.[147]

Lesbianism began to be presented as the means of discovering one's real identity as a woman through a more fulfilling alternative sexuality. Many lesbian feminists also saw their sexual relationships as striking at the roots of male power. There were several snags: not all feminists wanted to be lesbians, not all lesbians wanted to be feminists and not all lesbian feminists agreed with separatist feminist politics. Both lesbian and heterosexual feminists discovered too that sex was not always susceptible to political will. Nor was a new identity an automatic consequence of sex with another woman. In 1979 Ti-Grace Atkinson reflected, 'I was disappointed that it was not more different from heterosexual relationships.'[148]

Living the perfect, nurturing, non-possessive, non-hierarchical fuck became a terrible strain. It also began to seem less and less sexy. An early rebel was the pioneering author of *Ruby Fruit Jungle*, Rita Mae Brown, who described in an essay, 'Queen for a Day: A Stranger in Paradise', going to a gay bathhouse in male drag: 'I want the option of random sex with no emotional commitment when I need sheer physical relief.'[149] Were women seeking a new sexual identity which was completely different from existing forms of sexuality or breaking down the taboos against women exploring the sexual options which men took for granted? Lesbian feminists struggled with both approaches in a decade in which gay and lesbian sexuality came out of the closet and defied guilt and self-hatred.

The politicization of sexuality was equally important for the new right, whose answer to women's quest for self-realization also promised revelation and renewal. However, in marked contrast to radical feminism, the right-wing version of redemption was possible through surrender to authority, and authority was necessarily male. Unhappy wives were advised not to rebel by Ruth Carter Stapleton in *The Gift of Inner Healing* in 1976 but to imagine that their husbands returning from work were Jesus. Anita Bryant described in the same year how she had been able to yield to her husband only by practising 'yielding to Jesus'.[150]

Phyllis Schlafly shifted the viewfinder in *The Power of the Positive Woman* in 1977 by reworking the theme of women's essentially different power:

The new generation can brag all it wants about the new liberation of the new morality, but it is still the woman who is hurt the most. The new morality isn't just a 'fad' – it is a cheat and a thief. It robs the woman of her virtue, her youth, her beauty, and her love – for nothing, just nothing. It has produced a generation of young women searching for their identity, bored with sexual freedom, and despondent from the loneliness of living a life without commitment. They have abandoned the old commandments, but they can't find any new rules that work.[151]

The new right's effort to channel and contain women's sexuality tended on the whole to bring it into the anti-abortion camp. In contrast, the demand for abortion had been part of a wider vision of women's rights as individuals and as social citizens within the early self-help Women's Liberation health groups. Carol Downer, for example, a mother of six in the Los Angeles group which initiated the suction method, said that she believed 'a woman has the right to her own body,' adding, 'If she has children [she has the right] to expect this society to take responsibility to make sure the child has good schools to go to, to support her in all the ways that anybody deserves support for their children to grow up healthy and happy.'[152]

Initially the Women's Liberation movement's position was 'total repeal of all anti-abortion laws and free abortion on demand', later modified to 'the right to choose'. However, the legal victory *Roe* v. *Wade* (1973) gained abortion on the narrower and abstract basis of the right to privacy in one's own person. This obscured the fact that real

individuals existed in specific social circumstances. The story of Jane
Roe, a pseudonym for Norma McCorvey, illustrates the complexity
behind the rights of choice and autonomy. Norma McCorvey's parents
were poor and they divorced. She was in a reform school and, when
she married, she was beaten by her husband. The marriage broke up
and she began to be attracted to women. Her mother tricked her into
signing away custody of her daughter when she was drunk and she had
two more babies who were adopted. Her frantic search for an abortion
led her to a lawyer, Sarah Weddington, who was looking for a way
of overturning the law on abortion. So Jane Roe entered history
as a constitutional symbol, while Norma McCorvey worked as a
cleaner.

The emphasis upon control, choice and personal liberty which came
to predominate in the abortion campaign led by N O W was important
in countering the approach of population-control groups which dismissed the individual but did not take into account the wider questions
of reproductive rights. Poor women were more likely to be sterilized,
very often under pressure, with threats that their Medicaid would be
withdrawn. Racist eugenics continued to influence ideas of who were
unfit mothers. Ten Mexican-American women unsuccessfully brought
a case in 1978 against doctors at USC Medical Center who had got
them to sign their consent papers while actually in labour. In *Women,
Race and Class*, Angela Davis described how sterilization of black,
Native American Indian, Puerto Rican and chicana women persisted
throughout the 1970s.

Control over one's body and person actually had a more complex
range of meanings than simply birth control and abortion. Having a
baby, as Carol Stack discovered in her study of the Flats, could, in
circumstances which offered few options, bring adult status. Overcrowding made the privileges of 'a bed to be shared only with their
infant'[153] a relative gain in terms of privacy. Caring for a child would affect
the rest of their lives, but motherhood caused them to be recognized as
an individual with a certain authority who had rights within the networks
of kin. Recognition of the social and economic contexts in which many
black women made choices about fertility led black feminists to press
for wider social reproductive rights.

Both individual and social rights were to be explicitly contested when

466

the new right successfully targeted Medicaid abortions in the Hyde Amendment in 1977. The claim that poor women and teenagers seeking abortions were selfish, getting away with a 'free ride' – with a licence for pleasurable illicit sex – at the tax-payers' expense, proved one of the most politically effective weapons in the new right's arsenal. It played on a feeling that those without money should pay for sexual enjoyment and the delights of mothering with suffering, presenting a secular version of fire and brimstone. It was to be the basis for a broader assault on all those dependent on social welfare programmes. Dependence was being branded with guilt. As Rosalind Petchesky notes, 'Anti-abortion politics played midwife to the neo-conservative state and its business-oriented economic policies.'[154] But for some anti-abortion campaigners the politicians were going too slowly. In 1979 a firebomb destroyed the Bill Baird Abortion Clinic in Hempstead, Long Island, New York.

Control over women's bodies was also at issue in feminists' campaigns over rape. In the early 1970s Susan Griffin argued that rape was a form of control, and a version of this argument was developed by Susan Brownmiller. In 1975 in *Against Our Will*, she hypothesized that men had discovered their genitalia could 'serve as a weapon to generate fear', using rape as 'a conspicuous process of intimidation by which *all men* kept *all women* in a state of fear'.[155] It was an historical speculation which struck a contemporary chord amidst a widespread fear of violence in American cities. She went on to argue for an ideological challenge to 'rape culture'[156] – the assumption that the raping of women was normal, as were the patriarchal rights of men to protect women as property. Feminist activists contested the related conviction that husbands should be exempted from the charge of rape and the prejudiced ideas that some women deserved rape because of previous sexual activity.

Extending the definition of rape, in 1974 Robin Morgan declared, 'Pornography is the theory and rape the practice,'[157] when feminists had begun to take direct action against bookshops which stocked and films which showed pornography. By the late 1970s some separatist feminists had taken the trope further and maintained that all sex with men was pornographic. Many feminists disagreed with this reduction of all power relations to sexual coercion, the assumption that all men were equally powerful and the equation of male sexuality with violence. There was unease too about the attempt to ban pornography and the line that straight women, in Ellen Willis's phrase, 'consort with the beast'.[158] She noted in 1979 that the politics of Women Against Pornography went along with the myth that women were 'morally superior to men ... Self-righteousness has always been a feminine weapon, a permissible way to make men feel bad.'[159] Outrage against male vice did not threaten male power.

The curious convergence between some strands of feminism and the moral right marked a turn away from the belief that sexual freedom was the key to contentment. By 1979 the family was being rediscovered as a personal refuge from a competitive and dangerous society by some liberals and radicals – including feminists. This idealization of the family was as much an over-simplification as the 1960s sexual revolutionaries' attack on the family as the source of all oppression. Families were, after all, part of the wider society, as well as being the structures in which intimacy was experienced.

The tensions around the site of intimacy, the battles over women's bodies and the politicization of reproduction can be seen as part of a wider conflict around the boundaries of the personal and public spheres. As many aspects of life which had been defined as personal shifted on to the public, political agenda, there were counter-movements to reclaim them for privacy. These were accompanied by swings between communalism and individualism on the radical left and the radical right.

Somehow, in the furore of politics, women's sexual pleasure drifted off over the horizon and the possibility of reflection about the complexity and ambiguity of desire closed up. In 1979 Ellen Willis compared her generation of feminists to explorers caught camping out on a peninsula which the rising tide had turned into an island and seemed to be threatening to reduce to a sandbar.

All that existential angst about identity which clustered around sexuality – the fear of separation, the terror of abandonment, the desire for autonomy, the longing for love, the dread of dependency – returned to the shadowland of consciousness. Feminists sought healing through spirituality or understanding through psychology, but few claimed with confidence that the restless dissatisfactions which so many women continued to express could all be calmed by an effort of will, resolved by a consciousness-raising group, settled by an amendment or simply assuaged via the clitoris.

Chapter 9

THE 1980s

BRITAIN

In Two Minds

'We work bloody hard for our money,'[1] announced the woman at the Golden Masked Charity Ball to journalist Yvonne Roberts in 1987. She was collecting for the bone marrow unit at Westminster Children's Hospital and wearing 'a beautifully tailored long evening dress clutching a pink satin cock cover, shaped like an elephant's trunk with little beady eyes that wobble'.[2] Reward for individual effort was the message of the 1980s. Diane Charles, a part-time voluntary worker and housewife, told Beatrix Campbell that she was a Conservative 'because I like to see people get their achievements.'[3] Jean Brown, a cleaner doing three jobs, said she was a Conservative because 'they stand for everything we want . . . our own place, our own luxuries and the work that we need'.[4] Some Tory women believed this meant expanded opportunities for women. For Sonia Copland, a Conservative councillor at the Greater London Council (GLC): 'The chequebook and the pill have been very liberating and that's probably among the reasons women can break from marriage and cope on their own.'[5]

Josephine Hart, a successful theatre producer, married to advertising man Maurice Saatchi, was invigorated by the enterprise ethic: 'I find business thrilling. Business attracts brains.'[6] The emphasis on individual achievement had, however, differing meanings for women depending on their circumstances. Gina Giorgiou, who at twenty-seven had become the junior director of a clothing business in Islington, north London, in 1985, was equally passionate about her work. Her inspiration was her Greek-Cypriot father, who had taught her 'respect yourself:

if you have your own self-respect you are free to do anything'.[7] Self-respect was given a specific gender meaning by Rankin Ann, who became a DJ and reggae singer in the early 1980s: 'No call me chick, no call me bitch/Mi no use that label, and mi no take no stick.'[8]

Equal opportunities could mean self-expression and self-respect, not just getting on. Corinne Maine, a black housewife, went on a government clerical training course after being a housewife for twenty years. Her doctor prescribed it as a cure for depression and it worked. It made her 'really appreciate the notion of equal opportunity',[9] which she interpreted as black women as a group having more chances for equality and control over their lives.

The individualistic emphasis of the 1980s could release women from inhibiting constraints and duties, but it also brought confusion, removed customary protections and left an undertow of unease. When Beatrix Campbell went to interview Conservative women in the mid-1980s for her book *The Iron Ladies*, she found them in two minds about the implications of the sexual autonomy Sonia Copland connected with the pill. Sex was 'too easy' but 'Victorian values' were hypocritical.[10] Diane Charles was unhappy about women going back to work after they had had children: 'We're made to feel guilty for staying at home, because of all the opportunities available for mothers to work now. I want respect – this is what we have lost.'[11] Respect for her was not seen as something asserted or won but as an entitlement of women who were caring at home.

Moreover, there was frequently a gap between the powerful feeling that opportunities beckoned and actuality. Diane Charles had 'tried to do everything properly, to stay at home and bring up the children because society said you should. Society was wrong.'[12] Faith in individual action made it hard to explain why many people's lives did not fit the high-flying images. It could also make failure seem a personal not a social matter. The poet Amryl Johnson, who came to Britain from Trinidad when she was eleven, challenged 'The Loaded Dice' of race, class and gender:

> Yuh say we hol 'we fate in we own han'
> Is we own fault dat we cahn get on.[13]

471

A few might rise, but many didn't; this was the downside of individualism. Throughout the decade a muffled chorus of women's voices murmured about what individual endeavour forgot – the importance of human connection and interaction. On the right, this meant traditional values and the family. On the left, interconnection tended to be presented as defence of wider communities: 'You can't kill the spirit . . . She's like the mountain,' sang women from the coalfields. A curious sea-change occurred: as more women on the right adopted a language of individual assertion, women on the left were to be heard giving expression to a thwarted yearning for a longer-term responsibility for conserving – communities, human life, resources.

A new kind of subversion was brewing in some surprising places. Reading *Bunty*, a girls' magazine, in 1988, Sarah Benton noted the indignation of Marie, a socially minded nine-year-old rabbit-owner from St Helens, Lancashire: 'I am writing to tell you how angry I am about testing make-up products on animals.'[14] And young Shirley from Leven sent in a poem about seals and toxic waste which ended with the line, 'It's up to us to save the day.'[15]

Politics

'Nothing will ever be the same again,'[16] declared Emma Nicholson, one of the Conservatives who made the shift from Edward Heath to Margaret Thatcher. The 'seismic shock' had 'happened' in the person of Margaret Thatcher. There she was, Britain's first woman Prime Minister, who managed to win three elections and dominate the decade.

The fact that a woman could become Prime Minister had a symbolic meaning; modern women, it seemed, could do anything now. However, like many of her generation, Margaret Thatcher, born in 1925, really did not want to be seen as a woman in politics. She preferred to be a politician who happened to be a woman and she had little sympathy with the post-war generation's preoccupation with women's rights and wrongs. In contrast to her defence of working mothers in the 1950s, by the 1980s she was more likely to idealize the housewife and the mother at home. In this she was consistent with the Conservatives' tendency to talk of the family, rather than women as a group. The female sex thus merged with an ahistorical ideal of hearth and home – the site of personal moral authority.

The dramatic changes in women's lives were, however, stretching such cosy certainties even in the Conservative Party and the presence of a woman Prime Minister did serve to cast some time-honoured Conservative gender assumptions into new relief. 'The best compliment they can give a woman is that she thinks like a man,' she grumbled to admiring journalist Brian Walden in 1988. 'I say she does not, she thinks like a woman.'[17] Towards the end of her long period in office, Margaret Thatcher herself was inclined to attribute opposition to her as male prejudice. She told Walden:

The House of Commons is still very much male-dominated and there is something about them, a sort of 'little women' thing. It would have been all right if I had gone into what they would regard as one of the traditional professions. All right if I had followed Florence Nightingale. All right, you know, if I had gone into teaching.'[18]

However, she had made her way up through the Conservative Party, not by asserting any special claims as a woman but by skilfully spanning both male and female worlds. To survive she had had to manoeuvre the established meanings of gender and she brought this ability to Number 10. As Prime Minister she asserted her authority in Cabinet and then appeared shopping with a Lea and Perrins Worcestershire sauce bag. The symbolism of public office changed. The Falklands War in 1982 provided a new kind of photo opportunity: the Prime Minister popping out of a clump of soldiers, embodying Vera Lynn and Winston Churchill rolled into one. Anthony Barnett records how she evoked the Napoleonic saga of winter and ice, and then changed tack to explain to George Gale in a *Daily Express* interview:

It may just be that many, many women make naturally good managers. You might not think of it that way, George, but each woman who runs a house is a manager and an organizer. We thought forward each day, and we did it in a routine way, and we were on the job 24 hours a day.[19]

Adept at turning weaknesses into strength, she took the lower-middle-class woman's acute sense of the importance of appearances into party politics. Barbara Castle observed the effectiveness of 'the marketing

Body and Image

The individual had the power now: she could don her leotard for aerobics, jog painfully round the park, run in the GLC's London Marathon or take on the male sporting establishment. Elena Bond took up Olympic weight-lifting in 1984. Sue Atkins became the (unofficial) featherweight women's boxing champion, fighting in pubs and hotels from the Isle of Man to the Isle of Sheppey, with Watford in between. They were in the minority, but in 1984 2.7 million Britons were tuning into the 'Green Goddess' and 'Mad Lizzie' for TV aerobics. Keep-fit was a booming business; Cindy Gilbert's aerobics classes expanded from a suburban church hall to become a business by the early 1980s. Manufacturers of running treadmills as well as bran were hitting the big time. The exercise craze seemed to be calming down by the middle of the decade but not the yearning for health. Contamination of meat from Chernobyl, salmonella and unease about British water were accompanied by an expanding market in health products, mainly vitamins and slimming pills. Annabel Ferriman noted in the *Observer* in 1988, 'British consumers now spend £6.7 billion on health products, almost a third of the cost of the NHS.'[20]

Looking good in the 1980s meant hard work, because the leotard did not lie. It was not all about muscles, however. Carolyn Miller, Image Consultant, made her living by getting Brits to realize the body was an investment. 'Dress your assets' was her motto: 'Really we're more like America now: anyone can make it economically . . . Most of us . . . are climbing our way up and we can't afford to have a door slammed in our face. Understanding image teaches us how not to antagonize by our dress.'[21] Her American boss, Ashley Crystal, pointed to Margaret Thatcher in 1987: 'She used to have that mousy look and now she's a woman with impact.'[22] Carolyn Miller had three don'ts: no scent (most men don't like it), no unnaturally coloured hair and no dangly earrings. The last two had become marks of subcultural deviance and the 'loony left' feminists on radical Labour Councils – the antithesis of power dressing.

The young were subverting dress codes: monkey boots were worn with fishnets and suspenders now. An anxious feminist mother wrote to *City Limits* from Hampstead in 1986, worried because her daughter, brought up to be independent and now nearly seventeen, 'thinks I'm reactionary and prudish when I express my displeasure at her wearing make-up, short skirts and "feminine" clothes. She says she wears them because they give her pleasure and that the days of dull dungarees are out. I don't want to see her exploited or sexually abused.'[23] *City Limits* told her not to worry: 'There is no catalogue of correct feminist dress, and Madonna has shown that femininity can be used in an assertive, independent and self-fulfilling way.'[24]

The concern with image was, it is true, particular to an era when the making of self assumed a central importance as established structures crumbled. But some things did not change. The emphasis on individual assertion accentuated old anxieties. Sex, like all forms of power, contained its opposite, the loss or lack of power. Reflecting on ageing when she was approaching fifty, Julie Christie said, 'To people who've been looked at and considered beautiful, particularly women who relied on it so much . . . age is quite a challenge. The thing which you've always used, a power, is taken away from you.'[25] She had the actress's professional understanding of self-representation: 'There's nothing wrong with being the picture you want to be, but you can only be that once you've decided who you're trying to please. The issue is control.'[26]

✳

Cheers for Margaret Thatcher, who survived an IRA bomb planted in the
Grand Hotel during the Conservative Party conference at Brighton, 1984.

of Margaret'[27] by the advertising firm Saatchi and Saatchi. Britain's first
woman Prime Minister was not at all nonchalant about power; she
worked at being Margaret Thatcher and it was visibly an effort. The
result was to be a grating self-consciousness, an air of unreality. Not
only the voice is contrived; her whole body can be seen in permanent
tension, shifting across the borders of femininity and masculinity. Beatrix
Campbell noted a characteristic gesture: 'She tilts her head in that
gesture which is placatory but superior.'[28] Class as well as gender made
Margaret Thatcher an outsider. If the voice was a careful imitation of
upper-class English, the language was that of the Grantham shop. She
was not airy-fairy, she had no time for moaning Minnies, her mission
was the salvation of a nation that had had the stuffing knocked out of
it. This was not the customary discourse of Whitehall, but it enabled
her to put over ideas and policies as if she were a kind of highly
developed 'one of us' coming to the rescue.

When Ronald Reagan was inaugurated President of the United
States in 1981, Margaret Thatcher gained a political ally on the far right
and, at a time when her popularity was at a low ebb in Britain, was
able to make a triumphant progress through Washington. The Tory
grandee Lord Carrington followed in her wake, neutralizing her enthusiasm for Reagan's schemes, and Hugo Young records his response when

asked how the visit had gone: 'Oh, very well indeed. She liked the Reagan people very much. They're so vulgar.'[29] Along with the similarities in political outlook, both politicians were outsiders in the world of upper-class European diplomacy. They were upstarts who understood that appearances and images communicated politically. They shared Protestant religious influences in their backgrounds too, Methodism in hers and the Disciples of Christ in his. Yet there were differences between Reaganomics and Thatcherism. *The Economist* in 1987 called them 'Lord Wishful and Lady Rigorous'.[30] He did not share her horror of borrowing. Their personalities were dissimilar too. In contrast to the laid-back President, Margaret Thatcher was obsessive about details, forever going through her 'boxes' and prepared to intervene at every level, from large sweeps of policy to the school history curriculum. Her famous diligence, along with the tacit nature of British political structures which she simply ignored, meant that she faced fewer constraints than Reagan, and busily set about increasing the secret powers of the Cabinet and the state, abolishing whole tiers of local government, privatizing the public sector and nationalized industries, and intervening directly in the media and the education system in an unprecedented manner.

In the process she unsettled British Conservatism, which was accustomed to an authority embedded in custom which could fade into the dull texture of the everyday. Her explicit righteousness, the kind that none but Zion's children know, scorched the smugly unstated power of Toryism with its zeal. She persisted in announcing that her mission was to save Britain from multiple evils: inflation, socialism, the welfare state, the nationalized industries, along with civil servants, intellectual snobs in the chattering classes and politicians who did not say what they meant. She was continually telling people that she was right, that she was honest – which implied that her opponents were not. She banished doubt, ennobled endeavour and disliked deference, though she expected her ministers, her party, Parliament and the country to defer to her, increasingly adopting the royal 'we'. 'We are a grandmother,'[31] she announced when her son, Mark, became a father. Like the Queen, her person merged with the nation. If Winston Churchill and *Our Island Story* skulked in the wings, the ghosts of queens beckoned from long ago. Hugo Young notes the renewed popularity of J. E. Neale's biography of Queen Elizabeth I during the 1980s. Indeed, her public persona resembled the theatrical royalty of British cinema classics from the 1930s to the early 1950s: Queen Bess bringing order, Queen Victoria doing her duty, Henry V fighting for England's glory. For the young, and others who were not inclined to nostalgia and heritage, she promised a society where enterprise would find its just rewards and the shops would always be open.

Margaret Thatcher presented her political perspectives as a coherent system, with herself at the helm, steering a straight and unflinching course. In the words of her speech writer Ronald Millar at the Conservative Party conference in 1980, 'The lady's not for turning.'[32] She was certainly aware of the power of ideas among her foes, the socialists, and a pot-pourri of theorists, Friedrich Hayek, Roger Scruton and Ferdinand Mount, were assembled to do battle. She was, however, a politician, not an intellectual, and she drew her concepts, like her quotations, out of a metaphorical handbag to serve the occasion. At one moment she was extolling voluntary service, at another the buccaneering spirit. She invoked individualism and self-help in one breath and the virtues of subordinating the individual will to authority in the next. This puzzled her liberal and left-wing interpreters and irritated the intellectual establishment, but it appealed to large sections of England who wanted to make money fast, who believed that freedom was a fat bank account, who thought that unions were too powerful and that law and order were best maintained by a heavy hand. This was an England which felt no long-term patrician stewardship or liberal unease. She gave them her name, Thatcherites, and endorsed their ambitions. Not the types to see power as hegemonic or to probe deeply into motives, when they saw riots and looting, like her, they pitied the shopkeepers, deplored wickedness and demanded that somebody put the boot in.

Despite the remarkable power that she was to exercise during the decade, her ministers were not entirely Thatcherite and not entirely in agreement, opposing her on Europe, on welfare and on women's role, as well as on economic policy. Patrick Jenkin and Norman Tebbit might put emphasis on women's place being in the home, but this was not the approach of the pragmatic Sir Geoffrey Howe (with Lady Howe to answer to at home), or of a more spiky kind of modern Conservative woman like Edwina Currie. Tory family policy had to adapt to various pressures, including the Conservative Women's Organization, which stubbornly resisted attempts to abolish child benefits and opposed family credit being added to the male wage packet. Though child benefits were cut by 5 per cent in 1985 and frozen in 1987 and 1988, incredibly a universal benefit survived the Thatcher era.

A minority lobby, which included Emma Nicholson, sought to apply the Thatcherite emphasis upon individual endeavour to a limited endorsement of equal opportunities. While the Conservatives did not openly oppose equal opportunities, the rights established by European legislation could be an irritating check to the freedom of market forces, and the government had to be chivvied and threatened into conceding them. At the same time, Tory employment legislation curtailed social rights like maternity provision and cuts in social spending meant that child-care provision remained woefully inadequate. In practice neither women nor poor families were favoured by Thatcherism.

It was not simply a matter of the government's policies towards women but their policies towards everything else which had repercussions. For example, the withdrawal of free milk and school meals affected low-waged families, and low-paid workers were made more vulnerable during the 1980s through the weakening of trade unions with unemployment and the privatization of public services. These were accompanied by a series of measures which assailed the low-paid as wage earners. On the other hand, the cuts in direct taxation during the early 1980s and the impact of unemployment on inflation added to the prosperity of families with high incomes, while women who were in a position to buy property, rise in one of the better-paid professions or the media, or set up their own businesses could do well.

From the mid-1950s the Conservatives had attracted more female than male votes, but their advantage narrowed in the 1960s and 1970s. In 1979, 1983 and 1987 the Conservatives no longer had this preferential vote. In *Power and Prejudice: Women and Politics*, Anna Coote and Polly Pattullo show that differences among women of various classes were evident. In 1983 and 1987, while professional, managerial and white-collar women (and men) were registering a preference for the Conservatives, skilled and unskilled manual women swung away from the Tories. In 1983 34 per cent of women manual workers voted Labour; by 1987 this had risen to 43 per cent. In 1987 young women (between eighteen and twenty-four) evinced an 11 per cent preference for Labour, while older women (over sixty-five) were slightly less keen on the Tories than men in their age group.

There was, moreover, a gender gap on issues of nuclear and military policy. In 1983 67 per cent of women opposed Cruise missiles from the United States coming to Britain and in 1986 65 per cent of women were opposed to the use of bases in Britain for the US raid on Libya. These included Conservative women from the southern shires, who took the unprecedented step of demonstrating after pictures of wounded children were shown on television.

While Margaret Thatcher inspired admiration among some women as a strong leader who told people to stand on their own feet, her policies also aroused intense opposition from others. Dealing with this kind of resistance was to prove extremely difficult for her, perhaps because she had little interest in women or in women's networks and was completely lacking in the ability to empathize imaginatively with women who neither resembled herself nor fitted her stereotypes. Such women were to be driven to take extraordinary action during her period in office and to show a tenacity and resolve which equalled hers. While she exercised unprecedented power at the centre of politics, she stirred up unprecedented forms of resistance from groups of people who had not been key players in the left-wing movements of the 1970s but who found that politics had somehow landed on their own doorsteps.

In *The Long Road to Greenham*, Jill Liddington describes the first small march in protest against Margaret Thatcher's acceptance of Cruise missiles 'as the pebble that started the avalanche'.[33] The original pebble was Ann Pettit, who, after participating in the women's movement and struggles over housing, had gone to live in Dyfed, Wales, with her baby and partner. She became aware of the implications of Cruise when she read a pamphlet by E. P. Thompson, 'Protest and Survive', and organized a march of thirty people, predominantly women with small children, from Cardiff to the base at Greenham in August 1981. These pioneers who took on the great powers of the world came from Fishguard and Luton, from Llanwrtyd Wells and Chester. They were sheltered by Methodist halls (that other Methodism of peace activism and social commitment) and welcomed in the villages and market towns of Avon and Wiltshire. The London-based media ignored them – women protesters tramping 120 miles was not a story; they had 'done' peace. So, as the little band approached Greenham, after much discussion, some of them decided to chain themselves to the gates in a suffragette-style defiance of the military. This was to be the origins of the Greenham camp, a new kind of protest which refused to go away. They evoked old freedoms to use the common land and sent out schoolgirl-style chain letters inviting women to Embrace the Base in the autumn of 1982. Women responded in thousands. On 13 December 1982 the *Daily Mirror*'s headline was 'PEACE! The plea by 30,000 women who joined hands in the world's most powerful protest against nuclear war.' It was not simply their ability to touch large numbers of people in many countries; their presence, as Jill Liddington says, represented an 'alternative icon'[34] to Thatcherite values. Against the free market, they symbolized a web of human life.

The Conservatives were caught off balance by Greenham and by the mass peace movement in which many women, including Joan Ruddock, Helen John, Lynne Jones, Dorothy Thompson and Meg Beresford, played an important role. Greenham grit appealed to some Tories, and the campers disturbed even their inveterate opponent Lady Olga Maitland, who noted with surprise that they 'were not what you'd call riff-raff dropouts'.[35] Her efforts at counter-demonstrations evoked alarm among Tories, who feared being called to don woolly hats and jeans and congregate in Trafalgar Square. She eventually gave up, to concentrate on the political indoctrination she decided was going on in schools.

The Thatcherite right responded by extending the definition of subversion in an effort to control the media and the legal system and redefining the meaning of national security to include protest groups like CND. This provoked resistance. Sarah Tisdall, a clerk in the private office of the Foreign Secretary, for instance, decided that the public had a right to know about Ministry of Defence arrangements for the arrival of Cruise missiles and forwarded details to the press in 1983. She was sent to prison for six months. In 1985 MI5 agent Cathy Massiter blew the whistle on TV, revealing that CND, the National Council for Civil Liberties and trade unions were defined as subversive and subjected to surveillance. The British courts refused to handle CND's complaint but the European Commission of Human Rights

One of the twenty-six women from the Greenham Common women's
peace camp who cut their way into the US military base, 1984.

ruled in 1988 that the government had to answer allegations of MI5
surveillance of two former NCCL officers, Patricia Hewitt and Harriet
Harman. The branding of trade unionists as potential threats to national
security also aroused antagonism in the civil service union, the Civil
and Public Service Association, many of whom were precisely those
respectable white-collar women workers who might normally be Conservatives. In 1984 they took to the streets in protest against the banning
of trade unions at the government information centre, GCHQ. The
threat to civil liberties also led to a new awareness among the intellectual
and professional middle class of the need for constitutional reform,
resulting in the Charter 88 movement.

Groups who were in vulnerable positions because they could be isolated as not 'one of us' experienced the full force of Thatcherite authoritarianism. In *Decade of Decline: Civil Liberties in the Thatcher Years*, Peter Thornton shows how the 1981 British Nationality Act restricted the meaning of British citizenship by reclassifying some citizens (mainly black) British overseas citizens and saying they had no right of entry. Jaswinder Kaur, Anwar Ditta, Nasreen Akhtar, Nasira Begum and Cynthia Gordon, along with many other Asian and Afro-Caribbean women, were transformed from private citizens into community campaigners in anti-deportation protests. Throughout the decade the government both made the immigration laws tighter and also restricted the right to protest against deportations.

When violence broke out in several cities in the early 1980s the behaviour of the police provoked hostility not only from young women who were among those beaten up, but from many black mothers and

The Sari Squad picket protesting against the government's immigration policy during the Conservative Party conference at Blackpool, 1983.

483

pensioners who saw them as an army of occupation exercising an arbitrary power. Asian and black women were beginning to gain a public political voice. They tended to be Labour: for example, Merle Amory was elected council leader in Brent, north-west London, and Diane Abbott became Britain's first black woman MP, representing Hackney in east London. However, Shreela Flather, an upper-middle-class Asian, was a Conservative who became the first Asian mayor of Windsor in 1986. Black women in both parties contested racist attitudes and Shreela Flather condemned the culture of the police as 'sexist and racist and not at all welcoming'.[36]

During the long and bitter miners' strike of 1984–5 a section of the white working class found, like black Britons, that they too were being classified as outside society. Women in the mining communities played a crucial part in challenging the attempt to isolate miners. No mere strike, this became a contest with a government that wanted to break a key section of the labour movement. Its meaning went way beyond the issue that provoked resistance – pit closures. Women mobilized initially because they had no money to feed their families and needed to find out about welfare rights. In May 1984 the Women's Action Groups called a rally. They expected a small demonstration in Barnsley but instead 10,000 women arrived as if from nowhere. That summer 50,000 women marched through London. Jean McCrindle, who became the treasurer of Women Against Pit Closures, commented, 'It clearly wasn't any longer about wages or even just jobs. It was about who's got the right to decide really how you live.'[37]

As Pauline Radford from Blidworth, near Mansfield, said, 'If the pits closed, we lost our whole way of life. Our children's future was at stake and the villages we called home.'[38] But the exceptional circumstances of violent pickets, roadblocks, phone-tapping and villages surrounded and invaded by police meant 'home' changed. Ann Suddick, a clerical worker from the Durham collieries became an opponent of nuclear weapons and aware of how the control over natural resources was an international struggle. It was not all economics either. As one Castleford woman put it, 'I never knew there was a life after marriage.'[39]

Even after defeat some of them kept going, helping other women set up women's support groups during the printers' strike at Wapping, east London, in 1986 and the seafarers' strike in 1988 against a new shift system which they feared would endanger crew and passengers. The links with CND were sustained when, in 1986, women demonstrated against nuclear power outside electricity showrooms. So was support for their former allies, gays and lesbians, and some miners' wives moved into the Labour Party and were elected to local councils.

One of the unintended consequences of 'Thatcherism' was the revitalization of local government. The attempts to reduce social welfare met resistance from a 'town hall socialism', which demonstrated that an alternative was not just talk but could mean new kinds of democratized services, from mobile crèches to advocacy during pregnancy for women who spoke English as a second language. Feminists played an important part in linking representative democracy with direct participation in community projects, especially at the Greater London Council. The GLC also used its resources to help vulnerable groups of workers, many of whom were Asian and black women, to resist privatization or the closure of hospitals. Its alternative economic strategy for London included cleaners, hotel workers and home-workers, as well as domestic labour.

The GLC and other local authorities introduced equal-opportunities policies on the American model to push individuals up through the structures of local government and to open up employment in exclusively male occupations like the fire brigade. These could also involve the expansion of opportunities for equality in a more general sense: for example, the provision of open-ended education for GLC canteen and cleaning staff.

By revealing the claims of women as a group, the particular claims of, say, lesbians, older women, women with disabilities, ethnic minorities and so on, were also raised. Irish women, for example, traced their history in Britain, pointing to the work and settlement patterns which had affected their lives. Jewish women in London started an archive of interviews and photographs which was to lead to the publication of a book, *Generation of Memories: Voices of Jewish Women*, in 1989.

The GLC was abolished by the Conservatives in 1986, but some of the innovations in local government survived elsewhere. By 1986 there were equal-opportunities policies in over 200 local authorities; institutions like the NHS, universities and colleges, and the police were to follow. Women's committees modelled on the GLC's began to appear, particularly in Labour boroughs, and brought women's needs on to local government agendas. An Asian women's centre was funded in Leeds; Wakefield investigated the conditions of homeworkers; Oxford set up a workplace crèche and studied the impact of pollution on children after the deregulation of buses; Chesterfield hosted International Women's Day in the town hall. Cuts and a barrage of propaganda against 'loony left' politics were, however, to restrict what could be done. By 1989 the number of women's committees was down to fifty.

Scotland, however, resolutely resisted 'Thatcherism'. Feminists in Scotland had found it hard to make headway during the 1970s, but Labour-controlled councils meant that 'town hall feminism' was actually expanding in the late 1980s and women like Alice Mosely in Glasgow for People and Ruth Gillett in the Save the Kelvingrove Park Campaign were becoming leading figures in a range of campaigns.

In Northern Ireland the women's movement showed a remarkable resilience. Despite the often violent rift between Republicans and Unionists, which reached an overwhelming intensity when ten hunger-strikers died in 1981, feminists developed a terrain outside sectarian politics from the 1980s by focusing on common interests: domestic violence, rape, child-care, conditions at work and health. Women in the North thus managed to maintain links with the South and cautiously make connections which crossed over the Catholic–Protestant divide.

Anne Speed, from the South of Ireland, described the women's movement as 'a creature of ebb and flow'.[40] Another image being used in the late 1980s in England was that of an underground stream. Whether there was really a women's movement any more was a question that puzzled feminist meetings at the end of the decade. There were certainly still women meeting and feminist ideas were reaching outwards.

Versions of feminism had percolated through the media; women's studies courses were appearing in universities, colleges and schools. Gender awareness hit religious organizations from the liberal wing of Judaism to the Anglican Church. Feminist ideas were having a noticeable impact on the battered trade unions. The pressure groups for civil liberties, against poverty and for welfare provision had all taken on a 'women's agenda'. Some of them were women-led by 1989: for example, Sheila McKechnie at Shelter and Fran Bennett at the Child

Poverty Action Group had both been active socialist feminists in the 1970s.

Political parties, not just Labour and Conservatives but the Liberals, Social Democrats and the new Green Party, were all forced to respond, just as the smaller left groups had been in the 1970s. Many feminists turned to the Labour Party, where considerable energy was consumed in debates about party structure. Labour promised a Ministry of Women and Jo Richardson kept a women's lobby together in Parliament, where women still faced the dilemmas which had troubled earlier generations in politics. As Harriet Harman remarked in the late 1980s, 'You certainly don't get swept into the shadow cabinet on the basis of your devotion to the under-fives or school holiday play schemes.'[41] Women in fact were not being swept into Parliament at all. In 1989 the Conservatives had only seventeen women MPs, Labour twenty-two and the SLD, the SDP and the Scottish Nationalists had one each. Thus 52 per cent of the population were represented by a tiny minority in Parliament. Power politics proved to be resolutely resistant to feminist pressure.

Margaret Thatcher, in contrast, was exercising an unprecedented degree of power and taking politics into more and more areas of social existence. A corrosive fear silenced criticism of the effect of Tory policies in the media and in public institutions. In the process, however, she was also treading on some powerful toes. Tory ministers, dumped or threatened, were licking their wounds. A growing body of well-heeled resisters were coalescing in the professions, as university teachers, lawyers, top hospital doctors and civil servants became exasperated by changes which upset both their privileges and their pride in their work. The majority of people in Britain had not voted for her return and, when Labour and the Greens did well in the European elections in June 1989, she looked suddenly less invincible. The mood in the press shifted. She seemed remote, bolstered by the paraphernalia of security, out of touch, unreal. 'She has become a fictional character,' wrote Victoria Glendinning in the *Sunday Correspondent*. 'Will the real Mrs Thatcher please sit down.'[42]

It is doubtful whether the Prime Minister heard. She had retired behind the security gates which she had ordered to be erected in Downing Street.

Work

Between 15 and 20 per cent of the country's manufacturing base was to vanish in the early 1980s. Unemployment, which at the end of 1979 was 1.4 million, had reached over 3 million by the end of 1982. Manufacturing decline was not new, but the acceleration which resulted from monetarist policies was. These coincided with the global restructuring of production and the impact of new technology. The consequences for women, especially in the manufacturing sector, were disastrous. The US firm Vanity Fair pulled out of Lee Jeans in Greenock, Scotland, in January 1981, partly because of the high value of sterling. The women occupied and managed to get a buyer, but this was rare. Claire Callender points out in Caroline Glendinning and Jane Millar's book *Women and Poverty in Britain: The 1990s* that while male unemployment rose by 146 per cent in the period 1979–86, female unemployment went up by 276 per cent. When unemployment began to decline between 1987 and 1990, the trend was to be reversed because women were moving into the low-paid service jobs which expanded in this period.

The rise in unemployment created an atmosphere of fear. Ann Butler from the West Indies had worked at Smith's factory in west London since 1964. In 1982 she was made redundant because the firm moved to Wales: 'When this Welsh lady came down and sat down beside me, I had to teach her the work, though it was going to take my job away. That really took it out of me.'[43] She was eating only one meal a day and worrying about bills; she rarely went out. Unemployed women simply faded from view.

Firms were putting pressure on workers with jobs to increase productivity and to accept lower rates of pay. Christina, a Greek-Cypriot clothing worker with twenty years' experience in the industry, was one of those who kept her job in the early 1980s at a price. She told Philip Pearson she was producing more dresses for less pay than eight years before: 'My friends say, "Forget the time as it used to be." These days it doesn't matter how much you push yourself . . . Chinese, Turkish or Indian ladies are working at home now, so all the work from the factory is going to these people.'[44] The sections of the clothing industry which were producing cheaper garments were in fact competing with

Third World women's labour. One consequence noted by Swasti Mitter in her study of the impact of the global movement of capital on women's work, *Common Fate, Common Bond*, was that a Third World could be seen growing amidst the First.

As jobs declined and conditions worsened, more and more women took service jobs in the private or public sector. But here too the rise in unemployment and the growth of contract work through privatization meant that this already vulnerable section of the workforce faced added pressure. The shift from the public sector had gender implications, because this was an area where women had had some social benefits and security of employment.

Economic restructuring was accompanied by legislative policies which undermined not only recent Labour measures to protect the low-paid but ones established from the late nineteenth century. The 1980 repeal of the right of workers to claim the 'going rate' for the job under the Employment Protection Act, the 1983 removal of the Fair Wages Resolution from government contracts and the 1986 exclusion of young workers from the Wages Councils, which fixed minimum rates in low-paid industries, all hit low-paid women. Then in 1988 the Local Government Act stopped local authorities adopting the practice of contract compliance, which had sought to ensure that the firms they dealt with paid fair wages and had equal-opportunities policies.

From the mid-1980s the percentage of workers in the low-paid category steadily mounted. Carol Buswell records that by 1990 the 'decency threshold' specified by the Council of Europe was £178 a week or £4.76 per hour: 'In that year, within the hotel and catering industries, 88 per cent of manual and 34 per cent of non-manual women workers in "other services" (shops, hairdressers, etc.) and 40 per cent of women in the banking and finance sector also came into this category.'[45] By the end of the decade over half the low-paid full-time workers and 80 per cent of part-time workers were women. In the first half of the 1980s women continued to move into paid employment, though the rate of increase had slowed down from the period 1973–9. The proportion of those doing full-time jobs, however, actually declined from 34 per cent to 33 per cent between 1979 and 1985. The numbers of part-timers continued to grow.

'Flexibility' was the watchword of economic development during

Dinner ladies: public sector service workers in vulnerable
low-paid jobs were being hit by privatization despite ingenious attempts to
create their own co-operative alternatives.

the 1980s. Feminist writers like Ursula Huws noted that this invariably
meant the casualization of women's work. Other terms were 'Americanization' or 'Brazilization'. Similar tendencies were operating in other
economies, but in Britain employers were able to adapt the custom of
part-time women's employment. They also had a government which
did not simply regard low pay as a regrettable economic necessity
but appeared to believe it was something that should be positively
encouraged by legislation and policies. The 1986 Wages Act removed
500,000 workers from the protection of Wages Councils. The poverty
lobby met deaf government ears. Only pressure from larger employers
who feared competition saved the Wages Councils from outright
abolition.

'Privatization', contracting out public services, made them more
'flexible', because workers lost legal protections, sick pay and pensions.
For groups like women cleaners, these were crucial, for pay was already
low. They were also unlikely to be unionized when they became
contract workers because cleaning companies could move them around
and employ them by the day or night. Many were also classed as

part-time. The argument was that this was convenient for women because of child-care, but when Jane Paul interviewed London cleaners in the mid-1980s she found that the opposite was often the reality. Some women did several 'part-time' jobs; Asian women at Heathrow airport complained that they were put on irregular shifts which meant they did not know when they would have to work. They were so desperate to earn enough to survive that they were fitting their families around their work, not the other way round.

From the early 1980s groups like the Leicester Outwork Campaign and several Homeworking Groups funded by the GLC in London were pointing to the spread of low-paid homework. Child-care was one important factor in deciding to take up homework; others were race and ethnicity. Swasti Mitter observed in 1986 that Bangladeshi women homeworkers in London's East End were constrained in their choice of employment not simply by 'the wrath of their own men' or familial patterns of employment, but by the 'pattern of immigration, racialism in the host country, and the subsequent level of unemployment among immigrant men'.[46] Homeworkers were outside the official statistics and estimates of the numbers were thus hard to assess; researchers discovered how prevalent it had become by doing house-to-house surveys. Not only clothing but electronic assembly work, food-packaging, toy-making, cracker stuffing and many more kinds of work were being 'put out'. Conditions could be dangerous, there was no job security and the rates could be extremely low. A 1988 report from Birmingham, for example, described Saroja doing a fifty-six-hour week for between £20 and £25.

Conservative economic policies were not particularly successful in developing the British economy, but they were effective in making people feel that the changes which were devastating daily life were inevitable. 'There is no alternative' was repeated like a refrain by the Prime Minister, earning her the nickname TINA. It was not true that all contrary thinking had been eliminated. The problem was that, apart from local government, there was no way of implementing it. In the first half of the decade there was an ongoing debate about a socialist alternative to 'TINA' and feminists such as Anna Coote, Anne Phillips and Hilary Wainwright, among others, raised women's social needs, as well as gender equality. They examined the broader implications of equality, questioning the organization of work and domestic activity, and the social choices in how new technology was designed and used. These issues in turn raised questions about the meaning of work, the appropriation of time and the value of caring, leading to proposals about how economic alternatives needed to take on the conditions of livelihood as a whole and the quality of relationships between people. They had obvious relevance to men as well as women, for conditions were becoming more hazardous and stressful in many jobs and people were working longer hours.

Even in the Tories' third term, when more equitable and democratic economic strategies were looking like pie in the sky, pockets of working-class women were still battling against market-led economic arguments which turned all human values into cash transactions. Marsha Marshall led a successful campaign to save Darfield Main colliery in 1988; when the miners found themselves facing a six-day working week, Mary from Derbyshire Women's Action Group remarked in *Coalfield Women*, 'It's a bit of a bugger if my granddad and dad thought a five-day week was a step forrard for miners all them years ago an' all this wunderful technology can do is put more hours on't day an't working week.'[47]

Barnsley Women Against Pit Closures protest against the pit closure plans of the American chairman of the National Coal Board, Ian McGregor, summer 1984.

The case for equal opportunities also continued to be made right through the decade and the Equal Opportunities Commission, under pressure not just from women's groups but from older organizations like the Fawcett Society, the Townswomen's Guild and the British Federation of University Women, was becoming more combative. Valerie Amos was able to bring more awareness of race and the European Community gave the EOC some leverage. In 1982 the Conservative government was found guilty of failing to comply with the requirement that it should make provision for women to claim equal pay for work of equal value, agreed in the Treaty of Rome. Nor had it provided redress for women who challenged job-evaluation schemes for hidden or overt discrimination. In 1983 the Equal Pay regulations were amended as a result. The 1983 Equal Value (Amendment) Regulations laid the basis for a few successful equal-value claims in the mid-1980s: for example, by Cammell Laird cook Julie Heyward and women fish workers at Hull. Ford's sewing machinists also finally won equal grading rights (seventeen years after their famous 1968 strike). These were all symbolically important, though large numbers of women were not affected.

The European Court repeatedly forced the British government to modify its policies, though the Tories retaliated on several occasions by restricting the implications of legal equal-rights victories. Helen Marshall took a case to Europe because she did not want to retire at sixty; when she won, the government introduced the 1986 Sex Discrimination Act, which made it illegal to dismiss women in the public sector at sixty and extended sex discrimination into small undertakings and private households. But the government used this as an opportunity to repeal laws preventing women working at night.

Similarly a case taken to the European Court by Jacqueline Drake for her right as a married woman to claim Invalid Care Allowance when she gave up her job to look after her disabled mother caused the government to concede £23 a week to married carers like her but restrict the right in general by redefining it as severe disablement allowance.

Recognition that the male culture of many workplaces could be overtly abusive or exclude women from informal networking was growing during the 1980s. Pressure from the Women's Conference led to the TUC producing guidelines on sexual harassment in 1983. These distinguished between 'social relationships *mutually* entered into, and sexual harassment which is the *imposition* of unwelcome attention or action on one person by another in a superior position'.[48] Sexual harassment became illegal in 1986. Women in male-dominated jobs were more prepared to speak out. A former policewoman complained to Melissa Benn in 1983, 'You get chipped away. You have to take all the insults, all the wind-ups. I resented being called a "fucking cunt"'.[49]

Women were slowly moving into the police force during the 1980s in larger numbers. They also were appearing in 'male' jobs. There were visible minorities driving buses, working on the railways, being fire fighters, customs officials and security guards. Most visible of all were the women who were emerging through the media. Kate Adie, for example, broke through the gender barrier against women news reporters covering dangerous topics when, by chance, she was sent to cover the siege of the Iranian embassy in London in 1980. She later upset the Tories by her report of the US bombing of Libya in 1986 and provided moving coverage of events in Tiananmen Square, Beijing, in 1989. Women were rising behind the scenes too on TV. Some moved up via the traditional supportive role. Sarah Radclyffe, co-founder of the production company Working Title, which made the successful film *My Beautiful Laundrette* (1985), had started as a secretary, was then Derek Jarman's production assistant on *The Tempest* (1979) and went on to produce the popular *Comic Strip* TV series. Other routes into the media were through the alternative press, publishing, films and theatre, which in London got its last spasm of funding with the GLC.

English metropolitan culture was not the only place women could be found making their mark in the arts. In *Women in Focus*, Pat Murphy and Nell McCafferty documented through photographs 'the new energy at work' among Irish women in 'the creative arts'.[50] In Scotland too a growing number of women artistic directors and administrators, and women writers like Liz Lochhead and Aileen Ritchie, were becoming well known. The 1980s saw a creative explosion in Afro-Caribbean theatre, ranging from Winsome Pinnock's play about Claudia Jones to Jackie Kay's *Chiaroscuro* (1985), which used dance and ritual. Other new voices were Nandita Ghose, with a play about girls in an Asian bhangra band, and Su-Lin Looi's *All Sewn Up*, which described the lives of three generations of Chinese women in London. Much of this new work was developing through co-ops and community theatre, but funding was becoming increasingly hard to find by the late 1980s. In England public money was much reduced and businesses were often not interested.

British business remained a man's world. Male financial institutions were inclined to be sceptical of women in business. Stephanie Cooper, a designer with work featured in *Vogue* and *Woman's Own* in the mid-1980s, had been refused a loan when she got her first order for £6,000 worth of garments. The manager said she was too high a risk because she had no security, no collateral and no rich parents. Even Anita Roddick, who developed the Body Shop from what Stuart Cosgrove and Dave Hill call a 'hippie crunchy Granola outfit' to an international chain of 366 shops in the late 1980s, selling everything from Japanese washing grains to banana hair conditioner, found, 'When the Body Shop was in its infancy the government didn't give a toss, they gave us no help whatsoever. It was only when we were deemed successful that financial doors opened up for us. The idea of Thatcherism helping the small business community is a fallacy.'[51]

Angela Coyle's research showed that in 1988 women occupied 15 per cent of management or management-related posts. This was a 5 per cent increase on the previous decade, but expansion was mainly in junior management in retail, hotels, catering and local government. Top women were a tiny minority. Yet there was a powerful perception that women had 'made it': women's magazines were increasingly career-oriented and articles on post-feminism proliferated on the women's pages of national newspapers. West End theatre producer Josephine Hart's irritation with whingeing about women's oppression was widespread among media women by 1987: 'It's nonsense to say there are no prominent women. Today women are on boards everywhere.'[52] She was commenting on a new visibility rather than a mass movement. In 1988 women made up only 6 per cent of directors and 10 per cent of senior managers in Britain.

The enterprise culture was full of contradictions for women, both ideologically and practically. An unfettered market-oriented individualism clashed head on with the moral authority of hearth and home in Conservative ideology. In real life children meant the crunch came.

Funny Women

All women comedians shared a problem: they were expected to be the joke not the joker. Men from groups which were the butt of prejudice had found ways of turning the tables, but it was more complicated for women. Funny among themselves, at home or in the hairdressers, they were still exceptions on the stage and screen. Marti Caine was unusual in having her own TV show. Those who made it tended to be comedy actresses rather than stand-up comics.

The 1980s saw the emergence of a group of women comedians with a new style of comedy. An important origin was the 'alternative circuit', which in turn was linked to radical theatre through Roland and Claire Muldoon, who launched CAST Variety with funding from the GLC early in the decade. Jo Brand, Pauline Melville, Jenny Le Coat, Jenny Eclair, Angie Lemar and Hattie Heyridge (later the lugubrious blonde in *Red Dwarf*) were among those who found an opening through the circuit, working in clubs and halls, for benefits and socials. Dawn French and Jennifer Saunders, who were still drama students, joined Claire Muldoon in political sketches.

Television variety was in the doldrums and looking for talent. The success of *Comic Strip*, *The Young Ones* and Lenny Henry showed there was an audience desperate to laugh its way through the 1980s. There was to be a continuing process of crossover between alternative comedy, which flourished in venues like London's Hackney Empire, and a new genre of mainstream humour.

Other routes in were theatre and TV itself. Victoria Wood, who had won the 1975 *New Faces* competition, was a pioneer on television and worked with actress Julie Walters. By 1984 she had her first solo West End show, *Lucky Bags*. Pamela Stephenson was one of the stars in the satirical *Not the Nine O'Clock News*. Sheila Steafel, from South Africa, made her name on Channel 4 with 'Aunt Kitty', the ultimate bigot.

They were going against the grain. Pamela Stephenson, born in New Zealand and raised in Australia, thought it was partly because the British ideal woman 'doesn't make waves' and Sheila Steafel told Diana Simmonds that Bette Midler could never have made it in Britain. Glamour helped to get you noticed, but it also stuck you in the passive role. Sex was a problem too. In 1982 Pamela Stephenson thought it was still the case that 'if women start to tell lewd jokes and so on, it's automatically assumed they're either very free sexually or they're unhappy,' adding, 'Women are under enormous pressure to maintain the kind of stabilizing influence they're supposed to have on society and their families. Meanwhile, they go quietly crazy. Look at the national Valium bill.'[53]

Women began to demonstrate some ingenious ways of being funny, subverting the narrow option of being pitied or punished. Victoria Wood's skill was in bringing quiet craziness out into the open. She learned her humour from her mother, who taught her to eavesdrop on women's conversations on buses and in cafés. She made the women in her audience allies, drawing together upper working class and lower middle class in a po-faced complicity. As Suzanne Moore remarked in 1988, 'She laughs with as well as at *Freemans* catalogue culture.'[54]

Jenny Le Coat, in contrast, positioned herself on the edge of accepted femininity, with male 'dick' humour from the other side. She got her laughs by shattering the shock barriers of what could be said. But there was, under the veneer, a recognizable theme: women's complaints about men. Suzanne Moore describes another kind of hard-edged humour, the style of Ruby Wax and Joan Rivers from the United States, who played on 'an aberrant femininity, a butch masquerade with a butch persona which requires a certain amount of femme glam to pull it off'.[55] Dawn French and Jennifer Saunders shifted away from the full-frontal political attack in the late 1980s and began to capture the absurdities in the gap between aspiration and reality, where more and more women lived daily. They made their humour from all the bits of women that didn't fit – the bits that looked backwards, the fat bits and the ball-breaking bits. They were mean, sneaky, ambitious, randy, weedy and sulky. They made fun of the unspoken observations of characters who were both recognizable to women and out the other side.

It was Sue Townsend who chronicled the 1980s, though, in the unlikely person of a thirteen-and-three-quarters adolescent whom she described as 'solidly out of step with the world he lives in . . . an outsider and an observer'.[56] Adrian Mole's *Diary* began as a book, made it to Wyndhams Theatre and became a TV series. Young Adrian Mole (a descendant of *Just William*), appalled by his 1960s parents, educated by radical Miss Elf at school, measuring his 'thing' (in centimetres), suffering in his hopeless passion for Pandora Braithwaite, just couldn't match up to the 1980s. Even his humdrum purity of purpose was affected by the glitzy hype. 'Well, the ego got him in the end,'[57] was his creator's comment.

Maternity rights were weakened; the Social Security Act of 1986 abolished the universal maternity grant and single payments for maternity items to women on income support. Some 94,000 women lost their maternity allowance when the system of payment was changed. The government seemed to be fighting a veritable vendetta against under-fives. Families on income support were not allowed to deduct child-care payments. The 1980 Education Act meant that local authorities no longer had to provide nursery care for three- to five-year-olds, and cuts in council funding made it harder for them to meet the demand for provision. Under pressure from nursery campaigners some employers, especially in the public sector, began providing workplace nurseries. However, despite the opposition of the Equal Opportunities Commission, in 1985 the Inland Revenue started taxing parents who used these nursery places on the grounds that they were a perk. This hit not so much the very poor but middle earners who were full-time workers.

Even those positioned just under the much-discussed 'glass ceiling' of women achievers were beginning by the late 1980s to wonder whether competitive individualism, which was increasingly equated with 'feminism', was all it had been cracked up to be. *Today* newspaper reported in October 1989 that Linda Kelsey was quitting *Cosmo* for *She*, 'a magazine for women who have to go to school plays and wipe children's noses as well as attend board meetings'.[58]

Changes in the economy and in working practices were occurring so fast that feminists in the trade unions were realizing that demands which had been radical were being overtaken by events. Ruth Elliott, an official in the health workers' union COHSE, noted uneasily in the late 1980s that the application of the equal-value principle to recognition of the underrated skills of groups like home helps was, in practice, just redividing the low-paid cake. 'The check list of women's demands' was, she said, looking 'very '70s. What did improved part-time working opportunities, improved legal rights, job sharing, maternity agreements and child-care leave mean to women facing privatization, casualization or social security changes which made it not worth having a job?'[59]

As for the much-vaunted British miracle, manufacturing productivity grew dramatically between 1979 and 1989, but manufacturing output increased by less than 1 per cent per annum. Investment in the late 1980s went mainly into services and the City, where much of it was squandered on property development. TINA triumphed, its expenses paid by a shadowy host of homeworkers, hotel chambermaids, lavatory attendants and fast-food workers whose destinies were shrouded in the elusive statistics of government agencies.

Daily Life

In December 1988 Eileen Thompson was taking orders in Possil, north Glasgow. Christmas was approaching and there was quite a demand for TVs and videos, as well as the usual school uniforms, children's clothes and food. The bulky items presented a few problems to her but she tried to keep her clients happy. The extra income was vital. She had an income of £70 a week from social security and four children under four to support. So every day she took the bus into Glasgow, walked into the shops and stole.

Strathclyde had the fourth highest unemployment rate in Britain, though the government's statistical changes made precise calculations difficult. The Low Pay Unit estimated that 60 per cent of the women who had jobs were low-paid. Yet when Glasgow hosted the 1988 Garden Festival, thriving Thatcherite Britain bustled past the unseen and forgotten poor. Eradicated from view and banished from memory, they became creatures who had fallen from that state of grace – the new times. The stark contrasts were everywhere. In 1987 *The Economist* noted that 'bonus-fuddled yuppies' at Saatchi and Saatchi who had sprayed water and foam over 'their colleagues and other over-priced equipment' at the office party in 1986 had been warned that they would be fined £200 for 'unruly behaviour'.[60] These sums were, the magazine commented, 'little more than small change . . . to them'.[61]

Meanwhile, an unemployed woman in Wales whose husband was disabled made a decision which left them frighteningly isolated. Unable to pay the telephone bill of £24, they had their phone disconnected. Poverty cut off the means of communication. It immobilized people and left them cold in the effort to save on heating bills. It meant living with no treats, outings or holidays. In her study of the impact of unemployment on a group of women in South Wales in the mid-1980s, Claire Callender reported how anxiety accumulated as they made 'hard decisions and choices as to what expenditure to cut or what bill could be postponed for yet another week. They dreaded the unanticipated bill or unforeseen expenditure.'[62] One of the women interviewed said she could no longer buy biscuits, cake or meat. Women frequently did without within the household group. One woman said she bought half a pound of stewing meat, which she gave to her husband and children, 'then I just have the gravy'.[63] Another told how she went without food for three or four days. Cutting back was one thing over a short period; as a way of life it created a kind of depressed, dull desperation: 'We're not living on the dole. We're just existing,'[64] stated one woman on benefit who had gone to the butcher to ask for bones, pretending they were for the dog. Poverty had become shameful.

The punitive approach to benefits taken by the government accentuated the sense of being a pariah. The widows' allowance was abolished and the qualifying age for their pensions was raised. The State Earnings Related Pensions Scheme, which Labour had introduced in 1975, had allowed women's pensions to be calculated over their twenty highest-earning years. This went in the 1986 Social Security Act. The same act not only contributed to homelessness by excluding sixteen- to eighteen-year-olds but reduced income support for items like fuel and stopped one-off emergency payments. The poor could receive assistance only after they had gone to charities and their families. Those who were seen as responsible for leaving work could not get benefit for six months. The 1988 Social Security Act restricted benefit to those with two years' consecutive employment before making a claim (a ruling which was particularly bad for women with families). The 1989 act that followed meant that social security was confined to those who made themselves available for full-time work. Women who wanted only part-time jobs could thus have their unemployment benefit or income support reduced or withdrawn.

Yet despite the stringent legislation, the cost of unemployment offset the government's cuts in welfare provision. Ironically, dependence on the state increased and the mass of regulations lengthened the process. In May 1988 Shyama Perera reported in the *Guardian* from the queue at the Lisson Grove Department of Health and Social Security in north-west London. It began at 6.10 a.m.; by 9.30 several hundred people had arrived, but the offices closed at 10.30 because the staff could not cope with the overload of work. A mother of three who had arrived the previous day at 11.30 – four hours before the official closing time – had been turned away and told to try again tomorrow: 'Her pleas, "I have not even got the money to buy my children milk," were ignored.' As Shyama Perera commented, 'Collecting money from Lisson Grove is now a full-time job.'[65]

Some stole, others borrowed. More poor women were getting into debt. David Vincent records, 'Four single-parent families in ten had at least one problem debt at the end of the 1980s and one in seven were in serious trouble with three or more outstanding commitments.'[66] Others turned to their families. Women were the shock-absorbers of the economic and social system. Hilary Graham shows that both couples and single mothers were relying increasingly on female relatives, mothers or partners' mothers and grandmothers for sustenance. The General Household Survey of 1985 also revealed a surprising number of single women who were caring for parents or relatives – 29 per cent of unmarried women in the forty-five to sixty-four age group were carers, compared with 24 per cent of married women and 16 per cent of men. So, amidst all the talk of expanded choice, familial obligations actually became heavier.

Margaret Thatcher sought to reintroduce the distinction between the deserving and the undeserving poor, and a great deal of money was spent investigating cases for signs of 'scrounging'. Such boundaries have always been blurred and the lines drawn are inevitably arbitrary and subject to personal prejudice. Over the course of the decade, poverty and the poor *en bloc* became somehow reprehensible. The most 'deserving' acquired a hang-dog air.

Because the poor simply did not go away, they could hardly be regarded as news. Poverty made increasingly bad copy. Survey after survey showed that people (including the poor themselves) believed the impoverished suffered not from a simple lack of income but as a result of their own financial ineptitude. Some of the unemployed continued loyally to vote Conservative.

It followed that the increasing inequality was not generally resented, and nor was the new wealth which was so visible from house sales, property development, contracting, private services, finance, the media or whatever. People felt that the rich had worked for their money or had just had a lucky break. When the government privatized nationalized industries, working-class housewives happily invested their part-time

Waiting for the lift: tenants of Divis flats, Belfast, demanded demolition and rehousing, 1987.

earnings and dreamed along with the rest. Borrowing and credit became the way life was lived.

Everyone (apart from the poor) was shopping. Children and men were discovered as potentially expanding markets; new needs for garages that turned into space stations and sports gear were fostered. A booming market in Next and Jigsaw medium-priced clothes took off and men's suits made a flourishing business for the Paul Smith shops. Shop till you drop became a kind of patriotic duty, especially at Christmas. A fall in retail figures was of more gloomy import than a rise in unemployment – the unemployed, after all, helped to keep prices down. Britain's industrial base was too battered to meet the demand, so the goods were largely imports. Shopping quite simply made people feel good. The decline in social services was less immediately noticeable than the new consumer goods which made people believe that they were prospering and that things were on the up. By the 1980s televisions and refrigerators had ceased to be luxuries, and as the gap closed in some goods, it opened up in others. The poor were less likely to have washing machines, telephones and freezers. Ownership of videos, microwaves and dishwashers were the signs of being better off. Ownership of home computers was also restricted.

Private consumption did not mean just having more things; it increasingly became the way people did things. The forms of communication were being reshaped by the fax machine, private express deliveries and Sky television, as well as the computer. You had to have money to access these types of communication. The supermarkets which sprouted out of town with their expanded range of goods and the big Do-It-Yourself stores were designed for people with cars, yet even in London in the mid-1980s the majority of women did not drive. In country areas the deregulation of transport left many people without bus services. The foreign holidays of the discriminating tourist became more daring, but a large section of the population, especially outside the South-East, had no holiday at all. As schools budgets were cut, it became harder to take children on outings and on trips unless their families could pay. Leisure centres opened, but they were often private and cost money to join. Local councils were closing pools and libraries. Municipal pleasures and free shared enjoyment seemed to be anathema to the Thatcherite

GLC-funded catering co-op stall at the massive 'Jobs for a
Change' festival in Battersea, south London, 1985.

spirit. Indeed, a group who were repeatedly hounded and attacked by
the government were the New Age travellers, who roamed the land
seeking a simpler life and spiritual solace at the Stonehenge solstice.
Their main crime seems to have been their rejection of shopping and
soap.

In contrast, the 'yuppies', like Margaret Thatcher, were acutely
conscious of appearances, though they called it 'style' and spent a lot
of money in achieving it. The astute cultural commentator Judith
Williamson described this restless quest for things as 'congealed longing,
the final form of an active wish'.[67] She added that the shape in which
fulfilment was being offered came to configure the wish itself. In Lynval

Golding's song 'Do Nothing' for the Specials, the future was not to be found and 'fashion'[68] was the only culture.

The end result was not a more stable country but a disintegratory sense that survival, success or cardboard city was a matter of chance. In 1987 Yvonne Roberts described 'Thatcher's New Woman' in the Volkswagen advertisement: a well-groomed woman walks towards us; we see her throw

her pearls, a brooch and a fur coat into various dustbins and [she] is about to fling 'his' car keys down the drain too when she hesitates . . . Instead she climbs into a Volkswagen Golf GTI and roars off into the night. 'If only everything in life was as reliable as a Volkswagen.'[69]

And just in case people didn't notice how much you'd spent on your clothes, you could buy an 'I am rich' badge to tell them.

It was only partly the case that Thatcher 'brought new values into play',[70] which was designer Vivienne Westwood's view of 'Thatcherism'. It was rather that Margaret Thatcher expressed and legitimated attitudes which already existed and provided certainties which some people wanted reaffirmed amidst dramatic economic and social changes. In *Divided Britain*, Ray Hudson and Allan M. Williams suggest that she 'appealed to popular reactions *against* . . . new movements'.[71] Some of this antagonism went towards the poor, homosexuals, lesbians, the unemployed, the homeless, New Age travellers and the black and Asian communities, and some towards the new public-sector middle class, the Beveridge babies who had been marching since the 1960s. Amidst the hostility and the fear, she pulled off a remarkable trick, and Barbara Castle, a close Thatcher watcher, spotted it:

Because her most influential allies were the wealthy and powerful she evolved the concept of the incentive society in which the rich were to be helped to become richer still, the medium-earners told to stand on their own feet and the poor at the bottom of the pile made to feel that it was their fault that they had failed. Her most remarkable quality was her ability to make this sound like a moral crusade.[72]

Sex

The voices of antique patriarchal authority could still be heard pronouncing upon sexual behaviour in the law courts. Judge Bertrand Richards, for instance, who fined a convicted rapist £2,000 in 1981, commented that his victim was 'guilty of a great deal of contributory negligence' – she had hitchhiked home. In another rape case the following year, Judge David Wild advised the jury that women who did not want sex kept their legs closed and struggled; marks of force would consequently be found if the woman had not consented. Yet judges displayed a contrasting consideration in cases where women were murdered by husbands or lovers, and in 1983 Judge Brian Gibbens told William Watson-Sweeney, who pleaded guilty to having intercourse with his friend's seven-year-old daughter, that he had 'considerable sympathy' with a case 'which strikes me as one of the kind of accidents which happen in life to almost anyone – although of a wholly different kind'.[73] The judges' views of life and its accidents were so evidently bizarre by the mid-1980s that one prominent male legal figure admitted to journalist Janet Watts that a gap had opened up between these judgements and contemporary attitudes. Yet, he maintained, 'The social standards of virtue for women tended to be higher than for men.'[74]

Changes in sexual behaviour, along with feminist pressures, made the assumptions of this old-style upper-class male conservatism look increasingly absurd. However, another kind of conservative voice was to be heard, asserting the need for protection against the contamination of a permissiveness which invaded the privacy of the home through the media with its revealing images and seduced the young at school with enthusiastic talk about sex and its pleasures. This moral right was joined by others with differing motives: by feminists who attacked sex shops and pornography, by community groups trying to clean up their neighbourhoods and by sections of the Labour Party. The existence of these very different kinds of campaigners demanding action from the state contributed to a new sensitivity about the relationship between law and sexual representation and behaviour. It was no longer just authoritarian patriarchal control versus sexual freedom: the lines had blurred.

The new moral climate was not conducive to improving the conditions of sex workers like Lillie, aged twenty-eight, a prostitute and heroin addict in a Soho clip joint, and the free market did not offer her much by way of an alternative. She told Melanie McFadyean in 1982, 'I'd love to get out of it, but what could I do? How could I earn enough money?'[75] Instead, she worried what she would do in ten years' time and cultivated upper-class punters because of their lack of interest in sex: 'They get off on being humiliated, beaten, dominated.'[76] A local community campaign to reduce the spread of strip clubs, pornography shops and clip joints in Soho was soon to lead to police raids, and these resulted in prostitutes moving to other areas. Their arrival in Bayswater brought angry protests and kerb-crawling became a crime in the 1985 Sexual Offences Act. In practice, however, as long as prostitutes were not too visible, there was little moral outcry. By now the contact magazines were largely left alone by the police. 'Mandy, in comfy home, Humberside, wearing nurse's uniform' plied her trade and the 'away-day girls' continued to work the trains, catering to commuters with an early-morning appetite for sex in the lavatories.[77] The booming tourist trade created a market for clubs, which had become increasingly organized, taking credit cards and offering a taxi service. In Paul Ferris's words, 'The obloquy had passed to porn.'[78] In 1981 in Leeds groups of feminists attacked sex shops. The following year the Local Government (Miscellaneous Provisions) Act gave local authorities the power to refuse licences to sex shops. Restrictions on visual displays and on cinema clubs were also introduced. The Video Recordings Act of 1984 imposed controls and set up a licensing system.

Opponents of pornography, like Mary Whitehouse and the National Viewers' and Listeners' Association, along with evangelical Christians, were more influential than feminists in Parliament. They had links with Conservative MPs who favoured censorship and were part of a 'pro-family' lobby. However, Women Against Violence Against Women (WAVAW), influenced by the political lesbianism of the revolutionary feminists, did have an impact on Labour. The result was to be some strange alliances which included left Labour women Jo Richardson, Clare Short and Dawn Primarola. Clare Short, exasperated when Tory male MPs who were pro-family supporters of tighter obscenity laws named their favourite Page 3 nude pin-ups in the *Sun*, introduced a bill to ban female nudity in newspaper pin-ups. She received many letters from women which endorsed her stand, was lampooned in the tabloids and barracked in the House of Commons by Tory men. The Labour women consulted with American anti-pornography campaigner Andrea Dworkin, but balked at her inclusion of works of art, literature and science. They did, however, adopt her wide definition of pornography as the depiction of women as objects, or in 'sexually humiliating or degrading poses or being subjected to violence'.[79] Dawn Primarola brought a bill before Parliament on these lines in 1989, introducing the civil rights ideas of American anti-pornography campaigners into British politics. But Britain had no written Constitution, simply a male-dominated legal system which believed that higher moral standards applied to women than to men and was, as feminist film-maker Mandy Merck pointed out, 'more characteristically interested in restricting sexual representation' than in resisting 'sexual discrimination'.[80]

She and other feminists opposed to W A V A W's simple fit between pornography and male violence were feeling increasingly exasperated as the label 'feminist' came to be equated with anti-porn censorship. In 1987 in *Is the Future Female?*, Lynne Segal observed that the correlation between pornography and violence against women was unproved and pointed out the difficulty of determining pornographic images amidst the wider spectrum of cultural representation. She warned that Winston Churchill's 1986 bill to 'clean up television'[81] was aimed at radical gay films like Derek Jarman's *Jubilee* rather than violence against women.

Mandy Rose, an independent film-maker aware of the course of the anti-pornography debate in the United States, opposed the extension of censorship on the grounds that pornography might be a flawed means of expression but it was the 'only sphere that exists for a non-moralistic exploration of women's sexual fantasy and desire'.[82] Attempts to close it were likely to lead to 'the creation of yet more silences and suppression about sex'.[83]

Melissa Benn's examination of porn shops revealed a clue to the outcry against pornography. It was not just that it had expanded to meet the market; it was no longer a discreet zone of compartmentalized sleaze but nestled next to such items of everyday life as Douglas Hurd's spy thriller *Send Him Victorious* and colour-pic biographies of Prince Andrew. In turn, raunchy sex magazines had settled in newsagents. But clearing them off the shelves and banning pin-ups in newspapers would still not restore the old boundaries and return pornography to its secret life under the carpet in the lavatory. Its stylized accoutrements, its routines of control and abandonment, and its frozen iconography of desire had migrated to popular culture. As the young woman's magazine *Undercoats* put it in March 1985, 'Body paupers' dreams are made of these.'[84]

Art, fashion and design all played with porn as a symbolic language for the contortions in relations between the sexes. The repetition of tried responses and sensations was reassuring, while their appearance in incongruous settings shifted the connotations. Leather dog collars were worn by young women on the bus going for a night out and bondage gear appeared in modern dance at Sadler's Wells. The ethos of choice brought the impermissible into the open. S&M clubs opened in London in the early 1980s and their PR offered women greater choice. By 1987 what had been slightly risqué a few years before had become a fashion motif. Women's clothes became provocative as fear about AIDS intensified, though the prevalence of boots contained a hint that this was an invitation to voyeurism not action.

In part it was a romantic individualism. In rebellion against the woolly socks and understated dowdiness of 1970s radical collectivity, porn was embraced and taken home as style. The excess of the outrageous became an expression of discontent in a conservative era when rebellion seemed to go nowhere. A conscious aesthetic of glamour created a space for self-expression which went against the new conventions of Thatcherite conformity, epitomized by shiny sports-gear *Sun* readers. Glamour, of course, also made money, gave distinction and, in its turn, fed the persuasive market values which were coming to seem all-powerful.

The contradictions were evident not only in visual images of sex but in behaviour. Neither divorce, illegitimacy nor adultery carried much stigma. Cohabitation had become so common that parents had more or less given up protesting and the number of single mothers was rising. It was a sign of the times when, in the TV soap *EastEnders*, the teenage Michelle, played by Susan Tully, kept her baby. She received sympathetic letters from women who had been unable to make such a choice, even though, as she put it, the series didn't 'paint it like a rose trellis box'.[85]

Yet the decade which invented the uncomplicated bouncy word 'bonking' was also beset by fears. In the early 1980s the Ripper murders spread terror throughout the north of England. After the murder of the third victim, Jacqueline Hill, in November 1980, the police advised women not to go out alone. Margaret Thatcher wanted to go up to Leeds and take personal control of the case – a course which Willie Whitelaw discouraged, telling her that the government would be blamed if the Ripper was not caught. By the mid-1980s the panic generated because of AIDS had contributed to a mood of sexual conservatism which stressed the connection between sex and danger. Always an undercurrent in the traditional women's magazines, this spread to the modern glossies and was also setting the tone of health-education literature and sex education in schools. Some lesbian feminist writing also implied that the only safe sex was no sex, while on the right AIDS became the retribution meted out for the permissive 1960s and was persistently associated in the popular media exclusively with homosexuality. In 1989 Margaret Thatcher personally intervened to cancel public funding for research into how heterosexual behaviour spread AIDS.

Sex education in schools had been subjected to a barrage of publicity and criticism from the late 1970s. Mention of masturbation and the clitoris became increasingly taboo and right-wing pressure for a positive endorsement of chastity, monogamy and family values shifted from the wacky margins to the centre. Many schools simply avoided subjects like lesbianism, which could cause controversy, or reduced sex education to a series of warnings. Valerie Riches, a former social worker who ran a group called the Responsible Society, drew up a spider's-web chart linking the Inner London Education Authority (ILEA) with other bodies which she identified as still endorsing liberal permissive values, including the Family Planning Association, the Abortion Law Reform Association and the British Council of Churches. ILEA was to follow the GLC into oblivion and in 1988 the Local Government Act's Clause 28 made it illegal for schools maintained by the state or for other local authority-funded bodies to promote homosexuality or teach it as a possible family relationship. Clause 28, however, by making explicit attitudes which had operated through rumour and innuendo, produced a vigorous campaign in resistance from lesbians and gays. The implications for theatre groups and libraries disturbed a wider liberal group. Clause 28 was in fact to restrain more through self-censorship than direct prosecution.

In 1987 a concerted defence of abortion rights also defeated the Catholic Liberal MP David Alton's attempt in a bill supported by the Society for the Protection of the Unborn Child and LIFE to bring down the time limit in which abortions could be performed to eighteen weeks. Pro-abortion campaigners managed to overcome their disagreements on whether to campaign for reproductive rights as a whole or focus on abortion and FAB (Fight the Alton Bill) was set up, drawing in a new generation of young women through students' unions and left groups. In Parliament Jo Richardson used her considerable experience in defending abortion rights to impressive effect. Alton's bill was defeated on the final reading. A new element was the formation of Tories for the Abortion Act of 1967 (TACT), a sign that the Conservatives were divided on abortion. Margaret Thatcher and Health Minister John Moore believed that the limit should be the twenty-four weeks advocated by the British Medical Association. The government refused to allow more time for Alton's bill, although in January 1989 Margaret Thatcher promised Ann Widdecombe, a Tory supporter of Alton, that the government would debate the reduction in the abortion time limit at a later date.

In practice the Conservatives did not pursue a completely consistent moral line, despite much talk about family values and Victoria Gillick's campaign to prevent young girls getting contraceptive advice without parental consent. Though Margaret Thatcher was sympathetic, other leading Conservatives like Kenneth Clarke were not and the Conservative Women's Organization came out against her. Moreover, legislation under Thatcher reduced the time limit for divorce (1984 Family Proceedings Act) and eliminated some of the legal disadvantages of illegitimacy (1987 Family Law Reform Act). When, using new and contested means of detection, social workers in Cleveland took large numbers of children into care because they found signs of sexual abuse, amidst protests from the parents and a furore in the press, the government listened carefully to evidence on both sides before passing the 1989 Children Act. The act tried to balance the need for state intervention to protect children with respect for the rights of families not to be painfully separated because outside agencies mistakenly suspected abuse.

Moreover, the Tories were never able to appear convincingly as the party of virtue because they were too scandal-prone themselves. Cecil Parkinson, one of Margaret Thatcher's favourite ministers, told her in 1984 that he was thinking of marrying his former secretary Sara Keays, who had become pregnant. Adultery and divorce were no bar to government office, but the Prime Minister was adamantly opposed. He suggested that when the affair became known there might be some damage to the Tory endorsement of Victorian values, to which she replied, 'What could be more Victorian than keeping the family together?'[86] An angry Sara Keays refused to keep quiet and serialized her book in the *Daily Mirror* during the 1985 Tory conference, causing them some embarrassment. It was not just that illicit sex at the top made the moral posturing of the right look silly; Sara Keays also challenged the secret power operating within the Thatcher government, and, though a Conservative, she expressed sympathy for the Greenham protesters.

The personal evidently was political, but it was also always personal too and as such could not be contained in laws, policies or political pronouncements. Undeniably a shift in gender relations and sexual interaction was occurring. The certainties of male sexual control had been dented, leaving an ambiguity in sexual etiquette. There was a certain androgyny in style and a prevalent cool in outward behaviour among young women. The new glamour juxtaposed masculine and feminine in incongruous ways. There was a choice and the option of saying no. Yet along with the new 1980s style fears about danger in the street and anxiety about AIDS went very old ones about desirability and rejection. Autonomy was there all right, but what about connection? When he said it was great and that he had to go to work, Sheena Easton's 'Modern Girl' knew the score. Freedom could come down to 'getting by'.[87] Yet through it all sex kept its charm. In the autumn of 1989 Marcelle d'Argy Smith took over at *Cosmopolitan*. She decided it was time to bring sex back and up went the sales.

THE UNITED STATES

Mothers and Others

Teddi Holt, a white American from Georgia, was in her late twenties in March 1980 when she 'sat down at a kitchen table' along with 'three other homemakers' and discovered 'we prayed with one accord'.[88] She told Robyn Rowland that this was the origin of Mothers on the March (MOM), 'a non-profit-making corporation . . . to preserve and strengthen the home'.[89] MOM's creed was:

I AM MOTHER . . . The Creator of this universe chose me to be His instrument to bring all future human beings into His world . . . Lying dormant in me, to arise when needed to protect my young, is the fierceness of God Himself. I AM MOTHER. The world should hope that it never hears me roar, for if I do I WILL SHAKE THE FOUNDATIONS OF THE EARTH.[90]

MOM spoke in tongues which evoked the Bible, Helen Reddy and country music. Teddi Holt, who had had a sales job and been a secretary before she married, had become involved in politics a few years before when the International Women's Year Conference was held in Georgia. Worried about Communists and the United Nations, which she saw as plotting, along with feminists, to send women out to work, she was an opponent of the Equal Rights Amendment, gay parents' rights and health insurance for abortion. She felt threatened as 'a free citizen of the US', as 'a homemaker and a Christian mother'.[91]

Higher up the social scale, 'Mary Donnelly' — the pseudonym of a Catholic supporter of Reagan interviewed by Rebecca Klatch in *Women of the New Right* — was similarly opposed to the ERA and abortion. A former college graduate, married to a prosperous husband in insurance, she had had seven children. If Teddi Holt's God was fierce, Mary Donnelly's demanded obligation, service and duty. She had learned from her mother that 'nothing worthwhile comes easy . . . the future belongs to those who prepare for it . . . and sweet are the uses of adversity'.[92] She did not, however, describe herself in the physical terms used by the MOM as God's 'instrument'. Instead she stressed the skills of 'homemaking as a great responsibility, a vocation that tapped a woman's mental and physical faculties and demanded creativity

. . . a selfless occupation in which a woman made constant material and emotional sacrifices but also reaped many spiritual rewards.'[93]

Mary Donnelly's involvement in politics had begun in opposition to abortion during the early 1970s and was motivated by moral duty and a fear that 'women's lib'[94] would defeminize women by mixing up gender roles. She remembered the father at her Catholic College who had warned her, 'Beware of the guy who likes to hang curtains. Look for the masculine guy.'[95] Masculinity was about support; femininity about nurture – and curtains.

A *laissez-faire* conservative, 'Dora Remington', also interviewed by Rebecca Klatch, was not impressed: 'I mean, hell, how can you spend twenty years in the kitchen today. I mean, everybody's got a Cuisinart or something else . . . You can only vacuum the house so many times before you start sucking up the carpet.'[96] She was not at all keen on duty, authority, the state or patriarchal masculinity telling her what to do with her body or to 'get back there and do the dishes'.[97] The important and liberating aspect of Reaganism was his economic policies. The social issues were just 'smoke screens'; she reckoned, 'People vote with their pocket books.'[98] The ERA was not a personal threat to her, just a gift to Phyllis Schlafly: 'Who really cares about the ERA? Do you think it would really make one bit of difference one way or the other? It might screw up everything but that's about all it would do.'[99]

The National Organization for Women, in defending the ERA, had focused increasingly on individual equal rights; their success could be seen in the fact that even inveterate anti-feminists like Teddi Holt and Mary Donnelly supported some degree of equal rights. However, against the prevailing terms of a liberal feminism which pursued a strategy of equality with men in the world as it was, other strands of 1980s feminism were arguing that women were indeed different from men. This meant searching for alternatives to a competitive, materialistic, male-dominated society. There were spiritual ecologists, Jewish women rediscovering the female spirit of God, Shekinah, Goddess worshippers and white-witch healers, busy weaving webs and invoking spells in protests against nuclear power. They emphasized not individual equal rights but women's collective power as redeemers of the earth.

Paula Gunn Allen, a Keres Pueblo Indian, also expressed a view of connectedness in the image of the sacred hoop. Inspired by Native

American culture, she explained, 'When I was small, my mother often told me that animals, insects, and plants are to be treated with the kind of respect one customarily accords to high-status adults. "Life is a circle, and everything has a place in it," she would say.'[100] The sacred hoop might appear a long way from white suburban life in Love Canal, New York, but Lois Gibbs's stand against a toxic waste dump which seriously harmed her children's health in the late 1970s inspired many other women to get involved in campaigns for environmental justice. A few used the image of being 'mothers of the earth', but they were more inclined to be matter of fact about land use, the power of big companies and the distorted use of scientific evidence. Their involvement, which often began as defence of their children and their homes, frequently led to alliances with civil rights groups, trade unions, community groups and Greenpeace rather than with MOM.

Citizenship, mothering, connection and autonomy, communalism and individualism were invoked by women on the right *and* on the left during the 1980s. As in Britain, behind the divisions similar social forces can be seen pulling at the boundaries of what was regarded as personal or public.

Politics

Jane Byrne, the first woman mayor of Chicago, NOW President Eleanor Smeal and leading African-American Democrat Jesse Jackson were among the speakers at a rally of 90,000 people in favour of the ERA in Grant Park in 1980. It marked the swing of the pendulum. That year the Democratic Convention voted to deny National Committee funds to candidates who opposed ERA and Medicaid abortions for poor women. In contrast, right-wing Republicans were successful in making their party come out against the ERA, despite protests from pro-ERA Republican women who demonstrated outside the party's convention, dressed in white like the earlier suffrage campaigners. Pro-ERA Republican women voters continued to campaign for the passage of the amendment in their states. Former First Lady Betty Ford became an honorary co-chair of the ERA Countdown Campaign, and rallies, with supporters wearing green and white, were held in cities all

George Lucas from Petersburg, Virginia, arguing with a
pro-choice supporter outside the Supreme Court in Washington, DC, in 1984,
when *Roe* v. *Wade* was being reconsidered.

over the country in 1981. But regardless of a tremendous campaign
across party divisions, when the extension gained in 1979 ran out
in June 1982, Alabama, Arizona, Arkansas, Florida, Georgia, Illinois,
Louisiana, Mississippi, Missouri, Nevada, North Carolina, Oklahoma,
Utah and Virginia had not ratified.

How was it that the ERA, which had seemed unstoppable in the
early 1970s, had suffered defeat? One factor certainly was Phyllis Schlafly,
who alarmed conservatives with her prognosis of the draft of eighteen-
year-old girls, federal funds for abortion and mandatory gay and lesbian
rights. By mobilizing grass-roots women, the new right made it evident
that women were divided on the ERA. However, as Jane Mansbridge
points out in *Why We Lost the ERA*, the sweeping general terms of
the amendment made it an excellent target for the right: 'Because ERA
activists had little of an immediate, practical nature to lose if the ERA
was defeated, they had little reason to describe it in a way that would
make it acceptable to middle-of-the-road legislators.'[101]

It was not only supporters of Reagan like Teddi Holt and Mary

Donnelly who came to fear that the ERA threatened their identity as women. Democrats like Mrs Marilyn Lloyd wanted a measure which opposed discrimination, but would not 'rend the fabric of family life' or violate 'personal modesty' in public institutions through integrating the sexes.[102] The idea had got around that the ERA was about changing gender identity, and by 1982 its actual support was in decline.

The irony was that the changes which could be effected by legislation would have been far less extensive in practice than either its adherents or its detractors claimed. Jane Mansbridge shows that the opposition to the ERA enabled the new right 'to forge a coalition of the traditional radical right, religious activists, and that previously relatively apolitical segment of the non-cosmopolitan working and middle classes that was deeply disturbed by the cultural changes – especially the changes in sexual mores – in the second half of the twentieth century'.[103] It had become the symbol of an attitude, not just a piece of legislation.

Reagan in office threatened more than the ERA. Civil rights, abortion and social welfare were all under attack from 1980. His economic policies stressed individual self-help and his foreign policy aimed to restore America's military power and prestige. The *New York Times/ CBS News* Poll during the 1980 elections revealed that while 54 per cent of men voted for Reagan, only 46 per cent of women supported him. Susan Hartmann argues that this did not mean that women were becoming more liberal or more pro-Democratic, but that men were more likely to support Republicanism and conservative values. The sexes divided on 'issues of peace, the environment, the economy, and the government's responsibility for social welfare'.[104] As these were issues on which men and women had differed in the 1950s, it is difficult to conclude how much the women's movement affected women's resistance to Reaganism. However, the existence of women's groups and a feminist consciousness did recast the meaning of gendered political attitudes. This polarization was accentuated by Reagan's species of conservatism and by the fact that the right-wingers who regarded his administration with hope lost no time in mounting a challenge to feminist demands. Paul Weyrich's Heritage Foundation set out a 'Mandate for Leadership' in 1981, warning against the influence of feminists, who were blamed for everything from divorce rates to lack of jobs. Despite protests from Margaret Heckler, Leslie Wolfe, a civil servant who was director of the Women's Educational Equity Act programme, was personally hounded out of office during Reagan's first term and the staff were replaced by members of Phyllis Schlafly's Eagle Forum.

Right-wing Republicans also ruthlessly attacked the candidature of the personable vice-presidential Democrat candidate Geraldine Ferraro, even though she soft-pedalled feminist issues and seemed to embody family values. Unable to find scandal in her life, the new right media questioned the business deals of her husband, John Zaccaro. The rest of the press joined the hunt; they even investigated her father and her husband's father. These smears and witch-hunts not only damaged Ferraro but made other Democratic women reluctant to run. Sara Evans records that when Congresswoman Patricia Schroeder considered running for the presidency in 1987, the press wanted to know what Mr Schroeder would have for supper while she governed the country and why she was running 'as a woman'. Her favourite answer was, ' "Do I have any choice?" '[105]

Several new right women were given political appointments on sexual and domestic policy. For example, the charismatic Beverley LaHaye was on the Family Advisory Board, anti-abortion campaigner Marjory Mecklenburg was made responsible for the 'squeal rule' – Reagan's policy proposal to make clinics reveal the identities of teenage girls who came for abortions without their parents' permission – and Jo Ann Gasper, a conservative journalist, was given the job of closing domestic violence programmes. Right-wing women were, however, thwarted by a profound resistance to women in public office, which made them vulnerable to personal criticism: for example, Jeane Kirkpatrick, who was UN Ambassador, was accused in 1985 of being 'too temperamental to hold higher office' – a 'classic male sexist charge,' she retorted.[106]

Nancy Reagan, on the other hand, exerted considerable influence over her husband. Bill Casey, campaign manager and later CIA chief, noted, 'The looks, the voices, the glances, the subtle deference told one story: Nancy.'[107] She always claimed, of course, that she was just protecting 'Ronnie'. But this was an extensive brief and the boundaries blurred. The CIA had a weekend log on Nancy Reagan's social calls, for, as Bob Woodward put it in *Veil*, 'Some of Nancy's activities often drifted into the President's orbit.'[108] Indeed, she had an impact on

Salute to Nancy Reagan: Republican convention, 1984.

both posts and policies, as women as well as men learned to their cost.

Nancy Reagan was preoccupied with appearances. Her designer clothes and liking for the jet set became a joke, even among White House staff, who referred to her as 'the Hairdo with Anxiety'.[109] A bad press made her eager to be accepted by the liberal Democratic élite in Washington – people like Katherine Graham, editor of the *Washington Post*. The moral new right increasingly came to be a social embarrassment. Editing Reagan's 1987 State of the Union message, she rang Donald Regan, Chief of Staff, to say that while it should be patriotic and show that the President was in charge, 'the parts about abortion have got to come out . . . I don't give a damn about the right-to-lifers'.[110] Barbara Ehrenreich commented in 1989, 'As Ronnie slipped into personal reverie or the prodromal phase of Alzheimer's, she was making her stealthy advance on the presidency . . . Behind the dizzying camouflage of borrowed gowns and extorted china, Mrs Reagan carried on brilliantly.'[111]

The gender gap continued to have an important impact on voting patterns throughout Reagan's terms in office. It was not just the traditional issues of peace, welfare and crime either. Ann Smith, director of the Congressional Caucus for Women's Issues, which co-ordinated legislative information affecting women, told Anne Costain in 1984, 'There is a new political base out there . . . When women are working, they know what is coming or not coming in their pay check. They recognize problems in pension systems. With so many single heads of household, they know what is involved in trying to take care of a family.'[112]

Despite the conservatism of American society on many issues, there remained considerable support for women's rights. The experience of women lobbyists, combined with the organizational strength of the League of Women Voters and the National Federation of Business and Professional Women's Clubs, along with NOW and several new groups, the Older Women's League and the National Women's Health Network, meant that a determined resistance was maintained through-out the decade. A combination of all these factors checked the President's inclinations. Despite the right-to-life movement, a determined onslaught on affirmative action and the Supreme Court's restriction of Title IX (the constitutional right to educational equity) in 1984, Reagan could not dismantle all the rights gained in the 1970s.

Moreover, he was compelled to come up with policies aimed at women: for instance, pension reform making it easier for women to qualify for private pension schemes and sterner methods of collecting child support. Nor was he able to cut back all aspects of state funding: for instance, battered women's shelters still got money, much to the annoyance of Schlafly's Eagle Forum, which complained that the National Coalition Against Domestic Violence was a 'subversive group of radical lesbian feminists'.[113] Her Coalition for Abused Women was accordingly given $625,000 to research the effects of domestic violence on 'traditional women'.[114]

Reagan made some symbolic concessions by appointing a few women, notably Sandra Day O'Connor to the Supreme Court, and after 1986 he was prepared to mark such events as American Business Women's Day. Such symbolism was not without significance, but it was, as Johanna Brenner observes, the demands which required 'increases in government spending'[115] which were really hit. Policies addressing the needs of poor and working mothers – child-care, demands for a higher minimum wage and welfare benefits – were uniformly unsuccessful.

'Reform' of welfare under Reagan meant shifting the burden of poverty towards the poor. The National Congress of Neighborhood Women, the National Welfare Rights Union, the National Black Women's Health Project and women of colour in the Coalition of Labor Union Women protested, but, along with NOW, they were marginalized. These groups were to coalesce in the Rainbow Coalition around Jesse Jackson in 1988. But while many white liberal feminists in NOW came to pay lip service to racial and ethnic 'diversity', the admission that a key component in the resistance to Reaganism involved the connection of 'women's issues' with social inequality as a whole was a much harder fight to win.

The ideological centre moved to the right in the 1980s pushing even moderate liberal opposition to the margins. In the process the moral right conjured an America in their own image. As Barbara Ehrenreich says, 'Sometime in the eighties, Americans had a new set of "traditional values" installed.'[116] The Democrats borrowed these family values from the Republicans for the 1988 election contest against George Bush. This idyll of the family dissolved the needs of actual individuals in real families and marginalized women who were outside the bounds – single

Gwen Craig from San Francisco demonstrating at the Democratic convention, 1980.

521

mothers and lesbians. But the Republicans won yet again and President
Bush, who had disdained mention of 'women's issues' during the
election, vetoed a bill approved by the House and Senate in 1989
to grant Medicaid funds for abortions even for victims of 'promptly
reported'[117] rape or incest.

Yet amidst the social conservatism a wide range of women's movements developed in opposition to Reaganism. A women's peace movement was stirring internationally and there were close links between
the US and Greenham women; in 1983 Seneca Women's Peace
Encampment was established and peace women demonstrated against
the Nevada test site. Environmental movements proliferated and their
social base widened. The African-American activist Cora Tucker said
of her campaign against a uranium-mining project in Halifax, Virginia,
'Nothing in the world is more bread and butter than clean air to breathe
or having good water to drink.'[118] Marta Salinas's struggle against
pesticides in a Latino agricultural community began when she found
her daughter crying over a shoebox filled with flowers: 'She said her
Barbie doll died of cancer, and she came up and told me, "Mom, if I
die of cancer I want to die with my kittens so I can die hugging
them." '[119]

The women's health movement also reached out to poor women of
colour after the formation of the National Black Women's Health
Project in 1981 and the creation of the Native American Community
Board on a South Dakota reservation by Charon Asetoyer in 1985. It
dealt with birth control, child development, AIDS, alcohol-related
problems and domestic violence. The following year Luz Alvarez
Martinez set up the National Latina Health Organization. They all
stressed the wider social and economic context of reproductive
rights.

Local community movements began to coalesce against Reaganism
in ad-hoc radical coalitions which were to be the basis of a national
rainbow alliance. For example, in San Antonio, Texas, Communities
Organized for Public Service, in which women played a leading part,
produced an alternative development plan for their city, elected an
Hispanic mayor and, by activating women's local networks, made new
social demands on public life. Despite the Reaganite attack on trade
unions, women continued to join unions like the American Federation

of State, County and Municipal Employees. The demand for comparable worth, which sought to close the gap between low-paid women's jobs and male employment, was to be implemented in many US states as well as local government during the 1980s.

Lesbian women were under intense political pressure as the antithesis of the cardboard cutout the right called the 'traditional woman'. One consequence was a consolidation of the lesbian and gay communities around AIDS, which led to a recognition of the need for public health care. Lesbians had considerable impact upon academia, NOW and trade unions. In 1988 the National Women's Studies Association convention had its first plenary on lesbian studies. The American Association of University Women recognized its first lesbian caucus in 1989. NOW held its first national Lesbian Conference in the same year and trade unions were to change their position on gay and lesbian rights. The massive lesbian and gay mobilization on the 1987 National March on Washington for Lesbian and Gay Rights, when 650,000 demonstrators chanted slogans like, 'We're one country, one people – we're part of the fabric of life in our country,' testified to a resistance which refused to be marginalized and cowed.

Feminism jettisoned its Utopian vision of transforming the whole of society but refused to go away during the 1980s; so did the problems which brought it into being. As the decade ended, a new wave of young feminists was mobilizing in defence of reproductive rights. Moreover, after a decade of propaganda against working mothers and women's equality in the media, the gender gap in political and social attitudes actually became more marked. In Susan Faludi's words:

By the end of the decade, the National Opinion Research poll was finding that nearly twice the proportion of women as men thought a working mother could be just as good a parent as a mother who stayed at home. In 1989, while a majority of women in the *New York Times* poll believed American society had not changed enough to grant women equality, only a minority of men agreed.[120]

Work

Women were presented with two clear-cut images in the 1980s. One was the model of competitive success – the business suit made a surprise comeback; the other was a pastiche of a 1950s apple-pie mom in a crisp white apron. While American women were reaching the boardroom and Sally Ride was going up in space, Susan Faludi describes how journalists made careers with articles written in a tone of strangled agony about women giving up too much. Meanwhile, advertisers doggedly celebrated high-earning, assertive women who did not clutter their lives with sentiment. Women were being told that their problem was that they loved too much, at the same time as being rebuked because they did not love enough. Neither polarity fitted most American women's predicament.

Yet the family wage ideal of the American family was dissolving. Blue-collar men who were losing jobs might have blamed global economic restructuring, but women were closer to hand: 'Go back home and be more submissive,'[121] said the preachers. Resentment went higher up the scale. George Gilder's *Wealth and Poverty* (1981), written with help from Reagan's campaign manager Bill Casey, accused women of holding back men from making money and Allan Bloom's *The Closing of the American Mind* (1987) declared that feminists were blocking talented men (like himself) from academic careers.

Though the dust never really settled about what women should or should not be doing, they kept moving into paid employment. Families increasingly needed two incomes and more and more women were heads of households. Women's representation in the workforce increased from 51 to 57 per cent and reached 70 per cent in the twenty-five to forty-four age group during the 1980s. The numbers of working mothers were still rising – by 1989 73.2 per cent of married women with children between six and seventeen were in paid employment, and women's unemployment rates were lower than men's. A few women executives did make a lot of money, but they were the exceptions. Low pay was still characteristic of women's work and, as low earners already, they suffered because from 1981 the Reagan administration had refused to increase the minimum wage. Though the hourly earnings of full-time women workers had increased slightly between 1980 and 1985, and the proportion of women earning over $30,000 had inched up to 10.3 per cent by 1986, nearly two-thirds (63.4 per cent) of minimum-wage workers were women in 1989. Disparity between women, as well as between women and men, was also marked, as was the race–ethnicity hierarchy, which had shifted but not diminished. Women were in there, but very few were able to set the terms. The workforce had been 'feminized', but feminization, as labour economist Teresa Amott points out, meant low pay, lack of benefits and worsening conditions.

The economy, meanwhile, continued to be structured with men in mind. Discrimination, sexual harassment, low cultural evaluation of women workers' skills and lack of support for women's needs as mothers at work combined with inadequate social provision to create what came to be called the 'glass ceiling' – an invisible barrier that checked women moving up at every level of the job market.

American women found it hard to make much headway with the kind of social rights which were regarded as basic in many European countries. In the mid-1980s only five states – California, Hawaii, New Jersey, New York and Rhode Island – had the partially paid maternity leave with a guaranteed return to work customary in Europe. There was an acute shortage of child-care and it was frequently of an inferior quality. While private nursery schools for those who could pay were geared to stimulating and enriching childhood, public day-care had a custodial ethos. Nor did child-care solve the continuing needs of older children. Lack of public transport and fear of danger meant children had to be ferried around and schools had high expectations of mothers as fund-raisers.

Most women muddled through, like Cathy Collins, a black middle-class supervisor at New York's cardiology unit. In 1988 the *New York Times* magazine reported that she got up at five, gave her family breakfast in Teaneck, New Jersey, caught two buses, dealt with phones, paperwork and photocopying, mediated in disputes and responded to crises. Back home at 6.30 p.m. to family hassles, the stress bleeper fixed to her arm registered anxiety. Her blood pressure at 9.34 was higher than it had been at work. The intensification of work, combined with domestic work (still mainly done by women), resulted in a time crisis. In *The Second Shift: Working Parents and the Revolution at Home*, Arlie Hochshild interviewed working wives who were 'getting by' and

Women Composers

Diane Peacock Jezic began *Women Composers: The Lost Tradition Found* in 1986 while ill with cancer. It was to be published posthumously in 1988. She paid tribute to twenty-five women composers of Western music since medieval times. Among them were six contemporary US composers: Katherine Hoover, Ellen Taaffe Zwilich, Ruth Schonthal, Barbara Kolb, Marga Richter and Judith Lang Zaimont. The Festivals of Women's Music organized by Katherine Hoover in New York between 1977 and 1981 were her inspiration. However, while these led to a reawakening of interest in women's music, publicity and money were problems. As Katherine Hoover remarked, they 'were . . . musically rewarding and under-attended', adding that ignorance about the work done by women was a 'mark of the sad twisted history of women's compositions'.[122]

The problems were evident in the women composers' own lives. Ellen Taaffe Zwilich was the first woman to win the Pulitzer Prize in Music Composition in 1983 for her Symphony No. 1; it was composed in a one-bedroom apartment in the Bronx. Ruth Schonthal, a refugee from Fascism, had survived by playing in clubs and cocktail lounges before teaching, telling Diane Peacock Jezic in 1986 that it had 'been a tremendous struggle to find time and energy to compose'.[123] Barbara Kolb, who in 1969 had been the first US woman to gain the Prix de Rome, was frequently congratulated for making it in her profession. Her response in the late 1980s was that she was not sure if she had: 'I mean, I don't even have a job . . . Recognition is fine, but I'm at a point in my life where remuneration means something.'[124]

It was not simply their position as women composers within the profession but the cultural implications of femininity which troubled them. Marga Richter, whose *Landscapes of the Mind* was inspired by the paintings of Georgia O'Keeffe, was convinced that women expressed emotions through music differently from men. Judith Lang Zaimont, the youngest composer in the group, was looking beyond the Western tradition for women's songs in other cultures. However, Ellen Taaffe

Zwilich articulated a universal artistic responsibility, despite the experience of 'evil and pain in this country', when she described the role of the artist as expressing the other reality – 'beauty, joy, nobility and love'.[125]

✳

sleeping less: 'These women talked about sleep the way a hungry person talks about food.'[126] Juliet Schor estimated that women in full-time jobs increased their total annual hours of work by approximately 160 hours between 1969 and 1989. This amounted to an extra month each year. The increase in labour-market hours was 305 hours. Household work went down by 145 hours. For every hour a woman worked outside the home, she cut down on half an hour's housework. It tended to be the mopping and the dusting that diminished, for, as Juliet Schor remarked, 'It's easier to cut back on scrubbing the floor than it is to cut back on child-care, laundry or meal preparation.'[127]

The prevalence of shift work in the faster-growing occupations – among clerks and cashiers in stores, nurses, nursing aides, workers in fast food or gas stations – affected health and stress levels and presented particular problems for women with children. Alison McClure, a postal worker, often had to work overtime. This meant collecting her three-year-old daughter from her mother at 1 a.m., doing housework, getting to bed at 3 or 4 a.m. and then getting up to send her daughter to nursery school at 6.45 a.m. Shift work was unregulated and Reagan's policies stressed less regulation and social provision, not more.

Even highly paid professional women with families faced a dilemma. New right theorist Connie Marshner, who drafted the Family Protection Act (1980), continued to work until she was pregnant with her fourth child in 1987. The death of her baby daughter, born with congenital heart defects in 1984, contributed to her decision to give up her post as vice-president of the Free Congress Foundation. She became a homeworker, writing against day care. Connie Marshner's 'solution' was well-paid homework – a rare thing. In fact, homework did not necessarily reduce the pressures, it just concentrated them in one place. Betty Beach cites 'Mrs E.', a homeworker in rural Maine, who also provided day care for five children. She did roughly eleven hours' work a day lacing shoes, which could spread over into the weekends. Her daughters helped her sometimes and accepted her 'grouchiness'[128] when she was tired.

By the 1980s the growth of low-waged casualized work was so noticeable that it could hardly be regarded as marginal any more. Work in the bargain basement could mean homework in electronics production in Silicon Valley or among the automobile dashboard-plate makers in New York State or as clerical workers in insurance in Wisconsin. The homeworkers could be illegal Hispanic or Asian immigrants in Silicon Valley, middle-class suburbanites in the New York area or the white rural poor. The *Christian Science Monitor* in August 1986 reported one success story of a rural business employing 150 homeworkers sewing appliquéd designs on jogging suits. The company expected sales of $3.5 million by the end of the year. Women accepted the conditions because they were illegals, had a disability or were old, but mainly because they had families. New technology gave homework a new lease of life because it made decentralized production more possible. Big firms like Kodak and Magnavox used electronics homeworkers and finance companies began to employ 'teleworkers', professional and clerical computer-based homeworkers. But the real attraction for employers was that homeworkers provided a flexible and cheap workforce, they could be easily shed and employers saved on wages and running costs like electricity.

In *America's Working Women*, Rosalyn Baxandall and Linda Gordon show how, 'As globalization of the big corporations began to deindustrialize the United States, even privileged white men with skilled jobs were laid off, and as they began to seek lower-paying service sector jobs, the relatively disadvantaged position of poor women increased.'[129] In the low-paid service sector married women worked alongside young and single workers, scooping French fries in McDonald's or BurgerKing, waitressing or working at the check-out counter of the convenience stores which competed for the trade of the poor and immobile shoppers. These 'flexible' service workers were expected to keep smiling regardless and the mealy-mouthed 'Have a nice day' ethos could breed either deference or anarchic rage. Melinda Gebbie was a receptionist in a fancy San Francisco pet hospital. Neither the pets nor the pay impressed her. The final straw was being expected to 'extend this motherly attitude not only to the furry parasites . . . but to their owners and the doctors as well'.[130]

Sex work was the disreputable and sometimes illegal end of the service sector. But as Linda Thomas, who was a sex worker and then a 'temp' in insurance, remarked, both working experiences were 'firmly rooted in the same money market'.[131] It was a very big money market too. Rosalyn Baxandall and Linda Gordon point out that by the mid-1980s men were spending around $40 million a day on prostitutes. Despite the danger of violence and AIDS, women took risks because of the money. In a 1980 radio discussion, Lou observed, 'Unfortunately more women are going into prostitution because the economic situation is getting worse. You got two little kids. Welfare isn't enough and it's humiliating besides.'[132] Annie added that there was as much sexual indignity in waitressing at Steak 'n' Eggs. Male customers would just drink a coffee and 'pinch you on the ass'.[133] Why shouldn't she charge them $50 instead?

The introduction of new technology in distribution and clothing as well as the clerical sectors made new ways of structuring jobs possible and enabled employers to extend control from afar, as Barbara Garson found out when she became a data-entry clerk in 1981:

I entered the Office of the Future through a door that led into a windowless basement where dozens of women sat spaced apart, keying with three fingers of one hand. I felt like Dorothy stepping into Oz, only in this version the movie turned from color to black and white.[134]

Instead of the wicked witch, the young man in the glass booth materialized to tell her that she was way behind on her keystrokes. New technology made some tasks unnecessary; it was also demanding more new skills. Its impact on women's work thus varied. By 1988 Barbara Garson noted differentiation among social workers: 'When a front-line service job, the rank that first meets the customer, is reduced to a clerical function, it's often necessary to create a smaller second rank of better-treated and better-trained workers.'[135]

Just as in Britain, things were changing so fast that the strategies of the unions and the women's movement were hardly able to keep up. Women's desire for flexibility and for work they could combine with caring for their families remained an unresolved dilemma. In the early 1980s a New England knitter, Audrey Pudvah, challenged the 1942 Fair Labor Standards Act, which banned industrial homework in knitted outerwear. While trade unionists simply opposed homeworking as sweated labour, Reaganite politicians took up the knitters' cause as good mothers with the right to free enterprise; their cause fitted into 'back to the home' and economic deregulation rhetoric. Behind the ideological battle were women who saw work at home as their best chance of a livelihood. One Massachusetts woman, whose husband had a pre-ulcer condition, said she wanted to be at home with her children: 'There are many women like me. We want to be productive not just reproductive.'[136] A former factory worker in Maine said she preferred homework to the polluted minimum-wage mills and factories in the woollen, paper, plastic and shoe industries: 'I know mothers and fathers who only see their babies when they are asleep in their cribs.'[137]

During the 1980s the attempt to extend equal rights and the argument that women had different needs clashed head on. In fact, neither strategy had all the answers. Pay equity was never accepted at the federal level, but some private employers and state and local governments did adopt comparable-worth guidelines, which resulted in crucial gains for state and municipal workers. However, equity at the workplace did not deal with the fact that women might want time off work when they had children; nor did it address the extra hours they spent in cooking and child-care. Some feminists tried to offset the limitations of demanding equality with men by a renewal of the claim that women's differing experience of domestic life could be the basis for a more caring society. But, the line that women's differing approach to work could counter a commercial world had a bitter twist to it for women at Sears Roebuck, who lost their fight to work on jobs which brought higher commissions in 1984, and for women employees of the firm American Cynamid, which, when reproductive hazards were revealed, actually demanded that women employees be sterilized and then fired them anyway.

Some important changes were occurring, however, in the law and in the unions, which recognized differences while demanding equality.

New York's first female sanitation workers, Carlen Sanderson and
Anne Pabon, 1986.

In 1986 the Supreme Court ruled that sexual harassment did violate civil rights. The movement for disabled rights was revitalized during the 1980s. Lesbians and gays were forming rank and file committees in unions which combined with gay communities to care for union members with AIDS. They also got union contracts changed to include health insurance for domestic partners and children in Santa Cruz, West Hollywood and Berkeley.

Pressure for a broader social unionism and attempts to cut across the workplace/community divide were coming from many sources. Cecilia Rodriguez, a chicana garment worker and union activist, helped form a women's centre in El Paso which organized around problems sweatshop workers faced with benefits and transport. They went on to set up a co-operative food-buying scheme and established adult education courses. Community groups in ACORN, Association of Community Organizations for Reform Now, banded together in Detroit, Philadelphia, New Orleans and Boston to try to raise the wages of young workers in 'fly by night' jobs. Co-operation in the decade of competition adapted to new times. Teresa Amott records the formation of Co-operative Home Care Associates, started in the South Bronx in 1985 to provide health and various domestic services for the homebound on a contract basis to hospitals and health service agencies. It employed many African-American and Latino women.

The movements of the 1980s, like those of the 1970s, were about empowerment. During the Pittston miners' strike against job losses women mobilized in support, gaining confidence from choosing the name Daughters of Mother Jones. Mexican and chicana women frozen-food workers of Watsonville, Santa Cruz County, struck for the right to unionize in 1985. And their rebellion had an impact on relationships at home: 'This kind of change is especially important for Latino men,' said Margarita, one of the strikers. 'They're so used to their women waiting on them hand and foot.'[138] They found that their efforts to achieve equality could be blocked and their assertion of difference turned against them. However, they took action with much less hope of victory and with little sense of any other possible economic system.

'We want alternatives,'[139] Lou the prostitute had said in 1980. But if anybody knew how low-paid women workers were to get them, they were not letting on.

Daily Life

Ronald Reagan's half-million-dollar campaign film for the 1984 election, *The New Beginning*, presented a world bathed in sunlight: the children were smiling and people were hugging, getting married and working. Joanne Morreale comments, 'All of these images have appeared time and again on greetings cards, on television, in movies. They invoke knee-jerk associations with the way people "remember" it to be, or, more likely, with the way that they would like it to have been.'[140] The Reagans themselves were contrary and complementary symbols: *Time* magazine reported in 1980 that though Reagan was worth 'as much as $4 million'[141] he had 'to be prodded into buying a new suit'.[142] The austere hero with his air of being at ease with 'just folks' contrasted with the archetypal feminine consumer Nancy with her $5,000 dresses. Stuart and Elizabeth Ewen contrast 'the rigors of thrift' with 'the guilt of leisure, consumption, and the tangible symbols of an "upper class".'[143]

During the 1980s reality became hard to find among the images of the Reaganite good life; the movie took over. Here was a world in which the sun always shone and nobody grew old – you only had to look at the President and his diet-conscious wife. The diet was the clue, for while the chosen were predestined to be happy, this destiny involved individual endeavour. There was so much to eat in the refrigerators of the fortunate that they were beset by the responsibility of fitness. Not only did America take up healthy jogging and aerobics in a big way in order to slip lithely into the new stylish jeans which had become family wear, they were also buying diet foods and diet therapies. *Glamor* magazine surveyed 33,000 women in 1984 about their bodies. Most of them thought that they were too fat; those who were underweight saw themselves as overweight. Laxatives were used by 18 per cent to purge themselves; 15 per cent induced vomiting. Girls of five were reported to be in tears about being too fat. Writing in *Psychology Today*, J. Kevin Thompson observed, 'Many women see themselves as round-faced and pudgy, even when nobody else does.'[144] Great-shape Barbie set everyone an example with her leotard, leg-warmers and hard-outline definition. Real-life Jane Fonda seemed to defy the adage that beauty must fade.

The frenzy of individual control among those in the sunny side up of America fended off the dark side of the street. Threatening chaos was contained as 'the other' – the people who were not quite people, the ones who had failed. Then the Iran–Contra scandal in 1986 and financial chicanery and corruption broke through the conservative fantasy of style, well-being and virtue rewarded. Evil, it seemed, was there in the suburbs. The film *Blue Velvet* (1986) captured this new mood. You could never be sure of being among the good, you could never really be safe. Bush's campaign in 1988 marshalled negative images of fear of the horrors which could be released. As Stuart and Elizabeth Ewen remark, 'If Reagan's campaign had plucked Americans' heart-strings, George Bush's . . . mined mean-spirited anxieties.'[145]

Popular papers like the *National Enquirer* reported danger everywhere: LOVERS SLAIN IN LOVERS' LANE, CAR TRAPS WOMAN IN HER BED.[146] Films like *The Terminator* (1984) and *Total Recall* (1990) were metaphors of danger and revenge. Women figured both as victims and scapegoats in these scenarios of terror and retribution. The gender images of the 1980s were marked by ambiguity. The autonomous single woman in *Fatal Attraction* (1987) might be punished, but in *Desperately Seeking Susan* (1985) women got freedom to roam. On television the round and abrasive *Roseanne* replaced the sleek and bitchy soap heroines

Caring Krystle is countered by power-dressing Alexis in *Dynasty*, 1981.

of the early 1980s ('I hate the word "housewife". I prefer to be called "domestic goddess".'[147]) There was a plethora of images and any number of styles – and of course these meant new markets. The *Wall Street Journal* announced in the late 1980s that Yale University had 'a growing number of special-interest [lesbian] factions': there were radical chic 'lipsticks', and 'crunchies', who were 'granola dykes who have old-fashioned Utopian ideas about feminism', along with 'assimilationists'.[148] Trend journalism, meanwhile, added to the confusion about the conflicting virtues of individualist go-getters and 'family value'-style mothers devotedly tending to husbands and offspring. Advertisements slogged out the social meaning of gender – the gourmet kitchen equipment for the creative homemaker versus the microwave for the working mother. Meanwhile, the popular media battled for its niche – traditionalist magazines like *Family Circle* and *Good Housekeeping* versus the modernizing *New Woman* and *Ms.*

The soundbites and the images folded fiction and fantasy into fact, obscuring the real-life consequences of the over-simplified dichotomies of 'personal' and 'political', of 'modernizing' and 'traditional', of 'individual' and 'social'. Anti-abortion campaigners, for instance, claimed that women did not as individuals have the right to decide whether to bear a child or not; society had to intervene to protect the rights of the foetus to be born. Some of these opponents of abortion were prepared to take direct action. For example, in 1983 an arsonist set fire to the Hillcrest Clinic in Norfolk, Virginia, with kerosene. Violence escalated from 1984 and there were growing numbers of arson and bombing attacks, not only in the South or in rural areas but in big Northern cities as well – in 1986, for example, a Manhattan clinic was bombed, injuring two pedestrians. By 1988 'Operation Rescue' demonstrations were blocking the entrances of abortion clinics. In response, the National Organization of Women began to mobilize women on a mass scale to defend abortion rights. Feminists lined up alongside the opponents of abortion in dramatic confrontations which brought a new generation into contact with NOW.

Despite Reagan, the 1983 Supreme Court decision that the government could not interfere with women's right to abortion was a setback to the anti-abortionists, and they also had difficulty in getting anti-abortion measures through at state level. However, the Hyde

Amendment prohibiting the use of Medicaid and other federal health programme funds for abortion, restriction of grants to Planned Parenthood, the insistence that teenage girls needed parental consent and the general cuts in health care made abortion much more difficult, especially for young or poor women. In 1988 Becky Bell, aged seventeen, died after an illegal abortion because she did not want to get parental consent. It was the new right during the 1980s who were politicizing the personal – even though they claimed it was sacrosanct. The era also saw what Amy Kesselman describes as 'a swollen emphasis on the political implications of personal behaviour'.[149] Issues which were psychologically complex and emotionally painful exploded into the public arena. The focus was on personal dilemmas rather than on social problems.

The case of Baby M, which hit the headlines in 1987, is an example. The biological mother, Mary Beth Whitehead, agreed to have a baby for $10,000 and then changed her mind and said she wanted to keep the baby after pregnancy. The couple who had contracted with her to bear the child, the Sterns, claimed that the contract was binding – a deal was a deal. Moreover, Dr Stern's sperm was implicated. Who had the best claim on the baby? The case became a metaphor for much deeper confusions about mothering, class (the biological mother was working class) and the acceptable penetration of market values.

As divorces soared, frequently initiated by women, alimony, custody and child support became all-consuming battles. The media attacked 'Deadbeat Dads' who did not pay child support, but also depicted them as tragic heroes harried by anxieties – the long-term worries of the women left with the children did not make such good copy. A 1984 federal law enabled states to take child-support payments from an absent father's pay cheque. The amounts due were sometimes calculated on a flat-rate basis, sometimes as a proportion of the parents' incomes. Pressure did force some men to pay more, but chasing individual fathers was costly and time-consuming. It also could reach an impasse. The incomes of the majority of black working-class men were extremely low and a growing number of young white working-class male workers with low and irregular earnings were being marginalized. Moreover, as Teresa Amott notes:

If all women received all the child support they were due, only a quarter of the gap between their income and the poverty threshold would be closed. A far greater portion of the gap would be closed by increasing women's earnings and income support from the government, rather than focusing on the individual father.[150]

The outcry about divorced wives or welfare mothers was less bothered with solutions for the women involved than with blaming. Nora Ephron declared bitterly in *Heartburn*, 'Wives went out into the world free at last, single again and discovered the horrible truth: that they were sellers in a buyer's market and that the major concrete achievement of the women's movement in the 1970s was the Dutch Treat.'[151]

Under Reagan, relationships of reciprocity narrowed to members of one's immediate family. It was the common sense about the good life which, Nancy Fraser points out, 'omitted such essential elements of a decent life as a clean, safe, and sustainable environment; a vibrant public culture; and the entire gamut of public goods and services that had been included along with income in the idea of *the social wage*'.[152] Concepts of equality and social provision increasingly seemed like mere chimeras. As people were forced to protect 'their own', she describes them 'jettisoning their stake in public goods and services, which were increasingly viewed as benefiting others'.[153]

The consequences were disastrous for poor women. Teresa Amott shows that Reagan's measures not only cut AFDC recipients off but meant that the value of benefits was reduced in real terms. The end result was to be that everyone, except the very rich, paid more tax.

Reaganism was politically opportunistic rather than ideologically coherent. If an extreme individualism upheld the rights of Dr Stern's middle-class sperm, a patriarchal authoritarianism denied poor women the individual right to choose to be mothers. Bearing children came to be equated with causing poverty. As poverty was clearly the fault of the poor themselves, the organization of society was conveniently exonerated from responsibility. This punitive spirit was evident in the approach to low-income mothers who took drugs and drank alcohol. From 1987 they were prosecuted, fined and even jailed, and their babies could be removed at birth. As many poor women were black, these policies had a racist component too. Instead of being seen as individuals with legitimate needs as carers, they were treated as inadequate, inefficient reproducers who deserved retribution.

The mix of authoritarian communalism and the individualism of the competitive work ethic enabled Reagan to cobble together big-business interests and right-wing populism. Gary Bauer, head of family policy in the Education Department under Reagan, talked much about values. He announced there was 'a lot of research' which indicated that they were 'much more important, say, than the level of welfare payments'.[154] The difference was, of course, that values did not buy you or your children breakfast. Again reality had slipped behind the image of make-believe. Gary Bauer thought the answer to America's welfare miasma was *The Cosby Show*, which featured glamorous black professional life. The programme was one of Reagan's favourites too.

'Values', however, had gone sour for anti-gay campaigner Anita Bryant. She was divorced, without a job and disowned by the church which had made thousands of dollars from her name. She began to comprehend the people she had once despised as perverted: 'Fundamentalists have their head in the sand.... Some pastors are so hard-nosed about submission and insensitive to their wives' needs that they don't recognize the frustration – even hatred – within their own households.'[155] Rosalind Petchesky makes the point that the new right traditionalists also had their heads in the sand about the main reason women were poor – those low-paid, high-turnover service jobs which were an integral part of Reaganomics.

Disintegration and devastation, accompanied by tragic and unnecessary death and suffering, took a destructive toll; lack of adequate health care, bad housing, homelessness, AIDS, the impact of crack and gang warfare were just some of the accumulative problems facing poor women. It was as if they were living through a war. Martine Barrat took a portrait photograph of Vickie Alvarez, who died of AIDS in 1993. She was the sixth child of Irene Alvarez Perito to die between 1985 and 1993. 'She was so dear to my heart,'[156] Vickie's mother told the photographer. Richard Younge, an African-American doctor working in a community health centre in the Bronx, where 'the AIDS statistics all had people's faces',[157] related the story of 'Mrs M.', a woman in her fifties, caring for her daughter's baby, Anthony. Her daughter had died of AIDS in 1989 and there was a likelihood that the child would be HIV-positive, but, 'She will be there for him no matter what his HIV status may be.'[158]

Amidst the social crisis of the poor, Temma Kaplan noted a new communalism – movements placing 'human survival and improving the quality of life rather than ideological struggles at the forefront of politics'.[159] Poor people fought for basic needs – for housing, health care and an unpolluted environment – and in the process came up against the arbitrary power of the market. For example, in 1988, when tenants in East 136th Street in the Bronx resisted eviction from an old building they had renovated, the stakes were high for them as many faced homelessness: 'Our homes are just trading chips to these guys,' said tenants' leader Bertha Lewis. 'It's like they're playing some huge Monopoly game.'[160] The claim for social rights was resuscitated out of bitter experience. In 1984 in Massachusetts welfare mothers and their supporters slept at the State House to protest against lack of housing. In Brooklyn activists organized families in welfare hotels who barricaded themselves in. In New Hampshire groups such as Parents for Justice and others set up an independent state commission to determine the real costs of raising children. The National Welfare Rights Union was established in 1987.

In the same year a report, 'Toxic Waste and Race in the United States', produced by the United Church of Christ Commission for Racial Justice, pointed to the sites of hazardous waste and identified 'environmental racism'.[161] In 1988 a series of Great Louisiana Toxics Marches, initiated by the Gulf Coast Tenants' Project in New Orleans, brought together tenants, trade unionists, church members and civil rights activists with Greenpeace and the Sierra Club in massive demonstrations through Louisiana's 'Cancer Alley'. These multiracial coalitions transformed the class base of the National Toxics Campaign. Jessie Deer-in-Water, who became involved in the environmental justice movement, was part Irish-American and part Native American. She recalled, 'I was born not knowing anything but a racial memory of struggling.'[162] When campaigner Cora Tucker was called 'an hysterical housewife', she threw it right back: 'If men don't get hysterical, there's something wrong with them.'[163]

All these rebels were up against a system of power which castigated

Journeys

The author of the biographical *Migrations of the Heart: A Personal Odyssey* (1983), Marita Golden, stated that an important element in her writing was women 'who find themselves in negotiating the tension between personal and political choices and are compelled to leave home to further their self-definition'.[164]

Leaving home had a metaphorical as well as literal significance in the literature of the 1980s. For several black women writers it involved an exploration of the past. Toni Cade Bambara, Gloria Naylor, Maya Angelou, Alice Walker and Toni Morrison all looked back autobiographically or historically in a search for understanding and identity. Octavia Butler's *Wild Seed* (1980) unusually brought the historical experience of slavery into science fantasy. Anyanwu, a powerful healer, is appropriated by Doro, a genetic breeder. She escapes, after bearing his children, by shape-changing and remains in the crevices of the world, shifting identity. Recaptured, she eventually leaves home by choosing death.

The sense of enclosure and the impossibility of effective active resistance permeates the Canadian author Margaret Atwood's *Bodily Harm* (1983) and *The Handmaid's Tale* (1985), while *Life before Man* (1983) is set in the Royal Ontario Museum – a labyrinth in which all the maps are out of date. During the 1960s and 1970s women's Utopian science fantasy had frequently featured rural communities, without hierarchy or government. Some of these motherist worlds harboured an oppressive irrationalism and essentialism which could smother deviance, but the much gloomier dystopias of the 1980s suggested that the only hope was grim survival. The world had assumed the oppressive ethos of a shopping mall with the exits blocked, transforming into a junkyard at the end of history.

Escape in such circumstances assumed a high priority. But if the imagination was leaving home, it was not heading for the localism of 1970s-style alternative culture. It was going into the mainstream. As bell hooks remarked of black women's creativity, it was not so much absence as audience that had been the problem: 'our speech' had been 'soliloquy . . . talk in thin air'.[165] Black American women were reaching a mass audience in the United States and internationally. A notable example was Alice Walker's novel *The Color Purple*, which became a popular film in 1985, starring Whoopi Goldberg.

Suzette Elgin, author of *Native Tongues*, thought about writing in *Family Circle* but decided that science fiction was to be her chosen medium. Her aim was to 'reach a wider audience'.[166] Science fiction/fantasy and thrillers were two popular genres through which powerful female characters reached a mass audience in the 1980s. They were frequently outsiders, like the witch/prophetess or the female aliens drawn from 1950s pulp fiction or the 1930s hard-boiled investigator, maintaining integrity amidst urban rot. Sara Paretsky's Polish-Irish V. I. Warshawski was a female version of the loner detective.

Female power in both popular genres was increasingly presented as an individual quest, a psychological process of self-discovery, a journey inwards. Freedom became symbolic space, which meant vacating real life, sometimes breaking with the body and biology altogether, and the key to transformation was language. Suzette Elgin speculated that if a language expressing 'the perceptions of women' could be introduced into American culture, it would 'destruct and change radically'.[167] The poet Denise Levertov suggested, 'A line of peace might appear/if we restructured the sentence our lives are making'.[168] Others, less sure that a women's culture was in abeyance, saw no exit except by subverting through the imagination, collecting by chance the metaphors dumped as junk.

✳

them as dysfunctional people. Writing in the *Black Scholar* in 1988, Julianne Malveaux commented:

The poor no longer come to us as supplicants on one knee, willing to do anything for a little welfare change. Some stand before us as angry as the agitators of the sixties, speaking of the homeless unions, jobless unions and dignity. In response, many who write about public policy recoil and talk about 'behavior'.[169]

One group who knew all too well about the power of definitions was lesbians. Less prepared than in the 1970s to say how lesbianism should be lived, many knew how important it was to create shelter. Lillian Faderman quotes one thirty-six-year-old woman, 'I'm much closer to my lesbian friends than I am to my family . . . Most of my friends I've known for ten or twelve years. We're really family.'[170] In America in the late 1980s, there were family values and there were family values.

Sex

In 1982 at Barnard College, New York, a feminist conference, 'Towards a Politics of Sexuality', was held. It proved to be a traumatic event; the politics of sexuality divided feminists so bitterly that the conference was picketed by the Coalition for a Feminist Sexuality and Against Sadomasochism (Women Against Violence Against Women, Women Against Pornography and New York Radical Feminists). Lynne Segal comments, 'Participation in the event proved a near disaster for some speakers. Individual women were denounced and condemned, their employers contacted, careers and livelihoods threatened, as their feminist opponents deployed straightforwardly McCarthyite tactics to try to silence them.'[171]

The co-ordinator, Carole Vance, tried to steer through two polarities which had been present throughout the long struggle of women to redefine and determine their sexuality: 'To focus only on pleasure and gratification ignores the patriarchal structure in which women act, yet to speak only of sexual violence and oppression ignores women's experience of sexual agency and choice and unwittingly increases the sexual terror and despair in which women live.'[172]

It was to be an extremely difficult route to pursue. On the side of permission were the promises of fulfilment in advertising images which presented an increasingly sophisticated iconography of desire, sex manuals which promised success in bed and the multifarious and ingenious ramifications of the sex business. The voice of prohibition, on the other hand, was that of fundamentalist Christianity and the new right. As Teddi Holt put it, 'It is Satan who stands behind these two movements in our nation, and he seeks to destroy the "Home", God's first institution.'[173] It really amounted to a choice between the devil and the deep blue sea.

One escape route seemed to be to dump all the earnest 'personal is political' stuff of the 1970s. The term 'post-feminism'[174] was coined by journalist Susan Bolotin in 1982 and it stuck. Journalists, ever in the business of finding new trends, were happy to consign feminism to the 1970s, and some young women agreed it was a bore: 'Girls Just Want to Have Fun' sang Cyndi Lauper in 1983. However, this was easier said than done as the female punk band the Runaways discovered. When they were interviewed, singer Joan Jett remembers, 'The first question would be, "I heard you girls are all sluts, right?"'[175] The old 'Madonna/whore' divide still lurked behind both the permissive and the prohibitive attitudes to women's sexuality, leaving no space for irony, as Madonna discovered in the early 1980s. Her Boy Toy slogan on the belt buckle positioned on her then raunchy and slightly podgy bare midriff was denounced by other women performers as reactionary. 'They didn't get the joke,'[176] she complained to *Cosmopolitan* magazine.

But women still could not just simply be sexy and call the shots. One wing of the feminist movement, including Gloria Steinem, decided that girls' fun was different from boys'. Women were turned on not by pornography but by erotica. This cleaned-up aesthetic-type dirt, more democratic, more equal, might be a political compromise, but the problem was that inconveniently not all women found it sexy. A defiant minority were left proclaiming the existence of a split between lust and liberal permission. Cindy Patton worked on the lesbian pornography magazine *Bad Attitude* and she told Sue O'Sullivan in 1990 that they had aimed 'to give women space to talk about their sexuality and develop a language, not impose one'.[177] In contrast, feminist opponents of pornography, like Catherine MacKinnon and Andrea Dworkin, believed that it was inherently oppressive – part of the culture of subordination which objectified and degraded women. They stressed themes of violence and control, and Andrea Dworkin made a further connection in *Pornography: Men Possessing Women* (1981) to human beings' control over animals. Both Dworkin and MacKinnon argued that pornographic images contributed to the continuing oppression of women and that fantasies of domination were part of a continuum of male violence. In Minneapolis in 1983 they invoked civil rights to ban pornography and convinced the civil council. Pornography was defined as 'the sexually explicit subordination of women, graphically depicted'.[178] Other cities followed, amidst furious disputes. Conservative opponents of sexually explicit images, which they saw as inciting lust and crime, were denouncing CBS and Coca-Cola and also trying to extend the obscenity laws. The Meese Commission began public hearings in six US cities in 1985 and women's sexuality came out, along with porn, into a courtroom, where it was put on trial. Bizarre scenes ensued as the conservative panellists tried to get a ban on vibrators, rejected the case made by the US Prostitutes' Collective and COYOTE for decriminalization and listened to Andrea Dworkin and Catherine MacKinnon testifying against pornography. Carole Vance observes, 'Witnesses alternated between chronicling the negative effects of pornography and making sensationalized presentations of "it". Taking a lead from feminist anti-pornography groups, everyone had a slide show: the FBI, the US Customs Service, the US Postal Service and sundry vice squads.'[179] The Meese Report sold like hot cakes, though the Supreme Court in 1986 rejected the case for discrimination.

The political passion aroused by pornography made it difficult to consider more calmly the relationship between sexual fantasies and culture. The inspiration gained from the new left slogan 'the personal is political' had run into troubled ground by the 1980s. Muriel Dimen commented in 1986, 'The psyche is not a microcosm of social life, nor is the world a psyche writ large.'[180] She argued for interaction rather than for collapsing one into the other.

Conflict between feminists coincided with a profoundly conservative backlash repudiating the optimistic hope that human beings could experience relationships which were more equal, less guilty or more pleasurable. Amidst the sexual crisis, which accompanied the social crisis among America's abandoned citizens, it seemed that danger was everywhere. The fear of violence in the cities was accompanied by the fear and guilt which AIDS evoked. AIDS emerged first as an epidemic among homosexual and bisexual males, but spread rapidly in poor communities. People suffering from AIDS thus often had unequal access to care. Moreover, men were much more visible than women with the HIV virus – 'a forgotten group'[181] in the words of physicians Kathryn Anastos and Carola Marte. They showed in their article 'Women: The Missing Persons in the AIDS Epidemic' in 1989 that women's symptoms were being interpreted differently from men's 'because women are not expected to have AIDS'[182] and that the effect of AIDS symptoms on gynaecological disease was largely unknown.

The difficulties in dealing with the AIDS epidemic were accentuated by the collapse of welfare services, including health care, by homelessness, unemployment, drug addiction and despair. The right's suspicion of sex education also made safe-sex information more difficult to disseminate. But there were also powerful cultural prejudices operating which defined AIDS as a sexual punishment. It became associated with people branded as outcasts because of their sexual

Delia, a mother with AIDS, reading to her daughter,
Lower East Side, New York. Delia died in 1989.

choice, because they used drugs, were homeless or were prostitutes. Of course, women could become HIV-positive because of their partners, because they were raped or had blood transfusions, but the stereotypes remained. They concealed individuals, like Delia, an African-American mother of five children who became infected through drug use. She lived in a shantytown in New York's Lower East Side in a shack she built with her boyfriend Michael. She mourned Michael's death, before dying herself on 30 December 1989, aged thirty-six. Her name, along with those of her neighbours, was inscribed on the wall of her shelter, the marks of the people America wanted to forget. The consequences of ostracism were to be tragic. By 1988 AIDS was the ninth leading cause of death among children aged one–four and the seventh among young people aged fifteen–twenty-four.

By the late 1980s the drug economy had taken hold of many poor areas, providing the only hope of employment for many young black men. The crack epidemic contributed to crime and to prostitution. Young women and teenage girls exchanged sex for a dollar or a 'hit' in the crack houses, and their partners could well be men who used needles to inject drugs. The organization formed to stop drug abuse, ADAPT, the Association for Drug Abuse and Treatment, reported that some prostitutes were as young as ten, passing for seventeen. Sexual exploitation was thus embedded in a scenario of social disintegration which neither the moral right's rhetoric nor the demands formulated by the women's movement from the 1970s addressed.

Photographers and film-makers recorded and bore witness. GIRLTALK, a film made by Kate Davis and Alyson Denny in 1989, looked at the lives of three young women as the decade ended. Pinky, fourteen, a truant and runaway from a brutal home, was living on the street, sleeping in an alley with rats. Mars, raped by her stepfather at twelve and gang-raped by six men, was at thirteen strip-teasing in a bar dressed as a child, saying 'Thank you, Daddy' after simulating sex with her father. Martha, the oldest, abused by her adoptive father sexually and physically, had left home at twelve and had a baby at eighteen. The Women's Crisis Line in Oregon objected to the film as 'exploitative'.[183] Martha wrote to them, saying, '[What we] wanted was someone to listen to us and accept us despite our pasts, our problems and the ways we chose to deal with them' and that the film-makers had done this;

she added, 'GIRLTALK is a film about inspiration and desperation. It poses many questions that only society can answer. Yes, GIRLTALK is disturbing – it's supposed to be. Reality is often disturbing, with no clear explanation.'[184]

Sex workers had their own job hierarchies and were far from all being helpless victims. Women who became prostitutes in their twenties were more likely to see themselves as making choices within certain confines. AIDS did add to the perils of their work, but they were adamant that they wanted improvement of conditions through decriminalization, not state regulation. One consequence of AIDS, obscured in an atmosphere of moral panic, was that it contributed to a more diversified sex business. While prostitutes were being branded as carriers of AIDS, other aspects of the sex trade were being normalized. Not only did sex therapies and sexual experts blossom but, as Rosalyn Baxandall noted, so did 'non-contact sex: telephone sex, 900 numbers, sex cable stations, mail-order porn, home-made pornographic videos and so on'.[185] 'Look but don't touch,' sang rapper Roxanne.

Pleasure, then, was as present as danger. Carole Vance argues that the 'hallmark of sexuality is its complexity: its multiple meanings, sensations and connections'.[186] It was to be primarily lesbian women like Joan Nestle who found the outlaw courage to explore where the further parameters of pleasure might lead. For despite all the hearings and declarations, the voices of heterosexual women were barely present within feminist discussion of sexual pleasure. Occasionally they speak from the wings: 'I like penetration because it feels warm and sweet and mutual', 'It's an intimate closeness, one is kind of enfolding the other person.'[187] But these testimonies appeared in *The Hite Report on Female Sexuality* under the heading 'Sexual Slavery'! As Lynne Segal points out, Shere Hite's focus on physiology, in the tradition of behaviourist sex studies, obliterated sensual sensibility. Nuances of sexual feeling and the emotional complexities facing American women in relationships were being deposited with poets and novelists. Here questions could be asked without offering easy answers. In *A Woman's Place* (1986), for instance, Marita Golden's character Serena ponders, 'How do women survive being considered superfluous yet claimed as indispensable?'[188]

Chapter 10

1990–95

BRITAIN AND
THE UNITED STATES

The British media increasingly took its cue from US-style opinion journalism by the early 1990s. Consequently not only were fact and fiction being scrambled as 'info-tainment' but the British received a version of themselves from a mid-Atlantic perspective. If it was happening (or said to be happening) in the United States, then it was news in Britain too in the 1990s. As a result, distinguishing between the actual similarities or differences structuring women's lives in the two countries increasingly resembles an archaeological dig through half-truths. Moreover, in both countries the media invariably treated the position of women as a separate agenda, whereas the destinies of women were, as ever, bound up with wider economic changes and affected by political choices. The extent of social provision and the manner in which the public sector was regarded, for instance, impinged upon women's lives in both countries.

In November 1990 Margaret Thatcher was forced to resign. John Major, her successor, faced a deepening economic recession: home-owners could not afford their mortgage payments, businesses collapsed and government revenues had fallen. The Thatcherite economic miracle was rapidly appearing as a disaster; Margaret Thatcher was inclined to think that her greatest achievement had been 'changing attitudes'.[1]

Attitudes, however, are notoriously mercurial: the *British Attitudes Survey* of 1991, for instance, found that support for state provision of welfare had increased. The British remained particularly attached to their health service and more people said they would be prepared to pay

Living rough, Waterloo Station, south London: thousands of
homeless people sleep on the streets of Britain's cities.

more taxes to keep the public provision of services. A high proportion
favoured government intervention in industry and there was growing
acceptance of redistribution through taxation to help the have-nots.
Women wanted nurseries, holiday-care arrangements, workplaces able
to adjust to family responsibilities and more help at home from men.
Those with young children would on the whole have preferred to stay
at home. In 1992 John Major and the Conservatives were once more
elected. The new leader was an unknown factor who seemed to be
mildly sympathetic to child-care, to women getting on, to anti-racism
and to gays. He did allow child benefits to rise with inflation but broadly
continued the restrictive policies of the Thatcher years towards welfare
and the workplace. A diffuse commitment to social welfare among the
British public, however, checked him, as it had Margaret Thatcher,
from completely dismantling the welfare state.

Despite the convergence in right-wing policies, the context was not
the same in the two countries. In the United States the argument for
even minimal social entitlement had always been harder to make. In
1992, when Bill Clinton replaced George Bush, it seemed as if there

was at last a chance for a social health scheme. The Democrats again had attracted more women voters than men. Women were still more inclined to favour social measures than men, and with a certain amount of pushing, the new President did appoint several women to important administrative positions. Among them was his wife, Hillary Clinton.

Both Clinton and Major were to be diverted from domestic social problems by the Gulf War and by challenges from a resurgent right. In Britain this took the form of opposition to closer integration in Europe and pressure to continue privatization despite its unpopularity. In the United States it manifested itself in an extreme hostility to social welfare and to government. By 1994 any aroma of care had been wafted away and President Clinton's plans for health had been shredded by the powerful insurance-company lobby. In November the Republican sweep signalled discontent with Clinton and the Democrats, particularly among white men, though the Republican right did have support from women too. A group of women in their twenties and thirties, for instance, played a high-profile role in the Republican victory on the National Congressional Committee: Maria Cino, Ann McCord, Julie Wadler and Susan Tyndall.

The tensions around gender and race occupied centre-stage in US politics; in Britain they impinged on society from the wings. As Republicans took control of both the House and the Senate, Newt Gingrich orchestrated a veritable panic about affirmative-action programmes, social welfare and crime. The scapegoating of vulnerable groups held responsible for the taxes of those who were better off was to falter slightly by 1995 after the shock of the bombing of the Ohio child-care centre by a right-wing extremist. The cuts were also bringing home how the middle classes, and not just the poor, benefited from public funding. The right had, however, touched a profound chord of anxiety about identity and gender relations. A sense of loss, of disempowerment, of the need to recast manhood, was appearing from differing places in American cultures. This was not only expressed in articles and books such as Robert Bly's *Iron John*; in July 1994 52,000 men each paid $75 (nearly £50) to sit in the Folsom Stadium in Boulder, Colorado. The Promise Keepers braved temperatures of 95 degrees, not to watch some vital football match but to meet God and find a new role as male heads of the household. In the words of Pastor Tony Evans of Texas, 'a spiritually pure man' was one who sat down with his wife to say, 'Honey, I've made a terrible mistake. I've given you my role. I gave up leading this family and I forced you to take my place. Now I must reclaim that role.'[2]

The following year saw the million-men march converging on Washington mobilized by Louis Farrakhan of the Nation of Islam. Both white and black men in these groups stressed a crisis in personal behaviour as the problem. However, in an article entitled 'Can We Still Win the War Against Poverty?' in the magazine *Dollars and Sense* in 1995, Marc Breslow pointed to an interesting material factor: 'Since 1972 the median income of all men aged 25–34 (adjusted for inflation) has dropped by an astounding 26%. The wages of fully one-third of men in this age group are below the poverty line in a family of four.'[3] Women's earnings were thus crucial in keeping families out of poverty. But women's wages were low and the pressure to take paid work ignored looking after children. The Luxembourg Income Study Group found that American women were slower to return to work after childbirth than Europeans because of the lack of inexpensive high-quality child-care. It also revealed that poor children in the United States were poorer than those in other Western industrialized countries (apart from Ireland), because the gap between the rich and poor was more marked and welfare less generous.

The emphasis on behaviour was also evident in the scapegoating of welfare mothers for social breakdown. This obscured the way in which poverty was structured into the core of society because of low wages. It also distorted the significance of welfare payments. In a powerful advertisement in the *New York Times* in August 1995, the Women's Committee of One Hundred, a group of scholars and activists, pointed out that welfare to single mothers made up 'just 1% of the federal budget – 3% if food stamps are included'.[4] There was a particular focus on teenage single mothers after President Clinton, in an unpleasant bid to outdo the right by a spasm of moral authoritarianism, announced that they should be made to go home to their parents. This not only ignored the uncomfortable fact that many of them had not left home sweet home but violent and abusive adults; it was also, as the Women's Committee of One Hundred noted, not an extensive problem in terms of welfare. Only 8 per cent of welfare mothers were teenagers in 1995.

The numbers of single mothers had certainly risen, but fewer than a third were under nineteen. In *Dubious Conceptions*, Kristin Luker documented how a crisis of social inequality was being cloaked in rhetoric of hypocritical moral indignation about the supposed sexual profligacy of the young.

Britain had been moving during the 1980s in a similar direction to the United States as the disparity in wealth became more marked. By the early 1990s, Jane Millar and Caroline Glendinning pointed out, 12 million people, or around one in five, lived 'in poverty or in circumstances so constrained and restricted that poverty is just a step away'[5] – ten years before the figure had been 5 million. Poverty and inequality had increased partly because of structural changes in the labour market but also because of government policies. Unemployment, the decline in public provision and the shift towards privatization had all materially affected the quality of people's lives and resulted in a pervasive sense of social disintegration and decay.

As in the United States, there was a powerful inclination to blame the poor rather than to challenge the distribution of economic and social resources. During 1994 several religious figures, prominent

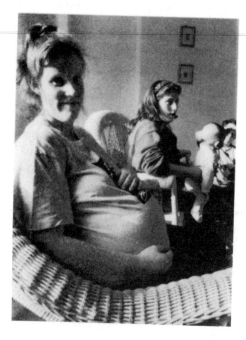

Practical help instead of punitive values: teenage mothers' safe house, Leeds.

Conservatives and the new Labour leader Tony Blair, taking their cue from the United States, deplored the prevalence of single-parent families. The press took up the issue of young, poor single mothers who were defrauding the country of its council housing by presuming to breed. There were more single mothers, but many were employed and though there had been a slight increase of teenage pregnancies between 1980 and 1990, in the early 1990s the numbers actually fell again. As in the United States, the sexuality of the young became a political gambit to attack a group whose circumstances made it difficult for them to retaliate. The issue did, however, provoke an interesting division in the Conservative Party. Peter Lilley on the right wanted tough and punitive measures; Virginia Bottomley disagreed. So did a Conservative council-lor in Shrewsbury, Eileen Sandford, who accused her own party and Labour leader Tony Blair of a 'lack of understanding of the real prob-lems facing young and older lone mothers'; having been on the bor-ough council for twelve years, she said, she had 'not met one young mother who deliberately had a baby in order to obtain a house'.[6]

The state's intervention in the realm of moral responsibility hit sticky ground in the attempt to make fathers pay for their children. There was an evident injustice in the way in which the cost of bringing up children was being disproportionately borne by women, but the Child Support Act (1991) was more concerned with cutting state benefits by compelling women to name fathers. Modelled on Reagan's measure, it disregarded US evidence of the problems and costs of implementation. It was guided by the same ideological conviction that families should bear all the cost and responsibility of children with no help from the rest of society. The real needs of children were not the main concern. The act was supported by some women because they thought men ought to pay more towards their children's upbringing, but others opposed it because they did not want an enforced dependence. The cost of administering the search for fathers was considerable and those who could be traced tended to be the ones who were already paying. It provoked a furious reaction, not only from fathers, who were faced with higher maintenance, but from second wives. In October 1994 the feminist journalist Angela Phillips argued that the Child Support Agency was in fact a means of 'easing lone parents into work'[7] which tended to be low-paid and not necessarily an improvement in the lives of the children. The debate in Britain began to echo that in the United States in which the reproductive inclinations of the poor were increasingly being branded as the cause of economic and social problems.

The crucial difference, however, was that the emotion generated against AFDC was accompanied in the United States by the escalating violence of the anti-abortion campaigners. The issue of control over reproduction thus occupied an antipodal political terrain. Attacks on clinics, violent picketing and the murder of a doctor were resisted by mass mobilization of pro-choice activists and by the tenacious resolve of some workers in the clinics to continue despite death threats. In 1992 the Supreme Court did uphold Roe by a narrow 5–4 decision, but with the proviso that states could introduce a mandatory waiting period which would block early abortions. By 1995, however, the threat of direct action from extremist anti-abortion groups like Operation Rescue meant that fewer centres were in existence; the risk was too great. Even in New York, which had been crucial in the Women's Liberation agitation for legal abortion, many hospitals no longer trained gynaecology students to perform abortions. Norma McCorvey (the real Jane Roe)

Around 800,000 people marched to Washington, DC, to campaign for safe, legal and accessible abortion and reproductive freedom, April 1992.

had gone to work in an abortion clinic but, upset by late terminations and drawn to the evangelical ethos of care she encountered in Operation Rescue groups, was baptized by Philip Benham amidst a blaze of publicity. The fact that she lived in a lesbian relationship of twenty-five years' standing and was still in favour of early abortion made her an unconventional convert.

Though Operation Rescue sent members to agitate in Britain, the situation was very different. Anja Hohmeyer, writing on the National Abortion Campaign, cited a 1991 Harris poll in which '81% of the adult population agreed that women should make their own decision on abortion'.[8] The great majority of abortions were performed within thirteen weeks. The main problem was that cuts in the health service meant that many women were paying all or some of the cost in order to avoid delay. In Ireland, however, abortion was still a divisive issue. Thousands of women continued to come to England from the South of Ireland, where, despite the efforts of campaigners, abortion was still illegal, and from the North, where the 1967 act did not apply and abortions were difficult to obtain. Despite the feeling in the South about the case of a young girl who was raped and the evidence of sexual abuse within the Catholic hierarchy, the Catholic Church's opposition to abortion continued to prevent a change in the law.

In the early 1990s the impressive mobilization against the anti-abortionists and anger against the treatment of Anita Hill when she testified against Clarence Thomas's sexual harassment in 1990 led to a revival in US feminist organizations. There was widespread awareness of a backlash against women's equal rights and sexual autonomy and NOW decided to focus on political pressure. In an article on US feminism in the 1990s published in the *New Left Review* in 1993, Johanna Brenner notes that the feminist ' "Emily's List" (Early Money is Like Yeast)'[9] had raised a record $6 million for women Democratic candidates during 1992. In 1992 many more women (108) ran for Congress and there was an improvement in the numbers in both the Senate and the House of Representatives, though women were still only 6 per cent of the total in the former and 11 per cent in the latter. Clinton appointed five women to the Cabinet, and though the inner circle of advisers remained male, the evident feminist sympathies of Hillary Clinton contributed to a renewed hope that the pendulum was swinging back towards a pro-women's rights policy.

John Major, like his predecessor, had not initially promoted women. But in 1991 he endorsed Opportunity 2000, which aimed to encourage the appointment of women to prominent positions. Gillian Shephard was made Employment Secretary in 1992 with responsibility for women. Labour's Betty Boothroyd became the first woman Speaker in the House of Commons in 1992. The Liberal Democrats and Greens nominated more women candidates, though these were, of course, unlikely to win elections. A determined effort by Labour women resulted in a target of 50 per cent being set for the year 2000 and Labour adopted women-only lists of candidates in an effort to make the Commons more representative. (This was later declared to be illegal, ironically because of sex-discrimination legislation.) The scale of lobbying for equal opportunities in Britain was never as great as that in the United States, but the early 1990s did see two very different women in high public office. Stella Rimington was made head of MI5 and the prominent feminist and socialist Helena Kennedy was made a QC.

In Britain as well as in the United States, there was talk of a 'backlash' against women in the early 1990s. However, in Britain liberal feminism had never made the same impact on mainstream institutions, though it had acquired support in the liberal media. The problem with demands which would have improved the lives of the majority of women was the isolation and powerlessness of trade unions and the left inside and outside the Labour Party. This made it more difficult to challenge injustice and inequality of all kinds or to present realistic alternatives. Moreover, in both countries, the modest gains of a minority of women in the political public arena were accompanied by a resurgent cultural conservatism which set strict limits on the terms of political debate. 'PC', a term which had been used by feminists in the 1980s against sexual puritanism within women's groups, was appropriated by the right in the United States to challenge the minimal gains in equal rights made by blacks, women and gays. In Britain it was used against left-wing arguments for social equality which had made headway in local government. It was not simply a matter of ridiculing cant and arrogance (as evident on the right as on the left after all); 'PC' was used as an effective ploy against any defiance of prejudice and inequality. In this context, organizations which had dwelt in the moderate centre, such as the Fawcett Society, rooted in early-twentieth-century liberal feminism, or local voluntary groups, such as the Low Pay Units, assumed an increasingly strategic position. It was the Fawcett Society which raised the inequality in women's pensions, for instance, low-pay campaigners who backed the demand for the minimum wage and women in local homeworking groups who publicized the conditions of homeworkers. In the media a notable survivor of serious investigative journalism through the Thatcher years had been *Woman's Hour*, in the 1990s Jenni Murray continued to present a fair-minded pro-woman programme which had a broad and democratic appeal.

Gender inequality did, however, hit the most conservative institutions in the first half of the 1990s. For example, in the United States women in the CIA took an action suit out against their employer for denying them advancement and the US army was embarrassed by a charge of forced sodomy by a woman serving in the Gulf War. In Britain the Ministry of Defence was compelled to pay out large sums because women had been forced illegally to resign from the armed forces when they became pregnant and there were accusations of sexual harassment and rape in the legal profession.

But while issues of equal opportunity, discrimination and sexual harassment became news, there were new problems emerging. The arrival of more women in the executive and managerial jobs, which had typified the women-on-top ethos of the 1980s, was not to be a simple success story. In both countries discrimination in pay levels with their male counterparts increased in the higher echelons. Also their relative privilege was far from secure. In 1993 the percentage of women in management in Britain fell from 10.2 to 9.5. Women who had made it into moderately well-paid posts in the finance sector in London were the first to go as the economy slumped in 1993. These graduate middle managers were surplus to requirements.

The tendency for inequality between women workers continued. The restructuring of clerical employment made possible by new technology was changing the type of work in offices and the way it was distributed. While it had created a stratum of lower-grade managers, it was also eliminating some clerical jobs. The increase in low-paid service

Low-paid ancillary workers in Unison picketing at Hillingdon Hospital, west London, 1996: several of the women involved in the lengthy strike against pay cuts had resisted privatization in the early 1980s.

jobs, evident in the 1980s, also continued, despite Britain's recession. The case for a minimum wage was countered by claims from employers that this would create only more unemployment and set back Britain's economic recovery. Thus after the abolition of the Wages Councils in January 1993, Britain had no regulatory mechanism to prevent wages being pushed down, and women, of course, were still concentrated in low-paid employment. In autumn 1995 cleaners at Hillingdon Hospital in west London went on strike after a contract cleaning firm, Pall Mall, cut their already low wages. In December 1995 the National Home-working Group reported that women were packing tights at home for 36p an hour. In the United States the minimum wage had fallen in value and was being evaded. In 1995, for example, seventy-two Thai women in a Los Angeles clothing sweatshop were discovered working eighteen hours a day in slave-like conditions. Yet the US model of private-sector jobs was presented by the Conservatives as the answer to unemployment and economic growth.

Not only pay but the issue of time was of crucial significance for women. By 1995 the British, who had the longest working week in

Europe, were moving towards the pattern in the United States, where the hours worked had greatly increased from the 1970s. Women's entry into the labour force and the introduction of new technology were not accompanied by reduced hours for men. The result was, as Juliet Schor pointed out in *A Sustainable Economy*, that 'families are experiencing a sharp time squeeze'.[10] If some people had too much to do, others had too little because they were unemployed. The decline in the British economy had been a long, slow process; in the United States it was a more recent occurrence. The poor, labelled as the 'under class' and contained in urban ghettos or trailer parks, were joined by a new poor comprising working-class people for whom male unemployment brought fear of poverty and dread of old age. The shock of a decline in living standards provoked a bitter hostility among Americans which was frequently aimed at those most vulnerable. The absence of social provision meant this was a terrible country in which to become poor.

Unemployment remained high, however, in Britain and as public provision was reduced, poor urban areas were beginning to resemble

Home is a converted bus in Greenwood, West Virginia.

the devastation of US inner cities. Crime became a major concern and in 1991 riots exploded in Cardiff, Oxford and Tyneside. 'I need a job, me, I really do,'[11] declared Tracy Grafton from the Thorntree Estate, Middlesbrough, in 1992. Aged twenty-one, she had been on the dole since losing her job as a cleaner. She and her friends spent their time sitting in each other's houses. When they could afford it they went to the pub: 'Once in a blue moon we go nightclubbing. We go out as a group of lasses, have a laugh and mess around. I was going out with a lad for two years. He got put away for burglary and twocs [stolen cars]. He's on the run now.'[12]

A noticeable change from the 1980s was that poverty and homelessness were matters of public concern again in Britain. Wealth was no longer something to boast about. The fashionable were dressing down in the 1990s. *The Times* quoted Lisa Armstrong from *Vogue* in November 1994:

The charity-go-round in London is . . . one of the few contexts in which a black tie and real evening gowns are still the norm . . . British women, so often racked with guilt when it comes to spending money on their wardrobe, don't seem to suffer the same qualms when it's all in a good cause.[13]

While the upper-class Sloanes headed off to Calcutta to work with Mother Teresa, an uneasy realization was dawning among those in the middle stratum of both societies that market values offered a viable lifestyle only to a minority of the very rich. A new ethical tone in politics appeared to be the order of the day. Prime Minister Major declared it was time to get back to basics, while President Clinton and the Democrats competed with the Republicans as the upholders of family values – though a series of sexual scandals made the high moral stance difficult to sustain. New Labour, clean-cut and besuited, borrowed from the Democrats an air of scrubbed virtue and talk of values, moral and communal. Some of these were not new at all, being part of Labour's ethical socialist traditions, while others had originated more ominously in the 1980s think tanks of the US new right.

There were, however, powerful forces in both societies which were leading towards atomization. More women and men were living alone than twenty years before. Insurance companies and advertisers, realizing that single middle-class people were the ones with money to spare, targeted them as prime consumers. Unlike spinsterhood, which implied failure, the 1990s *femme seule* was the successful one, which perhaps explains why *Thelma and Louise* (1991) was the surprise hit film of the early 1990s. The trend towards individual autonomy had been assimilated by the young and there were signs of shifts in gender attitudes which had both positive and negative results. In 1991, when Sue Sharpe returned to interview British schoolgirls for a new edition of *Just Like a Girl*, one told her, 'I don't want to get married. I don't see the point in getting married. You could live with someone, then if it broke up it's easier than going through divorce, half this and half that.'[14]

A nationwide *New York Times/CBS News* poll of 1,055 teenagers found that 55 per cent of the girls would consider becoming a single parent and that girls were more inclined to be in favour of divorce than boys. Girls were more confident and motivated at school. By the mid-1990s teachers were anxiously searching for the causes of *boys'* not girls' under-achievement. At the same time, a 1994 study in Britain undertaken by Manchester University's Social Work and Social Policy Unit found that girls aged fifteen–seventeen were more likely to have tried cannabis and Ecstasy than boys of the same age. There was evidence too that British women were drinking more. By the mid-1990s, men were the ones more likely to be calling the Samaritans than women, while the tabloids discovered girl gangs in November 1994 when actress Liz Hurley was mugged. The Peckham Rude girls and the Chippies emulated US gangs like the Los Angeles Lady Rascal Gangsters.

The incongruence in gender identity was reaching down the age range. In 1994–5 eleven- to twelve-year-old girls in both Britain and the United States customarily departed to children's parties clad in dresses which resembled petticoats and hefty black boots. A 1990 survey on gender stereotypes in advertising conducted by Aston University provides the clue to the nature of the changes which had occurred. Georgina Henry reported in the *Guardian* on 21 November 1990 that men were to be seen doing housework now on prime-time TV, but it was likely to be cooking, not the cleaning or the washing. Twenty years of agitation and an employment structure which had turned inside-out had modified notions of gender but left some parts untouched. Slippage seemed to produce an exaggerated reworking of earlier idioms of masculinity and femininity.

Identity was chameleon-like in the first half of the decade. The early 1990s fashionable waif turned into the dandy and by the mid-1990s the sheath dress and shirt-waister were heading back via Jackie Kennedy to Doris Day. Moreover, nationality, ethnicity and race, so crucial in US culture, were assuming a new significance in Britain. What did it mean to be Scottish or Welsh? Who was black British? Who was black English? No one was sure any more what being English meant. The old symbols had taken on new meanings. The Union Jack had been appropriated by Fascist-leaning football supporters, or was turned into boxer shorts or a motif on Oasis's electric guitar, while the Royal Family quarrelled about their affairs on TV. Diana, fed up with the fairy-tale princess image, came out in open rebellion against being an idyll.

Searching for a role on the charity-go-round: Princess Diana with Hillary Clinton at a White House breakfast for the Nina Hyde Center for Breast Cancer Research, September 1996.

Edward Verity, writing in the *Daily Mail* on 23 November 1995, suspected the feminist influence of therapist Susie Orbach after Princess Diana said she wanted to serve the country as an ambassador in her controversial TV interview that autumn. The nation divided for and against Di. Was she a courageous survivor or a malevolent manipulator? Princesses on public funding who spoke for themselves upset several applecarts and patriotic reflexes were firing off all over the place.

In the United States, confusion about what a leading lady should be entangled Hillary Clinton, who could do nothing right. Accused of being a feminist frump in glasses, she became a power-dresser and was immediately declared too bossy. She vamped it in black in *Vogue* and then donned white, making herself look a bit silly and a bit too good to be true. And through it all she remained suspect as intelligent. Amidst the confusion, the puzzled millions watched endless soaps in which rules and reliability had found their Valhalla. Here at least all conflict eventually unravelled into the next storyline and you could test out a wide range of people to be. Soaps knew no country. Though British exports like *EastEnders* were minority shows in the United States, the British were eclectically absorbing *Bel Air* and *Home Improvement* along with their own.

Diversity was the thing with 1990s female role models. Feisty Roseanne went from strength to strength, while the quite different shape of Pamela Anderson in *Baywatch* fascinated viewers of both genders. How could anyone impersonate Barbie so well? Real (or unreal) Barbies had become collectors' items by 1995 in the United States, fetching up to $500, and there were Barbie groups. Barbie had become an art object too. Maggie Robbins busily hammered nails into Barbie dolls to gruesome effect. Photographer Susan Evans Grove ruthlessly exposed Barbie to urban blight and environmental disaster. Barbie was portrayed experiencing homelessness, drug addiction and skin cancer. Mattel Toys did not like their all-American girl turning into a social document and responded with an exhibition of approved Barbie artwork in 1994. Even here, though, diverse identity crept in. German artist Elke Martensen showed a butch Barbie in leather helmet fondling the breast of another Barbie.

Change could just be fun. Paul O'Grady invented Lily Savage, a blonde streetwise bombshell: 'It's me with a wig on.'[15] He emphasized that he was a comedian in drag, not a transvestite: 'You can have a hoot with it [Lily] because it's like having a Barbie doll, where you can get all those leery cossies made . . . You think, "What can I make her do now? Who can I dress her in?"'[16] Journalist Rachel Newsome defined Lily Savage as 'an oxymoronic marriage between the pure and the defiled; she is both an archetypal slapper from hell and champion of the underdog'.[17]

Along with the oxymoron as a figure of the 1990s went the gender changer and the third sex. Kate Bornstein, American author of *Gender Outlaw: On Men, Women and the Rest of Us*, disliked rigid categories. She turned from heterosexual Albert Herman to heterosexual Kate and then identified as a lesbian. Before her sex change she said she had never felt 'like a man'; after her operation she had come to the conclusion that it was not 'worth the trouble trying to be a man and a woman' and dressed in 'transgendered' style.[18] Sally Potter's film of Virginia Woolf's *Orlando* added to the gender-as-costume confusion in 1993, with Tilda Swinton playing the nobleman who lives for 400 years and becomes a woman half-way through.

The state was confused by the bureaucratic implications of the new technological possibilities of sex changes – British transsexuals in 1995 were campaigning for their official records to be altered. Fantasy kept turning into reality. After test-tube babies and sperm banks came the extraction and preservation of sperm from a dead man (at the request of his wife) by a New York urologist.

Popular culture had absorbed a new common sense of gender. The British were slower off the mark than the Americans but by 1995 scriptwriters had sharpened the dialogue. 'I wish I'd known you were a copper. I really go for women in uniform,' announced a male character on *The Bill*. 'I hope you get a female judge then.' The media's reflections were one thing, but actual attitudes another. Oxymoron is an apt metaphor to express the coexistence of opposites. 'Karen's a little minx, isn't she?' said a mother to a small boy on the Manchester to London train in autumn 1995. Delighted with the new word, he announced, 'Dad's a little minx.' While Dad stared out of the window, an embarrassed mother explained, 'No, girls are minxes, not boys.' 'Dad girls are minxes,' declared the toddler in a valiant effort at male bonding. Dad kept his silence.

Attitudes to sex were as contrary as those towards gender identity. Family values were not particularly evident in the columns of *SF Weekly*'s 'Woman Seeking Man' section in 1994. One wanted a 'vampire gentleman', while a mysterious 'Sweater girl' stated, 'Girl of many fine wovens seeks SM for late evening dry-cleaning trips. Fluff and fold OK, several hours of martinizing preferred.'[19] Dogs and cats were assets, but atomized purity was specified by one advert seeking a male between thirty-five and forty-five: 'Must be smoke, drug and child free.'[20]

Sex was projected on music videos on the electronic screens of New York's Times Square and in the British pub. Upfront sex that took the direct tack was back: 'Hello, boys,' said the Wonderbra adverts. Eva Herzigova, the model, was photographed in a raunchy style reminiscent of late-1960s images, which was where Women's Liberation had come in. But thirty years on she had a more mischievous look. The poster resulted in a 41 per cent increase in sales. Sex was a money-spinner in the women's glossy magazines in Britain. Readers were curious to find out why their men masturbated and kept mistresses, and what a week in a prostitute's life was like. Younger readers (aged ten upwards) in both Britain and the United States were reading a new-style teen magazine which carried offbeat fashion, pin-ups and advice about life and love. Anorexia, lesbianism, deciding when you were ready for it, were being considered young. Men's magazines in Britain, meanwhile, were intrigued by what women wanted in bed – the women grumbled about men's preoccupation with their own anatomy and their failure to realize how rude women were.

Yet along with such modernity, tradition got a new wind. British tabloids juxtaposed titillation with moral opprobrium in a time-honoured manner. The cheating wife and the straying husband were still cards to be drawn. In both countries a sexually explicit media dug out some old favourites, the madam and the mistress, though they had adapted to new market forces. A Hollywood madam, when found guilty of procuring, ingeniously marketed her brand of underwear. *Marie Claire* carried a story in 1994 about a mistress kept on the company payroll at middle-management rates. Madonna, who had made a fortune baring all, was puzzled by 1994: 'I didn't know I couldn't talk about sex,' she intoned into the microphone on her album *Bedtime Stories*.

An American writer, Gay Talese, announced this was the era of 'sex without fingerprints'.[21]

Talk was one thing, doing another. Empirical surveys revealed that among heterosexuals it was the ones who were married or living together who had sex more frequently than the autonomous and fancy-free. The British survey *Sexual Behaviour in Britain* (1994) found those cohabiting were having slightly more than those who were married but the key factor was the length of the relationship. There was a tendency for convergence in behaviour between men and women (though women in their late fifties were having less sex than men of the same age). The American study *Sex in America* (1994) was a national random survey of 3,432 people and it reported that two-thirds of those interviewed had sex with a partner only several times a month. Around three-quarters of the married men and 80 per cent of the married women said they had been completely faithful. The majority of people had had relatively few partners.

Only a small percentage of the British said they had had relationships outside marriage too. Casual sex was not well regarded, especially by women. But the authors of *Sexual Behaviour in Britain* found:

Acceptance of sex before marriage is now nearly universal. Only 8.2 per cent of men and 10.8 per cent of women believe it to be always or mostly wrong. In this respect the British public is markedly more permissive than the American public – according to the latest survey, 36 per cent in the US view premarital sex as always or mostly wrong.[22]

In both countries there was a long-term decline in sex with prostitutes. With this went a tendency for young women to have sexual relationships. Donna, a twenty-four-year-old architectural student interviewed in the British survey, had slept with a boy when she was fifteen (under age; he was seventeen). They stayed together for two years until she was going to college. Since then she had had 'half a dozen relationships', but never 'unprotected sex with a person I don't know'.[23] In *Straight Sex* Lynne Segal pointed out that despite AIDS, sex was less likely to be fraught with fears that were impossible to voice than in the previous generation. In both Britain and the United States young people were more likely to have sex and less likely to talk about it in romantic terms than their parents had been. Curiosity now could be cited, not just

Feminist and funny.

passion, for the loss of virginity. Female virginity – the old symbol of male power – had 'disappeared as an issue for most groups of women and men'.[24] However, young people were inclined to disapprove of infidelity; they had presumably watched their elders floundering in confusion and muddle.

Yet sexuality continued to be both a problematic and a politically emotive area. The pressure to restrict sex information and make the lives of teenage mothers as unpleasant as possible was a continuing preoccupation of a moral right in the United States and Britain. Young single mothers faced tremendous practical problems over work, money and housing. So did divorced older women. Changes in sexual patterns still occurred within an unequal balance of power between men and women. The shift to no-fault divorce and mediation was not always to women's advantage, especially if there was a history of domestic violence. Despite the alienating character of the legal system, its rituals provided some protection. Disagreement continued among women about how to respond to sexual harassment and pornographic images.

In the United States the new wave of feminist activism on abortion again raised issues of sexual politics which had contributed to the origins of the Women's Liberation movement. In her pamphlet *Women and Abortion: The Body as Battleground*, Rosalyn Baxandall made a passionate plea for 'exploration of the body, curiosity, intimacy, sensuality, excitement and human connection'.[25] The proliferating young girl groups producing girlzines, pioneered by Riot girls, were all for exploration and cheerful outrage. As *Girl Jock* magazine put it, 'Fuck the well of loneliness, goodbye to all that. We're here to have fun.'[26]

No equivalent single issue mobilized women in Britain. However, the Gay Pride marches, which had begun as a few hundred people, were becoming major events. The 1995 demonstration was a massive 200,000, rivalling the numbers at the VE celebrations, and was sponsored by big business – Virgin, Evian and Levi's. Alex Duval Smith described how, as they passed Downing Street, 'there was a call to "Free Beth Jordache" [the lesbian jailed in the popular soap *Brookside*].'[27]

Though there was not a single identifiable 'women's movement' in either Britain or the United States, sexual politics continued in women's activism around, for example, health groups, campaigns to decriminalize prostitution and agitation against inequalities in the treatment of breast cancer. In 1991 in Britain rape in marriage was judged to be a crime. During the first half of the 1990s Southall Black Sisters and Justice for Women also took up the cases of several women in prison for murdering violent husbands. An important ally in both issues was the mass organization of the Women's Institute. Beryl Sutton from Clare in Suffolk, who moved the resolution to change the law on provocation after reading of the imprisonment of an Asian woman, said that the Women's Institute movement was becoming more radical because rural women felt excluded from the political process. They were 'under-resourced and under-supported. Women are bearing the brunt of a lot of political decisions – in this village we practically look after everybody.'[28]

In both countries women were playing a prominent part in a whole series of struggles around the rights of groups shunted to the margins and in grass-roots attempts to challenge the unequal and destructive use of resources. The clampdown on migrant labour from Mexico, Resolution 187, brought young chicana women in schools and universities into a struggle which Dolores Huerta from the farm workers' union described in 1994 at the University of Santa Cruz as 'a new civil rights movement'. The right wing in the Conservative Party in Britain in the same period were also using migrant labour as an argument against closer European union, and in 1993 black and ethnic minority women in London formed a network which aimed to span Europe. Young women were prominent in demonstrations for civil liberties in Britain in 1994. Maria Hutt, manager of the rock band the Levellers, said it was belief in 'human civil rights'[29] which led her to resist the Criminal Justice Bill. She told the magazine for the homeless, *Big Issue*, in 1994 that she thought 'the Government has shot itself in the foot in trying to clamp down on youth culture, it has brought everyone together'.[30]

In Britain animal rights resulted in an extraordinary uprising early in 1995 when protesters picketed against the export of live animals, including calves that were to be slaughtered for fresh veal. They included pensioners and members of the Royal Society for the Prevention of Cruelty to Animals, as well as a thirty-one-year-old single mother, Jill Phipps, who died in February when she fell under a lorry on the picket line at Coventry airport. At her funeral, her partner, Justin Timson, affirmed her love for her nine-year-old son and also 'the earth, the trees, the sun and all the creatures of the earth'.[31] The grass-roots

The politics of food: protesting against the misery miles imposed by the
deregulation of the European meat trade, Shoreham, January 1995.

direct-action spirit of these movements, along with the resistance to
road-building, was nurturing alternative views about rights and values.
In the United States Feminists for Animal Rights, formed in the early
1980s as a strand within eco-feminism, were making similar political
connections.

By the 1990s the campaigns for environmental justice in the United
States had become multicultural and multiracial coalitions which had
extended beyond the dumping of toxic waste. Environmental justice
challenged how decisions were made about the environment and questioned the use of scientific evidence and resources. In the magazine
Everyone's Backyard, Lois Gibbs pointed out in August 1992 that this
movement was led 'for the most part by women . . . from a variety of
backgrounds . . . moms, full-time homemakers, family farmers and
other workers'.[32] They encountered formidable opposition. One of the
activists, Sonja Anderson, a scientist from Kennewick, Washington,
had had to contend with fifty break-ins, phone taps, threats and the
loss of her job. The Citizens' Clearinghouse for Hazardous Waste,
which produced *Everyone's Backyard*, was internationalist in scope,

reporting, for instance, on toxic waste in Britain and an anti-road protest in Hawaii in 1992 when Hawaiian women camped in the jungle in protest against the H-3 military highway.

In 1992 a massive demonstration in Britain which the unions said numbered 200,000 people marched in the pouring rain on the issue of jobs and resources in the coal industry. In 1993 Anne Scargill led a group of coalfield women in a sit-in down a mine to try to stop the pit closures. The burst of resistance slowed down but did not alter Conservative energy policy. However, the memory of the miners' strike and the women's mobilization of the 1980s and early 1990s left a permanent mark on the forms of labour movement organizing. When the dockers in Liverpool opposed casualization in 1995 the women formed their own group, Women of the Waterfront. That the nature of work was the concern of the community and not simply an economic question had become rooted in the responses of people whose lives and livelihoods were devastated and disregarded.

In the United States a series of grass-roots initiatives could be observed which made similar connections between employment and communities. For example, in Baltimore in 1993 the American Federation of State, County and Municipal Employees linked with a community group BUILD, Baltimoreans United in Leadership, to fight poverty through an association of low-paid workers. In July 1994 representatives from twenty workers' centres met in New York to discuss new kinds of association against poverty. They included Young Shin from the Asian Immigrant Women's Advocates in Oakland and Maria del Carman from La Mujer Obrera in El Paso, who were confronting the problem of garment work in slave-like compounds with workers terrified of reprisals and repatriation. Jo Ann Lunn from the Chinese Staff and Workers' Association in New York described their attempts to organize workers in restaurants earning 70c. an hour and clothing workers on $1 an hour. The Association connected workplace issues to health, schools and gay and lesbian concerns. The vulnerability of low-paid Mexican migrant workers in California meant that many of the young protesters saw rights and livelihood as inseparable issues.

Several radical economic initiatives were asserting an economy geared to needs and rejecting the low-waged option. In Milwaukee the Campaign for a Sustainable Milwaukee, launched in January 1995, had revived the idea of a living wage. In 1990 child-care workers, through the Worthy Wage Campaign, expanded the idea of comparable worth to a wider questioning of how work was valued. Going against the whole basis of market economics, they defined work as activity which had a social purpose. In 1995 one family-care provider in Wisconsin said she only kept on working in child-care because the Worthy Wage movement reminded her of her ideals when she entered the field:

I still believe that because of my education and skills, I can influence the lives of the next generation. I can be part of creating a community where individuals care for and about each other and are valued simply for what they are. A community where gender, race, physical abilities and economic status do not define one's potential – a community where life is fair.[33]

In both Britain and the United States many women were becoming aware that this challenge to dominant economic values and the extension of the meaning of human rights were global struggles which involved women in Asia, Africa and Latin America, as well as in the richer countries. The vast gathering at Beijing in autumn 1995 was the visible sign of global networking among women which ranged from issues of domestic violence to homework. There was uncertainty in the mid-1990s about what name fitted the new movements for individual and social rights which sought an economy geared to need and a caring community, and these were not the kinds of concern that grabbed the headlines. However, name or no name and despite differences, new connections have been coming into being. In 1995 Debjani Chatterjee from the Bengali Women's Support Group in Sheffield said:

Many of us would rather not make artificial choices between the individual and the group, between femininity and feminism, and there is a perception that Western feminism has required that such choices be made . . . Within our sisterhood, there is room for many different points of view and a variety of approaches. Our arms are wide.[34]

Whose values? Protest at Home Secretary Michael Howard's
home in Folkestone against the Criminal Justice Act's curbs on civil
liberties, November 1994.

CONCLUSION

'Women Face the '90s. In the '80s they tried to have it all. Now they've just plain had it. Is there a future for feminism?' *Time* magazine's announcement on 4 December 1989 was typical of the media's tone during the late 1980s and early 1990s. The immediate riposte from feminists was likely to be a list of political and legal rights, with an emphasis on women's greater cultural visibility, the impact women had made on existing institutions from education and the churches, to sport and the trade unions. They might point to a less tangible influence in popular culture and a shift in attitudes to sex. They could demonstrate that the trend for mothers to enter paid employment had continued and that the achievements of girls at school were improving.

Yet somehow the question would never get answered and variations would recur again and again. The reason is, of course, that such questions are like hoops and the complexity of women's lives and hopes can never be crammed through them. The dimensions of women's experience are too extensive to fit a simplistic linear model. They range from conditions of employment, relationships in the family and child-bearing to state policies which impinge on welfare benefits, the built environment, time for leisure and much more. Moreover, individuals can perceive similar circumstances in divergent ways and particular groups of women have experienced varied conditions in life. Consequently contrasts are apparent not just between Britain and the United States but within both countries, because of class, race and ethnicity, along with region, age and disability. All this makes for a much more muddled picture – and a far more interesting history.

Instead of a series of generalizations, an historical approach provides a way of looking at how such similarities and differences emerge, unfold, shift and move. The long view of history presents a different way of considering what is happening by seeking to know how change arises. The story that unfolds when we look at this century as a whole is neither a straightforward march of progress nor one in which débâcle is ever absolute. There is too a story that surfaces and one that has to be gleaned. Women's history in the twentieth century includes demands like the vote and equal pay, which are in the public arena, along with the glance of pleasure or the wild act of personal daring.

The passing of time is elusive and difficult to comprehend, yet it is only by going in pursuit of its passing that we can begin to see how things move at many levels. History is about tracing reflections, looking behind mirrors, rediscovering lost passages and digging among roots. Take, for example, that extraordinary tendency which emerges decade after decade for women with children to enter paid employment with very little corresponding alteration in the structure of either British or American society. Women have lived this incongruity of being expected to be in two places at once as an apparently insoluble dilemma, yet what has appeared as a law of nature has been in reality the result of particular social arrangements. Neither of the two cultures has seemed able to make up its mind about how women are meant to fit into an achievement-oriented economy while sticking society together as 'mum' (or 'mom').

It is hardly surprising really that women's claims for freedom and justice have oscillated between equality with men and improvements in their daily lives at home. Hence the continuing tug among feminists over whether to aim for equal rights with men or for reforms based on women's difference. It becomes evident when these divergent perspectives are considered within an historical context that neither in itself can provide a complete remedy. Advantages and disadvantages have accrued around both strategies, whether they have been for legislative protection at work, the needs of mothers and children, equal access in employment or equal divorce. Indeed, if the answer to whether it was to be equality or difference were easy, it would most evidently have been resolved long ago. Attempts to combine them have been tried, but the choice of emphasis is still a difficult calculation which has to be made in each specific case. Such choices have been complicated by the fact that the gains of one era can turn into the problems of the next. Not all repercussions can be calculated. The demand for flexible employment, for instance, in the expansive early 1970s has become more problematic with high unemployment and growing inequality in pay.

The span of 100 years can also throw light on the reasons for the resistance to change, whether it has been from female opponents of suffrage or the women of the new right. The long trek into (almost) equal citizenship in the public sphere has been perceived differently by women. For some it has meant opportunity and respect, for others it has looked like a mug's game – and for many it has seemed like a bit of both. Women have experienced the fracturing of feminine identity in the course of this century and somehow accommodated to living the split. It is the real-life contrariness of these shifting boundaries between personal and public worlds which has resulted in contrasting responses, not some innate psychological incapacity among women to make up our minds. Both women and men grew up in one world and have found themselves in another as the century draws to its close.

The ways in which men are men, the ways women are women and the manner in which we regard one another and ourselves do not take place in a vacuum. Gender relations are an integral part of other relationships in society, so attitudes and perceptions of gender identity cannot be considered in watertight compartments. Changes affecting women's destinies in both the United States and Britain have also been processes in the society at large. The last quarter of the century has seen a profound global restructuring of production and distribution and a changing relation between the market and the state. In both countries this has occurred amidst growing social inequality and has been accompanied by efforts to shift the cost, both economic and psychological, away from the public domain to the private individual. Many women have been caught within this transformation as low earners and as mothers whose lives make them dependent on social resources, not just on the wage.

The political and social responses of women and men to these dilemmas of the late twentieth century will have a crucial effect on the shape of life in the twenty-first century. There could be a new impetus for rethinking work, time, the social forms of technology, the utilization and distribution of resources and power, the role of the state, the bringing up and educating of children – or the feeding of an anger that lashes out at scapegoats. As the twentieth century draws to a close, there are signs of both.

Hopefully absorbing the past might make us pause. One of the contributions of history is to lay out possibilities by drawing on a deeper knowledge of the roots of present-day circumstances. This involves an eerie catching of echoes. Women who had tried to have it all were being told they had had it in 1929 as well as 1989, for example. It can also challenge a tendency to panic over red herrings. The 1990s scare over the sexuality of teenage girls has its precedents, after all – in the 1900s, the 1920s and the 1940s. A gender crisis has a habit of substituting for a knot of other social problems. Taking the long historical view might calm that propensity for moral panics to which US society – as if in fear of constant dissolution – has been particularly prone. Since 1900 the family thus appears so frequently under threat from Bolsheviks, Europeans, gigolos, feminists, teenagers, blacks, gays and whatnot that it is impossible not to notice a certain repetition. Britain, for its part, has been inclined to catch social and sexual anxieties in a milder form – and blame the Americans for exporting the cakewalk, ragtime, their divorce rates and delinquent teenagers, pulp fiction, Hollywood, rock 'n' roll and stroppy feminists.

It is a platitude, and only part of the truth, to say that US culture has put a much greater emphasis on individuals standing up for themselves, while the British have had a greater acceptance of solidarities and collectivity. This obscures how the United States has had its undertow of powerful communalisms of the left and of the right and how aspects of British culture, long before Thatcher, have valued self-help. Nonetheless, these broad parameters have affected the differing cultures of womanhood in the two countries. They have also influenced the organizational forms and assumptions of feminism, of workplace and community organizing, and of women's involvement in right-wing politics. It is not just that the religious right has much greater resonance in US society; an evangelical mind-set pervades the culture. The absolute moral stands, the emphasis on personal testimony and witnessing, which appear in many guises in the United States continue to meet with profound resistance in Britain.

There are obvious differences in the political structures of the two countries; this is not just a matter of Britain's feudal remains such as the House of Lords or the formal Constitution of the United States. A peculiar feature of US politics is the relative disengagement of large sections of its population from politics in the formal sense of party politics, accompanied by the extraordinary proliferation of movements within society. Social movements such as Civil Rights, Women's and Gay Liberation have proved capable of responding to grievances more sensitively than the formal political arena within the United States.

These movements, initiated in America, have had an impact all round the world, including Britain. They have not only affected the structure of politics; they have shifted ways of seeing. The very existence of such a book as this is a sign of how the emergence of new ways of looking leads to the retelling and rediscovery of the past – a process which itself is never static. 'Women's history' developed out of the Women's Liberation movement and, in the early heyday of hope and activism, initially focused on the obvious – the suffrage or workplace militancy. It was when things did not seem to change so fast that hanging on began to gain respect; studies of survival and women's culture followed. Women's history was barely conceived before it was challenged as an unproblematic unity. This assertion of the variety of women's experience has, in turn, revealed a much richer history – and much is still awaiting discovery. As Delia Jarrett-Macauley points out, in Britain, 'For all the hype and hyperbole which surrounds "black womanhood", we are still under-produced, under-explored, under-researched.'[35] Moreover, the recognition of various histories has, in the words of Paula Giddings, revealed that the entry points of inquiry necessarily affect what is asked and what is uncovered. The history of women is thus no more cut and dried than the circumstances of women.

Historical questions are always partly framed by contemporary preoccupations, and this applies to women's history as to any other. One consequence of living through the 1980s and 1990s, for instance, has been more studies of women's participation in conservative and extreme right-wing politics. The Primrose League and the Klan have their women's history as well as the Co-operative or trade union movements. Women have been for hierarchy and exclusion; exponents of 'women's values' have to face evidence that women can be as nasty as they have been nice. Belonging to a subordinated sex is not an automatic ticket to ride with the angels; reality in the twentieth century is not a moral tale of feminine virtue versus masculine evil. Equally, the recent participation of poor women in the United States in a range of struggles for social justice has alerted historians to movements around welfare and consumption which cannot be framed in the feminism of the 1970s or 1980s. The forms of women's protest have altered in response to circumstances.

The scope of women's history has also been affected by changes within history as a subject and the emergence of new disciplines like cultural studies. The last decade has seen a growing interest in interpreting changes in consciousness through popular culture – catching attitudes through the oblique codes of fantasy and not simply in the formally stated demand. The realization that history is made not only in the public spheres of politics or work but in the private zones and that change can be played out in culture when all appears silent in politics is a perception which has particular relevance for the history of women. It corrects over-simple views of progress or of women as the eternal victims of an unchanging patriarchy. More generally it illuminates the predicament of being pinioned and silenced as 'the other' in somebody else's fantasy. It does not make the writing of history easier though. The expression of desire, contrary and secretive, fragmentary and tentative, is never easy to marshal, and for women the traces are faint. That tremendous struggle for personal autonomy within culture and society has been frequently conducted in zones which evade the record. Women's history and gender history have contributed to a wider reassessment of sources which has been revitalizing social history.

The pursuit of history is driven partly by the sheer fascination of finding out. As the field of inquiry shifts and expands, the historical hunt is on for the nooks and crannies as well as clear-cut events. Any study of the past comes across coincidence and the momentary, flashing amidst forgetfulness, yet outside any known narrative. Sometimes, when such stuff is related to the longer term, it takes on an unexpected meaning – a realization which was not there before. And, of course, one thing leads to another, so the terms which set the first inquiry melt into more questions. The new histories which emerged from omissions are affected by this dynamic. So while the focus on women continues to be important because it challenges a common exclusion, women's history, like other categories of history, interacts and spills over its particular boundaries.

But can history tell us what should be done? The blunt answer has to be that it cannot, though this alchemical hope that the past might transmute into the future dies hard. Nonetheless, some of the energy that fuels the incessant discovering and rediscovering that are the historian's craft has always been a longing to satisfy more than the curiosity of the chronicler. My own search over the years has certainly been based on an effort to reveal suppressed possibilities – those understandings that time rushes past which can also be a means of releasing aspiration. Amidst all those voices echoing down the decades there is, for example, Crystal Eastman wondering in 1920 'how to arrange the world so that women can be human beings, with a chance to exercise their infinitely varied gifts in infinitely varied ways'.

I believe that women's possibilities for happiness as individuals and expansion as human beings are indeed linked to the wider society and its reshaping. Eleanor Roosevelt's recognition at the UN in 1947 of the need for a balance between individual and social rights seems to me a good guide for thinking about how this unknown alternative might develop: 'It is not that you set the individual apart from society but that you recognize in any society that the individual must have rights that are guarded.'

Such a balance between polarities can never be easy or likely to remain constant. A good book to remind us that the righting of wrongs is necessarily a dynamic process rather than a fixed solution is Ursula le Guin's *The Dispossessed*, in which a gifted individual flees a future world of collective co-operation because it inhibits him, only to struggle against another based on rampant competitive individualism. Rather than the image of linear progress or of those soundbite hoops, the history of women this century can be interpreted as a complex, sometimes conflicting quest for both personal and social balance. Balance, after all, is a word which contains a sense of justice, self-possession and equilibrium; it is also decisively affected by surrounding circumstance.

Biographies

The selection of biographies that follows is intended to provide more information on some of the women in the book. It has not been possible to include everyone, partly for reasons of space and partly because the necessary information does not exist.

Diane Abbott, 1953–
Labour MP. Educated at Cambridge University. Worked at the Home Office, as Race Relations Officer at the National Council for Civil Liberties, then for TV and as press and PR officer at the GLC and Lambeth Council. Joined the Labour Party in 1971; a Member of Westminster City Council, 1982–6, she became Britain's first black woman MP, representing Hackney North and Stoke Newington in 1987.

Grace Abbott, 1878–1939
Social worker. From a reform-minded middle-class family, she worked at Hull House. Supported Chicago garment workers, 1910–11. Active in suffrage movement and immigrants' rights. In 1917 joined Julia Lathrop at the Children's Bureau. Was able

through the Sheppard-Towner Act to open 3,000 child health and prenatal centres during the 1920s, but in 1929 failed to save act. In New Deal helped draft the Social Security Act and in 1938 contributed to the Fair Labor Standards Act, which partially banned child labour – a cause for which she had fought for many years.

Bella Abzug, 1920–
Democratic Party politician. Born in the Bronx into Russian-Jewish family. Went to Hunter College to study law, and later specialized in labour law and civil rights. Anti-war activist in 1960s. Helped form Women Strike for Peace. In 1970 elected Congress-woman for the 19th Congressional District in New York. Known as 'Battling Bella', she opposed the Vietnam War and supported the ERA.

Jane Addams, 1860–1935

Settlement worker and social reformer. From a prosperous Republican family in Illinois, she was influenced by visits to East London's Toynbee Hall social settlement. Started Hull House settlement in 1893 with Ellen Gates Starr. It encouraged many reform projects and was an example of learning from doing. She was involved in women's suffrage and was in 1915 president of the International Congress of Women. In 1919 she was first president of Women's International League for Peace and Freedom and in 1920 helped form American Civil Liberties Union. Supporter of Consumer League and protective legislation for women workers.

Kate Adie, 1945–

TV reporter. Read Scandinavian Studies at Newcastle University and taught in Arctic. Entered radio as a producer. Became a TV reporter on BBC news team. Covered Iranian Embassy siege in 1980 and US bombing of Libya in 1986. Won International News Story award in 1986. In 1989 reported from Tiananmen Square, Beijing, and in early 1990s covered Gulf War and conflict in former Yugoslavia.

Sally Alexander, 1943–

Historian. An actress for ten years, she studied at Ruskin College, Oxford. Helped organize first Women's Liberation conference there in 1970. Demonstrated against Miss World contest and active in Night Cleaners' Unionization Campaign. Taught in Workers' Educational Department and helped to develop women's history in Britain. Professor at Goldsmiths' College, London. Works include *Becoming a Woman* (1994).

Gracie Allen, 1895–1964

Comedienne. Born in San Francisco, she worked in vaudeville and met George Burns in 1922. They toured together and broadcast in US and UK. By 1940 their US radio show had 45 million listeners. Appeared on CBS TV in 1950 and became famous as the not-so-dizzy blonde.

Paula Gunn Allen, 1939–

Writer. Born in New Mexico. Her mother was part American Indian and her father was Lebanese-American. Educated at the University of Oregon. She has held several academic posts and written award-winning poetry and fiction, as well as *The Sacred Hoop: A Contemporary Indian Perception of American Indian Literature* (1986).

Jessie Daniel Ames, 1883–1972

Suffrage and anti-lynching campaigner. Widowed at thirty-one in Texas, she became active in suffrage movement. In 1920s involved in progressive social reform. Joined Woman's Committee of Texas Commission on Inter-racial Co-operation. Involved in inter-racial Christian groups in 1920s. In 1930 helped form Anti-Lynching Association of white Southern women. Worked through existing women's groups, especially in Methodist Church.

Marian Anderson, 1902–93

Concert and opera singer. From a poor black family in Philadelphia, she began singing in church. After a 1929 Carnegie Hall recital, she toured Europe and the USSR. When the Daughters of the Revolution prevented her singing in Constitution Hall, Washington, DC, instead, with Eleanor Roosevelt's support, she sang to a vast crowd of 75,000 at the Lincoln Memorial on Easter Sunday, 9 April 1939. In 1955 she was first black soloist to perform at the Metropolitan Opera House, New York City. President Eisenhower made her a delegate to the UN in 1958. Autobiography, *My Lord, What a Morning*, published in 1956.

Maya Angelou, 1928–

Writer and film director. Raised by her grandmother, a storekeeper in Arkansas, and later by her mother, an entertainer in San Francisco. Her memoir *I Know Why the Caged Bird Sings* (1970) established her reputation as a writer. She has worked in film and for TV and theatre, written poetry and lectured in universities.

Anna Mae Picton Aquash, 1945–76

Micmac Indian rights activist. Born in Nova Scotia and brought up in Picton's Landing Northumberland Strait in poverty. In early 1970s teacher for Training and Research in Bicultural Education in Maine. Member of American Indian Movement. Involved in 1972 occupation of Bureau of Indian Affairs in Washington, DC, and in 1973 at Wounded Knee, South Dakota, occupation. Pursued by FBI for information on a case. Found shot on Pine Ridge Reservation, South Dakota.

Elizabeth Arden, c. 1878–1966 (*Florence Nightingale Graham*)

Beautician and businesswoman. Born in Ontario, Canada. Went to New York in 1908 and worked as an assistant in a cosmetics shop. Set up own salon in 1909 as Elizabeth Arden. Sold make-up and creams and started health resorts, becoming a worldwide name. She was a conservative Republican.

Pat Arrowsmith, 1930–

Peace campaigner. Educated at Cambridge University. In 1952–3 worked as a community worker in Chicago, later doing community and welfare work with children. From 1958 to 1968 she was organizer for CND and the Committee of One Hundred. Imprisoned eleven times for direct-action protests.

Bea (Beatrice) Arthur, c. 1926–

Actress and comedienne. Starred in US TV series *Maude*, breaking the formula for soaps during the 1970s. Starring in *The Golden Girls* during the 1980s, she was popular in the US and UK as the sassy older woman.

Margery Corbett Ashby, 1882–1981

Feminist and Constitutional Suffragist. Active in Liberal Party. In 1907 she was secretary of National Union of Women's Suffrage Societies and in 1920 secretary of the International Alliance of Women. Involved in international peace movement in the 1930s and after the Second World War.

Dame Peggy Ashcroft, 1907–91
Actress. Famous from the 1930s for her work in Shakespearian drama. Also acted in work by modern dramatists, including Samuel Beckett. Supported CND and other radical causes. She was awarded the DBE in 1956 and won an Oscar for her film role in *A Passage to India* in 1984.

Laura Ashley, 1925–85
Designer and businesswoman. From Welsh Baptist family. Worked in the War Office and WRNS during war. Involved in National Federation of Women's Institutes. In 1953 began designing and selling scarves and later dresses from home. In 1967 opened first shop in Kensington. Expanded in 1970s and 1980s in Britain, Europe and the US.

Lady Nancy Astor, 1879–1964
American Conservative politician. In 1906 married Waldorf Astor, the son of an American millionaire who had been made a British peer in 1906. In 1919 elected MP for Plymouth after he became a Viscount. She was thus the first woman to take her seat in the House of Commons. A Christian Scientist from 1914 and pro-temperance, she supported social reforms for women and children. In favour of appeasement in the 1930s; for German right but anti-Hitler. In war protested about conditions of homeless in Plymouth and women's exclusion from Foreign Office. Opposed agitation for continued

imprisonment of British Fascist leader, Sir Oswald Mosley, in 1943.

Katherine Marjory, Duchess of Atholl, 1874–1960
Scottish Conservative politician. In 1899 married future 8th Duke of Atholl, becoming Duchess in 1917. Did charitable work for troops in Boer and First World War. Anti-women's suffrage, she was elected MP for Kinross and Perthshire in 1923. From 1924 to 1929, first Conservative woman minister as parliamentary secretary to the Board of Education. Defended poor children's education. Opposed to European non-intervention in Spanish Civil War; produced *Searchlight on Spain*. In 1938 opposed Munich agreement and attacked as 'Red Duchess'. Worked with refugees after Second World War.

Margaret Atwood, 1939–
Novelist and poet. Born in Ottawa, educated in Canada and US. Has held academic posts in US, Canada and Australia. Novels include *Surfacing* (1972), *The Handmaid's Tale* (1986, filmed 1990). Has also written *Survival: A Thematic Guide to Canadian Literature* (1972).

Alice Bacon, 1911–
Labour MP. Educated at Stockwell College. Worked as a teacher. MP for Leeds North East in 1945–55; subsequently elected for Leeds South East. Interested in industrial and social questions. Critical of Housewives' League but opposed bread rationing, 1945. In 1964 Minister of State Home Office; 1967–70 Department of

Education and Science. She was awarded the CBE in 1953 and made Deputy Lieutenant of West Yorkshire in 1974.

Joan Baez, 1941–
Singer. Her mother was of English and Scottish descent and her father was Mexican. Began singing in Cambridge (Mass.) coffee bars. Involved in civil rights in early 1960s and opposed war in Vietnam. In 1974 began giving concerts in Californian prisons.

Ella Baker, 1903–86
From North Carolina. Educated at Shaw University. In Harlem during Depression. Joined Young Negroes Co-operative League, founded in 1930, to gain economic power through consumer co-operation. Employed on Workers' Educational Project of the Works Progress Administration. Organized with domestic workers and housewives. Wrote for *West Indian News* and in 1943–6 became director of National Association for the Advancement of Colored People branches. In 1950 organized parents against discrimination in schools. In 1960s active in Civil Rights movement. Helped form Student Non-Violent Co-ordinating Committee and Mississippi Freedom Democratic Party. Inspired Students for a Democratic Society.

Josephine Baker, 1906–75
Entertainer. From St Louis, of African and Spanish descent, she was in vaudeville as a child. In *Shuffle Along* at Plantation Club, New York, 1921.

Went to Paris with *La Revue Nègre*, becoming symbol of the jazz era. Worked for Red Cross and Resistance in the Second World War. Active in Civil Rights movement. Made comeback in 1970s as a singer.

Lucille Ball, 1910–89
Comedienne. From New York, she was a child performer. Worked as a model and chorus girl before acting in Hollywood B movies. Became a hit in the *I Love Lucy* series, which began on US TV in 1951 and was also shown in UK.

Toni Cade Bambara, 1939–95
Novelist. Brought up in Harlem, she was influenced by her mother, who had been involved in the Harlem Renaissance. She graduated from Queens and City College, New York. Worked in welfare and community jobs and then lectured in women's studies. Active in radical politics during the 1970s. Novels include *The Salt Eaters* (1980). From 1986 worked with young film-makers at Scribe Video Center in Philadelphia. In 1994–5 she was co-ordinating writer on a documentary about life of W. E. B. DuBois.

Tallulah Bankhead, 1903–68
Actress. A rebel from a prominent political family in Alabama. Began acting after winning a beauty contest aged fifteen. In film *When Men Betray* (1918). Well known in London theatre, 1923–30. Plays included *The Green Hat* and *Fallen Angels*. Appeared in Lillian Hellman's *Little Foxes* in 1939 in US. Also worked in radio and TV.

Theda Bara, 1885–1955 (*Theodosia Goodman*)

Film actress. From a Jewish background, her exotic personality was created for studio publicity. Starred in *A Fool There Was* as 'the vamp' in 1915. Retired from films in 1926.

Djuna Barnes, 1892–1982

Writer. Lived in Greenwich Village, writing poetry. Went to Paris in 1919, mixing in a bohemian expatriate circle which included Natalie Barney. Her *Ladies Almanack* (1928) was a comic account of expatriate lesbians in Paris. Her novel *Nightwood* (1936) also explored lesbian relations.

Roseanne Barr, 1952–

Comedienne. Born into a poor Jewish family in Salt Lake City. Inspired by *The Ed Sullivan Show* and Richard Pryor. Appeared at the Comedy Works Club. Worked in Woman to Woman Bookstore. Developed her Domestic Goddess act and performed it in Kansas City. In 1988 this became the basis for the sitcom *Roseanne* about the working-class Connors family.

Daisy Bates, 1914–

Civil rights activist. From Arkansas. In 1945 produced newspaper with husband, L. C. Bates, exposing attacks on black Americans. In 1952 president of Arkansas State Conference of National Association for the Advancement of Colored People branches. Led move to test US Supreme Court ruling against Segregation (*Brown* v. *Board of Education*, 1954) in 1957 in Little Rock. Continued to be active in registration campaigns and community projects. Author of *The Long Shadow of Little Rock* (1962).

Rosalyn Fraad Baxandall, 1941–

Historian. From a New York Communist family, she studied at Wisconsin and Columbia. Became a community organizer on welfare rights in Lower East Side. Active in civil rights and in rent struggles in the 1960s. Early member of New York Radical Women, the first New York Women's Liberation group. Also in feminist guerrilla theatre group, WITCH. Helped set up co-operative day-care centre and the first women's history group, the Atlanta Patchwork Quilt. Involved in trade union work and issues around reproductive rights. Teaches women's studies and American studies at the State University of New York (Old Westbury). Works include *Words on Fire: The Life and Writing of Elizabeth Gurley Flynn* (1987).

Louie Bennett, 1870–1956

Irish trade unionist and suffrage supporter. Helped start Irish Women's Suffrage Federation in 1913. Supporter of strikers in Dublin lock-out the same year. Member of Women's International League, 1914–55. Anti-war during First World War. From 1916 organizer of Irish Women Workers' Union. First woman president of Irish Trades Union Congress, 1931–2. Active in Irish Labour Party in 1940s.

Meg Beresford, 1937–

Peace campaigner. Educated at Warwick University. She was a

community worker and then became organizing secretary for European Nuclear Disarmament, 1981–3. In 1985 she became General Secretary of CND. Active in the women's peace movement.

Mary McLeod Bethune, 1875–1955
Black American educator. Born in South Carolina, the fifteenth of seventeen children. Worked in cotton fields. Won scholarship to Scotia seminary. Involved in black educational projects and National Association for the Advancement of Colored Women (NACW). Member of Florida Federation of Colored Women's Clubs, 1917–24, and supported suffrage movement. Defied Ku Klux Klan in registering black women in 1920. President NACW, 1924. Challenged exclusion of black women from International Council of Women. Worked closely with Eleanor Roosevelt in New Deal as Director of Negro Affairs in the National Youth Administration, 1936–43. Accused of Communism in McCarthy era for role in New Deal.

Teresa Billington-Greig, 1877–1964
Suffragette socialist. Preston school-teacher. Joined Women's Social and Political Union (WSPU) in Manchester, 1903. Organized Manchester teachers to campaign for equal pay in 1904. Organizer for the Independent Labour Party, 1904–6. Established WSPU branches in Scotland. Resigned and helped form Women's Franchise League with Charlotte Despard. Advocated non-violent direct action. Journalist

between wars. In Second World War active in Women for Westminster, campaigning for the election of more women.

Harriot Stanton Blatch, 1856–1940
Suffrage campaigner. Daughter of pioneering feminist Elizabeth Cady Stanton. Lived in Britain for two decades; involved in suffrage movement and Fabian Society. In US formed Equality League of Self-Supporting Women in 1907, then the Women's Political Union in 1910. Campaigned for a constitutional amendment for women's suffrage. In First World War worked for Food Administration and Women's Land Army. Supported Alice Paul's campaign for ERA through National Woman's Party and Mothers' Pensions in 1920s.

Margaret Grace Bondfield, 1873–1953
Trade unionist and Labour politician. Active in shopworkers' union. Helped form National Federation of Women Workers. Left-wing pacifist in First World War. First woman chair of TUC, 1923. Labour MP, 1923–4 and 1926–31. Moved to the right as Minister of Labour from 1929 and introduced harsh unemployment policies. Chair of Women's Group on Public Welfare, 1939–49.

Laura Bonham-Carter (Grimond), 1918–94
Liberal Party activist. Daughter of Violet Bonham-Carter. In 1938 married Rt. Hon. Jo Grimond, later Liberal Party leader. Active also in Orkney local government.

Lady Violet Bonham-Carter, Baroness Asquith of Yarnbury, 1887–1969

Liberal politician. Daughter of Henry Asquith (Prime Minister, 1908–16). Married Sir Maurice Bonham-Carter, civil servant. Active in Liberal Party. Governor of BBC, 1941–6.

Betty Boothroyd, 1929–

Labour MP and Speaker of the House of Commons. Educated at Dewsbury Technical College. Became MP for West Bromwich in 1973 and Member of the European Parliament, 1975–7. Served on the National Executive of the Labour Party in 1981. MP for West Bromwich again in the 1980s, she was made the first woman Speaker in the Commons in 1992.

Virginia Bottomley, 1948–

Conservative MP and Minister. Educated at Essex University and London School of Economics. Researcher for Child Poverty Action Group and lecturer Further Education College, 1971–3. Worked as psychiatric social worker, 1973–84. Entered Parliament in 1984. Minister at the Department of the Environment, 1988–9. Minister of Health from 1989 and Secretary of State for Health from 1992. In 1995 became Secretary of State for National Heritage.

Margaret Bourke-White, 1906–71

Photographer. Studied at Columbia University, New York. Initially celebrating the machine age in her work, she changed tack from 1929 to cover the 'dustbowl' for *Fortune* magazine and document Southern sharecroppers for *Life* magazine. Produced *You Have Seen Their Faces* with Erskine Caldwell (1937). During Second World War her photographic record of conditions in the camps where Japanese-Americans were interned was suppressed. As a war correspondent photographed Buchenwald concentration camp. Post-war assignments included India and Korea.

Clara Bow, 1905–65

Film actress. Brought up in a Brooklyn tenement. Entered films via a Fame and Fortune contest in 1921. Became the symbol of the Hollywood flapper. Films include *Dancing Mothers* (1926) and Elinor Glyn's *It* (1927). Retired from films in 1933.

Bessie Braddock, 1899–1970

Labour politician. From left-wing socialist and feminist Liverpool family. Her mother, Mary Bamber, was active in the trade union movement and influenced her daughter. MP for Liverpool (Exchange division), 1945–70. On the right of the Labour Party, she fought for housing and education opportunities for her constituents.

Angela Brazil, 1868–1947

Writer. Famous for schoolgirl books with hearty heroines showing true British grit. From 1906 wrote fifty school stories.

Fanny Brice, 1891–1951

Vaudeville star. Born in New York's Lower East Side. Her father was a gambler and her mother ran a saloon. Appeared at Ziegfeld Follies in 1910 and was an instant hit as a comedienne. Famous for send-up of vamp Theda Bara and the song 'Second-hand Rose'. Her role as 'Baby Snooks' on radio made her a household name.

Vera Mary Brittain, 1893–70
Writer, feminist, pacifist and socialist. Her best-known works are *Testament of Youth* (1933) and *Testament of Friendship* (1940), a tribute to her friend Winifred Holtby. In Second World War she became vice-president of the Women's International League for Peace and Freedom, and in 1944 wrote *Seeds of Chaos* in protest at the bombing of German cities. Six years before she died her daughter Shirley Williams became a Labour MP.

Romaine Brooks, 1874–1970
English painter. Her mother was a wealthy American. Studied in Rome. Married John Brooks (marriage of convenience) in 1902. Went to Paris and had close relationship with Natalie Barney. Moved in bohemian and lesbian literary circles. Returned to US only once, in 1930s.

Helen Gurley Brown, 1922–
Writer and editor. Worked as copy-writer in Los Angeles in the late 1940s and 1950s. Became editor of US *Cosmopolitan* 1965. Has received many awards as a newspaper woman. Books include *Sex and the Single Girl* (1962) and *Having It All* (1982).

Rita Mae Brown, 1944–
Lesbian feminist and novelist. After trying to raise lesbianism in National Organization for Women in 1969,

formed radical women's group, The Furies, in 1971 in Washington, DC. Wrote *Rubyfruit Jungle* (1973). She founded a TV and film option company, American Artists, and continues to write.

Stella Browne, 1882–1955
Canadian campaigner for birth control and abortion. Educated in Britain at Oxford University and in Germany. Active in Malthusian League and linked to *Freewoman* before First World War. Member of Communist Party in its first two years, then joined Labour Party. Helped found Abortion Law Reform Association in 1936.

Susan Brownmiller, 1935–
Journalist and writer. Active in civil rights. In 1969 was a founder member of New York Radical Feminists. Best-known work is *Against Our Will* (1975).

Anita Bryant, 1940–
Entertainer. Influenced by Protestant fundamentalism. Campaigned against sexually permissive attitudes in the 1960s. Anti-gay campaigner in the early 1980s. Became disillusioned with male leadership of the churches.

Pearl S. Buck, 1892–1973
Novelist and journalist. Her parents were missionaries and she grew up in China. Married John Buck, an agricultural expert, in 1917 and returned to China. Her novel *The Good Earth* (1931) was a best-seller. First American woman to win Nobel Prize for Literature, 1938. Wrote on position of women in 1940s and 1950s. Formed Pearl S. Buck

Foundation in 1964 to help fatherless half-American children in Asia.

Jane Byrne, 1934–
Mayor of Chicago. From Chicago, her father was founder of Gordon-Burke Steel. Studied at the University of Illinois. In early 1960s involved in Anti-Poverty programme in Chicago. Mayor Richard J. Daley appointed her first commissioner of Chicago's Department of Consumer Sales, Weights and Measures. Active in the Democratic Party. Mayor of Chicago, 1979–83, the first woman to hold the post.

Rachel Carson, 1907–64
Environmental campaigner and biologist. Overcoming prejudice against women scientists, she studied zoology and in 1935 worked for US Bureau of Fisheries as a junior aquatic biologist. In 1962 *Silent Spring* published, exposing the danger of DDT.

Angela Carter, 1940–92
Novelist. From Sussex, but lived also with her grandmother in Yorkshire. In 1959 worked as a journalist. Studied English at Bristol University, 1962–5. Visiting Professor, Brown University, Providence, US, 1980–81, and writer in residence at University of Adelaide, 1984. Work includes *Shadow Dance* (1966), *The Magic Toyshop* (1967; awarded John Llewellyn Rhys prize) and *The Sadaian Woman* (1979). Her last novel was *Wise Children* (1991).

Dame Barbara Cartland, 1901–
Prolific romantic novelist. Active in charitable organizations. In Auxiliary Territorial Services (ATS) in Second World War. Lady Welfare Officer and librarian to all services in Bedfordshire, 1941–9. Critic of 1960s 'permissive society'.

Baroness Barbara Castle, 1911–
Labour politician. Educated at Oxford University. Was a journalist before becoming MP for Blackburn in 1945. Minister for Overseas Development, 1964–5; Transport Minister, 1965–8; Secretary of State for Employment and Productivity, 1968–70; Minister of Health and Social Security, 1974; Vice-Chair of Socialist Group in the European Parliament, 1974–84.

Irene Castle, 1893–1969
Dancer. From New Rochelle, New York. Married Vernon Castle, her dancing partner. Exhibition dancers and teachers famous for the Turkey Trot, the Castle Walk and the Hesitation Waltz.

Carrie Chapman Catt, 1859–1947
Suffragist. Worked as a teacher and superintendent of schools. Active in suffrage movement from 1887. President of National American Woman Suffrage Association (NAWSA) in 1900. Active in international feminist groups. Organizer in the New York area until 1915, when she succeeded Anna Howard Shaw as president of NAWSA. In 1920s worked on peace and disarmament.

Edith Louisa Cavell, 1865–1915
Nurse. Worked in Hackney, east London, before going to Belgium in First World War, treating all wounded soldiers regardless of their nationality. She also smuggled French and British soldiers out of Belgium. She was court-martialled and shot by the Germans in 1915.

Thelma Cazalet-Keir, 1899–1989
Conservative politician. Active in London local government, 1937–40. Parliamentary Secretary to Ministry of Education, 1942. Member of Committee of Inquiry into conditions in Women's Services, 1943. Chairman Equal Pay Campaign Committee, 1943–6. Also involved in transport, BBC and the arts. Works include *From the Wings* (1967), an autobiography, and an edited collection, *Homage to P. G. Wodehouse* (1973). In 1964 she was president of the Fawcett Society.

Cher, 1943–
Singer and actress. Became famous for 'I've Got You, Babe' with Sonny Bono in 1965, which led to *The Sonny and Cher Show* on TV. Worked in clubs and casinos in Las Vegas. In the early 1980s began new career, acting in Robert Altman's film *Come Back to the 5 and Dime, Jimmy Dean, Jimmy Dean*, and then in *Silkwood*, the film about Karen Silkwood (q.v.).

Judy Chicago, 1939–
Feminist and artist. Work includes *The Woman House* (1972), *Through the Flower Chrysanthemum* (1973) and *Female Rejection Drawing* (1974). She

has tried to find female imagery for her art.

Shirley Chisholm, 1924–
Democratic Party politician. From Brooklyn, her parents were from Barbados. Studied sociology at Brooklyn College, 1946–52. Childcare worker, 1960. Formed United Democratic Club and in 1964 was elected New York State Assembly woman for 55th District. Campaigned for domestic workers to get minimum wage. Active in National Organization for Women. Congresswoman for the 12th District, 1968–83, becoming first black woman to be elected to Congress. On Democratic National Committee, 1972–6. In 1972 ran for Democratic nomination for President. Campaigned for the rights of women, racial minorities and better conditions in the inner city.

Kate Chopin, 1851–1904
Writer. Began writing after the death of her husband, Oscar Chopin, in 1882. Her short stories and novels dealt with sexually taboo subjects. *The Awakening* (1899) is her best-known work.

Dame Agatha Christie, 1890–1976
Writer. Began writing detective stories in 1920. Creator of quirky sleuths Hercule Poirot and Miss Marple. Her play *The Mousetrap* opened in London in 1952 and became a record survivor. She was awarded the DBE in 1971.

Julie Christie, 1940–
Actress. Educated Brighton College of
Technology and Central School of
Speech and Drama. Films include
Billy Liar (1963), *Darling* (1964), for
which she won an Oscar, *In Search of
Gregory* (1969), *Memoirs of a Survivor*
(1981) and *Heat and Dust* (1983). Has
won many awards, including Motion
Picture Herald Award, 1967, for Best
Dramatic Actress. Active in peace
movement and in a wide range of
human rights causes.

Caryl Churchill, 1938–
Playwright. Brought up in Canada.
Educated at Oxford University,
where she was involved in student
drama. Plays include *Light Shining in
Buckinghamshire* and *Vinegar Tom*
(1976), *Cloud 9* (1979), and *Top Girls*
(1982).

Hillary Clinton, 1947–
America's First Lady and lawyer.
Studied at Wellesley College and
Yale. Worked in legal profession in
1970s. Chair of Committee on
Women in the Profession, American
Bar Association, 1987–81. Has won
many awards as a lawyer. Interests
include social policy issues, especially
health and women's employment,
including women's economic
initiatives in the Third World.

Jacqueline Cochran, 1910–80
Airwoman. Adopted and brought up
in poverty, she initially worked as a
beautician. Got licence to fly in 1933
and won Bendix Cup air race in
1938, flying a Seversky fighter plane.
Recruited US volunteers for UK in
Second World War. In charge of

Women Auxiliary Service Pilots
(WASP) when US entered war. In
1953 she was first woman to fly
through sound barrier. Tried
unsuccessfully to be nominated as a
Republican candidate for Congress.

Marie Corelli, 1855–1924
Popular sentimental novelist. Books
include *Eyes of the Sea* (1917). In 1907
she opposed women's suffrage as
unfeminine. She upheld traditional
sexual morality.

Ida Cox, *c.* 1889–1967
Singer. From the South, she sang first
in the church choir, running away to
tour in minstrel shows and vaudeville.
Sang with Jelly Roll Morton and
Louis Armstrong. Appeared at
Carnegie Hall concert 'From
Spirituals to Swing', 1939. In 1961
recorded *Blues for Rampart Street* with
Coleman Hawkins.

Jill Craigie, 1914–
Film-maker. Worked as a journalist.
Wrote filmscripts in 1940s and
became first woman film-maker in
Britain. First documentary was on
modern art in Second World War,
followed by *The Way We Live*, a
feature documentary. Worked at
Pinewood in 1940s and 1950s.
Member of Six Point Group. Married
Michael Foot (later leader of the
Labour Party) 1949. Compiled an
archive of suffrage history, which she
has researched and lectured upon.

Joan Crawford, *c.* 1906–77
Film actress. From Texas. Worked as
a dancer before making films from
mid-1920s. Best-known films include

A Woman's Face (1941), *Mildred Pierce* (1945) and *Whatever Happened to Baby Jane?* (1962).

Helen Crawfurd, 1877–1954
Socialist and feminist. From a Glasgow Protestant and Conservative family, she became involved in the Women's Social and Political Union. She was honorary secretary of Women's Peace Crusade, and was active with Agnes Dollan, Mary Barbour and Jessie Stephen in Glasgow rent strikes in 1915. Worked with Workers' International Relief Organization in the 1920s. She visited Ireland in 1922 and was pro-Home Rule. Active in anti-Fascist groups during the 1930s and as a left-winger in local government in Dunoon.

Nellie Cressall, 1882–1973
Suffragette and Labour activist. Born in Stepney, east London. Worked in a laundry in Whitechapel. Joined Limehouse Independent Labour Party in 1908. From 1912 active with Sylvia Pankhurst in suffrage movement. On Food Control Committee, 1914–18. Poplar councillor, 1919–65. Imprisoned in 1921 with other Poplar councillors for refusing to lower poor relief. Mayor of Poplar, 1943; Freeman of the Borough, 1959.

Constance Cummings, 1910–
Actress. Born in Seattle. Theatre career began in 1932. Plays include *Goodbye Mr Chips* (1938) and *Who's Afraid of Virginia Woolf?* (1964). Has appeared in both US and Britain. On Arts Council of Great Britain, 1965–71. Awarded the CBE in 1974.

Nancy Cunard, 1896–1965
Poet, writer and publisher. Daughter of American society hostess and English baronet. Moved in bohemian society in 1920s. Interested in Surrealism, Dada, African art and black American music. In 1934 published *Negro*, on black culture and politics. Supported Republican Spain.

Edwina Currie, 1946–
Conservative MP. Educated at Oxford University and the London School of Economics. Worked as a lecturer and was active in Birmingham local government before being elected to Parliament for Derbyshire South in 1983. Secretary of State for Education and Science, 1985–6, she was then Parliamentary Under-Secretary of State at the Department of Health, causing controversy with her outspoken views on healthy diet. Pro-European. Her first novel, *A Parliamentary Affair* (1994), was a best-seller.

Mary Daly, 1928–
Writer and feminist theologian. Fired from Boston College theology department in 1968 for her book *The Church and the Second Sex*. Rehired after students protested. Went on to write extensively on feminism and spirituality. Work includes *Beyond God the Father* (1973) and *Gyn/Ecology* (1978).

Angela Davis, 1944–
African-American activist and writer. From a middle-class family in Alabama. Influenced by civil rights, radical student movement and Third World anti-colonial movement. Studied under Herbert Marcuse and

593

joined Communist Party. In 1970 charged with kidnapping, conspiracy and murder when the brother of her friend, prisoner George Jackson, used her (legally owned) guns to try to free him. Her trial, 1971–2, was accompanied by an international campaign for her acquittal. She has continued to work with prisoners and is in the Black Women's Health Project. She has held academic posts in several universities in California. Work includes *Women, Race and Class* (1982).

Emily Wilding Davison, 1872–1913
Suffragette. Member of the Women's Social and Political Union (WSPU). A 'militant', she flung herself, wrapped in a WSPU flag, in front of George V's horse at the Derby in 1913 and died. Huge crowds attended her funeral.

Doris Day, 1924–
(*Doris von Kappelhoff*)
Actress. Began as a dancer and singer, becoming leading lady in *The Bob Hope Show*, 1948–50. Films include *Calamity Jane* (1953) and *Pillow Talk* (1954). Became a star in 1950s and early 1960s.

Dorothy Day, 1897–1980
Social reformer. Studied at University of Illinois, Urbana. Joined the Socialist Party. Wrote for the socialist *Call* and *The Liberator*. Joined Industrial Workers of the World. Converted to Catholicism in 1927. Opened Houses of Hospitality for the unemployed in the 1930s. Active in civil disobedience against nuclear

weapons, 1955–61. Opposed Vietnam War in the 1960s and supported the farm workers in the 1970s.

Simone de Beauvoir, 1908–86
French writer whose book *The Second Sex* (1949) challenged the sexual conservatism of the late 1940s and had a great influence in both Britain and the US from the 1950s. Through novels such as *The Mandarins* (1957) and several autobiographical works she presented a personal statement of women's emancipation and left-wing political commitment. She had a long-term relationship with the philosopher Jean-Paul Sartre.

Julia de Burgos, *c*. 1914–53
Poet and journalist. From a poor rural barrio in Puerto Rico, she studied at University of Puerto Rico, 1931–3. Became a teacher and worked in day care. Her poems, published 1937–9, won an award from the Institute of Puerto Rican Literature. In 1940 went to New York and worked as a journalist. Visited Cuba, 1941–2. Involved in the Circle of Ibero-American Writers and Poets, 1943–5. Worked for Pueblos Hispanicos. Influenced by Chilean poet Pablo Neruda.

Jessie Lopez de la Cruz, 1919–
Trade union organizer. Brought up by her grandmother in California. Lived in farm workers' labour camps. In 1965 joined the National Farm Workers' Association. Started organic farming co-operative in 1973 and helped to found National Land for People in 1974. In 1977 she studied at Farm Workers' Free University. She

was given an award by the League of Mexican American Women for her work for the farm workers in 1977.

Dame Ninette de Valois, 1898– (*Edris Stannus*)

Irish dancer and choreographer. Began dancing in a children's theatre company. Went on to work with Diaghilev's Ballets Russes. In 1931, with Lilian Baylis, formed Vic-Well's Ballet (later Sadler's Wells). Developed ballet in Turkey, Canada and Iran. Founded Royal Ballet in 1956 and was director until 1963. Awarded the CBE in 1947 and the DBE in 1957. In 1974 first woman to win the Erasmus Prize Foundation Award.

Shelagh Delaney, 1939–

Playwright. Born Salford, Lancashire. Best known for her 1950s play *A Taste of Honey*, which was turned into a film. She has also worked for TV and wrote the screenplay for the film *Dance with a Stranger* (1985).

Charlotte Despard, 1844–1939

Suffragette, socialist and supporter of Sinn Fein. From a prominent Anglo-Irish family. Broke with Women's Social and Political Union in 1907 and founded the Women's Freedom League. Continued to be active in Irish politics after the women's vote was won in Britain. In the 1930s she opposed Franco and spoke at an anti-Fascist demonstration in Hyde Park when she was ninety-one.

Bernadette Devlin (McAliskey), 1947–

Socialist and Republican politician. From a Catholic family in Cookstown, Northern Ireland. Became interested in Republican politics and socialism. Helped form the Civil Rights movement as a university student. In 1969 became youngest MP in House of Commons. Continued to be active in left politics in Ireland. She and her husband, Michael McAliskey, were seriously wounded in 1981 by Protestant gunmen.

Diana, Princess of Wales, 1961–

Daughter of 8th Earl Spencer. Worked as a nursery teacher after finishing school. In 1981 she married Prince Charles, becoming a popular media figure and supporter of many charities. In 1992 Andrew Morton's *Diana: Her True Story* told of her unhappiness in the marriage and in 1994 James Hewitt revealed their affair. In autumn 1995 Diana appeared in a controversial TV interview which was followed by divorce in 1996, instigated by the Queen.

Monica Dickens, 1915–92

Writer. After an upper-class upbringing in London, she did the season and then became a servant, before writing *One Pair of Hands* (1939). She wrote nearly fifty books and a column for *Woman's Own*, 1946–65. In 1950, after marrying an American Naval officer, Roy Stratton, she went to live in Cape Cod, Massachusetts, where she founded the US branch of the Samaritans.

Returned to Britain after her husband's death in 1985.

Babe Didrikson, 1914–56
(Mildred Zaharias)

Sportswoman. Daughter of a Norwegian carpenter from Texas. At fifteen broke two national records in Dallas with the javelin and basketball throw. Excelled as an athlete at the Olympics in 1932, winning gold medals in the javelin and hurdles. In 1938, took up golf, helped by her husband, George Zaharias, who became her manager. Won many tournaments in professional and amateur golf. In 1947 founded Ladies' Professional Golf Association.

Marlene Dietrich, 1901–92
(Maria Magdalene von Losch)

Actress. Born in Berlin, she acted in German films directed by Gerry Wilhelm Pabst and Alexander Korda, among others, before starring in Josef von Sternberg's The Blue Angel (1930). She worked in Hollywood in the 1930s and during the Second World War supported the Allies against Hitler, performing for the troops. Awarded the Medal of Freedom in 1947. There was still hostility towards her in Germany when she returned in 1960. Other films include Blonde Venus (1932), The Devil is a Woman (1935) and Destry Rides Again (1939).

Lady Agnes Dollan, 1887–1966

Trade union and community organizer. Brought up in Glasgow. Organized post office workers with Mary MacArthur. Joined Independent Labour Party and Women's Social and Political Union. In First World War

organized Glasgow Women's International League with Helen Crawfurd in opposition to war. Treasurer of Glasgow Women's Housing Association and active in rent strike of 1915. In Second World War involved in Women's Volunteer Service. Given an MBE in 1966.

Mary Dreier, 1875–1963

Social reformer. From comfortable New York Brooklyn family. Became involved in Women's Trade Union League. Supported 1909 shirt-waisters' strike. Supporter of suffrage movement and the Progressive Party. Friendly with President Roosevelt, she supported New Deal. Campaigned for Henry Wallace in 1948. Member of German Evangelical and later Presbyterian Church. In 1950s campaigned against nuclear weapons. Sister of Margaret Dreier Robins.

Peggy Duff, 1910–81

Peace campaigner. Educated at Bedford College. Member of Labour Party, 1945–67, resigning in protest against Labour government's policies over Vietnam War and Greek Junta. Organizing secretary for CND from its inception, she continued to be active in the peace movement and in the 1970s was General Secretary of the International Confederation for Disarmament and Peace.

Shiela Grant Duff, 1913–

Journalist. From a liberal family. Educated at Oxford University. Wrote for New Statesman in early 1930s about the rise of Hitler, then worked for the Observer. In the mid-1930s reported from Czechoslovakia and went to Spain. During Second World War worked in Foreign Office and BBC.

Isadora Duncan, 1877–1927
Dancer. Influenced by physical culture movement in San Francisco. Became famous as a symbol of freedom before First World War for her expressive style of dancing. Moved in radical bohemian circles in New York and Europe. Visited Soviet Union in 1921.

Andrea Dworkin, 1946–
Writer and feminist campaigner. Author of *Woman Hating* (1974). In 1983 drafted an anti-pornography ordinance with Catharine McKinnon for Minneapolis City Council. The US Supreme Court declared this unconstitutional in 1985. Continues to campaign on pornography and lesbian sexual issues.

Amelia Earhart, 1898–1937
Pioneer aviator. Flew across the Atlantic in 1932. She attempted a round-the-world flight from New Guinea in 1937 and vanished mysteriously, rapidly becoming a legend.

Crystal Eastman, 1881–1928
Social investigator, socialist and feminist writer. From a Congregationalist family. Educated at Vassar and Columbia. Studied law in New York. In 1907 joined the 'Pittsburgh Survey' and in 1910 published *Work Accidents and the Law*. Joined the Political Equality League and in 1913 helped Alice Paul start the Congressional Union for Woman Suffrage (later the National Woman's Party). She opposed the First World War and helped form the US Civil Liberties Bureau to defend conscientious objectors. Went to Britain 1921.

Gertrude Ederle, 1906–
Athlete. Won a gold medal in 1924 Olympic Games as a member of US 400-metre relay team and two bronze medals. In 1926 swam the English Channel in 14 hours 31 minutes, beating the existing men's record by nearly two hours.

Barbara Ehrenreich, 1941–
Journalist. Brought up in Butte, Montana, in a mining family. Studied at Reed College, Portland, Oregon. Became involved in anti-Vietnam War movement. Began writing on women's health in the early 1970s. In 1974 joined the socialist New American Movement. Journalist for *Ms.* and *The Nation*. Has written several books on women and social policy and a novel, *Kipper's Game* (1993).

Gertrude Elion, 1918–
Biochemist. From a Russian immigrant family, she was educated at Hunter College, New York. In 1940s worked on biochemistry of cancer cells. Her research on purines was vital in developing cancer treatment. In 1988 awarded Nobel Prize.

Elizabeth II, 1926–
Queen of the United Kingdom of Great Britain and Northern Ireland. She married Philip Mountbatten, who

was created Duke of Edinburgh, in 1947, and became Queen in 1952. Her Coronation took place in 1953. She travels widely and is particularly interested in the Commonwealth. In the 1990s she had to face a series of royal scandals and popular scepticism about the monarchy.

Elizabeth, Queen Mother, 1900–
Queen through marriage to George VI, upon abdication of Edward VIII in 1936. Born into an aristocratic Scottish family, the Bowes-Lyons, who were descended from Robert the Bruce. Married Prince Albert (Bertie), Duke of York, in 1924, and had two daughters, Elizabeth and Margaret. Became popular during the war for her work in the Blitz. Became Queen Mother in 1952. In 1979 she was made the 160th Warden of the Cinque Ports, the first woman to hold the post for 900 years.

Ruth Ellis, 1926–55
Nightclub hostess. Last woman to receive death penalty in Britain. From Rhyl, Wales. Shot her former lover, David Blakely, a racing driver, outside a pub in Hampstead because he had deserted her.

Lillian Evanti, 1891–1967
Singer. From an intellectual and musical black family in Washington, DC, she became well known as an opera singer in Paris in the 1920s. She performed at the Belasco Theater in Washington in 1934 and gave a command performance at the White House for the Roosevelts that year. Celebrated in Latin America in the 1940s. Gave concerts for US troops in

the war. Founded the National Negro Opera Company in Washington. Toured Africa during the 1950s.

Susan Faludi, 1959–
Journalist. From a New York Jewish family, she studied at Harvard and then worked for the *New York Times* and *Miami Herald* in the early 1980s. Wrote freelance for *Ms.* and *Mother Jones.* Her book *Backlash: The Undeclared War Against American Women* (1991) was an influential best-seller.

Jessie Fauset, 1882–1961
African-American novelist. Graduated from Cornell in 1905. Wrote for W. E. B. DuBois' journal *The Crisis.* Translated French-speaking black writers from Africa and the Caribbean. Novels include *The Chinaberry Tree* (1931).

Dame Millicent Garrett Fawcett, 1847–1929
Liberal feminist. President of National Union of Women's Suffrage Societies. Leading figure in constitutional suffrage movement. In 1914 supported the First World War.

Geraldine Ferraro, 1935–
Politician in Democratic Party. Worked as a schoolteacher and attended law school at night. Assistant District Attorney, 1974–8. In 1978 won a seat in Congress from 9th Congressional District (Queens New York). In 1981 sponsored Economic Equity Act. In 1984 first woman to be appointed as Chair of Democratic platform committee. Selected by Walter Mondale as vice-presidential

running mate in 1984, the first time a woman had been selected. They were defeated in November 1984.

Dame Gracie Fields, 1898–1979 (*May Stansfield*)

Singer and comedienne. From Rochdale, Lancashire. Beginning as a child performer in music hall, she became a popular star on radio, records, films and later television. Films include *Sally in Our Alley* (1931) and *Sing As We Go* (1934). Known as 'Our Gracie', she published her autobiography, *Sing As We Go*, in 1960, and in 1978 was made a DBE.

Shulamith Firestone, 1945–

Writer. From Canada, she studied at Art Institute of Chicago. Active in anti-Vietnam War protests and early Women's Liberation groups. In 1969 edited *Red Stockings*, a radical feminist journal. Her *Dialectic of Sex* (1970) was an influential book in the US and in Britain.

Ruth First, 1925–82

South African writer and Communist. Campaigned against conditions of black farm workers. Married to Joe Slovo, leader of the Communist Party. They were both tried and acquitted in treason trials of 1956. Imprisoned in 1963. Books include *The South African Connection: Western Involvement in Apartheid* (1972) and a biography of Olive Schreiner (with Ann Scott). Killed by a letter bomb while teaching at the Centre for African Studies, Mozambique.

Ella Fitzgerald, 1918–96

Singer. From Virginia, she was brought up in New York orphanage. Became a cabaret singer in 1940s. Developed 'scat singing'. Recorded with Cole Porter, Duke Ellington, Richard Rodgers, George Gershwin and Irving Berlin.

Zelda Fitzgerald, 1900–1948

Symbol of the Jazz Age. Belle of Montgomery, Alabama, she married Scott Fitzgerald in 1920. Tried to write and dance. Suffered a breakdown in 1930. Published *Save Me the Waltz* (1932), but spent most of her subsequent life in sanatoriums.

Baroness Shreela Flather, 1938–

Teacher and Conservative politician. Born in India and educated at London University. Called to the bar in 1962. Worked as a teacher in the 1960s and organized Maidenhead Ladies' Asian Club. Involved in Commission for Racial Equality. Active in local government, 1986–7, in Windsor and Maidenhead. First Asian woman to become a mayor. Member of Economic and Social Committee, 1987–90.

Eleanor Flexner, 1908–95

Historian. Influenced by her mother, a 'new woman', Anne Crawford Flexner. Graduated from Swarthmore College. Interested in left theatre and in 1938 wrote *American Playwrights, 1918–38*. During the 1940s organized office workers. Her *Century of Struggle: The Woman's Rights Movement in the United States* (1959) was written in the McCarthy era and contributed new insights about the role of working-class and African-American women.

Elizabeth Gurley Flynn, 1890–1964

'The Rebel Girl'. Labour organizer and Communist. From Irish-American family. Joined Industrial Workers of the World in 1906. Active in militant strikes at Lawrence, Massachusetts, 1912, and Paterson, New Jersey, 1913. Joined Communist Party in 1936 and wrote in CP publications. Persecuted in McCarthy era. Imprisoned in 1955–7, she went to Soviet Union in 1960.

Jane Fonda, 1937–

Actress. Born in New York, daughter of actor Henry Fonda. Went to Paris in the 1960s and married Roger Vadim, starring in his film *Barbarella* (1968). Returned to US, protested against Vietnam War. Active on women's rights, peace and ecology. Films include *Klute* (1971) and *Coming Home* (1978). In 1980s became famous for aerobics fitness routine.

Dame Margot Fonteyn, 1919–91 (*Margaret Hookham*)

Dancer. Joined Vic–Well's Ballet School as a snowflake in *Casse Noisette*. In 1940s became established as an outstanding dancer in *Coppelia* (1943) and *The Fairy Queen* (1946). Became president of the Royal Academy of Dancing in 1954 and Guest Artiste to the Royal Ballet in 1959. In 1962 began working with Rudolf Nureyev. Played an important part in popularizing ballet in Britain.

Betty Ford, 1918–

Former First Lady and organization executive. Worked as a dance instructor. Married Gerald R. Ford. Trustee of many organizations. Awarded Presidential Medal of Freedom in 1991.

Aretha Franklin, 1942–

Singer. From Memphis, Tennessee, she was brought up in a religious and musical family in Detroit. Began singing in a gospel choir. Inspired by Clara Ward, Mahalia Jackson and Dinah Washington, who were friends of the family. Signed with Atlantic Records in 1966. Songs include 'I Never Loved a Man (The Way I Loved You)', 1966, and 'Respect', 1967 – hits which made her known as the Queen of Soul. In the early 1980s she moved into rock and gospel. She has supported civil rights and the black movement, standing bail for Angela Davis.

Christine Frederick, 1883–1970

Scientific management theorist. Editor of *Ladies' Home Journal*. Founder of the League of Advertising Women in 1912. Applied ideas of scientific management to housework. Works include *The New Housekeeping* (1913) and *Selling Mrs Consumer* (1929).

Betty Friedan, 1921–

Feminist campaigner and writer. Graduated from Smith College, 1942. Studied at Berkeley. From 1946 to early 1950s wrote for trade union journal *UE News*. Began writing for women's magazines in the mid-1950s. Interest in predicament of housewives led to *The Feminine Mystique* (1963).

Went on to form National Organisation for Women in 1966, helped form National Women's Political Caucus, 1971, and first Women's Bank, 1973. Campaigned for the ERA and continued to write books and articles.

Greta Garbo, 1905–90
(*Greta Lovisa Gustafsson*)
Swedish and American film actress. From Stockholm working-class family. Worked as a salesgirl and appeared in a publicity film. Studied at Royal Dramatic Theatre School and worked in European films. Went to Hollywood in 1924. Appeared in silent film *The Torrent* (1926). Other films include *Grand Hotel* (1932), *Queen Christina* (1933) and *Ninotchka* (1939). Retired from acting in 1941.

Amy Ashwood Garvey, 1897–1969
Black political organizer. From Jamaica, she met black leader Marcus Garvey when she was seventeen. Became secretary of his Universal Negro Improvement Association (UNIA) in Jamaica. In 1918 she joined him in US to work on UNIA magazine the *Negro World*. They married in 1919. After marriage broke down she went to Britain. Helped form Nigerian Progress Union. From 1935 to 1938 her restaurant in west London was a Pan-Africanist centre frequented by C. L. R. James, George Padmore and Jomo Kenyatta among others. Chaired opening session of Pan-African Conference in Manchester in mid-1940s. Travelled between US, Britain, the Caribbean and Africa in 1950s and 1960s. Organized a community centre in London

after Notting Hill race riots in the late 1950s.

Amy Jacques Garvey, 1896–1973
Activist. From Kingston, Jamaica. Went to US in 1917. Joined Marcus Garvey's United Negro Improvement Association in 1918. Worked as his secretary and office manager. They married in 1922. While he was in prison for alleged mail fraud, she continued his work, editing 'Our Women and What They Think' in the *Negro World*, linking Pan-Africanism to the active political involvement of women. Accompanied Garvey to Jamaica after his release in 1927. Her writing, which included *Black Power in America* (1968), helped revive interest in the Garveyite movement.

Martha Gellhorn, 1908–
Journalist and novelist. Reported from Spain in the 1930s and worked for *Colliers* during Second World War, when she travelled widely in Europe and China. In 1983 she exposed torture in El Salvador and during the British miners' strike interviewed Welsh women in the coal fields. Books include *The Trouble I've Seen* (1936) and *The View From the Ground* (1989).

Lois Gibbs, 1951–
Environmental campaigner. Became aware of dangerous toxic waste dumped at Love Canal after her children became sick in 1978. Campaigned to evacuate homes. President Carter agreed in 1980. In 1990s still fighting to prevent resettlement. Active in Everyone's Backyard: The Citizens' Clearinghouse for Hazardous

Waste, the grass-roots movement for environmental justice.

Lillian Moller Gilbreth, 1878–1972
Theorist of scientific management. Educated at Berkeley and Columbia. Collaborated with husband Frank Gilbreth on application of time and motion study in industry. Brought up twelve children. Pioneered scientific management in the home. Influenced home economics and pioneered ergonomics. First woman to receive Hoover Medal for distinguished public service in engineering, 1966.

Charlotte Perkins Gilman, 1860–1935
Feminist writer. Related to the famous Beecher family but grew up in poverty. After divorce from Charles Stetson, an artist, in 1892, she began writing and lecturing to support herself. Was influenced by Bernard Shaw and the Webbs. In 1898 published *Women and Economics*, arguing for social planning. Supported suffrage movement and helped found Woman's Peace Party. Her theories about collective domestic services were influential in Britain as well as the US.

Victoria Glendinning, 1937–
Journalist and writer. Educated at Oxford and Southampton universities. Worked part-time as a teacher and then a social worker. Has written for *The Times, Times Literary Supplement, Times Education Supplement* and *Washington Post*. Work includes biographies of Elizabeth Bowen and Rebecca West.

Maria Goeppert, Mayer, 1906–72
German-born American physicist. Taught at Johns Hopkins University. Studied nuclear shell structure and developed theory of spin orbit coupling. Given Professorial Chair at University of California in 1960. Awarded (with Eugene Paul Wigner and Hans Jensen) Nobel Prize for Physics in 1963 for her research on nuclear shell structure.

Whoopi Goldberg, 1949–
Actress. Born in a New York housing project, she was active in civil rights during the 1960s. After a successful one-woman show she got the lead in the film of Alice Walker's *The Color Purple* (1985). Later films include *Jumpin' Jack Flash* (1986) and *Ghosts* (1990), which won her an Oscar. She was a founder of Comic Relief Benefit shows and has done a TV series based on the film *Baghdad Café*.

Emma Goldman, 1869–1940
Political activist. Born in Lithuania, she emigrated to US in 1885 and worked in a factory. Became an anarchist. Campaigned for workers' rights, women's emancipation and free love. Edited *Mother Earth*, 1906–17. Imprisoned 1893 and 1914 for giving birth-control information. Anti-First World War; imprisoned 1918–19 for opposition to the draft. Deported to Soviet Union in 1919. Criticized Bolsheviks for human rights abuses. Lived in exile in Europe and Canada. Supported anarchists in Spanish Civil War. Wrote extensively. Works include her autobiography, *Living My Life* (1931).

Maud Gonne, 1865–1953

Irish Nationalist and actress. Daughter of an English colonel. She edited *L'Irlande libre* in Paris, 1903. W. B. Yeats dedicated poems to her, and she played Cathleen ni Hoolihan in his play in Dublin. Married Major John MacBride, who fought against the British in the Boer War and in the Easter Rising. He was executed in 1916 and she became active in Sinn Fein. Sean MacBride, her son, was Foreign Minister in the Irish Republic, 1948–51.

Betty Grable, 1916–73

Film actress. Star of 1940s. Famous as pin-up in Second World War. In *How to Marry a Millionaire* with Marilyn Monroe and Lauren Bacall (1953).

Katherine Graham, 1917–

Newspaper executive. Studied at Vassar, 1934–6. Worked as a reporter on *San Francisco News*, 1938–9, then went to *Washington Post*, a paper her father bought in 1933. President of Washington Post Co., 1963–73, and then chief executive officer. Her paper exposed President Nixon in the Watergate affair.

Edith Green, 1910–87

Politician in Democratic Party. Worked as a teacher, radio announcer, freelance scriptwriter and operator of a trailer court. Entered Congress in 1954. Particular interests were education and equal pay. Authored Equal Pay Act of 1963.

Germaine Greer, 1939–

Writer and broadcaster. From Australia, she was educated at Melbourne and Cambridge universities. Taught English at Warwick University. Influenced by radical counter-culture of the late 1960s. Her book *The Female Eunuch* (1970) was very successful and she became a well-known figure in the media, speaking as well as writing on women. Her recent work includes *The Change* (1991).

Martha Griffiths, 1912–

Politician in the Democratic Party. Elected to US Congress 1954, she was a key figure in getting the ERA through Congress in 1972. Active in Women's Research and Education Institute. In 1983 became Michigan's first woman lieutenant governor.

Marguerite Radclyffe Hall, 1880–1943

Writer. Her most famous work was *The Well of Loneliness* (1928), which was banned. She lived with Una Troubridge for twenty-eight years and they created an image of 'the lesbian' in smartly tailored 1920s styles which had an impact far beyond Britain.

Fannie Lou Hamer, 1917–77

Civil rights activist. Born into poor rural Mississippi family, she worked in cotton fields. Tried unsuccessfully to register to vote in 1962 and became campaigner for voter registration. Field officer for Student Non-violent Co-ordinating Committee, 1963. One of the founders of Mississippi Freedom Democratic Party. In 1969 set up Freedom Farms Corporation to help poor families grow food. Became chair of the board of the Fannie Lou Hamer Day Care Center in 1970.

Alice Hamilton, 1869–1970

Physician and social reformer. Despite family objections, she studied bacteriology and pathology in Germany. Became professor of pathology at North Western University's Woman's Medical School, 1897, and worked at social settlement Hull House. Became interested in industrial diseases and campaigned for safety laws. By 1916 had become an authority on lead poisoning. In First World War accompanied Jane Addams to International Congress of Women at The Hague. Became a pacifist. Active in New Deal as a consultant to Department of Labor. In 1963 signed open letter opposing Vietnam War.

Lorraine Hansberry, 1930–65

Playwright. Studied at University of Wisconsin, where she integrated her dormitory. Supported Henry Wallace's campaign for the presidency in 1948. Worked as a journalist, 1951–3, on Paul Robeson's paper, *Freedom*. Married white theatre director Robert Nemiroff in 1953. Wrote *A Raisin in the Sun* and in 1959 was first black playwright to win New York Drama Critics' Circle Award. Supported Civil Rights movement. Wrote photoessay *The Movement: Documentary of a Struggle for Equality* (1964). After she died, her husband produced *To Be Young, Gifted and Black: Lorraine Hansberry in Her Own Words*. It was dramatized in 1968 and published in 1969.

Harriet Harman, 1950–

Labour MP. Educated at York University. Was legal officer for the National Council of Civil Liberties, 1978–82. She has focused on women, welfare issues, health and the economy since she was elected for Peckham in 1982.

Dame Judith Hart, 1924–91

Labour MP. Born in Burnley, Lancashire, she studied at the London School of Economics. Elected MP for Lanark in 1959. Chief area of interest was Third World development. Minister of Overseas Development, 1969–70, 1974–5 and 1977–9. Chairman of Labour Party, 1981–2. Active in CND.

Dame Caroline Haslett, 1845–1957

Engineer. Worked as a secretary in an engineering firm and in First World War trained as an engineer. Founded Women's Engineering Society in 1919. In 1947 appointed part-time head of British Electrical Authority and made a DBE. She encouraged women in engineering as a profession and also wrote on electricity in the home.

Goldie Hawn, 1945–

Actress. From Washington, DC. Began as chorus girl at the World's Fair, New York. Worked in theatre, film and TV. Films include *There's a Girl in My Soup* (1970) and *Private Benjamin* (1980), which was also a TV series.

Margaret Heckler, 1931–

Politician in the Republican Party. Became Representative for Massachusetts in 1967. Advocated day care in Congress. Supported women's credit rights with Democrat Edward Koch, leading to Equal Credit Opportunity Act in 1974. After International

Women's Year Conference of 1975, introduced legislation in Congress with Patsy Mink and Bella Abzug for the National Women's Conference at Houston, Texas, 1977. Under Reagan, supported funding of Women's Educational Equity Act programme, 1981–2.

Lillian Hellman, 1907–84
Playwright. Born in New Orleans, she was educated at New York and Columbia universities. Her plays include *The Little Foxes* (1939) and *Toys in the Attic* (1960). She reported on the Spanish Civil War and appeared before the Un-American Activities Committee. In the 1980s she sued Mary McCarthy for libel over the veracity of her memoirs *An Unfinished Woman* (1969) and *Pentimento* (1973).

Audrey Hepburn, 1929–93
(*Edda Van Heemstra Hepburn*)
Film actress. Worked as a model, dancer and actress. In 1951 a meeting with Colette led to her being given the lead in the stage version of one of Colette's books, *Gigi* (1952). This took her to Hollywood. Films include *Breakfast at Tiffany's* (1961). Worked on child poverty with UNICEF.

Katharine Hepburn, 1909–
Film and stage actress. Brought up by a feminist mother and educated at Bryn Mawr College. Films include *The Philadelphia Story* (1940), *The African Queen* (1951) and *Suddenly Last Summer* (1959). She made a successful transition into playing older women's roles in films.

Dame Barbara Hepworth, 1903–75
Artist and sculptor. Born in Wakefield, studied at Leeds School of Art and the Royal College of Art. Involved in radical artists' group Seven and Five Society. Her work became increasingly abstract in the 1930s, when she worked with Ben Nicholson, whom she married in 1939. Her work includes *Figures in a Landscape* and *Single Form* for the UN Building, New York (1964).

Margaret Herbison, 1907–
Labour MP and minister. Educated at Bellshill Academy and Glasgow University. Worked as a schoolteacher in Glasgow and also taught for National Council of Labour Colleges. Elected for North Lanark in 1945. Joint Under-Secretary for Scotland, 1950–51. Minister of Pensions and National Insurance from 1964.

Aileen Hernandez, 1926–
Administrator and feminist campaigner. From a Jamaican family, she grew up in Brooklyn. Studied at Howard University, Washington, DC. Equal Opportunities Commissioner, 1965, and in 1970 became president of National Organization for Women.

Patricia Hewitt, 1948–
Labour policy adviser. From Australia, she was educated at Cambridge University. Worked for Age Concern, 1971–3, and became Women's Rights Officer for the National Council of Civil Liberties, 1973–4, and General Secretary, 1974–83. From 1983 to 1988 she was a policy adviser

to Neil Kinnock. Since 1989 she has been at the Institute for Public Policy Research. Active in the Fabian Society. She has written on employment rights.

Shere Hite, 1943–
Social scientist. Works include *Sexual Honesty by Women for Women* (1974) and *The Hite Report: A Nationwide Study of Female Sexuality* (1976). Chosen by *Newsweek* as one of America's twenty-five most influential women in 1978.

Oveta Culp Hobby, 1905–
Newspaper proprietor, broadcasting executive and lawyer. Became director of Women's Army Auxiliary Corps (WAAC). In 1943 this gained military status as the Women's Army Corps. In 1953–4 was Secretary of Health, Education and Welfare under President Eisenhower. In the 1950s she worked in publishing, radio and TV and in 1970 became Chair of Broadcasting.

Dorothy Crowfoot Hodgkin, 1910–94
Scientist. Born in Egypt and studied at Oxford and Cambridge universities. Research Fellow, Somerville College, Oxford, 1936–77, and Wolfson research professor at the Royal Society, 1960–77. Distinguished crystallographer. In Second World War she worked on the structure of penicillin. In 1964 she was given the Nobel Prize for Chemistry for discoveries through the use of X-ray techniques of the structure of molecules, penicillin, vitamin B_{12} and insulin.

Billie Holiday, 1915–59 (*Eleanora Fagan*)
Singer. Started singing in Harlem bars in 1931. Recorded with Benny Goodman in 1933. Worked with Count Basie in 1937 and Artie Shaw in 1938–9. Was in Duke Ellington's *Symphony in Black* (1935), a film about African-American life. Songs include 'Strange Fruit', about lynching, and 'Lover Man Don't Explain'. Hospitalized in 1947 and then imprisoned on a narcotics charge. Sang at Carnegie Hall in 1948 and toured Europe in 1954. Addicted to heroin, she was admitted to the Metropolitan Hospital, New York, and was arrested for possessing illicit drugs.

Winifred Holtby, 1898–1935
Journalist and novelist. Educated in Scarborough. Member of Women's Auxiliary Corps in First World War. Studied at Oxford University, where she became friendly with Vera Brittain. Wrote for *Manchester Guardian*, *News Chronicle* and *Time and Tide*. Her novels include *Anderby Wold* (1923) and *South Riding* (1936), published posthumously. Her study of Virginia Woolf was published in 1932.

bell hooks, 1952– (*Gloria Watkins*)
Writer. From Kentucky, she has held several academic posts and written influential works on race and gender, including *Ain't I a Woman: Black Women and Feminism* (1981).

Katherine Hoover, 1937–
Composer and flautist. Studied at the, Eastman School, Bryn Mawr, and the Manhattan School of Music. Organ-

ized Women's Interart Center music festivals in New York, 1978–81.

Grace Hopper, 1906–92
Computer pioneer. From New York, she graduated from Vassar and then studied maths at Yale. In Second World War she joined Women Accepted for Voluntary Emergency Service. In 1944 she worked with the Bureau of Ordnance Computation Project at Harvard. Her basic programme language helped to simplify computing. She retired from the navy in 1960 but was recalled during the Vietnam War in 1967 to reorganize the navy's computers. She became the first woman to rise to the rank of Rear Admiral.

Lena Horne, 1917–
Singer and civil rights activist. Her mother was an actress. She was brought up partly by her grandmother, a former suffragette and member of the National Association for the Advancement of Colored People. She began singing and dancing while young. Starring role in *Blackbirds* (1939). Acted in all-black film *Cabin in the Sky* (1943). Appeared on *The Ed Sullivan Show* in 1950, but blacklisted under McCarthy as a radical and did not perform again until she did *The Perry Como Show* in 1959. Active in civil rights in the 1960s and continued her support for racial equality.

Karen Horney, 1885–1952
German-American psychoanalyst. Studied medicine at Göttingen. In First World War worked at Berlin Sanatorium military neuropsychiatric hospital. At Berlin Psychoanalytic Institute after war. Challenged Freud on penis envy. Went to USA 1932. Wrote on women and psychoanalysis and on neurosis. Challenged Oedipus complex. Became interested in Zen Buddhism and visited Japan.

Lady Elspeth Howe, 1932–
Equal Opportunities Commissioner. Educated at London School of Economics. Married Rt. Hon. Sir Geoffrey Howe in 1953. Active in Conservative women's politics, 1966–77. Particularly interested in legal matters. Deputy Chairman, 1975–9, Equal Opportunities Commission. Active in Pre-School Playgroups Association, 1979–83. In the 1980s she became a director in various companies. She was Chair of Hansard Society Commission on Women on Top, 1989–90, and from 1979 was president of the Women's Gas Federation.

Dolores Huerta, 1930–
Union organizer. Born in New Mexico. In 1955 worked for Community Service Organization and organized farm workers. In 1962 helped Cesar Chavez in organizing drive. In 1962 became member of United Farm Workers' Organizing Committee. Negotiated contract with Delano grape growers in 1970. Involved in lettuce boycott in 1970. A supporter of poor people's movements, in the early 1990s she organized against the denial of civil rights to immigrant workers from Mexico.

Charlayne Hunter-Gault, 1942–
Journalist. From a middle-class family in South Carolina, she was one of two black students to desegregate the Uni-

versity of Georgia, Athens, in 1961. Journalist on the *New Yorker* and the *New York Times*. Joined *The MacNeil/ Lennet News Hour* on CBS as national correspondent in 1978.

Margery Hurst, 1913–89

Businesswoman. Studied drama. Joined Auxiliary Territorial Service in Second World War. Founded Brook Street Bureau Mayfair Ltd in London in 1946, which made her a millionaire. Her non-profit-making social clubs for secretaries have expanded to many countries, including Australia and the US. Awarded Pimms Cup for Anglo-American business friendship in 1962. On American Committee of British National Economic Commission, 1967–70. Awarded Order of the British Empire in 1976. In 1970 she became one of the first women members of Lloyd's of London. First woman elected to the New York Chamber of Commerce. Her autobiography, *No Glass Slipper*, was published in 1967.

Zora Neale Hurston, 1901–60

Anthropologist and novelist. Born in all-black town, Eatonville, Florida, and educated at Hungerford School, established by supporters of black leader Booker T. Washington. Studied part-time at Howard University, where she met writer Alain Locke and poet Georgia Douglas Johnson. Gained scholarship to Barnard College in 1925. Studied with anthropologist Frank Boas at Columbia University. Wrote for black reviews and for academic journals. Studied folk culture and religious cults in Southern states, the Bahamas, Haiti and Jamaica.

Involved in Harlem Renaissance through friendship with Alain Locke and Langston Hughes. Novels include *Their Eyes Were Watching God* (1937).

Elsie Maud Inglis, 1864–1917

Doctor and suffragist. Born in India and studied at Edinburgh School of Medicine under pioneer doctor Sophia Jex Blake. Initiated Scottish Women's Hospital Units in First World War.

Mahalia Jackson, 1911–72

Singer. From New Orleans, she began singing in church. At sixteen went to Chicago, singing for Choir of the Salem Baptist Church and then for the Johnson Gospel Singers. Recording gospel songs from mid-1930s. Sang for Civil Rights movement in 1960s and performed at Martin Luther King's funeral in 1971. Featured in film *Jazz on a Summer's Day* (1959).

Storm Jameson, 1891–1986 (*Margaret*)

Novelist. Brought up in Whitby. Studied at Leeds University and as a graduate in London. Edited the *New Commonwealth* magazine and in the 1920s co-managed the British firm of Knopf publishers. Works include *The Clash* (1922) and *Women Against Men* (1933–7). First woman president of British section of the International PEN, 1939–45. Worked for refugee writers.

Alice Mae Lee Jemison, 1901–64

American Indian leader of Cherokee and Seneca Indian stock. Worked as an usher and beautician until she graduated from Silver Creek High

School. Concern about conditions on the Seneca reservation led her into politics. An upholder of Indian treaty rights, she was influenced by Pan-Indian leader Carlos Montezuma. Hostile to the Bureau of Indian Affairs and the New Deal, she found herself in alliance with right-wing groups.

Dorothy Jewson, 1884–1964
Labour politician. From a wealthy Norwich Liberal family. Educated at Cambridge University, where she became interested in socialism. Joined Independent Labour Party. Active in suffrage movement. MP for Norwich, 1923–4, president of Workers' Birth Control Group, 1924. Campaigned with Stella Browne and Dora Russell for birth control in welfare centres. Later supported peace movement and joined the Society of Friends.

Amy Johnson, 1904–41
Aviator. From Hull and educated at Sheffield University. Learned to fly at Brent, Middlesex. Famous for a long-distance flight from London to Australia in 1930. Joined Women's branch of the Air Transport Auxiliary in Second World War. Disappeared over the Thames Estuary on a flight in bad weather.

Georgia Douglas Johnson, 1886–1966
Poet and playwright. Born in Atlanta, Georgia, of mixed Indian and black ancestry. Studied at Atlanta University and Oberlin Conservatory of Music. Began to write poetry in the journal *Crisis* in 1916. Her collections *The Heart of a Woman* (1918), *Bronze: A*

Book of Verse (1922) and *An Autumn Love Cycle* (1928) brought her into contact with the Harlem Renaissance.

Claudia Jones, 1915–64
From Port of Spain, Trinidad. Her family emigrated to the US in 1924. Active in Communist Party during the 1930s. Wrote on black and women's issues. In 1955, during the McCarthy era, she was forced to leave for Britain, where, in 1958, she founded and edited the *West Indian Gazette*. Co-ordinator of the first Caribbean Carnival in London, which developed into the annual Notting Hill Carnival, the biggest in Europe.

Mary Harris (Mother) Jones, 1830–1930
Labour organizer. Born in Cork, Ireland. Family emigrated to US in 1835. Worked as dressmaker and teacher. Became active in labour organizing in 1880s. She led wives of striking miners against scabs in the early 1890s. Campaigned against coal owners after lock-out and massacre at Ludlow in 1914. Supported New York City street car and garment workers on strike in 1915–16 and the 1919 steel strike. She was sympathetic to socialism, but anti-suffrage.

Erica Jong, 1942–
Novelist. From New York, she was educated at Barnard and Columbia. After several academic posts, she began writing fiction. Works include *Fear of Flying* (1973) and *Fanny* (1979).

Janis Joplin, 1943–70
Singer. From Port Arthur, Texas. Inspired by Bessie Smith. Sang with

Big Brother and the Holding Company. Appeared at Monterey Festival in 1967. Albums include *Cheap Thrills* (1968).

Jackie Kay, 1961–

Poet and playwright. Born in Edinburgh. Brought up by white adoptive parents in Glasgow. Studied English at Stirling University. She has read her work and written for several collections. She co-edited *Charting the Journey: Writings by Black and Third World Women* (1988). Her sequence of poems *The Adoption Papers* was dramatized on Radio 3 in 1990.

Helen Adams Keller, 1880–1968

Social reformer. She lost sight and hearing when she was seventeen months old. Taught from the age of seven by Anne Sullivan. Graduated from Radcliffe College. Exposed industrial conditions causing blindness. She became a socialist and supporter of radical social reform. Friendly with Eleanor Roosevelt. Her triumph over her disabilities made her a celebrated figure.

Florence Kelley, 1859–1932

Social reformer. Translated Friedrich Engels's *Condition of the Working Class* (1887, New York). In 1891 became a resident at Hull House. Campaigned against child labour and low-paid sweated work. Became general secretary of the National Consumers' League in 1899. Worked towards protective labour laws. In 1909 helped form National Association for the Advancement of Colored People, and in 1919 the Women's International League for Peace and Free-

dom. Opposed the ERA in the 1920s.

Frances Oldham Kelsey, 1914–

Campaigner against thalidomide. Born in Canada. Worked on pharmacology in Chicago in 1930s. In 1960 began working for US Food and Drug Administration. Concern about thalidomide led to a battle in 1961 to get it banned. In 1962 awarded District Federal Civilian Medal under President Kennedy.

Helena Kennedy, 1950–

Lawyer. From Scottish working-class family. Educated Holyrood School, Glasgow and Gray's Inn, London. Involved in women's movement and Labour politics. Among her cases was the Guildford Four Appeal. Became a QC in 1991. Is Chancellor of Oxford Brooks University and chair of constitutional rights group Charter 88. Works include *Eve was Framed* (1992), on women and the criminal justice system.

Annie Kenney, 1879–1953

Lancashire suffragette. A mill worker and trade unionist active in the Clarion socialist group. She was a member of the Women's Social and Political Union (WSPU) in Manchester from 1905. Moved to London with the Pankhursts. Arrested, imprisoned and went on hunger strike many times for vote. In WSPU recruitment drive during First World War.

Ellen Key, 1849–1926

Writer. Swedish feminist whose views on motherhood and free love had an international influence. She pioneered anti-authoritarian teaching methods.

Billie Jean King, 1943–
Tennis player. Born in California. Went professional in 1967. Wimbledon Champion 1966–8, 1972–3, 1975; US Champion 1967, 1971–2, 1974. Won record twenty Wimbledon titles: six singles, ten doubles, four mixed. Top Woman Athlete of the Year in US in 1973. In 1981 named in International Tennis Hall of Fame.

Maxine Hong Kingston, 1940–
Novelist. Born in California of Chinese immigrant parents. Studied at the University of California, Berkeley, and then taught in high schools in California and Hawaii. Work includes *The Woman Warrior* (1975), which won the National Book Critics Circle Award, and *Through the Black Curtain* (1988).

Freda Kirchwey, 1894–1976
Journalist. From upper-class New York family. Educated at Barnard College. Active in suffrage. Supported striking garment workers. Joined *The Nation*, aged twenty-four, becoming editor in 1922. Bought it fifteen years later and ran it until 1955. Against Alice Paul's proposed ERA supporting trade union women who were for protective legislation. Campaigner for birth control and world peace.

Jeane Kirkpatrick, 1926–
Academic and diplomat. She did research at Government Affairs Institute, 1953–4, and at Human Resources Organization of George

Washington University, 1954–6. Held academic position at Trinity College, 1962–78, and at the Foundations of American Freedom and American Enterprise Institute, 1977–81. Appointed representative to the UN, 1981. Initially a member of the Democratic Party, she joined the Republicans in 1985 and became a well-known advocate of Reaganite foreign policy.

Melanie Klein, 1882–1960
Austrian psychoanalyst. Member of Training Committee of British Psychoanalytic Society and of the International Psychoanalytical Association. *The Psychoanalysis of Children* (1960) emphasized the baby's struggle with the mother in its first four months.

Dame Laura Knight, 1877–1970
Artist. Educated at Nottingham School of Art. Moved to Cornwall in the 1920s, where she painted circus performers and gypsies. During Second World War she depicted women's activities in wartime for the War Artists Advisory Committee and also painted the Nuremberg trials. In 1965 a major retrospective exhibition of her work was held.

Antoinette Konikow, 1869–1946
Birth-control campaigner. Born in Russia, she married a Jewish medical student and emigrated to Boston, US, in 1893. Helped found the Socialist Party of America in 1901. Graduated as a doctor in 1902 and worked in Boston, specializing in birth control.

Lee Krasner, 1908–84

Artist. From Russian-Jewish immigrant family. Won scholarship to New York's Cooper Union and studied at National Academy of Design. Joined Federal Arts Project in 1935. Worked in Hans Hofmann's studio, 1937–40. Influenced by the work of Mondrian. Married artist Jackson Pollock in 1945. Began to work in Abstract Expressionist style during the 1950s.

Cleo Laine, 1927–

Singer and actress. Brought up in Southall, the child of an English mother and Jamaican father. Began singing with jazz bands in Soho in the early 1950s and worked with Johnnie Dankworth, whom she later married. She has toured the world, and appeared in plays and musicals, including *Showboat*.

Elsa Lanchester, 1902–86

Actress. Brought up in a London socialist family. Her mother, Edith Lanchester, had defied convention to live in a free union with John Sullivan, her working-class father. Keen on dancing as a girl, she was influenced by Raymond Duncan, Isadora Duncan and Maud Allan. Founded Children's Theatre, Soho, 1918. In Independent Labour Party after the First World War. Married actor Charles Laughton and went to Hollywood in 1935. They were together for thirty-six years, despite his homosexuality. Her best-known role was in *The Bride of Frankenstein* (1935).

Dorothea Lange, 1895–1965

Photographer. Best known for her studies of migrant workers, sharecroppers and tenant farmers in south and west of US during the 1930s Depression, especially her 'Migrant Mother' (1936). Wrote *An American Exodus: A Record of Human Erosion* (1939) with her husband, economist Paul Taylor. In Second World War she photographed conditions in the internment camps for Japanese-Americans. In the 1950s she worked as a freelance photographer in Asia, South America and the Middle East.

Cyndi Lauper, 1953–

Singer and composer. Brought up in Queens, New York. Dropped out of college and lived on the street in Greenwich Village. Sang on club circuit during the 1970s. First solo album, *She's So Unusual* (1983), had sold 6 million copies by 1985. 'Girls Just Want to Have Fun' gave 'girl talk' songs a new feminist dimension.

Susan Lawrence, 1871–1947

Social reformer. Educated at Cambridge University. Active in London local government as a Conservative. Campaigned for equal pay for school cleaners. Joined Fabian Society in 1911 and Independent Labour Party in 1912. Labour candidate for South Poplar to London County Council, 1913–28. Imprisoned in 1921 with Poplar councillors for refusing to lower poor relief. MP East Ham North, 1923–4, 1926–31. Junior posts in first and second Labour governments.

Ursula K. le Guin, 1929–

Novelist. From Berkeley, California. Educated at Radcliffe College and Columbia University. Author of science fantasy which explores social issues. Work includes *The Left Hand of Darkness* (1967), about a race who are female some months and male the others. The 'Earthsea' trilogy began in 1968 and became a fantasy classic. Her novel *The Dispossessed* (1974) deals with the relation of the individual to the collective.

Baroness Jennie Lee, 1904–88

Scottish Labour politician. From a mining family, she was MP for Lanark in 1929. Married Aneurin Bevan in 1934 and they both were active in the Labour Party. MP for Cannock, 1945–70. Particular interest in education and culture. Played founding role in origins of the Open University. Books include *The Great Journey* (1963) and *My Life with Nye* (1980).

Vivien Leigh, 1913–67
(*Vivian Mary Hartley*)

Actress. Born in India and educated at RADA. Starred with Laurence Olivier in film *Fire Over England* (1937) and played Scarlett O'Hara in *Gone With the Wind* (1939). Married Laurence Olivier, 1940. During their stormy marriage she suffered from manic depression. Won Oscar for Blanche in *A Streetcar Named Desire* (1951). Worked at Stratford-upon-Avon in 1950s.

Margaret Leighton, 1922–76

Actress. Toured with Entertainments National Service Association (ENSA) in 1940. Appeared in theatre and films. Plays include *The Cocktail Party* (1950) and *Separate Tables* (1956), and she won the Best Supporting Actress Award of 1971 for her role in the film *The Go-Between*. Awarded the CBE in 1974.

Clara Lemlich (Shavelson), 1886–1982

Union activist. From New York Jewish immigrant family. Her passionate speech in 1909 inspired the shirtwaisters' strike. Helped form Wage Earners' League for women's suffrage. Formed United Council of Working Class Housewives, which helped striking workers raise money and get food and help with child-care. Led rent strikes, anti-eviction protests, meat and milk boycotts, sit-ins and marches. Summoned before House Committee on Un-American Activities in 1951. Protested against execution of the Rosenbergs in 1953. Opposed nuclear weapons.

Gerda Lerner, 1920–

Historian. Active in the US labour movement in the 1940s. Pioneer in women's studies and in black women's history. Work includes *The Majority Finds Its Past: Placing Women in History* (1979).

Doris Lessing, 1919–

Writer from Rhodesia (now Zimbabwe). Author of 'Martha Quest' series of novels set in southern Africa. Her 1962 *The Golden Notebook* was an influential statement of women's emancipation. Interest in radical psychiatry and Sufi mysticism contributed to a science fiction series, *Canopus in Argos: Archives*, between 1979 and 1983. Recent work includes *Love, Again* (1996).

Joan Littlewood, 1914–91

Stage director. Worked in radio in Manchester and in left theatre with Ewan MacColl, her husband, in the 1930s. In 1953 leased Theatre Royal, Stratford, east London, which became the centre of her radical Theatre Workshop. Committed to popular drama, she put on *The Quare Fellow* (1956), *A Taste of Honey* (1958), *Fings Ain't Wot They Used To Be* (1959) and, in 1963, *Oh! What a Lovely War.*

Marie Lloyd, 1870–1922 (*Matilda Alice Victoria Wood*)

Music-hall entertainer. From Hackney, east London. Best-known songs include 'The Boy I Love Sits Up in the Gallery', 'Oh, Mr Porter', 'My Old Man Said Follow the Van' and 'I'm One of the Ruins That Cromwell Knocked About a Bit'.

Lady Megan Lloyd George, 1902–66

Politician. Daughter of David and Dame Margaret Lloyd George. Liberal MP for Anglesey (campaigned in Welsh), 1929. Deputy Leader of Parliamentary Liberal Party, 1949. Campaigned for a Welsh Parliament, 1952–5. In 1955 joined Labour Party. Labour MP for Carmarthen, 1957.

Margaret Lockwood, 1911–90

Stage and film actress. Films include *Lorna Doone* (1934), *The Lady Vanishes* (1938) and *Stars Look Down* (1939). Awarded the CBE in 1981.

Marchioness of Londonderry, 1859–1959 (*Edith Vane-Tempest Stewart*)

Conservative public figure. From a prominent Conservative family. In First World War founder and director-general of the Women's Legion and the first woman to receive the DBE. Became a famous political hostess for her husband.

Dame Anne Loughlin, 1894–1979

Trade unionist. From a Leeds Irish family. Active in Tailors' and Garment Workers' Union from 1915. Involved in a strike of 6,000 workers in Hebden Bridge in 1916. Served on Trades Board fixing wage rates. In 1943 became first woman president of TUC. Served on commissions on holidays, equal pay, safety at work and unemployment. In 1948 first woman general secretary of a mixed union.

Mary Lowndes, 1857–1929

Stained-glass artist. Studied at the Slade, London. Designed heraldic shields and banners for suffrage demonstrations. Co-founder of Lowndes and Drury in 1897, which moved to The Glass House in 1906 and encouraged independent glass designers, including many women. Active in National Union of Women's Suffrage Societies. Chairman of Artists' Suffrage League. Involved in Women Welders' Union in First World War.

Clare Boothe Luce, 1903–87

Politician in Republican Party. From New York. Worked as journalist, playwright and novelist in 1930s. Edited *Vogue* in 1930 and then *Vanity Fair*. Plays include *Kiss the Boys Goodbye*

(1938). In 1935 married second husband, Henry Luce, millionaire owner of Time-Life Publications. Converted to Catholicism in 1946. Edited *Saints for Now* in 1952. First woman elected to Congress, representing Connecticut, 1943–7. Ambassador to Italy, 1953–7. In 1982 she was a member of the President's Foreign Intelligence Advisory Board. On right of Republican Party. Awarded Medal of Freedom in 1983.

Mabel Dodge Luhan, 1879–1962
Writer. Born into New York upper-class family. Ran literary salon in Greenwich Village, 1912–17, before moving to Taos in 1918, where she married her fourth (and last) husband, Antonio Lujan, a Pueblo Indian. Pioneer of America as a multicultural society. Work includes *Winter in Taos* (1936).

Loretta Lynn, 1935–
Country singer from poor rural Kentucky family. A hit with 'Honky Tonk Girl' started her singing career. Her autobiography, *Coal Miner's Daughter* (1976), was made into a film in 1979.

Dame Vera Lynn, 1917–
Singer. Brought up in East Ham, east London. Sang first in public aged seven. In 1935 began recording with Joe Loss, Charlie Kunz and the Ambrose Orchestra. Became 'Forces Sweetheart' in Second World War. Sang for troops in Burma. In the 1950s toured US. Her record of 'Auf Wiedersehen' sold over 12 million copies. Awarded the DBE in 1975.

Lady Constance Lytton, 1869–1923
Suffragette. Born in Austria, daughter of British Viceroy of India. Joined Women's Social and Political Union. Imprisoned and force-fed when disguised as a working-class woman. She suffered a stroke which caused permanent damage to her health. Despite becoming an invalid, she continued to work for women's suffrage.

Mary Reid Macarthur, 1880–1921
Scottish trade union organizer. Member of shop assistants' union. In 1903 became secretary of Women's Trade Union League. Formed National Federation of Women Workers in 1906. She led the Cradley Heath outworkers' strike in 1910 and was on the National Council of the Independent Labour Party, 1909–12.

Ann Macbeth, 1875–1948
Designer, embroiderer and illustrator. Trained at Glasgow School of Art, where she taught embroidery from 1900. Designed aesthetic clothes for women who were not well off. Produced banners for Women's Social and Political Union and hangings for churches. Written works include *Educational Needlecraft* (1911) with Margaret Swanson, a schoolteacher from Ayrshire, and *Countrywoman's Rug Book* (1929). She was influential in reviving craft skills and in the 1930s pioneered a waterproof trouser suit for walking in the rain.

Mary McCarthy, 1912–89
American novelist and critic. An orphan, she studied at Vassar College. Her second husband was essayist

Edmund Wilson, who encouraged her to write fiction. Her best-known work is *The Group* (1963), set in the 1930s. She also wrote three volumes of memoirs, the last of which, *Intellectual Memories*, was published in 1992.

Norma McCorvey (Jane Roe), 1947–

Became test case for abortion rights. A meeting with lawyer Sarah Weddington in 1969 led to her involvement in the abortion campaign. Under the pseudonym 'Jane Roe', her victory in the Supreme Court legalized abortion in the US in 1973. In 1994, while working at an abortion clinic, she was converted by Operation Rescue minister Philip Benham. In 1995 she said she opposed late abortion.

Jean McCrindle, 1937–

Teacher, writer and organizer. From Scottish Communist family. Tutor-organizer for Workers' Educational Association in Scotland and Extramural Department. Left the Communist Party in 1956. Helped start women's movement in Britain. Treasurer of Women Against Pit Closures, 1984–5. Work includes *Dutiful Daughters* (1977), edited with Sheila Rowbotham.

Floretta Doty McCutcheon, 1888–1967

Bowler. She began bowling after her husband put her in a team, becoming a champion in the 1920s and 1930s in what had been a men's sport. Defeated world champion Jimmy Smith in 1927. Instructed other women bowlers from the 1930s.

Inducted into Women's International Bowling Congress Hall of Fame, 1974.

Hattie McDaniel, 1895–1952

Singer and actress. Dropped out of high school to perform in minstrel shows and radio in Denver. Travelled as a blues singer in 1920s. In 1931 went to Los Angeles and got bit parts in films. Appeared in *Blonde Venus* (1932) with Marlene Dietrich and in *I'm No Angel* (1933) with Mae West. Her best-known role was Mammy in *Gone With the Wind* (1939).

Margaret Ethel MacDonald, 1870–1911

Socialist, active around women's issues. Campaigned for regulation of sweated work. Member of Women's Labour League and became its president in 1906. Married Ramsay MacDonald (later Labour Prime Minister) in 1896.

Margaret MacDonald Mackintosh, 1865–1933

Artist and designer. Trained and worked in Glasgow in the Glasgow style associated with her husband, Charles Rennie Mackintosh. Worked in watercolour and stained glass. Collaborated with her husband in much of his work.

Margaret McMillan, 1860–1931

Socialist educationalist. Born in New York and brought up in Inverness, Scotland. Involved in suffrage movement. Campaigned for school medical inspections in Bradford and for school clinics. In 1904 published *Education Through Imagination*. Ran camps for poor children. In 1913 founded an infants' school with her sister Rachel in Deptford, south London. It was finished in 1914 and called the Rachel McMillan Open-air Nursery School.

Rachel McMillan, 1859–1917
Socialist educationalist. Born in New York and brought up in Inverness, Scotland. Became a teacher of hygiene in London. Worked with her sister Margaret on poor children's medical and educational needs. The Rachel McMillan Open-air Nursery School embodied her ideas of healthy child-care in the open air.

Frances MacDonald MacNair, 1873–1921
Stained-glass artist, embroiderer, enameller and designer. Trained at Glasgow School of Art. Worked with her sister Margaret MacDonald Mackintosh, Charles Rennie Mackintosh and Herbert MacNair. Married Herbert MacNair in 1899.

Aimee Semple McPherson, 1890–1944
Evangelist. From a Canadian farming family. Converted in a Pentecostal mission in 1907 by evangelist Robert Semple, whom she married in 1908. After he died in 1910, she married Harold McPherson. She began travelling in 1918 as an evangelical preacher. During the 1920s she spoke at vast meetings. Vanished mysteriously in 1926, and said she had been kidnapped.

Mary MacSwiney, 1872–1942
Irish Nationalist political activist. Active in suffrage movement, 1912, and then Sinn Fein in Cork from 1915. Sister of Terence MacSwiney, imprisoned by British in 1920. Toured US to campaign for his release before he died as a result of hunger strike. Imprisoned and went on hunger strike herself. In 1933 helped form Mna na Poblachta (Women of the Republic), a right-wing nationalist group.

Olga Mader, 1915–
Union official. From coal-mining area in Pennsylvania. Went to Detroit with her family in 1933 and worked for Chrysler. Studied at Eastern Michigan University part-time. Joined recreation department of Union of Auto Workers (UAW) in 1944. Became director in 1947. In 1966 elected to executive of UAW. In 1970 and 1972 vice-president of the International Union. In 1974 first president of Coalition of Labor Union Women.

Madonna, 1958– (*Louise Veronica Ciccone*)
Film actress and singer. Songs include 'Burning Up' and 'Like a Virgin'. Films include *Desperately Seeking Susan* (1985) and *Evita* (1996). Records have sold over 50 million worldwide.

Lady Olga Maitland, 1944–
Conservative politician. Worked as journalist and gossip columnist. Active in local government in Islington, north London. Founded pro-NATO Families for Defence in 1983. Elected MP for Sutton and Cheam in 1992. Involved in law and order issues, education and defence. Voluntary work includes Conservative Disability Campaign and Conservative Family Group.

Sara Maitland, 1950–

Novelist. Brought up in Scotland. Studied English at Oxford University. Involved in the women's movement since 1970 and part of the Christian feminist movement from 1978. Her first novel, *Daughter of Jerusalem*, won the Somerset Maugham Award in 1979.

Jayne Mansfield, 1933–67

Film actress. Blonde bombshell comic and parody of Marilyn Monroe. Films include *The Girl Can't Help It* (1956) and *Will Success Spoil Rock Hunter?* (1957).

Katherine Mansfield, 1888–1923 (*Kathleen Mansfield Beauchamp*)

New Zealand writer. Part of Bloomsbury literary circle. Experimented with modernist style of fiction. *Bliss and Other Stories* (1920) is her best-known work.

Margaret, Princess, 1930–

Sister of Queen Elizabeth II. In 1955 her affair with Peter Townsend hit the news. They did not marry because he was divorced. Married to photographer Antony Armstrong-Jones, 1960–78. Interested in entertainment world, especially theatre.

Violet Markham, 1872–1959

Public administrator. Daughter of a wealthy colliery owner in Chesterfield. Liberal activist and social reformer in mining area. Anti-suffrage campaigner.

Countess Constance Markievicz, 1868–1927

Campaigner for Irish Nationalism and women's rights. Having married Polish painter Count Casimir Markievicz, she returned to Dublin with him in 1903. Joined Gaelic League and the Abbey Theatre. Helped found United Arts Club. Active in Sinn Fein. Imprisoned after the Easter Rising of 1916, narrowly escaping execution. Elected MP for a Dublin constituency in 1918 while in prison. On her release joined De Valera's Fianna Fáil party.

Helen Marot, 1865–1940

Labour reformer. From a Quaker family. Worked in the University Extension Society of Philadelphia in 1893. In 1897 formed a library for people interested in social and economic thought and published the *Handbook of Labor Literature* in 1899. Influenced by the British Fabian Society. She was sympathetic to Industrial Workers of the World and in 1916 was on the editorial board of the left-wing political and cultural journal *Masses*. Works include *American Labor Unions* (1914) and *Creative Impulse in Industry* (1918).

Catherine Marshall, 1880–1961

Suffragist and pacifist. Moved from involvement in Liberal politics to Labour. Opposed First World War. Involved in international peace movement and No Conscription Fellowship. Active in Women's International League for Peace and Freedom in 1920s and worked to help Jewish refugees in 1930s.

Una Marson, 1905–65

Journalist, poet and playwright. From Jamaica, she went to the US and then to Britain in 1932. Secretary of the League of Coloured Peoples in London and secretary to Emperor Haile Selassie of Ethiopia. Active in Women's International League for Peace and Freedom and the International Alliance of Women. In 1938 started *Caribbean Voices* BBC programme.

Hilda Matheson, 1888–1940

Broadcaster. Worked for army intelligence at the War Office in First World War. In 1919 became Nancy Astor's secretary. Went to work for John Reith at the BBC in 1926. In 1927 became Head of Talks. Resigned in 1932 because Reith would not allow Harold Nicolson to defend *Ulysses*. In 1939 returned to broadcasting and, with her lover Dorothy Wellesley, worked on *Britain in Pictures*.

Jessie Matthews, 1907–81

Actress. Began as a child dancer in *Bluebell in Fairyland* (1919) and went on to work in theatre and film in 1920s and 1930s. In Second World War worked for Entertainments National Service Association (ENSA) in Normandy. Toured Australia, South Africa and US in 1950s. Made numerous radio broadcasts, including six years in the serial *Mrs Dale's Diary*.

Victoria Earle Matthews, 1861–1907

Social worker and club woman. Born into slavery in Fort Valley, Georgia. Worked as a domestic servant. Began writing articles and a novel about slavery, *Aunt Lindy*, under the name Victoria Earle in 1893. In 1895 helped found the National Federation of Afro-American Women (later National Association of Colored Women). In 1897 started the White Rose Industrial Association, which helped young black women with training and work. It developed into the White Rose Mission, which ran mothers' clubs, a kindergarten and classes in black history.

Margaret Mead, 1901–78

Anthropologist. Studied at Barnard. Did fieldwork in Samoa and New Guinea. Work includes *Coming of Age in Samoa* (1928), *Sex and Temperament in Three Primitive Societies* (1935) and *Male and Female: A Study of the Sexes in a Changing World* (1949). Some of her research and conclusions have been subsequently challenged but she had an important influence in stressing the cultural aspects of gender relations.

Bette Midler, 1945–

Comic and singer. Named after Bette Davis. Appeared in plays and musicals from the late 1960s. Became known through cabaret in the 1970s. Films include *Down and Out in Beverly Hills* (1985) and *Ruthless People* (1986).

Lee Miller, 1907–77

Photographer. From a farm in Poughkeepsie. Went to Paris in 1925 and travelled in Egypt. Worked as a fashion model for *Vogue*. In 1932 began working as a photographer. From 1937 she was linked to the Surrealists and was friendly with Roland Penrose (whom she married), Eileen Agar, Max Ernst, Leonora Carrington and Pablo Picasso. Books include

Grim Glory (1941). In Second World War became a war reporter and photographed Dachau concentration camp.

Kate Millett, 1934–
Writer. Educated at the University of Minnesota, Oxford University and Columbia University. Her *Sexual Politics* (1970) had an important influence in the US women's movement and elsewhere. Involved in early Women's Liberation groups. Other works include *Flying* (1974) and *Sita* (1977).

Patsy Mink, 1927–
Politician in Democratic Party. From Hawaii. First woman of Japanese ancestry to be elected to the territorial House (1956) and then to the Senate (1958). In 1964 became first Japanese-American woman member in Congress. Introduced an equal pay for equal work bill in Hawaii's Senate. Campaigned for civil rights, women's rights and legislation for the disabled and old people.

Juliet Mitchell, 1940–
Psychoanalyst. From New Zealand, she was brought up in Britain and educated at Oxford University. Worked on *New Left Review*, where she published 'The Longest Revolution' in 1966. Helped form early Women's Liberation groups in London. Trained as an analyst at the Institute of Psychoanalysis in the 1970s. Books include *Women's Estate* (1972) and *Psychoanalysis and Feminism* (1974).

Margaret Mitchell, 1900–1949
Novelist. Worked as journalist on the *Atlantic Journal*. After an unhappy first marriage, married John Marsh in 1925. Her book *Gone With the Wind* (1936) made her internationally famous – the film appeared in 1939. It was banned by both the Nazis and the Communists. During the 1940s she became embroiled in legal disputes. She was militantly right-wing.

Naomi Mitchison, 1897–
Writer. Born in Edinburgh, the daughter of scientist John Scott Haldane. In 1916 married lawyer Gilbert Richard Mitchison, who became a Labour MP (1945–64). Books include *The Corn King and the Spring Queen* (1931) and *Memoirs of a Spacewoman* (1962). Stood as Labour candidate in 1935. In 1937 she moved to Carradale on the Mull of Kintyre, Scotland. Member of Argyll County Council, 1945–63. Travelled in Africa. In 1963 made Tribal Adviser and Mother to the Bakgatla of Botswana.

Jessica Mitford, 1917–96
Writer. Born into British aristocratic family. Eloped with cousin Esmond Romilly, a nephew of Winston Churchill, to Spain in the Civil War. Moved to US in 1939. Romilly killed in Second World War in 1942. Persecuted under McCarthy because of links with Communist Party. Books include *Hons and Rebels* (1960) and *The Making of a Muckraker* (1979).

Helena Molony, 1884–1967
Irish trade unionist and nationalist. Member of Maude Gonne's Daughters of Ireland, 1903. Edited *Bean na h Eireann* (*Women of Ireland*), 1908. Helped Constance Markievicz form Na Fianna youth movement. Member of Abbey Theatre Company. Secre-

tary of Irish Women Workers' Union, 1915, and member of James Connolly's Irish Citizen Army, 1916. Jailed for her part in Easter Rising of 1916. After 1921 Republican supporter and active in trade union movement.

**Marilyn Monroe, 1926–62
(*Norma Jeane Baker*)**
Film actress. Illegitimate daughter of Gladys Baker, who suffered from mental illness. Brought up in foster homes and orphanages. Married Jim Dougherty when she was fourteen. Worked in munitions in Second World War and began posing for photographs. In 1950 she had parts in *The Asphalt Jungle* and *All About Eve*, and went on to star in films which included *How to Marry a Millionaire* (1953), *The Seven Year Itch* (1955) and *Some Like It Hot* (1959). Married basketball star Joe DiMaggio in 1954 and from 1956 to 1961 was married to playwright Arthur Miller, who wrote *The Misfits*, her last film. Died from overdose of sleeping pills.

Maria Montessori, 1870–1952
Italian educational theorist and feminist. Particularly interested in educating backward slum children, her 'method', which stressed stimulation and creativity, had considerable influence in US and Britain from the 1920s.

Robin Morgan, 1941–
Writer. A child actress on TV. Active in anti-war movement and the Yippies. Joined New York Radical Women and took part in 1968 Miss America protest. Books include *Sister-*

hood is Powerful (1970). Adviser on gender for the UN, 1985–7.

Margaret Morris, 1891–1980
Dancer and sports therapist. Worked as choreographer. In 1915 started the Margaret Morris Dance Club. Interested in Greek movement and in yoga breathing techniques. After working in theatre, began to apply them to physiotherapy in the 1920s. In 1930 trained in massage and medical gymnastics. Applied them to sports training and tried to take ideas into the education system. Also advocated vegetarianism and was opposed to tea and coffee.

May Morris, 1862–1938
Designer, embroiderer, wallpaper and fabric designer, and jeweller. Trained by her father, William Morris. Ran his firm's embroidery department from 1885. Designed banner for Fabian women's group in 1908. Lecture tour of US in 1910 on embroidery, jewellery and clothes design. Taught embroidery at the Central School of Arts and Crafts, London.

Toni Morrison, 1931–
Writer. Her novels include *The Bluest Eye* (1970), *Sula* (1974), *Song of Solomon* (1977), *Tar Baby* (1981) and *Beloved* (1987), which won the Pulitzer Prize for fiction. In 1993 she was awarded the Nobel Prize for Literature. Her work explores black American history and experience, creating fiction from everyday speech.

Laura Mulvey, 1941–
Film-maker and critic. Educated at Oxford University. Involved in Women's Liberation movement. In 1975 her film *Riddles of the Sphinx*, with Peter Wollen, questioned the relation of the viewer to film. She returned to the theme of the masculine spectator in film criticism in *Screen*.

Dame Iris Murdoch, 1919–
Novelist and philosopher. Taught at St Anne's College, Oxford, 1948–63. Married critic John Bayley in 1956. Author of *Sartre: Romantic Rationalist* (1953). Linked with 'New Reasoner' group in the new left and supporter of CND in the 1950s. Novels include *Under the Net* (1954) and *The Flight from the Enchanter* (1955). In 1978 won the Booker Prize for *The Sea, The Sea*.

Gloria Naylor, 1950–
Writer. From New York, she was educated at Brooklyn College and Yale. Works include *Linden Hills* (1985) and *Mama Day* (1988).

Dame Anna Neagle, 1904–86 (*Marjorie Robertson*)
Went from the chorus into film. Married director Herbert Wilcox and established a reputation in British films like *Victoria the Great* (1937), *Nurse Edith Cavell* (1939) and *Odette* (1950). In the 1960s and 1970s appeared in popular stage productions, including *Charlie Girl* (1965–71).

Alice Neal, 1900–1984
Artist. Studied at Philadelphia School of Design. In 1932 moved to New York and worked through New Deal artists programmes. Joined Communist Party in 1935. Active in the Artists' Union. Critical of the ascendancy of Abstract Expressionists, she continued to paint portraits. In the 1970s her work began to be appreciated and a major retrospective was held at the Whitney Museum in 1974.

Joan Nestle, 1940–
Writer. Brought up in the Bronx, New York. Studied at Queens College, City University of New York. Work draws on Jewish, working-class, lesbian experience, challenging complacent moralism in the women's movement. Author of *A Restricted Country* (1987).

Margaret Morse Nice, 1883–1974
Ornithologist. Studied how small birds defended their territories by placing coloured numbered bands on their legs. Never held an academic post but became first woman president of American Ornithological Society in 1938.

Emma Nicholson, 1941–
Conservative and Liberal Democrat politician. Worked in computers and was director of fund-raising for Save the Children Fund. Active in Conservative Party and became MP in 1987. Interested in women's issues and penal system. Resigned the Tory whip in 1995 and joined the Liberal Democrats over Conservative policy on Europe.

Stella Nowicki, 1916–
Labour organizer. From a Polish-Catholic working-class family. In 1933 went to Chicago and became

involved in meat-packing industry. In 1934 involved in sit-down strike against unsafe working conditions. Joined Young Communist League. Organizer and adult educator in packing industry until 1945.

Edna O'Brien, 1932–
Writer. Left Ireland and settled in London in 1959. Novels include *The Country Girls* (1960) and *The Lonely Girl* (1962). She has also written for the theatre and for films. Her early work provoked uproar in Ireland and was censored because it was sexually frank.

Sandra Day O'Connor, 1930–
Lawyer and Republican Party politician. From El Paso, Texas. Educated at Stanford, she practised law and was assistant attorney-general for Arizona, 1965–9. Member of the Arizona Senate, 1969–75. She was elected Senate majority leader in 1972, serving on committees dealing with legal issues and women in the services. In 1974 she was elected a judge and served on Court of Appeals, 1979–81. In 1981 President Reagan appointed her an associate justice of the US Supreme Court, the first woman ever to serve in that capacity.

Kate Richards O'Hare, 1877–1948
Prison reformer and labour organizer. Worked as a machinist. Active in Socialist Party. In 1917 arrested for anti-war speech and convicted of espionage. Sentenced to five years in prison. Became friend of Emma Goldman in jail. Pardoned in 1920. Worked in adult education and campaigned for prison reform. In 1939

assistant director of California Department of Penology.

Georgia O'Keeffe, 1887–1986
Artist. Born on the plains of Wisconsin. Studied at Art Institute of Chicago. Influenced by photographer George Stieglitz, whom she married. During the 1920s she produced a series of paintings using close-up images of flowers. From 1929 was increasingly drawn to New Mexico, which influenced her later work.

Leonora O'Reilly, 1870–1927
Labour organizer. Born in New York City. A clothing worker, she joined the Knights of Labor in 1886 and formed the Working Women's Society. Worked as a teacher, 1902–7. In 1903 joined Women's Trade Union League, becoming vice-president of New York branch in 1909. Involved in support of 1909–10 shirt-waisters' strike. Investigated cause of Triangle Shirt-waist Co. fire. A founder of National Association for the Advancement of Colored People. Involved in suffrage movement.

Elsie Jeannette Oxenham, 1885–1960
Writer. Author of forty schoolgirl novels between 1914 and 1959 featuring the Abbey school, a world of intense friendships between young women of the upper classes.

Dame Christabel Pankhurst, 1880–1958
Suffragette. Formed Women's Social and Political Union in 1903. Initiated militant direct-action tactics. Arrested and went on hunger strike. Exiled to

Paris before First World War. Supporter of war. Converted to the Second Day Adventists in 1920. Settled in 1940 in US, where she died.

Emmeline Pankhurst, 1858–1928
Suffragette. Active in Manchester Socialist movement. Formed Women's Social and Political Union in 1903. Toured US in 1909 and 1911. She was arrested many times and went on hunger strike. In 1913 on a visit to the US she was detained on Ellis Island amidst a public outcry. When Britain went to war in 1914 she supported army recruitment. After the war she lectured on social purity and in 1926 joined the Conservative Party.

Sylvia Pankhurst, 1882–1960
Suffragette, artist and socialist. Formed Women's Social and Political Union (WSPU) in Manchester in 1903. Moved to east London, 1912, and set up the East London Federation of the Suffragettes. Imprisoned and force-fed many times. Christabel forced her to leave the WSPU and she developed a socialist and feminist group in the East End producing the *Women's Dreadnought* from 1914 (renamed *Workers' Dreadnought* 1917). Involved in the formation of the Communist Party, she clashed with Lenin and the British leadership. She continued to be active in the unemployed movement and in the 1930s was in the anti-Fascist struggle and a supporter of Ethiopia, where she settled a few years before she died.

Mollie Panter-Downes, 1906–
Journalist and novelist. Sent fortnightly letter from London to the *New Yorker* from September 1939 all through the war. Works include *One Fine Day* (1946) about the aftermath of war.

Dorothy Parker, 1893–1967
Writer. Contributed to the *New Yorker* and *Vanity Fair*. Member of the Algonquin Round Table, a group of writers who met in a Manhattan hotel in the early 1930s. Poetry includes *Enough Rope* (1926). Wrote script in 1937 for film *A Star is Born* with her second husband, Alan Campbell. Blacklisted in Hollywood as a Communist sympathizer under McCarthy.

Rosa Parks, 1913–
Civil rights activist. From Montgomery, Alabama. Worked as a seamstress. Her refusal to give up her seat on a bus in Montgomery in 1955 started a 381-day bus boycott which inspired the Civil Rights movement.

Alice Paul, 1885–1977
US feminist. Studied in Britain. Active in Women's Social and Political Union. Returned to US in militant wing of suffrage movement. Worked in National Woman's Party from 1918 for ERA. An uncompromising advocate of egalitarian feminism, she supported the emerging feminist movement in the 1960s and 1970s.

Frances Perkins, 1882–1965
Administrator. Worked as a social worker and teacher and then was con-

nected with Hull House. Joined New York Consumers' League as executive secretary. Worked for safety legislation. In 1919 made a member of New York State Industrial Commission. Director of the Council on Immigrant Education. Member of New York State Industrial Board in 1922 and in 1926 the chair. After becoming industrial commissioner of New York State, she was appointed Secretary of Labor in 1933.

Esther Peterson, 1906–

Labour organizer and administrator. Worked as a teacher before becoming an organizer for the American Federation of Teachers in 1936. In 1948–52 worked on Women's Committee of Swedish Confederation of Trades Unions. In 1961 Head of Women's Bureau and Vice-Chairman of President's Commission on the Status of Women and Assistant Secretary of Labor. In 1964 Special Assistant to President Johnson on Consumer Affairs.

Emmeline Pethick-Lawrence, 1867–1954

Suffragette. Joined Women's Social and Political Union. With her husband, Frederick Lawrence, she started the paper *Votes for Women* in 1907. Broke with the Pankhursts in 1912 and became involved in Women's Freedom League. Attended Women's Peace Congress at The Hague in 1915. Active in Women's International League for Peace and Freedom. After Second World War lobbied for a women's section of the UN.

Ann Petry, 1911–

African-American novelist. Studied pharmacy and then became a journalist. Worked on *People's Voice* in Harlem. Involved in the American Negro Theater. Published short stories in *The Crisis*. Worked as an education officer in Harlem. Novels include *The Street* (1947), which sold over a million copies, *The Narrows* (1951) and *Miss Muriel and Other Stories* (1971).

Marion Phillips, 1881–1932

Australian. Active in suffrage movement in Britain. Chief woman officer of Labour Party from 1918. Organized relief for miners' wives and children after general strike. Labour MP for Sunderland, 1929–31.

Mary Pickford, 1893–1979

Actress. Born in Toronto. A child actress, she began working with D. W. Griffith aged sixteen and starred in silent films, including *The Poor Little Rich Girl* (1917). Known as America's Sweetheart, she could not make it in the talkies. Formed United Artists Corporation in 1919 with Charlie Chaplin, D. W. Griffith and Douglas Fairbanks. Founded cosmetics company in 1937. In 1975 awarded Academy Award for work in films.

Mervyn Pike, 1918–

Conservative politician and company director. Educated at Reading University. Served in Women's Auxiliary Air Force, 1941–6. MP for Melton, 1956. PPS to Joint Parliamentary Under-Secretary of State, Home Office, 1958–9; Assistant Postmaster

General, 1959–63; Joint Under-Secretary of State, Home Office, 1963–4; Member of Robens Committee on Safety and Health of People at Work, 1970–72. Involved in Women's Royal Voluntary Service, 1974–81.

Stef Pixner, 1945–
Writer and therapist. Brought up in London. Active in women's movement. Contributed to *Spare Rib*. Poems appeared in *Smile, Smile, Smile, Smile* (Feminist Press, 1980).

Sylvia Plath, 1932–63
American poet and novelist. Studied at Smith College. Came to Britain on a Fulbright Fellowship. Married British poet Ted Hughes, 1956. Taught in US at Smith, 1957–8. Began publishing poems in 1960. Separated from Ted Hughes, 1962. *The Bell Jar* published 1963. She committed suicide in 1963 and her poems were published posthumously.

Sally Potter, 1949–
Film-maker. Work for TV and cinema, 1979–88, includes films on women in Soviet cinema. Her film *Orlando* (1993), based on Virginia Woolf's book, was a major success.

Pearl Primus, 1919–94
Dancer and choreographer. Born in Trinidad and brought up in New York, where she studied dance. First work was *African Ceremonial* (1944). *Like Strange Fruit* and *Shendo* (1947) were inspired by a visit to the South. She also worked on *Showboat* (1945) and *Emperor Jones* (1947). Lived in

Liberia in 1970s. Awarded National Medal of Arts in 1991.

Mary Quant, 1934–
Director of Mary Quant Group of Companies since 1955. Sells clothes and cosmetics. Has served on the British Design Council and been a member of the British/USA Bicentennial Liaison Committee. Won many awards, including the Maison Blanche Rex Award, US, 1964. In 1973–4 the London Museum put on an exhibition about her company. Wrote *Quant by Quant* (1966).

Ma Rainey, 1886–1939
(*Gertrude Pridgett*)
Singer. Sang in Southern minstrel shows from the age of fourteen. In teens star of Rabbit Foot Minstrels. Became a national star when she recorded blues with Paramount Records in 1923.

Dame Marie Rambert, 1888–1982
(*Cyria Rambam*)
Ballet dancer and choreographer. Born in Poland. Influenced by Isadora Duncan. Worked with Nijinsky and Diaghilev's Ballets Russes in 1912. Founded the Ballet Rambert in 1926 after settling in London. In 1972 she became Vice-President of the Royal Academy of Dancing.

Jeannette Rankin, 1880–1973
Pacifist, suffrage campaigner and Republican. From Montana. Became a social worker in Seattle. In 1916 Republican candidate for Montana and in 1917 first woman to enter the House of Representatives. Voted against US entry in First World War

and lost her seat. In 1940 elected to Congress. After Pearl Harbor cast only vote against US entering Second World War and lost seat in 1942. Opposed US role in Korea in the 1950s, and Vietnam in the 1960s, leading the Jeannette Rankin Brigade in a protest march in Washington in 1968.

Eleanor Rathbone, 1872–1946
Suffragist. Campaigner against sweated labour. Social reformer in Liverpool and London. Campaigned for family allowances. Succeeded Millicent Fawcett as president of the National Union of Societies for Equal Citizenship in 1919. Author of *The Disinherited Family* (1924). In the 1930s active in women's issues in India, opposed non-intervention in Spain and appeasement of Hitler. In the 1940s worked with Jewish refugees. Became a supporter of Zionism.

Stella Reading (Dowager Marchioness of), 1894–1971
Voluntary worker. Active in Red Cross in First World War. In 1938 appointed Chairman of Women's Voluntary Service. In Second World War helped with evacuation, rationing, and care of air-raid victims. Friend of Eleanor Roosevelt. After war worked in Women's Royal Voluntary Service. Made a DBE in 1941 and a life peeress, Baroness Swanbury, in 1958.

Nancy Davis Reagan, 1923–
Former First Lady and actress. Educated at Smith College. Film actress, 1949–56. Chosen Woman of the Year by *LA Times*, 1977. Permanent member of Hall of Fame of Ten Best Dressed Women in US. Publications include *My Turn* (1989).

Bernice Johnson Reagon, 1942–
Singer. From rural Georgia. Sang in Baptist church choir. Active in Student Non-violent Co-ordinating Committee during civil rights struggle and in Freedom Singers. Founded Sweet Honey in the Rock during the 1970s. Repertoire ranges from hymns to rap. Active in women's movement. Curator of the Smithsonian Institution and National Museum of American History's division on community life.

Helen Reddy, 1942–
Singer. From Australia. Won a trip to New York through a talent contest. Her 'I am Woman' became a million-seller and she became a well-known TV personality.

Amber Reeves, 1887–1981
New woman and teacher. Daughter of Maud Pember Reeves. Her affair with H. G. Wells in 1909 was one of the influences for his novel *Ann Veronica*. Married another Fabian, Rivers Blanco White. In First World War worked on women's wages in Ministry of Munitions. In 1920s reviewed for *Queen* and *Vogue* magazines and from 1928 taught Ethics and Psychology at Morley College, London. After Second World War she wrote fiction.

Maud Pember Reeves, 1867–1953
Social investigator. From New South Wales. Married to a New Zealand diplomat who later became Principal of London School of Economics. Member of Fabian Society, and the

Fabian Women's Group was founded in her house in 1908. Supported state allowances for mothers. Worked on diets in Ministry of Food in First World War. On Council of National Union of Women's Suffrage Societies in the 1920s. Works include *Round About a Pound a Week*, a study of poverty in London conducted between 1909 and 1913.

Viscountess Rhondda, 1883–1958 (*Margaret Haig Thomas*)

Suffragette. Born in South Wales. Editor and publisher. Joined Women's Social and Political Union. Visited US and was rescued from the sinking *Lusitania* in 1915. Successful businesswoman in father's firm. Founded *Time and Tide*, a political and literary journal, in 1920 and edited it in 1926.

Jo Richardson, 1923–94

Labour MP. Supported CND. Elected an MP in 1974. Played an important role in defending abortion rights through the 1970s and 1980s. She increasingly focused on women's equality issues and campaigned for a ministry of women.

Marga Richter, 1926–

Composer. Studied piano at the Juilliard School with Rosalyn Tureck and composition with William Bergsma and Vincent Persichetti. Influenced by the work of painter Georgia O'Keeffe and by Indian and Tibetan music. Work includes *Landscapes of the Mind* (1968–79) and *Quann* (1985).

Sally Ride, 1951–

Physicist and astronaut. From Los Angeles. Became a successful national tennis player at school. Studied at Stanford. Qualified at NASA in 1979 as a shuttle mission specialist. In 1983 became the first American woman in space in the shuttle *Challenger*. Worked at NASA until 1987. Resigned to work on arms control at Stanford. Head of the Space Science Institute at the University of California, San Diego, 1989.

Bridget Riley, 1931–

Artist. From London. Studied at Royal College of Art with Frank Auerbach and Peter Blake. Taught in a school and art colleges. In 1960s became known for 'Op' art – black and white patterns which seemed to move in the light. Large retrospectives in 1970s and 1980s.

Stella Rimington, 1935–

Former director of MI5. Educated at Edinburgh University. Joined Secret Service in 1969. Worked on domestic 'subversion', including miners' strike. Appointed Director General of Secret Service in 1991, becoming the first named head of MI5 when she took over in 1992. Retired in 1996.

Faith Ringgold, 1930–

Artist. Brought up in Harlem. Studied at City College, graduating in 1955. Studied African Art and in the 1960s was influenced by the black power movement. She did a mural at the woman's house of detention at Riker's Island, New York City, 1971–2 and began linking race and gender oppression in her work. Work includes *The Flag is Bleeding* and *The Family of Women*. In 1990 a major retrospective exhibition of her work toured the US.

Elizabeth Robins, 1862–1952
American actress and writer. Active in British suffrage movement. Co-founded the Actresses' Franchise League and was in the Women's Social and Political Union. Political plays include *Votes for Women* (1906).

Margaret Dreier Robins, 1868–1945
Social reformer. From prosperous German *émigré* family. Joined Women's Trade Union League in 1904. Active in suffrage movement and Progressive Party in 1916 and then the Republican Party. Supported Roosevelt's New Deal in the 1930s. President of the International Federation of Working Women. Sister of Mary Dreier.

Joan Robinson, 1903–83
Economist. Educated at Cambridge University, where she worked from 1931 to 1971. In group round Maynard Keynes and influenced by Marxism in late 1930s. In the 1960s was interested in China. Work includes *Accumulation of Capital* (1956) and *Economic Heresies* (1971).

Dame Flora Robson, 1902–84
Actress. Best-known films include *Fire Over England* (1931) and *Guilty* (1944). Also well known in theatre. Made a DBE in 1960.

Gertie Roche, 1912–
Trade union organizer. Brought up in Leeds. She went to work at Montague

Burton's clothing factory when she was sixteen and got involved in trade unionism. Active in the Communist Party until 1956, then in CND and the Labour Party. In 1970 played a leading role in the dramatic Leeds clothing strike when mass pickets brought out thousands of workers.

Anita Roddick, 1942–
Businesswoman. From Brighton, she started the Body Shop with her husband, Thomas Gordon, to sell cosmetics made from natural material. By the mid-1990s the Body Shop International Inc. had branches all over Britain and overseas, including the US.

Henrietta Rodman, 1878–1923
Feminist teacher. From New York. Educated at Columbia Teachers' College. Lived in Greenwich Village. Organized the Feminist Alliance in 1914. Concern about childcare and women's independence led her to plan a co-operative apartment house. Campaigned for married women teachers' maternity rights and hiring of married women. Supported Margaret Sanger's birth-control campaign and was pacifist in First World War. Opposed red scare.

Edith Nourse Rogers, 1881–1960
Republican politician. Volunteered in Red Cross during First World War. Involved in auxiliary organization of the America Legion. When her husband died in 1925 she ran for his seat. Became Republican Congresswoman for the 5th District in Massachusetts, serving for thirty-five years. Initiated Women's Army Corps Bill. For equal

pay but believed in the home and 'feminine' qualities. Awarded the Distinguished Service Medal by the American Legion in 1950.

Ginger Rogers, 1911–95
Film actress. Famous as a dancer in films with Fred Astaire. Films include *Top Hat* (1935) and *Kitty Foyle* (1940).

Eleanor Roosevelt, 1884–1962
Social reformer and politician in the Democratic Party. Niece of President Theodore Roosevelt. Married Franklin Delano Roosevelt, a distant cousin, in 1905. In 1921 joined League of Women Voters and Women's Trade Union League. From 1933 as First Lady supported New Deal social reform and defended black and women's rights. Supporter of women's services in Second World War. Became international ambassadress for US after war and was involved in the UN.

Diana Ross, 1944–
Singer. In the group the Supremes initially and then went solo in 1970. Films include *Lady Sings the Blues* (1972). Supported President Johnson's Youth Opportunity Program and civil rights. Has won many awards, including one from the National Association for the Advancement of Colored People in 1970.

Emma Rothschild, 1948–
Economist. Educated at Oxford University. Academic posts include associate professorship at MIT, 1979–88. Particular interests include technology and peace. In 1986 member of Olaf Palme Memorial Fund Board, Stock-

holm. Member of Royal Commission on Environmental Pollution. Works include *Paradise Lost: The Decline of the Auto Industrial Age* (1973).

Marsha Rowe, 1944–
Writer. From Sydney, Australia. In 'little push' with Richard Neville. Worked on Australian *Vogue*. Came to Britain and worked on *Oz* with Richard Neville and Louise Ferrier. Started feminist magazine *Spare Rib* with Rosie Boycott in the early 1970s. Active in women's groups and involved in Jungian therapy during the 1970s. Worked for publishers Serpent's Tail and edited a collection of short stories, *Sacred Space* (1992).

Helena Rubinstein, 1882–1965
Polish-born beautician. Emigrated to Australia in 1902. Sold face cream and advised on skin care in Melbourne. Opened salons in Paris, London and New York between 1908 and 1915 which expanded after First World War into an international business. Pioneered medicated skin creams and waterproof mascara. Active in philanthropic causes, especially in relation to Israel.

Joan Ruddock, 1943–
Labour MP. Educated at Imperial College, London. Worked for Shelter, National Campaign for the Homeless, 1968–73. Director of Oxford Housing Aid Centre, 1973–7. Worked with unemployed young people in the late 1970s. Organizer of Citizens' Advice Bureau in Reading, 1977–9. Chair of CND, 1981–5 and Vice-Chair 1985–6. Also active in anti-racist politics. Elected for Lewisham,

Deptford, in south-east London, in 1987.

Dora Russell, 1894–1986

Feminist writer and activist. Member of Independent Labour Party. Campaigned for birth control and sexual freedom. Married the philosopher Bertrand Russell in 1921. Formed Workers' Birth Control Group in 1924. Ran a libertarian school, Beacon Hill, near Petersfield, 1927–39. Books include *The Right to Be Happy* (1927). Active in the Campaign for Nuclear Disarmament. Inspired the 1958 Women's Caravan of Peace protest across Europe against the Cold War.

Jane Russell, 1921–

Film actress. Discovered by Howard Hughes. Films include *The Pale Face* (1948) and *Gentlemen Prefer Blondes* (1953).

Juanita J. Saddler

Leader of Young Women's Christian Association (YWCA). Graduated in 1915 from Fisk University. Worked for YWCA in 1920, developing inter-racial policies. In New Deal worked on integrating welfare programmes for young people. In 1950s organized Community Relations Committee in Cambridge (Mass.), which helped open nursing schools to young African-American women. In 1960s organized women's church group in New York on ecumenical and inter-racial lines.

Margaret Sanger, 1883–1966

Birth-control campaigner. Of Irish-American ancestry. Became involved in radical politics, supporting strikers and writing in left newspapers. Produced *The Woman Rebel* and became interested in sex radicalism and birth control. Influenced by English sex psychologist Havelock Ellis. Founded first birth-control clinic in Brooklyn, New York, for which she was imprisoned. Went on a world tour to promote birth control and married millionaire J. Noel Slee, who supported her work. Created international lobby for birth control. First president of the International Planned Parenthood Federation, 1953. In 1952 got backing for research on the pill in Puerto Rico.

Dorothy L. Sayers, 1893–1957

Writer. Educated at Oxford University. Creator of Lord Peter Wimsey detective character and independent semi-autobiographical Harriet Vane. Translated Dante's *Inferno* and wrote the influential religious drama *The Man Born to be King* (1941–2).

Miriam Schapiro, 1923–

Artist. Associated with Abstract Expressionists in 1950s. Influenced by Georgia O'Keeffe and Barbara Hepworth. In 1962 began working on shrine paintings. Interested in female imagery. Worked with Judy Chicago on Feminist Art Program at California Institute for the Arts in Valencia, renovating a dilapidated house as *Project Womanhouse* (1972). Started *Heresies* with Lucy Lippard, a collective and journal looking at relationship of art and society.

Phyllis Schlafly, 1924–
New right politician. Became involved in Republican politics in 1940s. Wrote on defence policy and anti-Communism in the 1960s. Attacked feminism in 1970s. Led campaign against ERA. Worked as journalist and broadcaster. Work includes *The Power of the Positive Woman* (1977).

Rose Schneiderman, 1882–1972
Labour organizer. From an Orthodox Jewish family that immigrated to New York in 1890. Worked in a department store and clothing factories. During the 1905 cap-makers' strike, joined Women's Trade Union League (WTUL). Active in the organizing drive of the International Ladies Garment Workers' Union, 1909–14, and in aftermath of 1911 Triangle factory fire. In peace groups in First World War. President of National WTUL in 1926. Influenced New Deal labour policies and as secretary of the New York State Department of Labor, 1933–44, introduced a minimum wage there in 1937.

Ruth Schonthal, 1924–
Composer and pianist. Born in Hamburg. Her family left Germany in 1934 and travelled in Europe and Mexico. She had a struggle to study and earn a living, but produced a great body of musical composition drawing on the poetry of Yeats and Whitman. From the 1980s she has created work exploring her identity as a woman.

Patricia Scott-Schroeder, 1940–
Democratic Party politician. Studied law at University of Minnesota.

Elected to Congress in 1972. Special areas are defence spending, the elderly, consumers, education, and women's and children's rights. Supporter of the ERA.

Vida Scudder, 1861–1954
Educationalist. Born in India. Teacher at Wellesley College. Member of Women's Trade Union League. Supported strikers at Lawrence, 1912. Helped found college settlement movement.

Baroness Nancy Seear, 1913–
Liberal politician. She has been particularly concerned with women's employment and with women carers of dependants. Work includes *The Re-entry of Women in Employment* (1971). Since 1988 she has been deputy leader of the Social and Liberal Democrats in the House of Lords.

Lynne Segal, 1943–
Writer. From Sydney, Australia. Part of anarchist 'big push' radical grouping. Came to Britain in early 1970s and was active in Women's Liberation and libertarian left community politics in London. Co-authored *Beyond the Fragments* in 1980. Other books include *Is the Future Female?* (1987) and *Straight Sex* (1994). She is Professor of Gender Studies at Middlesex University.

Anna Howard Shaw, 1847–1919
Suffrage leader. Born in Newcastle upon Tyne. Family went to US in 1851. Qualified as a minister in the Methodist Church and then as a physician, but became involved with the suffrage movement. An impressive ora-

tor, she became president of National American Woman Suffrage Association in 1904. Resigned in 1915. In First World War chair of the Woman's Committee of the United States Council of National Defense. In 1919 awarded the Distinguished Service Medal.

Hanna Sheehy-Skeffington, 1877–1946

Feminist and Irish nationalist. From Kenturk, Co. Cork, she became a teacher. Founded Irish Association of Women Graduates in 1901. Active in Irish suffrage movement with Countess Markievicz. Imprisoned in 1912 for protesting against exclusion of women from Home Rule Bill. Went on hunger strike in support of English suffragettes denied political status. In 1919 she petitioned President Wilson on behalf of Irish women to intervene in Ireland.

Mary Ryott Sheepshanks, 1872–1958

Feminist. Social reformer and pacifist. Did social work in Southwark and Stepney, south and east London. From 1897 to 1913 was Vice-Principal of Morley College for Working Men and Women. Lectured for constitutional suffragists. Edited *Jus Suffragii* and was International Secretary of Women's International League of Peace and Freedom. In 1929 organized first international scientific conference on modern methods of warfare and the protection of civilians.

Cindy Sherman, 1954–

Photographer. Influenced by performance art. Produced *Untitled Film Still*

series in 1977. Influential figure in the emergence of the fine art photograph. In 1987 the Whitney Museum showed a ten-year retrospective exhibition of her work.

Clare Short, 1946–

Labour MP. Educated at Keele and Leeds universities. Was active as a community worker in Handsworth, 1976–7. Director of Youth Aid, 1979–83. When she was elected for Birmingham Ladywood in 1983 she continued to focus on race relations, unemployment and low pay. She has been active in raising Irish human rights issues and is committed to women's rights. She became involved in the debate on pornography, advocating legislation on similar lines to American anti-pornography campaigners. She held several positions on the Opposition front bench from the mid-1980s.

Renee Short, 1914–

Labour MP. Educated at Manchester University. Joined the Labour Party in 1948. Worked as a freelance journalist. Member of National Union of Journalists and Transport and General Workers' Union. MP for Wolverhampton NE, 1964–87. Interests include social services, East/West trade, the arts and women's issues. Active campaigner for nurseries and abortion rights.

Karen Silkwood, 1946–74

Campaigner against industrial hazards. From Texas. In 1972 went to Oklahoma City and worked at Cimarron plutonium fuel plant of the Kerr-McGee Corporation. Joined Oil,

Chemical and Atomic Workers'
Union (OCAW). Became concerned
about hazardous working conditions.
She died on the way to a meeting
with a *New York Times* reporter and
OCAW official in a car accident.

Ruth Slate, 1884–1953
New woman and feminist. Worked as
a clerk. Her diaries and letters describe
lower-middle-class London radicalism
and record her close friendship with
Eva Slawson. They were published
posthumously by Tierl Thompson in
*Dear Girl: The Diaries and Letters of
Two Working Women, 1897–1917*
(1987).

Agnes Smedley, 1892–1950
Writer. From a poor family in the Colorado mining camps. Worked as a
teacher and socialist journalist. Active
in birth-control agitation and in
defence of Indian nationalists. Visited
China in 1928 as a special correspondent for *Die Frankfürter Zeitung* and
later for the *Manchester Guardian*.
Returned to join the Fourth Army.
Red-baited under McCarthy.

Bessie Smith, 1894–1937
Singer. Daughter of a Baptist preacher
from Tennessee. Toured with bands
including Ma Rainey and Fat Chap-
pelle's Rabbit Foot Minstrel Show in
the South. Began recording blues in
1923 and earned the title 'Empress of
the Blues'. Sexually attracted to
women and men. Died after a car accident, having been barred from an all-
white hospital.

Clara Smith, c. 1894–1935
Singer. Worked in Southern vaudeville from c. 1914. Sang in Harlem
clubs from 1933. Ran Clara Smith
Theatrical Club. Was in musical
revues and recorded blues with Columbia, 1923–32.

Margaret Chase Smith, 1897–1995
Republican Party politician. Worked
as a teacher and a business executive.
In 1930 married Clyde H. Smith, a
Maine State senator, and became
active in Republican Party. After her
husband died, she was elected to suc-
ceed him in 1940. Served in House of
Representatives until 1948. Co-
sponsored bill forming Women
Appointed for Voluntary Emergency
Service and the ERA. In 1948
elected to Senate. In 1950 her 'Declaration of Conscience' speech challenged McCarthy. Chair of
Conference of All Republican Sena-
tors in 1967, 1969 and 1971. First
woman to be placed in nomination
for presidency, 1964. Woman of the
Year in Politics, 1954 and 1957, she
received many honours.

Patti Smith, 1946–
Singer and songwriter. From New
Jersey, moved to New York in 1967
and began writing songs. By 1975 was
linking psychedelic rock with punk.
Recorded with Bruce Springsteen in
1978. Band dispersed in 1979. She has
written poetry and a play with Sam
Shepard.

Ruby Doris Smith, 1942–67
Left college to join Civil Rights movement in the South. Involved in Freedom Rides in Nashville and

Montgomerie. Helped organize voter registration in 1961. Active in Student Non-violent Co-ordinating Committee (SNCC) and critical of role of whites in organization. In 1966 executive secretary of SNCC.

Nancy Spain, 1917–64
Journalist, broadcaster and writer of detective fiction. Educated at Roedean, Sussex. Reviewed detective fiction for *Tribune*. Became a household name in TV series *What's My Line?* and *Juke Box Jury*. Killed in plane crash. Works include lesbian detective novel, *Poison for Teacher* (1949).

Anne Spencer, 1882–1975
Poet. From Virginia. Linked to Harlem Renaissance. Was only black librarian in Lynchberg, 1923–45. Opposed segregation in education and transport in early 1920s.

Mary Bagot Stack, 1883–1935
Founder of the League of Health and Beauty, 1930. Born in Dublin. Influenced by Indian yoga. Interest in health and dance developed in 1920s. Author of *Building the Body Beautiful* (1931). Daughter Prunella Stack continued the work of the League.

Gertrude Stein, 1874–1946
Writer. Went to Paris in 1903 and moved in bohemian and lesbian literary circles. Lived with Alice B. Toklas and in *The Autobiography of Alice B. Toklas* (1933) recorded their life together. Famous for experimental writing style.

Gloria Steinem, 1934–
Journalist. Educated at Smith College. Worked as a freelance writer. In the late 1960s and early 1970s founded *New York Magazine* and *Ms.* magazine. Active in Democratic politics and in feminist movement. Work includes *Outrageous Acts and Everyday Rebellions* (1983) and *Marilyn: Norma Jeane* (1986).

Marie Stopes, 1880–1958
Birth-control campaigner. From Edinburgh. First woman science lecturer at Manchester University, 1904. Works include *Married Love* (1916), *Wise Parenthood* (1918) and *Radiant Motherhood* (1920). Started birth-control clinic in Islington, north London, in 1921 with her second husband, Humphrey Verdon Roe.

Ray (Rachel) Strachey, 1887–1940
Feminist campaigner and writer. Brought up by a Quaker grandmother from Philadelphia with strong feminist views. Educated at Cambridge University. Active in National Union of Women's Suffrage Societies. Friend of Millicent Fawcett. Took up issues of women's employment in First World War. In 1935 ran Women's Employment Federation. Books include *The Cause* (1928) and *Our Freedom and Its Results* (1936).

Anna Louise Strong, 1885–1970
Socialist organizer. Studied at Oberlin and Bryn Mawr. Anti-First World War. Involved in general strike in Seattle. In 1921 went to Poland to help famine victims with American Friends Service Committee. Visited Soviet Union and China. Autobiogra-

phy, *I Change Worlds*, published 1935.

Baroness Edith Summerskill, 1901–80
Labour doctor and politician. Worked with London poor. Labour MP for West Fulham, 1938. Interests included preventive medicine, birth control, welfare and maternity services and equal pay. Responsible for Clean Milk Act under Labour in 1949. Chaired Labour Party, 1954–5. MP for Warrington, 1955–61. Member of Shadow Cabinet until 1957. Campaigned for Married Woman's Property Act (1964) and Matrimonial Homes Act (1967). Mother of Shirley Summerskill, also a doctor and Labour MP.

Helena Swanwick, 1864–1939
Suffragist and pacifist. Active in Women's Trade Union Council and Co-operative movement. Edited *The Common Cause*, 1909–14. Member of Union of Democratic Control in First World War. In Labour Party and League of Nations Union after the war.

Maud Swartz, 1879–1937
Labour leader. Born in Co. Kildare, Ireland. Educated but poor, she emigrated to New York City and worked as a governess and proof-reader. Became involved in suffrage movement and joined Women's Trade Union League, becoming president in 1922. In 1931 secretary of New York State Department of Labor under Frances Perkins.

Mary Talbert, 1866–1923
Campaigner for black rights. Studied at Oberlin College. Involved in the Baptist Church, the National Association for the Advancement of Colored People and the Phyllis Wheatley Club in Buffalo, which affiliated to the National Association of Colored Women (NACW). Worked on black women's issues with Mary Church Terrell and Anna Julia Cooper. President of NACW, 1920. Supported attempt to introduce a bill against lynching into Congress. Active in anti-lynching campaign, 1921.

Eva Tanguay, 1878–1947
Vaudeville star. From a French-Canadian background. Began touring aged eight. Before First World War she became known from one of her song titles as the 'I Don't Care Girl'. One of her most popular songs was 'It's All Been Done Before But Not the Way I Do It'. She earned large amounts of money between 1904 and 1915 but in the 1920s suffered from ill-health.

Gladys Tantaquidgeon, 1899–
Mohegan scholar of Algonquian Indian culture. Trained in tribal medicine and traditional learning by her great-aunt. Studied anthropology at University of Pennsylvania. Worked for Bureau of Indian Affairs as a community worker in 1934. Later became a specialist on Indian arts and crafts.

Mavis Tate, 1893–1947
Conservative politician and feminist. Unionist MP for West Willesden, 1931–5, and then for Frome, 1935–

45. In 1934 went to Berlin and obtained release from a concentration camp of the wife and baby of a former Socialist deputy. In 1941 tabled a motion in House of Commons condemning a judge who had condoned wife-beating. Active in equal pay campaign. In 1942 forced division on equal compensation for women with war injuries. She was an aeronautic enthusiast and flew her own plane in the 1930s. A virus contracted on a visit to Buchenwald at the end of the war undermined her health and spirit. She was found dead in a gas-filled room in 1947.

Shirley Temple, 1928–
Actress, dancer and later (as Shirley Temple Black) diplomat. Child star, became famous in *Curly Top* (1935) and *Dimples* (1936). Involved in Republican politics. Appointed US representative to the UN in 1969. Ambassador to Ghana, 1974–6. White House Chief of Protocol, 1976–7.

Mary Church Terrell, 1863–1954
Campaigner for African-American and women's rights. Born into upper-class black family in Memphis. President of National Association of Colored Women, 1892–8. In 1904 spoke at International Council of Women in Berlin in German and French on the problems of black women. Campaigned against lynching. Active in Republican Party politics, though she came to admire Eleanor Roosevelt in the 1930s. In 1949 she successfully pressurized the American Association of University Women to admit black women. In

1950 she began to take direct action against segregated restaurants and stores. In 1953 the Supreme Court ruled that restaurants must serve all. Active on human rights issues, she protested against the execution of the Rosenbergs in 1953.

Dame Ellen Terry, 1847–1928
Actress and theatre manager. Supporter of suffrage movement. Made several tours of the US. Her daughter Edith 'Edy' Craig was active in the suffrage movement.

Lady Margaret Hilda Thatcher, 1925–
Conservative politician and former Prime Minister. Born in Grantham, Lincolnshire. Educated at Oxford University. Worked in industry in 1947. In 1953 took bar finals. In 1959 became Conservative MP for Finchley, north London. Joint Parliamentary Secretary for the Ministry of Pensions and National Insurance, 1961–4. Secretary of State for Education and Science under Edward Heath. In 1975 elected leader of Conservative Party. In 1979 first woman Prime Minister in Britain. Applied monetarist economic policies, cut public spending and initiated privatization of public services. Directed a wide range of policy issues through Cabinet. Ousted by Tory coup in 1990 but continued to work on right of party.

Martha Carey Thomas, 1857–1935
Educationalist and feminist. From a prosperous Quaker family. In 1894 became president of Bryn Mawr women's college. Campaigned for

women's higher education, including working-class women. Active in suffrage movement.

Dorothy Thompson, 1923–
Historian. Was involved in the Young Communist League while at school. Educated at Cambridge University. Trained as a 'draughtsman' in Second World War. In 1947 worked on youth railway in Yugoslavia. Married E. P. Thompson in 1948 and went to live in Halifax, where she did extra-mural teaching. On the national executive of the National Assembly of Women. Left the Communist Party in 1956. Active in the Institute of Workers' Control and CND. Helped to form European Nuclear Disarmament in the early 1980s. She has written several books on the Chartist movement and a biography of Queen Victoria.

Dorothy Thompson, 1894–1961
Journalist. From a Methodist family. Studied at Syracuse University, 1912–14, and joined Syracuse Equal Suffrage League. She worked as a journalist in Berlin, Vienna and Warsaw. In 1927 toured Soviet Union. Interviewed Hitler in 1931. Expelled from Nazi Germany in 1934. In 1937 wrote monthly column in *Ladies' Home Journal*. Also wrote in *Herald Tribune* and *New York Post*. Supported Roosevelt. After Second World War became interested in Arab refugees. In 1952 supported Eisenhower.

Flora Thompson, 1876–1947
Writer and historian. Left school at fourteen. Ran a post office with her husband in Bournemouth. Produced the semi-autobiographical classic trilogy *Lark Rise to Candleford* in 1945, describing a rural community in Oxfordshire beginning to feel the impact of modern industrial society.

Willa Mae (Big Mama) Thornton, 1926–84
Singer. From Montgomery, Alabama. Her father was a minister. Learned drums and harmonica as a child. In 1953 topped R&B charts with 'Hound Dog', with Johnny Otis's band. In 1965 in Folk Blues Festival troupe. Her 'Ball and Chain', recorded with Muddy Waters, inspired Janis Joplin's version.

Grace Thorpe, 1921–
Campaigner for American-Indian rights. From Yale, Oklahoma, and a member of the Sauk-Fox tribe. Active in agitation for land rights from mid-1960s. Tried to develop economic opportunities on reservations. In 1970 took part in occupations of Alcatraz and Fort Lawton Museum in Washington State. In the late 1970s she was a legislative assistant to the US Senate Sub-Committee on Indian Affairs and was on the American Indian Policy Review Board, sponsored by US House of Representatives. In the early 1990s she was a part-time district court judge for the Five Tribes in Stroud, Oklahoma.

Vesta Tilley, 1864–1952 (*Matilda Alice Powles, later Lady de Frece*)
Music hall artiste and male impersonator. Appeared in first Royal Command Performance, 1912, and successfully toured in US. Famous

songs include 'Burlington Bertie' and 'After the Ball'.

Johnnie Tillmon (Tillmon-Blackston), 1926–95

Welfare rights activist. Born in Arkansas, she lived in Little Rock and then went to California in 1960. Worked as a shirt line operator. Became involved in a community group on her housing project. Forced to go on welfare after she was ill, she began to organize women on welfare in the early 1960s. This rapidly developed into a national organization linking poor black and white women. She continued to speak out on issues of social justice in Los Angeles.

Sue Townsend, 1946–

Writer. From Leicester, she has written about the Midlands in *The Secret Life of Adrian Mole Aged 13¾* (1982) and *The Secret Diary of Adrian Mole* (1985). She has also written several plays and a best-selling novel, *The Queen and I* (1992), which was made into a stage play (1994).

Una Troubridge, 1887–1963

Studied sculpture at Royal College of Art and did a bust of Nijinsky while he was performing in Diaghilev's Ballets Russes in London. Lived with Radclyffe Hall.

Lana Turner, 1920–95

Actress. From an Idaho mining family. Discovered in Hollywood ice-cream parlour aged fifteen. Married eight times. Known as 'the sweater girl'. Films include *The Postman Always Rings Twice* (1946) and *Peyton Place* (1957).

Dorothy Tutin, 1931–

Actress. Born in Surrey and trained at the Bristol Old Vic. Parts include Sally Bowles in *I am a Camera*, dramatized from Christopher Isherwood's *Goodbye to Berlin*, and St Joan in Christopher Fry's translation of Anouilh's work *The Lark*, along with many Shakespearian roles. She has appeared on the stage in US too.

Twiggy (Lesley Hornby), 1949–

Model and actress. Model from Neasden, north-west London, who became symbol of the Swinging Sixties. Went on to star in musical *The Boyfriend* (1971). Moved to Los Angeles. Has acted in films and on TV.

Mary Ure, 1933–75

Actress. Born in Glasgow. Studied at the Central School of Speech Training and Dramatic Art. Played Shakespearian roles. Was Alison in John Osborne's *Look Back in Anger* (1958) on the stage and in the film version. Also in *Sons and Lovers* (1975) and *Where Eagles Dare* (1968).

Marie Van Vorst, 1867–1936

Social reformer. From New York. Began writing novels and investigative reports about women's working conditions in the early 1900s. Campaigned against child labour. In 1914 volunteered to serve with the American Ambulance (field hospital) in France.

Glenna Collett Vare, 1903–89

Golfer. From an athletic family in Rhode Island, began to play golf at thirteen, winning championships from nineteen with her famous long drives. In 1975 World Golf Hall of Fame.

Dame Janet Vaughan, 1899–1993
Doctor. Worked as assistant clinical pathologist at University College Hospital, London, 1927–9. The shock of poverty in the Euston area made her a socialist. Studied in Boston on a Rockefeller Travelling Fellowship, 1929. Involved in Medical Aid to Spain in Civil War. Introduced method of storing blood for transfusions developed in Spain. Sent after war to help survivors of concentration camps. Studied effects of radiation, becoming Director of Medical Research Unit for Research on Bone-seeking Isotopes. Principal of Somerville College, Oxford, 1945–67.

Sarah Vaughan, 1924–90
Singer. From Newark, New Jersey. In the 1940s began singing with Earl Hines and Billy Eckstine. She later worked with Charlie Parker and Dizzy Gillespie and recorded both jazz and popular songs.

Pablita Velarde, 1918–
Painter. Taught traditional lore by her grandmother and father. Studied at Sante Fe Indian School. In the 1930s worked on Works Progress Administration art projects with Olive Rush. Taught arts and crafts at the Santa Clara Day School. She has won many awards for her work, which is displayed in the Indian Pueblo Cultural Center in Albuquerque.

Alice Drysdale Vickery, 1844–1929
Birth-control campaigner and physician. First woman to qualify as a chemist of the Royal Pharmaceutical Society. Also studied midwifery and medicine in London, Paris and Dublin. In 1904 formed Women's Branch of the New Malthusian League, becoming president in 1907. She linked birth control to women's economic and political independence and worked with the Women's Co-operative Guild on birth control.

Hilary Wainwright, 1949–
Writer and organizer. From a Leeds Liberal family. Educated at Oxford University. In radical student movement of the 1960s and involved in Women's Liberation movement. Head of Popular Planning Unit at the Greater London Council, 1983–6. Helped form the Socialist Society and the Socialist Movement in the 1980s, and edited *Red Pepper* magazine from 1994. Has written and broadcast widely on radical politics. Associate fellow at Manchester University's International Centre for Labour Studies.

Lillian D. Wald, 1867–1940
Social reformer. Graduated as a nurse and studied at Women's Medical College, New York, 1893. In 1893 set up Henry Street Settlement House. In 1904 helped form National Child Labor Committee with Florence Kelley. Developed idea for the Federal Children's Bureau, formed in 1912, and the district nursing branch of the American Red Cross, set up the same year.

Aida Overton Walker, 1880–1914
Entertainer. From New York. Worked in the ragtime musicals which replaced minstrel shows. She

had major parts in *Sons of Pan* and *In Dahomey*, which caused a furore in the Southern states. In 1903 the show was put on in London and she sang before the Royal Family. It made the Cakewalk a craze in London. Continued to work in vaudeville, starring in *Salome* in 1912.

A'lelia Walker, 1885–1931

Businesswoman, arts patron and socialite. Brought up by her mother, the successful businesswoman Madame C. J. (Sarah Breedlove) Walker, and her stepfather, Charles Walker, she inherited her mother's company and became a millionairess. She liked dancing, parties, jewels and clothes, and was a patron of Harlem writers, including Langston Hughes and Zora Neale Hurston. In 1928 she started 'The Dark Tower' salon, which later became a nightclub in Harlem.

Alice Walker, 1944–

Writer. Born into a poor rural family in Georgia. She lost vision in one eye in a gun accident. As a student she became involved in civil rights and in the welfare rights movement. Taught black studies at Jackson State College, 1968–9. Wrote poems and stories. Her first novel was published in 1970. *The Color Purple* (1982) won American Book Award and the Pulitzer Prize in 1983. It became an Oscar-winning film in 1985. Other writings include *In Search of Our Mothers' Gardens* (1983), which examines memory and identity and questions black women's relationship to feminism.

Madame C. J. (Sarah Breedlove) Walker, 1867–1919

Businesswoman. Born on a Delta Louisiana cotton plantation. Worked as a domestic and laundress. Married Moses McWilliams and had a daughter Lelia (later known as A'lelia Walker). Began selling hair products after he died and with her second husband, Charles Walker, started mail-order business in Denver. They travelled to advertise the products and set up beauty salons. Moved to Harlem, New York, as the business prospered. She contributed to the National Association for the Advancement of Colored People and was part of the campaign against lynching. First black American woman millionaire.

Maggie Lena Walker, 1867–1934

Banker. From Richmond, Virginia. Worked as an assistant cook. Became a schoolteacher. In 1886 married Armstead Walker. In 1903 elected president of a former co-operative insurance company, the St Luke Penny Savings Bank. In 1912 founded Richmond Council of Colored Women. Supported health and educational welfare projects in the black community. Received honorary degree from Virginia Union University of Richmond. In 1930 St Lukes became Consolidated Bank and Trust Company of Richmond.

Julie Walters, 1950–

Stage and film actress. Educated at Manchester Polytechnic. She won awards for her performances in play and film versions of *Educating Rita* (1980, 1983). She also appeared on British TV with Victoria Wood.

Sylvia Townsend Warner, 1893–1978

Poet, novelist, Communist and lesbian. She lived in Devon with Valentine Ackland and was active in left cultural and political movements during the 1930s and 1940s. Works include *Lolly Willowes* (1926).

Ethel Waters, 1896–1977

Singer and actress. From poor background in Chester, Pennsylvania. Toured in vaudeville. Recorded for Black Swan records, which did 'race recordings', in 1919. Began to appear in Broadway musicals in 1927. Toured Europe in 1930, opening at London Palladium. Was in *Blackbirds* (1930) and *Rhapsody in Black* (1931). Irving Berlin wrote songs for her and she became well known on the radio. In 1940 she sang 'Taking a Chance on Love' in *Cabin in the Sky* and played Berenice in Carson McCullers's *Member of the Wedding* (1950). After her religious conversion in late 1950s, she performed in Billy Graham Crusades.

Beatrice Webb, 1858–1943

Social investigator and reformer. Married Sidney Webb in 1892. Prominent member of Fabian Society. Beatrice and Sidney Webb's joint works include *Industrial Democracy* (1897) and *Soviet Communism: A New Civilization?* (1935). Beatrice Webb's autobiographical *My Apprenticeship* (1926) was followed by her posthumous *Our Partnership* (1948).

Sarah Weddington, 1946–

Lawyer and public administrator. Studied law at University of Texas. Presented abortion case of 'Jane Roe' which in 1973 resulted in Supreme Court decision overruling state abortion bans. In 1978 appointed by President Carter as special assistant in charge of women's issues. Worked for ERA ratification and on social security and affirmative action. Awarded honours from women's church and business organizations and from National Organization for Women.

Fay Weldon, 1931–

Novelist. From New Zealand, she came to Britain after Second World War. Worked in advertising. Novels include *Down Among the Women* (1971) and *Female Friends* (1975). She has also written for television. Active in the peace movement in the 1980s, she has also campaigned for writers around issues like Public Lending Rights and Minimum Terms Agreement.

Ida B. Wells, 1862–1931

Journalist and anti-lynching campaigner. From Mississippi, her parents were slaves and she worked to support the family after they died. In 1883 she became a teacher in Memphis and studied at Fisk University. Worked as a journalist, 1884–91. From 1893 campaigned against lynching and toured Britain. Active in Women's Club movement. Helped form National Association of Colored Women and National Association for the Advancement of Colored People, and active in suffrage movement before the war. In

1917–18 she reported on race riots in East St Louis, Arkansas and Chicago and defended African-Americans who had been arrested.

Mae West, 1893–1980
Actress and playwright. Began working in vaudeville and musical reviews before First World War. Acted in her own plays *Sex* (1926) and *Diamond Lil* (1928). In 1933 went to Hollywood, where her witty sexy one-liners became famous and upset the censor. Interested in boxing, wrestling and seances. UK tour in 1948 included Birmingham and Blackpool as well as London. By the 1960s she had become a cult figure in her own lifetime.

Rebecca West, 1892–1983
(*Cecily Isabel Fairfield*)
Suffragette, feminist critic, journalist and author. Wrote for the *Freewoman* and *Clarion*, 1911–12, and later for the *New Statesman*, *Daily Telegraph* and *New Yorker*. Had a child with H. G. Wells in 1914. Continued to work as a reporter in the 1940s and 1950s. Awarded the OBE in 1949 and DBE in 1959. Her non-fiction includes *The Meaning of Treason* (1949) and her novels include *The Birds Fall Down* (1966).

Vivienne Westwood, 1941–
Fashion designer. With Malcolm McLaren, she made and sold punk clothes in Chelsea, 1970–83. Solo career from 1984, opening her own shop in 1990. Has received many awards for her designs.

Alice Wheeldon, 1867–1919
Suffrage, anti-war and socialist organizer. Active in Derby Women's Social and Political Union and the Independent Labour Party. In anti-war network. Accused of conspiracy to kill Lloyd George by a police spy in 1916. Imprisoned until 1918. Died in influenza epidemic of 1919.

Eirene White, 1909–
Labour politician. Educated at Oxford University. Readers' adviser to New York Public Library. Civil servant and journalist for *Manchester Guardian*. Elected MP for East Flint, 1950. A Fabian socialist, she was particularly interested in education, child welfare, and overseas and industrial issues. She introduced Matrimonial Causes Bill in the early 1950s which led to a Royal Commission. Parliamentary Secretary to the Colonial Office, 1964; Minister of State at the Foreign Office, 1965. She was president of the National Council of Women (Wales).

Willye B. White, 1939–
Athlete. Educated at Tennessee State University. Excelled in long jump and as a sprinter. Won Olympic Silver Medal in 1956 for long jump and in 1964 for sprinting. Won Pan-Am Games long jump, 1963, and took US long jump record up to 21 feet 6 inches in 1964. In Black Sports Hall of Fame.

Mary Whitehouse, 1910–
Campaigner against sex in the media. Educated at Cheshire County Training College. Worked as a teacher in the 1930s and 1940s. Involved in moral rearmament movement.

Became concerned about sex education in schools. Formed National Viewers' and Listeners' Association in 1965. Co-founder Clean Up TV campaign in 1964. Outspoken critic of 'permissive society'. She was an influence on Tory Party thinking on sexual politics from the late 1970s.

Ann Widdecombe, 1947–
Conservative MP. Educated at Oxford University. Worked for Unilever in marketing, 1973–5, and was then a senior administrator at London University, 1975–87. Elected as MP for Maidstone in 1987. She has been particularly involved in issues of defence, crime and morality. In 1987 she supported David Alton's bill to reduce the period for legal abortion. Vice-Chairman and founder member with Lady Olga Maitland of Women and Families for Defence. In 1993 she opposed the ordination of women priests in the Anglican Church, and converted to Roman Catholicism. Minister of State at the Department of Employment, 1994–5. Minister of State at the Home Office, 1995.

Hazel Wightman, 1886–1974
Athlete. Born in Healdsbury, California. Won her first tennis tournament in 1902. In 1909, 1910 and 1911 she won all three national events: singles, doubles and mixed doubles. She won many awards, including Olympic Gold medals for doubles and mixed doubles in 1924. She also encouraged young tennis players. In 1973 presented the first equal pay cheque at the US National championships.

Ellen Wilkinson, 1891–1947
Socialist and feminist from a Manchester working-class family. Active in the Co-operative and trade union movement. Labour MP for Middlesbrough, 1924–31, and Jarrow, 1935. Member of Communist Party and on the left of the Labour Party. Known as 'Red Ellen'. She toured the US to fund-raise for the miners during the 1927 lock-out which followed the General Strike. In the 1930s she opposed Fascism and led the 1936 Hunger March from Jarrow. After Labour's victory in 1945 she became Minister of Education, the first woman to hold this position.

Baroness Shirley Williams, 1930–
Labour and Social Democratic Party (SDP) politician. Daughter of Vera Brittain. Studied at Oxford and Columbia universities. Worked as a journalist before becoming Labour MP for Hitchin, 1964–74, and Hertford and Stevenage, 1974–9. Minister of State for Education and Science, 1967–9; Home Office, 1969–70. A Catholic, she opposed liberalization of divorce laws and legalization of abortion. Campaigned for comprehensive schools as Education Minister. Resigned from Labour Party and formed Social Democratic Party with David Owen, Roy Jenkins and Bill Rodgers in 1982.

Helen Wills (Helen Wills Moody), 1905–
Tennis player. From California, she began to play tennis at school. Between 1923 and 1938 won eight Wimbledon singles titles – a record until Martina Navratilova reached

nine in 1990. Pioneered dress reform by wearing short tennis skirts. In 1959 Member of International Hall of Fame.

Elizabeth Wilson, 1936–

Writer. Worked as a social worker. Helped form lesbian group in Women's Liberation workshop in London. Founder member of *Feminist Review*. A socialist feminist, her writing has ranged from welfare to fashion. Work includes *Hallucinations: Life in the Post-modern City* (1988). She is Professor of Social Studies at the University of North London.

Audrey Wise, 1935–

Labour MP. Became a borough councillor aged twenty-one. Active in the shop workers' union, USDAW, and in the Institute of Workers' Control. Active in equal pay campaign in 1960s. Spoke at first Women's Liberation conference in 1970 and when elected to Parliament continued to take up women's issues, including abortion rights. Lost Coventry seat in 1974. On national executive of Labour Party, 1982–3. Elected MP for Preston, 1987.

Rose Witcop, 1890–1932

Anarchist and birth-control campaigner. Active in Jewish anarchist movement in east London. Lived in free union with anarchist and Communist Guy Aldred, 1907–12. Wrote about Jewish life in the East End in *Herald of Revolt*. Opposed First World War. Became friendly with Margaret Sanger in 1915 and campaigned for birth control. Published Sanger's *Family Limitation* in 1922. She was charged with obscenity, the resulting trial in 1923 publicizing birth control. Associated with beginnings of Workers' Birth Control Group in 1924, and opened birth-control clinic in 1925. Moved towards the Labour Party in the late 1920s and early 1930s. When she died the anarchist paper *Freedom* printed a Rose Witcop Memorial Number.

Elizabeth Wood, 1899–1993

Municipal official. Active in housing reform in the 1920s. Campaigned for better design in public housing in US cities.

Victoria Wood, 1953–

Comedienne. Studied drama at Birmingham University. Worked as a singer and songwriter. In 1981–2 did TV comedy series *Wood and Walters*. Went on to do her own show and has appeared on stage. She has won many awards.

Ellen Sullivan Woodward, 1887–1971

Administrator. Brought up in Mississippi. Involved in charities for children and hospitals during the 1920s. Became an official with the Mississippi State Board of Development in 1925. In 1933 director of the Federal Emergency Relief Administration. Believed in professionalization of social work and in work-based relief. Tried to strengthen Aid to Dependent Children. Worked on social security rights for farmers, domestic workers and the self-employed. From 1946 involved in UN and especially UNESCO.

Virginia Woolf, 1882–1941
Writer. Central figure in the Bloomsbury Group. Novels include *Jacob's
Room* (1922) and *Orlando* (1928).
Essays collected in *The Common
Reader* include a study of Mary Woll-
stonecraft. *A Room of One's Own*
(1929) and *Three Guineas* (1938) were
influential inter-war feminist state-
ments. Married writer Leonard Woolf
in 1912. Together they set up the
Hogarth Press in 1917. Intimate friend
of Vita Sackville-West, who influenced *Orlando*. She committed suicide
in 1941.

**Baroness Barbara Wootton,
1897–1988**
Social scientist. Educated at Cambridge University. Researcher for
Labour Party and TUC from 1922.
Principal of Morley College for Working Men and Women, 1926. Worked
in adult education at London University from the 1920s. Wrote widely on
economic and social policy.

Chien-Shiung Wu, *c.* 1912–
Nuclear physicist. Her father was a
pioneer of Chinese girls' education.
Educated at Berkeley. During Second
World War worked at Princeton University. In 1944 helped develop sensitive radiation detectors for atom
bombs. Best known for an experiment
on beta decay. Elected to National
Academy of Sciences, 1958.

Judith Lang Zaimont, 1945–
Composer. Studied at the Juilliard
School, Queens and Columbia.
Taught at several university colleges.
Work includes *From the Great Land*
(1982). She has also written on
women's music. *The Musical Woman:
An International Perspective* (1984),
Vol. III (1991), was awarded the
Pauline Alderman Prize for new
scholarship.

Ellen Taaffe Zwilich, 1939–
Composer and violinist. Studied at
Florida State University and the Juilliard School. Works include *Sym-
posium* (1973) and *Sonata in Three
Movements* (1974). Performed in 1982
by the American Composers' Orchestra, the latter won the Pulitzer Prize
in music composition, making her the
first woman to win the award. In the
1980s she wrote for the trombone, the
oboe and the horn.

Notes

INTRODUCTION

1. Bessie Delany in Sarah L. and A. Elizabeth Delany, with Amy Hill Hearth, *Having Our Say: The Delany Sisters' First 100 Years*, a Dell book, Bantam Doubleday Dell Publishing Group Inc., New York, 1994, p. 296
2. Ibid., pp. 298–9

CHAPTER I: 1900–1914

1. Patricia Stubbs, *Women and Fiction: Feminism and the Novel 1880–1920*, Harvester Press, Brighton, 1979, p. 184
2. H. G. Wells, quoted ibid.
3. Ellen Key, quoted in Constance Rover, *Love, Morals and the Feminists*, Routledge and Kegan Paul, London, 1970, p. 137
4. Quoted in Julie Holledge, *Innocent Flowers: Women in the Edwardian Theatre*, Virago, London, 1981, p. 58
5. Vera Brittain, *The Women at Oxford: A Fragment of History*, George G. Harrap and Co., London, 1960, p. 123
6. Ibid.
7. Vera Brittain, *Testament of Youth*, Arrow Books, London, 1960 (first edn 1933), p. 39
8. Ibid.
9. Antonia Raeburn, *Militant Suffragettes*, New English Library, London, 1974, p. 19
10. Millicent Garrett Fawcett, *What I Remember*, T. Fisher Unwin, London, 1924, p. 179
11. 'A Songbird in Holloway', obituary of Victoria Liddiard, *Guardian*, 12 October 1992
12. Kitty Marion, quoted in Holledge, *Innocent Flowers*, p. 58
13. *Glasgow Evening Citizen*, 22 July 1914, quoted in Elspeth King, *The Hidden*

History of Glasgow's Women, Mainstream Press, Edinburgh, 1993, p. 105

14. *Derby Daily Express*, 8 June 1914
15. Ibid., 17 June 1914
16. Beatrice Webb to Millicent Garrett Fawcett, 2 November 1906, quoted in Barbara Caine, 'Beatrice Webb and the "Woman Question"', *History Workshop: A Journal of Socialist and Feminist Historians*, 14, Autumn 1982, p. 35
17. Charlotte Despard, quoted in Andro Linklater, *An Unhusbanded Life: Charlotte Despard – Suffragette, Socialist and Sinn Feiner*, Hutchinson, London, 1980, p. 150
18. Jessie Stephen, quoted in Suzie Fleming and Gloden Dallas, 'Jessie', in Marsha Rowe (ed.), *Spare Rib Reader: 100 Issues of Women's Liberation*, Penguin Books, Harmondsworth, 1982, p. 559
19. Cicely Hamilton, *Marriage as a Trade*, Chapman and Hall, London, 1912, p. 107
20. Mabel Harding, 'Social Motherhood', *Daily Herald*, 19 April 1912
21. David Vincent, *Poor Citizens: The State and the Poor in Twentieth-century Britain*, Longman, London, 1991, pp. 34–5
22. Jessie Newbery, quoted in Liz Bird, 'Threading the Beads: Women in Art in Glasgow, 1870–1920', in Glasgow Women's Studies Group (ed.), *Uncharted Lives: Extracts from Scottish Women's Experiences, 1850–1982*, Pressgang, Glasgow, 1983, p. 109
23. Ibid., p. 99
24. Mary Macarthur, quoted in Sarah Boston, *Women Workers and the Trade Unions*, Lawrence and Wishart, London, 1980, p. 62
25. Ibid., p. 91
26. Hamilton, *Marriage as a Trade*, p. 96
27. Lady Violet Bonham-Carter, quoted in Paul Thompson, *The Edwardians: The Remaking of British Society*, Weidenfeld and Nicolson, London, 1975, p. 82
28. Harley Granville-Barker, quoted in Sylvia Strauss, *'Traitors to the Masculine Cause': The Men's Campaign for Women's Rights*, Greenwood Press, Westport, Connecticut, 1982, p. 164
29. Mrs Murray, quoted in Carol Adams, *Ordinary Lives: A Hundred Years Ago*, Virago, London, 1982, pp. 149–51
30. Ellen Ross, 'Survival Networks: Women's Neighbourhood Sharing in London before World War I', *History Workshop: A Journal of Socialist and Feminist Historians*, 15, Spring 1983, pp. 8–9
31. Naomi Mitchison, *All Change Here*, Bodley Head, London, 1975, p. 90
32. Grace Foakes, *My Part of the River*, Futura, London, 1976, p. 18
33. Kathleen Woodward, *Jipping Street*, Virago, London, 1983 (first edn 1923), pp. 19–20
34. Emily Wilson, quoted in Steve Humphries and Pamela Gordon, *Forbidden Britain: Our Secret Past, 1900–1960*, BBC Books, London, 1994, p. 150

35. Teresa Billington-Greig, quoted in Lucy Bland, *Banishing the Beast: English Feminism and Sexual Morality, 1885–1914*, Penguin Books, Harmondsworth, 1995, p. 299

36. Quoted in Ziggi Alexander, 'Black Entertainers', in Jane Beckett and Deborah Cherry (eds.), *The Edwardian Era*, Phaidon Press and the Barbican Gallery, London, 1987, p. 46

37. Arthur Hall, 'The Increasing Use of Lead as an Abortifacient', *British Medical Journal*, 18 March 1905, p. 586

38. Foakes, *My Part of the River*, p. 78

39. Bland, *Banishing the Beast*, p. 251

40. Paul Ferris, *Sex and the British: A Twentieth-century History*, Michael Joseph, London, 1993, p. 2

41. Peter Brent, *The Edwardians*, BBC Books, London, 1972, pp. 109–10

42. Quoted in Lucy Bland, 'Sex and Morality: Sinning on a Tiger Skin or Keeping the Beast at Bay', in Beckett and Cherry (eds.), *The Edwardian Era*, p. 88

43. Storm Jameson, *Autobiography of Storm Jameson: Journey from the North*, Vol. I, Virago, London, 1984, pp. 65–6

44. Kate Chopin, *The Awakening*, The Women's Press, London, 1978, p. 96

45. June Sochen, *The New Woman in Greenwich Village, 1910–1920*, Quadrangle Books, New York, 1972, p. 17

46. Jiu Jin, quoted in Elizabeth Croll, *Feminism and Socialism in China*, Routledge and Kegan Paul, London, 1978, p. 67

47. Irene Castle, quoted in Lewis A. Erenberg, *Steppin' Out: New York Nightlife and the Transformation of American Culture, 1890–1930*, University of Chicago Press, Chicago, 1984, p. 167

48. Barbara Woloch, *Women and the American Experience: A Concise History*, Overture Books, The McGraw-Hill Companies Inc., New York, 1996, p. 214

49. Ibid.

50. Ellen Carol DuBois, 'Harriot Stanton Blatch and the Transformation of Class Relations among Woman Suffragists', in Noralee Frankel and Nancy S. Dye (eds.), *Gender, Class, Race and Reform in the Progressive Era*, University Press of Kentucky, Lexington, 1991, p. 169

51. Sara M. Evans, *Born for Liberty: A History of Women in America*, The Free Press, Macmillan, New York, 1989, p. 165

52. Ellen Carol DuBois, 'Working Women, Class Relations and Suffrage Militance', in Ellen Carol DuBois and Vicki L. Ruiz (eds.), *Unequal Sisters: A Multicultural Reader in US Women's History*, Routledge, New York, 1990, p. 190

53. Evans, *Born for Liberty*, p. 153

54. Jane Addams, quoted ibid., p. 154

55. Jane Addams, quoted in Carol Hymowitz and Michaele Weissman, *A History of Women in America*, Bantam Books, New York, 1978, p. 273

56. Mary Ritter Beard, *Women's Work in Municipalities*, Arno Press, New York, 1972 (first edn 1915), p. 66

57. Dorothy Sterling, *Black Foremothers: Three Lives*, The Feminist Press, New York, 1988, p. 131

58. Elizabeth Ewen, *Immigrant Women in the Land of Dollars: Life and Culture on the Lower East Side, 1890–1925*, Monthly Review Press, New York, 1985, p. 260

59. Mollie Schepps, quoted in Rosalyn Baxandall and Linda Gordon (eds.), with Susan Reverby, *America's Working Women: A Documentary History, 1600 to the Present*, W. W. Norton, New York, 1995, p. 189

60. Elizabeth Gurley Flynn, 'Women in Industry Should Organize', in Rosalyn Fraad Baxandall, *Words on Fire: The Life and Writing of Elizabeth Gurley Flynn*, Rutgers University Press, New Brunswick, 1987, p. 95

61. Mary Heaton Vorse, quoted ibid., p. 46

62. Baxandall and Gordon (eds.), *America's Working Women*, p. 147

63. Elizabeth Beardsley Butler, *Women and the Trades: Pittsburgh, 1907–1908*, University of Pittsburgh Press, 1984 (first edn 1909), p. 83

64. Julia Lathrop, quoted in Molly Ladd-Taylor, *Mother-Work: Women, Child Welfare and the State, 1890–1930*, University of Illinois Press, Urbana, 1994, p. 33

65. Mrs Levy, quoted in Paula E. Hyman, 'Immigrant Women and Consumer Protest: The New York City Kosher Meat Boycott', in George E. Pozzetta (ed.), *Ethnicity and Gender: The Immigrant Woman*, Garland, New York, 1991, p. 93

66. Woloch, *Women and the American Experience*, p. 190

67. Charlotte Perkins Gilman quoted in Dolores Hayden, *The Grand Domestic Revolution*, MIT Press, Cambridge, Mass., 1984, p. 221

68. Susan Strasser, *Never Done: A History of American Housework*, Pantheon Books, New York, 1982, p. 91

69. Ibid., p. 285

70. Valeska Suratt, quoted in Shirley Staples, *Male–Female Comedy Teams in American Vaudeville, 1865–1932*, UMI Research Press, Ann Arbor, Michigan, 1984, p. 133

71. Ibid., p. 155

72. Joanne Meyerowitz, 'Sexual Geography and Gender Economy: The Furnished Room District of Chicago, 1890–1930', in Barbara Melosh (ed.), *Gender and American History since 1890*, Routledge, London, 1993, pp. 52–3

73. Kathy Peiss, '"Charity Girls" and City Pleasures', in Kathy Peiss and Christine Simmons (eds.), with Robert A. Padgug, *Passion, Power and Sexuality in History*, Temple University Press, Philadelphia, 1989, p. 59

74. Linda Gordon, *Pitied But Not Entitled: Single Mothers and the History of Welfare, 1890–1935*, The Free Press, Macmillan, New York, 1994, p. 30

75. Emma Goldman, *The Traffic in Women and Other Essays on Feminism*, Times Change Press, Washington, New Jersey, 1970, pp. 28–30

76. 'The Revolt of Decency', *New York Sun*, quoted in *Literary Digest*, 9 April 1913, p. 894

77. Christine Simmons, 'Modern Sexuality and the Myth of Victorian Repression', in Peiss and Simmons (eds.), *Passion, Power and Sexuality in History*, p. 159

78. Mary Murphy, 'The Private Lives of Public Women: Prostitution in Butte, Montana, 1878–1917', in Susan Armitage and Elizabeth Jameson (eds.), *The Women's West*, University of Oklahoma Press, Norman, 1987, p. 203

79. William Lee Howard, quoted in Carroll Smith-Rosenberg, 'Discourses of Sexuality and Subjectivity: The New Woman, 1870–1936', in Martin Duberman, Martha Vicinus and George Chauncey Jr (eds.), *Hidden from History: Reclaiming the Gay and Lesbian Past*, Penguin Books, Harmondsworth, 1991, p. 272

80. Cora Anderson/Ralph Kerwinieo, quoted in Jonathan Katz (ed.), *Gay American History: Lesbians and Gay Men in the USA*, Thomas U. Crowell Company, New York, 1976, p. 257

81. Linda Gordon, *Woman's Body, Woman's Right: A Social History of Birth Control in America*, Grossman, Viking Press, New York, 1976, p. 212

82. Ibid., pp. 221–2

83. Quoted in Sharon A. Glenn, *Daughters of the Shetl: Life and Labor in the Immigrant Generation*, Cornell University Press, Ithaca, 1990, p. 166

84. Rose Schneiderman, quoted in Ardis Cameron, *Radicals of the Worst Sort: Laboring Women in Lawrence Massachusetts, 1860–1912*, University of Illinois Press, Urbana, 1993, p. 117

CHAPTER 2: THE FIRST WORLD WAR AND ITS AFTERMATH

1. Roland, quoted in Vera Brittain, *Testament of Youth*, Arrow Books, London, 1960, p. 64

2. Ibid., p. 185

3. Ibid., p. 153

4. Ibid.

5. Ibid., p. 156

6. Ibid., p. 251

7. F. E. Smith, quoted in Sheila Rowbotham, *Friends of Alice Wheeldon*, Pluto, London, 1986, p. 58

8. Ibid., p. 56

9. Alice Wheeldon to Lydia Robinson, 26 February 1917; printed in *Derby Evening Telegraph*, 23 March 1983

10. Emmeline Pankhurst, quoted in Jill Liddington, *The Life and Times of a Respectable Rebel: Selina Cooper, 1864–1946*, Virago, London, 1984, p. 269

11. Millicent Fawcett, quoted in Diana Condell and Jean Liddiard, *Working for*

Victory? Images of Women in the First World War, 1914–1918, Routledge and Kegan Paul, London, 1987, p. 7

12. Cliona Murphy, '"The Tune of the Stars and Stripes": The American Influence on the Irish Suffrage Movement', in Maria Luddy and Cliona Murphy (eds.), *Women Surviving: Studies in Irish Women's History in the 19th and 20th Centuries*, Poolbeg Press, Dublin, 1900, p. 197

13. Hanna Sheehy Skeffington, quoted in Rosemary Cullen Owens, *Smashing Times: A History of the Irish Women's Suffrage Movement, 1889–1922*, Attic Press, Dublin, 1984, p. 110

14. Mary Sheepshanks, quoted in Margaret Kamester and Jo Vellacott (eds.), *Militarism Versus Feminism: Writings on Women and War*, Virago, London, 1987, p. 13

15. Anonymous, *WAAC: The Women's Story of the War*, T. Werner Laurie Ltd, London, 1930, p. 66

16. Quoted in Martin Pugh, *Women and the Women's Movement in Britain, 1914–1959*, Macmillan, London, 1992, p. 13

17. Ibid.

18. Quoted in E. S. Turner, *The Shocking History of Advertising*, Penguin Books, Harmondsworth, 1965, p. 169

19. Quoted in Pugh, *Women and the Women's Movement*, p. 14

20. *Punch*, 1917, quoted in E. Royston Pike, *Human Documents of the Lloyd George Era*, George Allen and Unwin, London, 1972, p. 185

21. Robert Roberts, *The Classic Slum: Salford Life in the First Quarter of the Century*, Penguin Books, Harmondsworth, 1973, p. 201

22. A. K. Foxwell, *Munition Lasses: Six Months as Principal Overlooker in Danger Buildings*, Hodder and Stoughton, London, 1917, p. 99

23. Ibid., p. 44

24. Gail Braybon and Penny Summerfield, *Out of the Cage: Women's Experiences of Two World Wars*, Pandora, London, 1987, p. 75

25. J. T. Murphy, *The Workers' Committee: An Outline of Its Principles and Structure*, Pluto, London, 1972 (first edn 1918), p. 18

26. Mary Macarthur, quoted in Sheila Lewenhak, *Women and Trade Unions: An Outline History of Women in the British Trade Union Movement*, Ernest Benn, London, 1977, p. 160

27. Ken Weller, *Don't Be a Soldier: The Radical Anti-War Movement in North London, 1914–18*, Journeyman Press, London, 1985, p. 32

28. *The Times*, 24 August 1918

29. Lloyd George, quoted in Sarah Boston, *Women Workers and the Trade Unions*, Lawrence and Wishart, London, 1980, p. 126

30. Dolly Scannell, *Mother Knew Best: An East End Childhood*, Pan Books, London, 1975, p. 59

31. *The Times*, 1 January 1917

32. James J. Smyth, 'Women in Struggle: A Study of the Political Activity of Working-class Women in Glasgow during the First World War', MA

thesis, Department of Sociology, University of Glasgow, March 1980, p. 25

33. Pugh, *Women and the Women's Movement*, p. 17
34. Mrs Layton, 'Memories of Seventy Years', in Margaret Llewellyn Davies (ed.), *Life As We Have Known It, by Co-operative Working Women*, Hogarth Press, London, 1931, p. 51
35. Mary Allen, quoted in Angela Woollacott, *On Her Their Lives Depend: Munitions Workers in the Great War*, University of California Press, Berkeley, 1994, p. 124
36. *The Girl's Friend*, quoted in Woollacott, *On Her Their Lives Depend*, p. 153
37. *Beryl of the Biplane*, quoted in Mary Cadogan, *Women with Wings*, Macmillan, London, 1992, pp. 63–4
38. E. Almaz Stout, quoted ibid., p. 63
39. Woollacott, *On Her Their Lives Depend*, p. 144
40. Ibid., p. 126
41. Sylvia Pankhurst, *The Home Front*, Hutchinson, London, 1932, p. 98
42. Roberts, *The Classic Slum*, p. 205
43. Woollacott, *On Her Their Lives Depend*, p. 146
44. Roberts, *The Classic Slum*, p. 215
45. Braybon and Summerfield, *Out of the Cage*, p. 111
46. Mary Allen, quoted in Woollacott, *On Her Their Lives Depend*, p. 175
47. Braybon and Summerfield, *Out of the Cage*, p. 109
48. Quoted in Lucy Bland, 'In the Name of Protection', in Julia Brophy and Carol Smart (eds.), *Women in Law: Explorations in Law, Family and Sexuality*, Routledge and Kegan Paul, London, 1985, p. 29
49. Braybon and Summerfield, *Out of the Cage*, p. 109
50. Scannell, *Mother Knew Best*, p. 75
51. Anonymous, *WAAC: The Women's Story of the War*, p. 87
52. Ibid., p. 104
53. Roberts, *The Classic Slum*, p. 206
54. Alison Neilans, 'Changes in Sex Morality', in Ray Strachey (ed.), *Our Freedom and Its Results by Five Women*, Hogarth Press, London, 1936, p. 223
55. Siegfried Sassoon, 'Glory of Women', in Jon Silkin (ed.), *The Penguin Book of First World War Poetry*, Penguin Books, Harmondsworth, 1979, p. 132
56. Pat Barker, *The Eye in the Door*, Penguin Books, Harmondsworth, 1993, pp. 279–80, Author's Note
57. Gwen Chambers, quoted in Jill Liddington, *The Long Road to Greenham: Feminism and Anti-Militarism in Britain since 1820*, Virago, London, 1989, pp. 130–31
58. Melvina Walker, 'My Impressions of the Women's Conference', *The Workers' Dreadnought*, 2 November 1918
59. Florence Farrow, Women's Guild Congress, *Derby Monthly Records*, October 1919 report
60. Sandra Holton, *Feminism and Democracy*, Cambridge University Press, Cambridge, 1986, p. 150

61. Virginia Woolf, quoted in Judith Hattaway, 'Virginia Woolf's *Jacob's Room*, History and Memory', in Dorothy Goldman (ed.), *Women and World War I: The Written Response*, Macmillan, London, 1993, p. 18

62. Katherine Mansfield, quoted in Lyn Bicker, 'Public and Private Choices: Public and Private Voices', ibid., p. 102

63. Sylvia Townsend Warner, quoted in Janet Montefiore, ' "Shining Pins and Wailing Shells": Women Poets and the Great War', ibid., p. 51

64. Anna Louise Strong, *I Change Worlds: The Remaking of an American*, Seal Press, Seattle, 1979 (first edn 1935), p. 57

65. Dorothy Sterling, *Black Foremothers: Three Lives*, The Feminist Press, New York, 1988, p. 145

66. Ibid.

67. Ibid., p. 144

68. Quoted in Aileen S. Kraditor, *The Ideas of the Woman Suffrage Movement, 1890–1920*, W. W. Norton and Co., New York, 1981, p. 26

69. Ibid., p. 24

70. Lillian Wald, 'Suffrage 1914', in Clare Coss (ed.), *Lillian D. Wald, Progressive Activist*, The Feminist Press, New York, 1989, p. 75

71. Angela Morgan, quoted in Barbara J. Steinson, ' "The Mother Half of Humanity": American Women in the Peace and Preparedness Movements in World War I', in Carol R. Berkin and Clara M. Lovett (eds.), *Women, War and Revolution*, Holmes and Meier, New York, 1980, p. 263

72. Crystal Eastman, quoted in Blanche Wiesen Cook (ed.), *Crystal Eastman: On Women and Revolution*, Oxford University Press, Oxford, 1978, p. 16

73. Lillian D. Wald to John Haynes Holmes, 25 February 1916, in Coss (ed.), *Lillian D. Wald*, p. 52

74. Inez Milholland, quoted in Cook (ed.), *Crystal Eastman*, p. 17

75. Quoted in Steinson, ' "The Mother Half of Humanity" ', in Berkin and Lovett (eds.), *Women, War and Revolution*, p. 269

76. Ibid., p. 264

77. *Four Lights*, quoted in Cook (ed.), *Crystal Eastman*, p. 19

78. Quoted in June Sochen, *The New Woman: Feminism in Greenwich Village, 1910–1920*, Quadrangle Books, New York, 1972, p. 101

79. Crystal Eastman, quoted in Cook (ed.), *Crystal Eastman*, p. 264

80. Emma Goldman, quoted in Alice Wexler, *Emma Goldman: An Intimate Life*, Virago, London, 1984, p. 234

81. Mary Marcy, 'The Real Fatherland', in Mary E. Marcy, *You Have No Country*, Charles H. Kerr, Chicago, 1984, p. 17

82. Vylla Poe Wilson, quoted in Steinson, ' "The Mother Half of Humanity" ', in Berkin and Lovett (eds.), *Women, War and Revolution*, p. 266

83. Eleanor Roosevelt, quoted in Blanche Wiesen Cook, *Eleanor Roosevelt: Volume One, 1884–1933*, Viking, New York, 1992, p. 214

84. Florence Luscomb, quoted in Ellen Cantarow (ed.), *Moving the Mountain:*

Women Working for Social Change, The Feminist Press and McGraw-Hill, New York, 1980, p. 22

85. Helen Marot, quoted in Janet Polansky, 'Helen Marot: The Mother of Democratic Technics', in Barbara Drygulski Wright (ed.), *Women, Work and Technology: Transformations*, University of Michigan Press, Ann Arbor, 1987, p. 260

86. Charles E. Knoeppel, quoted in Philip S. Foner, *Women and the American Labor Movement: From the First Trade Unions to the Present*, The Free Press, Macmillan, New York, 1979, p. 219

87. William M. Ashby, quoted ibid., p. 229

88. *Chicago Defender*, quoted ibid., p. 228

89. Quoted in Jacqueline Jones, *Labor of Love, Labor of Sorrow: Black Women, Work and the Family, from Slavery to the Present*, Basic Books, New York, 1985, p. 153

90. Ibid., pp. 152–3

91. Elizabeth Ewen, *Immigrant Women in the Land of Dollars: Life and Culture on the Lower East Side, 1890–1925*, Monthly Review Press, New York, 1985, p. 179

92. Ibid., p. 177

93. Ibid., p. 181

94. Ibid.

95. Quoted in Linda Gordon, *Heroes of Their Own Lives: The Politics and History of Family Violence, Boston, 1880–1960*, Virago, London, 1989, p. 19

96. Quoted in Gwendolyn Mink, 'The Lady and the Tramp: Gender, Race, and the Origins of the American Welfare States', in Linda Gordon (ed.), *Women, the State and Welfare*, University of Wisconsin Press, Madison, 1990, p. 109

97. Margaret Morse Nice, 'Research is a Passion with Me', in Jill Ker Conway (ed.), *Written by Herself: Autobiographies of American Women – an Anthology*, Vintage Books, New York, 1992, pp. 211–12

98. Ibid., p. 212

99. Ibid.

100. Charlotte Perkins Gilman, *Herland: A Lost Feminist Utopian Novel*, with an introduction by Ann J. Lane, Pantheon Books, New York, 1979 (first edn 1915), p. 68

101. Margaret Sanger, quoted in Linda Gordon, *Woman's Body, Woman's Right: A Social History of Birth Control in America*, Grossman, Viking Press, New York, 1976, p. 223

102. Agnes Smedley, quoted in Janice R. and Stephen R. Mackinnon, *Agnes Smedley: The Life and Times of an American Radical*, Virago, London, 1988, p. 48

103. Ibid., p. 49

104. Margaret Anderson, quoted in Richard Drinnon, *Rebel in Paradise: A Biography of Emma Goldman*, University of Chicago Press, Chicago, 1961, p. 143

105. Quoted in Jessie M. Rodrique, 'The Black Community and the Birth Control Movement', in Kathy Peiss and Christine Simmons (eds.), with Robert A. Padgug, *Passion, Power and Sexuality in History*, Temple University Press, Philadelphia, 1989, p. 145

106. Quoted in Elizabeth Fee, 'Venereal Disease: The Wages of Sin?', ibid., p. 195, footnote 5

107. Alan Dawley, *Struggles for Justice: Social Responsibility and the Liberal State*, The Belknap Press of Harvard University Press, Cambridge, Mass., 1991, p. 208

108. Quoted ibid., p. 209

109. Ibid.

110. Ibid., p. 208

111. Quoted in James R. McGovern, 'The American Woman's Pre-World War I Freedom in Manners and Morals', *Journal of American History*, Vol. IV, No. 2, September 1968, p. 323

112. Quoted in Jennifer Scanlon, *Inarticulate Longings: 'The Ladies' Home Journal', Gender, and the Promises of Consumer Culture*, Routledge, New York, 1995, p. 178

113. Dawley, *Struggles for Justice*, pp. 213, 210

114. Quoted in Carol Hymowitz and Michaele Weissman, *A History of Women in America*, Bantam Books, New York, 1978, p. 284

115. Margaret Dreier Robins, quoted in Philip S. Foner, *Women and the American Labor Movement*, p. 274

116. Quoted ibid.

117. Dana Frank, *Purchasing Power, Consumer Organizing, Gender, and the Seattle Labor Movement, 1919–1929*, Cambridge University Press, Cambridge, 1994, p. 117

118. Quoted in Mackinnon and Mackinnon, *Agnes Smedley*, p. 63

119. Emma Goldman, quoted in Wexler, *Emma Goldman*, p. 234

120. Georgia Douglass Johnson, quoted in Paula Giddings, *When and Where I Enter: The Impact of Black Women on Race and Sex in America*, Bantam Books, Toronto, 1985, p. 148

121. Cook, *Eleanor Roosevelt*, p. 239

CHAPTER 3: THE 1920S

1. Quoted in Anne Chisholm, *Nancy Cunard*, Penguin Books, Harmondsworth, 1981, p. 104

2. Mary Hutchinson, quoted ibid., p. 93

3. Dr Cecil Webb-Johnson, 'Discontented Wives', in Brian Braithwaite and Noëlle Walsh (eds.), *Things My Mother Should Have Told Me: The Best of 'Good Housekeeping', 1920–1940*, Ebury Press, London, 1991, p. 61

4. Quoted in Christopher Sykes, *Nancy: The Life of Lady Astor*, Panther, Granada Publishing, London, 1979, pp. 250–51

5. Bernard Shaw, quoted in Martin Pugh, *Women and the Women's Movement in Britain, 1914–1959*, Macmillan, London, 1992, p. 174

6. Margaret Wintringham, quoted ibid., p. 228

7. Ellen Wilkinson, quoted in Margaret Ward, *Unmanageable Revolutionaries: Women and Irish Nationalism*, Pluto, London, 1983, p. 143

8. Ellen Wilkinson, quoted in Pugh, *Women and the Women's Movement*, p. 158

9. Eleanor Rathbone, quoted in Jane Lewis, 'Beyond Suffrage: English Feminism in the 1920s', *Maryland Historian*, Spring 1975, p. 7

10. Winifred Holtby, quoted in Rosalind Delmar, Afterword, Vera Britain, *Testament of Friendship: The Story of Winifred Holtby*, Virago, London, 1980, p. 450.

11. P. S. O'Hegarty, quoted in Rosemary Cullen Owens, *Smashing Times: A History of the Irish Women's Suffrage Movement, 1889–1922*, Attic Press, Dublin, 1984, p. 131

12. Mary Agnes Hamilton, quoted in Sykes, *Nancy: The Life of Lady Astor*, p. 354

13. Stella Browne, 'The New Motherhood', *The New Generation*, July 1922, p. 14

14. Lavinia Swainbeck, in John Burnett (ed.), *Unequal Toil: Autobiographies of Working People from the 1820s to the 1920s*, Allen Lane, Harmondsworth, 1974, p. 221

15. Bessie Dickenson, quoted in Sarah Boston, *Women Workers and the Trade Unions*, Lawrence and Wishart, London, 1980, p. 175

16. Winnie Young, quoted in Miriam Glucksmann, *Women Assemble: Women Workers and the New Industries in Inter-War Britain*, Routledge, London, 1990, p. 97

17. Dolly Scannell, *Mother Knew Best: An East End Childhood*, Pan Books, London, 1975, p. 163

18. Mrs Dunne, 'Canteen Workers Canteen on the Quayside', *Women's Work on the Waterfront, 1916–1987*, Liverpool Women's History Women's Lives, Second Chance to Learn Group, Liverpool, c. 1987, p. 21

19. Robert Roberts, *The Classic Slum: Salford Life in the First Quarter of the Century*, Penguin Books, Harmondsworth, 1973, pp. 237–8

20. Rose Gamble, quoted in Sally Alexander, *Becoming a Woman and Other Essays in 19th and 20th Century Feminist History*, Virago, London, 1994, p. 224

21. Norah Kirk, quoted in Jean McCrindle and Sheila Rowbotham (eds.), *Dutiful Daughters: Women Talk About Their Lives*, Penguin Books, Harmondsworth, 1979, p. 189

22. Mary Malloy, 'The Happiest Days of My Life', *Women's Work on the Waterfront*, p. 25

23. Maud Wood, quoted in Steve Humphries and Pamela Gordon, *Forbidden Britain: Our Secret Past, 1900–1960*, BBC Books, London, 1994, p. 166

24. Vera Alsop, quoted in Huw Beynon and Terry Austrin, *Masters and Servants: Class and Patronage in the Making of a Labour Organization*, Rivers Oram Press, London, 1994, p. 183

25. Ibid.
26. Christian Miller, *A Childhood in Scotland*, John Murray, London, 1979, p. 19
27. Kathleen Woodroofe, *From Charity to Social Work in England and the United States*, Routledge and Kegan Paul, London, 1962, p. 147
28. Ibid.
29. Board of Education, *The Education of the Adolescent*, HMSO, London, 1926, p. 234
30. Ibid.
31. Rose Macaulay, quoted in Braithwaite and Walsh (eds.), *Things My Mother Should Have Told Me*, p. 14
32. Ibid., p. 88
33. Mabel Liddiard, quoted in Steve Humphries and Pamela Gordon, *A Labour of Love: The Experience of Parenthood in Britain, 1900–1950*, Sidgwick and Jackson, London, 1993, pp. 51–2
34. Ellen Wilkinson, quoted in Betty D. Vernon, *Ellen Wilkinson, 1891–1947*, Croom Helm, London, 1982, p. 98
35. Rose Luttrell, quoted in Humphries and Gordon, *A Labour of Love*, p. 29
36. Prunella Stack, *Zest for Life: Mary Bagot Stack and the League of Health and Beauty*, Peter Owen, London, 1988, pp. 101–2
37. Quoted in Braithwaite and Walsh (eds.), *Things My Mother Should Have Told Me*, p. 72
38. Ibid., p. 73
39. Dorothy Jewson, 'Socialism and the Family: A Plea for Family Endowment', ILP Publication (pamphlet), London, no date, pp. 6, 5
40. Dora Russell, 'The Long Campaign', *New Humanist*, December 1974, p. 260
41. Dr Halliday Sutherland, quoted in Keith Briant, *Marie Stopes: A Biography*, Hogarth Press, London, 1962, p. 153
42. Stella Browne, quoted in Sheila Rowbotham, *A New World for Women: Stella Browne – Socialist Feminist*, Pluto, London, 1977, p. 62
43. Ruth Adler, Jewish Women in London Group (ed.), *Generations of Memories: Voices of Jewish Women*, The Women's Press, London, 1989, p. 35
44. Elsie Friend, quoted in Barbara Brookes, *Abortion in England, 1900–1967*, Croom Helm, London, 1988, p. 34
45. Stella Browne, quoted in Rowbotham, *A New World for Women*, p. 69
46. Andrew Davies, *Leisure, Gender and Poverty: Working-class Culture in Salford and Manchester, 1900–1939*, Open University Press, Buckingham, 1992, p. 88
47. Humphries and Gordon (eds.), *Forbidden Britain*, p. 16
48. Ibid., p. 27
49. Dora Russell, *The Right to be Happy*, Harper Brothers, New York, 1927, p. 163
50. Ibid., pp. 163–4
51. Dora Russell, *The Tamarisk Tree: My Quest for Liberty and Love*, Elek/Pemberton, London, 1975, p. 203

52. Leonora Eyles, 'Unattached Woman', in Braithwaite and Walsh (eds.), *Things My Mother Should Have Told Me*, pp. 74–5

53. Virginia Woolf, *A Room of One's Own*, in Virginia Woolf, *A Room of One's Own and Three Guineas*, with an introduction by Hermione Lee, Chatto and Windus, Hogarth Press, London, 1984, p. 106

54. Russell, *The Tamarisk Tree*, p. 216

55. C. Lawton Campbell, quoted in Nancy Milford, *Zelda Fitzgerald: A Biography*, Bodley Head, London, 1970, p. 81

56. Scott Fitzgerald, quoted ibid., p. 77

57. Ibid., p. 275

58. Ibid., p. 274

59. Zelda Fitzgerald, quoted in Sara M. Evans, *Born for Liberty: A History of Women in America*, The Free Press, Macmillan, New York, 1989, p. 175

60. Freda Kirchwey, quoted in Elaine Showalter, Introduction, in Elaine Showalter (ed.), *These Modern Women: Autobiographical Essays from the Twenties*, The Feminist Press, New York, 1978, p. 6

61. Ibid., p. 14

62. Vicki L. Ruiz, *Cannery Women, Cannery Lives: Mexican Women, Unionization and the Californian Food Processing Industry, 1930–1950*, University of New Mexico Press, Albuquerque, 1992, p. 10

63. Hazel V. Carby, ' "It Jus Be's Dat Way Sometime": The Sexual Politics of Women's Blues', in Ellen Carol DuBois and Vicki L. Ruiz (eds.), *Unequal Sisters: A Multicultural Reader in US Women's History*, Routledge, New York, 1990, p. 240

64. Sarah L. and A. Elizabeth Delany, with Amy Hill Hearth, *Having Our Say: The Delany Sisters' First 100 Years*, A Dell book, Bantam Doubleday Dell Publishing Group Inc., New York, 1994, p. 188

65. Ibid., pp. 201, 200

66. Ibid., p. 202

67. Crystal Eastman, 'Now We Can Begin', in Blanche Wiesen Cook (ed.), *Crystal Eastman: On Women and Revolution*, Oxford University Press, Oxford, 1978, pp. 53–4

68. Alice Paul, quoted in Rosalind Rosenberg, *Divided Lives: American Women in the Twentieth Century*, Penguin Books, Harmondsworth, 1993, p. 78

69. Denver Klansmen, quoted in Edith L. Blumhofer, *Aimee Semple McPherson: Everybody's Sister*, William B. Eerdmans Publishing Company, Grand Rapids, Michigan, 1993, p. 187

70. Ibid.

71. Ruth Pickering, 'A Deflated Rebel', in Showalter (ed.), *These Modern Women*, p. 62

72. Lorine Pruette, quoted ibid., p. 13

73. Dorothy Dunbar Bromley, quoted in Glenda Riley, *Inventing the American Woman: A Perspective on Women's History, 1865 to the Present*, Harlan Davidson Inc., Arlington Heights, Illinois, 1986, p. 85

74. Barbara Bair, 'True Women, Real Men: Gender Ideology and Social Roles in the Garvey Movement', in Dorothy O. Helly and Susan M. Reverby (eds.), *Gendered Domains: Rethinking Public and Private in Women's History*, Cornell University Press, Ithaca, 1992, pp. 159, 163

75. Clara Jones, quoted in Stephanie J. Shaw, 'Black Club Women and the Creation of the National Association of Colored Women', *Journal of Women's History*, Vol. 3, No. 2, Fall 1991, p. 14

76. M. Carey Thomas, quoted in Rita Heller, 'Blue Collars and Blue Stockings: The Bryn Mawr Summer School for Women Workers, 1921–1938', in Joyce L. Kornbluh and Mary Frederickson (eds.), *Sisterhood and Solidarity: Workers' Education for Women*, Temple University Press, Philadelphia, 1989, p. 112

77. Lillian Harris Dean, quoted in Bruce Kellner (ed.), *The Harlem Renaissance: A Historical Dictionary of the Era*, Methuen, New York, 1987, p. 97

78. Carby, ' "It Jus Be's Dat Way Sometime" ', DuBois and Ruiz (eds.), *Unequal Sisters*, p. 247

79. Ibid.

80. Ibid., p. 248

81. Jacqueline Dowd Hall, 'Disorderly Women: Gender and Labor Militancy in the Appalachian South', in DuBois and Ruiz (eds.), *Unequal Sisters*, p. 311

82. Ibid.

83. Alice Kessler-Harris, *Out to Work: A History of Wage-earning Women in the United States*, Oxford University Press, Oxford, 1982, p. 229

84. Quoted ibid., p. 217

85. Bessie Edens, quoted in Dowd Hall, 'Disorderly Women', in DuBois and Ruiz (eds.), *Unequal Sisters*, p. 307

86. Stephanie L. Twin (ed.), *Women and Sports*, The Feminist Press, New York, 1977, p. 15

87. Ibid., p. 16

88. Dorothy Parker, 'Day Dreams', in Marion Meade, *Dorothy Parker, a Biography: What Fresh Hell is This?*, Heinemann, London, 1988, p. 97

89. Ruth Alice Allen, *The Labor of Women in the Production of Cotton*, Department of Economics, University of Chicago, Arno Press, New York, 1975, p. 36

90. Paul H. Nystrom, quoted in Annegret S. Ogden, *The Great American Housewife: from Helpmate to Wage Earner, 1776–1986*, Greenwood Press, Westport, Connecticut, 1986, p. 157

91. Christine Frederick, quoted ibid., p. 159

92. Mattie Mae Halford, quoted in Philip S. Foner, *Women and the American Labor Movement: From the First Trade Unions to the Present*, The Free Press, Macmillan, New York, 1979, p. 294

93. Mrs M. S., quoted in Molly Ladd-Taylor, *Mother-Work: Women, Child Welfare and the State, 1890–1930*, University of Illinois Press, Urbana, 1994, p. 158

94. Paul H. Nystrom, quoted in Stuart and Elizabeth Ewen, *Channels of Desire:*

Mass Images and the Shaping of American Consciousness, University of Minnesota Press, Minneapolis, 1992, p. 172

95. Ibid., p. 171
96. Quoted in Ruiz, *Cannery Women, Cannery Lives*, p. 12
97. Quoted in Rosalyn Baxandall and Linda Gordon (eds.), with Susan Reverby, *America's Working Women: A Documentary History, 1600 to the Present*, W. W. Norton, New York, 1995, p. 204
98. Ibid.
99. Sinclair Lewis, *The Job*, Jonathan Cape, London, 1926, pp. 68, 83
100. Margaret Mitchell, quoted in Darden Asbury Pyron, *Southern Daughter: The Life of Margaret Mitchell*, Oxford University Press, New York, 1991, p. 117
101. Dorothy Parker, 'Ballade at Thirty-five', in Meade, *Dorothy Parker*, p. 126
102. Blanche Wiesen Cook, *Eleanor Roosevelt: Volume One, 1884–1933*, Viking, New York, 1992, p. 297
103. Donald Clarke, *Wishing on the Moon: The Life and Times of Billie Holiday*, Penguin Books, Harmondsworth, 1995, p. 42
104. Bessie Smith, quoted in Carby, '"It Jus Be's Dat Way Sometime"', in DuBois and Ruiz (eds.), *Unequal Sisters*, p. 247
105. Ma Rainey, quoted ibid., p. 245
106. Ida Cox, quoted ibid., p. 247
107. Quoted in June Sochen, *Mae West: She Who Laughs, Lasts*, Harlan Davidson Inc., Arlington Heights, Illinois, 1992, p. 49
108. Ibid.
109. Carby, '"It Jus Be's Dat Way Sometime"', in DuBois and Ruiz (eds.), *Unequal Sisters*, p. 241
110. Nettie Reece, quoted in Dowd Hall, 'Disorderly Women', in DuBois and Ruiz (eds.), *Unequal Sisters*, p. 310
111. Ibid.

CHAPTER 4: THE 1930S

1. Mary Borden, 'Financial Independence for Wives: The Technique of Marriage, V', in Brian Braithwaite and Noëlle Walsh (eds.), *Things My Mother Should Have Told Me: The Best of 'Good Housekeeping', 1922–1940*, Ebury Press, London, 1991, p. 128
2. Leonora Eyles, 'Have You Failed?', ibid., p. 165
3. Virginia Woolf, *Three Guineas*, in Virginia Woolf, *A Room of One's Own and Three Guineas*, with an introduction by Hermione Lee, Chatto and Windus, Hogarth Press, London, 1984, p. 267
4. Lewis Grassic Gibbon, *Cloud Howe*, Jarrolds, London, 1933, p. 238
5. Rita Altman, quoted in Jewish Women in London Group (ed.), *Generations of Memories: Voices of Jewish Women*, The Women's Press, London, 1989, p. 121
6. Asphodel, quoted ibid., p. 195

7. Ellen Wilkinson, quoted in Jim Fryth (ed.), with Sally Alexander, *Women's Voices from the Spanish Civil War*, Lawrence and Wishart, London, 1991, p. 284

8. Shiela Grant Duff, quoted ibid., p. 268

9. Mrs Churches, quoted in Beatrix Campbell, *The Iron Ladies: Why Do Women Vote Tory?*, Virago, London, 1987, p. 67

10. Ibid.

11. Quoted in Martin Durham, 'Women in the British Union of Fascists', in Sybil Oldfield (ed.), *This Working-day World: Women's Lives and Culture(s) in Britain, 1914–1945*, Taylor and Francis, London, 1994, p. 102

12. Anne Brock Griggs, quoted ibid., p. 106

13. Charles Madge and Tom Harrison, *Britain by Mass-Observation*, Penguin Books, Harmondsworth, 1939, p. 101

14. Steve Humphries and Pamela Gordon, *Forbidden Britain: Our Secret Past, 1900–1960*, BBC Books, London, p. 122

15. Kate Reynolds, quoted ibid., p. 134

16. Sheila Lewenhak, *Women and Trade Unions: An Outline History of Women in the British Trade Union Movement*, Ernest Benn, London, 1977, p. 217

17. Ibid.

18. Gertie Roche, quoted in Ursula Huws, *Gertie Roche*, Policy Research Unit, Leeds Polytechnic, Leeds, 1992, p. 3

19. Quoted in Sarah Boston, *Women Workers and the Trade Unions*, Lawrence and Wishart, London, 1980, p. 170

20. Quoted ibid., p. 169

21. Quoted ibid., p. 170

22. Quoted ibid.

23. Quoted in Ellen Leopold, *In the Service of London: Origins and Development of Council Employment from 1889*, Industry and Employment Branch, GLC, London, 1985, p. 54

24. Miriam Glucksmann, *Women Assemble: Women Workers and the New Industries in Inter-War Britain*, Routledge, London, 1990, p. 117

25. Edith Boyd, quoted ibid., p. 34

26. Jessie McCullough, quoted in R. A. Leeson, *Strike: A Live History, 1887–1971*, George Allen & Unwin Ltd, London, 1973, pp. 130–31

27. Lewenhak, *Women and Trade Unions*, p. 233

28. G. D. H. and Margaret Cole, *The Condition of Britain*, Victor Gollancz, London, 1937, p. 25

29. Jessica Mitford, *Hons and Rebels*, Penguin Books, Harmondsworth, 1962, p. 95

30. Ibid.

31. Vivien Mosley, quoted in Angela Lambert, *1939: The Last Season of Peace*, Weidenfeld and Nicolson, New York, 1989, p. 108

32. Ibid., p. 110

33. Ibid., p. 109

34. Shiela Grant Duff, quoted ibid., p. 111
35. Ibid.
36. Margery Spring Rice, *Working-class Wives, Their Health and Conditions,* Penguin Books, Harmondsworth, 1939, p. 123
37. Allen Hutt, *The Condition of the Working Class in Britain,* Martin Lawrence, London, 1933, p. 143
38. Graham Greene, quoted in Peter Stead, *Film and the Working Class: The Feature Film in British and American Society,* Routledge, London, 1989, p. 108
39. David Shipman, *Cinema: The First Hundred Years,* Quality Paperbacks Direct, London, 1993, p. 140
40. Jean MacGibbon, *I Meant to Marry Him: A Personal Memoir,* Victor Gollancz, London, 1984, p. 128
41. Ibid., p. 127
42. Prunella Stack, *Zest for Life: Mary Bagot Stack and the League of Health and Beauty,* Peter Owen, London, 1988, p. 114
43. Beatrice Hamer, quoted in Jeffrey Richards and Dorothy Sheridan (eds.), *Mass-Observation at the Movies,* Routledge and Kegan Paul, London, 1987, p. 54
44. Ibid.
45. Quoted in Alison Light, *Forever England: Femininity, Literature and Conservatism Between the Wars,* Routledge, London, 1991, p. 103
46. Sally Alexander, *Becoming a Woman and Other Essays in 19th and 20th Century Feminist History,* Virago, London, 1994, p. 222
47. Ibid., pp. 221–2
48. Elizabeth Wilson, *Adorned in Dreams: Fashion and Modernity,* Virago, London, 1985, p. 111
49. John Osborne, quoted ibid., p. 112
50. Ann Schuster, quoted in Lambert, *1939,* p. 75
51. Peggy Wood, quoted in Jean McCrindle and Sheila Rowbotham (eds.), *Dutiful Daughters: Women Talk About Their Lives,* Penguin Books, Harmondsworth, 1979, p. 166
52. Alexander, *Becoming a Woman,* pp. 220–21
53. Quoted in Paul Ferris, *Sex and the British: A Twentieth Century History,* Michael Joseph, London, 1993, p. 136
54. Mrs Bramwell Booth, quoted ibid., p. 134
55. Peggy Wood, quoted in McCrindle and Rowbotham (eds.), *Dutiful Daughters,* p. 163
56. Stella Browne, quoted in Sheila Rowbotham, *A New World for Women: Stella Browne – Socialist Feminist,* Pluto, London, 1977, p. 68
57. Quoted in Ferris, *Sex and the British,* p. 129
58. Ibid., p. 128
59. Stella Browne, quoted in Rowbotham, *A New World,* p. 103
60. Peggy Wood, quoted in McCrindle and Rowbotham (eds.), *Dutiful Daughters,* p. 163

61. Vera Brittain, *Testament of Friendship: The Story of Winifred Holtby*, Virago, London, 1980 (first edn 1940), p. 118
62. Winifred Holtby, quoted ibid., pp. 338–9
63. Hellen Keller, quoted in Sybil Oldfield, *Women Against the Iron Fist: Alternatives to Militarism, 1900–1989*, Basil Blackwell, Oxford, 1989, p. 188
64. Ibid.
65. Ibid.
66. Eleanor Roosevelt, quoted in Carol Hymowitz and Michaele Weissman, *A History of Women in America*, Bantam Books, New York, 1978, p. 311
67. Ibid.
68. Lorena Hickok, quoted in Blanche Wiesen Cook, *Eleanor Roosevelt: Volume One, 1884–1933*, Viking, New York, 1992, p. 452
69. June Sochen, *Movers and Shakers: American Women Thinkers and Activists, 1900–1970*, Quadrangle/The New York Times Book Co., New York, 1973, p. 153
70. Rosalyn Baxandall and Linda Gordon (eds.), with Susan Reverby, *America's Working Women: A Documentary History, 1600 to the Present*, W. W. Norton, New York, 1995, p. 194
71. Gwendolyn Mink, *The Wages of Motherhood: Inequality in the Welfare State, 1917–1942*, Cornell University Press, Ithaca, 1995, p. 138.
72. Marian Anderson, 'My Lord What a Morning', in Jill Ker Conway (ed.), *Written by Herself: Autobiographies of American Women – an Anthology*, Vintage Books, New York, 1992, p. 87
73. Dorothy Parker, 'I Shall See Their Like Again', in Jim Fryth (ed.), with Sally Alexander, *Women's Voices from the Spanish Civil War*, Lawrence and Wishart, London, 1991, p. 346
74. Ibid.
75. Quoted in Robert L. Daniel, *American Women in the 20th Century: The Festival of Life*, Harcourt Brace Jovanovich, San Diego, 1987, p. 87
76. Jacqueline Jones, *Labor of Love, Labor of Sorrow: Black Women, Work and the Family from Slavery to the Present*, Basic Books, New York, 1985, p. 200
77. Juanita Loveless, quoted in Sherna Berger Gluck (ed.), *Rosie the Riveter Revisited: Women, the War and Social Change*, Twayne Publishers, a division of G. K. Hall and Co., Boston, 1987, p. 130
78. Patricia Wiseman, quoted in Nancy F. Gabin, *Feminism in the Labor Movement: Women and the United Auto Workers, 1935–1975*, Cornell University Press, Ithaca, 1990, p. 19
79. Patricia Cooper, 'The Faces of Gender and Sex Segregation and Work Relations at Philco, 1928–1938', in Ava Baron (ed.), *Work Engendered: Toward a New History of American Labor*, Cornell University Press, Ithaca, 1991, p. 348
80. Aunt Molly Jackson, quoted in Sheila Rowbotham, 'Mountain Woman Blues', *Spare Rib*, 27, September 1974, p. 45
81. Ruth Milkman, 'Gender and Trade Unionism in Historical Perspective', in

Louise A. Tilly and Patricia Gurin (eds.), *Women, Politics and Change*, Russell Sage Foundation, New York, 1990, p. 96

82. Mary Heaton Vorse, quoted in Elizabeth Faue, 'Paths of Unionization: Community, Bureaucracy and Gender in the Minneapolis Labor Movement of the 1930s', in Baron (ed.), *Work Engendered*, p. 296

83. Mrs H. E. C., quoted in Robert McElvaine (ed.), *Letters from the Forgotten Man*, University of North Carolina Press, Chapel Hill, 1983, p. 63

84. Mrs N. J. S., quoted ibid., p. 148

85. Quoted in Jones, *Labor of Love, Labor of Sorrow*, p. 198

86. Meridel LeSueur, quoted in Joyce L. Kornbluh, 'The She-She-She Camps: An Experiment in Living and Learning', in Joyce L. Kornbluh and Mary Frederickson (eds.), *Sisterhood and Solidarity: Workers' Education for Women*, Temple University Press, Philadelphia, 1989, p. 255

87. Ibid., p. 257

88. Stella Nowicki, 'Back of the Yards', in Alice and Staughton Lynd (eds.), *Rank and File: Personal Histories by Working Class Organizers*, Beacon Press, Boston, 1973, p. 69

89. William Stott, *Documentary Expression and Thirties America*, University of Chicago Press, Chicago, 1986

90. Joan Crawford, quoted in Jeanine Basinger, *A Woman's View: How Hollywood Spoke to Women, 1930–60*, Chatto and Windus, London, 1993, p. 238

91. Katharine Hepburn, quoted ibid., p. 49

92. Hattie McDaniel, quoted in Stephen Bourne, 'Denying Her Place: Hattie McDaniel's Surprising Acts', in Pam Cook and Philip Dodd (eds.), *Women and Film: A 'Sight and Sound' Reader*, Scarlett Press, Sight and Sound, c. 1993, p. 34

93. Fanny Christina Hill, quoted in Gluck (ed.), *Rosie the Riveter Revisited*, p. 341

94. Dorothy Parker, *The Standard of Living*, in Liz Heron (ed.), *Streets of Desire: Women's Fictions of the Twentieth-century City*, Virago, London, 1993, p. 92

95. Quoted in Philip S. Foner, *Women and the American Labor Movement: From the First Trade Unions to the Present*, The Free Press, Macmillan, New York, 1979, p. 302

96. Quoted in Vicki L. Ruiz, *Cannery Women, Cannery Lives: Mexican Women, Unionization and the Californian Food Processing Industry, 1930–1950*, University of New Mexico Press, Albuquerque, 1992, p. 38

97. Meridel LeSueur, quoted in Sara M. Evans, *Born for Liberty: A History of Women in America*, The Free Press, Macmillan, New York, 1989, p. 200

98. Quoted in Linda Gordon, *Woman's Body, Woman's Right: A Social History of Birth Control in America*, Grossman, Viking Press, New York, 1976, p. 323

99. Meridel LeSueur, quoted in Evans, *Born for Liberty*, p. 200

100. Margaret Bourke-White, 'Portrait of Myself', in Conway (ed.), *Written by Herself*, p. 440

101. Ibid.

102. Ibid., p. 428

CHAPTER 5: THE SECOND WORLD WAR
AND ITS AFTERMATH

1. *Girls' Own Paper*, quoted in Mary Cadogan, *Women with Wings*, Macmillan, London, 1992, p. 160
2. Ibid.
3. Ibid., p. 164
4. Ibid., p. 165
5. Christabel Leighton-Porter, quoted in Denna Allen, 'Jane's War: *Daily Mirror* D-Day Tribute', *Daily Mirror*, 6 June 1994
6. Cliff Parker, 'The Forces' Sweetheart', in *Jane at War*, Daily Mirror Newspapers, Wolfe, London, 1976
7. Gail Braybon and Penny Summerfield, *Out of the Cage: Women's Experiences of Two World Wars*, Pandora, London, 1987, p. 247
8. Martin Pugh, *Women and the Women's Movement in Britain, 1914–1959*, Macmillan, London, 1992, p. 276
9. Elizabeth Bowen, quoted in Jenny Hartley (ed.), *Hearts Undefeated: Women's Writing of the Second World War*, Virago, London, 1995, p. 78
10. Braybon and Summerfield, *Out of the Cage*, p. 165
11. Quoted in John Costello, *Love, Sex and War, 1939–1945*, Pan Books, London, 1986, pp. 213–14
12. Ministry of Food, quoted in Marguerite Patten, *We'll Eat Again: A Collection of Recipes from the War Years*, Hamlyn, in association with the Imperial War Museum, London, 1985, p. 7
13. Ibid.
14. Ibid.
15. Lesley A. Hall, 'Chloe, Olivia, Isabel, Letitia, Harriette, Honor and Many More: Women in Medicine and Biomedical Science, 1914–1945', in Sybil Oldfield (ed.), *This Working-day World: Women's Lives and Culture(s) in Britain, 1914–1945*, Taylor and Francis, London, 1994, p. 198
16. Quoted in Costello, *Love, Sex and War, 1939–1945*, p. 41
17. Quoted in Peter Fryer, *Staying Power: The History of Black People in Britain*, Pluto Press, London, 1984, p. 363
18. Costello, *Love, Sex and War*, p. 63
19. Quoted in Braybon and Summerfield, *Out of the Cage*, p. 202
20. Eve Sugden, quoted in Jane Waller and Michael Vaughan-Rees, *Women in Uniform, 1939–45*, Macmillan, London, 1989, p. 20
21. Quoted ibid., p. 15
22. Elizabeth Bowen, *The Heat of the Day*, quoted in Denise Riley, *War in the Nursery: Theories of the Child and Mother*, Virago, London, 1983, p. 123
23. Jean Mormont, quoted in Jean McCrindle and Sheila Rowbotham (eds.), *Dutiful Daughters: Women Talk About Their Lives*, Penguin Books, Harmondsworth, 1979, p. 142
24. Mrs Grossman, quoted in Braybon and Summerfield, *Out of the Cage*, p. 172

25. Riley, *War in the Nursery*, p. 130
26. Eleanor Roosevelt, quoted in Costello, *Love, Sex and War*, p. 223
27. Quoted in Braybon and Summerfield, *Out of the Cage*, p. 197
28. Quoted in Costello, *Love, Sex and War*, p. 210
29. Ibid., p. 208
30. Riley, *War in the Nursery*, p. 111
31. *British Medical Journal* (1942), quoted ibid., p. 112
32. *British Medical Journal* (1944), quoted ibid., p. 113
33. Barbara Nixon, quoted in Hartley (ed.), *Hearts Undefeated*, p. 85
34. Ibid.
35. Winnie Roberts, quoted in Liverpool City Council, *Liverpool Women at War: An Anthology of Personal Memories*, Picton Press, Liverpool, 1991, p. 11
36. Mickie Hulton Storie, quoted in Braybon and Summerfield, *Out of the Cage*, p. 193
37. Vera Lynn, quoted in Costello, *Love, Sex and War*, p. 103
38. Lale Andersen, quoted ibid., p. 107
39. Peggy Wood, quoted in McCrindle and Rowbotham (eds.), *Dutiful Daughters*, p. 173
40. Sadie MacDougal, quoted in Braybon and Summerfield, *Out of the Cage*, p. 253
41. C. M. Beith, quoted in Liverpool City Council, *Liverpool Women at War*, p. 71
42. Eileen Haligan, quoted ibid., p. 63
43. C. A. Lejeune, quoted in Hartley (ed.), *Hearts Undefeated*, p. 227
44. Ibid., pp. 227–8
45. Quoted in Costello, *Love, Sex and War*, pp. 311–12
46. Ibid., p. 309
47. Ibid., p. 313
48. Quoted in James Walvin, *Black and White: The Negro and English Society, 1555–1945*, Allen Lane, Harmondsworth, 1973, p. 213
49. Barbara Cartland, quoted in Costello, *Love, Sex and War*, p. 319
50. Jean Mormont, quoted in McCrindle and Rowbotham (eds.), *Dutiful Daughters*, pp. 142–3
51. Joan Stewart, quoted in Waller and Vaughan-Rees, *Women in Uniform*, p. 15
52. Ibid.
53. Quoted in Costello, *Love, Sex and War*, p. 23
54. Pugh, *Women and the Women's Movement*, p. 271
55. Quoted in Costello, *Love, Sex and War*, p. 277
56. Ibid., p. 280
57. Ibid.
58. Herbert Morrison, quoted in Terry Monaghan, 'D for Deleted', *Casablanca*, Summer 1994, p. 38
59. Costello, *Love, Sex and War*, p. 281

60. Quoted in Paul Ferris, *Sex and the British: A Twentieth-century History*, Michael Joseph, London, 1993, p. 147
61. Quoted in Robert Kee, *1945: The World We Fought For*, Cardinal, London, 1990, p. 237
62. Ibid.
63. Naomi Mitchison, quoted in Dorothy Sheridan (ed.), *Among You Taking Notes: The Wartime Diary of Naomi Mitchison, 1939–1945*, Victor Gollancz, London, 1985, p. 335
64. Sheila Rowbotham, interview with Betty Harrison, 1976
65. Zelma Katin, quoted in Braybon and Summerfield, *Out of the Cage*, p. 284
66. Barbara Davies, quoted ibid., p. 260
67. Joan Robinson, quoted in Riley, *War in the Nursery*, pp. 166–7
68. Geoffrey Thomas, quoted in Jane Lewis, *Women in England, 1870–1950*, Wheatsheaf Books, Sussex, 1984, p. 193
69. Riley, *War in the Nursery*, p. 170
70. William Beveridge, quoted in Pugh, *Women and the Women's Movement*, p. 294
71. Quoted in Riley, *War in the Nursery*, p. 163
72. William Beveridge, quoted in Pugh, *Women and the Women's Movement*, p. 294
73. Margaret Powell, *Climbing the Stairs*, Pan Books, London, 1971, p. 107
74. Barbara Cartland, quoted in Costello, *Love, Sex and War*, p. 276
75. Jane Lewis, *Women in Britain Since 1945: Women, Family, Work and the State in the Post-war Years*, Blackwell, Oxford, 1992, p. 24
76. Nancy Spain, quoted in Alison Hennegan, Introduction to *Poison for Teacher*, Virago, London, 1994, p. xv
77. Nancy Spain, ibid., p. 197
78. Melissa Dubakis, 'Gendered Labor', in Barbara Melosh (ed.), *Gender and American History Since 1890*, Routledge, London, 1993, p. 196
79. Barbara Melosh, 'Manly Work, Public Art and Masculinity in Depression America', ibid., p. 162
80. Norma Jeane (Marilyn Monroe), quoted in Donald Spoto, *Marilyn Monroe: The Biography*, Arrow Books, London, 1994, p. 100
81. Juanita Loveless, quoted in Sherna Berger Gluck (ed.), *Rosie the Riveter Revisited: Women, the War and Social Change*, Twayne Publishers, a division of G. K. Hall and Co., Boston, 1987, p. 135
82. Louis McSherry, quoted in Robert L. Daniel, *American Women in the 20th Century: The Festival of Life*, Harcourt Brace Jovanovich, Orlando, Florida, 1987, p. 140
83. Rosalind Rosenberg, *Divided Lives: American Women in the Twentieth Century*, Penguin Books, Harmondsworth, 1993, p. 132
84. Karen Beck Skold, 'The Job He Left Behind: Women in the Shipyards During World War II', in Carol R. Berkin and Clara M. Lovett (eds.), *Women, War and Revolution*, Holmes and Meier, New York, 1980, p. 59

85. Quoted in Daniel, *American Women in the 20th Century*, pp. 141–2
86. Alma Lutz, quoted ibid., p. 142
87. Georgia O'Keeffe to Eleanor Roosevelt, 10 February 1944, in Wendy Slatkin, *The Voices of Women Artists*, Prentice Hall, Englewood Cliffs, New Jersey, 1993, p. 230
88. Ibid.
89. Quoted in Costello, *Love, Sex and War*, p. 64
90. Ibid.
91. Ibid.
92. Ibid., p. 65
93. Ibid., p. 67
94. Ibid., p. 69
95. Ibid., p. 59
96. Quoted in Katherine Jellison, *Entitled to Power: Farm Women and Technology, 1913–1963*, University of North Carolina Press, Chapel Hill, 1993, p. 146
97. Mark H. Leff, 'The Politics of Sacrifice on the American Home Front in World War II', *Journal of American History*, Vol. 77, No. 4, March 1991, p. 1,296
98. Fanny Christina Hill, quoted in Gluck (ed.), *Rosie the Riveter Revisited*, p. 43
99. Sara M. Evans, *Born for Liberty: A History of Women in America*, The Free Press, Macmillan, New York, 1989, p. 226
100. Elizabeth Faue, *Community of Suffering and Struggle: Women, Men and the Labor Movement in Minneapolis, 1915–1945*, University of North Carolina Press, Chapel Hill, 1991, p. 185
101. Ibid.
102. Juanita Loveless, quoted in Gluck (ed.), *Rosie the Riveter Revisited*, p. 142
103. Quoted in Evans, *Born for Liberty*, p. 226
104. Quoted in Faue, *Community of Suffering and Struggle*, p. 179
105. Quoted in Susan Strasser, *Never Done: A History of American Housework*, Pantheon Books, New York, 1982, p. 267
106. Anne Firor Scott, 'One Woman's Experience of World War II', *Journal of American History*, Vol. 77, No. 2, September 1990, p. 558
107. Dr Leslie Hohman, quoted in Mary Beth Norton (ed.), *Major Problems in American Women's History: Documents and Essays*, D. C. Heath and Company, Lexington, Mass., 1989, pp. 354, 355
108. Dorothy Roosevelt, quoted in Rosalyn Baxandall, Linda Gordon and Susan Reverby (eds.), *America's Working Women: A Documentary History, 1600 to the Present*, Vintage Books, New York, 1976, p. 297
109. Fanny Christina Hill, quoted in Gluck (ed.), *Rosie the Riveter Revisited*, p. 39
110. Ibid.
111. Mrs Itsu Akiyama, quoted in Linda Tamura, *The Hood River Issei: An Oral History of Japanese Settlers in Oregon's Hood River Valley*, University of Illinois Press, Urbana, 1993, p. 166
112. Mrs Misuyo Nakamura, quoted ibid., p. 168

113. Mrs Itsu Akiyama, quoted ibid., p. 166
114. Teiko Tomita, quoted in Teresa L. Amott and Julie A. Matthaei, *Race, Gender and Work: A Multicultural Economic History of Women in the United States*, South End Press, Boston, 1991, p. 224
115. Mrs Masayo Yumibe, quoted in Tamura, *The Hood River Issei*, p. 169
116. Quoted in 'Working Women and the War: Four Narratives', *Radical America*, Vol. 9, Nos. 4–5, July–August 1975, p. 141
117. Ibid.
118. Ibid., p. 142
119. Quoted in Costello, *Love, Sex and War*, p. 188
120. Ibid.
121. Mary Cadogan, *Women with Wings*, Macmillan, London, 1992, p. 241
122. Quoted in Beth Bailey, *From Front Porch to Back Seat: Courtship in Twentieth Century America*, Johns Hopkins University Press, Baltimore, 1989, p. 35
123. Ibid., p. 36
124. Quoted ibid.
125. Quoted ibid., p. 95
126. Oveta Culp Hobby, quoted in Costello, *Love, Sex and War*, p. 90
127. Ibid., p. 86
128. Ibid., p. 93
129. Johnnie Phelps, quoted in Lillian Faderman, *Odd Girls and Twilight Lovers: A History of Lesbian Life in Twentieth-century America*, Penguin Books, Harmondsworth, 1992, p. 118
130. General Eisenhower, quoted ibid.
131. Ibid., p. 123
132. Quoted in Costello, *Love, Sex and War*, p. 96
133. Ibid.
134. Quoted in Faderman, *Odd Girls and Twilight Lovers*, p. 121
135. Ibid.
136. Ibid., p. 126
137. Juanita Loveless, quoted in Gluck (ed.), *Rosie the Riveter Revisited*, p. 140
138. Ibid.
139. Faderman, *Odd Girls and Twilight Lovers*, p. 126
140. Evans, *Born for Liberty*, p. 225
141. Lola Weixel, quoted in Ruth Milkman, *Gender at Work: The Dynamics of Job Segregation by Sex during World War II*, University of Illinois, Urbana, 1987, p. 103
142. Lena Horne, quoted in Jacqueline Jones, *Labor of Love, Labor of Sorrow: Black Women, Work and the Family from Slavery to the Present*, Basic Books, New York, 1985, p. 272
143. Eleanor Roosevelt, quoted in Joseph P. Lash, *Eleanor: The Years Alone*, New American Library, New York, 1972, p. 37
144. Ibid., p. 40
145. Ibid., p. 45

146. Ibid., p. 53
147. Ibid., p. 60
148. Ibid.
149. Westbrook Pegler, quoted ibid., p. 149
150. Eleanor Roosevelt, quoted ibid., p. 71
151. Margaret Busby (ed.), *Daughters of Africa: An International Anthology of Words and Writings by Women of African Descent from the Ancient Egyptian to the Present*, Jonathan Cape, London, 1992, p. 261
152. Claudia Jones, 'An End to the Neglect of the Problems of Negro Women', in Busby (ed.), *Daughters of Africa*, p. 265
153. Quoted in Joanne Meyerowitz, 'Beyond the Feminine Mystique: A Reassessment of Postwar Mass Culture, 1946–1958', *Journal of American History*, Vol. 7, No. 4, March 1993, p. 1,470, footnote 42
154. Mary McLeod Bethune, quoted in Paula Giddings, *When and Where I Enter: The Impact of Black Women on Race and Sex in America*, Bantam Books, Toronto, 1985, p. 244
155. Matilde Albert, quoted in Rosalyn Baxandall and Elizabeth Ewen, 'Picture Windows: The Changing Role of Women in the Suburbs', *Long Island Historical Journal*, Vol. 3, No. 1, Fall 1990, p. 94
156. Ibid., p. 93
157. Ann Petry, *The Street*, in Liz Heron (ed.), *Streets of Desire: Women's Fiction of the Twentieth-century City*, Virago, London, 1993, p. 145
158. Ibid., p. 151
159. Marynia Farnham and Ferdinand Lundberg, quoted in Bailey, *From Front Porch to Back Seat*, pp. 93–4
160. Jones, *Labor of Love, Labor of Sorrow*, p. 232
161. Nancy Reagan, quoted in Kitty Kelley, *Nancy Reagan: The Unauthorized Biography*, Bantam Books, Toronto, 1992, p. 95

CHAPTER 6: THE 1950S

1. Simone de Beauvoir, *The Second Sex*, New English Library, London, 1969 (first edn 1949), p. 9
2. Jackie Stacey, *Star Gazing: Hollywood Cinema and Female Spectatorship*, Routledge, London, 1994, p. 238
3. Ibid., p. 113
4. Patricia Ogden, quoted ibid., p. 203
5. Ibid.
6. Veronica Millen, quoted ibid., p. 138
7. Alison Hennegan, Introduction, in Nancy Spain, *Poison for Teacher*, Virago, London, 1994, p. xv
8. Alison Fell, 'Rebel with a Cause', in Liz Heron (ed.), *Truth, Dare or Promise: Girls Growing Up in the 50s*, Virago, London, 1985, p. 22
9. Ibid., p. 23

10. Rosemary Auchmuty, 'You're a Dyke, Angela! Elsie J. Oxenham and the Rise and Fall of the Schoolgirl Story', in Lesbian History Group (ed.), *Not a Passing Phase: Reclaiming Lesbians in History, 1840–1985*, The Women's Press, London, 1989, p. 137

11. 'The Silent Three at Farley's Folly', *School Friend Annual: 1954*, Fleetway House, London, 1954, p. 4

12. Dennis Duckworth, 'The True Story of Helen Keller', in *Girl Annual: No. 7*, Hulton Press, London, no date, p. 143

13. Marghanita Laski, quoted in Martin Pugh, *Women and the Women's Movement in Britain, 1914–1959*, Macmillan, London, 1992, p. 285

14. Thelma Cazalet-Keir, quoted ibid., p. 306

15. Jennie Lee, *My Life with Nye*, Jonathan Cape, London, 1980, p. 223

16. Ibid., p. 228

17. Pugh, *Women and the Women's Movement*, p. 306

18. Doris Lessing, *The Golden Notebook*, Penguin Books, Harmondsworth, 1964, p. 160

19. Beatrix Campbell, *The Iron Ladies: Why Do Women Vote Tory?*, Virago, London, 1987, p. 95

20. Ibid.

21. Ibid., p. 90

22. Kikue Ihara, quoted in Jill Liddington, *The Long Road to Greenham: Feminism and Anti-militarism in Britain since 1820*, Virago, London, 1989, p. 182

23. Sheila Rowbotham, interview with Margaret Widgery, August 1994

24. Rose Macaulay, quoted in Peggy Duff, *Left, Left, Left: A Personal Account of Six Protest Campaigns, 1945–65*, Allison and Busby, London, 1971, p. 121

25. V. M. Hughes, *Women in Bondage*, Torchstream Books, London, 1959, p. 158

26. Elizabeth Harrison, in Strong Words Collective (ed.), *But the World Goes on the Same: Changing Times in Durham Pit Villages*, Strong Words, Whitley Bay, Tyne and Wear, 1979, pp. 78, 80

27. Quoted in Angela Finlayson, 'Married Women Who Work in Early Motherhood', *British Journal of Sociology*, 14, 1963, p. 159

28. The Crowther Report, quoted in Sue Sharpe, *'Just Like a Girl': How Girls Learn to be Women*, Penguin Books, Harmondsworth, 1976, p. 20

29. Monica Dickens, quoted in Pugh, *Women and the Women's Movement*, p. 284

30. Janet Sayers, *Mothering Psychoanalysis: Helene Deutsch, Karen Horney, Anna Freud and Melanie Klein*, Hamish Hamilton, London, 1991, p. 263

31. Ibid., p. 264

32. John Bowlby, quoted in Pugh, *Women and the Women's Movement*, p. 296

33. Quoted in Denise Riley, *War in the Nursery: Theories of the Child and Mother*, Virago, London, 1983, p. 101

34. Stef Pixner, 'The Oyster and the Shadow', in Heron (ed.), *Truth, Dare or Promise*, p. 85

35. Margaret Thatcher, quoted in Pugh, *Women and the Women's Movement*, p. 297

36. Lee, *My Life with Nye*, pp. 227–8
37. Alva Myrdal and Viola Klein, *Women's Two Roles: Home and Work*, Routledge and Kegan Paul, London, 1956, p. 190
38. Ibid., p. 145
39. Ibid.
40. Liz Heron, Introduction, in Heron (ed.), *Truth, Dare or Promise*, p. 3
41. Michael Young and Edward Shils, quoted in E. P. Thompson, 'Outside the Whale' (from *Out of Apathy*, Stevens and Son, London, 1960) in E. P. Thompson, *The Poverty of Theory and Other Essays*, Merlin Press, London, 1978, p. 23
42. Princess Elizabeth, quoted in Richard Dimbleby, *Elizabeth Our Queen*, University of London Press, London, 1953, p. 38
43. E. P. Thompson, 'Outside the Whale', p. 23
44. Elizabeth Wilson, *Hallucinations: Life in the Post-modern City*, Radius, London, 1988, p. 6
45. Liz Heron, 'Dear Green Place', in Heron (ed.), *Truth, Dare or Promise*, p. 165
46. Stef Pixner, quoted ibid., p. 84
47. Mary Grieve, quoted in Pugh, *Women and the Women's Movement*, p. 292
48. Ibid.
49. Jennifer, 'The New Year at Sandringham', *The Tatler and Bystander*, 11 January 1956, p. 46
50. Jennifer, 'Fair Wind to Jamaica', *The Tatler and Bystander*, 7 March 1956, p. 385
51. Elizabeth Bowen, 'Criminal in the Family', *The Tatler and Bystander*, 11 January 1956, p. 64
52. Ibid., p. 65
53. Elizabeth Bowen, 'Dwellers in the Wilderness', *The Tatler and Bystander*, 27 June 1956, p. 697
54. Elspeth Grant, 'Spyglass on London', *The Tatler and Bystander*, 4 July 1956, p. 30
55. Ibid., p. 31
56. Ibid.
57. Elspeth Grant, 'Crusader Against the Linoleum Standard', *The Tatler and Bystander*, 13 February 1957, p. 288
58. Michael Young and Edward Shils, quoted in E. P. Thompson, 'Outside the Whale', p. 23
59. Catherina Barnes, quoted in Jean McCrindle and Sheila Rowbotham (eds.), *Dutiful Daughters: Women Talk About Their Lives*, Penguin Books, Harmondsworth, 1979, p. 102
60. Daisy Noakes, *Faded Rainbow: Our Married Years*, Queen Spark Books 8, Brighton, 1980, p. 44
61. Liz Heron, Introduction, in Heron (ed.), *Truth, Dare and Promise*, p. 6
62. Ursula Huws, 'Hiraeth', ibid., p. 184
63. Liz Heron, 'Dear Green Place', ibid., p. 154

64. Quoted in Ron Ramdin, *The Making of the Black Working Class in Britain*, Wildwood House, Aldershot, 1987, p. 225

65. Myrdal and Klein, *Women's Two Roles*, p. 157

66. Liz Heron, Introduction, in Heron (ed.), *Truth, Dare or Promise*, p. 3

67. Tricia Dempsey, quoted in Mary Chamberlain, *Growing Up in Lambeth*, Virago, London, 1989, p. 79

68. Ibid., pp. 79–80

69. Stef Pixner, 'The Oyster and the Shadow', in Heron (ed.), *Truth, Dare or Promise*, p. 101

70. Quoted in Jeffrey Weeks, *Sex, Politics and Society: The Regulation of Sexuality since 1800*, Longman, London, 1981, p. 238

71. Fay Weldon, *Down Among the Women*, Penguin Books, Harmondsworth, 1971, p. 106

72. Barbara Schreier, *Mystique and Identity: Women's Fashions of the 1960s*, Chrysler Museum, New York, 1984, p. 13

73. Angela Partington, 'Popular Fashion and Working-class Affluence', in Juliet Ash and Elizabeth Wilson (eds.), *Chic Thrills: A Fashion Reader*, Pandora, HarperCollins, London, 1992, p. 155

74. Christine Buchan, quoted in McCrindle and Rowbotham (eds.), *Dutiful Daughters*, p. 310

75. Ibid.

76. Sheila Francis, quoted in Kenneth and Valerie McLeish (eds.), *Long to Reign Over Us: Memories of Coronation Day and Life in the 1950s*, Bloomsbury, London, 1992, p. 56

77. Quoted in Lynne Segal, *Slow Motion: Changing Masculinities, Changing Men*, Virago, London, 1990, p. 5

78. David Morgan, *It Will Make a Man of You: Notes on National Service, Masculinity and Autobiography*, Studies in Sexual Politics, 17, University of Manchester, 1987, p. 48

79. Weeks, *Sex, Politics and Society*, p. 241

80. Jean McCrindle, 'Reading the Golden Notebook in 1962', in Jenny Taylor (ed.), *Notebooks/Memoirs/Archives: Reading and Rereading Doris Lessing*, Routledge and Kegan Paul, Boston, 1982, p. 51

81. Melanie McFadyean, 'Looking for Daddy', in Ursula Owen (ed.), *Fathers: Reflections by Daughters*, Virago, London, 1983, p. 201

82. Bessie, quoted in Rosalind Wilkinson, 'Report for the British Social Biology Council', in C. H. Rolph (ed.), *Women of the Streets: A Sociological Study of the Common Prostitute*, New English Library, 1961 (first edn 1955), p. 92

83. Quoted ibid., p. 19

84. Weeks, *Sex, Politics and Society*, p. 243

85. Quoted in Barbara Brookes, *Abortion in England, 1900–1967*, Croom Helm, London, 1988, p. 148

86. Mrs Amy Griffiths, quoted ibid.

87. Hughes, *Women in Bondage*, p. 67

88. Wilson, *Hallucinations*, p. 8
89. Thompson, 'Outside the Whale', p. 31
90. Ibid.
91. Donald Spoto, *Marilyn Monroe: The Biography*, Arrow Books, London, 1994, p. 274
92. Ibid.
93. Ibid.
94. Judith Crist, 'And DD Led All the Rest', *Herald Tribune*, 24 January 1965
95. Judith Williamson, 'Nice Girls Do', in *Consuming Passions: The Dynamics of Popular Culture*, Marion Boyars, London, 1986, p. 145
96. Marilyn Monroe, quoted in Spoto, *Marilyn Monroe*, p. 321
97. Ibid., p. 252
98. Ibid.
99. Hollis Albert, 'Enough Enough, SR Goes to the Movies', *Saturday Review*, New York, 17 November 1956
100. Sylvia Plath, *The Bell Jar*, quoted in Liz Heron (ed.), *Streets of Desire: Women's Fictions of the Twentieth-century City*, Virago, London, 1993, p. 177
101. Sally Belfrage, *Un-American Activities: A Memoir of the Fifties*, André Deutsch, London, 1994, p. 2
102. Westbrook Pegler, quoted in Joseph P. Lash, *Eleanor: The Years Alone*, New American Library, New York, 1972, p. 230
103. Margaret Chase Smith, quoted in Margaret Truman, *Women of Courage from Revolutionary Times to the Present*, William Morrow, New York, 1976, p. 216
104. Ibid., pp. 211–12
105. Dwight Eisenhower, quoted in Robert L. Daniel, *American Women in the 20th Century: The Festival of Life*, Harcourt Brace Jovanovich, Orlando, Florida, 1987, p. 207
106. Verta Taylor, 'The Continuity of the American Women's Movement: An Elite-Sustained Stage', in Guida West and Rhoda Lois Blumberg (eds.), *Women and Social Protest*, Oxford University Press, New York, 1990, p. 284
107. Ibid.
108. Arnold W. Green and Eleanor Melnick, quoted ibid., p. 282
109. Quoted in Marcia Cohen, *The Sisterhood: The True Story of the Women Who Changed the World*, Simon and Schuster, New York, 1988, p. 80
110. Barbara Gittings, quoted in Jonathan Katz, *Gay American History: Lesbians and Gay Men in the USA*, Thomas Y. Crowell, New York, 1976, p. 425
111. Lillian Faderman, *Odd Girls and Twilight Lovers: A History of Lesbian Life in Twentieth-century America*, Penguin Books, Harmondsworth, 1992, p. 149
112. Bernice Reagon, quoted in Dick Cluster (ed.), *They Should Have Served That Cup of Coffee*, South End Press, Boston, 1979, p. 38
113. Elizabeth Eckford, quoted in Daisy Bates, *The Long Shadow of Little Rock* (David McKay, New York, 1962), in Clayborne Carson et al. (eds.), *Eyes on the Prize: America's Civil Rights Years*, Penguin Books, New York, 1987, p. 72

114. Barbara Ransby, 'Ella Josephine Baker', in Mari Jo Buhle, Paul Buhle and Harvey J. Kaye (eds.), *The American Radical*, Routledge, New York, 1994, p. 293

115. Linda Gordon, 'How "Welfare" Became a Dirty Word', *Chronicle of Higher Education*, 20 July 1994, p. B2

116. Linda Gordon, 'What Future for Social Policy? Welfare Reform: A History Lesson', *Dissent*, Summer 1994, p. 326

117. Sara M. Evans, *Born for Liberty: A History of Women in America*, The Free Press, Macmillan, New York, 1989, p. 247

118. Lynn Y. Weiner, 'Reconstructing Motherhood: The La Leche League in Postwar America', *Journal of American History*, Vol. 80, No. 4, March 1994, p. 1,360

119. Mary Jane Brizzolara, quoted ibid., p. 1,362

120. Vera Norwood, 'Rachel Carson', in Buhle et al. (eds.), *The American Radical*, p. 317

121. Ibid., p. 315

122. Glenda Riley, *Inventing the American Woman: A Perspective on Women's History, 1865 to the Present*, Harlan Davidson, Arlington Heights, Illinois, 1986, p. 125

123. Quoted in Philip S. Foner, *Women and the American Labor Movement: From the First Trade Unions to the Present*, The Free Press, Macmillan, New York, 1979, p. 407

124. Ibid.

125. Reka Hoff, quoted in Tony Carabillo, Judith Menli and June Bundy Csida (eds.), *Feminist Chronicles, 1953–1993*, Women's Graphics, Los Angeles, 1993, p. 40

126. Hans Hofmann, quoted in Wendy Slatkin, *The Voices of Women Artists*, Prentice Hall, Englewood Cliffs, New Jersey, 1993, p. 145

127. Peter Wollen, *Raiding the Ice Box*, Verso, London, 1993, p. 87

128. Whitney Chadwick, *Women, Art and Society*, Thames and Hudson, London, 1990, p. 307

129. Lee Krasner, in Slatkin, *The Voices of Women Artists*, p. 244

130. Chadwick, *Women, Art and Society*, p. 307

131. Barbara Rose, quoted in Slatkin, *The Voices of Women Artists*, p. 240

132. Lee Krasner, quoted ibid.

133. Joanne Meyerowitz, 'Beyond the Feminine Mystique: A Reassessment of Postwar Mass Culture, 1946–1958', *Journal of American History*, Vol. 7, No. 4, March 1993, pp. 1,464–5

134. Ibid., p. 1,463

135. Elaine Tyler May, *Homeward Bound: American Families in the Cold War Era*, Basic Books, New York, 1988, p. 105

136. Ibid.

137. Quoted in Rosalyn Baxandall and Elizabeth Ewen, 'Picture Windows: The Changing Role of Women in the Suburbs', *Long Island Historical Journal*, Vol. 3, No. 1, Fall 1990, p. 98

138. Del Martin, quoted in Katz, *Gay American History*, p. 431
139. Faderman, *Odd Girls and Twilight Lovers*, p. 160
140. Ibid., p. 163
141. Ibid.
142. Ibid., p. 161
143. Weiner, 'Reconstructing Motherhood: The La Leche League in Postwar America', p. 1,363
144. Daniel, *American Women in the 20th Century*, pp. 204–5
145. Alice McDermott, quoted in Wini Breines, *Young, White and Miserable: Growing Up Female in the Fifties*, Beacon Press, Boston, 1992, p. 6
146. Ibid., pp. 136–7
147. Clare Boothe Luce, quoted in Gillian G. Gaar, *She's a Rebel: The History of Women in Rock 'n' Roll*, Cassell, London, 1993, p. 10
148. Ruth Brown, *Rolling Stone*, April 1990, quoted ibid., p. 1
149. Ibid., p. 3
150. Beth Bailey, *From Front Porch to Back Seat: Courtship in Twentieth Century America*, Johns Hopkins University Press, Baltimore, 1989, p. 80
151. Belfrage, *Un-American Activities*, p. 88
152. Alice Walker, 'In Search of Our Mother's Gardens', quoted in Breines, *Young, White and Miserable*, p. 15
153. Judy Grahn, quoted in Faderman, *Odd Girls and Twilight Lovers*, p. 139
154. Tyler May, *Homeward Bound*, p. 115
155. Breines, *Young, White and Miserable*, p. 10
156. Margaret Sanger, quoted in Rosalind Rosenberg, *Divided Lives: American Women in the Twentieth Century*, Penguin Books, Harmondsworth, 1993, p. 152
157. Quoted in Paul Ferris, *Sex and the British: A Twentieth-century History*, Michael Joseph, London, 1993, p. 202
158. Quoted in Bailey, *From Front Porch to Back Seat*, p. 71
159. Stuart and Elizabeth Ewen, *Channels of Desire: Mass Images of the Shaping of American Consciousness*, University of Minnesota Press, Minneapolis, 1992, p. 184
160. Margaret Mead, quoted in Ferris, *Sex and the British*, p. 151
161. Cher, quoted in Breines, *Young, White and Miserable*, p. 91
162. Ibid., p. 23
163. Carolyn Cassady, *Off the Road*, quoted in Ann Charters, *The Penguin Book of the Beats*, Penguin Books, Harmondsworth, 1993, p. 456
164. Maxine Hong Kingston, *The Woman Warrior*, in Linda K. Kerber and Jane Sherron De Hart, *Women's America: Refocusing the Past*, Oxford University Press, New York, 1995, p. 510
165. Ibid.
166. Quoted in Cohen, *The Sisterhood*, p. 89
167. Ibid., p. 95
168. Lorraine Hansberry, quoted in Katz, *Gay American History*, p. 425

CHAPTER 7: THE 1960S

1. Angela Carter, 'Truly, It Felt Like Year One', in Sara Maitland (ed.), *Very Heaven: Looking Back at the 1960s*, Virago, London, 1988, p. 210
2. Ibid.
3. Ibid., p. 212
4. Julie Christie, 'Everybody's Darling', ibid., p. 172
5. Terri Quaye, 'Taking It On the Road', ibid., p. 32
6. Moureen Nolan and Roma Singleton, 'Mini-Renaissance', ibid., p. 20
7. Quaye, 'Taking It On the Road', ibid., p. 34
8. Christie, 'Everybody's Darling', ibid., p. 170
9. Barbara Castle, 'No Kitchen Cabinet', ibid., p. 47
10. Ibid., p. 52
11. Ibid., p. 51
12. Ibid., p. 53
13. Beatrix Campbell, *The Iron Ladies: Why Do Women Vote Tory?*, Virago, London, 1987, p. 101
14. Mary Whitehouse, quoted ibid., p. 99
15. Ibid.
16. Sona Osman, '1968–88: Rivers of Blood', in Amanda Sebestyen (ed.), *'68, '78, '88: From Women's Liberation to Feminism*, Prism Press, Bridport, Dorset, 1988, p. 45
17. Campbell, *The Iron Ladies*, p. 102
18. Ibid.
19. Quoted in Jill Liddington, *The Long Road to Greenham: Feminism and Anti-militarism in Britain since 1820*, Virago, London, p. 190
20. David Widgery, *The Left in Britain, 1956–1970*, Penguin Books, Harmondsworth, 1975, p. 111
21. Leila Berg, 'All We Had was a Voice', in Maitland (ed.), *Very Heaven*, pp. 59–60
22. Peggy Duff, *Left, Left, Left: A Personal Account of Six Protest Campaigns, 1945–65*, Allison and Busby, London, 1971, p. 216
23. Personal memory, Sheila Rowbotham
24. Duff, *Left, Left, Left*, pp. 267, 447
25. Carter, 'Truly, It Felt Like Year One', in Maitland (ed.), *Very Heaven*, p. 211
26. *Black Dwarf*, quoted in Widgery, *The Left in Britain*, p. 392
27. Mary Kay Mullan, '1968: Burntollet Bridge', in Sebestyen (ed.), *'68, '78, '88*, p. 16
28. Ibid.
29. Frances Molloy, 'On Our Way to Derry' (extract from 'No Mate for the Magpie'), in Maitland (ed.), *Very Heaven*, p. 81
30. Ibid., p. 78
31. Sue O'Sullivan, 'From 1969', in Sebestyen (ed.), *'68, '78, '88*, p. 53

32. T. E. Chester, 'Growth, Productivity and Woman Power', *District Bank Review*, No. 143, September 1962, p. 30

33. Sabby Sagal, interview with Rose Boland, in Widgery, *The Left in Britain*, p. 297

34. Audrey Wise, quoted in Michelene Wandor (ed.), *Once a Feminist: Stories of a Generation*, Virago, London, 1990, p. 202

35. Mrs H. Sloane, TUC conference 1968, quoted in Sheila Rowbotham, *Woman's Consciousness, Man's World*, Penguin Books, Harmondsworth, 1973, p. 81

36. Miss J. O'Connell, quoted ibid., p. 96

37. Ibid.

38. Miss D. C. M. Nolan, quoted in TUC Women Workers' Conference 1969, 'Report of the 39th Annual Conference of Representatives of Trade Unions Catering for Women Workers', Trades Union Congress, London, 1969, p. 50

39. Ibid., p. 51

40. Nancy Seear, *The Position of Women in Industry*, HMSO, London, 1968, p. 16

41. Hannah Gavron, *The Captive Wife: Conflicts of Housebound Mothers*, Penguin Books, Harmondsworth, 1968, p. 39

42. Ibid., p. 145

43. Ibid., p. 150

44. Ibid.

45. Suzanne Gail, quoted in Ronald Fraser (ed.), *Work: Twenty Personal Accounts*, Penguin Books, Harmondsworth, 1968, p. 151

46. Wilson, *Adorned in Dreams*, p. 176

47. Ibid.

48. Alexandra Pringle, 'Chelsea Girl', in Maitland (ed.), *Very Heaven*, pp. 37–8

49. Nolan and Singleton, 'Mini-Renaissance', ibid., p. 24

50. Quoted in Sheila Rowbotham, *Dreams and Dilemmas*, Virago, London, 1983, p. 29

51. Ibid., p. 21

52. Elizabeth Wilson, *Adorned in Dreams: Fashion and Modernity*, Virago, London, 1995, p. 175

53. Mary Quant, quoted in ibid., p. 175

54. Nolan and Singleton, 'Mini-Renaissance', in Maitland (ed.), *Very Heaven*, p. 20

55. Norah Kirk, quoted in Jean McCrindle and Sheila Rowbotham (eds.), *Dutiful Daughters: Women Talk About Their Lives*, Penguin Books, Harmondsworth, 1979, p. 214

56. Irene McIntosh, quoted ibid., p. 338

57. Ibid., p. 349

58. Barbara Marsh, quoted ibid., p. 258

59. Quaye, 'Taking It On the Road', in Maitland (ed.), *Very Heaven*, p. 34

60. Nigel Fountain, *Underground: The London Alternative Press, 1966–74*, a Comedia book, published by Routledge, London, 1988, pp. 28–9

61. Michelene Wandor, 'In the Sixties', in Maitland (ed.), *Very Heaven*, p. 133

62. Carol Smart, 'Law and the Control of Women's Sexuality', in Bridget Hutter and Gillian Williams (eds.), *Controlling Women: The Normal and the Deviant*, Croom Helm, London, 1981, p. 51

63. Fountain, *Underground*, p. 8

64. Sara Maitland, '"I Believe in Yesterday" – an Introduction', in Maitland (ed.), *Very Heaven*, p. 7

65. Lord Silkin, quoted in Victoria Greenwood and Jock Young, *Abortion in Demand*, Pluto, London, 1976, p. 23

66. Lady Wootton, quoted ibid., p. 24

67. Lady Summerskill, quoted in Paul Ferris, *Sex and the British: A Twentieth-century History*, Michael Joseph, London, 1993, p. 215

68. Juliet Mitchell, 'The Longest Revolution', *New Left Review*, 40, November/December 1966, p. 21

69. Christie, 'Everybody's Darling', in Maitland (ed.), *Very Heaven*, pp. 169–70

70. Louise Ferrier, quoted in Fountain, *Underground*, p. 92

71. Christie, 'Everybody's Darling', in Maitland (ed.), *Very Heaven*, p. 171

72. Jane, 'Unwomanly and Unnatural – Some Thoughts on the Pill', in Maitland (ed.), *Very Heaven*, p. 152

73. Ibid.

74. Mary Quant, quoted in Lynne Segal, *Straight Sex: The Politics of Pleasure*, Virago, London, 1994, pp. 9–10

75. Marianne Faithfull, *Faithfull*, Michael Joseph, London, 1994, p. 210

76. Elizabeth Wilson, 'Memoirs of an Anti-heroine', in Elizabeth Wilson (ed.), *Hallucinations: Life in the Post-modern City*, Radius, London, 1988, p. 8, and Bob Cant and Susan Hemmings (eds.), *Radical Records: Thirty Years of Lesbian and Gay History, 1957–1987*, Routledge, London, 1988, p. 49

77. Faithfull, *Faithfull*, p. 210

78. Carter, 'Truly, It Felt Like Year One', in Maitland (ed.), *Very Heaven*, p. 213

79. Gina Adamou, 'My Nose Pressed Against the Window', ibid., p. 186

80. Ibid., p. 188

81. Quoted in Sheila Rowbotham, 'Cinderella Organizes Buttons', in Widgery, *The Left in Britain*, p. 417

82. Berg, 'All We Had Was a Voice', in Maitland (ed.), *Very Heaven*, p. 71

83. Marsha Rowe, 'Up from Down Under', ibid., p. 163

84. Wilson (ed.), *Hallucinations*, p. 3, and Cant and Hemmings (eds.), *Radical Records*, p. 49

85. Betty Friedan, *The Feminine Mystique*, Penguin Books, Harmondsworth, 1965, p. 19

86. Quoted ibid., p. 328

87. Paula Giddings, *When and Where I Enter: The Impact of Black Women on Race and Sex in America*, Bantam Books, Toronto, 1985, p. 299

88. Daniel Horowitz, 'Rethinking Betty Friedan and *The Feminine Mystique*: Labor Union Radicalism and Feminism in Cold War America', *American Quarterly*, Vol. 48, No. 1, March 1996, pp. 30–31

89. Susan J. Douglas, *Where the Girls Are: Growing Up Female in the Mass Media*, Penguin Books, Harmondsworth, 1995, pp. 55, 57–8

90. Ibid., pp. 123, 128

91. Ibid., p. 123

92. Quoted in Susan Seidelman, *Confessions of a Suburban Girl*, TV film, 1994

93. Friedan, *The Feminine Mystique*, p. 66

94. Diane di Prima, *Memoirs of a Beatnik*, Last Gasp, San Francisco, 1988 (first edn 1969), pp. 135–6

95. Ibid., p. 137

96. Alix Kates Shulman, *Burning Questions: A Novel*, Alfred A. Knopf, New York, 1978, p. 180

97. Joanne Meyerowitz, 'Beyond the Feminine Mystique: A Reassessment of Postwar Mass Culture, 1946–1958', *Journal of American History*, Vol. 79, No. 4, March 1993, p. 1,482

98. Quoted in Joseph P. Lash, *Eleanor: The Years Alone*, New American Library, New York, 1972, p. 293

99. John F. Kennedy, quoted ibid., p. 297

100. Quoted in Toni Carabillo, 'A Passion for the Possible', in Toni Carabillo et al., *Feminist Chronicles, 1953–1993*, Women's Graphics, Los Angeles, 1993, p. 5

101. Ibid.

102. Esther Peterson, quoted ibid., p. 3

103. Howard W. Smith, quoted in Carl M. Brauer, 'The "Old Feminism" and the Civil Rights Act of 1964', in Mary Beth Norton (ed.), *Major Problems in American Women's History: Documents and Essays*, D. C. Heath and Company, Lexington, Mass., 1989, p. 406

104. Fannie Lou Hamer, quoted in Clayborne Carson et al., (eds.), *Eyes On the Prize: America's Civil Rights Years*, Penguin Books, New York, 1987, p. 124

105. Ibid.

106. Quoted in Rhoda Lois Blumberg, 'White Mothers as Civil Rights Activists: The Interweave of Family and Movement Roles', in Guida West and Rhoda Lois Blumberg (eds.), *Women and Social Protest*, Oxford University Press, New York, 1990, p. 173

107. Casey Hayden and Mary King, quoted in Sara M. Evans, *Personal Politics: The Roots of Women's Liberation in the Civil Rights Movement and the New Left*, Alfred A. Knopf, New York, 1979, p. 86

108. Stokely Carmichael, quoted ibid., p. 87

109. Ella Baker, in Carson et al. (eds.), *Eyes On the Prize*, p. 87

110. Evans, *Personal Politics*, p. 101

111. Ibid.
112. Linda Gordon, 'How "Welfare" Became a Dirty Word', *Chronicle of Higher Education*, 20 July 1994, p. B2
113. Ruth Turner Perot, 'Black Power: A Voice Within', in Carson et al. (eds.), *Eyes On the Prize*, p. 198
114. Naomi Weisstein, 'Chicago '60s: Ecstasy as Our Guide', *Ms.*, September/October 1990, p. 66
115. Carabillo, 'A Passion for the Possible', in Carabillo et al. (eds.), *Feminist Chronicles*, p. 1
116. Weisstein, 'Chicago '60s', p. 65
117. Rosalyn Baxandall, quoted in Evans, *Personal Politics*, p. 203
118. Weisstein, 'Chicago '60s', p. 65
119. Quoted in Robert L. Daniel, *American Women in the 20th Century: The Festival of Life*, Harcourt Brace Jovanovich, Orlando, Florida, 1987, p. 299
120. Anne Koedt, 'The Myth of the Vaginal Orgasm', quoted in Alice Echols, *Daring to be Bad: Radical Feminism in America, 1967–1975*, University of Minnesota Press, Minneapolis, 1989, p. 111
121. Ibid.
122. Betty Friedan, quoted in Carabillo et al. (eds.), *Feminist Chronicles*, p. 53
123. Lillian Faderman, *Odd Girls and Twilight Lovers: A History of Lesbian Life in Twentieth-century America*, Penguin Books, Harmondsworth, 1992, pp. 194–5
124. Vicki L. Crawford, 'Beyond the Human Self: Grassroots Activists in the Mississippi Civil Rights Movement', in Vicki L. Crawford, Jacqueline Anne Rouse and Barbara Woods (eds.), *Women in the Civil Rights Movement: Trailblazers and Torchbearers, 1941–1965*, Carlson Publishing Inc., Brooklyn, New York, 1990, p. 51
125. Jane, quoted in Roderick Thorp and Robert Blake (eds.), *Wives: An Investigation*, Souvenir Press, London, 1972, p. 37
126. Jacqueline Jones, *Labor of Love, Labor of Sorrow: Black Women, Work and the Family, from Slavery to the Present*, Basic Books, New York, 1985, p. 299
127. Lesley Gore, quoted in Gillian G. Gaar, *She's a Rebel: The History of Women in Rock 'n' Roll*, Cassell, London, 1993, p. 52
128. Ibid., p. 56
129. Douglas, *Where the Girls Are*, p. 84
130. Ibid., p. 85
131. Quoted ibid., p. 147
132. Ellen Willis, *Beginning to See the Light: Pieces of a Decade*, Alfred A. Knopf, New York, 1981, p. 63
133. Ibid.
134. Ibid., p. 62
135. Donna Redmond, 'I'm Proud to be a Hillbilly', in Kathy Kahn (ed.), *Hillbilly Women*, Avon Books, a division of the Hearst Corporation, New York, 1974, p. 116

136. Aileen Clarke Hernandez, quoted in Carabillo, 'A Passion for the Possible', in Carabillo et al. (eds.), *Feminist Chronicles*, p. 13

137. Pauli Murray, quoted ibid., p. 14

138. American Social History Project, *Who Built America? Working People and the Nation's Economy, Politics, Culture and Society. Vol. Two: From the Gilded Age to the Present*, Pantheon Books, New York, 1992, p. 553

139. Dolores Huerta, quoted in Philip S. Foner, *Women and the American Labor Movement: From the First Trade Unions to the Present*, The Free Press, Macmillan, New York, 1979, p. 424

140. Quoted in Jones, *Labor of Love, Labor of Sorrow*, p. 300

141. Kahn (ed.), *Hillbilly Women*, p. 100

142. Jane and Michael Stern, *Sixties People*, Alfred A. Knopf, New York, 1990, p. 219

143. Douglas, *Where the Girls Are*, p. 119

144. Pauli Murray, 'The Liberation of Black Women', in Mary Lou Thompson (ed.), *Voices of the New Feminism*, Beacon Press, Boston, 1970, p. 567

145. Quoted in William K. Tabb, *The Political Economy of the Black Ghetto*, W. W. Norton, New York, 1970, p. 93

146. Quoted in Jones, *Labor of Love, Labor of Sorrow*, p. 307

147. Tabb, *The Political Economy of the Black Ghetto*, p. 91

148. Shirley Dalton, quoted in Kahn (ed.), *Hillbilly Women*, p. 35

149. Ibid., p. 38

150. Winifred Bell, cited in Tabb, *The Political Economy of the Black Ghetto*, p. 95, footnote 38

151. Patti Reagan, quoted in Kitty Kelley, *Nancy Reagan: The Unauthorized Biography*, Bantam Books, Toronto, 1992, p. 164

152. Ibid.

153. Stern, *Sixties People*, p. 8

154. Stuart and Elizabeth Ewen, *Channels of Desire: Mass Images and the Shaping of American Consciousness*, University of Minnesota Press, Minneapolis, 1992, p. 79

155. Douglas, *Where the Girls Are*, p. 96

156. Quoted ibid., p. 102

157. *Barbie Magazine*, quoted in Stern, *Sixties People*, p. 32

158. Ibid., p. 33

159. Stern, *Sixties People*, p. 24

160. Alice Rossi, quoted in Carabillo, 'A Passion for the Possible', in Carabillo et al. (eds.), *Feminist Chronicles*, p. 8

161. Douglas, *Where the Girls Are*, p. 151

162. Redmond, 'I'm Proud to be a Hillbilly', in Kahn (ed.), *Hillbilly Women*, p. 118

163. Stern, *Sixties People*, p. 224

164. Douglas, *Where the Girls Are*, p. 61

165. Gael Greene, *Sex and the College Girl*, quoted ibid., p. 70

166. Stern, *Sixties People*, p. 25
167. Ibid.
168. Segal, *Straight Sex*, p. 93
169. Douglas, *Where the Girls Are*, p. 98
170. Pamela, quoted in Thorp and Blake (eds.), *Wives*, p. 22
171. Ibid., p. 119
172. Harriet, quoted ibid., p. 66
173. Quoted in Linda Gordon, *Woman's Body, Woman's Right: A Social History of Birth Control in America*, Grossman, Viking Press, New York, 1976, p. 397
174. Alma Routsong, quoted in Jonathan Katz, *Gay American History: Lesbians and Gay Men in the USA*, Thomas Y. Crowell, New York, 1976, p. 436
175. Ibid., p. 440
176. Redmond, 'I'm Proud to be a Hillbilly', in Kahn (ed.), *Hillbilly Women*, p. 119
177. Seidelman, *Confessions of a Suburban Girl*, ibid.

CHAPTER 8: THE 1970S

1. April de Angelis, quoted in Trevor R. Griffiths and Margaret Llewellyn-Jones (eds.), *British and Irish Women Dramatists since 1958: A Critical Handbook*, Open University Press, Buckingham, 1993, p. 139
2. Ibid.
3. Alison Fell, 'Love Song – the beginning of the end of the affair', in Lilian Mohun (ed.), *One Foot on the Mountain: An Anthology of British Feminist Poetry, 1969–1979*, Only Women Press, London, 1979, p. 9
4. Nelly Kaplan, quoted in Barbara Halpern Martineau, 'Nelly Kaplan', in Claire Johnston (ed.), *Notes on Women's Cinema*, Screen Pamphlet 2, Society for Education in Film and Television, London, 1973, p. 22
5. Sheila Shulman, 'HARD WORDS, or Why Lesbians Have to be Philosophers', in Caroline Halliday, Sheila Shulman and Caroline Griffin (eds.), *Hard Words and Why Lesbians Have to Say Them*, Only Women Press, London, 1979, no page numbers
6. Griselda Pollock, 'Feminism, Femininity and the Hayward Annual Exhibition, 1978', *Feminist Review*, 2, 1979, p. 38
7. Ibid., p. 34
8. Angela Carter, 'Reflections', quoted in Lorna Sage, *Angela Carter*, Northcote House Publishers Ltd, Plymouth, 1994, p. 36
9. Doris Lessing, 'Some Remarks', *Shikasta*, Jonathan Cape, London, 1979, p. ix
10. Sally Alexander, quoted in Michelene Wandor (ed.), *Once a Feminist: Stories of a Generation*, Virago, London, 1990, p. 90
11. 'Missiles at the Miss World', *The Times*, 21 November 1970
12. Margaret Ward, 'The Women's Movement in the North of Ireland, Twenty

Years On', in Sean Hutton and Paul Stewart (eds.), *Ireland's Histories: Aspects of State, Society and Ideology*, Routledge, London, 1991, p. 152

13. 'Women Together: Edinburgh', *Spare Rib*, 27, September 1974, p. 17
14. Quoted in Ann Oakley, 'The Failure of the Movements for Women's Equality, *New Society*, 23 August 1979, p. 392
15. Joni Lovenduski and Vicky Randall, *Contemporary Feminist Politics: Women and Power in Britain*, Oxford University Press, Oxford, 1993, p. 186
16. Quoted in Melanie Phillips, 'Family Policy: The Long Years of Neglect, *New Society*, 8 June 1978, p. 531
17. Margaret Wynn, *Family Policy*, Penguin Books, Harmondsworth, 1970, quoted ibid., p. 531
18. Lady Howe, quoted ibid., p. 533
19. Ibid.
20. Michelene Wandor, quoted in Ann McFerran, 'Theatre's (Somewhat) Angry Women', *Time Out*, 21–27 October 1977, p. 13
21. Caryl Churchill, quoted ibid., p. 15
22. Ibid.
23. Mary O'Malley, quoted ibid.
24. Cherry Potter, quoted ibid.
25. Margaret Thatcher, quoted in Jeremy Seabrook, 'Winter of Resentment', *New Society*, 19 April 1979, p. 152
26. Barbara Castle, *Fighting All the Way*, Pan Books, London, 1994, p. 513
27. Beatrix Campbell, *The Iron Ladies: Why Do Women Vote Tory?*, Virago, London, 1987, p. 109
28. Castle, *Fighting All the Way*, p. 458
29. Hilary Wainwright, *Arguments for a New Left: Answering the Free-market Right*, Blackwell, Oxford, 1994, p. 60
30. Margaret Thatcher, *The Downing Street Years*, HarperCollins, London, 1993, p. 15
31. *Sunday Times*, Business News, 28 May 1972, in Carol Adams and Rae Laurikietis (eds.), *The Gender Trap: A Closer Look at Sex Roles*, Virago, London, 1976, p. 76
32. Rhona Churchill, 'What Every Secretary Bird Needs to Know', *Daily Mail*, 27 May 1970
33. David Vincent, *Poor Citizens: The State and the Poor in Twentieth-century Britain*, Longman, London, 1991, p. 183
34. Jayaben Desai, quoted in Beatrix Campbell and Valerie Charlton, 'Grunwick Women', in Marsha Rowe (ed.), *Spare Rib Reader*, Penguin Books, Harmondsworth, 1982, p. 210
35. Maggie Goodman, quoted in Ruth Inglis, 'Thoroughly Modern Mags', *Daily Express*, 13 September 1978
36. Beata Lipman, 'Wives Blockade Factory in Pollution Demo', *Observer*, 7 February 1971
37. Amrit Wilson, 'Women Against the Dust', *Spare Rib*, 49, August 1976

38. Sonia Jackson, 'Women in Poverty', *The Times*, 2 September 1970
39. Kirsten Cubitt, 'Playgroup in a Pensioned-off Bus', *The Times*, 18 November 1970
40. Dr Christine Pickard, 'Pre-marital Violence', *Sun*, 9 July 1970
41. Rebecca and Russell Dobash, quoted in Elizabeth Wilson, *What is to Be Done About Violence Against Women?*, Penguin Books, Harmondsworth, 1983, p. 84
42. Jane Lewis, *Women in Britain since 1945*, Blackwell, Oxford, 1992, p. 88
43. Sue Sharpe, *'Just Like a Girl': How Girls Learn to be Women*, Penguin Books, Harmondsworth, 1976, p. 108
44. Sue McCowan, quoted in Margaret Stacey and Marion Price, *Women, Power and Politics*, Tavistock Publications, London, 1981, p. 154
45. Elizabeth Wilson, *Adorned in Dreams: Fashion and Modernity*, Virago, London, 1995, p. 153
46. Ted Polhemus, *Street Style: From Sidewalk to Catwalk*, Thames and Hudson, London, 1995, p. 91
47. Germaine Greer, quoted in Lynne Segal, *Straight Sex: The Politics of Pleasure*, Virago, London, 1994, p. 27
48. Germaine Greer, quoted in Paul Ferris, *Sex and the British: A Twentieth-century History*, Michael Joseph, London, 1993, p. 227
49. Germaine Greer, quoted in Nigel Fountain, *Underground: The London Alternative Press, 1966–74*, a Comedia book, published by Routledge, London, 1988, p. 175
50. Jane Firbank, quoted in Linda Blandford, 'Women Shed Their Guilt', *Observer*, 28 May 1972
51. Anna Raeburn, quoted ibid.
52. Anna Raeburn, quoted in Len Richmond, 'Mentioning the Dreaded Word "Sex"', *Time Out*, 292, 17–23 October 1975, p. 13
53. Ibid.
54. Elinor Goodman, 'In Hot Pursuit of Today's Women', *Financial Times*, 29 September 1973
55. Lord Chief Justice Widgery, quoted in Ferris, *Sex and the British*, p. 226
56. Sir Keith Joseph, quoted in Jeffrey Weeks, *Sex, Politics and Society: The Regulation of Sexuality since 1800*, Longman, London, 1981, p. 278
57. Laura Mulvey, quoted in Segal, *Straight Sex*, p. 30
58. Phyllis Bowman, quoted in *Time Out*, 289, 26 September–2 October 1975, p. 7
59. Anna Coote and Beatrix Campbell, *Sweet Freedom: The Struggle for Women's Liberation*, Pan Books, London, 1982, p. 221
60. Ibid., p. 225
61. Mr Justice Slynn, quoted in Segal, *Straight Sex*, p. 56
62. Ray Gosling, 'Quite Contrary', *New Society*, 29 April 1976, p. 249
63. William Whitelaw, quoted in Ferris, *Sex and the British*, p. 250
64. Ibid., p. 246

65. Weeks, *Sex, Politics and Society*, p. 274

66. Quoted in Angela Neustatter and Gina Newson, *Mixed Feelings: The Experience of Abortion*, Pluto, London, 1986, p. 32

67. Linda Nochlin, quoted in Lynda Nead, 'The Female Nude: Pornography, Art and Sexuality', in Lynne Segal and Mary McIntosh (eds.), *Sex Exposed: Sexuality and the Pornography Debate*, Virago, London, 1992, p. 289

68. Toni Holt, quoted in Sandy Fawkes, 'Playgirl Toni Jets in to Hunt for the Naked Truth', *Daily Express*, 15 January 1974

69. Barbara Cartland, quoted in Rosalind Brunt, 'A Career in Love: The Romantic World of Barbara Cartland', in Christopher Rawling (ed.), *Popular Fiction and Social Change*, Macmillan, London, 1984, p. 143

70. Chris Hutchins and Peter Thompson, *Diana Confidential: The Nightmare and the Family*, Pocket Books, London, 1994, p. 74

71. Helen Reddy, quoted in Gillian G. Gaar, *She's a Rebel: The History of Women in Rock 'n' Roll*, Cassell, London, 1993, p. 123

72. Ibid.

73. Ibid., p. 127

74. Judy Chicago, quoted in Wendy Slatkin, *The Voices of Women Artists*, Prentice Hall, Englewood Cliffs, New Jersey, 1993, p. 285

75. Ibid.

76. Quoted in Michele Wallace, *Invisibility Blues: From Pop to Theory*, Verso, London, 1990, p. 35

77. Alice Walker, quoted in Mary Helen Washington, 'Teaching Black-eyed Susans: An approach to the Study of Black Women Writers', in Gloria T. Hull, Patricia Bell Scott and Barbara Smith (eds.), *All the Women are White, All the Blacks are Men, But Some of Us are Brave*, Black Women's Studies, The Feminist Press, Old Westbury, New York, 1981, p. 214

78. Anita Valerio, quoted in Cherríe Moraga and Gloria Anzaldúa (eds.), *This Bridge Called My Back: Writings by Radical Women of Color*, Kitchen Table: Women of Color Press, New York, 1981, p. 44

79. Cindy Sherman, quoted in Slatkin, *The Voices of Women Artists*, p. 312

80. Ibid., p. 309

81. Sara M. Evans, *Born for Liberty: A History of Women in America*, The Free Press, Macmillan, New York, 1989, p. 291

82. 'Guide to the Movement: Bread and Roses', *Women: A Journal of Liberation*, Spring 1970, p. 61

83. Alice Echols, *Daring to be Bad: Radical Feminism in America, 1967–1975*, University of Minnesota Press, Minneapolis, 1989, p. 175

84. Rosalyn Baxandall, 'Co-operative Nurseries', *Women: A Journal of Liberation*, Spring 1970, p. 44

85. Quoted in Paula Giddings, *When and Where I Enter: The Impact of Black Women on Race and Sex in America*, Bantam Books, Toronto, 1985, p. 345

86. Combahee River Collective, 'A Black Feminist Statement', in Moraga and Anzaldúa (eds.), *This Bridge Called My Back*, p. 210

87. Charlotte Bunch, quoted in Echols, *Daring to be Bad*, p. 234
88. June Arnold, quoted in Lillian Faderman, *Odd Girls and Twilight Lovers: A History of Lesbian Life in Twentieth-century America*, Penguin Books, Harmondsworth, 1992, p. 215
89. The Sarah Eisenstein Fund, *Commemorate and Carry On: Sarah Eisenstein, September 26, 1946–April 16, 1978*, New York, 1978, p. 10
90. Susan Brownmiller, quoted in Susan J. Douglas, *Where the Girls Are: Growing Up Female in the Mass Media*, Penguin Books, Harmondsworth, 1995, p. 168
91. Ibid., p. 169
92. Rosalind Rosenberg, *Divided Lives: American Women in the Twentieth Century*, Penguin Books, Harmondsworth, 1993, p. 225
93. Ibid.
94. American Social History Project, *Who Built America? Working People and the Nation's Economy, Politics, Culture and Society. Vol. Two: From the Gilded Age to the Present*, Pantheon Books, New York, 1992, p. 613
95. Johnnie Tillmon, quoted in Rosalyn Baxandall, Linda Gordon and Susan Reverby (eds.), *America's Working Women: A Documentary History, 1600 to the Present*, Vintage Books, New York, 1976, p. 335
96. Erica Jong, quoted in Barbara Ehrenreich, 'The Women's Movements, Feminist and AntiFeminist', *Radical America*, Vol. 15, Nos. 1 and 2, Spring 1981, p. 98
97. Ibid., p. 99
98. Phyllis Schlafly, 'The Power of the Positive Woman', in Mary Beth Norton (ed.), *Major Problems in American Women's History: Documents and Essays*, D. C. Heath and Company, Lexington, Mass., 1989, p. 429
99. Ibid., p. 434
100. Susan M. Hartmann, *From Margin to Mainstream: American Women and Politics since 1960*, Temple University Press, Philadelphia, 1989, p. 129
101. Alma M. Garcia, 'The Development of Chicana Feminist Discourse', in Ellen Carol DuBois and Vicki L. Ruiz (eds.), *Unequal Sisters: A Multicultural Reader in US Women's History*, Routledge, New York, 1990, p. 427
102. Carol Kleiman, *Women's Networks: The Complete Guide to Getting a Better Job, Advancing Your Career, and Feeling Great as a Woman Through Networking*, Ballantine Books, New York, 1980, p. 202
103. Colleen Dishon, quoted ibid., p. 206
104. Barbara Garson, *All the Livelong Day: The Meaning and Demeaning of Routine Work*, Penguin Books, New York, 1977, p. vii
105. Quoted in Toni Carabillo et al. (eds.), *Feminist Chronicles, 1953–1993*, Women's Graphics, Los Angeles, 1993, p. 81
106. Quoted in Garson, *All the Livelong Day*, p. 176
107. Ibid., p. 221
108. Ruth Milkman, 'Women Workers, Feminism and the Labor Movement since the 1960s', in Ruth Milkman (ed.), *Women, Work and Protest: A Century*

of US Women's Labor History, Routledge and Kegan Paul, Boston, 1985, p. 304

109. Laurie Coyle, Gail Hershatter and Emily Honig, 'Women at Farah: An Unfinished Story', in Joan M. Jensen and Sue Davidson (eds.), *A Needle, a Bobbin, a Strike: Women Needleworkers in America*, Temple University Press, Philadelphia, 1984, p. 261

110. Cathy Tuley, quoted in Milkman, 'Women Workers: Feminism and the Labor Movement since the 1960s', in Milkman (ed.), *Women, Work and Protest*, p. 308

111. Ibid.

112. Larry Hodgson, 'Women's Lob', *The Listener*, 24 June 1971, p. 808

113. Francie Kraker, quoted in Stephanie L. Twin (ed.), *Women and Sports*, The Feminist Press, New York, 1977, p. 105

114. Willye White, quoted ibid., p. 96

115. Cathy Tuley, quoted in Milkman, *Women, Work and Protest*, p. 310

116. Barbara Mayer Wertheimer, 'To Rekindle the Spirit: Current Education Programs for Women Workers', in Joyce L. Kornbluh and Mary Frederickson (eds.), *Sisterhood and Solidarity: Workers' Education for Women*, Temple University Press, Philadelphia, 1989, p. 287

117. Joyce Croy, quoted in Terri Suess, 'Klamath Tribes Challenge Illegal Restrictions', *Northwest Passage: Washington's Feminist Newspaper*, Vol. 19, No. 7, 19 September–9 October (*c.* 1978)

118. Lillian Rubin, *Worlds of Pain: Life in the Working-class Family*, Basic Books, a division of HarperCollins, 1992 (first edn 1976), p. 172

119. Ibid., p. 173

120. Glenda Riley, *Inventing the American Woman: A Perspective on Women's History, 1865 to the Present*, Harlan Davidson, Arlington Heights, Illinois, 1986, p. 141

121. Ellen Willis, *Beginning to See the Light: Pieces of a Decade*, Alfred A. Knopf, New York, 1981, p. 151

122. Carol B. Stack, *All Our Kin: Strategies of Survival in a Black Community*, Harper Colophon Books, Harper and Row, New York, 1974, p. 31

123. Johnnie Tillmon, quoted in Baxandall, Gordon and Reverby (eds.), *America's Working Women*, p. 357

124. Ibid.

125. Teresa L. Amott, 'Black Women and AFDC: Making Entitlement out of Necessity', in Linda Gordon (ed.), *Women, the State and Welfare*, University of Wisconsin Press, Madison, 1990, p. 290

126. Quoted in American Social History Project, *Who Built America?*, p. 615

127. Quoted in Rubin, *Worlds of Pain*, p. 178

128. Beverly, quoted in Roderick Thorp and Robert Blake (eds.), *Wives: An Investigation*, Souvenir Press, London, 1972, p. 204

129. Ibid., p. 207

130. Caroline Bird, quoted in Douglas, *Where the Girls Are*, p. 199

131. Ibid., p. 200

132. Quoted ibid., p. 202
133. Ibid., p. 208
134. Ibid., p. 209
135. Ibid., p. 240
136. Ibid.
137. Ibid., p. 242
138. Lillian, quoted in Thorp and Blake (eds.), *Wives*, p. 221
139. Ibid., p. 222
140. Quoted in Sheila Rowbotham, 'Mountain Woman Blues', *Spare Rib*, 27, September 1974, p. 46
141. Quoted in Rubin, *Worlds of Pain*, p. 139
142. Ibid., p. 143
143. Ibid.
144. Ibid.
145. Quoted in Robert L. Daniel, *American Women in the 20th Century: The Festival of Life*, Harcourt Brace Jovanovich, Orlando, Florida, 1987, p. 312
146. Alix Kates Shulman, quoted in Lynne Segal, *Straight Sex: The Politics of Pleasure*, Virago, London, 1994, p. 36
147. Quoted in Faderman, *Odd Girls and Twilight Lovers*, p. 209
148. Ti-Grace Atkinson, quoted in Echols, *Daring to be Bad*, p. 239
149. Rita Mae Brown, quoted in Faderman, *Odd Girls and Twilight Lovers*, p. 256
150. Anita Bryant, quoted in Sylvia Ann Hewlett, *A Lesser Life: The Myth of Women's Liberation*, Michael Joseph, London, 1987, p. 219
151. Schlafly, 'The Power of the Positive Woman', in Norton (ed.), *Major Problems in American Women's History*, p. 431
152. Carol Downer, quoted in Rosalyn Baxandall, *Women and Abortion: The Body as Battleground*, Open Magazine Pamphlet Series, Westfield, New Jersey, 1992, p. 2
153. Stack, *All Our Kin*, p. 7
154. Rosalind P. Petchesky, *Abortion and Woman's Choice*, Verso, London, 1986, p. 250
155. Susan Brownmiller, quoted in Hester Eisenstein, *Contemporary Feminist Thought*, Unwin Paperbacks, London, 1984, p. 29
156. Ibid., p. 32
157. Robin Morgan, *The Word of a Woman*, Virago, London, 1993, p. 88
158. Willis, *Beginning to See the Light*, p. 224
159. Ibid., p. 225

CHAPTER 9: THE 1980S

1. Quoted in Yvonne Roberts, 'If You've Got It, Flaunt It', *New Statesman*, 18 December 1987–1 January 1988, p. 10
2. Ibid.

3. Diane Charles, quoted in Beatrix Campbell, *The Iron Ladies: Why Do Women Vote Tory?*, Virago, London, 1987, p. 155

4. Jean Brown, quoted ibid., p. 203

5. Sonia Copland, quoted in Helena Blaker et al., 'Happiest Days of Our Lives?', *City Limits*, 8–14 March 1985, p. 11

6. Josephine Hart, quoted in Helen Birch et al., 'By Their Jargon Shall Ye Know Them', *City Limits*, 4–10 December 1987, p. 10

7. Gina Giorgiou, quoted in Blaker et al., 'Happiest Days of Our Lives?', *City Limits*, 8–14 March 1985, p. 10

8. Rankin Ann, quoted in Sheryl Garratt, 'Reggae Woman', *City Limits*, 1–7 June 1984, p. 17

9. Corinne Maine, quoted in Blaker et al., 'Happiest Days of Our Lives?', *City Limits*, 8–14 March 1985, p. 13

10. Sue Lake, quoted in Campbell, *The Iron Ladies*, p. 176

11. Diane Charles, quoted ibid., p. 154

12. Ibid., p. 155

13. Amryl Johnson, 'The Loaded Dice', in Amryl Johnson, *Long Road to Nowhere*, Virago, London, 1985, p. 55

14. Sarah Benton, 'Community Voices', *New Statesman*, 16 December 1988, p. 13

15. Ibid.

16. Emma Nicholson, quoted in Anna Coote and Polly Pattullo, *Power and Prejudice: Women and Politics*, Weidenfeld and Nicolson, London, 1990, p. 197

17. Margaret Thatcher, quoted in Brian Walden, 'Why I Can Never, Never Let Up', *Sunday Times*, 8 May 1988

18. Ibid.

19 Margaret Thatcher, quoted in Anthony Barnett, *Iron Britannia: Why Parliament Wages Its Falklands War*, Allison and Busby, London, 1982, p. 91

20. Annabel Ferriman, 'The Great Minerals Goldmine', *Observer*, 22 May 1988

21. Carolyn Miller, quoted in Helen Birch and Julia Pascal, 'Power Dressing', *City Limits*, 3–10 December 1987, pp. 13–14

22. Ashley Crystal, quoted ibid., p. 14

23. *City Limits*, 7–13 March 1986

24. Ibid.

25. Julie Christie, quoted in Beatrix Campbell, 'Miss Julie', *City Limits*, 17–24 September 1987, p. 11

26. Ibid.

27. Barbara Castle, *Fighting All the Way*, Pan Books, London, 1994, p. 535

28. Campbell, *The Iron Ladies*, p. 242

29. Lord Carrington, quoted in Hugo Young, *One of Us: A Biography of Margaret Thatcher*, Pan Macmillan, London, 1993, p. 252

30. 'Conservative Economics: Lord Wishful, Lady Rigorous', *The Economist*, 24–30 October 1987, p. 21

31. Margaret Thatcher, quoted in Young, *One of Us*, p. 491

32. Ibid., p. 209
33. Jill Liddington, *The Long Road to Greenham: Feminism and Anti-militarism in Britain since 1820*, Virago, London, 1989, p. 221
34. Ibid., p. 246
35. Lady Olga Maitland, quoted in Campbell, *The Iron Ladies*, p. 135
36. Shreela Flather, quoted ibid., p. 255
37. Sheila Rowbotham, interview with Jean McCrindle, ' "More Than Just a Memory": Some Political Implications of Women's Involvement in the Miners' Strike, 1984–5', *Feminist Review*, 23, Summer 1986, quoted in Sheila Rowbotham, *The Past is Before Us: Feminism in Action since the 1960s*, Penguin Books, Harmondsworth, 1990, p. 284
38. Pauline Radford, quoted in Coote and Pattullo, *Power and Prejudice*, p. 65
39. Ibid., p. 71
40. Anne Speed, quoted in Margaret Ward, 'The Women's Movement in the North of Ireland', in Sean Hutton and Paul Stewart (eds.), *Ireland's Histories: Aspects of State, Society and Ideology*, Routledge, London, 1991, p. 159
41. Harriet Harman, quoted in Coote and Pattullo, *Power and Prejudice*, p. 267
42. Victoria Glendinning, 'Will the Real Mrs Thatcher Please Sit Down', *Sunday Correspondent*, 15 October 1989
43. Ann Butler, quoted in *Jobs for a Change*, GLC, London, no. 13, c. 1983
44. Quoted in Philip Pearson, *Twilight Robbery: Trade Unions and Low-paid Workers*, Pluto, London, 1985, p. 36
45. Carol Buswell, 'Training Girls to be Low-paid Women', in Caroline Glendinning and Jane Millar (eds.), *Women and Poverty in Britain: The 1990s*, Harvester Wheatsheaf, New York, 1992, p. 87
46. Swasti Mitter, 'Industrial Restructuring and Manufacturing Home-work: Immigrant Women in the UK Clothing Industry', *Capital and Class*, 27, Winter 1986, p. 57
47. Quoted in 'Derbyshire: Activity Goes On', *Coalfield Women*, Women Against Pit Closures Newsletter, 6, January 1988
48. TUC, Sexual Harassment at Work (1983), quoted in Sarah Boston, *Women Workers and the Trade Unions*, Lawrence and Wishart, London, 1987 (first edn 1980), p. 338
49. Quoted in Melissa Benn, 'An Unsuitable Job for a Woman', *City Limits*, 23–29 September 1983, p. 10
50. Pat Murphy and Nell McCafferty, *Women in Focus: Contemporary Irish Women's Lives*, Attic Press, Dublin, 1987, p. 7
51. Anita Roddick, quoted in Stuart Cosgrove and Dave Hill, 'Ten Long Years', *New Statesman and Society*, 5 May 1989, p. 41
52. Helen Birch et al., 'By Their Jargon Shall Ye Know Them', *City Limits*, 4–10 December 1987, p. 11
53. Pamela Stephenson, quoted in Diana Simmonds, 'There is Nothing Like a (Funny) Dame', *City Limits*, 17–23 December 1982, p. 19

54. Suzanne Moore, 'Renaissance Woman', *New Statesman*, 11 November 1988, p. 40
55. Ibid.
56. Sue Townsend, quoted in Barney Bardsley, 'Teen Moles', *City Limits*, 14–20 December 1984, p. 17
57. Ibid., p. 16
58. Sian James, 'Cosmo Queen is She Who Must Be Obeyed', *Today*, 23 October 1989
59. Ruth Elliott, conference paper 'Women and the Economy Conference', North London Polytechnic, 1988, unpublished ms.
60. 'But Once a Year', *The Economist*, 19 December 1987, p. 30
61. Ibid.
62. Claire Callender, 'Redundancy, Unemployment and Poverty', in Glendinning and Millar (eds.), *Women and Poverty in Britain*, p. 143
63. Quoted in Hilary Graham, 'Budgeting for Health: Mothers in Low-income Households', ibid., p. 214
64. Quoted ibid., p. 215
65. Shyama Perera, 'A Full-time Job Claiming Social Security', *Guardian*, 6 May 1988
66. David Vincent, *Poor Citizens: The State and the Poor in Twentieth-century Britain*, Longman, London, 1991, p. 188
67. Judith Williamson, *Consuming Passions: The Dynamics of Popular Culture*, Marion Boyars, London, 1986, p. 12
68. Lynval Golding, quoted ibid., p. 203
69. Yvonne Roberts, 'Thatcher's New Woman Arriving in a Golf GTI', *New Statesman and Society*, 11 December 1987, p. 16
70. Vivienne Westwood, quoted in Cosgrove and Hill, 'Ten Long Years', *New Statesman and Society*, 5 May 1989, p. 42
71. Ray Hudson and Allan M. Williams, *Divided Britain*, Belhaven Press, London, 1989, p. 84
72. Barbara Castle, *Fighting All the Way*, Pan Books, London, 1994, p. 559
73. Judge Brian Gibbens, quoted in Janet Watts, 'Without Prejudice: Are Judges Unfair to Women?', *Observer*, 29 January 1984
74. 'Male legal figure', quoted ibid.
75. Quoted in Melanie McFadyean, 'On the Game: It's a Man's World', *City Limits*, 22–28 October 1982, p. 19
76. Ibid.
77. Quoted in Paul Ferris, *Sex and the British: A Twentieth-century History*, Michael Joseph, London, 1993, p. 249
78. Ibid., p. 248
79. Ibid., p. 247
80. Quoted in Mandy Merck, 'From Minneapolis to Westminster', in Lynne Segal and Mary McIntosh (eds.), *Sex Exposed: Sexuality and the Pornography Debate*, Virago, London, 1992, p. 54

81. Lynne Segal, *Is the Future Female? Troubled Thoughts on Contemporary Feminism*, Virago, London, 1987, p. 112

82. Mandy Rose, quoted in Melissa Benn, 'Adventures in the Soho Skin Trade', *New Statesman*, 11 December 1987, p. 23

83. Ibid.

84. *Undercoats*, quoted in Janice Winship, ' "A Girl Needs to Get Street-wise": Magazines for the 1980s', *Feminist Review*, 21, Winter 1985, p. 27

85. Barbara Rogers, interview with Sue Tully, 'The Reaction's Been Brilliant', *Everywoman*, August 1986, p. 12

86. Margaret Thatcher, quoted in Young, *One of Us*, p. 344

87. Sheena Easton, quoted in Williamson, *Consuming Passions*, p. 20

88. Teddi Holt, quoted in Robyn Rowland (ed.), *Women Who Do and Women Who Don't Join the Women's Movement*, Routledge and Kegan Paul, London, 1984, p. 53

89. Ibid.

90. Ibid., p. 54

91. Ibid., p. 52

92. 'Mary Donnelly', quoted in Rebecca Klatch, *Women of the New Right*, Temple University Press, Philadelphia, 1987, p. 166

93. Ibid.

94. Ibid., p. 168

95. Ibid.

96. 'Dora Remington', quoted ibid., p. 181

97. Ibid., p. 182

98. Ibid., p. 181

99. Ibid.

100. Paula Gunn Allen, quoted in Carolyn Merchant, *Radical Ecology: The Search for a Livable World*, Routledge, New York, 1992, p. 120

101. Jane Mansbridge, *Why We Lost the ERA*, University of Chicago Press, Chicago, 1986, p. 2

102. Mrs Marilyn Lloyd, quoted in Mary Frances Berry, *Why ERA Failed: Politics, Women's Rights and the Amending Process of the Constitution*, Indiana University Press, Bloomington, 1986, p. 103

103. Mansbridge, *Why We Lost the ERA*, p. 16

104. Susan M. Hartmann, *From Margin to Mainstream: American Women and Politics since 1960*, Temple University Press, Philadelphia, 1989, p. 156

105. Quoted in Sara M. Evans, *Born for Liberty: A History of Women in America*, The Free Press, Macmillan, New York, 1989, p. 312

106. Quoted in Toni Carabillo et al. (eds.), *Feminist Chronicles, 1953–1993*, Women's Graphics, Los Angeles, 1993, p. 114

107. Bill Casey, quoted in Bob Woodward, *Veil: The Secret Wars of the CIA, 1981–1987*, Simon and Schuster, New York, 1987, p. 38

108. Ibid., p. 336

109. Quoted in Kitty Kelley, *Nancy Reagan: The Unauthorized Biography*, Bantam Books, Toronto, 1992, p. 376

110. Nancy Reagan, quoted ibid., p. 577

111. Barbara Ehrenreich, *The Worst Years of Our Lives: Irreverent Notes from a Decade of Greed*, Pantheon Books, New York, 1990, p. 90

112. Ann Smith, quoted in Anne N. Costain, *Inviting Women's Rebellion: A Political Process Interpretation of the Women's Movement*, Johns Hopkins University Press, Baltimore, 1992, p. 174, footnote 16

113. 'Congressional Caucus on Women's Issues', *Update*, 20 October 1986, p. 11, quoted in Johanna Brenner, 'The Best of Times, the Worst of Times: US Feminism Today', *New Left Review*, 200, July–August 1993, p. 151

114. Ibid.

115. Ibid., p. 125

116. Ehrenreich, *The Worst Years of Our Lives*, p. 3

117. Quoted in Carabillo et al. (eds.), *Feminist Chronicles*, p. 132

118. Cora Tucker, quoted in Giovanna di Chiro, 'Defining Environmental Justice: Women's Voices and Grass-roots Politics', *Socialist Review*, Vol. 22, No. 4, October–December 1992, p. 115

119. Marta Salinas, quoted ibid., p. 114

120. Quoted in Lillian Faderman, *Odd Girls and Twilight Lovers: A History of Lesbian Life in Twentieth-century America*, Penguin Books, Harmondsworth, 1992, p. 295

121. Quoted in Susan Faludi, *Backlash: The Undeclared War Against Women*, Chatto and Windus, London, 1992, p. 264

122. Katherine Hoover, quoted in Diane Peacock Jezic, *Women Composers: The Lost Tradition Found*, The Feminist Press, New York, 1994, p. 167

123. Ruth Schonthal, quoted ibid., p. 187

124. Barbara Kolb, quoted ibid., p. 197

125. Ellen Taaffe Zwilich, quoted ibid., p. 176

126. Arlie Hochshild, *The Second Shift: Working Parents and the Revolution at Home*, Viking, New York, 1989, p. 87

127. Juliet Schor, quoted in Rosalyn Baxandall and Linda Gordon (eds.), with Susan Reverby, *America's Working Women: A Documentary History, 1600 to the Present*, W. W. Norton, New York, 1995, p. 303

128. Betty A. Beach, 'The Family Context of Home Shoe Work', in Eileen Boris and Cynthia R. Daniels (eds.), *Homework: Historical and Contemporary Perspectives on Paid Labor at Home*, University of Illinois Press, Urbana, 1989, p. 141

129. Baxandall and Gordon (eds.), *America's Working Women*, p. 289

130. Melinda Gebbie, 'Horrors of Pooper-Scooper U.', in Chris Carlsson and Mark Leger (eds.), *Bad Attitude: The Processed World Anthology*, Verso, London, 1990, p. 24

131. Linda Thomas, 'It's a Business Doing Pleasure with You', ibid., p. 243

132. Lou, quoted in Baxandall and Gordon (eds.), *America's Working Women*, p. 296

133. Annie, quoted ibid.

134. Barbara Garson, *The Electronic Sweatshop: How Computers are Transforming the Office of the Future into the Factory of the Past*, Penguin Books, New York, 1989, pp. 9–10

135. Ibid., p. 105

136. Quoted in Eileen Boris, 'Homework and Women's Rights', in Boris and Daniels (eds.), *Homework*, p. 242

137. Ibid.

138. Caitlin Manning and Louis Michaelson, 'Fire Against Ice: California Frozen Food Workers on Strike', in Carlsson and Leger (eds.), *Bad Attitude*, p. 131

139. Lou, in Baxandall and Gordon (eds.), *America's Working Women*, p. 296

140. Joanne Morreale, 'A New Beginning: A Textual Frame Analysis of the Political Campaign Film (New York 1990)', quoted in Stuart and Elizabeth Ewen, *Channels of Desire: Mass Images and the Shaping of American Consciousness*, University of Minnesota Press, Minneapolis, 1992, p. 216

141. Ibid., p. 107

142. Ibid., p. 230, footnote 58

143. Ibid., p. 107

144. J. Kevin Thompson, quoted in Stuart Ewen, *All-consuming Images: The Politics of Style and Contemporary Culture*, Basic Books, New York, 1988, p. 182

145. Ewen and Ewen, *Channels of Desire*, p. 217

146. Quoted ibid., p. 203

147. Roseanne Barr, quoted in John Lahr, 'Crazy All the Way', *Guardian*, 2 September 1995

148. Quoted in Faderman, *Odd Girls and Twilight Lovers*, p. 292

149. Amy Kesselman, quoted in Jesse Lemisch and Naomi Weisstein, 'Cornucopia isn't Consumerism', *Against the Current*, January/February 1992, p. 34

150. Teresa L. Amott, *Caught in the Crisis: Women in the US Economy Today*, Monthly Review Press, New York, 1993, p. 108

151. Nora Ephron, *Heartburn* (Pocket Books, New York, 1983), quoted in Sylvia Ann Hewlett, *A Lesser Life: The Myth of Women's Liberation*, Michael Joseph, London, 1987, p. 219

152. Nancy Fraser, 'Clintonism, Welfare and the Antisocial Wage: The Emergence of a Neoliberal Political Imaginary', in Antonio Callari, Stephen Cullenberg and Carole Biewener (eds.), *Marxism in the Post Modern World: Confronting the New World Order*, The Guilford Press, New York, 1995, p. 494

153. Ibid.

154. Gary Bauer, quoted in Faludi, *Backlash*, p. 297

155. Anita Bryant, quoted in Rosalind Petchesky, in Mary Beth Norton (ed.),

Major Problems in American Women's History: Documents and Essays, D. C. Heath and Company, Lexington, Mass., 1989, p. 452

156. Irene Alvarez Perito, quoted with photograph of Vickie Alvarez by Martine Barrat, in *A Century Apart: Images of Struggle and Spirit – Jacob Riis and Five Contemporary Photographers*, exhibition at the Museum of the City of New York, 19 January–3 September 1995

157. Richard Younge, 'Report from the Frontlines: Unsung Heroines of the AIDS Epidemic', *Health/PAC Bulletin*, Winter 1989, p. 16

158. Ibid., p. 18

159. Temma Kaplan, 'Impediments to the New Communalism', in Jeremy Brecher and Tim Costello (eds.), *Building Bridges: The Emerging Grassroots Coalition of Labor and Community*, Monthly Review Press, New York, 1990, pp. 209–10

160. Bertha Lewis, quoted in Michael Kamber, '22 Families Fight Mass Eviction in the South Bronx: A Photo Essay', *Z Magazine*, January 1989, p. 55

161. Quoted in di Chiro, 'Defining Environmental Justice', *Socialist Review*, Vol. 22, No. 4, October–December 1992, p. 99

162. Jessie Deer-in-Water, quoted in Karen Jan Stults, 'Hysterical Housewives (and Other Courageous Women)', *On the Issues*, XIII, 1989, p. 30

163. Cora Tucker, quoted ibid.

164. Marita Golden, quoted in Margaret Busby (ed.), *Daughters of Africa: An International Anthology of Words and Writings by Women of African Descent from the Ancient Egyptian to the Present*, Jonathan Cape, London, 1992, p. 818

165. bell hooks, quoted ibid., p. 842

166. Suzette Haden Elgin, 'Women's Language and Near-future Science Fiction: A Reply', *Women's Studies*, Vol. 14, No. 2, 1987, p. 181

167. Ibid., pp. 177, 178

168. Denise Levertov, quoted in Maria Lauret, *Liberating Literature: Feminist Fiction in America*, Routledge, London, 1994, p. 97

169. Julianne Malveaux, quoted in Teresa L. Amott and Julie A. Matthaei, *Race, Gender and Work: A Multicultural Economic History of Women in the United States*, South End Press, Boston, 1991, p. 183

170. Quoted in Faderman, *Odd Girls and Twilight Lovers*, p. 299

171. Lynne Segal, *Straight Sex: The Politics of Pleasure*, Virago, London, 1994, p. 64

172. Carole Vance, quoted ibid., p. 65

173. Teddi Holt, quoted in Rowland (ed.), *Women Who Do and Women Who Don't*, p. 53

174. Susan Bolotin, 'Voices from the Postfeminist Generation', *New York Times* magazine, 17 October 1982, cited in Alice Echols, *Daring to be Bad: Radical Feminism in America, 1967–1975*, University of Minnesota Press, Minneapolis, 1989, p. 365, footnote 34

175. Joan Jett, quoted in Gillian G. Gaar, *She's a Rebel: The History of Women in Rock 'n' Roll*, Cassell, London, 1993, p. 221

176. Madonna, quoted ibid., p. 333

177. Sue O'Sullivan, 'An Interview with Cindy Patton: Mapping – Lesbians, AIDS and Sexuality', *Feminist Review*, 34, Spring 1990, p. 132

178. Quoted in Merck, 'From Minneapolis to Westminster', in Segal and McIntosh (eds.), *Sex Exposed*, p. 53

179. Carole S. Vance, 'Negotiating Sex and Gender in the Attorney General's Commission on Pornography', ibid., p. 41

180. Muriel Dimen, *Surviving Sexual Contradictions*, Macmillan, New York, 1986, p. xv

181. Kathryn Anastos and Carola Marte, 'Women: The Missing Persons in the AIDS Epidemic', *Health/PAC Bulletin*, Winter 1989, p. 7

182. Ibid.

183. Quoted in Beverly Lowy, 'Girl Talk', *On the Issues*, XIII, 1989, p. 31

184. Ibid.

185. Rosalyn Baxandall, 'Marxism and Sexuality: The Body as Battleground', in Callari, Cullenberg and Biewener (eds.), *Marxism in the Post Modern World*, p. 243

186. Carole Vance, quoted in Segal, *Straight Sex*, p. 63

187. *The Hite Report*, quoted ibid., p. 107

188. Marita Golden, quoted in Busby (ed.), *Daughters of Africa*, p. 821

CHAPTER 10: 1990–95

1. Margaret Thatcher, quoted in Alan Sked and Chris Cook, *Post-war Britain: A Political History*, Penguin Books, Harmondsworth, 1993, p. 584

2. Pastor Tony Evans, quoted in Mark Tran, 'Be a Man, for God's Sake – Try Bonding', *Guardian*, 26 November 1994

3. Marc Breslow, 'Can We Still Win the War Against Poverty?', *Dollars and Sense*, July–August 1995, p. 40

4. Women's Committee of One Hundred, 'Why Every Woman in America Should Beware of Welfare Cuts', *New York Times*, 8 August 1995

5. Jane Millar and Caroline Glendinning, ' "It All Really Starts in the Family": Gender Divisions and Poverty', in Caroline Glendinning and Jane Millar (eds.), *Women and Poverty in Britain: The 1990s*, Harvester Wheatsheaf, New York, 1992, p. 3

6. Eileen Sandford, quoted in 'Top Tory Defends Young Mothers', *Shrewsbury Chronicle*, 29 August 1994

7. Angela Phillips, 'All Work and Low Pay', *Guardian*, 10 October 1994

8. Anja Hohmeyer, 'The National Abortion Campaign', in Gabriele Griffin (ed.), *Feminist Activism in the 1990s*, Taylor and Francis, London, 1995, p. 44

9. Johanna Brenner, 'The Best of Times, the Worst of Times: US Feminism Today', *New Left Review*, 200, July–August 1993, p. 130

10. Juliet Schor, *A Sustainable Economy for the 21st Century*, Open Magazine Pamphlet Series, Westfield, New Jersey, p. 9

11. Tracy Grafton, quoted in Kathy Marks, 'Voices from the Other England', *Independent on Sunday*, 23 August 1992

12. Ibid.

13. Lisa Armstrong, quoted in Rachel Kelly, 'Last Chance for the Chanel', *The Times*, 25 November 1994

14. Quoted in Sue Sharpe, *'Just Like a Girl': How Girls Learn to be Women*, Penguin Books, Harmondsworth, 1994, p. 299

15. Paul O'Grady, quoted in Rachel Newsome, 'Brains Make a Finer Flower', *City Life*, 29 March–13 April 1995, p. 14

16. Ibid.

17. Ibid.

18. Kate Bornstein, quoted in Julia Brosnan, 'Agenda Bender', *Red Pepper*, 9, February 1995, pp. 24, 25

19. Tele Club, *SF Weekly*, 5 January 1994, p. 32

20. Ibid.

21. Gay Talese, quoted in Michael Marriott, 'Not Frenzied, But Fulfilled', *Newsweek*, 17 October 1994, p. 70

22. Excerpt from Kaye Wellings et al., *Sexual Behaviour in Britain* (Penguin Books, Harmondsworth, 1994), quoted in 'Sex and the British', *Independent on Sunday*, 16 January 1994

23. Ibid.

24. Lynne Segal, *Straight Sex: The Politics of Pleasure*, Virago, London, 1994, p. 313

25. Rosalyn Baxandall, *Women and Abortion: The Body as Battleground*, Open Magazine Pamphlet Series, Westfield, New Jersey, 1992, p. 13

26. *Girl Jock*, 14, p. 1

27. Quoted in Alex Duval Smith, 'Rainbow Alliance for Party Politics', *Guardian*, 26 June 1995

28. Beryl Sutton, quoted in Katie Buchanan, 'Blessed are the Jam-makers', *Guardian*, 27 April 1994

29. Rosalind Powell, interview with Maria Hutt, *Big Issue*, 24 August 1994, p. 14

30. Ibid.

31. Justin Timson, quoted in David Ward, 'Bardot Pays Tribute to Coventry's Joan of Arc', *Guardian*, 15 February 1995

32. Lois Gibbs, 'Women Warriors', *Everyone's Backyard*, Citizens' Clearinghouse for Hazardous Waste, Vol. 10, No. 4, August 1992, p. 2

33. Quoted in Rosemary Vardell and Mary Whitebook, 'Worthy Work, Worthless Wages', *Dollars and Sense*, 201, September–October 1995, p. 38

34. Debjani Chatterjee, 'Harnessing Shakti: The Work of the Bengali Women's Support Group', in Griffin (ed.), *Feminist Activism in the 1990s*, p. 95

35. Delia Jarrett-Macauley, *Reconstructing Womanhood, Reconstructing Feminism*, Routledge, London, 1995, p. xii

Select Bibliography

The works listed below are either general surveys which I have drawn upon extensively over several decades or particular studies which provided source material not cited in the notes. This select bibliography is thus in part an acknowledgement of my debt to many authors. It also complements the notes and provides a guide to further reading, but it does not include either the numerous works of historical background used or original source material, because in a general survey like this such a list would be impossibly unwieldy.

Alexander, Sally, *Becoming a Woman and Other Essays in 19th and 20th Century Feminist History*, Virago, London, 1994

Alexander, Ziggi, 'Black Entertainers', in Jane Beckett and Deborah Cherry (eds.), *The Edwardian Era*, Phaidon Press and the Barbican Gallery, London, 1987

American Social History Project, *Who Built America? Working People and the Nation's Economy, Politics, Culture and Society. Vol. Two: From the Gilded Age to the Present*, Pantheon Books, New York, 1992

Amott, Teresa L., *Caught in the Crisis: Women in the US Economy Today*, Monthly Review Press, New York, 1993

Amott, Teresa L., and Matthaei, Julie A., *Race, Gender and Work: A Multicultural Economic History of Women in the United States*, South End Press, Boston, 1991

Armitage, Susan, and Jameson, Elizabeth (eds.), *The Women's West*, University of Oklahoma Press, Norman, 1987

Ash, Juliet, and Wilson, Elizabeth (eds.), *Chic Thrills: A Fashion Reader*, Pandora, HarperCollins, London, 1992

Bailey, Beth, *From Front Porch to Back Seat: Courtship in Twentieth-century America*, Johns Hopkins University Press, Baltimore, 1989

Banks, Olive, *Faces of Feminism: A Study of Feminism as a Social Movement*, Basil Blackwell, Oxford, 1986

Baron, Ava (ed.), *Work Engendered: Toward a New History of American Labor*, Cornell University Press, Ithaca, 1991

Basinger, Jeanine, *A Woman's View: How Hollywood Spoke to Women, 1930–1960*, Chatto and Windus, London, 1994

Bataille, Gretchen M. (ed.), *Native American Women: A Biographical Dictionary*, Garland Publishing, New York, 1993

Baxandall, Rosalyn Fraad, *Words on Fire: The Life and Writing of Elizabeth Gurley Flynn*, Rutgers University Press, New Brunswick, New Jersey, 1987

Baxandall, Rosalyn, Gordon, Linda, and Reverby, Susan (eds.), *America's Working Women: A Documentary History, 1600 to the Present*, Vintage Books, a division of Random House, New York, 1976; new edition revised and updated by Rosalyn Baxandall and Linda Gordon published by W. W. Norton, New York, 1995

Belen, Edna Acosta, *The Puerto Rican Woman: Perspective on Culture, History and Society*, Praeger, Westport, Connecticut, 1986

Belfrage, Sally, *Un-American Activities: A Memoir of the Fifties*, André Deutsch, London, 1994

Bentley, Joanne, *Hallie Flanagan: A Life in the American Theater*, Knopf, New York, 1988

Berkin, Carol R., and Lovett, Clara M. (eds.), *Women, War and Revolution*, Holmes and Meier, New York, 1980

Berkin, Carol Ruth, and Norton, Mary Beth (eds.), *Women of America: A History*, Houghton Mifflin Company, Boston, 1979

Beynon, Huw, and Austrin, Terry, *Masters and Servants: Class and Patronage in the Making of a Labour Organization*, Rivers Oram, London, 1994

Bird, Liz, 'Threading the Beads: Women in Art in Glasgow, 1870–1920', in Glasgow Women's Studies Group (ed.), *Uncharted Lives: Extracts from Scottish Women's Experiences, 1850–1982*, Pressgang, Glasgow, 1983

Black, Clementina, *Married Women's Work*, Virago, London, 1983 (first edn 1915)

Bland, Lucy, *Banishing the Beast: English Feminism and Sexual Morality, 1885–1914*, Penguin Books, Harmondsworth, 1995

Blee, Kathleen M., *Women of the Klan: Racism and Gender in the 1920s*, University of California Press, Berkeley, 1991

Bolt, Christine, *Feminist Ferment: 'The Woman Question in the USA and England, 1870–1940*, UCL Press, London, 1995

Boris, Eileen, 'Crafts Shop or Sweatshop? The Uses and Abuses of Craftsmanship in Twentieth Century America', *Journal of Design History*, Vol. 2, Nos. 2 and 3, 1989

——*Home to Work: Motherhood and the Politics of Industrial Homework in the United States*, Cambridge University Press, Cambridge, 1994

Boris, Eileen, and Daniels, Cynthia R. (eds.), *Homework: Historical and Contemporary Perspectives on Paid Labor at Home*, University of Illinois Press, Urbana, 1989

Boston, Sarah, *Women Workers and the Trade Unions*, Lawrence and Wishart, London, 1980

Braithwaite, Brian, and Walsh, Noëlle (eds.), *Things My Mother Should Have Told*

Me: The Best of 'Good Housekeeping', 1922–1940, Ebury Press, London, 1991

Branson, Noreen, *Poplarism, 1919–1925: George Lansbury and the Councillors' Revolt*, Lawrence and Wishart, London, 1979

Braybon, Gail, and Summerfield, Penny, *Out of the Cage: Women's Experiences of Two World Wars*, Pandora, London, 1987

Breines, Wini, *Young, White and Miserable: Growing Up Female in the Fifties*, Beacon Press, Boston, 1992

Brenner, Johanna, 'The Best of Times, the Worst of Times: US Feminism Today', *New Left Review*, 200, July–August 1993; revised and updated in Monica Threlfall (ed.), *Mapping the Women's Movement: Feminist Politics and Social Transformation in the North*, Verso, London, 1996

Brent, Peter, 'Marie Lloyd', in Peter Brent (ed.), *The Edwardians*, BBC Books, London, 1972

Brittain, Vera, *Testament of Friendship: The Story of Winifred Holtby*, Virago, London, 1980 (first edn 1940)

——*Testament of Youth: An Autobiographical Story of the Years 1900–1925*, Arrow Books, London, 1960 (first edn 1933)

——*The Women at Oxford: A Fragment of History*, George G. Harrap and Co., London, 1960

Brookes, Barbara, *Abortion in England, 1900–1967*, Croom Helm, London, 1988

Buhle, Mari Jo, *Women and American Socialism, 1870–1920*, University of Illinois Press, Urbana, 1983

Buhle, Mari Jo, Buhle, Paul, and Kaye, Harvey J. (eds.), *The American Radical*, Routledge, New York, 1994

Busby, Margaret, *Daughters of Africa: An International Anthology of Words and Writings by Women of African Descent from the Ancient Egyptian to the Present*, Jonathan Cape, London, 1992

Cadbury, Edward, Matheson, M. Cecile, and Shawn, G., *Women's Work and Wages: A Phase of Life in an Industrial City*, T. Fisher Unwin, London, 1909

Cadogan, Mary, *Women with Wings*, Macmillan, London, 1992

Callen, Anthea, *Angel in the Studio: Women in the Arts and Crafts Movement, 1870–1914*, Astragel Books, London, 1979

Cameron, Ardis, *Radicals of the Worst Sort: Laboring Women in Lawrence Massachusetts, 1860–1912*, University of Illinois Press, Urbana, 1993

Campbell, Beatrix, *The Iron Ladies: Why Do Women Vote Tory?*, Virago, London, 1987

Cantarow, Ellen (ed.), *Moving the Mountain: Women Working for Social Change*, The Feminist Press and McGraw Hill Publishing, New York, 1980

Carabillo, Toni, Meuli, Judith, and Csida, June Bundy, *Feminist Chronicles, 1953–1993*, Women's Graphics, Los Angeles, 1993

Carson, Clayborne, Garrow, David J., Harding, Vincent, and Hine, Darlene Clark, *Eyes On the Prize: America's Civil Rights Years*, Penguin Books, New York, 1987

Castle, Barbara, *Fighting All the Way*, Pan Books, London, 1994

Chamberlain, Mary, *Growing Up in Lambeth*, Virago, London, 1989

Charters, Ann (ed.), *The Penguin Book of the Beats*, Penguin Books, Harmondsworth, 1993

Chinn, Carl, *They Worked All Their Lives: Women and the Urban Poor in England, 1880–1939*, Manchester University Press, Manchester, 1988

Chisholm, Anne, *Nancy Cunard*, Penguin Books, Harmondsworth, 1981

Clarke, Donald, *Wishing On the Moon: The Life and Times of Billie Holiday*, Penguin Books, Harmondsworth, 1994

Cohen, Marcia, *The Sisterhood: The True Story of the Women Who Changed the World*, Simon and Schuster, New York, 1988

Collette, Christine, *For Labour and for Women: The Women's Labour League, 1906–18*, Manchester University Press, Manchester, 1989

Condell, Diana, and Liddiard, Jean, *Working for Victory? Images of Women in the First World War, 1914–1918*, Routledge and Kegan Paul, London, 1987

Conway, Jill Ker (ed.), *Written By Herself: Autobiographies of American Women – an Anthology*, Vintage Books, a division of Random House, New York, 1992

Cook, Blanche Wiesen, *Crystal Eastman: On Women and Revolution*, Oxford University Press, Oxford, 1978

——*Eleanor Roosevelt: Volume One, 1884–1933*, Viking Penguin, New York, 1992

Coote, Anna, and Campbell, Beatrix, *Sweet Freedom: The Struggle for Women's Liberation*, Pan Books, London, 1982

Coote, Anna, and Pattullo, Polly, *Power and Prejudice: Women and Politics*, Weidenfeld and Nicolson, London, 1990

Costello, John, *Love, Sex and War: Changing Values, 1939–1945*, Pan Books, London, 1985

Daniel, Robert L., *American Women in the 20th Century: The Festival of Life*, Harcourt Brace Jovanovich, Orlando, Florida, 1987

Davies, Andrew, *Leisure, Gender and Poverty: Working-class Culture in Salford and Manchester, 1900–1939*, Open University Press, Buckingham, 1992

Davies, Margaret Llewelyn (ed.), *Maternity: Letters from Working Women Collected by the Women's Co-operative Guild*, Virago, London, 1978 (first edn 1915)

Davis, Angela, *Women, Race and Class*, The Women's Press, London, 1982

Davis, Flora, *Moving the Mountain: The Women's Movement in America since 1960*, a Touchstone book, Simon and Schuster, New York, 1991

Dawley, Alan, *Struggles for Justice: Social Responsibility and the Liberal State*, The Belknap Press of Harvard University Press, Cambridge, Mass., 1991

Delany, Sarah L. and A. Elizabeth, with Amy Hill Hearth, *Having Our Say: The Delany Sisters' First 100 Years*, Bantam Doubleday Dell, New York, 1994

Dennis, Norman, Henriques, Fernando, and Slaughter, Cliff, *Coal is Our Life: An Analysis of a Yorkshire Mining Community*, Tavistock Publications, London, 1969 (first edn 1956)

Docherty, Mary, *A Miner's Lass*, Lancashire Community Press, Preston, 1992

Douglas, Susan J., *Where the Girls Are: Growing Up Female in the Mass Media*, Penguin Books, Harmondsworth, 1995

Duberman, Martin, Vicinus, Martha, and Chauncey Jr, George (eds.), *Hidden from History: Reclaiming the Gay and Lesbian Past*, Penguin Books, Harmondsworth, 1991

DuBois, Ellen Carol, and Ruiz, Vicki L., *Unequal Sisters: A Multicultural Reader in US Women's History*, Routledge, New York, 1990

Dyhouse, Carol, *No Distinction of Sex? Women in British Universities, 1870–1939*, UCL Press, London, 1995

Echols, Alice, *Daring to be Bad: Radical Feminism in America, 1967–1975*, University of Minnesota Press, Minneapolis, 1989

Ehrenreich, Barbara, *The Worst Years of Our Lives: Irreverent Notes from a Decade of Greed*, Pantheon Books, New York, 1990

Eisenstein, Sarah, *Give Us Bread But Give Us Roses: Working Women's Consciousness in the United States, 1890 to the First World War*, Routledge and Kegan Paul, London, 1983

Enstad, Nan, 'Dressed for Adventure: Working Women and Silent Movie Serials in the 1910s', *Feminist Studies*, Vol. 21, No. 1, Spring 1995

Erenberg, Lewis, A., *Steppin' Out: New York Nightlife and the Transformation of American Culture, 1890–1930*, University of Chicago Press, Chicago, 1984

Evans, Sara M., *Born for Liberty: A History of Women in America*, The Free Press, Macmillan, New York, 1989

Ewen, Elizabeth, *Immigrant Women in the Land of Dollars: Life and Culture on the Lower East Side, 1890–1925*, Monthly Review Press, New York, 1985

Ewen, Stuart, *All-consuming Images: The Politics of Style in Contemporary Culture*, Basic Books, New York, 1988

Ewen, Stuart and Elizabeth, *Channels of Desire: Mass Images and the Shaping of American Consciousness*, University of Minnesota Press, Minneapolis, 1992 (first edn 1982)

Faderman, Lillian, *Odd Girls and Twilight Lovers: A History of Lesbian Life in Twentieth-century America*, Penguin Books, Harmondsworth, 1992

Faludi, Susan, *Backlash: The Undeclared War Against Women*, Chatto and Windus, London, 1992

Faue, Elizabeth, *Community of Suffering and Struggle: Women, Men and the Labor Movement in Minneapolis, 1915–1945*, University of North Carolina Press, Chapel Hill, 1991

Ferris, Paul, *Sex and the British: A Twentieth-century History*, Michael Joseph, London, 1993

Fielding, Steven, Thompson, Peter, and Tiratsoo, Nick, *'England Arise!' The Labour Party and Popular Politics in 1940s Britain*, Manchester University Press, Manchester, 1995

Figes, Kate, *Because of Her Sex: The Myth of Equality for Women in Britain*, Macmillan, London, 1994

Foakes, Grace, *My Part of the River*, Futura Publications, London, 1976

Foner, Philip S., *Women and the American Labor Movement: From the First Trade Unions to the Present*, The Free Press, Macmillan, New York, 1979

Foner, Philip S., and Schultz, Reinhard, *The Other America: Art and the Labor Movement in the United States*, Journeyman Press, London, 1985

Fountain, Nigel, *Underground: The London Alternative Press, 1966–74*, a Comedia book, published by Routledge, London, 1988

Frank, Dana, *Purchasing Power, Consumer Organizing, Gender, and the Seattle Labor Movement, 1919–1929*, Cambridge University Press, Cambridge, 1994

Frankel, Noralee, and Dye, Nancy S. (eds.), *Gender, Class, Race and Reform in the Progressive Era*, University Press of Kentucky, Lexington, 1991

Fryer, Peter, *Staying Power: The History of Black People in Britain*, Pluto Press, London, 1984

Fyrth, Jim (ed.), *Labour's High Noon: The Government and the Economy, 1945–51*, Lawrence and Wishart, London, 1993

——*Labour's Promised Land? Culture and Society in Labour Britain, 1945–51*, Lawrence and Wishart, London, 1995

Fyrth, Jim, with Sally Alexander, *Women's Voices from the Spanish Civil War*, Lawrence and Wishart, London, 1991

Gaar, Gillian G., *She's a Rebel: The History of Women in Rock 'n' Roll*, Cassell, London, 1993

Gabin, Nancy F., *Feminism in the Labor Movement: Women and the United Auto Workers, 1935–1975*, Cornell University Press, Ithaca, 1990

Gentry, Curt, *The Madams of San Francisco: An Irreverent History of the City by the Golden Gate*, Ballantine Books, New York, 1964

Giddings, Paula, *When and Where I Enter: The Impact of Black Women on Race and Sex in America*, Bantam Books, Toronto, 1985

Glendinning, Caroline, and Millar, Jane, *Women and Poverty in Britain: The 1990s*, Harvester Wheatsheaf, New York, 1992

Glenn, Sharon A., *Daughters of the Shetl: Life and Labor in the Immigrant Generation*, Cornell University Press, Ithaca, 1990

Gluck, Sherna Berger (ed.), *Rosie the Riveter Revisited: Women, the War and Social Change*, Twayne Publishers, a division of G. K. Hall and Co., Boston, 1987

Glucksmann, Miriam, *Women Assemble: Women Workers and the New Industries in Inter-war Britain*, Routledge, London, 1990

Goldman, Dorothy (ed.), *Women and World War I: The Written Response*, Macmillan, London, 1993

Gordon, Linda, *Heroes of Their Own Lives: The Politics and History of Family Violence. Boston, 1880–1960*, Virago, London, 1989

——*Pitied But Not Entitled: Single Mothers and the History of Welfare, 1890–1935*, The Free Press, Macmillan, New York, 1994

——*Woman's Body, Woman's Right: A Social History of Birth Control in America*, Grossman Publishers, a division of the Viking Press, New York, 1976

Gordon, Linda (ed.), *Women, the State and Welfare*, University of Wisconsin Press, Madison, 1990

Graves, Pamela M., *Labour Women: Women in British Working-class Politics, 1918–1939*, Cambridge University Press, Cambridge, 1994

Greenwald, Maurine Weiner, 'Working-class Feminism and the Family Wage Ideal: The Seattle Debate on Married Women's Right to Work, 1914–1920', *Journal of American History*, Vol. 75, No. 1, June 1989

Griffiths, Trevor R., and Llewellyn-Jones, Margaret (eds.), *British and Irish Women Dramatists since 1958: A Critical Handbook*, Open University Press, Buckingham, 1993

Groneman, Carol, and Norton, Mary Beth (eds.), *'To Toil the Livelong Day': American Women at Work, 1780–1980*, Cornell University Press, Ithaca, 1987

Hartley, Jenny (ed.), *Hearts Undefeated: Women's Writing of the Second World War*, Virago, London, 1995

Hartmann, Susan M., *From Margin to Mainstream: American Women and Politics since 1960*, Temple University Press, Philadelphia, 1989

Hayden, Dolores, *The Grand Domestic Revolution*, MIT Press, Cambridge, Mass., 1984

Healey, Dorothy, and Isserman, Maurice, *Dorothy Healey Remembers: A Life in the American Communist Party*, Oxford University Press, New York, 1990

Heron, Liz (ed.), *Truth, Dare or Promise: Girls Growing Up in the 50s*, Virago, London, 1985

Hine, Darlene Clark, 'The Housewives' League of Detroit: Black Women and Economic Nationalism', in Nancy A. Hewitt and Suzanne Lebsock (eds.), *Visible Women: New Essays on American Activism*, University of Illinois Press, Urbana, 1993

Hine, Darlene Clark (ed.), *Black Women in America: An Historical Encyclopedia: Vols. 1 and 2*, Carlson Publishing, New York, 1993

Holledge, Julie, *Innocent Flowers: Women in the Edwardian Theatre*, Virago, London, 1981

Horowitz, Daniel, 'Rethinking Betty Friedan and "The Feminine Mystique": Labor Union Radicalism and Feminism in Cold War America', *American Quarterly*, Vol. 48, No. 1, March 1996

Hudson, Ray, and Williams, Allan M., *Divided Britain*, Belhaven Press, a division of Pinter Publishers, London, 1989

Humphries, Steve, and Gordon, Pamela, *Forbidden Britain: Our Secret Past, 1900–1960*, BBC Books, London, 1994

——*A Labour of Love: The Experience of Parenthood in Britain, 1900–1950*, Sidgwick and Jackson, London, 1993

Hutchins, Chris, and Thompson, Peter, *Diana Confidential: The Nightmare and the Family*, Pocket Books, London, 1994

Hymowitz, Carol, and Weissman, Michaele, *A History of Women in America*, Bantam Books, New York, 1978

Jarrett-Macauley, Delia, *Reconstructing Womanhood, Reconstructing Feminism: Writings on Black Women*, Routledge, London, 1996

Jayawardena, Kumari, *The White Woman's Other Burden: Western Women and South Asia During British Colonial Rule*, Routledge, New York, 1995

Jellison, Katherine, *Entitled to Power: Farm Women and Technology, 1913–1963*, University of North Carolina Press, Chapel Hill, 1993

Jewish Women in London Group (ed.), *Generations of Memories: Voices of Jewish Women*, The Women's Press, London, 1989

Johnson, Paul (ed.), *20th Century Britain: Economic, Social and Cultural Change*, Longman, London, 1994

Jones, Jacqueline, *Labor of Love, Labor of Sorrow: Black Women, Work and the Family from Slavery to the Present*, Basic Books, New York, 1985

Kelley, Kitty, *Nancy Reagan: The Unauthorized Biography*, Bantam Books, Toronto, 1992

Kelley, Robin D. G., '"We Are Not What We Seem": Rethinking Black Opposition in the Jim Crow South', *Journal of American History*, June 1993

Kellner, Bruce (ed.), *The Harlem Renaissance: A Historical Dictionary for the Era*, Methuen, New York, 1987

Kessler-Harris, Alice, *Out to Work: A History of Wage-earning Women in the United States*, Oxford University Press, Oxford, 1982

King, Elspeth, *The Hidden History of Glasgow's Women: The THENEW Factor*, Mainstream Publishing, Edinburgh, 1995

Klatch, Rebecca, *Women of the New Right*, Temple University Press, Philadelphia, 1987

Kleiman, Carol, *Women's Networks: The Complete Guide to Getting a Better Job, Advancing Your Career, and Feeling Great as a Woman Through Networking*, Ballantine Books, New York, 1980

Kraditor, Aileen S., *The Ideas of the Woman Suffrage Movement, 1890–1920*, W. W. Norton, New York, 1981 (first edn 1965)

Ladd-Taylor, Molly, *Mother-Work: Women, Child Welfare and the State, 1890–1930*, University of Illinois Press, Urbana, 1994

Laing, Adrian, *R. D. Laing: A Biography*, Peter Owen, London, 1994

Lambert, Angela, *1939: The Last Season of Peace*, Weidenfeld and Nicolson, New York, 1989

Lash, Joseph P., *Eleanor: The Years Alone*, a Signet book, New American Library, New York, 1972

Lauret, Maria, *Liberating Literature: Feminist Fiction in America*, Routledge, London, 1994

Lewis, Jane, *Women in Britain since 1945*, Blackwell, Oxford, 1992

Liddington, Jill, *The Life and Times of a Respectable Rebel: Selina Cooper, 1864–1946*, Virago, London, 1984

——*The Long Road to Greenham: Feminism and Anti-militarism in Britain since 1820*, Virago, London, 1989

Light, Alison, *Forever England: Femininity, Literature and Conservatism Between the Wars*, Routledge, London, 1991

Link, Arthur S., and McCormick, Richard L., *Progressivism*, Harlan Davidson Inc., Arlington Heights, Illinois, 1983

Lovenduski, Joni, and Randall, Vicky, *Contemporary Feminist Politics: Women and Power in Britain*, Oxford University Press, Oxford, 1993

Luker, Kristin, *Dubious Conceptions: The Politics of Teenage Pregnancy*, Harvard University Press, Cambridge, Mass., 1996

McCrindle, Jean, and Rowbotham, Sheila (eds.), *Dutiful Daughters: Women Talk About Their Lives*, Penguin Books, Harmondsworth, 1979

McElvaine, Robert (ed.), *Letters from the Forgotten Man*, University of North Carolina Press, Chapel Hill, 1983

McLeish, Kenneth and Valerie, *Long to Reign Over Us: Memories of Coronation Day and Life in the 1950s*, Bloomsbury, London, 1992

Madge, Charles, and Harrison, Tom, *Britain by Mass-Observation*, Penguin Books, Harmondsworth, 1939

Maitland, Sara, *Vesta Tilley*, Virago, London, 1986

Maitland, Sara (ed.), *Very Heaven: Looking Back at the 1960s*, Virago, London, 1988

Mansbridge, Jane, *Why We Lost the ERA*, University of Chicago Press, Chicago, 1986

May, Elaine Tyler, *Homeward Bound: American Families in the Cold War Era*, Basic Books, New York, 1988

Melosh, Barbara (ed.), *Gender and American History since 1890*, Routledge, London, 1993

Meyerowitz, Joanne, 'Beyond the Feminine Mystique: A Reassessment of Post-war Mass Culture, 1946–1958', *Journal of American History*, Vol. 79, No. 4, March 1993

Milkman, Ruth, *Gender at Work: The Dynamics of Job Segregation by Sex during World War II*, University of Illinois Press, Urbana, 1987

——'New Research in Women's Labor History', *Signs: Journal of Women in Culture and Society*, Vol. 18, No. 2, Winter 1993

Milkman, Ruth (ed.), *Women, Work and Protest: A Century of US Women's Labor History*, Routledge and Kegan Paul, Boston, 1985

Mink, Gwendolyn, *The Wages of Motherhood: Inequality in the Welfare State, 1917–1942*, Cornell University Press, Ithaca, 1995

Mitter, Swasti, *Common Fate, Common Bond: Women in the Global Economy*, Pluto, London, 1986

Morgan, Marguerite, *Part of the Main: Life of a Communist Woman*, People's Publications, London, 1990

Morris, Margaret, *My Life in Movement*, Peter Owen, London, 1969

Munt, Sally R., *Murder by the Book? Feminism and the Crime Novel*, Routledge, London, 1994

Norton, Mary Beth (ed.), *Major Problems in American Women's History: Documents and Essays*, D. C. Heath and Company, Lexington, Mass., 1989

Ogden, Annegret S., *The Great American Housewife: From Helpmate to Wage Earner, 1776–1986*, Greenwood Press, Westport, Connecticut, 1986

Oldfield, Sybil (ed.), *This Working-day World: Women's Lives and Culture(s) in Britain, 1914–1945*, Taylor and Francis, London, 1994

Orleck, Annelise, *Common Sense and a Little Fire: Women and Working-class Politics in the United States, 1900–1965*, University of North Carolina Press, Chapel Hill, 1995

Parry, Melanie (ed.), *Chambers Biographical Dictionary of Women*, Chambers, Edinburgh, 1996

Pawling, Christopher (ed.), *Popular Fiction and Social Change*, Macmillan Press, London, 1984

Peiss, Kathy, and Simmons, Christine (eds.), with Robert A. Padgug, *Passion, Power and Sexuality in History*, Temple University Press, Philadelphia, 1989

Polhemus, Ted, *Street Style: From Sidewalk to Catwalk*, Thames and Hudson, London, 1994

Pollitt, Katha, *Reasonable Creatures: Essays on Women and Feminism*, Vintage, London, 1995

Pollock, Griselda, 'Feminism, Femininity and the Hayward Annual Exhibition 1978, *Feminist Review*, 2, Summer 1979

Pugh, Martin, *The Tories and the People, 1880–1935*, Basil Blackwell, Oxford, 1985
——*Women and the Women's Movement in Britain, 1914–1959*, Macmillan, London, 1992

Ramdin, Ron, *The Making of the Black Working Class in Britain*, Wildwood House, Aldershot, Hants, 1987

Richards, Jeffrey, and Sheridan, Dorothy, *Mass-Observation at the Movies*, Routledge and Kegan Paul, London, 1987

Rigney, Barbara Hill, *Margaret Atwood*, Macmillan, London, 1987

Riley, Denise, *War in the Nursery: Theories of the Child and Mother*, Virago, London, 1983

Riley, Glenda, *Inventing the American Woman: A Perspective on Women's History, 1865 to the Present*, Harlan Davidson Inc., Arlington Heights, Illinois, 1986

Roberts, Elizabeth, *A Woman's Place: An Oral History of Working-class Women, 1890–1940*, Basil Blackwell, Oxford, 1984

Roberts, Robert, *The Classic Slum: Salford Life in the First Quarter of the Century*, Penguin Books, Harmondsworth, 1973

Roberts, Robin, *A New Species: Gender and Science Fiction*, University of Illinois Press, Urbana, 1993

Rolley, Katrina, 'Cutting a Dash: The Dress of Radclyffe Hall and Una Trowbridge', *Feminist Review*, 35, Summer 1990

Rose, Phyllis (ed.), *The Penguin Book of Women's Lives*, Viking, London, 1994

Rosen, Ruth, *The Maimie Papers*, The Feminist Press, New York, 1977

Rosenberg, Rosalind, *Divided Lives: American Women in the Twentieth Century*, Penguin Books, Harmondsworth, 1993

Rossiter, Ann, 'Bringing the Margins into the Centre: A Review of Aspects of Irish Women's Emigration', in Sean Hutton and Paul Stewart (eds.), *Ireland's Histories: Aspects of State, Society and Ideology*, Routledge, London, 1991

Rossiter, Margaret, *Women Scientists in America: Before Affirmative Action, 1940–1972*, Johns Hopkins University Press, Baltimore, 1995

——*Women Scientists in America: Struggles and Strategies to 1940*, Johns Hopkins University Press, Baltimore, 1982

Rowbotham, Sheila, *Friends of Alice Wheeldon*, Pluto, London, 1986

——*A New World for Women: Stella Browne – Socialist Feminist*, Pluto, London, 1977

——*The Past is Before Us: Feminism in Action since the 1960s*, Penguin Books, Harmondsworth, 1990

——*Woman's Consciousness, Man's World*, Penguin Books, Harmondsworth, 1973

——*Women, Resistance and Revolution*, Allen Lane, Harmondsworth, 1972

Rowe, Marsha (ed.), *Spare Rib Reader*, Penguin Books, Harmondsworth, 1982

Rowland, Robyn (ed.), *Women Who Do and Women Who Don't: Join the Women's Movement*, Routledge and Kegan Paul, London, 1984

Rubin, Lillian B., *Worlds of Pain: Life in the Working-class Family*, Basic Books, New York, 1992 (first edn 1976)

Savage, Mike, and Miles, Andrew, *The Remaking of the British Working Class, 1840–1940*, Routledge, London, 1994

Sayers, Janet, *Mothering Psychoanalysis: Helene Deutsch, Karen Horney, Anna Freud and Melanie Klein*, Hamish Hamilton, London, 1991

Scannell, Dolly, *Mother Knew Best: An East End Childhood*, Pan Books, London, 1975

Scharft, Virginia, *Taking the Wheel: Women and the Coming of the Motor Age*, University of New Mexico, Albuquerque, 1991

Sebba, Anne, *Battling for the News: The Rise of the Woman Reporter*, Hodder and Stoughton, London, 1994

Sebestyen, Amanda (ed.), *'68, '78, '88: From Women's Liberation to Feminism*, Prism Press, Bridport, Dorset, 1988

Segal, Lynne, *Straight Sex: The Politics of Pleasure*, Virago, London, 1994

Segal, Lynne, and McIntosh, Mary (eds.), *Sex Exposed: Sexuality and the Pornography Debate*, Virago, London, 1992

Seller, Maxine S., 'Beyond the Stereotype: A New Look at the Immigrant Woman, 1880–1924', in George E. Pozzetta (ed.), *Ethnicity and Gender: The Immigrant Woman*, Garland Publishing, New York, 1991

Shipman, David, *Cinema: The First Hundred Years*, Quality Paperbacks Direct, London, 1993

Showalter, Elaine (ed.), *These Modern Women: Autobiographical Essays from the Twenties*, The Feminist Press, New York, 1978

Sked, Alan, and Cook, Chris, *Post-war Britain: A Political History*, Penguin Books, Harmondsworth, 1993

Slatkin, Wendy, *The Voices of Women Artists*, Prentice Hall, Englewood Cliffs, New Jersey, 1993

Sochen, June, *Mae West: She Who Laughs, Lasts*, Harlan Davidson Inc., Arlington Heights, Illinois, 1992

——*Movers and Shakers: American Women Thinkers and Activists, 1900–1970*, Quadrangle/The New York Times Book Co., New York, 1973

Spoto, Donald, *Marilyn Monroe: The Biography*, Arrow Books, London, 1994

Stacey, Jackie, *Stargazing: Hollywood Cinema and Female Spectatorship*, Routledge, London, 1994

Stacey, Margaret, and Price, Marion, *Women, Power and Politics*, Tavistock Publications, London, 1981

Staples, Shirley, *Male–Female Comedy Teams in American Vaudeville, 1865–1932*, UMI Research Press, Ann Arbor, Michigan, 1984

Sterling, Dorothy, *Black Foremothers: Three Lives*, The Feminist Press, New York, 1988

Stern, Jane and Michael, *Sixties People*, Alfred A. Knopf, New York, 1990

Strachey, Ray (ed.), *Our Freedom and Its Results*, Hogarth Press, London, 1936

Strauss, Sylvia, *Traitors to the Masculine Cause: The Men's Campaigns for Women's Rights*, Greenwood Press, Westport, Connecticut, 1982

Summerfield, Penny, *Women Workers in the Second World War*, Croom Helm, London, 1984

Susman, Warren I., *Culture as History: The Transformation of American Society in the Twentieth Century*, Pantheon, New York, 1984

Sykes, Christopher, *Nancy: The Life of Lady Astor*, Panther, Granada Publishing, London, 1979

Tandberg, Gerily G., 'Sinning for Silk: Dress-for-Success Fashions of the New Orleans Storyville Prostitute', *Women's Studies International Forum*, Vol. 13, No. 3

Thatcher, Margaret, *The Downing Street Years*, HarperCollins, London, 1993

Thompson, Flora, *Lark Rise to Candleford*, Oxford University Press, London, 1965

Thompson, Paul, *The Edwardians: The Remaking of British Society*, Weidenfeld and Nicolson, London, 1975

Thompson, Tierl, *Dear Girl: The Diaries and Letters of Two Working Women, 1899–1917*, The Women's Press, London, 1987

Thornton, Peter, *Decade of Decline: Civil Liberties in the Thatcher Years*, National Council for Civil Liberties, London, 1989

Tickner, Lisa, *The Spectacle of Women: Imagery of the Suffrage Campaign, 1907–14*, Chatto and Windus, London, 1987

Tilly, Louise A., and Gurin, Patricia (eds.), *Women, Politics and Change*, Russell Sage Foundation, New York, 1990

Twin, Stephanie (ed.), *Women and Sports*, The Feminist Press, New York, 1977

Uglow, Jenny (ed.), *The Macmillan Dictionary of Women's Biography*, Macmillan Reference Books, London, 1989 (first edn 1982)

Vincent, David, *Poor Citizens: The State and the Poor in Twentieth-century Britain*, Longman, London, 1991

Waller, Jane, and Vaughan-Rees, Michael, *Women in Uniform, 1939–45*, Macmillan, London, 1989

Wandor, Michelene, *Once a Feminist: Stories of a Generation*, Virago, London, 1990

Ward, Colin, and Hardy, Dennis, *Goodnight Campers! The History of the British Holiday Camp*, Mansell Publishing, London, 1986

Ward, Margaret, *Unmanageable Revolutionaries: Women and Irish Nationalism*, Pluto, London, 1983

Weeks, Jeffrey, *Sex, Politics and Society: The Regulation of Sexuality since 1800*, Longman, London, 1981

Weller, Ken, *'Don't be a Soldier': The Radical Anti-war Movement in North London, 1914–1918*, Journeyman Press, London, 1985

West, Guida, and Blumberg, Rhoda Lois (eds.), *Women and Social Protest*, Oxford University Press, New York, 1990

Wexler, Alice, *Emma Goldman: An Intimate Life*, Virago, London, 1984

Wheeler, Adade Mitchell, *The Roads They Made: Women in Illinois History*, Charles H. Kerr, Chicago, 1977

Wicks, Harry, *Keeping My Head: The Memoirs of a British Bolshevik*, Socialist Platform on behalf of Logie Barrow, London, 1992

Williamson, Judith, *Consuming Passions: The Dynamics of Popular Culture*, Marion Boyars, London, 1986

Willoughby, Martin, *A History of Postcards*, Bracken Books, London, 1994

Wilson, Elizabeth, *Adorned in Dreams: Fashion and Modernity*, Virago, London, 1995

Winship, Janice, '"A Girl Needs to Get Street-Wise": Magazines for the 1980s', *Feminist Review*, 21, Winter 1985

Winslow, Barbara, *Sylvia Pankhurst: Sexual Politics and Political Activism*, UCL Press, London, 1996

Wolmark, Jenny, *Aliens and Others: Science Fiction, Feminism and Postmodernism*, Harvester Wheatsheaf, Hemel Hempstead, Herts, 1993

Woloch, Barbara, *Women and the American Experience: A Concise History*, Overture Books, The McGraw-Hill Companies, New York, 1996

Woollacott, Angela, *On Her Their Lives Depend: Munitions Workers in the Great War*, University of California Press, Berkeley, 1994

Young, Hugo, *One of Us: A Biography of Margaret Thatcher*, Pan Books, London, 1993

Zinn, Howard, *A People's History of the United States*, A Harper Perennial, a division of HarperCollins, New York, 1990

Permissions

Grateful acknowledgement is made to publishers and individuals for permission to reprint the following: Michelene Wandor for lines from 'In the Sixties' in Sara Maitland (ed.), *Very Heaven*, Virago, London, 1988; Amryl Johnson for lines from 'The Loaded Dice' in *Long Road to Nowhere*, Virago, London, 1985, currently in print in the anthology of her poems *Tread Carefully in Paradise*, Cofa Press, 1991; Alison Fell for lines from 'Love Song – the beginning of the end of the affair' in Lilian Mohin (ed.), *One Foot on the Mountain: An Anthology of British Feminist Poetry 1969–1979*, Onlywomen Press, London, 1979; Sheila Shulman for fragments from 'Hard Words', which was originally published in *One Foot on the Mountain*; to Wynwood Music Company, Broad Run, VA, for lines from 'Custom Made Woman Blues', sung by Hazel Dickens and Alice Gerrard on Rounder Records, Boston; Carcanet Press for lines from Sylvia Townsend Warner, *Collected Poems of Sylvia Townsend Warner*, Claire Herman (ed.), Manchester 1982; New Directions Publishing Corporation and Gerald Pollinger Ltd for a quotation from Denise Levertov, 'Making Peace', from *Breathing the Water*, copyright © 1987 by Denise Levertov; 'Glory of Women' from *Collected Poems of Siegfried Sassoon* by Siegfried Sassoon, copyright 1918, 1920 by E. P. Dutton, copyright 1936, 1946, 1947, 1948 by Siegfried Sassoon, used by permission of George Sassoon and by permission of Viking Penguin, a division of Penguin Books USA Inc.; excerpt from 'Day-Dreams', copyright 1924 by Dorothy Parker, first appeared in *Life* magazine, reprinted by permission of Penguin Books USA, Inc.; 'Ballade at Thirty-Five' by Dorothy Parker, copyright 1926, renewed © 1954 by Dorothy Parker, from *The Portable Dorothy Parker* by Dorothy Parker, introduction by Brendan Gill, used by permission of Viking Penguin, a division of Penguin Books USA Inc., and by permission of Gerald Duckworth & Co. Ltd.

Index